MANAGING YOUR PERSONAL FINANCES

SECOND EDITION

JOAN S. RYAN

Business Instructor
Lane Community College
Eugene, Oregon

FH03BA
PUBLISHED BY
SOUTH-WESTERN PUBLISHING CO.
CINCINNATI, OH   WEST CHICAGO, IL   DALLAS, TX   LIVERMORE, CA

PREFACE

MANAGING YOUR PERSONAL FINANCES, Second Edition, is a multidisciplinary approach to personal financial management for high school students. The text incorporates a variety of topics in business, economics, law, business education, and social studies. This edition incorporates new economics materials to meet personal finance and economics curriculum needs that broaden the scope and depth of the course. Current technology terms are used throughout the textbook. The result is a text that offers high school students a comprehensive coverage of basic financial and economic concepts valuable in today's changing world.

The approach to the study of personal finance and consumer economics offered in MANAGING YOUR PERSONAL FINANCES, Second Edition, focuses on the student's role as citizen, student, family member, consumer, and active participant in the work and business world. The intent is to inform students of their various economic and financial responsibilities and to provide opportunities for self-awareness, expression, and advancement in a progressive and highly competitive society.

STRUCTURE Unit One, Employment and Income, covers individual goals and advancement concepts, including employment and income. Unit Two, Money Management, introduces students to financial planning, investing, and risk management. Unit Three, Credit, is a comprehensive coverage of credit. In Unit Four, Consumer Rights and Responsibilities, students explore the important role of the consumer in the marketplace. Unit Five, Purchasing Goods and Services, provides in-depth guidance for making personal and family decisions. Unit Six, Microeconomics and You; Unit Seven, Macroeconomics and the U.S. Economy; and Unit Eight, The World Economy, represent an expansion of the economic concepts presented in the first edition and now include the global concepts of international economics.

The Appendix has been expanded and a Glossary containing all vocabulary terms provides easy reference for study and review of the important concepts introduced in each chapter.

LEARNING ASSISTS IN THE TEXTBOOK

Learning objectives at the beginning of each unit draw together related chapters of study. Learning objectives at the beginning of each chapter are fulfilled by studying the chapter narrative, responding to end-of-chapter activities, and completing the workbook activities and comprehensive testing program. Vocabulary, review questions, applications, and case problems at the end of each chapter provide a variety of opportunities for students to apply the concepts presented.

Chapter study is enhanced by vocabulary terms printed in bold, with other important terms and concepts printed in italics. Margin notes draw attention to important concepts presented throughout each chapter.

STUDENT SUPPLEMENT

MANAGING YOUR PERSONAL FINANCES, Student Activities, Second Edition, provides additional opportunities for students to explore and enhance learning in practical assignments. Each workbook chapter includes vocabulary, review questions, and activities. New activities have been added throughout.

TEACHER SUPPLE- MENTARY ITEMS

The Manual accompanying MANAGING YOUR PERSONAL FI- NANCES, Second Edition, has been expanded extensively. Included are detailed course schedules, grading suggestions, lists of reference materials by unit, and suggestions for integrating the Student Activities and testing program with the textbook. Each Manual chapter contains Objectives, an Objectives Matrix, Teaching Suggestions, and Answers to End-of-Chapter and Student Activities. Two transparency masters for each chapter are now in the back of the Manual. Included also are additional blank federal income tax forms for duplication and classroom use.

TESTING PROGRAM

A comprehensive testing program accompanies MANAGING YOUR PERSONAL FINANCES, Second Edition. Student progress can be tracked with pretests and comprehensive tests over the first and second halves of the textbook, chapter tests, and a final examination. IBM and Apple computer versions of the testing program are available on MicroExam.

MESSAGE TO THE STUDENT

Effective consumers are aware of the significance of their role as consumers, from selection of personal purchases to understanding world economic problems and trends. After studying MANAGING YOUR PERSONAL FINANCES, you will have a better grasp of your responsibilities to yourself and society and you will better understand your own wants, needs, and values, and how these affect personal financial decisions. Understanding the basic economic concepts presented in this text will enable you to make wise decisions that will affect your financial future and make you a better citizen.

Joan S. Ryan

CONTENTS

UNIT ONE EMPLOYMENT and INCOME

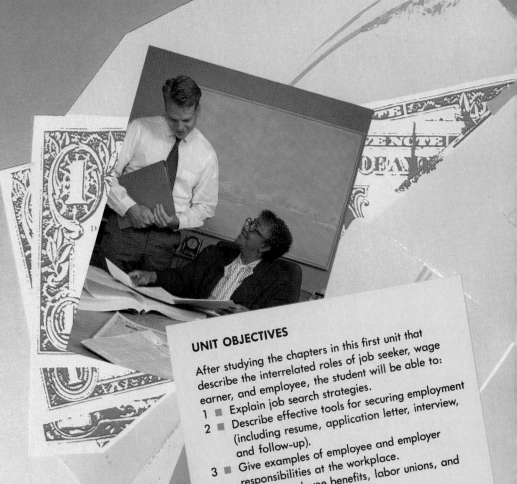

UNIT OBJECTIVES

After studying the chapters in this first unit that describe the interrelated roles of job seeker, wage earner, and employee, the student will be able to:

1 ■ Explain job search strategies.
2 ■ Describe effective tools for securing employment (including resume, application letter, interview, and follow-up).
3 ■ Give examples of employee and employer responsibilities at the workplace.
4 ■ Discuss employee benefits, labor unions, and professional organizations.

Chapter 1

YOUR JOB, YOUR FUTURE

◆◆◆◆◆◆◆◆◆◆◆◆◆◆◆◆◆◆◆◆◆◆◆◆◆◆

OBJECTIVES

1. List factors that determine career choices.
2. Identify and describe good career planning techniques.
3. List sources of job opportunity information.
4. Formulate a personal plan of action to get the desired job.
5. Itemize and explain good job search techniques.

WHY PEOPLE WORK

◆◆◆◆◆◆◆◆

Most of you will work at sometime during your life. After completing high school and other forms of additional training or education, many of you will work for twenty-five to forty years. Today it is common to see two-income families, teenagers with part-time jobs, and family members with more than one job.

Two-income families are common.

People work to meet their needs, wants, and goals. They work to provide themselves with everything from food, clothing, and shelter to vacations, education, and luxuries. If working does not make it possible for a person to meet personal goals, that person is likely to become frustrated or unhappy in his or her job.

2

Illustration 1-1
A person's employment gives a sense of identity and dictates a certain lifestyle.

Work is a central life activity.

Work provides more than a paycheck and income to meet financial goals. A person's employment gives a sense of **identity** — of who and what he or she is. Because work is most often a person's central activity, it often becomes a way of life, or a person's main identity in life. For example, as a student, your main activities center around school. Your identity is that of student. When you are asked what you do, you describe activities, classes, grades in school, and events related to your education. When you are out of school, your main identity will be based on your career. When adults are introduced, the first question asked is usually "What do you do for a living?" When one person answers, "I'm a financial analyst," and another says, "I'm a sports announcer," two entirely different images come to mind.

FACTORS AFFECTING CAREER CHOICE

Because your career will have an impact on nearly every part of your life, the choice of a career is a very important decision. Many factors affect your career decision; some of these are values and life-style choices, aptitudes and interests, and personal qualities and traits.

VALUES AND LIFE-STYLE

Values are the beliefs in life that are important to you. While you are living at home, your values will probably reflect your parents'. During your years

in high school, you begin to form values of your own — keeping many of
your parents' values and rejecting others. For example, you may retain your
parents' value that it is improper to dress casually while attending a religious
service. But you may reject their belief that modern music is worthless.

Life-style may be defined as the way people choose to live their lives,
based on the values they have chosen or rejected. Your life-style is
communicated to others by the clothes you wear and by the things you buy,
rent or use, do, enjoy, and feel. A career is considered an important value in
most people's lives because it dictates life-style. With careful planning, a
career can be rewarding and satisfying and also provide the money needed to
support the life-style you desire.

APTITUDES AND INTERESTS

An **aptitude** is a natural physical or mental ability that permits you to do
certain tasks well. Examples of aptitudes include *finger dexterity*, the ability
to use your fingers to move small objects quickly and accurately, and
manual dexterity, the ability to move your hands skillfully. Certain types of
work require certain aptitudes. Aptitude tests are valuable tools in career
planning because they help you to become aware of your strengths and
weaknesses. Aptitude tests can be taken through counseling or career
guidance departments of most high schools.

In addition to your aptitudes, you might also think about your interests —
the things you like to do — and the reasons why you enjoy them. By
examining the types of things you enjoy, you can better choose a career that
involves similar activities and that will be satisfying and enjoyable. For
example, a person who enjoys being with large groups of people and helping
others will likely prefer a job working with others rather than one working
alone. Consider the options listed in Figure 1-1.

Figure 1-1
Types of Work Ac-
tivities

Which of these work activities appeal to you?	
indoor work	outdoor work
physically active work	physically inactive work
various tasks	same tasks
manual work	thinking work
working with machines	working with others
working alone	leading and directing
following directions	creating and designing
helping others	presenting or speaking
self-motivated work	analyzing and recording

PERSONAL QUALITIES AND TRAITS

Your **personality** consists of the many personal qualities and traits that make you unique. Personal qualities include such things as your appearance, intelligence, creativity, sense of humor, and general attitude. Many times a certain position requires an individual with a particular set of personal qualities and traits. For example, a person who represents a company to the public or to potential customers needs a different set of personal qualities and traits than does a machine operator. Examining your personal qualities and traits can help you to choose a career that's right for you. How many of the traits listed in Figure 1-2 apply to you?

Your personality is a job qualification.

Figure 1-2
Personality Traits

Personality Traits

1. Has a good attitude toward own work and toward others' work.
2. Shows courtesy and respect toward others.
3. Is dependable and will do what is promised.
4. Has a desire to succeed and do a good job.
5. Has enthusiasm for the job and for life.
6. Is clean and has a healthy appearance.
7. Is friendly and helpful.
8. Has a good sense of humor and cares about others.
9. Desires and respects giving a full day's work for a full day's pay.

CAREER PLANNING

◆◆◆◆◆◆◆◆

The average worker spends 86,000 hours on the job.

Planning your future career is an important task. Consider the total time spent in life's central activity of working: Eight hours a day, five days a week, 50 weeks a year, totals 2,000 hours each year. If you work the average career span of 43 years (from age 22 to age 65), you will have spent 86,000 hours on the job. In addition, you will have spent time in traveling to and from work, in getting ready for work, in overtime (paid and unpaid), and in other work-related activities performed away from the workplace. Because your work will likely take so much of your time, you need to choose and plan for your career — your future — carefully.

STEPS IN CAREER PLANNING

Effective career planning involves careful investigation and analysis — a long process that may take years to complete. Career planning involves self-assessment, research, a plan of action, and reevaluation.

Self-Assessment.   Using resources available to you (at schools, employment offices, testing services, etc.) you can explore personal factors that relate to your career choice. You should:

1. Determine your wants and needs.
2. Determine your values and desired life-style.
3. Assess your aptitudes and interests and how they match job descriptions and activities.
4. Analyze your personal qualities and traits — those you have and those you need to improve.

What is your desired life-style?

Research.   Based on a good self-assessment, you can determine which careers interest you most and which suit you best. You should:

1. Seek information in books, pamphlets, articles, and other resources available from libraries, counseling centers, and employment offices.
2. Compare some of your values, interests, abilities, and personal qualities with job descriptions and requirements. Most careers can fit into one of the nine classifications shown in Figure 1-3. Can you choose one or more of these areas that you might want to pursue in which you would be able to meet the requirements? Can you decide which cluster the job of your choice would fit into?
3. Interview people in the fields of work you find interesting.
4. Observe occupations, spend time learning about jobs and companies, and seek part-time work to get direct exposure and experience.

Plan of Action.   After you have done some job research, you will need to develop a plan of action that will eventually bring you to your career goals.

Set a plan to meet your goals.

1. Use good job search techniques: Get organized, make a plan, follow through, and don't give up.
2. Develop necessary skills by taking courses and getting exposure to the areas in which you want to pursue a career.
3. Seek a part-time or volunteer job to gain experience. Your work experience coordinator or counselor at your school can help you find work-study positions and work sites.
4. Talk to workers in your career choice — observe them on the job, ask their advice, and discuss your plans with them. Make your decision a well-thought-out, carefully laid plan.

Reevaluation.   Because the world around us is changing so rapidly, we all need to prepare ourselves to meet the changes and challenges ahead.

JOB CLASSIFICATION	DESCRIPTION OF ACTIVITIES	TRAINING NEEDED	WORKING HOURS	BEGINNING SALARY	EXAMPLES
Clerical/Secretarial	Work in office setting. Involves contact with people and machines. Must type, have telephone skills, etc.	High school diploma plus special training in typing, shorthand, accounting, etc.	40 hours/week during normal business hours	$800+/month	Secretary, typist, word processor operator
Professional	Involves use of highly specialized knowledge. Often stressful. High-level responsibility implied.	4+ years of college. May require special training and/or apprenticeship.	40 hours/week during normal business hours plus overtime	$15,000/year to unlimited	Physician, lawyer, teacher, accountant
Skilled Labor	Emphasis on use of highly specialized skill. Special clothing required. Involves use of tools, machines, etc.	High school diploma plus special training, apprenticeship, licensing, or bonding.	40 hours/week plus overtime	Minimum wage to set salary. $1,000–1,200/month	Builder, mechanic, construction worker
Sales and Marketing	Emphasis on persuading others to buy products and services. Salesperson represents company, self.	High school diploma plus special training. License usually required.	Varied. Often seasonal.	Commission. Often self-employed.	Real estate agent, insurance agent, retail salesperson
Service	Involves labor that does not produce a material good. May or may not involve personal contact.	None to specialized 2-year degree program	Varied. Split shift, as needed	Minimum wage to $1,000/month	Custodian, barber, chef, police officer
Management	Emphasis on supervision of operations, decision making, and direction giving.	College degree plus in-service training.	40 hours or more/week.	$2,000/month or salary plus percentage of profits	Store manager, bank officer, supervisor
Semiskilled and Unskilled Labor	Involves assembly line and other manual work. Physical fitness and good health needed.	In-service training or vocational diploma.	40 hours/week plus overtime	Minimum wage. $10–$15/hour when advanced.	Assembly worker, farm laborer
Entertainment and Recreation	Emphasis on entertaining people. Special quality or talent needed.	None required. Dancing, singing, and music lessons helpful.	Varied. Often under contract.	$0 to unlimited.	Singer, dancer, athlete
Military Service	Emphasis on defense of the country. Discipline and training stressed. Ability to follow orders needed. Must fulfill minimum service requirement.	High school diploma usually required.	Daily during set number of years' commitment.	$7,000/year and up, depending on rank.	Armed Forces service people

Figure 1-3
Job Clusters

Reconsider your
choices and plans.

Once you have begun your journey toward the career of your choice, you may encounter new obstacles that cause you to reconsider your decisions and directions. A tool that you might find useful is a *self-evaluation inventory*, which lists your strong points and your weak points and gives you an idea of what you might do to better prepare yourself for changes. By keeping aware of what is going on in the world and what you need to do to keep up with technological changes, you will not be stranded in a career that is no longer rewarding.

Figure 1-4 is a self-evaluation inventory that lists a young person's assets, liabilities, and plans for action. Can you complete a similar inventory based on your personal qualifications? Completing the inventory should help you identify areas that you can work on so that you will be prepared for both the expected *and the unexpected* changes that will come.

Identify your
strengths and weak-
nesses.

Figure 1-4
Self-Evaluation In-
ventory

Self-Evaluation Inventory

ASSETS (STRENGTHS)	LIABILITIES (WEAKNESSES)	PLAN OF ACTION
Education: High school diploma; took business courses	Education: Weak in office skills	Take extra keyboarding classes to build speed and accuracy
Experience: Cooperative job office—part-time summer job as clerk; volunteer office work in church	Experience: Need computer application	Look for work experience with computers
Aptitudes/Abilities: Good hand-eye coordination; work well with people	Aptitudes/Abilities: Poor speaker; shy around opposite sex	Practice speaking in front of small groups; lead class at church; attend more social events
Appearance: Neat and clean; short, well-groomed hair	Appearance: Wardrobe needs more professional clothes	Start buying clothes appropriate for work

A comprehensive self-evaluation will help you determine areas that need attention. You might also ask another person, such as an employment counselor, to assess objectively your strengths and weaknesses. Another person's point of view can help clarify your self-evaluation. This inventory is useful at various stages in your career, not just in the beginning. Few people will work for only one employer, in one job, for their entire lifetimes. Most of us can count on updating, retraining, and planning for career changes every five to ten years. The rapid rate of technological change will oblige us to maintain an awareness of our strengths and weaknesses and to make plans to stay prepared for new opportunities.

Choosing and planning for a career using this four-step process (self-assessment, research, plan of action, and reevaluation) may seem confusing and complicated. Most people, however, do follow this method, either consciously or unconsciously. People who do not adequately consider career choice and planning often spend years in a job not really suited for them before they finally discover their error. Even after realizing their mistake, they are sometimes unable to correct it.

Be prepared for change.

Don't get locked into a job.

THE IMPORTANCE OF GOALS

A **goal** is an end toward which efforts are directed. People need to have goals to have a sense of direction and purpose in life. There are three types of goals: short-term goals, intermediate goals, and long-term goals.

A *short-term goal* is one that is set to happen within the next few days or weeks. You will work consistently and with certainty to achieve it because you will have to account for the results in a very short time. A short-term goal could be preparing to pass a math test next week — you know you must either study for the test or suffer the consequences.

Intermediate goals are those you wish to accomplish in the next few months or years. Some examples are graduation from high school, a trip you would like to take, or your plans for the coming summer.

Long-term goals include college, career, marriage, and family planning goals. All are activities or plans that will materialize in five to ten years or longer.

If they are to be meaningful, goals should be defined and worked on every day. If goals are to give direction to your life, they must be carefully considered, clearly outlined and actively sought in an organized manner. Many people find a checklist a handy way to stay on target. For example, your goals, which you would look at and work on daily, might be listed as in Figure 1-5.

You might want to make your own checklist form and include your own short-term, intermediate, and long-term goals. Remember: If you don't know where you're going, you'll probably end up somewhere else.

Short-term goals take care of daily living.

Work on your goals every day.

A checklist keeps you current on your goals.

Figure 1-5
Checklist

CHECKLIST

Week of _____

Short-term goals (today/this week)   Accomplished

    1.   Buy birthday gift for Mom.   _____

    2.   Get haircut (Saturday).   _____

    3.   See counselor about computer class.   _____

Intermediate goals (next month/year)

    1.   Get a C or better on computer test
        (test in two weeks).   _____
    2.   Prepare for SAT test (test in
        October).   _____
    3.   Finish term report (due November
        9).   _____
    4.   Complete college admission forms
        (by January 15).   _____

Long-term goals (future)   Things to do now

    1.   Graduate from college.
                        ____ Extra work on computer
                        ____ Bring up GPA to a 3.5
    2.   Begin full-time job.   ____ Update placement folder
    3.   Buy a car.   ____ Get part-time job (save
                                 $50 a month)

MAKING THE RIGHT CHOICES

How do you know what kind of job will be best for you? How can you possibly decide now, while in high school, what you will want to do for the rest of your life? You may not be able to decide. Yet, unfair as it may seem, the fact is that what you do now can greatly affect what you will do in the future.

What you learn to do, you gain *experience* doing — knowledge, skills, and practice from direct participation in a certain area. Furthermore, the more experience you gain, the more qualified you become, and the more you learn. The more experience and expertise you gain in one area, the more desirable you become as an employee in that area. You can, in effect, set yourself up for a career in a certain field, make yourself worth more to an employer, and increase your earnings by continuing in that field. Then you must design your life-style around that work and salary.

Experience makes you a valuable employee.

Unfortunately, the longer you work at one type of job, the greater the chance of becoming *locked in* a job — a feeling that you cannot switch to another type of work because you (and your life-style) cannot afford to take the cut in pay that may accompany starting over. This is true even of part-time work. If you take a job as a clerk, for instance, rather than a job that would pay less but would prepare you for your preferred career, you are in the process of locking into the clerk career. Taking a temporary position to earn a living while you are preparing for your chosen career is a common practice. However, to achieve your career goals, you must continue to pursue jobs in your field.

Look for jobs that will enhance your future plans.

Through careful self-assessment, research, a good plan of action, well-defined goals, and reevaluation throughout your career, you will be able to choose the right career and stay in the right career field for you.

SOURCES OF JOB OPPORTUNITY INFORMATION
◆◆◆◆◆◆◆◆

There are several sources of job opportunity information available: word of mouth and personal contacts; school counseling and placement services; periodicals, books and other publications; public and private employment agencies; and newspaper, telephone book, and private job listings.

WORD OF MOUTH AND PERSONAL CONTACTS

Most job openings are filled by word of mouth.

Many job openings are filled before they are ever advertised. They are filled from within the company, or by people outside the company who have been privately informed of the opening by a friend or other contact within the company. Each of you has a certain amount of exposure to a **contact**. Relatives, friends, people you have worked for, and others may be able to provide you with inside information and leads about job openings. The process of using your own connections or sources of information is called **networking**. You can begin to build your own effective network now, while you are in high school, and continue to develop it throughout your life. A network provides personal as well as professional (career) support and information needed to make wise decisions in your personal and work life. Therefore, the more people you know, the better your chances of hearing about a job opening before it is made public and of getting the job because you had a contact.

A network will last a lifetime.

If you are seeking a job in an area in which you have no contacts, you'll have to work harder. You'll want to make contacts — set up a network — in that area in order to find out about openings. If, for example, you want to work in a bank, you will find it to your advantage to get to know people who work in banks and make yourself known to managers and other key employees. You can do this through acquaintances and friends in business, through professional organizations, through community activities, and through school-sponsored visits, observations, job fairs or other activities.

SCHOOL COUNSELING AND PLACEMENT SERVICES

Many schools have programs to assist students in preparing for careers, in making career choices, and in securing part-time and full-time work. One such program is the *cooperative work experience program*. Students receive high school credits for on-the-job experience that directly relates to classroom studies in a chosen career area. Students placed in work situations are given grades on their work and are paid minimum wages for their efforts. Employers often receive tax credits or other incentives for providing such training.

Employers get tax credits for some wages paid.

School counselors and teachers are also good sources of job opportunity information. They may know about specific job openings, and are asked by employers to recommend students for openings. If you are interested in an office job, you should talk to counselors and business teachers as you complete business courses. Colleges and universities (and some high schools) offer a **placement service**. A placement service helps students find employment, usually free of charge. These services include keeping a placement folder on each student that contains school records usually requested by employers, such as attendance, academic, and discipline records. Job openings are posted at the school and qualified students are given information so that they can apply. When employers ask for information about a student, they are given copies of the information kept in the student's placement folder. If your school offers a placement service, perhaps through the counseling center, you should examine your folder and ask teachers and other adults to write recommendations to put in your folder. You should also check to see that all school records are in the folder.

Employers ask about attendance.

Be sure to check at your school to see what other types of assistance are available to you.

PERIODICALS, BOOKS, AND OTHER PUBLICATIONS

Your library has much information about jobs.

Your local public library and your school library are good resource centers where you can find information about jobs. You can find facts about which jobs will and will not be available in the future. You can also read about job descriptions, opportunities for employment, benefits, and requirements.

One good job sourcebook is the *Occupational Outlook Handbook*, published yearly by the U.S. Department of Labor. This book contains current information about most jobs throughout the country. At the library you will also find many government and industry publications that present information about job trends, kinds of jobs, employment possibilities, skills needed, and education requirements. Your librarian can assist you in finding and using such publications.

In addition, many current periodicals contain timely information about selected occupations. You might want to look at magazines such as *Time, U.S. News & World Report, Fortune,* and *BusinessWeek*. The library's *Guide to Current Periodicals* or *Guide to Business Periodicals* will assist you in locating information by topic, article title, or author.

PUBLIC AND PRIVATE EMPLOYMENT AGENCIES

Employment agency fees vary greatly.

All major cities have private and public employment agencies whose business is to help you find jobs for which you are qualified and to help employers locate the best applicants for job openings. Private employment agencies may or may not charge a fee for their services. Such fees vary from agency to agency, so you should compare prices before you sign with an agency. Some of these private agencies charge a fee to the employer, others charge the job-seeker a fee when a job is found, and still others divide the fee between the employer and the person hired. The state employment office does not charge a fee because it is a government agency.

At the state employment office, you can also obtain information about government job training assistance programs, YES (Youth Employment Service), Youth Corps, Civil Service (state and federal), and other employment programs that are sometimes available. You may qualify for one or more of these types of work programs.

Illustration 1-2
Libraries are good
resource centers
where you can find
information about
jobs.

NEWSPAPER, TELEPHONE BOOK, AND PRIVATE JOB LISTINGS

Job openings are often advertised.

The *help-wanted ads* in the classified section of your local newspaper consist of job openings in your area. Brief descriptions of the positions are given, often with salary ranges specified. By keeping a close watch on these ads, you can tell when a new job enters the market and be quick to respond. Both employers and employment agencies advertise job openings to attract qualified applicants. You may be asked to send a letter of application and a resume to an employer before you will be granted an interview. In the next chapter you will learn how to prepare a letter of application and a resume.

The Yellow Pages of the telephone book is an alphabetic subject listing of businesses advertising their services. If you are looking for a job in a certain field, determine the subject heading under which that type of work might be classified. Under that heading, you will find a list of companies to help you begin your job search. You may want to send letters of application and resumes to all those listed, asking to be considered for the next opening.

Many companies, government offices, and schools place job opening announcements on bulletin boards, circulate them within the company, and post them in other special locations. Checking in these places may give you inside information to apply for a position at the right time. The first persons to apply for a job opening often have an advantage over those who apply at the last minute.

JOB SEARCH TECHNIQUES
◆◆◆◆◆◆◆◆

Finding and getting the right job does not happen by accident. It takes hard work, careful planning, and often a great deal of time. Nevertheless, it is important that you put in sufficient time and effort to ensure that you get a job you enjoy and can stay with. Dissatisfaction leads to frequent job changing, which may damage your employment chances in the future. Your **work history**, a record of the jobs you have held and how long you stayed with each employer, will be important to future employers. If your record shows that you changed jobs six times in six months, you will appear immature and unstable to future employers. In this example, your work history will hurt your chances of getting a job you might want very much.

Job search techniques that will help you find and get the right job are discussed in the following paragraphs.

Your work history should show stability.

GET ORGANIZED

After you have decided what kind of job you want, the first step is to get organized. Gather all the information you will need about the type of work you want to do. Prepare a list of prospective companies for which you would like to work. Check your sources of information and research job descriptions, skills and aptitudes needed, and other requirements. Make lists of personal contacts, places to go, and people to see. Type a current resume and letter of application. Ask previous employers, teachers, or others to write letters of recommendation for you. Update your placement folder at school. You may want to prepare a checklist of things to do and check them off as they are completed.

Gather all the information you can about a job.

MAKE A PLAN

A plan is important to the success of your job search because it keeps you organized, shows what you have done, and indicates what you need to do in the immediate future. A good plan lists all your goals and shows a time frame for getting them done. As each step or goal is accomplished, it should be checked off. A plan you might want to follow is shown in Figure 1-6.

A good plan lists all your goals in a time frame.

Figure 1-6
Plan to Get a Job

Plan to Get a Job

Job Leads: — State employment office
— Help wanted ads (newspaper)
— School placement office
— Marketing teacher

Contacts: — Uncle Henry (knows the manager of local Penney's)

Time Line—Week 1
Day 1: — Type resume and letter of application
— Check help wanted ads
— Make list of local stores from Yellow Pages

Day 2: — Send two application letters
— Get two personal references
— Call Uncle Henry to set a date for lunch

Note: Any planned activities that are not completed this week should be brought forward to next week's plan.

FOLLOW-THROUGH

This difficult step is the most important. After you have contacted a potential employer by letter or by filling out a job application, after you have met a personnel manager or had an interview, it is important that you follow through. This means checking back from time to time to say that you are still interested in the job. Call back in a day or two to check on the job and remain courteous and optimistic. The employer needs to know that you want the job very much and that you are still interested and available.

DON'T GIVE UP

Before you finally get a good job, you will probably be turned down for several other jobs for which you have applied. When your first and second efforts appear to be fruitless, remain calm and courteous, and keep checking back for openings. Try all your employment leads. Thank your contacts, especially those in your network. Be prepared at all times, so that if you are called to come in for an interview on short notice — even on the same day — you can do so. Continually check the want ads for new openings. Call back

Check with your con-
tacts frequently.

when you have established a contact, and check with your contacts frequently. Although a thorough job search may take several weeks or months, it will pay off. With careful planning and research, you can find the job that will meet your needs, wants, and goals.

VOCABULARY

Directions: Can you find the definition for each of the following terms used in Chapter 1?

identity	goal
values	contact
life-style	networking
aptitude	placement service
personality	work history

1. The beliefs in your life that are important to you.
2. A natural physical or mental ability.
3. Personal qualities and traits that make you unique.
4. A person you know in a business to give you inside information about a job.
5. The record of jobs you have held.
6. A description of who and what you are.
7. The way you choose to live your life, based on your values.
8. An end toward which efforts are directed.
9. A service that sends out school records and other information used to help students secure employment.
10. The process of maintaining information sources; a personal and professional support system.

ITEMS FOR DISCUSSION

1. Why do people work?
2. What is your identity at this time in your life? (You may have more than one.)
3. Define *values*. List three of your parents' values and three of your own.
4. Why is choice of a career considered to be an important decision?
5. What is manual dexterity? Why might it be important to you to know if you have manual dexterity?
6. What is meant by *personal traits*? List three.
7. What are the four major steps in good career planning?
8. Why do people need to set goals in life?

9.   What are (a) short-term, (b) intermediate, and (c) long-term goals?
10.   What is meant by the term *locked in*?
11.   How can you establish personal contacts within a business where you don't know anyone?
12.   What is meant by *networking*?
13.   What are placement services? What types of placement services are available at your school?
14.   Who publishes the *Occupational Outlook Handbook*? What does it contain?
15.   Why should you compare different private employment agencies before signing up with one of them?
16.   Describe the Yellow Pages of your telephone book. What does it contain? How is the information listed?

APPLICATIONS

1.   From Figure 1-1, list the activities that appeal to you. Can you think of several occupations that offer these types of activities?
2.   Make a list of personality traits that would be important in three different types of work (for example, secretary, accountant, mechanic). Your best source of information is someone in these types of work. Ask which personality traits are more successful.
3.   Describe the life-style you hope to be enjoying ten years from now. Include the things you want to have and what you want to be. Consider such factors as marriage, family, housing, and job title. Will the job you want to work at support the life-style you desire?
4.   Research three different types of careers, using the resources available to you. (Suggestions: *Occupational Outlook Handbook* and current periodicals.) For each occupation, list job description, job requirements (including education), working hours, salary range, and other information.
5.   Using Figure 1-4 as an example, prepare your personal self-evaluation inventory, listing your strengths, weaknesses, and plans of action.
6.   Using Figure 1-5 as an example, prepare a checklist that contains short-term, intermediate, and long-term goals. At the end of the week, check to see what you have accomplished.
7.   Cut these types of want ads from the classified section of your local newspaper: three ads by private employers, three ads by private employment agencies, one ad for someone to make a cash investment, one ad for someone in a sales position (to work on commission rather than for a salary), and one ad that gives the beginning salary in a dollar amount.

8. Using your telephone book, list ten private employment agencies, their addresses, and their phone numbers. Also list the address and phone number of the state employment office. Call one of the private agencies and ask a counselor the fee for a job that would pay approximately $1,000 a month, and ask who would pay the fee.

9. Write a paragraph describing your work history. It can be current or what you would like it to be in ten years.

10. List and describe the four steps in an effective job search.

11. Using Figure 1-6 as an example, prepare a plan to get yourself a job using a one-week timetable. List your job leads, your contacts (or potential ones), and a daily plan to accomplish several things each day.

12. Define the term *follow-through*.

CASE PROBLEMS AND ACTIVITIES

1. Give five or more activities (see Figure 1-1) that would be a part of the work involved in each of the following occupations: carpenter, forest ranger, teacher, social worker.

2. Using the *Occupational Outlook Handbook* and the format shown on p. 20, prepare a career report for one occupation you are interested in.

3. Robbie Goodman has decided that his long-term goal in life is to become an astronaut. He is now a sophomore in high school and hasn't done any planning. His grades are average; he is active, outgoing, and bright. What can Robbie do now, in the next few years and beyond, to prepare himself for a career as an astronaut?

4. Using Figure 1-3 as a guide, classify each of the following job titles into one of the nine job classifications. You may have to do some research to determine types of activities performed, skills and education required, working hours, and beginning pay.

   a. log scaler
   b. court reporter
   c. sheet-metal worker
   d. technical writer
   e. building custodian
   f. underwriter
   g. mechanical engineer
   h. sonar operator
   i. cosmetologist
   j. physical therapist
   k. computer programmer
   l. radio announcer
   m. singer
   n. infantry officer
   o. administrative assistant
   p. FBI agent
   q. tailor

5. Maria Ramos wants to be an accountant when she completes high school. She is taking accounting courses and is working part-time at

CAREER REPORT

Name of career:_____

Year of handbook:_____ Info. located on pp.:_____

1. What is the nature of the work?_____

_____

_____

2. Describe the average working conditions._____

_____

3. List possible places of employment. _____

_____

4. What training is needed for this type of work?_____

_____

5. What is the employment outlook for this career across the country?_____

_____

6. What salary can you expect to earn as a beginning worker in this career?__

_____

7. What personality traits are needed for success in this career?_____

_____

_____

8. Where can you find additional information about this career?_____

_____

_____

the ice cream store. What should Maria be doing to prevent herself from becoming locked into her job at the ice cream store?

6. Tom Reynolds would like to work as a merchandising manager for a large department store. He has all the qualifications, education, and skills necessary, but Tom doesn't know anyone in any large stores, and most openings are filled before he even knows they exist. What can Tom do to find out about job openings in the large department stores?

7. A networking notebook is a project you could start now and work on throughout your life. It is an organized method for keeping track of such things as what you've done, who your friends are and how to contact them, business associates (you might collect business cards), addresses, and telephone numbers. A suggested table of contents might include the following sections: business card file; names and

addresses of personal friends; up-to-date resume; letters of reference; self-evaluation inventory; checklist of short-term, intermediate, and long-term goals; and career reports using the *Occupational Outlook Handbook*. Can you list the sections you would insert into a notebook that you might start now and keep updated through the years?

8. Sarah Maxwell is a sophomore in high school. She plans to use the placement service of her high school to get a part-time job in her senior year. What should Sarah do between now and her senior year to be sure her placement folder is complete when she is ready to find a job?

9. Ron Kensey has worked part-time after school for the past two years. He worked for two weeks as a cook, but rarely got to work on time and was fired. He worked for two months as a busboy but quit because he didn't get enough tips. Ron also worked for three weeks as a janitor but was laid off. Finally, he worked for four months as a plumber's assistant but quit because the work hurt his back. What is Ron's record of job changes called? What does it say to potential employers? Would you hire Ron? Why or why not?

Chapter 2

GETTING THE JOB

◆◆◆◆◆◆◆◆◆◆◆◆◆◆◆◆◆◆◆◆◆◆◆◆◆◆◆

OBJECTIVES

1. Prepare the necessary job application tools (letter of application, resume, letter of reference, application form, and thank-you letter).
2. Identify and describe appropriate job interview techniques.
3. Understand the steps in successful job application and the proper time to use the application tools.

LETTER OF APPLICATION

◆◆◆◆◆◆◆◆

Your initial job application should consist of a letter of application and a resume. The **letter of application** is an important tool in the application process: it introduces you to the potential employer and gives you a chance to "sell" your qualifications.

PREPARING THE LETTER OF APPLICATION

Generally, the letter of application should be typed on white, standard size (8½- by 11-inch) paper of good quality. The mailing envelope should be of

Illustration 2-1
Employers carefully
review all applica-
tion materials to
find the best person
for the job.

A letter of reference
helps your applica-
tion.

the same color and quality. You may also use personal letterhead stationery with matching envelope. Use Figure 2-1A as a guide when you type your own letter of application.

You may wish to enclose a copy of your school records or a letter of reference with your letter of application and resume. Remember to refer to all enclosures within the body of the letter. Enclosures should also be listed at the end of the letter in a separate notation.

If a handwritten letter of application is required, be sure to follow the same guidelines. Use standard size plain white paper and leave the same amount of space between parts so that spacing on the final product looks very much like a typed letter.

PARTS OF THE LETTER OF APPLICATION

There are five basic parts to a letter of application. They are the return address, the inside address, the salutation, the body, and the complimentary close.

Return Address.   The **return address** shows your address to the person you are writing so that he or she can write back. The return address contains your complete address and the date of the letter, but it *does not* contain your name.

Inside Address.   The **inside address** contains the name and address of the person or company you are writing. It should be a complete address. You should make every effort to determine the name and title of the person you are writing, avoiding the use of "Personnel Manager" whenever possible. If you are unable to determine whether the person you are writing is male or female, you may wish to use the less personal style of business letter — the AMS Simplified version — as shown in Figure 2-1B.

Salutation. Also known as the greeting, the **salutation** addresses your letter to the particular person you want to read the message. The person's name or other form of address is followed by a colon. "Dear Mr. Smith:" and "Dear Sir or Madam:" are examples of salutations. You should avoid using the words "To Whom it May Concern" in an application letter. Notice that there is no salutation in the Simplified format. Instead, there is a subject line. This makes the letter less personal and more businesslike.

Body. The **body** of the letter contains four basic parts and should be three or four paragraphs long. These paragraphs should attract the employer's attention, state your interest in the company and position, arouse the employer's desire to interview you, and request that the employer take action in the form of an interview. These parts of the body are often referred to as AIDA — attention, interest, desire, and action.

Complimentary Close. After you have stated your business, a **complimentary close** of "Sincerely yours" or some other appropriate phrase courteously ends your letter. Your name is typed below the closing to allow space for signing the letter. The Simplified format does not include the complimentary close, but goes directly to your name, again eliminating the personal touch.

Below your typed name, make notations for enclosures that will accompany the letter.

Find out all you can about the interviewer.

Consider the purpose of the letter.

RESUME
◆◆◆◆◆◆◆◆

A **resume**, also called a personal data sheet, biographical summary, professional profile, or vita, is a concise summary of personal information. It briefly describes your work experience, education, abilities, and interests. The resume can be a valuable tool for getting a job because it tells the employer neatly and concisely who you are, what you can do, and what your special interests are. You can also list references (names and addresses) on the resume — people who can tell a prospective employer about your work habits, character, and skills. It is a good idea to prepare a typed resume and have it ready to send or give to potential employers. Figure 2-2 shows a commonly used resume style.

Your resume sells you to an employer.

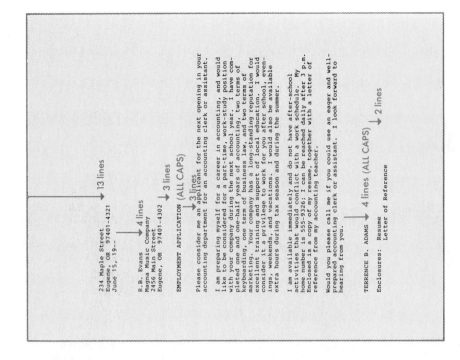

Figure 2-1B   AMS Simplified Version

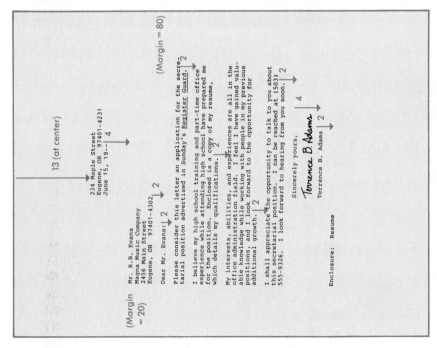

Figure 2-1A   Letter of Application

Figure 2-2
Resume

```
                    TERRENCE B. ADAMS
                     234 Maple Street
                  Eugene, OR  97401-4321

                      (503) 555-9326

                    CAREER OBJECTIVE

An office administration or accounting position that provides
challenge, increasing responsibility, and opportunity for growth
and advancement.

                       EDUCATION

1985-88  Madison High School, Eugene, Oregon  GPA 3.00 and higher
         Major course of study:  Business and college preparatory
1983-85  Wilson Junior High School, Eugene, Oregon  GPA 3.5 and
         higher

                        SKILLS

Typing (70 wpm)   Meeting the public   IBM Personal Computer
Filing            Public speaking      Software:  word
Accounting        Ten-key calculator     processing and
Telephone use     Scientific calculator  electronic spreadsheet

                 EXTRACURRICULAR ACTIVITIES

Member of National Honor Society; President, senior year (1987-88)
Senior class student council representative
Member of debate team, junior year (1986-87)
Secretary of FBLA (Future Business Leaders of America), sophomore
     year (1985-86)
Competitor at FBLA district and state events in business law and
     accounting

                      EXPERIENCE

Assistant File Clerk, Farwest Truck Center, Eugene Oregon (June
     1987-present)
     Duties include filing, typing, operating a word processor
     (IBM Personal Computer with Word Star 2000 software).

Office Assistant, Coast Carloading, Eugene, Oregon (1986-87)
     Duties included running errands, some typing and filing,
     greeting customers, and answering the telephone.

Host/Cashier, Pancake House Restaurant, Eugene, Oregon (1985,
     summer)
     Duties included greeting and seating customers, operating
     cash register (part-time work).

Part-time summer and weekend jobs (1983-85) including mowing
     lawns, paper route, and volunteer camp counselor at Day Star
     Camp Grounds (supervising eight-year-olds).

                      REFERENCES

Provided on request.
```

GENERAL GUIDELINES

Keep the following guidelines in mind when planning and preparing your resume:

Keep your resume short.

1. Keep your resume to one page, if possible, by carefully arranging the information you choose to include.
2. Include all information pertinent to the job for which you are

applying.   Be honest, but emphasize your strong points.

3.   Unless a particular employer requests otherwise, type the resume on good quality, 8½- by 11-inch paper.

4.   Use a format that is attractive and that displays the information in an easy-to-read fashion. Place the most important items in the upper one-third of the page.

5.   Proofread the finished copy — there should be no errors. Make corrections with care. You might want to use a letter quality printer, carbon ribbon typewriter, or other clear typestyle. The resume you present to a potential employer should not contain poor erasures or messy correction fluid blotches.

PARTS OF THE RESUME

You may arrange your resume according to your preference. In general, there are six basic parts to a simple resume. It should include limited personal information, career objective, education, work experience, additional qualifications and skills or special items of interest, and references. People often choose to list their references on the resume until they have adequate other data to replace them. When references are not listed on a resume, it is desirable to say: "Provided on request" so that prospective employers know that such information is readily available.

Notify your references that you are using their names.

Personal Information.   This section should be placed first on the resume. Information usually includes name, address, and phone number. You may also wish to include other data, such as message telephone or social security number. Information such as age, sex, marital status, number of dependents, and ethnic background cannot lawfully be demanded by potential employers (although you may offer it if you wish). Generally, such personal information is omitted from resumes.

Career Objective.   Below the personal information, you should place a short, assertive statement indicating your career goal (for example, a goal to obtain a particular position title). Make the statement forward-looking, interesting, and specific. This statement helps the employer identify with your plans while revealing your interest and enthusiasm for the job and for your future. Avoid weak and unimpressive statements such as, "Any type of work in the office."

Make the objective statement clear and forceful.

Education.   List all secondary and post-secondary schools you have attended, starting with the most recent. You may wish to include major areas of study, grade point average, extracurricular activities, scholastic honors, specific courses that apply to the job opening (such as marketing), or any other pertinent facts that you think will create a favorable impression on the employer. Extracurricular activities tell an employer that you are a well-rounded person and possess many different abilities, interests, and aptitudes. Listing any offices held in school organizations or clubs will show the employer that you have leadership ability. Be sure to include dates or years of attendance for each school.

Work Experience. List all jobs, paid and unpaid, that you have held, including assisting at school functions, working as a teacher's aide, and any part-time or full-time summer or vacation jobs (such as camp counselor or errand person). You may want to write this section of your resume in paragraph or outline form. Include information such as name and address of employer, job title, work duties, and specific achievements while with this employer. Emphasize your work rather than dates of employment or name of employer.

> Volunteer and un-paid work also count.

Additional Qualifications. Educational and employment records present an overview of your personal and professional qualifications. However, you may have additional skills and abilities that you wish to bring to a potential employer's attention. You may want to list special equipment you have learned to operate, languages you know, or special talents you have (such as playing the piano), or you may call attention to an especially high typing or shorthand speed. You can also list honors you have received or contests you have won. All of these things give an employer a more complete picture of your personality and your achievements.

> Emphasize your special qualifications.

References. **References** are persons who have known you for at least one year, and who can provide information about your character and achievements. References should be over age 18 and not related to you. The best types of references include teachers, school counselors, former employers, and adults in business. Be sure to ask permission of the people you wish to list as references before including them on your resume. If you choose not to list references on your resume, you should nevertheless have names, addresses, and telephone numbers ready for employers who ask for them.

LETTER OF REFERENCE

◆◆◆◆◆◆◆◆

> Ask for letters of reference now.

A **letter of reference** is a statement, in letter form, written by someone who can be relied upon to give a sincere report on your character, abilities, and experience. When you ask someone to write a letter of reference for you, be sure to give the person enough time to compose and type the letter. It is also helpful to give them a copy of your current resume or a short summary of your accomplishments and background. Be sure to ask a business reference to type the letter on letterhead stationery. A sample letter of reference is shown in Figure 2-3.

Figure 2-3
Letter of Reference

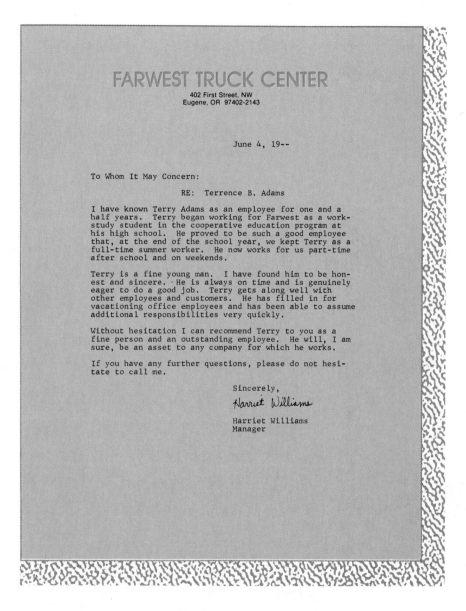

FARWEST TRUCK CENTER

402 First Street, NW
Eugene, OR 97402-2143

June 4, 19--

To Whom It May Concern:

RE: Terrence B. Adams

I have known Terry Adams as an employee for one and a half years. Terry began working for Farwest as a work-study student in the cooperative education program at his high school. He proved to be such a good employee that, at the end of the school year, we kept Terry as a full-time summer worker. He now works for us part-time after school and on weekends.

Terry is a fine young man. I have found him to be honest and sincere. He is always on time and is genuinely eager to do a good job. Terry gets along well with other employees and customers. He has filled in for vacationing office employees and has been able to assume additional responsibilities very quickly.

Without hesitation I can recommend Terry to you as a fine person and an outstanding employee. He will, I am sure, be an asset to any company for which he works.

If you have any further questions, please do not hesitate to call me.

Sincerely,

Harriet Williams

Harriet Williams
Manager

When you receive the letter of reference, make several photocopies of the original to give to employers along with your resume and letter of application. Keep the original letter of reference for your files because you may need additional copies for other job applications.

APPLICATION FORM
◆◆◆◆◆◆◆◆

Fill out the applica-
tion carefully.

When you visit a company to interview or to inquire about a job opening, you will probably be asked to complete an **application for employment**. When completing an application for employment, you should follow these steps:

1. Type your answers, or print them neatly using a black or dark blue pen that does not skip or blot. Keep your responses in the space provided.
2. Fill in all the blanks. When you cannot answer a question, write N/A (information not available or not applicable), or use a broken line (- - - -) to indicate to the employer that you have not skipped or ignored the question.
3. Be truthful. Give complete answers. Do not abbreviate unless the meaning of the abbreviation is clear.

Take needed infor-
mation with you.

4. Have with you all information that might be requested on the application form, such as social security number, telephone numbers, driver's license number, or work permit number. Calling later with the rest of the needed information inconveniences the employer.

A completed application for employment is shown in Figure 2-4.

JOB INTERVIEW
◆◆◆◆◆◆◆◆

During the job interview, an employer will have your completed job application, together with your resume, letter of application, letter(s) of reference, and any other information you have provided. A **job interview** is a procedure in which you may be questioned about statements you have made on the application for employment, or about information contained in the resume and letters. Therefore, you should spend at least as much time and effort in preparing for the interview as you did in obtaining the appointment.

Figure 2-4
Application of Employment

APPLICATION FOR EMPLOYMENT

PLEASE PRINT WITH BLACK INK OR USE TYPEWRITER   AN EQUAL OPPORTUNITY EMPLOYER

NAME (LAST, FIRST, MIDDLE INITIAL)	SOCIAL SECURITY NUMBER	DATE
Adams Terrence B.	643-27-1364	6/24/—

ADDRESS (NUMBER, STREET, CITY, STATE, ZIP CODE)	TELEPHONE NUMBER
234 Maple Street Eugene, OR 97401-4231	(503) 555-9326

IN CASE OF EMERGENCY, NOTIFY:	NAME Thomas and Rita Adams	RELATIONSHIP Parents
	ADDRESS same as above	

EDUCATION

	SCHOOL NAME	CITY AND STATE	YEARS ATTENDED
HIGH SCHOOL	Madison High School	Eugene, Oregon	1985-1988
JUNIOR HIGH SCHOOL	Wilson Junior High School	Eugene, Oregon	1983-1985
OTHER	Lane Community College	Eugene, Oregon	1988-1989

SKILLS

TYPING	SHORTHAND	ACCOUNTING	FILING
70 wpm	No	Yes (1½ yrs.)	Yes

OTHER SKILLS (LIST) Telephone Use

MACHINES YOU CAN OPERATE (LIST) Calculator, Ten-Key Adding Machine, IBM Word Processor, Copier, Cash Register

WORK HISTORY (LAST POSITION FIRST)

FROM	TO	EMPLOYER NAME/ADDRESS	POSITION	ENDING PAY	REASON FOR LEAVING
June, 1987	Present	Farwest Truck Center Eugene, Oregon	Assistant File Clerk	$4.35/hr	Desire More Responsibility
December 1986	June, 1987	Coast Car loading Eugene, Oregon	Office Helper	Minimum wage	More Responsibility
June, 1985	August, 1985	Pancake House Restaurant Eugene, Oregon	Host/ Cashier	Minimum wage	More Time For School

REFERENCES

NAME	ADDRESS	OCCUPATION	TELEPHONE NUMBER
Ms. Grace Lawton	Eugene, Oregon	Manager/Valley Title	(503) 555-6121
Mr. Patrick Bailey	Eugene, Oregon	Business Teacher	(503) 555-0731
Miss Frances Bishop	Eugene, Oregon	Work Experience Coordinator	(503) 555-0731

I understand and agree that any false statements on this application may be considered sufficient cause for dismissal.

Terrence B. Adams
SIGNATURE OF APPLICANT

PREPARING FOR THE INTERVIEW

Preparation is essential to a successful interview. First, you should review your resume so that all your personal information and qualifications will be fresh in your mind. Be prepared to state this information briefly during the interview.

It is also important to learn something about the company. Find out what the company makes or sells, where its plants and branch operations are

Rehearse before the
actual interview.

located, how rapidly it has grown, and what its prospects are for the future. Think of questions you might ask the interviewer about the company and about the position for which you are applying. The prospective employer will be more interested in you as an employee if you show that you are interested in the company. Be prepared for certain questions that are inevitable, such as "Tell me about yourself," or "Why do you want to work for us?"

Plan your interview strategy.

Information about companies can be obtained from such sources as these:

1. The Yellow Pages of the telephone directory, which may have an advertisement that will list products or services
2. The company itself (simply call and request the information you need)
3. A friend who works for the company and can give you good information
4. Annual reports (usually kept on file at public and university libraries), which describe the company and its financial resources
5. Current periodicals and newspaper articles, which may discuss the company's economic health or plans for expansion and growth

MAKING A GOOD FIRST IMPRESSION

Several important details should be remembered in preparing to make a favorable impression:

Arrive early for the interview.

Arrive on Time.   Better yet, arrive five to ten minutes early so you have time to check your appearance and compose yourself. Never be late to an interview: The interviewer will consider your tardiness an indication of your expected job performance. Time your travel route before the day of the interview, then allow extra time for traffic and parking.

Dress Appropriately.   If you are seeking work in a bank, dress like those already employed at the bank. Whatever you wear, be neat and clean. Do not overuse jewelry, perfume, or after-shave. Be modest and conservative in dress, hair style, and appearance. In other words, look like you already have the job.

Go Alone.   Do not bring along a friend or relative. Only you will perform the job if hired; therefore, the interviewer wishes to talk to you alone.

Be Prepared.   Have copies of your resume, reference letters, and school transcripts with you. All should be typed neatly and accurately. Take with you a pad of paper and one or two good pens, articles you have found at the library concerning the company, and other information you may need or find useful. Bring such papers in a briefcase or some type of carrying folder to keep them neat and organized.

Illustration 2-2
Poised, self-confident people make the best impressions at job interviews.

Appear Poised and Self-Confident. It is normal to be nervous, but don't let your emotions control you. It is important to appear relaxed and comfortable. Maintain good eye contact with the interviewer. Do not chew gum, smoke, or display nervous habits. An occasional smile shows you are relaxed and feel good about yourself. Avoid chattering to fill quiet times; allow the interviewer to lead the discussion.

Smile to show self-confidence.

Be Courteous. Even if you are asked to wait, respond with courtesy and understanding. Convey an attitude of composure and congeniality. Use "please" and "thank you."

Think Before You Answer Each Question. Be polite, accurate, and honest. Use correct grammar; be especially careful of verb tenses. Speak slowly and clearly.

Speak slowly and pause before answering questions.

Emphasize Your Strong Points. Talk about your favorite school subjects, grades, attendance, skills, work experience, activities, and goals in a positive manner. Negative comments are inappropriate and reflect badly on your personality.

Be Enthusiastic and Interested in the Company and the Job. Show that you are energetic and able to do what is asked with a willing attitude. Let the interviewer know that you are interested in the company, in the job and career, in your future, and in what's going on in the world. Above all, let common sense be your guide throughout the interview; look for nonverbal and other cues from the interviewer, listening carefully, and seeking to understand the needs and wants of the company that is hiring.

Leave copies, not originals, for the employer.

When the interview is over, thank the interviewer for his or her time. Say you will check back later, then do it. Leave a copy of your resume, letters of reference, and other information with the interviewer. Exit with a smile and an I-look-forward-to-working-for-this-company type of comment.

THANK-YOU LETTER

◆◆◆◆◆◆◆◆

When your job interview is completed and the employer is left to make a decision, a **follow-up** is essential. Positive contact with the employer after the interview will remind the employer of your appearance, personality, and qualifications, and should improve your chance of getting the job. A **thank-you letter** is an excellent follow-up tool to remind the interviewer of your interest in and desire to work for the company.

Reaffirm your interest with a letter.

A brief thank-you letter should be written to the employer to express your appreciation for having been given the interview. This letter will also reaffirm your interest in the job and give you an opportunity to restate some of your qualifications for the position. See Figure 2-5 for a sample thank-you letter.

BASIC RULES

Keep the thank-you letter short and interesting.

The thank-you letter should be short and simple. Follow the same format and typing guidelines that you used in preparing your letter of application. You may want to enclose an additional letter of reference or some information that may help convince the interviewer to hire you. Remember to address the interviewer by name. If more than one person interviewed you during your visit, write a brief letter to each person.

BODY OF THE LETTER

The content of the thank-you letter is very important. The first paragraph should remind the interviewer of your interview by making reference to it. A good way to begin is as follows: "Thank you for giving me the opportunity to speak with you on (date and time of interview) concerning. . . ."

The second paragraph reminds the interviewer of your interest in and desire to work for the company. At this point, you could also remind the

Figure 2-5
Thank-You Letter

```
                              234 Maple Street
                              Eugene, OR  97401-4231
                              June 25, 19--


          Mr. R. B. Evans
          Magna Music Company
          2456 Main Street
          Eugene, OR  97401-4302

          Dear Mr. Evans:

          Thank you for the time you spent with me during our inter-
          view yesterday.  I enjoyed the opportunity to meet you
          and some of your office staff.

          Your description of the secretarial position sounded very
          interesting to me.  I am sure this is a position for
          which I am qualified, and I would enjoy working for your
          company.  You can be assured I am a very dependable and
          conscientious worker.  If there is any additional infor-
          mation that I can supply for you, please do not hesitate
          to call me.  I plan to make a career in the office admin-
          istration area and am, therefore, available for long-
          term employment.

          I look forward to hearing from you soon.

                              Sincerely yours,

                              Terrence B. Adams

                              Terrence B. Adams
```

Remind the interviewer of your strengths.

interviewer of your abilities, goals, and qualifications in a subtle, modest manner. You might add the times when you are available and the number where you can be reached.

The final paragraph should express courteously your eagerness to hear from the interviewer when he or she has reached a decision. This paragraph should end on a positive note.

Keep your letter short and to the point, and make sure it is error-free. Your final opportunity to represent yourself to the potential employer through a thank-you letter may make the difference that will get you the job.

VOCABULARY

Directions: Can you find the definition for each of the following terms used in Chapter 2?

letter of application   references
return address   letter of reference
inside address   application for employment
salutation   job interview
body   follow up
complimentary close   thank-you letter
resume

1. The part of a letter that shows the writer's street address, city, state, ZIP Code, and date of the letter.
2. The greeting, using a person's name followed by a colon.
3. The part of a letter that shows the name and address of the person or company to whom you are writing.
4. A summary of personal information, education, experience, additional qualifications, and references of a person seeking a job.
5. The main portion of a letter having four main parts.
6. People over 18, not related to you, who have known you for at least one year and can report on your character and achievements.
7. A written statement from someone who knows you; it should be typed.
8. A form you fill out when you apply for a job.
9. A procedure whereby you are asked questions about yourself, your work experience, and your education, and you respond orally.
10. A letter to an employer asking for a job interview.
11. The appropriate phrase which courteously ends a personal business letter.
12. A tool to remind the employer of your interest in the job, written after the job interview.
13. A final contact, usually a thank-you letter, made after a job interview and before the interviewer makes a decision.

ITEMS FOR DISCUSSION

1. What is the purpose of a letter of application? What action is desired? What do the letters AIDA stand for?
2. What size paper should you use for a letter of application or a thank-you letter?
3. List and describe briefly the five basic parts of a letter of application.

4.   When would you use the AMS Simplified letter format for a letter of application?
5.   What is a resume? Describe the parts you will include in your own resume.
6.   Why should you list extracurricular activities on your resume?
7.   Which kinds of people should be used as references on a resume?
8.   List four rules for filling out an application for employment.
9.   What is meant by the term *follow-up*?
10.   What is the content of the body of the thank-you letter?
11.   Why is it important for you to type your resume, letter of application, and thank-you letter?

APPLICATIONS

1.   Using Figure 2-1A or 2-1B as an example, prepare a letter of application to a business or company that you would like to work for. Read the instructions on pages 22-24 carefully. (Figure 2-1A shows the point of contact as a newspaper ad; Figure 2-1B shows an unsolicited letter of application.)
2.   Using Figure 2-2 as an example, prepare your resume, or prepare a resume of your own design. Include all information that applies to you, emphasizing your strong points.
3.   Call, write, or speak directly to each person listed on your resume as a reference (or would use when asked for references), and ask permission to use their names on your resume or for job interview purposes. Ask one person to write a letter of reference for you to use in seeking a job.
4.   Obtain from a local business an application for employment, such as the one shown in Figure 2-4, and complete it.
5.   Write a thank-you letter for a job interview, using Figure 2-5 as an example. Assume you were interviewed by the person to whom you sent your letter of application (see Question 1). You should know the interviewer's name now. Address the person by name and title.

CASE PROBLEMS AND ACTIVITIES

1.   Prepare a basic example of a letter of application, so that when you actually do apply for a job you will have the content outlined for actual use. In red pen, write in the directions for vertical spacing, margins, and letter parts. Use Figures 2-1A and B as examples.
2.   Mike Smith wants to work as a forest ranger when he graduates from college. At present, he knows of no openings, but does know the address of the local Bureau of Land Management, which

occasionally hires students during summers to help in the forest. Mike takes science courses and does well. He is available to work all summer, and could even work without pay if his living expenses were covered. Because you are Mike's friend, you have offered to help him write a letter of application. Make up a return address, inside address, salutation (or use Simplified format), body, and complimentary close, using the letters of application in Figures 2-1A and B as guides.

3. Naomi Moothart must provide a resume in order to answer an advertisement in the local newspaper. Write in outline form a summary of the basic rules of writing a resume. On another piece of paper, sketch a resume and label its parts. You do not need to insert fictional information — just describe what kinds of information Naomi should use.

4. Pam Olefson tells you that she has a job interview tomorrow. She has never been on a job interview before, and she is very nervous. Pam asks you to point out to her what she should and should not do during her interview. On a piece of paper, make a list for Pam of at least five things she should be sure to do and five things she should avoid during her job interview.

5. Lee O'Leary has just completed a job interview. The interviewer will see six more applicants over three days before she makes a decision. Lee knows that his competition is tough, but believes he stands a good chance of getting the job because he is available to work right away, his grades are high, and he has taken three marketing courses. Would you advise him to write a follow-up (thank-you) letter? What might he say in such a letter?

Chapter 3

KEEPING YOUR JOB

◆◆◆◆◆◆◆◆◆◆◆◆◆◆◆◆◆◆◆◆◆◆◆◆◆◆◆

OBJECTIVES

1. Understand and complete appropriate work forms, such as W-4, social security application, and work permit application.
2. Understand and recall employee responsibilities and employer responsibilities to employees.
3. List and define provisions of basic employment laws enacted for protection and security of workers.
4. Understand and describe effective human relations skills for survival in organizations.

WORK FORMS
◆◆◆◆◆◆◆◆

When you begin your first paying job, you will need to be aware of a number of forms. Most of these ask for information that employers are required by law to keep. Some of these forms can be obtained prior to beginning work (social security card and work permit, if you are under 16), while others are completed by you when you begin working (W-4) and by the employer after you have worked during the year (W-2). Immigration laws require that employers obtain information from all workers hired after January 1, 1987, to prove that each worker is legally entitled to work. This required information includes birth certificate and social security card, or photo identification and proof of eligibility to work.

FORM W-4, EMPLOYEE'S WITHHOLDING ALLOWANCE CERTIFICATE

When you first report to work, you will be asked to fill out a **Form W-4, Employee's Withholding Allowance Certificate**. Form W-4 is for income tax withholding purposes and remains in effect until you make a change. On this form you declare your total number of allowances. An **allowance** is a person who is dependent on your income for support. The more allowances you can claim, the less tax you will have withheld. You may automatically claim yourself. Other allowances can be claimed for spouse, children, or if your itemized deductions allow less money to be withheld from your paycheck. You fill out the worksheet that accompanies the W-4 certificate, giving the employer only the certificate that is shown in Figure 3-1. You may also claim **exempt** status and not have any federal tax withheld from your paycheck, if you qualify, by writing *exempt* as shown in Figure 3-1. You may claim to be exempt if you will not earn enough money to owe any federal tax. The amount of maximum earnings varies as new tax laws are passed. Exemption may be claimed if last year you owed no federal tax and had a right to receive a full refund and if this year you do not expect to owe any federal tax and expect a full refund.

Claim exempt status if you qualify.

Figure 3-1
Form W-4, Employee's Withholding Allowance Certificate

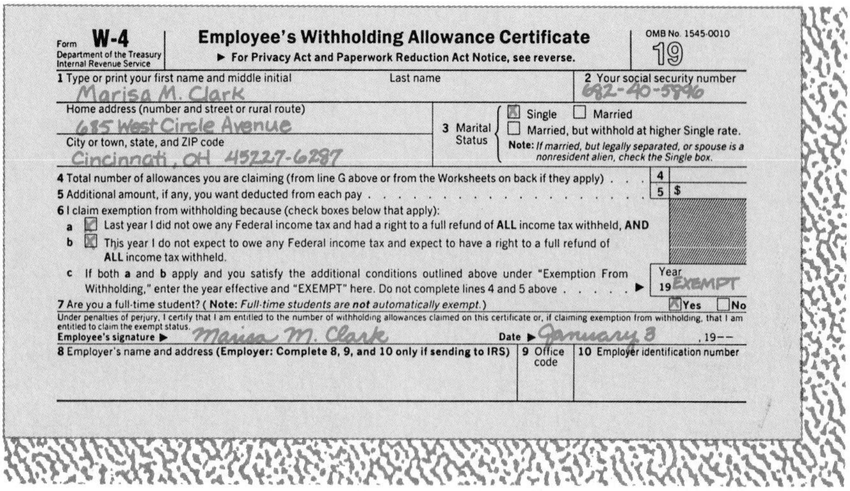

Form **W-4**
Department of the Treasury
Internal Revenue Service

Employee's Withholding Allowance Certificate
▶ For Privacy Act and Paperwork Reduction Act Notice, see reverse.

OMB No. 1545-0010
19

1 Type or print your first name and middle initial — Marisa M. | Last name — Clark | 2 Your social security number — 682-40-5896

Home address (number and street or rural route) — 685 West Circle Avenue

City or town, state, and ZIP code — Cincinnati, OH 45227-6287

3 Marital Status: ☒ Single ☐ Married ☐ Married, but withhold at higher Single rate.
Note: *If married, but legally separated, or spouse is a nonresident alien, check the Single box.*

4 Total number of allowances you are claiming (from line G above or from the Worksheets on back if they apply) . . . 4

5 Additional amount, if any, you want deducted from each pay . . . . 5 $

6 I claim exemption from withholding because (check boxes below that apply):
a ☒ Last year I did not owe any Federal income tax and had a right to a full refund of **ALL** income tax withheld, **AND**
b ☒ This year I do not expect to owe any Federal income tax and expect to have a right to a full refund of **ALL** income tax withheld.
c If both **a** and **b** apply and you satisfy the additional conditions outlined above under "Exemption From Withholding," enter the year effective and "EXEMPT" here. Do not complete lines 4 and 5 above . . . . . ▶ Year 19 EXEMPT

7 Are you a full-time student? (**Note:** *Full-time students are **not** automatically exempt.*) ☒ Yes ☐ No

Under penalties of perjury, I certify that I am entitled to the number of withholding allowances claimed on this certificate or, if claiming exemption from withholding, that I am entitled to claim the exempt status.

Employee's signature ▶ Marisa M. Clark **Date ▶** January 8, 19--

8 Employer's name and address (**Employer: Complete 8, 9, and 10 only if sending to IRS**) | 9 Office code | 10 Employer identification number

SOCIAL SECURITY FORMS

Because most workers in the United States must pay a social security tax from wages earned, all persons must obtain a **social security number**. Your social security number is your permanent work identification number. While you are working, your employers withhold social security taxes from your pay and contribute matching amounts. Throughout your working life, the amounts you earn and the amounts contributed for social security are credited by the Social Security Administration to your account under your assigned number. When you become eligible, benefits are paid to you monthly based upon how much you have paid into your account.

Social security isn't just for retirement. If a parent covered by social security dies or becomes disabled, minor children may be eligible for payments. Persons who become severely disabled (unable to work for a year or more) are paid benefits until they are able to return to work. If disability coverage is needed for more than two years, payments are continued under Medicare.

Figure 3-2 is an application for a social security card. This application must be filled out completely and sent to the Social Security Administration. You are then assigned one social security number for your lifetime, and are issued a card bearing this number. If the original card bearing the assigned number is lost or destroyed, you can obtain a duplicate without charge.

From time to time — every few years — you should check to see that your earnings have been properly credited to your account. The Social Security Administration in Baltimore, Maryland, provides a handy card for you to complete for this purpose (see Figure 3-3). Within 30 days you should receive a report that lists your income according to the Social Security Administration's records. Any mistakes should be reported immediately.

Withholdings are credited to your account.

Disability benefits are available.

Check your social security records periodically.

WORK PERMIT APPLICATION

Federal and some state laws require that a **minor**, a person under the age of legal majority, obtain a *work permit* before being allowed to work. The work permit is signed by the parents or legal guardian of persons under 16 years of age. Application for a work permit is obtained from the Department of Labor, a school counseling center, or work experience coordinators. There is usually no charge for obtaining the card, but the applicant will have to provide his or her social security card and proof of birth, and have a parent's or legal guardian's signature. Additional information may be required in

A parent must sign the work permit application.

DEPARTMENT OF HEALTH AND HUMAN SERVICES
SOCIAL SECURITY ADMINISTRATION

Form Approved
OMB No. 0960-0066

FORM SS-5 — APPLICATION FOR A SOCIAL SECURITY NUMBER CARD (Original, Replacement or Correction)

Unless the requested information is provided, we may not be able to issue a Social Security Number (20 CFR 422-103(b))

INSTRUCTIONS TO APPLICANT ▶	Before completing this form, please read the instructions on the opposite page. Type or print, using pen with dark blue or black ink. Do not use pencil. SEE PAGE 1 FOR REQUIRED EVIDENCE.

NAA	NAME TO BE SHOWN ON CARD	First *Marisa*	Middle *Melanie*	Last *Clark*

NAB **1**	FULL NAME AT BIRTH (IF OTHER THAN ABOVE)	First	Middle	Last

ONA	OTHER NAME(S) USED			

STT **2**	MAILING ADDRESS	(Street/Apt. No., P.O. Box, Rural Route No.) *685 West Circle Avenue*

CTY	CITY (Do not abbreviate) *Cincinnati*	STE	STATE *Ohio*	ZIP	ZIP CODE *45227-6287*

CSP **3**	CITIZENSHIP (Check one only)	SEX **4**	SEX	ETB **5**	RACE/ETHNIC DESCRIPTION (Check one only) (Voluntary)
	☒ a. U.S. citizen		☐ MALE		☐ a. Asian, Asian-American or Pacific Islander (Includes persons of Chinese, Filipino, Japanese, Korean, Samoan, etc., ancestry or descent)
	☐ b. Legal alien allowed to work				☐ b. Hispanic (Includes persons of Chicano, Cuban, Mexican or Mexican-American, Puerto Rican, South or Central American, or other Spanish ancestry or descent)
	☐ c. Legal alien not allowed to work		☒ FEMALE		☐ c. Negro or Black (not Hispanic)
	☐ d. Other (See instructions on Page 2)				☐ d. Northern American Indian or Alaskan Native ☒ e. White (not Hispanic)

DOB **6**	DATE OF BIRTH	MONTH *8*	DAY *21*	YEAR *68*	AGE **7**	PRESENT AGE	PLB **8**	PLACE OF BIRTH	CITY (Do not abbreviate) ▶ *Cincinnati*	STATE OR FOREIGN COUNTRY (Do not abbreviate) *Ohio*	FCI ☐

MNA **9**	MOTHER'S NAME AT HER BIRTH	First *Mary*	Middle *Grace*	Last (Her maiden name) *Jacobs*

FNA	FATHER'S NAME	First *Richard*	Middle *Allen*	Last *Clark*

PNO **10**	a. Has a Social Security number card ever been requested for the person listed in item 1? ☐ YES(2) ☒ NO(1) ☐ Don't know(1)	b. Was a card received for the person listed in item 1? ☐ YES(3) ☐ NO(1) ☐ Don't know(1)

▶ IF YOU CHECKED YES TO A OR B, COMPLETE ITEMS C THROUGH E; OTHERWISE GO TO ITEM 11.

SSN	c. Enter the Social Security number assigned to the person listed in item 1.	☐☐☐ – ☐☐ – ☐☐☐☐

NLC	d. Enter the name shown on the most recent Social Security card issued for the person listed in item 1.	PDS	e. Date of birth correction (See Instruction 10 on page 2)	MONTH	DAY	YEAR

DON **11**	TODAY'S DATE	MONTH *01*	DAY *08*	YEAR *--*	**12**	Telephone number where we can reach you during the day. Please include the area code.	HOME ▶ *(513) 555-8681*	OTHER

ASD	WARNING: Deliberately furnishing (or causing to be furnished) false information on this application is a crime punishable by fine or imprisonment, or both.

IMPORTANT REMINDER: WE CANNOT PROCESS THIS APPLICATION WITHOUT THE REQUIRED EVIDENCE. SEE PAGE 1.

13	YOUR SIGNATURE *Marisa M. Clark*	**14**	YOUR RELATIONSHIP TO PERSON IN ITEM 1 ☒ Self ☐ Other (Specify)
	WITNESS (Needed only if signed by mark "X")		WITNESS (Needed only if signed by mark "X")

DO NOT WRITE BELOW THIS LINE (FOR SSA USE ONLY)			
DTC (SSA RECEIPT DATE)	NPN		DOC
NTC	CAN	BIC	IDN	ITV	☐ MANDATORY IN PERSON INTERVIEW CONDUCTED
TYPE(S) OF EVIDENCE SUBMITTED		SIGNATURE AND TITLE OF EMPLOYEE(S) REVIEWING EVIDENCE AND/OR CONDUCTING INTERVIEW
		DATE
	DCL	DATE

Figure 3-2
Application for a
Social Security
Number Card

Figure 3-3
Request for Social Security Statement of Earnings

(Please read instructions on reverse before completing)

REQUEST FOR SOCIAL SECURITY STATEMENT OF EARNINGS

Your social security number

682	40	5896

Date of Birth

Month	Day	Year
08	21	68

Print Name and Address in ink or use typewriter

Please send a statement of my social security earnings to:

Name Marisa M. Clark

Number & Street 685 West Circle Avenue

City & State Cincinnati, OH Zip Code 45227-6281

Sign Your Name Here Marisa M. Clark
(Do Not Print)

I am the individual to whom the record pertains. I understand that if I knowingly and willingly request or receive a record about an individual under false pretenses I would be guilty of a Federal crime and could be fined up to $5,000.

If you ever used a name (such as a maiden name) different from the one above, on a social security card, please print name here: ____________________

FORM SSA 7004 PC (3-81)
(PRIOR EDITIONS MAY BE USED UNTIL SUPPLY IS EXHAUSTED)

some states. Figure 3-4 is an example of a work permit application. The form must be filled in completely and clearly. Processing of the work permit application takes three to six weeks, so early application is advisable.

FORM W-2, WAGE AND TAX STATEMENT

When you have worked for a business or company during the year, you will receive a **Form W-2, Wage and Tax Statement**, which lists income you earned during the year and all amounts withheld by the employer in your behalf. These amounts include federal income tax, state income tax, and social security tax. Figure 3-5 is a completed Form W-2. Your W-2 should be compared to payroll slips received with each paycheck to be sure that the right amounts have been reported.

Compare the Form W-2 with your payroll slips.

The employer must provide a Form W-2 to you no later than January 31 of the year following the one in which you were employed. This is true even if you only worked part of the year and were not working as of December 31. If you do not receive a W-2 from your employer (and all employers you may have worked for during the year) you should contact the employer to get the W-2 to attach to your income tax forms. Former employers may not have a current address for you.

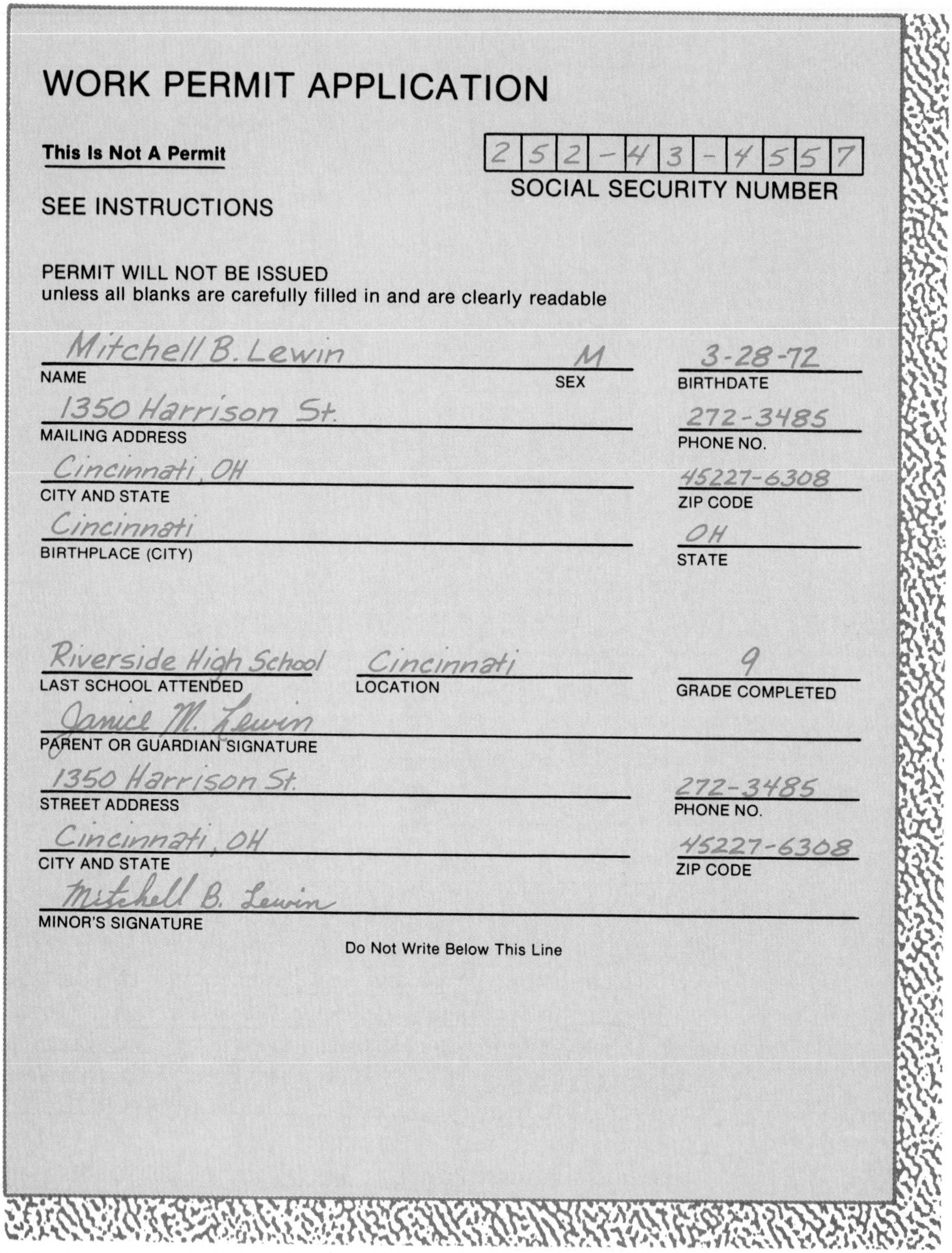

WORK PERMIT APPLICATION

This Is Not A Permit

SEE INSTRUCTIONS

| 2 | 5 | 2 | – | 4 | 3 | – | 4 | 5 | 5 | 7 |

SOCIAL SECURITY NUMBER

PERMIT WILL NOT BE ISSUED
unless all blanks are carefully filled in and are clearly readable

Mitchell B. Lewin   *M*   *3-28-72*
NAME   SEX   BIRTHDATE

1350 Harrison St.   *272-3485*
MAILING ADDRESS   PHONE NO.

Cincinnati, OH   *45227-6308*
CITY AND STATE   ZIP CODE

Cincinnati   *OH*
BIRTHPLACE (CITY)   STATE

Riverside High School   *Cincinnati*   *9*
LAST SCHOOL ATTENDED   LOCATION   GRADE COMPLETED

Janice M. Lewin
PARENT OR GUARDIAN SIGNATURE

1350 Harrison St.   *272-3485*
STREET ADDRESS   PHONE NO.

Cincinnati, OH   *45227-6308*
CITY AND STATE   ZIP CODE

Mitchell B. Lewin
MINOR'S SIGNATURE

Do Not Write Below This Line

Figure 3-4
Work Permit Application

Figure 3-5
Form W-2, Wage
and Tax Statement

1 Control number	22222	For Paperwork Reduction Act Notice, see back of Copy D. OMB No. 1545-0008	For Official Use Only ▶		
2 Employer's name, address, and ZIP code		3 Employer's identification number 93-81256791		4 Employer's state I.D. number OH44422	
Hanson Motors 85 Briar Street Cincinnati, OH 45230-5162		5 Statutory employee □ Deceased □ Pension plan □ Legal rep. □	942 emp. □	Subtotal □ Deferred compensation □	Void □
		6 Allocated tips		7 Advance EIC payment	
8 Employee's social security number 682-40-5896	9 Federal income tax withheld	10 Wages, tips, other compensation $2,084.00		11 Social security tax withheld $139.63	
12 Employee's name (first, middle, last) Maria M. Clark		13 Social security wages $2,084.00		14 Social security tips	
		16 (See Instr. for Forms W-2/W-2P)		16a Fringe benefits incl. in Box 10	
685 West Circle Avenue Cincinnati, OH 45227-6287		17 State income tax $14.04	18 State wages, tips, etc. $2,084.00	19 Name of state Ohio	
15 Employee's address and ZIP code		20 Local income tax $41.60	21 Local wages, tips, etc. $2,084.00	22 Name of locality Cincinnati	
Form W-2 Wage and Tax Statement		Copy A For Social Security Administration		Dept. of the Treasury—IRS	

EMPLOYEE RESPONSIBILITIES

◆◆◆◆◆◆◆◆

Plan to meet your job responsibilities.

As a new employee, you will want to do the best possible job. In order to be successful, you will have a number of responsibilities to meet.

RESPONSIBILITIES TO EMPLOYERS

Your employer hires you and pays you at predetermined intervals. In return for this pay and other benefits you may receive, the employer expects certain things from you.

Competent Work.   You should do your best to produce the best possible finished product for your employer. The product needs to be **marketable;** that is, of such quality that the employer can sell it or represent the company by use of your product. If, for example, you type a letter that has so many mistakes and erasures that it cannot be mailed, the letter is not a marketable product.

Thrift.   When using an employer's materials, you should be as thrifty as possible, conserving supplies and materials with care and diligence as though they were your own. Supplies and other materials are expensive to an employer.

Be thrifty with your employer's supplies.

Punctuality.   Workers should consistently arrive at work on time, take allotted breaks, and leave at quitting time. Being punctual means being ready to go to work at the appointed time — not rushing through the door at the last minute.

Illustration 3-1
Employers value
employees who are
pleasant and easy to
work with.

Loyalty displays re-
spect for the employ-
er.

Be aware of your
weak points.

Pleasant Attitude.   On any job, it is important to be pleasant and easy to get along with. You should be willing to follow orders and take directions.
Loyalty and Respect.   While working for a company, you should never be guilty of spreading rumors or gossiping about your employer or job. As long as you are on the "company team," you are expected to be loyal to the company. Loyalty includes showing respect to the employer and the company on and off the job.
Dependability.   When you say you will do something, follow through. The employer should be able to depend on you to do what you are hired to do.
Initiative.   You should not have to be told everything to do. Employees who stand idle after a specific job is completed are of very little value to employers. **Initiative** means that you do things on your own without being told to; you're a self-starter.
Interest.   It is important for you to show an interest in your job and your company. You should project an attitude of wanting to learn all you can and of giving all tasks your best possible effort. An enthusiastic attitude demonstrates to an employer your sincere interest in being a cooperative and productive worker.
Self-Evaluation.   The ability to take criticism and to assess your own progress is important to both you and the employer. Everyone has strong points and weak points, but the weak points cannot be improved unless you are willing to admit that they exist and begin to work on them. Employers must evaluate employees' work to determine raises and promotions.

Similarly, employees should recognize their own strong points and limitations and do a realistic self-evaluation of their job performance.

RESPONSIBILITIES TO OTHER EMPLOYEES

In addition to the responsibilities that you owe your employer, you also have duties to your fellow workers. These include the following:

Teamwork. You are part of a team when you work with others in a company, and you need to do your share of the work. Employees must work cooperatively in order to produce a quality product; when friction and personality problems occur, the productivity and efficiency of the whole company decrease.

Do your share of the work.

Thoughtfulness. Be considerate of fellow workers to promote a good work atmosphere for everyone, including customers. Having a pleasant attitude will result in a more enjoyable time for yourself and for others. Personal problems and conflicts should not be brought to work.

Loyalty. In addition to being loyal and supportive of your employer, you should also be loyal toward fellow employees. This means not spreading rumors about them. Gossiping leads to a breakdown of teamwork.

RESPONSIBILITIES TO CUSTOMERS

As an employee, you represent the company. To the customer who walks in the front door, you *are* the company. Your attitude toward a customer often determines whether or not he or she returns for future products or services. Therefore, remember that you have the responsibility to greet the customer with an attitude of helpfulness and courtesy.

Attitude is very important.

Helpfulness. When customers come to your employer's place of business, they expect to be given reasonable help in finding or deciding what to purchase. It is the employee's responsibility to help customers find what they want or to do what is needed. An attitude of helpfulness reflects well on the company and is an important part of any job.

Courtesy. Whether or not you like a customer, that customer actually pays your wages — by keeping your employer in business. Without the customer, the business could not exist. Therefore, your attitude toward the customer should always be respectful and courteous, never hostile or unfriendly. Customer loyalty to business is often built by friendly, helpful employees.

Being helpful is good for business.

EMPLOYER RESPONSIBILITIES
◆◆◆◆◆◆◆◆

Employers also have responsibilities to employees. Some responsibilities are required by law; others are simply good practices to follow for keeping employees happy and on the job. Failure to meet these responsibilities can result in an employer being fined for unfair labor practices, or a high turnover rate, higher premiums for unemployment insurance, and costly expenses in connection with the continual need to hire new employees. Some employer duties include adequate supervision, fair personnel policies, safe working conditions, open channels of communication, recognition of achievement, and compliance with civil rights and laws.

ADEQUATE SUPERVISION

Employees need to be supervised properly to be sure they are learning to do a good job on assigned work. Supervision includes providing appropriate instruction in the use of equipment and safety standards, and spending enough time with new employees to train them adequately to do the assigned work.

FAIR PERSONNEL POLICIES

Know what is expected of you.

Hiring and firing policies, salary advancement policies, and procedures for resolving employee disputes are some of the policies that need to be fair and well communicated. Employees should know clearly what is acceptable and unacceptable performance, what the standards are for advancements and raises, and what constitutes grounds for suspension or discharge.

SAFE WORKING CONDITIONS

All employees must be provided safe equipment, a safe working environment, and adequate training for working under dangerous conditions. Special protective equipment, clothing, warning signs, and adequate lighting must be provided to employees working under dangerous conditions. Working conditions must be safer for minors than adults in some industries.

OPEN CHANNELS OF COMMUNICATION

Employers need to communicate with employees so that all employees have the opportunity to express concerns, ask questions, and make suggestions. The lack of open communication can result in poor morale of workers and low work output. Employees need to know they are an important part of the company and that their opinions are valued.

RECOGNITION OF ACHIEVEMENT

Rewards are work incentives.

Employers need to provide some form of reward for performance by employees. Merit pay raises, as well as advancement on a regularly established schedule, provide encouragement for workers to do their best possible work. When achievement is not recognized, employees lose the desire to be as productive as possible. All human beings need to be rewarded and encouraged from time to time; a salary bonus or raise is an excellent method of encouragement.

COMPLIANCE WITH CIVIL RIGHTS AND LAWS

Employment laws protect workers' rights.

Employers must obey state and federal laws designed to protect workers from discrimination in employment on the basis of race, color, sex, national origin, religion, and, in some cases, age. In the next section we will learn about some of the employment laws enacted to protect workers from unfair labor practices. The employer is responsible for respecting workers' rights. Failure to do so can result in severe penalties for the employer. Complaints of employment discrimination may be filed with the Equal Employment Opportunity Commission. Some states have civil rights commissions through which all complaints must be filed.

EMPLOYMENT LAWS

◆◆◆◆◆◆◆◆

In the last fifty years many laws have been enacted to provide various protections for American workers. Laws enacted are generally enforced by government agencies, such as the Department of Labor or the Social Security Administration.

Major employment acts are called *administrative laws*. An **administrative agency** is given the authority to enforce administrative laws. Administrative agencies were established by Congress and authorized by the executive branch of government. The Department of Labor is responsible for overseeing several important labor acts and their provisions.

All workers receive benefits.

The main provisions of the laws will generally be in one or more of the following areas *for all workers*:

1. To establish a minimum wage
2. To provide regular working hours
3. To provide unemployment, disability, and retirement insurance benefits
4. To provide equal employment opportunities and eliminate discrimination
5. To establish and maintain safe working conditions

Other laws have provisions for specific workers that do not apply to all workers. Minors are given several special provisions:

1. Specific safety precautions and working conditions that are more extensive than for adults
2. Maximum number of hours to be worked and times during which minors can work during the school year
3. Requirement for those under age 16 to obtain a work permit

Legal recourse is available.

If any employee believes that he or she has not received benefits as required by law, *recourse*, or remedy, is available. If you think that you have a legitimate complaint, you should call the state Department of Labor, which will assist you without charge. Employers found in violation of labor laws are subject to fine, payment of damages to employees, and other penalties determined by a court of law.

Sexual harassment is an area in which protection is provided through the Equal Employment Opportunity Commission (EEOC). *Sexual harassment*

Illustration 3-2
Employment laws
protect workers'
rights.

refers to "unwelcome advances, requests, or other verbal or physical conduct of a sexual nature" where such conduct affects an individual's opportunities for employment or advancement, or interferes with work performance. The guidelines of the EEOC state that such sexual harassment is a violation of the Civil Rights Act. All such complaints are investigated by the EEOC, and if sexual harassment is found, the victim can be awarded back pay, promotion, reinstatement, or other remedies.

SOCIAL SECURITY ACT

Benefits depend on
contributions.

Originally called the Federal Insurance Contributions Act of 1935, the **Social Security Act** was the first national social insurance program, enacted to provide federal aid for the elderly and for disabled workers. In 1965 the Medicare provision (hospital and medical insurance protection) for elderly retired workers and other qualified persons was added. Five basic types of benefits are paid: (a) disability, (b) survivor, (c) retirement, (d) hospital, and (e) medical. Benefits received depend on the amount of contributions made. Self-employed workers pay their social security contributions when they pay their income tax. For employees in occupations covered by social security, contributions are mandatory. Social security protection is not yet available for some types of employment. Your local social security office will know if your employment is covered. Social security (FICA) is deducted from your gross pay and sent to the Internal Revenue Service for proper crediting to your social security account.

UNEMPLOYMENT COMPENSATION

An important part of the Social Security Act provides that every state must have an **unemployment insurance** program that provides benefits to workers who lose their jobs through no fault of their own. After a waiting period, laid-off or terminated workers may collect a portion of their regular pay for a certain length of time. Premiums for unemployment insurance are generally paid by employers. Rates vary according to employers' records of turnover, or how often they hire and fire employees. The more often employers let workers go, the higher the premium rate they will pay. Each state has its own regulations as to waiting period, maximum benefits, deadlines for filing claims, and premium rates. Unless otherwise extended by provision of the state legislature, benefits are paid for a maximum of 22 weeks, through the local state employment office.

Waiting periods are necessary.

FAIR LABOR STANDARDS ACT

Popularly known as the *Wage and Hour Act,* the Fair Labor Standards Act of 1938 provided that persons working in interstate commerce or a related industry could not be paid less than a minimum wage of 25 cents an hour. A *minimum wage* is the legally established lower limit on wages employers can pay. The minimum wage reached $3.35 an hour in January 1981. Another provision of the act states that hourly wage workers cannot be employed for more than 40 hours a week. Hours worked in addition to the regular hours are considered *overtime* and must be paid for at one and one-half times the regular rate.

Wage laws are enforced.

Each state enforces wage and hour laws, which include federal provisions and additional state regulations. These laws, which are regulated by the state Departments of Labor, provide that regular paydays must be established and maintained by every employer. For example, in Oregon, payment of wages to new employees must begin no later than 35 days after the first work day. When an employee quits, wages due must be paid within 48 hours of the final day worked. When an employee is discharged, all wages are due immediately. Any employee who requests that his or her paycheck be mailed is entitled to have it mailed to an address designated by the employee. An itemized statement of deductions from wages must be furnished to employees with their regular paychecks. The maximum number of hours that minors may work varies according to state laws. Tips are not considered wages and may not be calculated in the amount of minimum wage due.

Any employee who is unduly charged fees or denied any of the preceding legal rights provided by the Fair Labor Standards Act may file an appeal with the nearest office of the Department of Labor. Employees may not be discharged because of a pending wage claim.

The minimum wage law has an exception — those businesses whose annual sales do not exceed $250,000 are exempt from paying the minimum wage. Also exempt are nonprofit and governmental offices that provide employment as part of a training program.

Tips are not part of minimum wage.

WORKERS' COMPENSATION

Workers' compensation is the name for statutes (laws) that give financial security to workers and their families for on-the-job injury, illness, or death that occurs as a result of the job or working conditions. Stress has, in some cases, been recognized as a work-related illness. The worker's compensation law is often labeled "liability without fault" because the employer is responsible for employee injuries and illnesses that are the result of employment, even though the employer may have done nothing to cause the injury or illness. Today all 50 states have workers' compensation statutes. In some states, the SAIF (State Accident Insurance Fund), or other designated state insurance agency, collects a premium from each working person. The fee is usually based on the number of days worked during a pay period. Employers pay the workers' compensation premium in many states. However, in some states, employees are required to pay all or part of the premium. The premiums are used to pay benefits to injured workers. Benefits include payments to doctors and hospitals, payment to the employee for temporary or permanent disability, and payment of benefits to survivors in the event of death.

Employers are responsible for work injuries.

Employers may also elect to maintain their own workers' compensation insurance program, if they qualify. Upon proof that an employer can meet the expenses of such a liability, a private company will establish the fund on behalf of the employer to insure against the loss. Large companies may provide their own workers' compensation insurance program (self-insured) within the company benefits program.

Employers may provide their own insurance.

HUMAN RELATIONS SKILLS

◆◆◆◆◆◆◆◆

Keeping your job also includes another valuable skill — **human relations,** the art of getting along with others. There are many important lessons to remember, as affirmed by experienced workers who have sometimes learned the "hard way." These lessons in work survival are beneficial to all workers in all types of organizations, from the two-person office to the international conglomerate. Whenever two or more people must work together in an organizational setting to accomplish some joint purpose, human relations skills are important. The following list provides some helpful guidelines for good human relations skills that are also good office politics skills.

Office politics exists at all work sites.

1. *Make a good first impression.* People will form perceptions of you in the early stages of your employment. Once established, these perceptions are difficult to change.
2. *Choose work friends wisely.* Work friendships can sometimes affect your future with a company, either positively or negatively.
3. *Maintain confidentiality.* It is important to keep private and confidential information to yourself. Once you have revealed information to one person, you have begun the information chain.
4. *Use good public relations and sales habits.* Every job is a sales job; every employee represents his or her company to the public. In addition, you are always representing yourself and selling your skills and employability.
5. *Follow the hierarchy.* The **hierarchy** is the formal communication and power structure that exists in all organizations. When you communicate, go through proper channels; don't skip over your immediate supervisor and go to his or her boss with a problem, suggestion, or concern.
6. *Respect the grapevine.* A **grapevine** is the informal communication channel that exists in all organizations. Because people are people, they seek information about others and about what's going on. News travels fast in the grapevine, and it is usually pretty accurate. It is important to respect the power of the grapevine and be aware of how it operates.
7. *Work a full day.* To be truly valuable to your employer, always do your best, give a full day's work for a full day's pay, and go the extra mile — willingly and pleasantly.
8. *Think and act positively.* Employers value employees who express positive thoughts about themselves, their company, and others.

A good reputation is built slowly and carefully.

Be forward looking and positive at work.

Many other experienced workers could add to this list. Perhaps you have learned some truths such as these from your years as a student. Understanding and observing these truths can save you from costly mistakes as you build your career.

VOCABULARY

Directions: Can you find the definition for each of the following terms used in Chapter 3?

Form W-4   administrative agency
allowance   Social Security Act
exempt   unemployment insurance
social security number   workers' compensation
minor   human relations
Form W-2   hierarchy
marketable   grapevine
initiative

1. A person who is dependent on your income for support.
2. Your permanent work identification number.
3. A form completed by your employer and mailed to you no later than January 31.
4. Quality of product that allows an employer to sell it.
5. A person under the age of legal majority.
6. Authorized by Congress to enforce administrative laws.
7. Enacted in 1935, it was our first national insurance program to provide financial help for elderly and disabled workers.
8. A part of the Social Security Act, ensuring that benefits are paid to workers who lose their jobs.
9. One of the forms you will fill out when you begin working, on which you claim a number of allowances to determine taxes withheld from your paycheck.
10. Persons who will not incur any federal tax liability may claim this status on their Form W-4.
11. The willingness to do things without being told.
12. Benefits to protect workers from loss due to on-the-job illness or injury.
13. The formal channel of communication that exists in all organizations.
14. The informal channel of communication that exists wherever two or more people are employed.
15. The art of getting along with others.

ITEMS FOR DISCUSSION

1. What is the purpose of Form W-4?

2. Why do you need to have a social security number before you begin work?

3. Besides retirement income, what other benefits are provided by social security?

4. Why is it important that your employer have your correct social security number?

5. Where can you obtain a work permit application?

6. Besides yourself, who must sign your work permit application if you are under age 16?

7. What information is listed on Form W-2?

8. By what date must your employers for the past year provide you a Form W-2? Why do you need it?

9. What should you do if your employers during the past year do not send you a Form W-2?

10. List at least five responsibilities that an employee has to an employer.

11. List at least three responsibilities that an employee has to other employees at work.

12. What responsibilities do employees have to the employer's customers?

13. List and describe three responsibilities that employers have to their employees.

14. What is an administrative agency?

15. What are some of the provisions of the Social Security Act?

16. What is unemployment insurance?

17. List the major provisions of the Fair Labor Standards Act.

18. What is meant by the expression *liability without fault*?

19. What is meant by human relations?

20. How is the grapevine different from the hierarchy in an organization?

APPLICATIONS

1. Obtain a Form W-4 from the closest office of the Internal Revenue Service and complete it properly, claiming exempt status if you are entitled to do so.

2. Obtain an application for a social security number card from your local Social Security Administration office. Complete the form with the appropriate information.

3. Look up in your telephone directory the address of your nearest Department of Labor office. Go there and pick up a work permit application and fill it in. (Your counseling center or work experience coordinator will probably have these forms also.)

4. Ask your parent or another working person to list employee responsibilities to employers in order of importance. Then, if possible, ask an employer to list in order what she/he considers important responsibilities that employees have to employers. Compare the two lists.

5. Interview a person who is working full-time and ask what responsibilities he or she thinks employers should have to employees, besides the regular payment of wages earned.

6. Look up the Social Security Act in an encyclopedia or historical reference book in your library. Obtain this information: (a) why social security was deemed necessary by the president in 1935; (b) who was the president at the time; (c) the history of benefits, paycheck deductions, and purpose of social security.

7. Obtain from your state Department of Labor the provisions of state laws regarding employment of minors. Include (a) maximum hours per week that can be worked, (b) latest hour in the evening that a minor can work, (c) work permit requirements for workers under 16, (d) any other provisions that protect you as a minor while working part-time or full-time.

8. From your state Department of Labor or from an employer obtain information as to how workers' compensation insurance is handled in your state. Is it by a state agency or private insurance program? What types of benefits are available? How much are premiums and who pays them? Because all states have workers' compensation laws, determine all you can about the laws in your state.

9. Ask a full-time worker in an occupation you might choose to list some important human relations skills he or she has learned while working for any employer or employers for over a year. Ask the worker to share with you the company's organization chart (formal hierarchy). Draw arrows to show how communication lines are intended to flow within the company. Ask how the grapevine differs from the formal communication hierarchy.

10. Interview a general manager of a department store or other retail business and ask how all employees use public relations skills and are in "sales" positions for the company. Ask what personal characteristics are desired in employees who wish to work for the company.

CASE PROBLEMS AND ACTIVITIES

1. Your friend Frank has discovered that the amount of wages paid to him during the year appears to be different from the amount listed on

the W-2 sent to him by his employer. He asks you what to do. What is your advice?

2. Alan Willson worked for three employers last year. It is now February 1 of the following year, and he has received Form W-2 from only two of those employers. He asks you what he should do about it. What should you tell him?

3. Because last year Bill did not earn enough money on his part-time job to have to pay any federal taxes, his employer has asked him if this year he would like to claim "exempt" status on his W-4. Explain to Bill how he can claim to be exempt and what it means to him.

4. Consuela, 14, has decided that she wants to work part-time this summer, doing whatever kind of work she can find to earn money to buy school clothes. Tell her what she should do now, several months before summer, to obtain appropriate numbers and cards she may need to go to work. Also tell Consuela what forms she may have to complete when she begins work.

5. Connie Clark just received her W-2 form from her employer and has noticed that her social security number is wrong on the form. What should she do? What can happen if she does nothing?

6. Jack Anderson worked for over a year for the same employer, then was laid off because business was slow. He is looking for another job, but needs income to pay his rent. You told Jack that he may be eligible for unemployment insurance payments. Explain how he could qualify and whom he should see to learn about unemployment benefits.

7. Your friend Kim has just been hired to work for a large company doing office work and running errands. If she does a good job, it could lead to a permanent position. What advice can you offer her to build successful human relations skills and to make a good impression the first year on the job?

Chapter 4

EMPLOYEE BENEFITS

◆◆◆◆◆◆◆◆◆◆◆◆◆◆◆◆◆◆◆◆◆◆◆◆◆◆◆◆◆◆◆

OBJECTIVES

1. Compute payroll deductions and net pay from information and tables provided.
2. Identify optional and required employee benefits and recognize their value as additions to net pay.
3. Understand the role of labor unions and professional organizations in this country.

GROSS PAY, DEDUCTIONS, NET PAY

◆◆◆◆◆◆◆◆◆

Gross pay is the total pay before deductions.

When people work, they agree to perform certain tasks in exchange for financial remuneration and benefits. **Gross pay** is the total or agreed upon rate of pay or salary, before any deductions are made. If a person is working for $800 a month agreed upon salary, that is his or her gross pay. For people who work for an hourly wage or work overtime hours, computations must be made to determine the amount of gross and net pay.

HOURLY WAGE

Perhaps you will be paid for each hour you work. A record is kept of hours worked, and the number of hours is multiplied by the rate to determine the amount of gross pay. For example, a person paid $3.35 an hour and works 40 hours during the week will earn gross pay of $134 ($3.35 multiplied by 40 hours).

OVERTIME

Overtime is defined as hours worked in addition to regular hours of work. A standard workday is eight continuous hours with allowed breaks plus an unpaid lunch period. A standard workweek is 40 hours in a five-day period of eight hours each day. According to the Fair Labor Standards Act, overtime is paid at the rate of one and one-half times the regular rate of pay. If the regular rate of pay is $4.00 an hour, the overtime rate is $6.00 an hour ($4.00 times 1½). For example, a person may work a regular workweek of 40 hours at $3.50 an hour, plus one hour of overtime each day. Gross pay would be computed as follows:

Overtime pay is required by law.

$$
\begin{aligned}
40 \text{ hours} \times \$3.50 \text{ an hour (regular pay)} &= \$140.00 \\
5 \text{ hours} \times 5.25 \text{ an hour (overtime pay)} &= \underline{26.25} \\
\text{Gross pay} &= \$166.25
\end{aligned}
$$

MONTHLY SALARY

Perhaps you will be paid a set amount per month. In most cases you will work regular hours, but you will not receive additional pay for any overtime work. In the event you work overtime on a regular basis, then your employer could, if he or she wished, pay an agreed upon overtime rate computed from your monthly salary. For example, your salary is $800 a month. The agreed upon rate might be $6.82 an hour for overtime ($800 a month divided by 22 average working days a month, divided by 8 hours a day, times 1½). Thus, if you worked a total of 20 hours overtime in one month, your total gross pay would be $800 plus $136.40 (20 hours times $6.82 an hour).

Overtime pay is added to regular pay.

ANNUAL SALARY

Perhaps you will agree to an *annual*, or yearly, salary. Annual pay is usually divided into equal amounts paid each month. For example, you agree to work for $10,800 a year. Your monthly gross pay will be $900 ($10,800 divided by 12).

Illustration 4-1
Workers are often paid overtime for extra hours spent on the job.

DEDUCTIONS

Amounts subtracted from your gross pay are known as **deductions**. Some deductions, such as social security, federal income tax, and state income tax (if your state has an income tax), are required by law. Other deductions are optional and you may choose them, such as an automatic deduction to be sent to your savings account, or to your credit union for a car payment.

Records are kept by employers.

Employers are required to keep detailed records of wages earned and hours worked for inspection by the Department of Labor. With each paycheck, you must also receive a detailed list of all deductions taken from your gross pay. Deductions may not, except by court order, be withheld from your pay without written consent. This, of course, does not apply to taxes, social security, and other deductions required by federal and state laws. *child support/garnishments*

NET PAY

When all deductions are taken out of your gross pay, the amount left is called **net pay**. This is the amount of your paycheck, or what you can actually spend. Net pay is often called *take-home pay* because it is really what you have left over to "take home" or do with as you wish.

Regular wages (or salary) + Overtime = Gross Pay
Gross pay × Deductions = Net Pay

Figure 4-1 is an Employee Withholding Sheet, which lists gross pay, deductions, and net pay. By law, an explanation of the net pay computations — including gross pay, deductions, and net pay — must be provided with each paycheck. It is important to save the Employee Withholding Sheet or other form of itemization of withholdings from your gross pay so that you can check the accuracy of the W-2 your employer gives you the following January to file with your income tax return.

To compute gross pay on the Employee Withholding Sheet, the number of regular hours worked is multiplied by the hourly rate. Any overtime hours are multiplied by the overtime rate. Gross pay includes either hourly wages

Explanations of withholdings are required.

Figure 4-1
Employee Withholding Sheet

EMPLOYEE WITHHOLDING SHEET

Employee Name _Shari Gregson_   Social Security Number _898-40-7426_

Pay Period: ☒ weekly   ☐ bimonthly   ☐ monthly

Number of Allowances: _1_   ☐ married   ☒ single

GROSS PAY

1. Regular Wages: _40_ hours at $ _4.00_/hr. = $ _160.00_

or

2. Regular Salary: =   _____

3. Overtime: _4_ hours at $ _6.00_/hr. =   _24.00_

GROSS PAY ....$ _184.00_

REQUIRED DEDUCTIONS

4. Federal Income Tax (use tax tables) ....$ _23.20_

5. State Income Tax (use tax tables) .... _11.00_

6. Social Security Tax (use 7.51%) times gross pay) .... _13.82_

OTHER DEDUCTIONS

7. Insurance .... _____

8. Union Dues .... _8.00_

9. Credit Union .... _20.00_

10. Savings .... _____

11. Retirement .... _____

12. Charity .... _____

13. Other: _____ .... _____

_____ .... _____

TOTAL DEDUCTIONS (total lines 4 through 14) ....$ _76.02_

NET PAY (subtract total deductions from gross pay) ....$ _107.98_ plus overtime, or salary plus overtime.

Required deductions include federal, state, and local taxes, and social security withheld. The tax withholding amounts are determined from tax tables such as those shown in Figures 4-2 through 4-5. The more allowances an employee claims on her or his W-4 statement, the less the amount of income taxes the employer will withhold from gross pay. The social security deduction is withheld at the rate of 7.51 percent of the first $53,400 earned. This ceiling amount, as well as the interest rate, will continue to rise as Congress passes new laws to ensure adequate funding for the program. As

Withholding amounts are taken from tables.

Weekly payroll period (Oregon)
Amount of tax to be withheld

WAGE		SINGLE		MARRIED							SINGLE OR MARRIED							
AT LEAST	BUT LESS THAN	0	1	2	0	1	2	3	4	5	6	7	8	9	10	11	12	13	14+
0--	20	0	0	0	0	0	0	0	0	0	0	0	0	0	0	0	0	0	0
20--	40	1	1	0	1	1	0	0	0	0	0	0	0	0	0	0	0	0	0
40--	60	2	2	1	2	2	1	0	0	0	0	0	0	0	0	0	0	0	0
60--	80	4	3	2	3	3	2	1	0	0	0	0	0	0	0	0	0	0	0
80--	100	6	4	3	4	4	3	2	1	0	0	0	0	0	0	0	0	0	0
100--	120	7	6	4	5	5	4	3	2	1	0	0	0	0	0	0	0	0	0
120--	140	9	7	6	6	6	5	4	3	2	1	0	0	0	0	0	0	0	0
140--	160	10	9	7	8	7	6	5	4	3	2	1	0	0	0	0	0	0	0
160--	180	12	10	9	9	8	7	6	5	4	3	2	1	0	0	0	0	0	0
180--	200	14	12	11	11	9	8	7	6	5	4	3	2	1	0	0	0	0	0
200--	220	15	14	12	13	11	10	8	7	6	5	4	3	2	1	0	0	0	0
220--	240	17	15	14	14	13	11	10	8	7	6	5	4	3	2	1	0	0	0
240--	260	18	17	15	16	15	13	11	10	8	7	6	5	4	3	2	1	0	0
260--	280	20	18	17	18	16	15	13	11	10	8	7	6	5	4	3	2	1	0
280--	300	22	20	19	20	18	16	15	13	12	10	8	7	6	5	4	3	2	1
300--	320	23	22	20	21	20	18	16	15	13	12	10	8	7	6	5	4	3	2
320--	340	25	23	22	23	21	20	18	17	15	13	12	10	8	7	6	5	4	3
340--	360	26	25	23	25	23	21	20	18	17	15	13	12	10	9	7	6	5	4
360--	380	28	26	25	26	25	23	22	20	18	17	15	13	12	10	9	7	6	5
380--	400	29	28	27	28	26	25	23	22	20	18	17	15	14	12	10	9	7	6
400--	420	31	29	28	30	28	27	25	23	22	20	18	17	15	14	12	10	9	7
420--	440	32	31	29	31	30	28	27	25	23	22	20	19	17	15	14	12	10	9
440--	460	34	32	31	33	31	30	28	27	25	23	22	20	19	17	15	14	12	11
460--	480	35	34	32	34	33	31	30	28	27	25	24	22	20	19	17	15	14	12
480--	500	36	35	34	36	34	33	32	30	29	27	25	24	22	20	19	17	16	14
500--	520	38	36	35	37	36	34	33	32	30	29	27	25	24	22	21	19	17	16
520--	540	39	38	36	39	37	36	35	33	32	30	29	27	25	24	22	21	19	17
540--	560	41	39	38	40	39	37	36	35	33	32	30	29	27	26	24	22	21	19
560--	580	43	41	39	42	40	39	38	36	35	33	32	30	29	27	26	24	22	21
580--	600	45	43	41	43	42	40	39	38	36	35	33	32	31	29	27	26	24	22
600--	620	47	45	43	45	43	42	41	39	38	36	35	33	32	31	29	27	26	24
620--	640	50	48	46	46	45	43	42	41	39	38	36	35	34	32	31	29	27	26
640--	660	52	50	48	48	46	45	44	42	41	39	38	36	35	34	32	31	29	28
660--	680	54	52	50	50	48	46	45	44	42	41	39	38	37	35	34	32	31	29
680--	700	56	54	52	53	50	48	47	45	44	42	41	39	38	37	35	34	32	31
700--	720	58	56	54	55	53	51	49	47	45	44	42	41	40	38	37	35	34	32
720--	740	60	58	56	57	55	53	51	49	47	45	44	42	41	40	38	37	35	34
740--	760	63	61	58	59	57	55	53	51	49	47	45	44	43	41	40	38	37	35
760--	780	65	63	61	61	59	57	55	53	51	49	47	45	44	43	41	40	38	37
780--	800	67	65	63	63	61	59	57	55	53	51	49	47	46	44	43	41	40	38
800--	820	69	67	65	65	63	61	59	57	55	53	51	49	47	46	44	43	41	40
820--	840	71	69	67	68	66	64	61	59	57	55	53	51	49	47	46	44	43	41
840--	860	73	71	69	70	68	66	64	62	60	57	55	53	51	49	47	46	44	43

NUMBER OF WITHHOLDING ALLOWANCES — TWO OR LESS / THREE OR MORE

10.8 PERCENT OF EXCESS OVER 3560 PLUS --

| 860--OVER | 74 | 72 | 70 | 71 | 69 | 67 | 65 | 63 | 61 | 59 | 57 | 54 | 52 | 50 | 48 | 46 | 45 | 44 |

Figure 4-2   State Tax Withholding Table — Weekly Payroll

more Americans grow older, more money will be needed to pay for their retirement incomes. Unfortunately, as the working population decreases (lower birth rates), working people will be required to pay even more into social security to maintain the fund.

In addition to required deductions, those deductions that an employee has authorized will also be subtracted from gross pay. The most common of these deductions are insurance payments, union dues, credit union payments, savings account deposits, retirement contributions, and charity deductions. These types of deductions cannot be withheld from an employee's pay without her or his written consent (or by a court order).

Additional withholdings may be authorized.

Monthly payroll period (Oregon)
Amount of tax to be withheld

WAGE		TWO OR LESS					THREE OR MORE SINGLE OR MARRIED											
		SINGLE			MARRIED													
AT LEAST	BUT LESS THEN	0	1	2	0	1	2	3	4	5	6	7	8	9	10	11	12	13	14+
0--	40	0	0	0	0	0	0	0	0	0	0	0	0	0	0	0	0	0	0
40--	80	3	0	0	3	0	0	0	0	0	0	0	0	0	0	0	0	0	0
80--	120	5	1	0	5	1	0	0	0	0	0	0	0	0	0	0	0	0	0
120--	160	7	3	0	7	3	0	0	0	0	0	0	0	0	0	0	0	0	0
160--	200	9	5	1	9	5	1	0	0	0	0	0	0	0	0	0	0	0	0
200--	240	11	7	3	11	7	3	0	0	0	0	0	0	0	0	0	0	0	0
240--	280	13	9	5	13	9	5	1	0	0	0	0	0	0	0	0	0	0	0
280--	320	16	11	7	15	11	7	3	0	0	0	0	0	0	0	0	0	0	0
320--	360	19	13	9	17	13	9	5	0	0	0	0	0	0	0	0	0	0	0
360--	400	22	16	11	19	15	11	7	2	0	0	0	0	0	0	0	0	0	0
400--	440	26	19	12	21	17	13	9	4	0	0	0	0	0	0	0	0	0	0
440--	480	29	22	16	23	19	15	11	6	2	0	0	0	0	0	0	0	0	0
480--	520	32	25	19	25	21	17	13	8	4	0	0	0	0	0	0	0	0	0
520--	560	35	29	22	27	23	19	15	10	6	2	0	0	0	0	0	0	0	0
560--	600	38	32	25	29	25	21	17	12	8	4	0	0	0	0	0	0	0	0
600--	640	42	35	28	31	27	23	19	14	10	6	2	0	0	0	0	0	0	0
640--	680	45	38	32	35	29	25	21	16	12	8	4	0	0	0	0	0	0	0
680--	720	48	41	35	38	31	27	23	18	14	10	6	2	0	0	0	0	0	0
720--	760	51	45	38	41	34	29	25	20	16	12	8	4	0	0	0	0	0	0
760--	800	54	48	41	45	38	31	27	22	18	14	10	6	2	0	0	0	0	0
800--	840	58	51	44	48	41	34	29	24	20	16	12	8	4	0	0	0	0	0
840--	880	61	54	48	52	45	38	31	26	22	18	14	10	6	1	0	0	0	0
880--	920	64	57	51	55	48	41	34	28	24	20	16	12	8	3	0	0	0	0
920--	960	67	61	54	58	51	44	37	30	26	22	18	14	10	5	1	0	0	0
960--	1000	70	64	57	62	55	48	41	34	28	24	20	16	12	7	3	0	0	0
1000--	1040	74	67	60	65	58	51	44	37	30	26	22	18	14	9	5	1	0	0
1040--	1080	77	70	64	69	62	55	47	40	33	28	24	20	16	11	7	3	0	0
1080--	1120	80	73	67	72	65	58	51	44	37	30	26	22	18	13	9	5	1	0
1120--	1160	83	77	70	75	68	61	54	47	40	33	28	24	20	15	11	7	3	0
1160--	1200	86	80	73	79	72	65	58	51	44	37	30	26	22	17	13	9	5	1
1200--	1240	90	83	76	82	75	68	61	54	47	40	33	28	24	19	15	11	7	3
1240--	1280	93	86	80	86	79	72	64	57	50	43	36	30	26	21	17	13	9	5
1280--	1320	96	89	83	89	82	75	68	61	54	47	40	33	28	23	19	15	11	7
1320--	1360	99	93	86	92	85	78	71	64	57	50	43	36	30	25	21	17	13	9
1360--	1400	102	96	89	96	89	82	75	68	61	54	46	39	32	27	23	19	15	11
1400--	1440	106	99	92	99	92	85	78	71	64	57	50	43	36	29	25	21	17	13
1440--	1480	109	102	96	103	96	89	81	74	67	60	53	46	39	32	27	23	19	15
1480--	1520	112	105	99	106	99	92	85	78	71	64	57	50	43	36	29	25	21	17
1520--	1560	115	109	102	109	102	95	88	81	74	67	60	53	46	39	32	27	23	19
1560--	1600	118	112	105	113	106	99	92	85	78	71	63	56	49	42	35	29	25	21
1600--	1640	122	115	108	116	109	102	95	88	81	74	67	60	53	46	39	32	27	23
1640--	1680	125	118	112	120	113	106	98	91	84	77	70	63	56	49	42	35	29	25
1680--	1720	127	121	115	123	116	109	102	95	88	81	74	67	60	53	45	38	31	27
1720--	1760	130	125	118	126	119	112	105	98	91	84	77	70	63	56	49	42	35	29
1760--	1800	133	127	121	130	123	116	109	102	95	88	80	73	66	59	52	45	38	31

Figure 4-3   State Tax Withholding Table — Monthly Payroll

WAGE-BRACKET WITHHOLDING TABLES

WEEKLY Payroll Period — Employee NOT MARRIED

And the wages are—		And the number of withholding allowances claimed is—										
At least	But less than	0	1	2	3	4	5	6	7	8	9	10 or more
		The amount of income tax to be withheld shall be—										
$27	28	$.10	$0	$0	$0	$0	$0	$0	$0	$0	$0	$0
28	29	.20	0	0	0	0	0	0	0	0	0	0
29	30	.30	0	0	0	0	0	0	0	0	0	0
30	31	.40	0	0	0	0	0	0	0	0	0	0
31	32	.50	0	0	0	0	0	0	0	0	0	0
32	33	.70	0	0	0	0	0	0	0	0	0	0
33	34	.80	0	0	0	0	0	0	0	0	0	0
34	35	.90	0	0	0	0	0	0	0	0	0	0
35	36	1.00	0	0	0	0	0	0	0	0	0	0
36	37	1.10	0	0	0	0	0	0	0	0	0	0
37	38	1.30	0	0	0	0	0	0	0	0	0	0
38	39	1.40	0	0	0	0	0	0	0	0	0	0
39	40	1.50	0	0	0	0	0	0	0	0	0	0
40	41	1.60	0	0	0	0	0	0	0	0	0	0
41	42	1.70	0	0	0	0	0	0	0	0	0	0
42	43	1.90	0	0	0	0	0	0	0	0	0	0
43	44	2.00	.20	0	0	0	0	0	0	0	0	0
44	45	2.10	.30	0	0	0	0	0	0	0	0	0
45	46	2.20	.50	0	0	0	0	0	0	0	0	0
46	47	2.30	.60	0	0	0	0	0	0	0	0	0
47	48	2.50	.80	0	0	0	0	0	0	0	0	0
48	49	2.60	.90	0	0	0	0	0	0	0	0	0
49	50	2.70	1.00	0	0	0	0	0	0	0	0	0
50	51	2.80	1.10	0	0	0	0	0	0	0	0	0
51	52	2.90	1.20	.20	0	0	0	0	0	0	0	0
52	53	3.10	1.40	.40	0	0	0	0	0	0	0	0
53	54	3.20	1.50	.70	0	0	0	0	0	0	0	0
54	55	3.30	1.70	.90	0	0	0	0	0	0	0	0
55	56	3.40	1.80	.90	0	0	0	0	0	0	0	0
56	57	3.50	2.00	1.00	0	0	0	0	0	0	0	0
57	58	3.70	2.10	1.20	.30	0	0	0	0	0	0	0
58	59	3.80	2.30	1.40	.50	0	0	0	0	0	0	0
59	60	3.90	2.40	1.50	.70	0	0	0	0	0	0	0
60	62	4.10	2.60	1.70	.80	0	0	0	0	0	0	0
62	64	4.40	2.80	1.90	1.00	.30	0	0	0	0	0	0
64	66	4.70	3.10	2.20	1.30	.50	0	0	0	0	0	0
66	68	5.00	3.40	2.40	1.50	.80	0	0	0	0	0	0
68	70	5.30	3.70	2.70	1.70	1.00	0	0	0	0	0	0
70	72	5.70	4.00	3.00	2.10	1.20	.40	0	0	0	0	0
72	74	6.00	4.30	3.20	2.30	1.40	.60	0	0	0	0	0
74	76	6.30	4.70	3.50	2.50	1.60	.80	0	0	0	0	0
76	78	6.60	5.00	3.80	2.80	1.90	1.00	0	0	0	0	0
78	80	7.00	5.30	4.20	3.10	2.10	1.20	0	0	0	0	0
80	82	7.30	5.60	4.50	3.40	2.40	1.50	.50	0	0	0	0
82	84	7.60	6.00	4.80	3.70	2.70	1.70	.80	0	0	0	0
84	86	7.90	6.30	5.20	4.00	2.90	1.90	1.00	.20	0	0	0
86	88	8.20	6.60	5.50	4.30	3.20	2.20	1.20	.40	0	0	0
88	90	8.50	6.90	5.80	4.60	3.50	2.40	1.50	.60	0	0	0
90	92	8.80	7.30	6.10	5.00	3.80	2.80	1.80	.90	0	0	0
92	94	9.20	7.60	6.40	5.30	4.10	3.10	2.10	1.10	.30	0	0
94	96	9.60	7.90	6.80	5.60	4.50	3.40	2.30	1.40	.50	0	0
96	98	9.80	8.30	7.10	6.00	4.80	3.70	2.60	1.60	.70	0	0
98	100	10.10	8.60	7.40	6.30	5.10	4.00	2.90	1.90	1.00	.60	0
100	105	10.70	8.90	7.70	6.60	5.40	4.30	3.20	2.20	1.20	1.50	0
105	110	11.50	9.80	8.60	7.10	6.20	5.30	4.00	2.70	1.80		
110	115	12.30	10.60	9.40	8.30	7.00	5.80	4.70	3.50	2.40		
115	120	13.10	11.40	10.20	9.10	7.80	6.60	5.40	4.30	3.10		
120	125	13.90	12.20	11.00	9.90	8.70	7.50	6.30	5.20	4.00		
125	130	14.70	13.00	11.80	10.70	9.50	8.30	7.10	6.00	4.80		
130	135	15.50	13.80	12.60	11.50	10.30	9.10	8.00	6.80	5.60		
135	140	16.30	14.60	13.40	12.30	11.10	9.90	8.80	7.60	6.40		
140	145	17.10	15.40	14.20	13.10	11.90	10.70	9.60	8.40	7.20		
145	150	17.90	16.20	15.00	13.90	12.70	11.50	10.40	9.20	8.00		
150	160	19.10	17.40	16.20	15.10	13.90	12.70	11.60	10.40	9.20		

WEEKLY Payroll Period — Employee NOT MARRIED

And the wages are—		And the number of withholding allowances claimed is—										
At least	But less than	0	1	2	3	4	5	6	7	8	9	10 or more
		The amount of income tax to be withheld shall be—										
$160	170	$20.70	$17.60	$14.60	$11.50	$8.40	$5.30	$2.70	$.40	$0	$0	$0
170	180	22.50	19.20	16.20	13.10	10.00	6.90	5.40	2.80	1.70		
180	190	24.50	20.80	17.80	14.70	11.60	8.50	7.00	4.00	2.80		
190	200	26.50	22.80	19.40	16.30	13.20	10.10	7.00	5.60	2.90	.60	
200	210	28.50	24.60	21.00	17.90	14.80	11.70	8.60	5.80	4.10	1.80	0
210	220	30.50	26.60	22.80	19.50	16.40	13.30	10.20	7.20	5.70	3.00	.70
220	230	32.50	28.60	24.80	21.10	18.00	14.90	11.80	8.80	7.00	5.20	1.90
230	240	34.50	30.60	26.80	22.90	19.60	16.50	13.40	10.30	8.90	5.80	3.10
240	250	36.60	32.60	28.80	24.90	21.20	18.10	15.00	12.00	10.50	7.40	4.30
250	260	39.00	34.60	30.80	26.90	23.10	19.70	16.60	13.60	10.50		
260	270	41.40	36.80	32.80	28.90	25.10	21.30	18.20	15.20	12.10	9.00	5.90
270	280	43.80	39.20	34.80	30.90	27.10	23.20	19.80	16.80	13.70	10.60	7.50
280	290	46.20	41.60	37.00	32.90	29.10	25.20	21.40	18.40	15.30	12.20	9.10
290	300	48.60	44.00	39.40	34.90	31.10	27.20	23.40	20.00	16.90	13.80	10.70
300	310	51.00	46.40	41.80	37.20	33.10	29.20	25.40	21.60	18.50	15.40	12.30
310	320	53.40	48.80	44.20	39.60	35.10	31.20	27.40	23.50	20.10	17.00	13.90
320	330	55.80	51.20	46.60	42.00	37.40	33.20	29.40	25.50	21.70	18.60	15.50
330	340	58.20	53.60	49.00	44.40	39.80	35.20	31.40	27.50	23.70	20.20	17.10
340	350	61.80	56.10	51.40	46.80	42.20	37.60	33.40	29.50	25.70	21.80	18.70
350	360	64.80	59.10	53.80	49.20	44.60	40.00	35.40	31.50	27.70	23.80	20.30
360	370	67.80	62.10	56.30	51.60	47.00	42.40	37.80	33.50	29.70	25.80	22.00
370	380	70.80	65.10	59.30	54.00	49.40	44.80	40.20	35.50	31.70	27.80	24.00
380	390	73.80	68.10	62.30	56.50	51.80	47.20	42.60	37.90	33.70	29.80	26.00
390	400	76.80	71.10	65.30	59.50	54.20	49.60	45.00	40.30	35.70	31.80	28.00
400	410	79.80	74.10	68.30	62.50	56.80	52.00	47.40	42.70	38.10	33.80	30.00
410	420	82.80	77.10	71.30	65.50	59.80	54.40	49.80	45.10	40.50	35.90	32.00
420	430	85.80	80.10	74.30	68.50	62.80	57.00	52.20	47.50	42.90	38.30	34.00
430	440	88.80	83.10	77.30	71.50	65.80	60.00	54.60	49.90	45.30	40.70	36.00
440	450	92.30	86.10	80.30	74.50	68.80	63.00	57.20	52.30	47.70	43.10	38.50
450	460	95.70	89.20	83.30	77.50	71.80	66.00	60.20	54.70	50.10	45.50	40.90
460	470	99.10	92.60	86.30	80.50	74.80	69.00	63.20	57.50	52.50	47.90	43.30
470	480	102.50	96.00	89.50	83.50	77.80	72.00	66.20	60.40	54.90	50.30	45.70
480	490	105.90	99.40	92.90	86.50	80.80	75.00	69.20	63.40	57.70	52.70	48.10
490	500	109.30	102.80	96.30	89.70	83.80	78.00	72.20	66.40	60.70	55.10	50.50
500	510	112.70	106.20	99.70	93.10	86.80	81.00	75.20	69.40	63.70	57.90	52.90
510	520	116.10	109.60	103.10	96.50	90.00	84.00	78.20	72.40	66.70	60.90	55.30
520	530	119.50	113.00	106.50	99.90	93.40	87.00	81.20	75.40	69.70	63.90	58.20
530	540	122.90	116.40	109.90	103.30	96.80	90.30	84.20	78.40	72.70	66.90	61.20
540	550	126.70	119.80	113.30	106.70	100.20	93.70	87.20	81.40	75.70	69.90	64.20
550	560	130.40	123.20	116.70	110.10	103.60	97.10	90.50	84.40	78.70	72.90	67.20
560	570	134.10	126.80	120.10	113.50	107.00	100.40	93.90	87.40	81.70	75.90	70.20
570	580	137.80	130.50	123.50	116.90	110.40	103.80	97.30	90.70	84.70	78.90	73.20
580	590	141.50	134.20	127.20	120.30	113.80	107.20	100.70	94.20	87.70	81.90	76.20
590	600	145.20	137.90	130.90	123.90	117.20	110.60	104.10	97.50	91.00	84.90	79.20
600	610	148.90	141.70	134.60	127.50	120.60	114.00	107.50	101.00	94.40	87.90	82.20
610	620	152.60	145.40	138.30	131.20	124.10	117.40	110.90	104.40	97.80	91.30	85.20
620	630	156.30	149.10	142.00	134.90	127.80	120.80	114.30	107.80	101.20	94.70	88.20
630	640	160.00	152.80	145.70	138.60	131.50	124.40	117.70	111.20	104.60	98.10	95.00
640	650	163.70	156.50	149.40	142.30	135.20	128.10	121.10	114.60	108.00	101.50	95.00
650	660	167.40	160.20	153.10	146.00	138.90	131.80	124.60	118.00	111.40	104.90	98.40
660	670	171.10	163.90	156.80	149.70	142.60	135.50	128.40	121.30	114.80	108.30	101.80
670	680	174.80	167.60	160.50	153.40	146.30	139.20	132.10	124.90	118.20	111.70	105.20
680	690	178.50	171.30	164.20	157.10	150.00	142.90	135.80	128.60	121.60	115.10	108.60
690	700	182.20	175.00	167.90	160.80	153.70	146.50	139.50	132.30	125.20	118.50	112.00
700	710	185.90	178.70	171.60	164.50	157.40	150.30	143.20	136.00	128.90	121.90	115.40
710	720	189.60	182.40	175.30	168.20	161.10	154.00	146.80	139.70	132.60	125.50	118.80
720	730	193.30	186.10	179.00	171.90	164.80	157.70	150.60	143.40	136.30	129.20	122.10
730	740	197.00	189.80	182.70	175.60	168.50	161.40	154.30	147.10	140.00	132.90	125.80
$740 and over		198.80	191.70	184.60	177.50	170.30	163.20	156.10	149.00	141.90	134.80	127.60

37 percent of the excess over $740 plus—

Figure 4-4 Federal Tax Withholding Tables — Weekly Payroll

WAGE-BRACKET WITHHOLDING TABLES

MONTHLY Payroll Period — Employee MARRIED

And the wages are-		And the number of withholding allowances claimed is—										
At least	But less than	0	1	2	3	4	5	6	7	8	9	10 or more
		The amount of income tax to be withheld shall be—										
$0	$200	$0	$0	$0	$0	$0	$0	$0	$0	$0	$0	$0
200	204	.20	0	0	0	0	0	0	0	0	0	0
204	208	.70	0	0	0	0	0	0	0	0	0	0
208	212	1.20	0	0	0	0	0	0	0	0	0	0
212	216	1.70	0	0	0	0	0	0	0	0	0	0
216	220	2.20	0	0	0	0	0	0	0	0	0	0
220	224	2.60	0	0	0	0	0	0	0	0	0	0
224	228	3.10	0	0	0	0	0	0	0	0	0	0
228	232	3.60	0	0	0	0	0	0	0	0	0	0
232	236	4.10	0	0	0	0	0	0	0	0	0	0
236	240	4.60	0	0	0	0	0	0	0	0	0	0
240	248	5.30	0	0	0	0	0	0	0	0	0	0
248	256	6.20	0	0	0	0	0	0	0	0	0	0
256	264	7.20	0	0	0	0	0	0	0	0	0	0
264	272	8.20	0	0	0	0	0	0	0	0	0	0
272	280	9.10	0	0	0	0	0	0	0	0	0	0
280	288	10.10	.10	0	0	0	0	0	0	0	0	0
288	296	11.00	1.00	0	0	0	0	0	0	0	0	0
296	304	12.00	2.00	0	0	0	0	0	0	0	0	0
304	312	13.00	3.00	0	0	0	0	0	0	0	0	0
312	320	13.90	3.90	0	0	0	0	0	0	0	0	0
320	328	14.90	4.90	0	0	0	0	0	0	0	0	0
328	336	15.80	5.80	0	0	0	0	0	0	0	0	0
336	344	16.80	6.80	0	0	0	0	0	0	0	0	0
344	352	17.80	7.80	0	0	0	0	0	0	0	0	0
352	360	18.70	8.70	0	0	0	0	0	0	0	0	0
360	368	19.70	9.70	0	0	0	0	0	0	0	0	0
368	376	20.60	10.60	.60	0	0	0	0	0	0	0	0
376	384	21.60	11.60	1.60	0	0	0	0	0	0	0	0
384	392	22.60	12.60	2.60	0	0	0	0	0	0	0	0
At least	But less than	0	1	2	3	4	5	6	7	8	9	10 or more
392	400	23.50	13.50	3.50	0	0	0	0	0	0	0	0
400	420	25.20	15.20	5.20	0	0	0	0	0	0	0	0
420	440	27.60	17.60	7.60	0	0	0	0	0	0	0	0
440	460	30.00	20.00	10.00	0	0	0	0	0	0	0	0
460	480	32.40	22.40	12.40	2.40	0	0	0	0	0	0	0
480	500	34.80	24.80	14.80	4.80	0	0	0	0	0	0	0
500	520	37.40	27.20	17.20	7.20	0	0	0	0	0	0	0
520	540	40.60	29.60	19.60	9.60	0	0	0	0	0	0	0
540	560	43.80	32.00	22.00	12.00	2.00	0	0	0	0	0	0
560	580	47.00	34.40	24.40	14.40	4.40	0	0	0	0	0	0
580	600	50.20	36.80	26.80	16.80	6.80	0	0	0	0	0	0
600	640	55.00	41.60	30.40	20.40	10.40	.40	0	0	0	0	0
640	680	61.40	48.00	35.20	25.20	15.20	5.20	0	0	0	0	0
680	720	67.80	54.40	41.10	30.00	20.00	10.00	0	0	0	0	0
720	760	74.20	60.80	47.50	34.80	24.80	14.80	4.80	0	0	0	0
760	800	80.60	67.20	53.90	40.60	29.60	19.60	9.60	0	0	0	0
800	840	87.00	73.60	60.30	47.00	34.40	24.40	14.40	4.40	0	0	0
840	880	93.40	80.00	66.70	53.40	40.00	29.20	19.20	9.20	0	0	0
880	920	99.80	86.40	73.10	59.80	46.40	34.00	24.00	14.00	4.00	0	0
920	960	106.20	92.80	79.50	66.20	52.80	39.50	28.80	18.80	8.80	0	0
960	1,000	112.60	99.20	85.90	72.60	59.20	45.90	33.60	23.60	13.60	3.60	0
1,000	1,040	119.60	105.60	92.30	79.00	65.60	52.30	39.00	28.40	18.40	8.40	0
1,040	1,080	127.20	112.00	98.70	85.40	72.00	58.70	45.40	33.20	23.20	13.20	3.20
1,080	1,120	134.80	119.00	105.10	91.80	78.40	65.10	51.80	38.40	28.00	18.00	8.00
1,120	1,160	142.40	126.60	111.50	98.20	84.80	71.50	58.20	44.80	32.80	22.80	12.80
1,160	1,200	150.00	134.20	118.30	104.60	91.20	77.90	64.60	51.20	37.90	27.60	17.60
1,200	1,240	157.60	141.80	125.90	111.00	97.60	84.30	71.00	57.60	44.30	32.40	22.40
1,240	1,280	165.20	149.40	133.50	117.70	104.00	90.70	77.40	64.00	50.70	37.40	27.20
1,280	1,320	172.80	157.00	141.10	125.30	110.40	97.10	83.80	70.40	57.10	43.80	32.00
1,320	1,360	180.40	164.60	148.70	132.90	117.10	103.50	90.20	76.80	63.50	50.20	36.80
1,360	1,400	188.00	172.20	156.30	140.50	124.70	109.90	96.60	83.20	69.90	56.60	43.20
1,400	1,440	195.60	179.80	163.90	148.10	132.30	116.40	103.00	89.60	76.30	63.00	49.60
1,440	1,480	203.20	187.40	171.50	155.70	139.90	124.00	109.40	96.00	82.70	69.40	56.00
1,480	1,520	210.80	195.00	179.10	163.30	147.50	131.60	115.80	102.40	89.10	75.80	62.40
1,520	1,560	218.40	202.60	186.70	170.90	155.10	139.20	123.40	108.80	95.50	82.20	68.80

MONTHLY Payroll Period — Employee MARRIED

And the wages are-		And the number of withholding allowances claimed is—										
At least	But less than	0	1	2	3	4	5	6	7	8	9	10 or more
		The amount of income tax to be withheld shall be—										
$1,560	$1,600	$227.80	$210.20	$194.30	$178.50	$162.70	$146.80	$131.00	$115.20	$101.90	$88.60	$75.20
1,600	1,640	237.40	217.80	201.90	186.10	170.30	154.40	138.60	122.80	108.30	95.00	81.60
1,640	1,680	247.00	227.00	209.50	193.70	177.90	162.00	146.20	130.40	114.70	101.40	88.00
1,680	1,720	256.60	236.60	217.10	201.30	185.50	169.60	153.80	138.00	122.10	107.80	94.40
1,720	1,760	266.20	246.20	226.20	208.90	193.10	177.20	161.40	145.60	129.70	114.20	100.80
1,760	1,800	275.80	255.80	235.80	216.50	200.70	184.80	169.00	153.20	137.30	121.50	107.20
1,800	1,840	285.40	265.40	245.40	225.40	208.30	192.40	176.60	160.80	144.90	129.10	113.60
1,840	1,880	295.00	275.00	255.00	235.00	215.90	200.00	184.20	168.40	152.50	136.70	120.90
1,880	1,920	304.60	284.60	264.60	244.60	224.60	207.60	191.80	176.00	160.10	144.30	128.50
1,920	1,960	314.20	294.20	274.20	254.20	234.20	215.20	199.40	183.60	167.70	151.90	136.10
1,960	2,000	324.20	303.80	283.80	263.80	243.80	223.80	207.00	191.20	175.30	159.50	143.70
2,000	2,040	335.00	313.40	293.40	273.40	253.40	233.40	214.60	198.80	182.90	167.10	151.30
2,040	2,080	345.80	323.30	303.00	283.00	263.00	243.00	223.00	206.40	190.50	174.70	158.90
2,080	2,120	356.60	334.10	312.60	292.60	272.60	252.60	232.60	214.00	198.10	182.30	166.50
2,120	2,160	367.40	344.90	322.40	302.20	282.20	262.20	242.20	222.20	205.70	189.90	174.10
2,160	2,200	378.20	355.70	333.20	311.80	291.80	271.80	251.80	231.80	213.30	197.50	181.70
2,200	2,240	389.00	366.50	344.00	321.50	301.40	281.40	261.40	241.40	221.40	205.10	189.30
2,240	2,280	399.80	377.30	354.80	332.30	311.00	291.00	271.00	251.00	231.00	212.70	196.90
2,280	2,320	410.60	388.10	365.60	343.10	320.60	300.60	280.60	260.60	240.60	220.60	204.50
2,320	2,360	421.40	398.90	376.40	353.90	331.40	310.20	290.20	270.20	250.20	230.20	212.10
2,360	2,400	432.20	409.70	387.20	364.70	342.20	319.80	299.80	279.80	259.80	239.80	219.80
2,400	2,440	443.60	420.50	398.00	375.50	353.00	330.50	309.40	289.40	269.40	249.40	229.40
2,440	2,480	456.40	431.30	408.80	386.30	363.80	341.30	319.00	299.00	279.00	259.00	239.00
2,480	2,520	469.20	442.50	419.60	397.10	374.60	352.10	329.60	308.60	288.60	268.60	248.60
2,520	2,560	482.00	455.30	430.40	407.90	385.40	362.90	340.40	318.20	298.20	278.20	258.20
2,560	2,600	494.80	468.10	441.40	418.70	396.20	373.70	351.20	328.70	307.80	287.80	267.80
2,600	2,640	507.60	480.90	454.20	429.50	407.00	384.50	362.00	339.50	317.40	297.40	277.40
2,640	2,680	520.40	493.70	467.00	440.40	417.80	395.30	372.80	350.30	327.80	307.00	287.00
2,680	2,720	533.20	506.50	479.80	453.20	428.60	406.10	383.60	361.10	338.60	316.60	296.60
2,720	2,760	546.00	519.30	492.60	466.00	439.40	416.90	394.40	371.90	349.40	326.90	306.20
At least	But less than	0	1	2	3	4	5	6	7	8	9	10 or more
2,760	2,800	558.80	532.10	505.40	478.80	452.10	427.70	405.20	382.70	360.20	337.70	315.80
2,800	2,840	571.60	544.90	518.20	491.60	464.90	438.50	416.00	393.50	371.00	348.50	326.00
2,840	2,880	584.90	557.70	531.00	504.40	477.70	451.00	426.80	404.30	381.80	359.30	336.80
2,880	2,920	599.70	570.50	543.80	517.20	490.50	463.80	437.60	415.10	392.60	370.10	347.60
2,920	2,960	614.50	583.60	556.60	530.00	503.30	476.60	450.00	425.90	403.40	380.90	358.40
2,960	3,000	629.30	598.40	569.40	542.80	516.10	489.40	462.80	436.70	414.20	391.70	369.20
3,000	3,040	644.10	613.20	582.40	555.60	528.90	502.20	475.60	448.90	425.00	402.50	380.00
3,040	3,080	658.90	628.00	597.20	568.40	541.70	515.00	488.40	461.70	435.80	413.30	390.80
3,080	3,120	673.70	642.80	612.00	581.20	554.50	527.80	501.20	474.50	447.80	424.10	401.60
3,120	3,160	688.50	657.60	626.80	596.00	567.30	540.60	514.00	487.30	460.60	434.90	412.40
3,160	3,200	703.30	672.40	641.60	610.80	580.10	553.40	526.80	500.10	473.40	446.80	423.20
3,200	3,240	718.10	687.20	656.40	625.60	594.70	566.20	539.60	512.90	486.20	459.60	434.00
3,240	3,280	732.90	702.00	671.20	640.40	609.50	579.00	552.40	525.70	499.00	472.40	445.70
3,280	3,320	747.70	716.80	686.00	655.20	624.30	593.50	565.20	538.50	511.80	485.20	458.50
3,320	3,360	762.50	731.60	700.80	670.00	639.10	608.30	578.00	551.30	524.60	498.00	471.30
3,360	3,400	777.30	746.40	715.60	684.80	653.90	623.10	592.30	564.10	537.40	510.80	484.10
3,400	3,440	792.10	761.20	730.40	699.60	668.70	637.90	607.10	576.90	550.20	523.60	496.90
3,440	3,480	806.90	776.00	745.20	714.40	683.50	652.70	621.90	591.00	563.00	536.40	509.70
3,480	3,520	821.70	790.80	760.00	729.20	698.30	667.50	636.70	605.80	575.80	549.20	522.50
3,520	3,560	836.50	805.60	774.80	744.00	713.10	682.30	651.50	620.60	589.80	562.00	535.30
3,560	3,600	851.30	820.40	789.60	758.80	727.90	697.10	666.30	635.40	604.60	574.80	548.10
3,600	3,640	866.10	835.20	804.40	773.60	742.70	711.90	681.10	650.20	619.40	588.60	560.90
3,640	3,680	880.90	850.00	819.20	788.40	757.50	726.70	695.90	665.00	634.20	603.40	573.70
3,680	3,720	895.70	864.80	834.00	803.20	772.30	741.50	710.70	679.80	649.00	618.20	587.30
		37 percent of the excess over $3 720 plus—										
$3,720 and over		903.10	872.20	841.40	810.60	779.70	748.90	718.10	687.20	656.40	625.60	594.70

Figure 4-5 Federal Tax Withholding Tables — Monthly Payroll

BENEFITS

◆◆◆◆◆◆◆◆

A benefit that employers must provide is time off for national holidays. Full-time employees who receive a salary are entitled to have off, with pay, those holidays designated as *paid holidays*. These include Christmas, Thanksgiving, Fourth of July, Labor Day, and Memorial Day. Other holidays that are considered paid holidays by many companies include New Year's Day, Veterans' Day, and Presidents' Day. An employee cannot be required to work on a national holiday, and, if he or she does, the compensation is double or more than double the regular rate of pay.

Many employers provide one or more of the following *fringe (optional) benefits.*

Pay for work on national holidays is usually double.

PROFIT SHARING

Profit sharing is usually a plan whereby employees are allowed to receive a portion of the company's profits at the end of the corporate year: the more the company makes (profits), the more the company has to share with employees. Most companies who offer profit sharing consider it an **incentive**, which is a way to encourage employees to do more and better quality work. An incentive pays off financially for both the company and the worker.

Incentives encourage better performance.

PAID VACATIONS

Most businesses provide full-time employees with a set amount of paid vacation time. While you are on vacation, you are paid as usual. It is common to receive a week's paid vacation after a year, two weeks after two years, and three weeks after five years' employment, and so on. Most businesses also offer unpaid leaves to employees for short periods of time, so long as you have a good reason and make arrangements in advance.

DISCOUNTS

Many companies offer their employees discounts on merchandise sold or made by the company. For example, if you work at a clothing store that allows employee discounts, you can purchase your clothing for a reduced price. A usual discount is 10 percent or more. Service businesses often provide free services to employees (such as free food or entertainment) or give employees the private use of company space and equipment.

SICK PAY

Many businesses also provide an allowance of days each year for illness, with pay as usual, for full-time workers. It is customary to receive three to ten days a year as "sick days" without deductions from pay. Employers often have sick leave policies that do not permit sick pay for the days immediately before or after a holiday (such as Christmas or Thanksgiving) or vacation. In other words, you may not be allowed to take sick time so that it extends your other paid time off work.

Sick pay is available to full-time workers.

LEAVE OF ABSENCE

Some employers allow employees to leave their jobs (without pay) for certain events, such as having children or completing education, and to return to their jobs at a later time. In some cases, the company pays for such leaves. A **sabbatical** is a leave that benefits the company as well as the employee, and is funded partly or wholly by the employer. Generally, when an employer specifically asks you to take time away from your present job to complete more education or special training, the employer will pay for your time off. Of course, a sabbatical is not always "fun" and often involves specified courses of job-related study or training.

INSURANCE

Most large companies provide group health insurance plans for all employees. Some plans are paid entirely by the employer as a part of employee compensation, with full family coverage. Other plans require paycheck deductions if employees elect to participate in the plan. Other plans are called **cafeteria-style** because employees are allowed to choose the amounts and types of coverage they desire. If chosen coverages exceed some limit, the employee must pay the difference. The advantage of cafeteria-style insurance is that a family's needs change (children are born or children leave home) and therefore different coverages are required.

Coverages vary according to plans purchased.

Insurance plans typically include hospitalization, major medical, dental, vision, and life insurance. A typical health insurance plan has a $150 deductible per person, then pays 80 percent of most doctor bills and prescriptions, and 100 percent of hospitalization charges and emergency bills. Many insurance plans will not cover routine physical examinations because they are not classified as illness or injury. Chapter 10 provides more detailed health insurance information.

BONUSES

Bonuses are employee incentives.

Bonus plans include stock options or salary incentive plans based on quality of work done, years of service, or company profits. Typically, companies like to give bonuses at Christmas time or other special events such as company anniversaries or at the end of a big selling season. Once again, the more profitable a company is, the more individual employees will be paid in bonuses.

RETIREMENT PLANS

Some employers provide retirement plans whereby employees contribute a percentage of gross pay, which may or may not be matched by the employer. When an employee retires, he or she receives a monthly check that is partially or wholly taxable. In some cases, an employee may borrow against the account, withdraw it early in part or in full, or retire early and begin collecting benefits. Retirement accounts are generally considered to be owned by the employee, although in many plans employees are not allowed to withdraw funds while they are employed by the company.

TRAVEL EXPENSES

Mileage is allowed when you drive your own car.

Companies that require employees to travel in the course of their work often provide company cars or mileage allowances if employees use their own cars. Often car insurance, gasoline, and repair and maintenance expenses for the company automobile are also provided. While out of town, employees may be paid a daily allowance, or have their motel and meals paid, as well as other travel expenses. Some employees have an **expense account**, which allows them to charge travel and entertainment expenses to the company's account rather than pay for them first and be reimbursed by the company later.

Many of these optional benefits are of great value to employees. Optional benefits generally are not taxable to employees (except bonuses and some benefits paid in cash), yet they provide coverages and advantages. Generally, large companies provide more extensive optional benefit packages than smaller companies.

LABOR UNIONS AND PROFESSIONAL ORGANIZATIONS

◆◆◆◆◆◆◆◆

Membership in unions is sometimes required.

Many employment opportunities also involve union membership or participation in a professional organization as a requirement of employment. A **union** is a unit or group of people joined together for a common purpose. A **labor union** is a group of people who work in the same or similar occupations, organized for the benefit of all employees in these occupations.

HISTORY OF UNIONS

Unions were organized in the United States as early as the late 1800s. The first unions were local units organized by skilled craftspeople to protect themselves from competition of untrained and unskilled workers. In 1886 the American Federation of Labor (AFL) was organized by Samuel Gompers, who served as its president for 37 years.

Unions had a slow and painful start.

Early unions had very little power until 1935 when the National Labor Relations Act (Wagner Act) gave unions the right to organize and bargain with employers. In 1938 John L. Lewis became the first president of a new union — the Congress of Industrial Organizations (CIO). Unions continued to grow in number, power, and size until 1947, when Congress passed the Labor Management Relations Act, commonly called the Taft-Hartley Act. This act was passed to limit the powers of unions and to curb strikes. In 1955 the AFL and the CIO merged under the leadership of George Meany and became the largest and most powerful union in the United States.

FUNCTIONS OF UNIONS

The importance of labor unions in American life cannot be measured by the number of workers in unions. Many nonunion employers are influenced by

Illustration 4-2
Many American
workers benefit
from the activity of
labor unions.

the standards set by union agreements with other employers; and many employees reap the benefits of unionization even though they do not belong to a union. Labor unions have four major functions: (a) recruitment of new members; (b) collective bargaining; (c) support of political candidates who are favorable to the union; and (d) provision of support services for members, including employment, job transfer, membership and employment credentials, and education.

Large unions are usually powerful.

Unions exercise power through large numbers of members. Therefore, new employees in occupations that have unions are strongly urged, if membership is not mandatory, to join the union. Political candidates who express opinions favorable to a particular union may receive campaign funds and/or endorsements from union leaders. These endorsements usually mean large numbers of union members, locally and nationally, will vote for the candidate. Unions provide support for their members by helping to keep their members employed, negotiating job transfers, providing credentials for job-seeking employees, and providing education necessary to obtain and keep jobs held by union members.

Unions negotiate employment contracts.

The major function of unions is **collective bargaining,** which is the process of negotiating the terms of employment for union members. Terms of the agreement are written in an employment contract. The contract is usually quite detailed and is divided into these major sections: wages and benefits; workers' rights on the job; union rights in relation to the employer; management rights in relation to the union; and the grievance procedures when a provision of the contract has not been honored.

The contract stipulates wages to be paid for certain jobs and types of work. Paid holidays, vacations, overtime rates, and hours of work are also specified in the contract. Most contracts list the **fringe benefits,** which are optional or extra benefits provided for employees. Health insurance, sick leave, and pensions are considered fringe benefits. Union contracts usually provide for seniority rights, which state that the last ones hired should be the first ones laid off. **Seniority** refers to taking precedence because of the length of time one has worked for a company in a particular position, or in a particular department. In other words, the longer you work, the more job security you are entitled to have. Seniority may be used to determine transfers, promotions, and vacation time according to most union contracts.

Seniority rights are stated in contracts.

When agreement as to the meaning of a contract provision cannot be reached between the union and the employer through a grievance procedure, the dispute can go through additional steps. **Negotiation** is the process whereby the employer meets with union representatives to work out an agreement satisfactory to both sides. When this fails, the next step is called mediation. Under **mediation,** a neutral third party is chosen to assist the parties in reaching a decision. Under the most often used process, called **arbitration,** the decision of the neutral third party is binding on the parties, a condition that is agreed upon before the process begins. If the union and the employer do not agree to binding arbitration, and cannot agree on the terms of a new contract, the labor union may make the decision to **strike,** a process whereby the members of the union refuse to work until an agreement is reached.

The collective bargaining process has many steps.

TYPES OF UNIONS

Unions are classified into three types: craft unions, industrial unions, and public employee unions.

Various occupations have different unions.

Craft Unions. Membership in craft unions is limited to those who practice in an established craft or trade, such as bricklayers, carpenters, or plasterers. Major craft unions include those of the building, printing, and maritime trades, and of railroad employees.

Industrial Unions. Membership in industrial unions is composed of skilled, semiskilled, or unskilled workers in a particular place, industry, or group of industries. Examples include the AFL-CIO, Teamsters, and United Auto Workers.

Public Employee Unions. Municipal, county, state, or federal employees such as firemen, teachers, and policemen may organize public employee unions.

Unions are self-governing organizations. Major decisions are made by elected leaders. Of the four functions of unions, the most significant is collective bargaining. Many unions have developed a high degree of professionalism and power. Union leaders often devote full time to their positions. Unions often employ their own lawyers, doctors, economists, educators, and public relations officials; dues collected from the members provide the basis for the services of these professionals. Because unions collect large sums from members yearly, their funds are often invested in large companies and industries and provide unions with high visibility and importance in the American economy.

Powerful unions now exist.

PROFESSIONAL ORGANIZATIONS

Dues are used to fund professional organizations.

Professional organizations also collect dues from members and provide support services. A **professional organization** is an organization formed to serve the professional interests of members of a particular profession. In some cases, membership in a professional organization may be compulsory. The most notable professional organizations include the American Bar Association (required) for lawyers and the American Medical Association (optional) for doctors. Each state bar association provides the testing procedures by which lawyers who pass are "admitted to the bar." Attorneys can be severely disciplined, or "disbarred," which means they can no longer practice law.

Purposes of professional organizations are (a) to establish and maintain professional standards, including procedures for self-improvement; (b) to support legislation and political action that is beneficial to the profession (known as **lobbying**); (c) to encourage individual growth and achievement; (d) to publish a professional journal or magazine; (e) to provide pension, retirement, and insurance benefits for members, and (f) to keep members up-to-date on current information and procedures. Because most doctors and lawyers are self-employed, they are not regulated as to professional behavior except through membership in these organizations and/or through court procedures. Exams, accreditations, admission procedures, and other standards are administered through these professional organizations.

Unions benefit all employees.

Another professional organization, sometimes called a union (the largest one nationwide), is the National Education Association (NEA). Dues are *unified*, which means that an educator who joins a local association must also join the state and national associations. Each branch of the NEA charges dues, just as do the national, state, and county bar associations.

VOCABULARY

Directions: Can you find the definition for each of the following terms used in Chapter 4?

gross pay	collective bargaining
deductions	fringe/optional benefits
net pay	seniority
incentive	negotiation
sabbatical	mediation
cafeteria-style	arbitration
expense account	strike
union	professional organization
labor union	lobbying

1. Similar to labor unions, but membership is required for persons in certain occupations.
2. A process whereby employees refuse to work until an agreement is reached.
3. An effort to support legislation that would benefit a certain group.
4. The total agreed upon salary or pay before deductions.
5. A leave of absence that will benefit both employer and employee, and which usually has some compensation for the employee during the time off.
6. Amounts subtracted from gross pay, some required and some optional.
7. Also known as the amount of the paycheck.
8. Added benefits that are not required by law, but are provided by employers as a part of the total wage package.
9. A benefit for employees who are able to charge their expenses to the company's account rather than pay for them and be reimbursed.
10. Groups of people in the same or similar occupations, organized for the benefit of all.
11. The process whereby unions and employers negotiate terms of employment.
12. Taking precedence because of length of time worked.
13. Encouragement plan to get employees to do more and better work.
14. An insurance program whereby employees may choose desired coverages.
15. The employer and union representatives meet and work out an agreement satisfactory to both sides.
16. A neutral third party is chosen to assist the employer and the union reach an agreement.

17. The decision of a neutral third party is legally binding on the parties.
18. A unit or group of people joined together for a common purpose.

ITEMS FOR DISCUSSION

1. How is gross pay different from net pay?
2. List five optional deductions you may elect to have withheld from your gross pay.
3. What is required when an employee has worked more than the maximum regular workweek?
4. What is a leave of absence? How is it different from a sabbatical?
5. What are the four major functions of labor unions?
6. What are the three types of labor unions?
7. How are labor unions funded; that is, how are labor unions able to operate — who pays for the services that are provided?
8. What is collective bargaining?
9. What is seniority?
10. What was the significance of the Wagner Act to American labor?
11. What is a strike?
12. Name a professional organization.
13. Explain lobbying.

APPLICATIONS

1. Compute gross pay for these situations:

   a. Regular hours worked: 40
       Overtime hours worked: 5
       Regular rate of pay: $3.85 an hour

   b. Regular salary: $800 a month
       Overtime hours agreed upon: 8 a week (four weeks)
       Overtime rate of pay agreed upon: $6.82 an hour

   c. Total hours worked: 43 (in 5 days)
       Regular rate of pay: $4.10

   d. Annual salary: $18,000
       Compute gross pay (monthly)

2. Using the payroll income tax withholding tables on pages 63-66, find the following answers:

    a. For a single person, two allowances, who made $110 last week:

        State withholding tax: _____
        Federal withholding tax: _____

    b. For a single person, no allowances, who made $222 last week:

        State withholding tax: _____
        Federal withholding tax: _____

    c. For a married person, two allowances, who made $1,120 last month:

        State withholding tax: _____
        Federal withholding tax: _____
        Social security tax: _____

    d. For a married person, six allowances, who made $1,479 last month:

        State withholding tax: _____
        Federal withholding tax: _____
        Social security tax: _____

CASE PROBLEMS AND ACTIVITIES

1. Rudy Valdez, social security number 484-40-9876, works for a weekly paycheck. He is single and claims no allowances. Last week he worked five days, for a total of 44 hours. His regular rate of pay is $6.60 an hour. In addition to federal income tax, state income tax (use tables shown in Figures 4-2 through 4-5), and social security tax, Rudy has insurance of $16 a week withheld and puts 6 percent of his gross salary into his retirement account.

    Compute Rudy's gross pay, deductions, and net paycheck.

2. Maureen Chin, social security number 444-33-2121, works for a weekly paycheck. She is single and claims one allowance. Last week she worked five days, for a total of 48 hours. Her regular rate of pay is $6.80 an hour. In addition to required deductions, Maureen also has $10 a week sent to her credit union account and gives $5 a week to United Way (charity).

    Compute Maureen's gross pay, deductions, and net paycheck.

3. John Rubenstein, social security number 644-30-2929, works for a monthly salary. He is married and claims four allowances. Last

month John worked 22 days. He does not get paid for overtime. His monthly salary is $1,780. In addition to required deductions, John also pays insurance premiums of $23 a month and sets aside for retirement 6 percent of his gross monthly pay.

Compute John's gross pay, deductions, and net paycheck.

4. Andrea Newton, social security number 331-84-3139, works for a monthly paycheck. She is married and claims two allowances. Her yearly salary is $14,700. Last month she worked 21 days, without overtime. In addition to required deductions, Andrea also contributes $14 a week (assume a four-week month) to the Heart Fund and sets aside $50 a month, paid directly to her savings account.

   Compute Andrea's gross pay, deductions, and net paycheck.

5. Bill Webb, social security number 414-31-3245, works for a monthly salary. He is married and claims no allowances. His monthly salary is $1,500. When Bill works overtime it is at an agreed hourly rate of $12.75. Last month he worked 10 hours that will be paid overtime. He worked 23 days. Bill has only the required deductions.

   Compute Bill's gross pay, deductions, and net paycheck.

6. Interview three employees (or employers) in your local area. Choose one from a small business with 10 or fewer employees, the second from a medium-sized company, and the third from a large corporate employer. Try to find similar jobs, if possible. Ask these employees (or employers) what types of fringe benefits are supplied for the employees. Compare the three. Do you note similarities? Differences?

7. Your friend Sally is considering two job openings. One will require her to join a union. The other does not require a union, but has similar pay and benefits. Explain to Sally the advantages and disadvantages of belonging to a union.

UNIT TWO
MONEY MANAGEMENT

UNIT OBJECTIVES

After studying the chapters in this second unit that illustrate the decisions that contribute to financial stability and personal satisfaction, the student will be able to:

1 ■ Prepare financial planning documents and describe types of contracts.

2 ■ Prepare documents used with checking accounts, and compare consumer banking services.

3 ■ Understand purposes, types, and history of taxes, and prepare a short form tax return.

4 ■ Give examples of savings options, discuss the need for and purpose of savings, and compute interest on savings.

5 ■ Discuss investment options, the need for and purpose of investments, and the criteria for choosing investments.

6 ■ Identify principles of risk management, understand insurance terminology, and describe types and benefits of major types of insurance.

Chapter 5

FINANCIAL PLANNING AND LEGAL DOCUMENTS

◆◆◆◆◆◆◆◆◆◆◆◆◆◆◆◆◆◆◆◆◆◆◆◆◆◆◆◆◆

OBJECTIVES

1. Analyze and understand the budgeting process.
2. Prepare personal and case study budgets.
3. Understand the purpose of personal record keeping.
4. Prepare a personal net worth statement and a personal property inventory.
5. Explain the elements of legal contracts and negotiable instruments.
6. Understand and explain consumer rights and responsibilities when entering into agreements.

BUDGETING INCOME AND EXPENSES

◆◆◆◆◆◆◆◆◆

How would you like to have unlimited resources to buy all the things you want or need? Unfortunately, for most people personal financial management is not that easy. Careful budgeting and planning are needed to enable you to meet your financial goals. That is why you need to study financial planning and budgeting — so that you will be able to make the most of your financial resources.

IMPORTANCE OF FINANCIAL PLANNING

Your **disposable income** is the money you have to spend as you wish — after taxes, social security, and other required and optional deductions have been withheld from your gross pay. In order to use this income to your best ability, you will need to create a financial plan.

All the money you receive is spent, saved, or invested. You may spend it for things you need or want, save it for future needs, or invest it to earn more money. **Financial planning** is an orderly program for spending, saving, and investing the money you earn. You may already understand the need to save part of your income for the future. Financial planning is important because it helps you to do the following:

1. Determine and evaluate how wisely you are using your money
2. Get the most from your income
3. Prevent careless and wasteful spending
4. Organize your **financial resources** (sources of income) so that you can maintain a plan of personal financial fitness
5. Avoid money worries and problems by understanding the proper methods of saving, spending, and borrowing money

Eliminate waste through planning.

The first step in financial fitness is to set up a plan. A **budget** is an organized plan whereby you match your expected income to your expected out-flow. The purpose of budgeting is to plan your spending and saving so that you won't have to borrow money to meet your needs. Careful budgeting will enable you to stretch your money to provide for your present and future needs and satisfy your wants.

Budgeting allows for better financial planning.

PREPARING A BUDGET

Figure 5-1 shows a high school junior's budget plan for one month. This student expects to receive a total of $260, and plans to use the money for certain needs and wants and to save part of it as well.

The first step in setting up a budget is to estimate total expected disposable income for a certain time. Include all money you expect to receive. You may wish to use a weekly, biweekly, or monthly budget — whichever best matches how often you expect to receive income (money).

The second step is to decide how much of your income you want to save — to set aside for future needs. Most financial experts advise saving at least 10 percent of your disposable income each pay period. By saving at least 10

Set aside for savings each month.

Figure 5-1
Simple Budget

Budget for September

Income
	Work (part-time)...	$220.00
	Allowance (household chores)................................	10.00
	Lunch money..	30.00
	Total income...	**$260.00**

Expenses
	Savings (monthly)..	$195.00
	Daily lunches...	20.00
	Miscellaneous: supplies.......................................	12.00
	snacks...	14.00
	other..	19.00
	Total expenses..	**$260.00**

percent, you will have money to pay for future needs, both expected and unexpected. We'll take Benjamin Franklin's famous saying a step further: A penny saved is *better* than a penny earned because it has already been taxed.

The third step is to estimate your expenses, or money you will need for day-to-day purchases, for example, lunches, fees, personal care items, clothing, and so forth.

■■■■   A TYPICAL MONTHLY BUDGET   ■■■■

Figure 5-2 represents the monthly budget of Diane and Bill Blacke, a recently married couple. Diane and Bill have no children, and both are working. The Blackes estimate their expected income by adding together their two take-home incomes (paychecks). They have decided to save at least 20 percent every month, invest some of their income in a home, and use the rest as shown. To further refine their budget, Diane and Bill could divide their expenses into two groups: fixed expenses and variable expenses.

Fixed expenses are those that remain constant, and to remove or change them will require a major revision in life-style. Examples are savings, house payments, utilities, car payments, average gasoline and car maintenance costs, and insurance premium payments. These expenses are fixed in the short run, but can be altered in the long run by careful planning.

Variable expenses will change according to needs and short-term goals. Sufficient money should be allowed to cover these expenses, because they can change frequently. Usually the change is relatively small, although

Fixed expenses are difficult to change.

major events (such as emergencies) can cause one or more variable expenses
to change drastically in a month. Examples are telephone, TV cable service,
groceries, dental or medical bills not covered by insurance, entertainment
expense, recreation, charge account purchases, investments, and miscellaneous purchases.

Figure 5-2
Budget for Married
Couple

Budget
Diane and Bill Blacke

	Month	Year
Income (monthly)...	$1,800	$21,600
Expenses		
Savings..	$ 200	$ 2,400
House payment..	450	5,400
Utilities (average).......................................	80	960
Car payment..	150	1,800
Gasoline..	100	1,200
Car maintenance..	15	180
Insurance		
Car...	30	360
Life and Health..	50	600
Telephone..	45	540
Cable television..	25	300
Groceries...	200	2,400
Entertainment and recreation.......................	100	1,200
Vacation fund...	75	900
Charge accounts (clothing)...........................	200	2,400
Miscellaneous..	80	960
Total expenses...	$1,800	$21,600

PERSONAL RECORDS
◆◆◆◆◆◆◆◆

Efficient personal records are important. They make planning a budget easier; they assure improved long-range financial planning; and they are a basis for properly completing income tax returns, credit applications, and other needed forms. Basically, there are four types of personal records that most families will want to keep: records of income and expenses, a statement of net worth, a personal property inventory, and tax records.

Keep important records in a safe place.

RECORDS OF INCOME AND EXPENSES

W-2 statements sent by employers each January show money earned and deductions made by the employer during the year. The W-2s prove that you had social security withheld. You may need the W-2s later when you want to collect social security benefits. Other records of income include bank statements of interest earned on savings, or other IRS forms showing miscellaneous money earned or received by you. Expense items include receipts listing any charity contributions, medical bills, or work-related expenses. All this information will be needed when preparing budgets and tax returns. These receipts and statements are often called *documents* and can be used as *proof*, or evidence, of income and expenses. These documents should be stored in a safe place for future reference.

Keep receipts for tax return information.

STATEMENT OF NET WORTH

A net worth statement, such as shown in Figure 5-3, is a list of items of value, called *assets*, that a person owns; amounts of money that are owed to others, called *liabilities* or debts; and the difference between the two, known as *net worth*. If your assets are greater than your liabilities, you are said to be *solvent*, or in a favorable credit position. But if your liabilities are greater than your assets (you owe more than you own), you are said to be *insolvent*, or in a poor credit position.

Solvent means you're a good credit risk.

Net worth information (lists of assets and liabilities) is often required when you ask for a loan or apply for credit. The bank or other financial institution will want you to be solvent and a good risk who will likely pay back the loan. How does your personal net worth statement compare to the one shown in Figure 5-3?

Figure 5-3
Net Worth State-
ment

Net Worth Statement
Janice Wilson
January 1, 19—

ASSETS		LIABILITIES	
Checking account......	$ 58.00	Loan at bank on car...	$ 600.00
Savings account........	80.00	Loan from Mother.....	80.00
Car value...............	1,000.00	Total Liabilities.........	$ 680.00
Personal property (inventory attached)	2.000.00		
		NET WORTH	
		Assets – liabilities.......	$2,458.00
Total Assets..............	$3,138.00	Total.....................	$3,138.00

PERSONAL PROPERTY INVENTORY

The personal property inventory (Figure 5-4) is a list of all the personal property a person owns. Personal property is usually all items inside the home — clothing, furniture, appliances and so forth. A personal property inventory is especially useful in the event of fire, theft, or property damage, as proof of possession and value. As a further safeguard, a person or family may photograph items of value, attach the photographs to the inventory, and keep this information in a safe-deposit box or other safe place to use as evidence in the event the property is damaged, lost, or stolen. As new items are purchased and others disposed of, the inventory should be revised.

An inventory is proof of property ownership.

TAX RECORDS

All taxpayers must keep copies of their tax returns, W-2 statements, and other receipts verifying income and expenses listed on tax returns for six years. Information used in preparing tax returns should be kept in a safe place in the event of an **audit**, which is the examination of your tax records by the Internal Revenue Service (IRS). The IRS has the legal right to examine your tax returns and supporting records for six years from the date of filing the return (longer if fraud or intentional wrongdoing on your part can be proved).

Your records are subject to IRS audit.

Figure 5-4
Personal   Property
Inventory

	Personal Property Inventory Janice Wilson January 1, 19—		
Item	**Year Purchased**	**Purchase Price**	**Approximate Current Value**
Acme stereo turntable with speakers in cabinet, Model XJ (SN 54J213)	1985	$ 600	$ 600
Bedroom furniture (bed, dresser, lamp, clock)	1976	800	200
Clothing and jewelry	1985-86	app. 2,000	1,000
Marvel "Cruiser" 10- speed bicycle (SN 5482164)	1988	120	120
TKO microcassette tape recorder, Model II, (SN 81426)	1988	(gift)	80
Total (photographs attached)		$ 3,520	$ 2,000

The four types of personal records discussed are important because they enable you to (a) evaluate your family or individual spending; (b) provide information for tax returns; (c) analyze your financial picture and plan for the future; (d) provide a basis for determining future goals; and (e) provide a basis for maintaining an effective, updated budget.

LEGAL DOCUMENTS
◆◆◆◆◆◆◆◆

To manage personal finances, you often need to enter into agreements, fill out forms and applications, and provide personal information and records. It is difficult to function successfully in today's society if you do not understand these important documents.

CONTRACTS AND AGREEMENTS

A **contract** is a legally enforceable agreement between two or more parties to do or not to do something. We all have many transactions in our daily lives that can be properly classified as contracts, or lawful agreements. Contracts are involved in personal business situations even though one may or may not be aware that contracts exist. If you buy a suit and it needs an alteration, a ticket is filled out by the sales clerk. The needed change and the promised completion date are written on the ticket. This ticket is evidence of the contract under which you, the consumer, promise to pick up the suit and pay for the alteration when it is completed satisfactorily. The store promises to do the work as promised and present the suit to you on the agreed upon date for the stated price of the alteration.

Entering into contracts is a common practice.

Other examples of situations requiring agreements are (a) retail credit plans, whereby customers agree to pay for purchases by monthly payments or open a charge account at a store; (b) buying a home and paying for it over a number of years by means of mortgage payments; or (c) renting an apartment, a duplex, or a house. In each of these cases there is generally an agreement between two or more persons known as an *express contract*. Express contracts can be oral or written: what makes them *express* is that the terms have been agreed upon between the parties.

Written contracts are required for large purchases.

Figure 5-5 shows a charge application a retail store may require. In addition to providing certain requested information, you are asked to agree to certain conditions before opening the account. Attached to the application will be an explanation of finance charges and how they are computed. You will sign the application to show that you understand the finance charges and agree to pay them if your balance is not paid in full each month. Be sure you have read everything contained in the agreement *before* you sign it. If something is not clear, be sure to ask for an explanation so that you can understand your rights and responsibilities *before* you enter into the contract.

In addition to written agreements, there are also many unwritten agreements. If you possess a driver's license, a social security card, a work permit, or any of many such items, you have made an **implied agreement**. Whether or not you realize it, you have agreed to certain things by your acceptance of a license or card. When you are issued a driver's license, you agree to abide by laws, drive in a safe and responsible manner, and have the license with you when driving. A violation of one of these unwritten agreements can result in the loss of your license, a fine, imprisonment, or all of these.

By accepting certain items you enter into implied agreements.

ESSENTIALS OF AN ENFORCEABLE CONTRACT

To accomplish its purpose, a contract must be binding on all persons who enter into it. Some contracts *must* be in writing and signed by all persons

Figure 5-5
Charge Application

CHARGE APPLICATION

Please print clearly

ACCOUNT IN NAME OF:
First *Arthur* Initial *B.* Last *Davis*
Address *45 Front Street #8*
City *Portland* State *OR* ZIP *97201-1072*
Phone *(503) 221-1181* How long at this address? *4 years*

Check one: ☐ Own ☐ Lease ☒ Rent ☐ Live with parents ☐ Other*
*Explain

Previous address if less than three years
How long?

Employer *O'Toole Paper Co.* How long? *4 years*
Employer's Address *Portland, OR 97214-4179* Phone *221-8342*
Occupation *Administrative Assistant* Salary *$342* ☒ Weekly ☐ Monthly

COMPLETE SECTION FOR JOINT ACCOUNT:
Name First *N/A* Initial Last
Employer How long?
Employer's Address Phone
Occupation Salary ☐ Weekly ☐ Monthly

Other income: Source Amount

CREDIT REFERENCES:
Name of Bank *First Bank* Bank Address *Portland, OR* ☒ Checking ☒ Savings
Name of Creditor *Meier & Frank* Account Number *818 424961* Address *Portland*
Creditor *JC Penney* Number *489 1248369* Address *Portland*
Creditor Number Address

NEAREST RELATIVE NOT LIVING WITH YOU:
Name *Harry Washington* Address *614 Chevy St., Portland, OR 97216-6172*

I understand the terms and conditions of this credit application, including service charges and fees, which will be charged to this account as explained on the reverse side of this application. I have read it completely and agree to all conditions. I testify that all information contained in this application is true and complete.

APPLICANT'S SIGNATURE *Arthur B. Davis* Social Security Number *481-32-8194* Date *4/1/--*

involved in order to be legally binding. Examples of contracts that must be written are contracts for the purpose of sale of real property (homes and land); contracts that cannot be fully performed in less than a year; contracts involving $500 or more; and contracts in which one person agrees to pay the debts of another.

To be legally binding, enforceable agreements, contracts must have all of the following elements:

1. Mutual assent
2. Consideration
3. Competent parties

To be enforceable, some contracts must be in writing.

Illustration 5-2
Attorneys can advise you about the validity of a contract.

4. Lawful objective
5. An agreed upon period of time
6. Legal format

Mutual Assent.   A contract has **mutual assent** when it is offered and accepted. If there is any disagreement, the contract is not legally enforceable. In order to prove mutual assent, two conditions are required by law: a valid offer and acceptance of that exact offer. One person makes the offer, another person accepts the offer. When one person makes an offer and another person changes any part of it, the second person is making what is known as a *counteroffer*. The counteroffer is a new offer and must be accepted (or rejected) by the first person.

Consideration.   The price involved is called **consideration**. Consideration may be in the form of an object of value, money, a promise, or a performed act. If one person is to receive something but gives nothing in return, the contract is not enforceable. The idea behind consideration is that each party to the agreement receives something of value. When you buy a pair of shoes, you get the shoes and the store gets your money. The shoes and the money are items of consideration.

Consideration is something of value.

Competent Parties.   *Competent parties* are persons who are legally able to give sane and intelligent assent. Those who are unable to protect themselves because of mental deficiency or illness, or who are otherwise incapable of understanding the consequences of their actions, cannot be held to contracts. They are protected from entering into agreements that may prove to be against their best interests. Minors are not considered competent parties and therefore cannot be held to contracts, with exceptions. Generally, any person 18 or older who is not mentally deficient

Minors are not considered competent parties.

is considered competent. Married persons under age 18 are also considered competent to enter into agreements. Furthermore, all persons 18 or older are considered to be legally competent unless they are declared incompetent by a court of law.

Lawful Objective.   The purpose of a legally enforceable contract must be of a lawful nature. A court of law will not require a person to perform an agreed upon act if it is illegal. Without a lawful objective, the agreement has no binding effect on any person.

Agreed Upon Period of Time.   Within the contract, there must be a stated length of time for which the contract is to exist. For example, if the contract is to purchase a home, the agreed upon period of time is as long as money remains due and owing. When the last payment is made, then the contract is considered fulfilled.

Legal Format.   State laws provide that contracts must contain the necessary information to be enforceable. The contract may be a printed form, may be drawn up by attorneys, or it may be in some other readable and understandable form. It must state the date, duration of contract, persons involved, consideration, terms of agreement, and other necessary information to explain the purpose and intentions of the persons entering into the contract. In some cases, the contract, or a memorandum of contract, must be **recorded** or made a public record. A photocopy is stored by the county recorder. Before a document can be recorded, it must meet specific requirements that are set out by state law.

Contracts must be in proper format.

VOID AND VOIDABLE CONTRACTS

There are basically three types of contracts: valid, void, and voidable.

Valid Contracts.   *Valid contracts* are those that contain all of the essential elements — mutual assent, consideration, competent parties, lawful objective, agreed upon period of time, and legal format. These contracts are legally enforceable.

Void Contracts.   *Void contracts* are those that are missing one or more of the essential elements. These contracts are null and void, and are not enforceable in a court of law. An example of a void contract is one that will require doing something illegal. In other words, if you enter into an agreement and later learn that you will be doing something against the law, you cannot be forced to fulfill your part of the contract. In fact, in doing so you would put yourself in legal jeopardy.

An illegal purpose causes a void contract.

Voidable Contracts.   *Voidable contracts* contain an element within them that makes them void. If that element is not acted upon by the innocent party, the contract will become valid. An example of a voidable contract is an agreement entered into by a minor. A minor may declare the voidable contract *void* because contracts with minors do not meet the competent party test of a legally binding contract. However, if the minor continues to make payments on the contract after reaching age 18, he or she has made that contract valid and becomes legally responsible for fulfilling the contract.

Certain actions can make a voidable contract valid.

CONSUMER RESPONSIBILITIES IN AGREEMENTS

As a consumer, you have the following responsibilities regarding the contracts and agreements you enter into:

1. Understand all clauses and terms contained in the agreement. Do not sign it until you have read it. By signing, you are acknowledging that you have read and understood the contract.
2. Keep a copy of the agreement. Put it in a safe place. You may need it at a future date.
3. Be sure the agreement is correctly dated.
4. Be sure all blank spaces are filled in or marked out and that no changes have been made after you sign. Your initials at the bottom of each page will prevent substitution of pages when there is more than one page.
5. Be sure all provisions agreed upon are clearly written. Because interpretation may vary, vague phrases are often not enforceable.
6. Be sure all dates, amounts, and other numbers are correct and clearly written.
7. Be sure proper disclosure is made by the seller. The buyer is entitled to proper and complete information about such things as the rate of interest, total finance charges, and cash payment price.
8. Be sure all cancellations and adjustments are made in accordance with the contract.

Check a contract carefully before signing.

Although consumers are protected by numerous consumer protection laws, specific legal services are occasionally required. Legal services, in one form or other, are available to every citizen. But your best protection is to guard yourself in advance by understanding the agreement.

Protect yourself in the beginning.

NEGOTIABLE INSTRUMENTS

When referring to contract law, the word *negotiable* means legally collectible. A **negotiable instrument** is a document that contains promises to pay monies and is legally collectible. The kinds of negotiable instruments most people are likely to use are checks (discussed in Chapter 6) and promissory notes. A negotiable instrument is legally collectible if it meets the following conditions:

Checks are negotiable instruments.

1. It must be in writing and be signed by the maker (cannot be oral).
2. It must contain an unconditional promise to pay a definite amount of money.
3. It must be payable on demand or on a fixed or determinable future date.
4. It must be payable to the order of a particular person or to the holder of the note.
5. It must be delivered to the payee.

If any one of the above conditions is missing, the document is not a negotiable instrument; it is no longer legally collectible.

A *promissory note* is a written promise to pay a certain sum of money to another person or to the holder of the note on a specified date. A promissory note is a legal document, and payment can be enforced by law. An example of a promissory note is found in Figure 5-6.

Figure 5-6
Promissory Note

PROMISSORY NOTE

$ _400.00_   _January 15_   , 19--

I (we) _Marilyn Huykamp_ _____, jointly and severally, do agree and promise to pay to _Emerald Furniture Co._ _____ the sum of _Four hundred and ⁰⁰/₁₀₀_ ~~~~~~~ dollars with interest at the rate of _18_ % from _January 15, 19--_ , payable in monthly installments of $_72.67_ beginning _February 1_ , 19-- and on a like day each month until paid in full, the last payment due _July 1_ , 19--. Said payment shall include interest. In the event of default, the maker hereof agrees to pay attorneys' fees and court costs in collection of this note.

Marilyn Huykamp
Maker

The person who creates and signs the promissory note, agreeing to pay it on a certain date, is called the **maker**. The person to whom the note is made payable is known as the **payee**. The promissory note is normally used when borrowing a large sum of money from a financial institution, such as a bank or a credit union.

In some cases creditors (those extending credit) will require cosigners as additional security for repayment of a note. A **cosigner** is a person who is established (has a good credit rating) and who promises to pay the note if the maker fails to pay. The cosigner's signature is also on a note. Young people and persons who have not established a credit rating are often asked to provide a cosigner for their first loan.

Cosigners make payments when the debtor fails.

WARRANTIES

A **warranty**, also called a guarantee, is an assurance of product quality or of responsibility of the seller. The warranty may be in writing or assumed to exist by the nature of the product. However, a warranty is not a safeguard against a poor buying decision.

Read warranties before you buy.

All products contain implied warranties, and some have written guarantees as well, expressing responsibilities that the manufacturer will strictly enforce. A product is supposed to do what it is made to do, whether or not standards are expressed in writing. For example, a tennis ball must bounce. If it does not bounce, it is dead. You can return the defective ball, even if there is no written warranty.

Specific written warranties often guarantee that a product will perform to your satisfaction for a certain period of time. Many written warranties state that you may return a product for repair or replacement if it ceases to work because of a defect. Warranties will not, however, protect against normal wear and tear of the product.

An extended warranty provides added protection.

Many companies offer an *extended warranty* which protects you after your written warranty has expired. For example, you may purchase an extended warranty (service) contract on your car, washer and dryer, or other major appliance. Sometimes it may be beneficial to purchase an extended warranty or service contract because needed repairs and maintenance can be extensive as a product gets older.

Figure 5-7 illustrates a limited warranty that might be found when purchasing a home product. Read it carefully to determine what the manufacturer is and is not guaranteeing.

Figure 5-7
Limited Warranty

12 Y 845

Limited Warranty

This product is guaranteed for one year from the date of purchase to be free of mechanical and electrical defects in material and workmanship. The manufacturer's obligations hereunder are limited to repair of such defects during the warranty period, provided such product is returned to the address below within the warranty period.

This guarantee does not cover normal wear of parts or damages resulting from negligent use or misuse of the product. In addition, this guarantee is void if the purchaser breaks the seal and disassembles, repairs, or alters the product in any way.

The warranty period begins on the date of purchase. The card below must be received by the manufacturer within 30 days of purchase or receipt of said merchandise. Fill out the card completely and return it to the address shown.

Owner's Name: _____

Address: _____

City, State, ZIP: _____

Date of Purchase: _____

Store Where Purchased: _____

Return to: TIPTON MACHINERY, INC.
42 West Cabana
Arlington, VA 23445-2909

Serial No. **12 Y 845**

VOCABULARY

Directions: Can you find the definition for each of the following terms used in Chapter 5?

- disposable income
- financial planning
- financial resources
- budget
- expenses
- audit
- contract
- implied agreement
- mutual assent
- consideration
- recorded
- negotiable instrument
- maker
- payee
- cosigner
- warranty

1. Agreement by two or more persons to the terms of a contract.
2. An unwritten statement that nevertheless exists.
3. Sources of income and money on which you base a budget.
4. A price to be paid, or a promise to pay, or to do something or not do something.
5. Debts you have agreed to pay.
6. A person who promises to pay a note if the maker fails to pay.
7. An assurance of product quality or of responsibility of the seller.
8. An orderly program for spending, saving, and investing your income.
9. An organized plan of matching income and expenses.
10. A legally enforceable agreement.
11. A piece of paper containing written promises to pay.
12. One who signs a note and agrees to pay it on a certain date.
13. Person to whom a note is made payable.
14. An examination of your tax records by the Internal Revenue Service.
15. The money you have left over after required deductions, which you can spend or save as you wish.
16. Makes a document, such as a contract, a matter of public record.

ITEMS FOR DISCUSSION

1. Why should consumers prepare a budget and be concerned about financial planning?
2. What is the difference between fixed and variable expenses?
3. Which are the four types of personal records all consumers should prepare and keep in a safe place?
4. Why is it important to maintain these four types of personal records?
5. Besides the obvious use for obtaining credit, what is another good reason for preparing a personal property inventory?
6. Why should taxpayers save copies of their tax returns and supporting receipts and evidence?
7. How is an implied contract different from an express contract?
8. In order to be enforceable in a court of law, contracts must contain six elements. Briefly define each.
9. Give three examples of contracts that must be in writing in order to be enforceable in a court of law.
10. What is the difference between a void contract and a voidable contract?
11. What is the most commonly used form of negotiable instrument?
12. List the five conditions of negotiable instruments that make them legally collectible.

13. List five consumer responsibilities when entering into contracts.
14. What is an *extended warranty*? On what types of products might you consider purchasing extended coverage?

APPLICATIONS

1. Using Figure 5-1 as a model, prepare a simple budget for yourself, listing expected income, savings, and expenses for a month. How much will you set aside for savings?
2. How will your budget change in the next few years? (What are your short-term and intermediate goals?)
3. Using Figure 5-3 as a model, prepare a net worth statement, listing as assets those items of value you possess and any debts for which you are responsible. Compute your net worth. How can you use this information?
4. Using Figure 5-4 as a model, prepare a personal property inventory, listing items of personal property in your room at home. Why should you and your family keep a record such as this?
5. After examining Figure 5-5 (credit application), list the kinds of information requested by a retail store. Why do you think a store needs or wants this type of information?
6. Following the example of Figure 5-6, write out in longhand form a promissory note from you to John Doe, payable in one year of monthly payments, in the amount of $50 with interest at 15 percent, and monthly payments of $4.79. Are you the maker or the payee? (Note: This form of note is legally collectible and valid. A *printed* form is not necessary.)
7. Bring to class an express warranty from a product you or your family recently purchased. What does the manufacturer specifically promise to do in the warranty? List any restrictions (exceptions) that the manufacturer has placed in the warranty.
8. Has anyone in your family (or a relative or friend) recently purchased an extended warranty contract? If so, for what product? Ask what kinds of benefits are promised by the extended protection; also ask the cost. Do you know of anyone who has declined to purchase an extended warranty? Ask them why they chose to do so.

CASE PROBLEMS AND ACTIVITIES

1. Based on the information given, prepare a monthly and yearly budget for Dan and Alice Burke. Use Figure 5-2 as a model. INCOME: Net paychecks total $1,800 monthly.

Expenses:	Rent payment.....	$350	Savings.............	$150
	Utilities.............	100	Car payment......	110
	Gasoline...........	100	Car repairs.........	30
	Insurance..........	90	Telephone.........	30
	Groceries...........	200	Entertainment....	100
	Clothing...........	100	Vacation fund....	100
	Investment fund..	140	Miscellaneous.....	200

2. Dan Burke has decided to return to college for two years to obtain his degree. He will work part-time instead of full-time, thereby reducing the Burkes' take-home pay by $600 a month. Tuition will be $400 each term ($1200/year); books will cost $300 a year. Revise the Burkes' monthly budget.

3. Based on the information given, prepare a monthly and yearly budget for Bonnie Vowells. Follow Figure 5-2.

    INCOME: Net monthly paycheck is $1,200.

Expenses:	Rent Payment.....	$210	Savings.............	$120
	Insurance..........	60	Telephone.........	15
	Utilities.............	50	Car payment......	150
	Gasoline...........	60	Car repairs.........	20
	Clothing...........	60	Groceries...........	150
	Entertainment....	150	Miscellaneous.....	155

4. Revise Bonnie's budget when she agrees to share her apartment with a friend. Some expenses can be shared, but the car payment, insurance, and car repairs remain fixed. You will need to adjust her other expenses accordingly. What will you have her do with the added funds?

5. Based on the information given, prepare a net worth statement for Steve Plumber. Follow Figure 5-3. Steve owns a car worth about $3,000, but owes $1,500 to the bank. He has $500 in savings and $100 in checking. His personal property totals $3,000, and he also owes $90 to the credit union.

6. Based on the information given, prepare a personal property inventory for Steve Plumber. Follow Figure 5-4. Steve has these furnishings in his apartment: JWA stereo system, Model 252, SN 975923, bought last year for $500 (still worth $500); sofa, present worth about $800; Bright alarm clock (SN 630AM) and Blare radio (Model 2602, SN 413T) bought years ago, total worth about $200. Steve also has the following personal items: miscellaneous clothing and jewelry, present worth about $800; Quantex wrist watch, present worth about $100; coin collection, valued last year at $600. Steve has photographs and receipts for all of these items.

Chapter 6

CHECKING ACCOUNTS AND BANKING SERVICES

◆◆◆◆◆◆◆◆◆◆◆◆◆◆◆◆◆◆◆◆◆◆◆◆◆◆◆

OBJECTIVES

1. Understand the purpose, uses, and advantages of a personal checking account.
2. Prepare checking account documents, including signature card, checks, deposit slips, checkbook register, and bank reconciliation.
3. Explain check endorsements and describe the types of checking accounts available to consumers.
4. Define the various banking services available and fees charged to consumers.

PURPOSE OF A CHECKING ACCOUNT

◆◆◆◆◆◆◆◆

Financial institutions such as banks, credit unions, and savings and loan associations offer a number of different services. A **checking account** is a banking service wherein money is deposited into an account and checks, or **drafts**, can be written to withdraw money from the account as needed. This type of account is also known as a **demand deposit**, because you can demand portions of your deposited funds at will. Only you, the depositor or

Illustration 6-1
Writing a check for
large purchases is
often safer than
using cash.

drawer *(maker)*, can write checks on the account. Financial institutions usually charge a fee for checking services, or require that a minimum balance be kept in the account. In shopping for a checking account, you will find a wide variety of services, fees, and other choices to make.

A checking account can be a useful and convenient tool. Writing a check is often safer than using cash, especially when making major purchases in person, or when paying bills or ordering merchandise through the mail. **Canceled checks** (checks the bank has processed) can be used as proofs of purchase or payment in the event a dispute arises. Checking accounts also have built-in record keeping systems to help you keep track of money received and spent; thus, they are a great help in personal budgeting and record keeping. Finally, as a checking account customer, you have access to other banking services, such as instant loans, use of the day and night teller, and free traveler's checks.

In exchange for the convenience of using a checking account, you must accept certain responsibilities. First, you must write checks carefully and keep an accurate record of checks written and deposits made. Second, you must reconcile your account with your bank statement promptly each month. Third, you must keep canceled checks as proofs of purchase or payment and for income tax records. Canceled checks should be kept in a safe place, such as a safe-deposit box.

In addition, you must maintain sufficient funds in your account to cover all checks written. A check that cannot be covered by the funds in your account is called a **NSF (not sufficient funds) check** or **overdraft**. The check will bounce — go to your bank and then come back to you for payment. When you realize your account contains insufficient funds, but you write a check anyway in the hope that you can make a deposit before the check is

Checking accounts
are safer than cash.

Safeguard your can-
celed checks.

cashed, you are **floating a check**. Floating a check is more difficult to do in the computer age when the processing of checks and deposits is faster and more efficient. Overdrawing your account and floating a check are illegal practices in most states. These acts are felony crimes that can result in a fine, imprisonment, or both. In addition, the bank will charge a fee of $5 to $15 for each NSF check written.

Intentional overdrafts are unlawful.

OPENING YOUR CHECKING ACCOUNT

To open a checking account, a depositor must fill out and sign a signature card, such as the one shown in Figure 6-1.

The signature card provides the bank with important information and an official signature to compare with subsequent checks written. In Figure 6-1, Ardys Johnson completed and signed the left side of the card. The right side is for a joint account holder. Ardys also listed her mother's full name (including maiden name) for use in identification. Anyone forging Ardys's signature is not likely to know her mother's maiden name when questioned by a teller.

The signature card is a safety precaution.

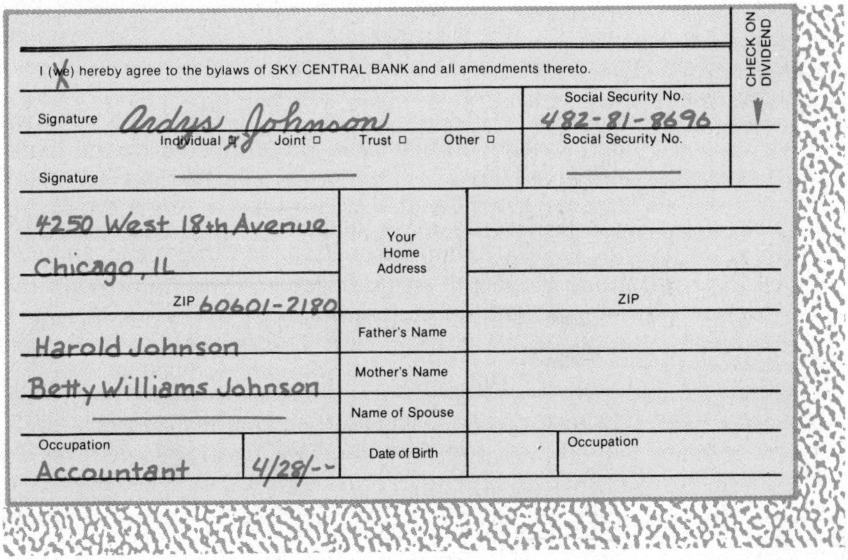
I (we) hereby agree to the bylaws of SKY CENTRAL BANK and all amendments thereto.
CHECK ON DIVIDEND
Signature Ardys Johnson
Social Security No. 482-81-8696
Individual Joint Trust Other
Social Security No.
Signature
4250 West 18th Avenue
Chicago, IL
ZIP 60601-2180
Your Home Address
ZIP
Harold Johnson
Father's Name
Betty Williams Johnson
Mother's Name
Name of Spouse
Occupation
Accountant
4/28/--
Date of Birth
Occupation

Figure 6-1
Signature Card

USING YOUR CHECKING ACCOUNT

Checking accounts can help you to manage your personal finances — but only if you use them correctly. Careless or improper use of a checking account can result in financial losses. Some tips on using a checking account follow.

PARTS OF A CHECK

A check consists of ten parts. Figure 6-2 illustrates these parts.

Figure 6-2
Check

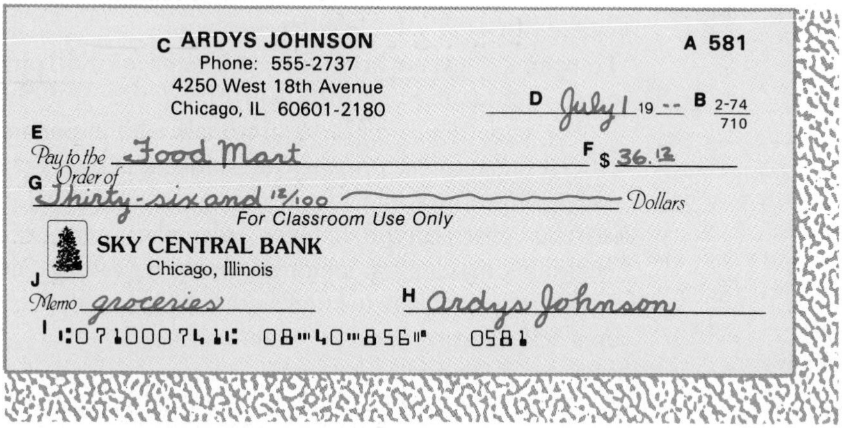

Check Number.   Checks are numbered for easy identification. In Figure 6-2, Check 581 has been prenumbered by the bank (see Part A).

ABA Number.   The "American Bankers Association number" appears in fraction form in the upper right corner of each check (see Figure 6-2, Part B). The top half of the fraction identifies the location and district of the bank from which the check is drawn. The number on the bottom half of the fraction helps in routing the check to the specific area and bank on which it is drawn.

Maker's Preprinted Name and Address.   Most checking account owners prefer to have their name, address, and telephone number preprinted on the top left of each check (see Figure 6-2, Part C). Many businesses are reluctant to accept a check unless it is preprinted with this information.

Date.   The first item to be filled in is the date on which the check is written (see Figure 6-2, Part D). Do not *postdate* checks; that is, do not write in a future date. Most banks process checks when they are presented, or charge a fee for holding them. Checks over six months old may not be honored by the bank.

Postdated checks are not held by banks.

Payee.   The *payee* is the person or company to whom a check is made payable. Food Mart is the payee in Figure 6-2 (Part E).

Numeric Amount.   The numeric amount is the amount of dollars and cents being paid, written in figures (see Figure 6-2, Part F). The amount should be neatly and clearly written, placed as close as possible to the dollar sign, with the dollars and cents distinctly readable. Many people raise the cents above the line of writing, as shown in Figure 6-2, and insert a decimal point between the dollar and cent amounts.

Written Amount.   The written amount shows the amount of dollars and cents being paid, written in words. The word "dollars" is preprinted at the end of the line (see Figure 6-2, Part G). The word "and" is handwritten to separate dollar amounts from cents; it replaces the decimal point. Always begin writing at the far left of the line, leaving no space between words, and draw a wavy line from the cents to the word "dollars," as shown. In Figure 6-2, the fraction 12/100 means that 12 cents out of 100 is to be paid.

Drawer or Maker.   The drawer/maker is the person authorized to write checks on the account. Ardys Johnson is the maker of the check in Figure 6-2 (see Part H) because she is the person who opened the checking account and who deposits money into it. The bank has a copy of Ardys's signature on file so that they can stop someone attempting to forge Ardys's name to one of her checks.

Account Number.   The account number appears in bank coding at the bottom of each check. In Figure 6-2 (see Part I), Ardys's checking account number is 08 40 856.   The number 581 refers to the preprinted check number at the top of the check.

Memo.   A Memo line is provided at the bottom left of each check so that the maker can write the purpose of the check (see Figure 6-2, Part J). This line does not have to be filled in; it is provided for the account holder's convenience.

   Some banks provide free "stock" checks to customers, but many customers prefer to order checks with special designs or colors rather than use the plainer stock checks. You will be charged for special design checks at rates from $5 to $15 for 200 checks. In addition, you may order special checkbook covers that match or coordinate with check designs (also at extra cost).

The decimal point separates dollars from cents.

Checks have special electronic coding.

■ WRITING CHECKS ■

When writing checks, remember to follow these important guidelines in addition to the hints already given:

1.   Always use a pen, preferably one with dark ink that does not skip or blot.
2.   Write legibly. Keep numbers and letters clear and distinct, without any extra space before, between, or after them.

Write checks in dark ink.

3. Sign your name exactly as it appears on the check and on the signature card you signed when you opened the account (see Figure 6-1).

4. Avoid mistakes. When you make a mistake, you should void (cancel) the check and write a new one. To cancel a check, write the word VOID in large letters across the face of the check. Save the voided check for your records.

Save your "voided" checks.

5. Be certain adequate funds have been deposited in your account to cover each check that you write. A check is a negotiable instrument that contains your written promise to pay a certain amount to the payee when the check is cashed.

MAKING DEPOSITS

Just as you need a form to withdraw money from your checking account, you need to complete a form each time you deposit money to the account. Figure 6-3 illustrates this form, which is called a deposit slip.

To prepare a deposit slip, follow these guidelines:

1. Insert the date of the transaction.
2. Write in the amount of currency (paper money) and coin to be deposited.
3. If any checks are being deposited, write in the amount of each check, together with the ABA check number (top part of fraction).
4. Total the currency, coin, and check amounts. Write this figure on the subtotal line.
5. If you wish to receive some cash at the time of your deposit, you should fill in the desired amount on the Less Cash Received line. Subtract this amount from the subtotal. Write in the final amount of the deposit on the Net Deposit line. Write your signature on the line above the words "Sign here for less cash in teller's presence."

Sign for cash in the teller's presence.

6. Keep one copy of this deposit slip as proof of the amount of your deposit. Financial institutions have been known to make errors in crediting an account.

Carefully total your deposit slip.

When writing deposit slips, you should carefully count the currency and coins you are depositing and recheck all addition and subtraction. Make sure all checks being deposited are properly endorsed (see pages 106-108). Hand the deposit slip to the teller with the currency, coins, and checks you are depositing. Deposits can also be made at automatic teller machines (see pages 113-114).

Figure 6-3
Deposit Slip

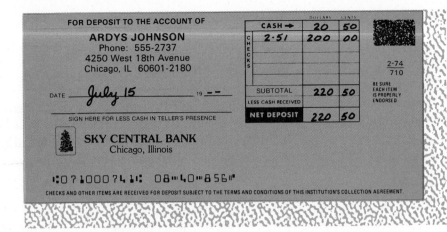

USING A CHECKBOOK REGISTER

A **checkbook register** is a record of deposits to and withdrawals from a
checking account. Figure 6-4 depicts a page from the checkbook register of
Ardys Johnson. Through use of her checkbook register, Ardys can keep track
of all checks written, service fees paid, interest earned, and deposits made to
the account.

Figure 6-4
Checkbook Register

ITEM NO.	DATE	PAYMENT ISSUED TO OR DESCRIPTION OF DEPOSIT	AMOUNT OF PAYMENT	✓	(-) CHECK FEE (IF ANY)	AMOUNT OF DEPOSIT	BALANCE FORWARD 800 00
		PLEASE BE SURE TO DEDUCT ANY PER ITEM CHARGES OR SERVICE CHARGES THAT MAY APPLY TO YOUR ACCOUNT					
581	7/1	To Food Mart / For Groceries	36 12		.20		Payment or Deposit −36 32 / Balance 763 68
/	7/15	To Deposit / For Paycheck				220 50	Payment or Deposit +220 50 / Balance 984 18
/	7/16	To Withdrawal / For Automatic Teller	20 00				Payment or Deposit −20 00 / Balance 964 18
/	7/31	To Service Charge / For mth. of July	5 00				Payment or Deposit −5 00 / Balance 959 18
		To / For					Payment or Deposit / Balance
		To / For					Payment or Deposit / Balance

To fill out a checkbook register, follow these simple guidelines:

1. Write the preprinted check number in the first column. If you are
    not writing a check, draw a diagonal slash in this column, or use
    another distinctive notation.

2. Write the month and day of the transaction in the Date column.
3. Enter the name of the payee on the first line of the Description section. On the second line, if one is provided, write the purpose of the check.
4. Enter the amount of the check, service charge, or other withdrawal in the column headed by a minus sign. If the transaction is a deposit, write this amount in the column headed by a plus sign.
5. Transfer the amount withdrawn or deposited to the top line of the Balance column. Subtract this amount from or add it to the previous balance, then write the new balance on the second line of the column.
6. The column headed by a check mark is provided so that you can check off each transaction when it appears on your monthly bank statement. The check mark shows that the transaction has been cleared by the bank and is no longer outstanding.

Keep the balance column in your checkbook register up-to-date.

Always keep your checkbook register handy so that you can write down the necessary information at the time each transaction is made. Prompt and correct notations will help you keep track of your personal finances.

RECONCILING YOUR CHECKING ACCOUNT

◆◆◆◆◆◆◆◆

Financial institutions that offer checking accounts provide each customer with a regular (usually monthly) *statement of account*. This statement lists checks received and processed by the bank, plus all other withdrawals and deposits made, service charges, and interest earned.

Statements are provided to check your account.

Most financial institutions return your canceled checks with your bank statement. Canceled checks serve as records of purchases and as proofs of payment. *Check safekeeping* (also called *truncating*) is a practice of some financial institutions whereby canceled checks are not returned to the customer. Microcopies are made of the processed checks; the checks themselves are then destroyed by the bank. If necessary, copies of canceled checks may be made from the microform for a small fee ($5 to $10 each).

The process of matching your checkbook register with the bank statement is known as **reconciliation**. The back of the bank statement is usually printed with a form to aid you in reconciling your account. Figure 6-5 represents both sides of a typical bank statement.

Reconciling is the process of matching.

On the left in Figure 6-5 is a simple statement of the bank's record of activity in the checking account. Canceled checks and other types of withdrawals are listed and are subtracted from the balance. Deposits are listed and are added to the balance. Bank service charges are subtracted from

Bank Statement

SKY CENTRAL BANK

Ardys Johnson
4250 West 18th Avenue
Chicago, IL 60601-2180

For month ended July 31, 19--:

Checks		Deposits	Balance
	7/1		800.00
32.00	7/1		768.00
36.12	7/5		731.88
22.00	7/8		709.88
	7/15	220.50	930.38
40.00	7/20		890.38
10.00	7/25	400.00	1280.38
1.00 SC*			1279.38

Ending balance			1279.38

*Service charge of 20 cents per check
 processed

Other charges and deductions: none

Bank Reconciliation

1. Write ending balance as
   shown on bank statement: <u>1,279.38</u>

2. Add credits or deposits
   made that do not appear on
   statement: <u>100.00</u>

3. Total lines 1 and 2: <u>1,379.38</u>

4. Write total checks outstanding (not processed): <u>139.90</u>

Check No.	Amount	
586	14	—
591	30	—
602	85	90
604	10	—

5. Subtract line 4 from line 3 and
   write balance (should agree with
   checkbook balance): <u>1,239.48</u>

Figure 6-5   Bank Reconciliation

the balance, and an ending account balance is given.

It is likely that the balance your checkbook register shows will not be identical to the ending balance shown on the bank statement. In this case, you can reconcile your account by following these guidelines:

Follow the directions
on the back of the
statement.

1. Use the reconciliation form printed on the back of your bank statement.
2. Write the ending balance as shown on the front of the statement.
3. List any deposits made that do not appear on the bank statement (they should be listed in your checkbook register).
4. Add the ending bank balance to the deposits made but not yet entered. Write down this subtotal.
5. List all checks you wrote or other withdrawals you made that do not appear on the bank statement.
6. Subtract the total checks outstanding from the subtotal. This should be the same as the balance shown in your checkbook register.

If your attempt at reconciliation is unsuccessful, check your addition and subtraction. Next, go through your checkbook register and check all addition and subtraction for the period covered by the statement. Finally, make certain that you have deducted service charges from and added any interest earned to your register balance. If you still cannot reconcile your account, report to the bank for help in discovering where the error lies. Usually you need to telephone ahead and make an appointment. Be sure to take your checkbook, canceled checks, and bank statement with you. There usually is no charge for this service.

The bank will help you if you can't reconcile your account.

Reconciliation must be done immediately upon receipt of the bank statement. Any errors or differences should be reported to the bank as soon as possible. Occasionally the bank does make an error, which it will be happy to correct when you report the error immediately.

ENDORSEMENTS

◆◆◆◆◆◆◆◆

It is necessary to endorse a check before cashing it.

A check cannot be cashed until it has been endorsed. To *endorse* a check, the payee named on the face of the check simply signs the back of the check in black or blue ink no more than one and one half inches from the left edge. There are four major types of endorsements: the blank endorsement, the special endorsement, the restrictive endorsement, and the joint endorsement.

BLANK ENDORSEMENT

A **blank endorsement** is simply the signature of the payee written exactly as his or her name appears on the front of the check.

✗(Note: If Donald's name had been written incorrectly on the face of the check, he would correct the mistake by endorsing the check with the misspelled version first, then with the correct version of his name, as shown here.)

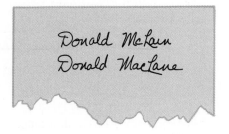

■■■ **SPECIAL ENDORSEMENT** ■■■

A **special endorsement**, or an endorsement in full, is written when the payee signs over a check to a third person. In the following illustration, for example, Donald MacLane uses a check written to him to pay a debt owed to Diane Jones. By using a special endorsement, Donald avoids having to cash the check before repaying Diane. The purpose of the special endorsement, then, is to specifically name the next payee who shall be entitled to cash the check.

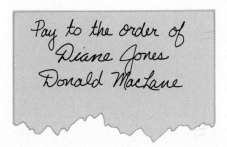

■■■ **RESTRICTIVE ENDORSEMENT** ■■■

A **restrictive endorsement** restricts or limits the use of a check. For example, a check endorsed with the words "For Deposit Only" above the payee's signature can be deposited only to the account specified.

The restrictive endorsement is safer than the blank endorsement for use in mailing deposits, in night deposit systems, or in other circumstances that may result in loss of a check. If a check with a restrictive endorsement is lost, it cannot be cashed by the finder.

JOINT ENDORSEMENT

A **joint endorsement** is necessary when there is more than one person named as payee on the face of the check. Each payee must endorse the check before it can be cashed.

TYPES OF CHECKING ACCOUNTS

♦♦♦♦♦♦♦♦

There are many types of accounts — both checking and savings — available at banks, savings and loan associations, and credit unions. Savings accounts are discussed in Chapter 8.

At most financial institutions, you will have a choice between several types of checking accounts. You should carefully study your options, because a wise choice can save you money. Some current options include the special account, the standard account, the joint account, the interest-bearing (NOW) account, the free account, and the share draft account.

Choose your account wisely; costs do vary.

SPECIAL ACCOUNTS

Most banks offer a *special checking account* to customers who will write only a small number of checks each month. No minimum balance is usually required for this type of account. Service fees are charged at a low flat rate per month with an additional fee for each check written. (For example, $3.00 per month, plus 15 cents for each check cashed). These customers also may be charged service fees only when the number of checks written in a month exceeds the set limit (such as more than 10 checks in a given month). If you write only a few checks each month (like many college students), this plan might be for you.

STANDARD ACCOUNTS

A *standard account* usually has a set monthly service fee of between $5 and $8, but no per-check fee. Often, if you are able to maintain a minimum balance, you can avoid service fees entirely. Many banks give extra services for this type of account, such as free traveler's checks, a teller machine card, or a free safe-deposit box. Some banks offer reduced interest rates on credit card balances to customers who also have checking, savings, and other accounts at their bank.

JOINT ACCOUNTS

A *joint account* is a survivorship account.

A *joint account* is opened by two or more persons. Such an account is called a *survivorship account* because any person who signs on the account has the right to the entire amount deposited. If one person using the account dies, the other (the survivor) then becomes the sole owner of the funds in the account. All of the accounts discussed in this chapter can be joint accounts.

INTEREST (NOW) ACCOUNTS

Most financial institutions offer what are called *interest checking accounts*. With these accounts, interest is paid if you maintain a certain minimum balance. Minimum amounts may vary greatly among different institutions.

NOW *(Negotiable Order of Withdrawal) accounts* are designed to provide the convenience of a checking account with short-term savings gains. With a NOW account, however, there are pluses and minuses. This type of account may not be for everyone. While you do receive interest on money deposited in a NOW account, you must put up with certain disadvantages. Minimum balance requirements may be as high as $2,500 or more, for example. If you fall below the minimum balance at any time during the month, you are automatically charged the full service fee, which may be higher than that charged for a standard account. Also, not only are you charged a service fee when your account drops below the minimum balance, but most likely you will not receive any interest for that month.

Interest rates on NOW accounts, set at 5¼ percent when the accounts first began, are likely to rise and fall with economic conditions. When overall interest rates drop, you will receive 4¼ percent; when overall interest rates rise, you might expect 6 or 7 percent. Keeping money in a low-interest account can cost you money in interest lost because you could have invested elsewhere. NOW accounts are often known as *market interest accounts* and vary widely among financial institutions. Check the options carefully before selecting one.

To earn interest, you need a minimum balance.

FREE ACCOUNTS

Most banks still offer *free checking* (no service fees) if you maintain a minimum balance. These minimum balances may be lower than for NOW accounts, because the bank pays no interest on deposits to free accounts. Free checking is available to senior citizens, nonprofit groups, and to others during special bank promotions, such as the opening of a new bank or branch.

Free accounts are available but limited.

SHARE DRAFT ACCOUNTS

Most credit unions offer *share draft accounts*. These are checking accounts with low (or no) minimum balance requirements, no service fees, and interest payments based on your lowest monthly balance. If you are eligible for credit union membership, this type of account may be the least expensive and most convenient checking method for you.

BANKING SERVICES AND FEES
◆◆◆◆◆◆◆◆

A *full-service bank* is one that offers every possible kind of service, from checking accounts to credit cards, 24-hour banking machines, safe-deposit boxes, loans, and electronic funds transfers. Some other services commonly offered are certified checks, cashier's checks, money orders, and debit cards. One service that most banks offer is FDIC (Federal Deposit Insurance Corporation) insurance, which protects customers' deposits against loss up to $100,000 per account.

Many services are available to depositors.

CERTIFIED CHECKS

A **certified check** is a personal check that the bank guarantees or certifies to be good. In effect, the bank puts a hold on that amount in the drawer's account so that the money will be there when the certified check is presented for payment.

CASHIER'S CHECK

A **cashier's check** is a check written by a bank on its own funds. You can pay for a cashier's check through a withdrawal from your savings or checking account, or in cash.

Cashier's checks are generally used to pay a person or firm when a cash payment is not desirable. A cashier's check might also be requested instead of a personal check when the payee questions your credit standing or you do not have a credit history established. A cashier's check can also be used for transactions in which you wish to remain anonymous, because the bank is listed as the maker of the check, and your identity need not be revealed.

Cashier's checks do not reveal the identity of the maker.

MONEY ORDERS

Banks sell *money orders* to those who do not wish to use cash or do not have a checking account. A money order is used like a check, except that it can never bounce. There is a charge for purchasing a money order. This charge ranges from 50 cents to $5 or more, depending on the size of the money order. You can also purchase money orders through the post office and local merchants.

DEBIT CARDS

Debit cards allow immediate deductions from a checking account to pay for purchases. The debit card is presented at the time of purchase. When the merchant presents the debit card receipt to the bank, the amount of the purchase is immediately deducted from the customer's checking account and paid to the merchant. The debit card transaction is similar to writing a check to pay for purchases. The issuing bank may charge an annual fee for the card or a fee for each transaction. (Note: There is no credit extended to you when you are using a debit card.)

Debit cards are like checks — deducted immediately.

SAFE-DEPOSIT BOXES

Safe-deposit boxes are available at most financial institutions for a yearly fee that is based on the size of the box. Rental fees may be between $8 and $20 for a small box to $40 or more for a large box. The customer is given two keys for the box and is allowed to store valuables and documents in the box. Private rooms are available to customers to use when opening boxes to add or remove items. Documents commonly kept in a safe-deposit box are birth certificates, marriage and death certificates, deeds and mortgages, stocks and bonds, contracts, tax returns and receipts, and insurance policies. Jewelry, coin collections, and other small valuables are also commonly stored in safe-deposit boxes. Keeping important papers and other items in a safe-deposit box insures that the items won't be stolen, lost, or destroyed. When you rent a safe-deposit box, you will fill out a signature card similar to that used for opening a checking account. Then each time you enter your safe-deposit box, you will sign a form so that your signature is compared to the one on file. This procedure prevents unlawful entry to your box by an unauthorized person.

Guard your valuable documents in a safe-deposit box.

Illustration 6-2
Keeping valuables in a safe-deposit box insures against their loss.

LOANS AND TRUSTS

Financial institutions also make loans to finance the purchase of cars, homes, vacations, home improvements, and other items. Large banks have loan departments that assist with loans, as well as provide advice for planning estates and trusts. Banks also act as trustees of estates for minors and others. As a bank customer, you may wish to open a *pre-established line of credit*, which means you fill out a credit application and a limit is established which you can use when you need it. There is no fee or interest charge until you actually borrow the money. Use of a pre-established line of credit will save you time when you are preparing for making a major purchase.

A line of credit is convenient and time-saving.

DISCOUNT BROKERAGE SERVICES

Many larger banks offer discount brokerage services to their depositors. You may buy and sell stocks and bonds through the brokerage service, at reduced rates. But you receive no advice or counseling. The purchases and sales are "cleared" through your checking or savings accounts with the bank.

Discount brokerage is a service of many banks.

BANK CREDIT CARDS

You can apply to a full-service bank for a *bank credit card* such as VISA or MasterCard. If you meet the requirements, the card you are issued can be used instead of cash at any business that will accept it. Banks offering national credit cards usually charge both an annual fee for use of the card and interest on the unpaid account balance.

ELECTRONIC FUNDS TRANSFERS

Certain transactions, such as the paying of bills, can be made through an *electronic funds transfer (ETF)*, using an automated teller machine and an automated teller card. Customers may make cash withdrawals from any of their accounts; make cash advances from their bank's VISA or MasterCard account; make deposits to any of their accounts; make payments on loans; and transfer funds from their accounts to pay their credit card, utility, and retail store accounts. With a Touch-Tone telephone, customers can also check balances and pay bills from their homes or offices. To use 24-hour

Cash withdrawals can be done electronically.

bank machines, you must have a card that is electronically coded (such as a check guarantee card or bank credit card). You also must know your *personal identification number (PIN)*, which usually is some combination of four or more numbers or letters. For safety, memorize your personal identification number; do not write it down and keep it with your bank card.

STOP PAYMENT ORDERS

A **stop payment order** is a request that the bank not cash or process a specific check. The usual reason for stopping payment is that the check has been lost or stolen. By issuing a stop payment order, the drawer can safely write a new check, knowing that the original check cannot be cashed if it is presented to the bank. Most banks charge a fee (usually $10 or more) for stopping payment on a check.

BANK FEES

Banks make loans from customers' deposits.

Customers' savings and deposits are the bank's primary sources of money for loans. Bank assets also come from demand deposits, from stockholders' investments, and from investments made by the bank. In addition, banks charge fees to their customers to cover costs of operation. For example, when you apply for a loan and it is granted, you are charged a loan fee. When the bank acts as a trustee, it charges a fee for this service.

Banks also charge noncustomers for services such as check cashing. If you want to cash a check at a bank where you do not have an account, the bank may charge you a fee for this service. Nondepositors pay for other services that may be free to depositors, such as traveler's checks, certified checks, and notary services.

VOCABULARY

Directions: Can you find the definition for each of the following terms used in Chapter 6?

11 checking account
12 drafts
10 demand deposit
4 canceled checks
13 NSF check/overdraft
1 floating a check
7 checkbook register
3 reconciliation

5 blank endorsement
8 special endorsement
6 restrictive endorsement
15 joint endorsement
9 certified check
14 cashier's check
2 stop payment order

1. A banking term to designate that there are insufficient funds to cover a check that has been written.
2. To have payment stopped on a check after the check is lost.
3. To compare your checkbook register with the bank statement each month.
4. Checks that have been processed by the bank and returned to you.
5. An endorsement that consists only of the payee's signature.
6. An endorsement, such as the words *For Deposit Only*, that restricts use of the check.
7. Your personal record of checking account transactions.
8. An endorsement signing a check over to a third party.
9. A check guaranteed by the bank to be good.
10. A type of bank account that allows you to withdraw your money at will.
11. A banking service in which money is deposited and checks written.
12. A form of check for withdrawing money from a demand account.
13. Writing a check on an account that doesn't have enough money in it at the time you write the check.
14. A check written by a bank on its own funds.
15. Required endorsement when two or more payees are listed on a check.

ITEMS FOR DISCUSSION

1. What are reasons for having a checking account?
2. What responsibilities do customers (depositors) have when using a checking account?
3. Why is a checking account called a demand deposit?
4. Explain what is meant by the phrase *floating a check.*
5. What is a canceled check, and why is it important to a depositor?
6. Why do you need to reconcile your checking account promptly when you receive the monthly bank statement?
7. List at least four banking services provided by financial institutions.
8. Why would you be asked your mother's maiden name when opening a bank account?
9. What is a survivorship checking account?
10. How is a bank debit card different from a bank credit card?
11. What is the purpose of a *pre-established line of credit?*
12. What is the purpose of a PIN (*personal identification number*)?

APPLICATIONS

1. List the names, addresses, and telephone numbers of five financial

institutions in your community, and list the services provided by each.

2. Using Figure 6-2 (check) as an example, and following the rules on pages 100-101, write these checks:

    a. Check No. 12 to Melvin Quigly for $34.44, written today
    b. Check No. 322 to Save-Now Stores for $18.01, written today
    c. Check No. 484 to M. A. Bales for $91.10, written today

3. Using Figure 6-3 (deposit slip) as an example, and following the rules on page 102, prepare these deposit slips:

    a. Today's date; currency $40.00; coins $1.44; Check No. 18-81 for $51.00; no cash retained
    b. Today's date; Check No. 40-22 for $300.00 and Check No. 24-12 for $32.00; $20.00 cash retained

4. Determine your ending reconciled checkbook balance when all of the following six conditions exist:

    a. Your ending checkbook balance is $311.40 (before the service fee is deducted).
    b. You made an error, resulting in $30.00 less showing in your account than should be.
    c. The service fee is $6.00.
    d. The ending bank balance is $402.00.
    e. Outstanding deposits total $100.00.
    f. Outstanding checks total $166.60.

5. Determine your ending reconciled checkbook balance when all of the following six conditions exist:

    a. Your checkbook ending balance is $800.40 (before the service fee is deducted).
    b. The service fee is $3.00.
    c. The ending bank balance is $1,100.00.
    d. Outstanding deposits total $50.00.
    e. Outstanding checks total $352.60.

6. List four types of endorsements and give a written example of each.
7. Write out on plain paper the appropriate information needed for a signature card, as shown in Figure 6-1.
8. List the banking services you would like to have when you open a checking account.
9. Which type of account will you choose? Why?
10. Explain the difference between a cashier's check and a certified check.

CASE PROBLEMS AND ACTIVITIES

1. Find the errors in the following check.

2. The deposit slip shown is to deposit the check in Question No. 1. Can you find the errors on the deposit slip?

3. Complete the given bank reconciliation form by first finishing the checkbook register and entering the service charge and then computing balances. (Use another piece of paper)

BANK STATEMENT
Hometown Bank

For month ended March 31, 19--

Beginning balance $100.00

Checks cashed		Deposits	Date	Balance
$24.75			3/7	$75.25
13.00		$30.00	3/8	92.25
10.00	$3.80		3/11	78.45
1.20 SC				77.25
Ending balance				$77.25

BANK RECONCILIATION

Ending balance as shown on bank statement $_____

Add deposits not shown on bank statement $_____

_____   _____

Subtract checks written but not shown
on bank statement   _____

_____   _____

Adjusted balance (should be same as
ending balance in checkbook) $_____

PLEASE BE SURE TO DEDUCT ANY PER ITEM CHARGES OR SERVICE CHARGES THAT MAY APPLY TO YOUR ACCOUNT

ITEM NO.	DATE	PAYMENT ISSUED TO OR DESCRIPTION OF DEPOSIT	AMOUNT OF PAYMENT	√	(-) CHECK FEE (IF ANY)	AMOUNT OF DEPOSIT	BALANCE FORWARD	
								100 00
101	3/1	To Grocery Mart / For Groceries	24 75	.			Payment/Deposit	24 75
							Balance	75 25
102	3/3	To Independent Phone Co. / For Feb. charges	13 00	.			Payment/Deposit	13 00
							Balance	42 25
	3/5	To Deposit / For				30 00	Payment/Deposit	30 00
							Balance	92 25
103	3/8	To Local High School / For Band donation	10 00	.			Payment/Deposit	10 00
							Balance	82 25
104	3/10	To Alan's Bakery / For Bread	3 80				Payment/Deposit	3 80
							Balance	78 45
105	3/15	To Grocery Mart / For Groceries	18 20				Payment/Deposit	18 20
							Balance	60 25
	3/18	To Deposit / For				42 00	Payment/Deposit	42 00
							Balance	102 25
106	3/20	To Acme Hardware / For Hammer	4 18				Payment/Deposit	4 18
							Balance	98 07
		To					Payment/Deposit	

Chapter 7

INCOME TAX

◆◆◆◆◆◆◆◆◆◆◆◆◆◆◆◆◆◆◆◆◆◆◆◆◆◆◆◆◆

OBJECTIVES

1. Understand the purpose of taxes and the different types of taxes.
2. Briefly outline a history of taxes in the United States, including why and how taxes evolved, and how taxes are determined today.
3. Define tax terminology.
4. Understand how to prepare Forms 1040EZ and 1040A U.S. Individual Income Tax returns.

OUR TAX SYSTEM

◆◆◆◆◆◆◆◆◆

Income taxes are the largest source of government revenue.

In the democratic, free enterprise society found in the United States, money is collected by the government from citizens and companies in the form of taxes. This money, or **revenue**, is redistributed according to needs and priorities determined by Congress. The largest source of government revenue is income taxes. Other taxes providing government revenue include social security tax, unemployment insurance tax, inheritance and estate tax, automobile license tax, driver's license fees, motel and hotel room tax, long-distance telephone call excise tax, business license tax, import duties, gasoline tax, liquor and tobacco tax, utility tax, and personal property tax.

Of all net revenue received by the U.S. Treasury, individual income taxes constitute the most.

There are three types of taxes in the United States. **Progressive taxes** are those that increase in proportion to increases in income. Income taxes are progressive taxes because as you earn more, you pay more in taxes. **Regressive taxes** are those that decrease in proportion as income increases. Sales taxes are regressive taxes, because those who can least afford to pay the tax are assessed the greatest amount of tax in proportion to their income. **Proportional taxes** are those for which the tax rate remains constant, regardless of the amount of income. Property taxes (called *ad valorem* taxes) are proportional taxes, because all those owning property of a certain value pay the same tax amount.

Income taxes are progressive taxes.

Taxes collected are used to provide services such as education; parks and recreation; streets and roads; and police, fire, and health departments on a local level. On the national level, taxes provide salaries for Congress and funds for national defense, highways, parks, welfare, foreign aid, etc.

Taxes provide services for everyone.

Most services (local, state, and national) are provided for the general welfare of all citizens, although individual citizens may not seem to benefit directly. For instance, through national student loan and grant programs, the entire country benefits because many citizens are able to obtain college educations, which increases the quality of the country's work force.

HISTORY OF TAXES

◆◆◆◆◆◆◆◆

While our country was a colony of England, the British government imposed certain taxes. However, after the Revolutionary War brought independence, there was no direct income tax imposed on individuals. The Constitution drawn in 1787 included the option to tax, but not to tax individuals directly. **Excise taxes** (levied against the manufacture, sale, or consumption of a commodity) and customs duties produced enough revenue to meet the nation's needs at that time.

Temporary income taxes paid for wars.

The Revolutionary War was financed by contributions from sympathetic countries such as France. The War of 1812 necessitated a temporary income tax; but when the war debts were paid, the tax was dropped. When the Civil War became an economic burden, an income tax to finance the war became necessary. In 1862 President Lincoln signed into law a bill that provided for progressive income taxes on wages earned only to pay off war debts; the tax then expired.

Congress introduced the first permanent income tax through the 16th Amendment to the Constitution in 1909. The amendment was ratified by three-fourths of the states by 1913, but only nominal taxes were levied as a result of the 16th Amendment.

Before the Great Depression of 1929, the government provided few services and collected few taxes. After the onset of the Depression, however, people suffered badly without government assistance — many had lost their jobs and unemployment or welfare benefits did not exist. When life savings were lost through bank failures, people had to start over without any assistance. But President Roosevelt's New Deal brought economic recovery through taxation and redistribution of income. In 1935, the Social Security Act was signed into law, creating the *Internal Revenue Service* (IRS). The IRS was designed to collect taxes and turn them over to the government for the payment of debts, commitments, and benefits. Money withheld from wages for social security is deposited with the U.S. Department of the Treasury.

People lost life savings during the Depression.

During World War II, taxes were increased to finance the war. This increase set a precedent for the increasing tax rates we know today. Rates are increased to pay for the growing services and needs of the government to provide for the general welfare of the people.

THE IRS

The Internal Revenue Service is an administrative agency of the Department of the Treasury, with headquarters in Washington, D.C. Each of seven regional offices is a major data processing center that oversees at least ten district and local offices. The main functions of the IRS are to collect income taxes and enforce tax laws.

The IRS collects taxes.

In local offices, IRS employees assist taxpayers in finding tax information and forms. Brochures and pamphlets to aid taxpayers in preparing their returns, and toll-free tax information lines are available at local IRS offices. Tax information and instruction booklets are furnished free to schools and colleges by the IRS. Auditors employed by the IRS examine returns selected for audit based on a computer check procedure.

THE POWER TO TAX

The power to levy taxes rests with the Congress of the United States. The Constitution provides that "all bills for raising revenue shall originate in the House of Representatives." Proposals to increase or decrease taxes may come from the president, the Department of the Treasury, or from a congressman or woman representing the interests of a geographic group of people. The House Ways and Means Committee studies the proposals and makes recommendations to the full House. Revenue bills must pass a vote in

Congress has the power to raise taxes.

Illustration 7-1
All bills for raising
taxes originate in
the House of Repre-
sentatives.

both the House and the Senate and then be signed by the president before
they become law.

PAYING YOUR FAIR SHARE

The ability to pay is the basic principle behind the tax laws of this country.
Our income tax system is based on **voluntary compliance**, which means that
all citizens are expected to prepare (or have prepared) and file income tax
returns. Responsibility for filing a tax return and paying taxes rests with the
individual. Willful failure to pay taxes is called **tax evasion**, which is a
felony, punishable by fine and/or imprisonment.

DEFINITION OF TERMS
◆◆◆◆◆◆◆◆

Before you can understand how to prepare tax returns, you need a working
knowledge of the tax vocabulary. The terms described in the following
paragraphs are found on income tax returns, in IRS instruction booklets,
and on forms and schedules you will work with.

FILING STATUS

There are five different ways to file a tax return: (a) as a single person (not
married on December 31); (b) married filing jointly (even if only one had

Filing status determines which tax table is used.

income); (c) married filing separate returns; (d) head of household (unmarried but with one or more dependents); or (e) qualifying widow(er) with dependent children.

EXEMPTIONS

An **exemption** is an allowance a taxpayer claims for each person dependent on the taxpayer's income. Each taxpayer is automatically allowed one exemption for self, one for spouse, and one for each dependent claimed. Figure 7-1 is a list of who can be claimed as a dependent.

Figure 7-1
Dependents

Child (natural, adopted, stepchild)	Father-in-law
Parent	Brother-in-law
Grandparent	Sister-in-law
Brother	Son-in-law
Sister	Daughter-in-law
Stepbrother	If related by blood:
Stepsister	Aunt
Stepmother	Uncle
Stepfather	Nephew
Mother-in-law	Niece

The amount of personal exemption changes.

Each exemption claimed on the tax form excludes a certain amount from a person's taxable income ($2,000 for 1989 returns); beginning in 1990 exemption amounts are indexed for inflation. You cannot claim an exemption on your tax return for a person claimed on another tax return. For example, two children may share the expense for taking care of an aging parent. Only one child (who contributes more than half) may claim the exemption. Students attending school full time may no longer claim themselves if they are claimed as exemptions on their parents' returns.

For all dependents over five years of age, you must furnish a social security number. Children of divorced or separated parents are claimed on the tax return of the custodial parent unless there is a written agreement or divorce decree providing otherwise.

GROSS INCOME

Gross income is all the taxable income you receive, including wages, tips, salaries, interest, dividends, unemployment compensation, alimony, and so forth. Certain types of income are not taxable and are not reported as income, such as child support, gifts, inheritances, scholarships, life insurance benefits, workers' compensation benefits, and veterans benefits. Social security benefits become taxable when income from all sources exceeds $25,000 (single) or $32,000 (married filing jointly). One half of the amount that exceeds $25,000 or $32,000 is fully taxable and is added to gross income.

Nontaxable income is not reported on a tax return.

Wages, Salaries, and Tips.   These items are monies received through employment, as shown on Form W-2, Wage and Tax Statement, supplied by the employer each year. Also reported on the W-2 are contributions to 401K, 401B (TSA), or other deferred compensation plans. These amounts are subtracted from gross earnings and will be taxed at a later date.

Interest Income.   Interest earned on savings accounts, certificates of deposit, and loans to others, whether or not you actually received it, is included in gross income. If interest income exceeds $400, a Schedule B must be filled out. It lists each source and amount of interest income. You should save the 1099-INT forms mailed to you by your bank and others who paid or accumulated interest in your behalf.

In addition, you must report any tax-exempt interest income (such as interest received on state and municipal bonds or as a shareholder in a mutual fund), even though it is not taxed.

Dividend Income.   Dividends are monies paid to stockholders from the profits of a corporation. They are fully taxable. You will receive Form 1099-DIV from the payer.

Unemployment Compensation.   Payments you receive while unemployed are fully taxable. Form 1099-G shows total unemployment compensation paid to you.

Unemployment compensation is taxable.

Child Support.   Money paid to a former spouse for support of dependent children is called **child support**. This income is not taxable for the one receiving it, nor is it deductible for the one paying it.

Alimony.   Money paid to support a former spouse is called **alimony**. It is taxable for the person receiving it, and it is deductible for the person paying it. (The long Form 1040 is required.)

Other Income.   In addition to the above, other miscellaneous types of income are also taxable, such as self-employment income; income from rents or royalties; prizes, awards, and gambling winnings (including lotteries); income tax refunds from state returns or previous years' federal returns; fees received for jury duty; and amounts recovered on bad debts.

ADJUSTMENTS TO INCOME

If you itemize deductions (use Form 1040) you can deduct reimbursed employee business expenses (the employer reported the income on your

W-2, so you include those expenses here); deductible IRA contributions, Keogh or SEP plans; penalties on early withdrawal from savings; and alimony paid. When these expenses are deducted from gross income, the result is **adjusted gross income**. Adjusted gross income is important, because percentages of this number will be taken later if you itemize deductions.

ITEMIZED DEDUCTIONS

Deductions are expenses the law allows taxpayers to subtract from gross income. You can deduct the full dollar amount for state and local taxes, property taxes, interest on home mortgages, and charitable contributions. Deductions for medical expenses and employee business expenses (miscellaneous deductions) are subject to limitations. Only medical expenses that exceed 7.5 percent of adjusted gross income, or employee business expenses that exceed 2 percent of adjusted gross income, are deductible. You cannot deduct these expenses if you do not itemize (use Form 1040) deductions. If you do not itemize deductions, you can take the **standard deduction**, which is an amount you can deduct depending on your filing status. The standard deductions are as follows:

Single or head of household... $2,540
Married filing jointly or Qualifying widow(er)........................ $3,760
Married filing separately.. $1,880

In addition, the standard deduction contains special rules if you are age 65 or older or blind. A single person, who is 65 or older or blind would have a standard deduction of $3,750 or, if both 65 or older and blind, $4,500. Figure 7-2 shows the standard deduction amounts for people who claim age 65 or blind, or both spouses.

Once deductions and exemptions are subtracted from adjusted gross income, what remains is **taxable income** — this amount determines the **tax liability** (taxes assessed against income) to be taken from the tax tables.

CREDITS

Some tax credits are available, such as child and dependent care expenses, credit for elderly and permanently disabled, and foreign tax credit. Special forms and schedules must be prepared to claim these credits.

Figure 7-2
Standard Deductions for Age 65 or Blind

Filing Status	Additional Checks On Form 1040		Standard Deduction Amount
Single	1	(age 65)	$3,750
	2	(blind)	4,500
Married filing	1	(age 65)	$5,600
jointly, or	2	(blind)	6,200
Qualified	3	(both are 65 and one blind)	6,800
widow(er)	4	(both are blind and 65)	7,400
Married filing	1	(age 65)	$3,100
separately	2	(blind)	3,700
	3	(both are 65 and one blind)	4,300
	4	(both are blind and 65)	4,900
Head of	1	(age 65)	$5,150
household	2	(blind)	5,900

The standard deduction is based on filing status.

OTHER TAXES

In addition to income taxes withheld and due, you may also owe self-employment tax, social security tax on tips not included in your W-2, or taxes due on IRAs you cashed in early. Again, special forms and schedules are required to report this money due.

PAYMENTS

You are given credit for taxes withheld from your paycheck (as shown on the W-2 statement, which must be attached), estimated tax payments, and other forms of prepayment. When payments made are compared to taxes due, you determine whether you have overpaid taxes and therefore have a *refund* due, or whether you owe an additional amount.

PREPARING TO FILE

♦♦♦♦♦♦♦♦

Begin preparing your tax return early.

Once income and expense records are ready, you can rough draft your tax return. You should also study the tax booklet that accompanies tax forms and other printed material that explains new tax laws and changes to old

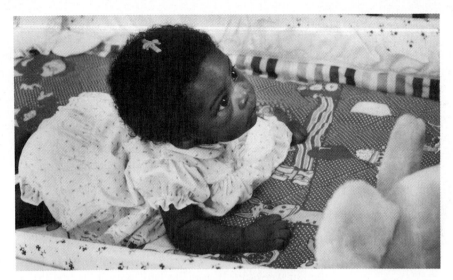

Illustration 7-2
Tax credits for child care expenses are available to some taxpayers.

laws. Read through tax returns carefully to be sure you are using the appropriate form, taking advantage of every possible deduction, and reporting all taxable income. A 1040EZ form may require only 15 minutes to prepare; the long form 1040 may require several days after all information has been gathered. In addition to a federal tax return, you may have to file a state income tax return.

WHO MUST FILE

You must file a tax return if you are:

You must file if you earn a certain amount.

	and:	with gross income of:
Single (or widowed)	under 65	$ 4,440
	under 65 and blind	4,900
	65 or over	5,650
Married, filing jointly	under 65 (both spouses)	7,560
	under 65 (both spouses, one blind)	8,800
	65 or over (one spouse)	9,400
	65 or over (both spouses)	10,000
Married, filing separately	any age	1,900
Head of household	under 65	4,400
	under 65 and blind	6,300
	65 or over	7,050

You may also have to file a return if claimed as a dependent on another person's return, if you owe any special taxes (such as social security tax on tips), if you earned $400 or more from self-employment after business expenses are deducted, or if you earned $100 or more from an organization exempt from social security taxes (such as a church).

Persons who did not earn enough to owe taxes, but had taxes withheld from their paychecks, should file a return to reclaim moneys withheld. If you do not file, you will not get a refund.

WHEN TO FILE

You must file by April 15.

You must file no later than April 15 of the year after you earned income. If April 15 falls on a weekend or holiday, your tax return is due on the next regular weekday. If you file late, you are subject to penalties and interest charges.

SHORT FORM OR LONG FORM

There are three tax forms from which to choose.

You must decide whether to fill out a short form (1040EZ or 1040A) or to itemize your deductions, using the long form (1040).

1. *Use Form 1040EZ* if you are single (not over 65 or blind); will claim no more than one personal exemption; have taxable income of less than $50,000; have income from wages, salaries, tips, and interest of $400 or less; and have no adjustments to income, no itemized deductions, no other taxes, and no tax credits.

2. *Use Form 1040A* if you are single, married (filing jointly or separately), or head of household; have taxable income of less than $50,000; have income from wages, salaries, tips, interest, dividends, and unemployment compensation (no limits); have a deductible IRA contribution; have no itemized deductions; and have tax credits only for child and dependent care expense and earned income credit.

3. You must *use Form 1040* as a qualifying widow(er) with dependent child; if your income exceeds $50,000; if you received taxable social security or railroad retirement benefits, self-employment earnings, rents and royalties, or income from pensions and annuities; if you had taxable state and local tax refunds, capital gains, gain from sale of your house, alimony income, or income from other sources; if your adjustments to income include alimony paid, penalty for early

withdrawal of savings, reimbursed employee business expenses, or other adjustments; if you wish to itemize deductions such as state and local income taxes, real estate taxes, interest paid, charitable contributions, medical and dental expenses, casualty and theft losses, moving expenses, and miscellaneous deductions; if any other taxes are due (self-employment, minimum tax, social security tax on tips, all other taxes); and if tax credits include foreign tax credit, credit for elderly, and so on.

Generally speaking, you should use Form 1040 only if your itemized deductions exceed the standard deduction, or if you must file it because you meet some condition that requires you to file the long form. After you have filed your first tax return, you will automatically receive the same forms and information booklets in the mail the next year.

WHERE TO BEGIN

During the year, save all receipts and proofs of payment for your itemized deductions. You will need these receipts to prove the accuracy of your tax return if you are audited. Save all employee withholding records. When you receive your Form W-2, Wage and Tax Statement, from each of your employers (by January 31), compare it with your records and check it for accuracy. Any discrepancy between the Form W-2 and your records should be reported immediately to the employer and corrected.

Everyone who works must pay social security taxes.

If you earned more than the maximum amount of earnings taxed for social security purposes, more social security tax (FICA) than the maximum may have been withheld. The excess amount of social security tax withheld can be added to taxes withheld on the tax form to reduce tax liability or increase tax refund. Figure 7-3 shows how social security taxes have progressed since they began in 1937.

Mail your return early.

It is wise to prepare your tax return early — as soon as you receive your W-2 (Wage and Tax Statement), 1099-INT (Statements for Recipients of Interest Income) forms from banks and savings institutions, and any other 1099 forms you may receive, and gather all other necessary information. If you owe additional taxes, mail your return and amount due in enough time to have the envelope postmarked by April 15. If you have a refund coming, the sooner you file, the sooner you will receive it. If you wait until April, your refund may be delayed for months. You will not receive interest on refunds.

Once you have gathered all your information, prepare both the short and the long form to determine whether you can save money by itemizing

Figure 7-3
Progression of So-
cial Security Taxes

Year	Maximum Amount of Earnings	Rate	Maximum Tax
1937	$ 3,000	1%	$ 30.00
1963	4,800	3.6%	172.80
1971	7,800	5.2%	405.60
1981	29,000	6.65%	1,975.00
1987	43,800	7.15%	3,131.70
1988	45,000	7.51%	3,379.50
1989	46,800*	7.51%	3,514.68
1990	50,100*	7.65%	3,832.65

(*Projected amounts, subject to change by Congress.)

deductions. Read all directions carefully and fill out all schedules completely.

If you did not have enough taxes withheld during the year, and you owe the government money when taxes are due, you may be subject to a penalty and have to increase the amount withheld for the next year. If you receive a large refund, you should increase your exemption status to have less withheld during the year.

You can amend your
tax return.

If you discover you made an error in a tax return after it has been filed, you may file an amended return (Form 1040X) in order to claim a refund or credit, or to pay additional taxes.

Save copies of the tax returns you file, together with all supporting evidence (receipts) for six years. Tax returns should be kept in a safe-deposit box, together with copies of W-2s and other supporting information.

PREPARING INCOME TAX RETURNS
◆◆◆◆◆◆◆◆◆

The federal income tax return must be completed in ink or typed with no errors or omissions. The booklets provided by the IRS have line-by-line instructions that explain each section and type of income or deduction. The preparation of tax returns is a simple process of following instructions and inserting appropriate information. An unsigned tax return will be returned to the taxpayer before a refund is issued. If a joint return is prepared, both spouses must sign it.

FORM 1040EZ

Line-by-line instructions for filling out Form 1040EZ are on the back of the form. Highlights of the instructions are described in the following paragraphs.

Step 1: Name and Address. Fill in your name, address, and social security number. Check the Yes box if you want $1 to go to the Presidential Election Campaign Fund. The dollar will come out of taxes already withheld; it is not an additional tax.

Step 2: Reporting Income. On line 1 enter total wages, salaries, and tips, as shown on your W-2 statement(s). Copies of the W-2s must be attached to the return. On line 2 enter taxable interest income (cannot be more than $400). Add lines 1 and 2 and enter the total on line 3.

> You must have taxable income of less than $50,000 to use Form 1040EZ.

For line 4, check whether you are a dependent on another person's tax return. If so, check Yes. You then complete the worksheet on the back of the form to determine the amount of standard deduction allowed. If No, enter the amount of your standard deduction ($2,540). For line 5, subtract line 4 from line 3.

For line 6, if you answered Yes for question 4, you get no exemption. If you answered No, enter $1,900 (in 1987), $1,950 (1988), or $2,000 (1989 and beyond, plus an amount indexed for inflation). This is your personal exemption amount.

For line 7, subtract line 6 from line 5. This is your taxable income.

Step 3: Figuring Tax. On line 8, enter the amount of federal income tax withheld, as shown on the W-2 statement. For line 9, enter the amount of tax liability, using the tax tables.

Step 4: Refund or Amount Due. If line 8 is larger than 9, you will receive a refund (you paid in more than your tax liability). Enter the amount of the refund on line 10. If line 9 is larger than 8, you owe the amount on line 11. You must write a check to the Internal Revenue Service and attach it to your return.

> Tax returns must be signed.

Sign your return. Make sure your W-2 statement(s) and check (if applicable) are attached to the completed return and mail the return to the nearest regional IRS office. The instruction pamphlet will provide an address to use.

FORM 1040A

Form 1040A is printed on the front and back of one piece of paper. Line-by-line instructions are available in booklet form. Schedule 1 must be completed and attached to Form 1040A if you claim child and dependent care expenses, have over $400 of taxable interest income, or have over $400 of dividend income.

Step 1: Name and Address.   Enter the name, address, social security number, and occupation of all persons filing the return. Each person can elect to give or not to give to the Presidential Election Campaign Fund.

Step 2: Filing Status.   In this section you check only one box, indicating your filing status. If married filing separately or filing as head of household, you must enter the spouse's name and social security number, or the dependent's name in the space provided.

Step 3: Exemptions.   You get an exemption for yourself and your spouse. (5a and 5b) You can also claim dependents who lived with you and meet the tests of dependency, as explained in the tax booklets. For children five or over, you must also list their social security numbers. You may not list a child of whom you do not have custody unless you have a pre-1985 agreement stating you are allowed to claim the exemption. Special rules apply. The total number of exemptions claimed is entered in 5(e).

Step 4: Total Income.   On line 6, enter wages, salaries, tips, etc. This amount is verified by W-2s. On line 7a, enter taxable interest income. If it exceeds $400, you must complete Schedule 1, Part II, where you list each payer and amount (as shown on 1099-INT or other 1099 forms). On line 7b, enter tax-exempt interest income, explained earlier, but do not add it to taxable income. On line 8, dividends are entered. If over $400, you must complete Schedule 1, Part III, where you list each payer and amount (as shown on 1099-DIV or other 1099 forms). On line 9, enter unemployment compensation received, as shown on Form(s) 1099-G or 1099-UC. On line 10, enter the total of lines 6, 7a, 8, and 9. This is your total income.

Step 5: Adjusted Gross Income.   On line 11a, enter your IRA deduction (if you are eligible), and your spouse's IRA deduction on 11b (if eligible). For 11c, the total is entered. For line 12, you subtract line 11c from total income, leaving adjusted gross income.

Step 6: Standard Deduction and Taxable Income.   On the top of the back of the page, line 13, you bring forward the amount from line 12 (adjusted gross income). For line 14a, you check boxes if you or your spouse is 65 or over or blind. These checks will allow you a larger standard deduction. For line 14b, check the box if you are claimed on another return (such as your parents'); on line 14c, check the box if you are married filing separately. These two lines will reduce your standard deduction amount. If you checked any of the boxes (14a, 14b, or 14c), you must read the directions in the tax booklet to figure the amount of standard deduction. Otherwise, based on your filing status from the front page, enter the applicable standard deduction amount on line 14d. This amount is subtracted from line 13 and entered on line 15.

For line 16, multiply $1,900 (1987), $1,950 (1988), or $2,000 (1989 and beyond, plus amount indexed for inflation) times the number of exemptions

claimed. For line 17, subtract line 16 from line 15. This is taxable income.
Step 7: Figuring Tax. On line 18, enter the amount of tax due, using the tax table. On line 19, enter the credit for child and dependent care expenses. To do so, fill out Schedule 1, Part I. To qualify for this credit, you

Child care expenses
require Schedule 1,
Part 1.

must have earned income (from wages, salaries, or tips). If two people are working, the lower income is considered, and you will receive from 20 to 30 percent of the amount of such expenses incurred to enter on line 19. On line 20, subtract the child care credit (line 19) from tax liability on line 18.

On line 21a, enter total federal income tax withheld, as shown on your W-2 statement(s). Earned income credit is entered on line 21b, as explained in the tax booklet. To qualify, you must have total earned income (line 13) of less than $15,432. The smaller the earned income, the larger the credit.

On line 22 enter the total tax payment.

Step 8: Figuring Tax Due. If line 22 is larger than 20 (more taxes paid than due), you get a refund, which is entered on line 23. But if line 20 (tax liability) is greater than line 22 (tax payments) then you must write a check

Taxes due must be
paid when you file.

for that amount (line 24) and attach the check to your return.

You must sign and date your return, and list your occupation. Your spouse must also sign and date the return, and enter his or her occupation. The taxpayer and spouse must both sign a joint return, even though only one may have earned or received income.

SAMPLE TAX RETURNS

Figure 7-4 shows Mary M. Belknap's Form W-2 Wage and Tax Statement. Figure 7-5 shows her completed Form 1040EZ tax return. Ms. Belknap is

Figure 7-4
Sample Form W-2
Wage and Tax
Statement

1 Control number	22222	For Paperwork Reduction Act Notice, see back of Copy D. OMB No. 1545-0008	For Official Use Only ▶		
2 Employer's name, address, and ZIP code			3 Employer's identification number 93-10298348	4 Employer's state I.D. number 44-18	
Mid-Valley Plumbing Co. 123 West 34th Place Springfield, OR 97477-1331			5 Statutory employee ☐ Deceased ☐ Pension plan ☐ Legal rep. ☐	942 emp. ☐ Subtotal ☐ Deferred compensation ☐	Void ☐
			6 Allocated tips	7 Advance EIC payment	
8 Employee's social security number 465-84-9138	9 Federal income tax withheld $2,301.00		10 Wages, tips, other compensation $18,330.00	11 Social security tax withheld $1,351.80	
12 Employee's name (first, middle, last) Mary M. Belknap			13 Social security wages $18,330.00	14 Social security tips	
			16 (See Instr. for Forms W-2/W-2P)	16a Fringe benefits incl. in Box 10	
335 Alder Street, #12 Springfield, OR 97477-1331			17 State income tax $933.28	18 State wages, tips, etc. $18,330.00	19 Name of state Oregon
15 Employee's address and ZIP code			20 Local income tax None	21 Local wages, tips, etc. None	22 Name of locality Lane
Form W-2 Wage and Tax Statement			Copy A For Social Security Administration	Dept. of the Treasury—IRS	

Department of the Treasury - Internal Revenue Service

Form **1040EZ**

Income Tax Return for
Single filers with no dependents (O)

OMB No. 1545-0675

Name & address

Use the IRS mailing label. If you don't have one, please print.

▸ Mary M. Belknap
Print your name above (first, initial, last)

335 Alder St. #12
Present home address (number and street). (If you have a P.O. box, see instructions.)

Springfield, OR 97477-1331
City, town, or post office, state, and ZIP code

Please print your numbers like this:

0 1 2 3 4 5 6 7 8 9

Your social security number

4 6 5 8 4 9 1 3 8

Please read the instructions for this form on the reverse side.

Presidential Election Campaign Fund
Do you want $1 to go to this fund?

Note: Checking "Yes" will not change your tax or reduce your refund.

Yes No
✓

	Dollars	Cents

Report your income

1 Total wages, salaries, and tips. This should be shown in Box 10 of your W-2 form(s). (Attach your W-2 form(s).)   **1**

18,330.00

2 Taxable interest income of $400 or less. If the total is more than $400, you cannot use Form 1040EZ.   **2**

100.00

Attach Copy B of Form(s) W-2 here

3 Add line 1 and line 2. This is your **adjusted gross income.**   **3**

18,430.00

4 Can you be claimed as a dependent on another person's return?
☐ Yes. Do worksheet on back; enter amount from line E here.
☐ No. Enter 2,540 as your standard deduction.   **4**

2,540.00

5 Subtract line 4 from line 3.   **5**

15,890.00

6 If you checked the "Yes" box on line 4, enter 0.
If you checked the "No" box on line 4, enter 1,900.
This is your **personal exemption.**   **6**

1,900.00

7 Subtract line 6 from line 5. If line 6 is larger than line 5, enter 0 on line 7. This is your **taxable income.**   **7**

13,990.00

Figure your tax

8 Enter your Federal income tax withheld. This should be shown in Box 9 of your W-2 form(s).   **8**

2,301.00

9 Use the **single** column in the tax table on pages 32–37 of the Form 1040A instruction booklet to find the **tax** on the amount shown on **line 7** above. Enter the amount of tax.   **9**

2,024.00

Refund or amount you owe

Attach tax payment here

10 If line 8 is larger than line 9, subtract line 9 from line 8.
Enter the **amount of your refund.**   **10**

277.00

11 If line 9 is larger than line 8, subtract line 8 from line 9.
Enter the **amount you owe.** Attach check or money order for the full amount, payable to "Internal Revenue Service."   **11**

Sign your return

I have read this return. Under penalties of perjury, I declare that to the best of my knowledge and belief, the return is true, correct, and complete.

Your signature   Date

Mary M. Belknap   april 1, 19--

For IRS Use Only—Please do not write in boxes below.

For Privacy Act and Paperwork Reduction Act Notice, see page 31.   Form **1040EZ**

Figure 7-5   Sample Form 1040EZ

single and claims one exemption. Her wages are found on the W-2 that she previously checked for accuracy. She earned $100 interest on savings accounts.

On the tax tables, Mary locates taxable income (line 7) in the Single column. Her tax liability is shown. When her tax liability is subtracted from taxes withheld (line 8), the difference is her refund.

Married persons filing jointly may choose to file Form 1040A. Figures 7-6A and 7-6B show the W-2 Wage and Tax Statements for Thomas B. and Wilana A. Henderson. Figure 7-7 is the Hendersons's joint return (1040A).

Tom and Wilana claimed the standard deduction for filing status "married, filing jointly," and claimed $1,900 for each exemption. (Note: This amount changes each year — check the directions for the current amount.) To claim the credit for child and dependent care expenses (line 19) they had to complete Schedule 1 as shown in Figure 7-8. The Hendersons cannot claim charitable deductions using 1040A, nor can they deduct interest or taxes paid, and other types of deductions that they might have if they file the long form 1040. Their tax liability is smaller than taxes withheld, so they will receive a refund. Federal tax tables, which taxpayers use to determine the amount of their income tax, are shown in Figure 7-9, pages 140-142.

Figure 7-6A
Sample Form W-2
Wage and Tax
Statement

1 Control number	22222	For Paperwork Reduction Act Notice, see back of Copy D. OMB No. 1545-0008	For Official Use Only ▶		
2 Employer's name, address, and ZIP code			3 Employer's identification number 91-1432343		4 Employer's state I.D. number 33-211
A Art Studios 48 East 143 Street Des Plaines, IL 60601-3132			5 Statutory employee Deceased Pension plan Legal rep. 942 emp. Subtotal Deferred compensation Void		
			6 Allocated tips		7 Advance EIC payment
8 Employee's social security number 333-12-6832	9 Federal income tax withheld $1,581.33		10 Wages, tips, other compensation $12,486.22		11 Social security tax withheld $937.72
12 Employee's name (first, middle, last) Wilana A. Henderson			13 Social security wages $12,486.22		14 Social security tips
321 East 13th Avenue Chicago, IL 60605-5214			16 (See Instr. for Forms W-2/W-2P)		16a Fringe benefits incl. in Box 10
			17 State income tax	18 State wages, tips, etc.	19 Name of state
15 Employee's address and ZIP code			20 Local income tax	21 Local wages, tips, etc.	22 Name of locality

Form **W-2 Wage and Tax Statement**   Copy A For Social Security Administration   Dept. of the Treasury—IRS

Figure 7-6B
Sample Form W-2
Wage and Tax
Statement

1 Control number	22222	For Paperwork Reduction Act Notice, see back of Copy D. OMB No. 1545-0008	For Official Use Only ▶		
2 Employer's name, address, and ZIP code			3 Employer's identification number 92-0186848		4 Employer's state I.D. number 33-261
A & W Welding Supply 85 West Bensington Blvd Chicago, IL 60615-1538			5 Statutory employee Deceased Pension plan Legal rep. 942 emp. Subtotal Deferred compensation Void		
			6 Allocated tips		7 Advance EIC payment
8 Employee's social security number 411-86-3215	9 Federal income tax withheld $1,801.33		10 Wages, tips, other compensation $14,311.21		11 Social security tax withheld $1,074.77
12 Employee's name (first, middle, last) Thomas B. Henderson			13 Social security wages $14,311.21		14 Social security tips
321 East 13th Avenue Chicago, IL 60605-5214			16 (See Instr. for Forms W-2/W-2P)		16a Fringe benefits incl. in Box 10
			17 State income tax	18 State wages, tips, etc.	19 Name of state
15 Employee's address and ZIP code			20 Local income tax	21 Local wages, tips, etc.	22 Name of locality

Form **W-2 Wage and Tax Statement**   Copy A For Social Security Administration   Dept. of the Treasury—IRS

Form
1040A

Department of the Treasury—Internal Revenue Service

U.S. Individual
Income Tax Return

Step 1
Label

Use IRS
label.
Otherwise,
please print
or type.

OMB No. 1545-0085

Your first name and initial (if joint return, also give spouse's name and initial)   Last name
Thomas B. and Wilana A.   Henderson

Your social security no.
411 : 86 : 3215

Present home address (number and street). (If you have a P.O. Box, see page 9 of the instructions.)
321 East 13th Avenue.

Spouse's social security no.
333 : 12 : 6832

City, town or post office, state, and ZIP code
Chicago IL 60605-5214

For **Privacy Act and Paperwork Reduction Act Notice, see page 31.**

Presidential Election Campaign Fund

Do you want $1 to go to this fund?.................. ☑ Yes ☐ No
If joint return, does your spouse want $1 to go to this fund?. ☑ Yes ☐ No

Note: *Checking "Yes" will not change your tax or reduce your refund.*

Step 2
**Check your
filing status**
(Check only one)

1 ☐ Single (See if you can use Form 1040EZ.)
2 ☑ Married filing joint return (even if only one had income)
3 ☐ Married filing separate return. Enter spouse's social security number above
   and spouse's full name here. _____
4 ☐ Head of household (with qualifying person). If the qualifying person is your child but not
   your dependent, enter this child's name here. _____

Step 3
**Figure your
exemptions**

(See page 12 of
instructions.)

Caution: If you can be claimed as a dependent on another person's tax return (such as your parents'
return), do not check box 5a. But be sure to check the box on line 14b on page 2.

5a ☑ Yourself   5b ☑ Spouse

No. of boxes
checked on 5a
and 5b   **2**

c Dependents: 1. Name (first, initial, and last name)	2. Check if under age 5	3. If age 5 or over, dependent's social security number	4. Relationship	5. No. of months lived in your home in 1987
Andy A. Henderson	✓		son	12
Cathy B. Henderson		541 : 80 : 3182	daughter	12

No. of children
on 5c who
lived with you   **2**

No. of
children on 5c
who didn't
live with you
due to divorce
or separation

No. of parents
listed on 5c

No. of other
dependents
listed on 5c

If more than 7
dependents,
attach
statement.

Attach Copy B of
Form(s) W-2 here.

d If your child didn't live with you but is claimed as your dependent
   under a pre-1985 agreement, check here . . . . ▶ ☐
e Total number of exemptions claimed. (Also complete line 16.)

Add numbers
entered on
lines above   **4**

Step 4
**Figure your
total income**

Attach check or
money order here.

6 Wages, salaries, tips, etc. This should be shown in Box 10 of your W-2
   form(s). (Attach Form(s) W-2.)   6 | 26,797 | 43

7a **Taxable** interest income (see page 17). (If over $400, also complete
   and attach Schedule 1, Part II.)   7a | 486 | 01

b **Tax-exempt** interest income (see page 17).
   (DO NOT include on line 7a.)   7b | —0—

8 Dividends. (If over $400, also complete and attach Schedule 1, Part III.)   8 | 120 | —

9 Unemployment compensation (insurance) from Form(s) 1099-G.   9 | —0— | —

10 Add lines 6, 7a, 8, and 9. Enter the total. This is your **total income.** ▶ 10 | 27,403 | 44

Step 5
**Figure your
adjusted
gross
income**

11a Your IRA deduction from applicable Worksheet. New
   rules for IRAs begin on page 18.   11a | —0— | —

b Spouse's IRA deduction from applicable Worksheet.
   New rules for IRAs begin on page 18.   11b | —0— | —

c Add lines 11a and 11b. Enter the total. These are your **total
   adjustments.**   11c | —0— | —

12 Subtract line 11c from line 10. Enter the result. This is your **adjusted
   gross income.** (If this line is less than $15,432 and a child lived with
   you, see "Earned Income Credit" (line 21b) on page 27 of instructions.) ▶ 12 | 27,403 | 44

Form **1040A**

Figure 7-7   Sample 1040A Joint Return

Form 1040A

Page 2

Step 6	**13** Enter the amount from line 12.	**13**	27,403 44

Figure your standard deduction,

14a Check if: ☐ **You** were 65 or over ☐ Blind ⎫ Enter number of
☐ **Spouse** was 65 or over ☐ Blind ⎬ boxes checked ▶ 14a ☐

b If you can be claimed as a dependent on another person's return (such as your parents' return), check here . . . . ▶14b ☐

c If you are married filing separately and your spouse files Form 1040 and itemizes deductions, check here . . . . ▶14c ☐

d Standard deduction. If you checked a box on line 14a, b, or c, see page 22 for amount to enter on line 14d. If no box is checked, enter amount shown below for your filing status.

Filing status from page 1 ⎰ Single or Head of household, enter $2,540
⎱ Married filing joint return, enter $3,760
Married filing separate return, enter $1,880

	14d	3760 —

Exemption amount, and

15 Subtract line 14d from line 13. Enter the result. | **15** | 23,643 44

16 Multiply $1,900 by the total number of exemptions claimed on line 5e. Or, figure your exemption amount from the chart on page 24 of the instructions. | **16** | 7,600 —

Taxable income

17 Subtract line 16 from line 15. Enter the result. This is your **taxable income.** ▶ **17** | 16,043 44

If You Want IRS To Figure Your Tax, See Page 24 of the Instructions.

Step 7

Figure your tax, credits, and payments (including advance EIC payments)

Caution: If you are under age 14 and have more than $1,000 of investment income, see page 24 of the instructions and check here . . . ./ . . . . ▶ ☐

18 Find the tax on the amount on line 17. Check if from: ☑ Tax Table (pages 32–37); or ☐ Form 8615, Computation of Tax for Children Under Age 14 Who Have Investment Income of More Than $1,000. | **18** | 2,284 —

19 Credit for child and dependent care expenses. Complete and attach Schedule 1, Part I. | **19** | 483 21

20 Subtract line 19 from line 18. Enter the result. (If line 19 is more than line 18, enter -0- on line 20.) This is your **total tax.** ▶ **20** | 1,800 79

21a Total Federal income tax withheld. This should be shown in Box 9 of your W-2 form(s). (If line 6 is more than $43,800, see page 26.) **21a** 3382 66

b Earned income credit, from the worksheet on page 28 of the instructions. Also see page 27. **21b** —0—

22 Add lines 21a and 21b. Enter the total. These are your **total payments.** ▶ **22** | 3382 66

Step 8

Figure your refund or amount you owe

23 If line 22 is larger than line 20, subtract line 20 from line 22. Enter the result. This is the **amount of your refund.** | **23** | 1581 87

24 If line 20 is larger than line 22, subtract line 22 from line 20. Enter the result. This is the **amount you owe.** Attach check or money order for full amount payable to "Internal Revenue Service." Write your social security number, daytime phone number, and "19-- Form 1040A" on it. | **24** |

Step 9

Sign your return

Under penalties of perjury, I declare that I have examined this return and accompanying schedules and statements, and to the best of my knowledge and belief, they are true, correct, and complete. Declaration of preparer (other than the taxpayer) is based on all information of which the preparer has any knowledge.

Your signature | Date | Your occupation
X *Thomas B. Henderson* | 4/1/-- | Welder
Spouse's signature (if joint return, both must sign) | Date | Spouse's occupation
X *Wilana A. Henderson* | 4/1/-- | Accountant

Paid preparer's use only

Preparer's signature | Date | Preparer's social security no.
X
Firm's name (or yours if self-employed) | Employer identification no.

Check if self-employed ☐

Address and ZIP code

Figure 7-7   Sample 1040A Joint Return (continued)

Schedule 1 (Form 1040A)

OMB No. 1545-0085

Name(s) as shown on Form 1040A

Thomas B. and Wilana A. Henderson

Your social security number

411 :86 :3245

You MUST complete and attach Schedule 1 to Form 1040A only if you:

- Claim the credit for child and dependent care expenses (complete **Part I**)
- Have over $400 of taxable interest income (complete **Part II**)
- Have over $400 of dividend income (complete **Part III**)

Part I

Credit for child and dependent care expenses (see page 24 of the instructions)

Complete this part to figure the amount of credit you can take on Form 1040A, line 19. Attach Schedule 1 to Form 1040A.

Note: *If you paid cash wages of $50 or more in a calendar quarter to an individual for services performed in your home, you must file an employment tax return. Get **Form 942** for details.*

1	Enter the number of qualifying persons who were cared for in 19--. (See the instructions for the definition of a qualifying person.)	1	*2*	
2	Enter the amount of **qualified** expenses you incurred and actually paid in 19-- for the care of the qualifying person. (See the instructions for which expenses qualify for the credit.) DO NOT enter more than $2,400 ($4,800 if you paid for the care of two or more qualifying persons).	2	*2301*	*—*
3 a	You **must** enter your earned income on line 3a.	3a	*14,311*	*21*
b	If you are married, filing a joint return for 19--, you must enter your spouse's earned income on line 3b. (If spouse is a full-time student or is disabled, see the instructions for amount to enter on this line.)	3b	*12,486*	*22*
c	If you are married, compare the amounts on lines 3a and 3b, and enter the **smaller** of the two amounts on line 3c.	3c	*12,486*	*22*
4 ●	If you were unmarried at the end of 19--, compare the amounts on lines 2 and 3a, and enter the **smaller** of the two amounts on line 4.			
●	If you are married, filing a joint return for 19--, compare the amounts on lines 2 and 3c, and enter the **smaller** of the two amounts on line 4.	4	*2,301*	*—*
5	Enter the percentage from the table below that applies to the amount on Form 1040A, line 13.			

If line 13 is:		Percentage is:	If line 13 is:		Percentage is:
Over—	But not over—		Over—	But not over—	
$0—10,000		30% (.30)	$20,000—22,000		24% (.24)
10,000—12,000		29% (.29)	22,000—24,000		23% (.23)
12,000—14,000		28% (.28)	24,000—26,000		22% (.22)
14,000—16,000		27% (.27)	26,000—28,000		21% (.21)
16,000—18,000		26% (.26)	28,000		20% (.20)
18,000—20,000		25% (.25)			

		5	*2301* × *.21*
6	Multiply the amount on line 4 by the percentage on line 5. Enter the result here and on Form 1040A, line 19.	6 =	*483* *21*

Figure 7-8   Sample Schedule 1 (Form 1040A)

Schedule 1 (Form 1040A)

OMB No. 1545-0085

Name(s) as shown on Form 1040A. (Do not complete if shown on other side.)
Thomas B. and Wilana A. Henderson

Your social security number
411 : 86 : 3215

Part II **Interest income** (see page 17 of the instructions)

Complete this part and attach Schedule 1 to Form 1040A if you received over $400 in taxable interest income.

Note: *If you received a Form 1099-INT or Form 1099-OID from a brokerage firm, enter the firm's name and the total interest shown on that form.*

1 List name of payer

List name of payer	Amount	
Security Savings and Loan	$	400 —
State Teachers Credit Union	$	86 01
	$	
	$	
	$	
	$	
	$	
	$	
	$	
	$	
	$	
	$	
	$	
	$	
	$	
	$	
	$	
	$	
	$	
	$	

2 Add amounts on line 1. Enter the total here and on Form 1040A, line 7a. **2** 486 01

Part III **Dividend income** (see page 18 of the instructions)

Complete this part and attach Schedule 1 to Form 1040A if you received over $400 in dividends.

Note: *If you received a Form 1099-DIV from a brokerage firm, enter the firm's name and the total dividends shown on that form.*

1 List name of payer

List name of payer	Amount	
	$	
	$	
	$	
	$	
	$	
	$	
	$	
	$	
	$	
	$	
	$	
	$	
	$	
	$	
	$	
	$	
	$	
	$	
	$	
	$	

2 Add amounts on line 1. Enter the total here and on Form 1040A, line 8. **2**

Figure 7-8 Sample Schedule 1 (Form 1040A) (continued)

Page 32

Tax Table

Based on Taxable Income

For persons with taxable incomes of less than $50,000

Example: Mr. and Mrs. Green are filing a joint return. Their taxable income on line 17 of Form 1040A is $23,270. First, they find the $23,250-23,300 income line. Next, they find the column for married filing jointly and read down the column. The amount shown where the income line and filing status column meet is $3.371. This is the tax amount they must write on line 18 of Form 1040A.

At least	But less than	Single (and 1040EZ filers)	Married filing jointly	Married filing separately	Head of a household
		Your tax is—			
→ 23,200	23,250	4,247	3,364	4,674	3,413
23,250	23,300	4,261	(3,371)	4,691	3,427
23,300	23,350	4,275	3,379	4,709	3,441
23,350	23,400	4,289	3,386	4,726	3,455

If 1040A, line 17, OR 1040EZ, line 7 is—		And you are—			
At least	But less than	Single (and 1040EZ filers)	Married filing jointly	Married filing separately	Head of a household
		Your tax is—			
$0	$5	$0	$0	$0	$0
5	15	1	1	1	1
15	25	2	2	2	2
25	50	4	4	4	4
50	75	7	7	7	7
75	100	10	10	10	10
100	125	12	12	12	12
125	150	15	15	15	15
150	175	18	18	18	18
175	200	21	21	21	21
200	225	23	23	23	23
225	250	26	26	26	26
250	275	29	29	29	29
275	300	32	32	32	32
300	325	34	34	34	34
325	350	37	37	37	37
350	375	40	40	40	40
375	400	43	43	43	43
400	425	45	45	45	45
425	450	48	48	48	48
450	475	51	51	51	51
475	500	54	54	54	54
500	525	56	56	56	56
525	550	59	59	59	59
550	575	62	62	62	62
575	600	65	65	65	65
600	625	67	67	67	67
625	650	70	70	70	70
650	675	73	73	73	73
675	700	76	76	76	76
700	725	78	78	78	78
725	750	81	81	81	81
750	775	84	84	84	84
775	800	87	87	87	87
800	825	89	89	89	89
825	850	92	92	92	92
850	875	95	95	95	95
875	900	98	98	98	98
900	925	100	100	100	100
925	950	103	103	103	103
950	975	106	106	106	106
975	1,000	109	109	109	109
1,000					
1,000	1,025	111	111	111	111
1,025	1,050	114	114	114	114
1,050	1,075	117	117	117	117
1,075	1,100	120	120	120	120
1,100	1,125	122	122	122	122
1,125	1,150	125	125	125	125
1,150	1,175	128	128	128	128
1,175	1,200	131	131	131	131
1,200	1,225	133	133	133	133
1,225	1,250	136	136	136	136
1,250	1,275	139	139	139	139
1,275	1,300	142	142	142	142
1,300	1,325	144	144	144	144
1,325	1,350	147	147	147	147
1,350	1,375	150	150	150	150
1,375	1,400	153	153	153	153

If 1040A, line 17, OR 1040EZ, line 7 is—		And you are—			
At least	But less than	Single (and 1040EZ filers)	Married filing jointly	Married filing separately	Head of a household
		Your tax is—			
1,400	1,425	155	155	155	155
1,425	1,450	158	158	158	158
1,450	1,475	161	161	161	161
1,475	1,500	164	164	164	164
1,500	1,525	166	166	167	166
1,525	1,550	169	169	171	169
1,550	1,575	172	172	174	172
1,575	1,600	175	175	178	175
1,600	1,625	177	177	182	177
1,625	1,650	180	180	186	180
1,650	1,675	183	183	189	183
1,675	1,700	186	186	193	186
1,700	1,725	188	188	197	188
1,725	1,750	191	191	201	191
1,750	1,775	194	194	204	194
1,775	1,800	197	197	208	197
1,800	1,825	200	199	212	199
1,825	1,850	204	202	216	202
1,850	1,875	207	205	219	205
1,875	1,900	211	208	223	208
1,900	1,925	215	210	227	210
1,925	1,950	219	213	231	213
1,950	1,975	222	216	234	216
1,975	2,000	226	219	238	219
2,000					
2,000	2,025	230	221	242	221
2,025	2,050	234	224	246	224
2,050	2,075	237	227	249	227
2,075	2,100	241	230	253	230
2,100	2,125	245	232	257	232
2,125	2,150	249	235	261	235
2,150	2,175	252	238	264	238
2,175	2,200	256	241	268	241
2,200	2,225	260	243	272	243
2,225	2,250	264	246	276	246
2,250	2,275	267	249	279	249
2,275	2,300	271	252	283	252
2,300	2,325	275	254	287	254
2,325	2,350	279	257	291	257
2,350	2,375	282	260	294	260
2,375	2,400	286	263	298	263
2,400	2,425	290	265	302	265
2,425	2,450	294	268	306	268
2,450	2,475	297	271	309	271
2,475	2,500	301	274	313	274
2,500	2,525	305	276	317	277
2,525	2,550	309	279	321	281
2,550	2,575	312	282	324	284
2,575	2,600	316	285	328	288
2,600	2,625	320	287	332	292
2,625	2,650	324	290	336	296
2,650	2,675	327	293	339	299
2,675	2,700	331	296	343	303

If 1040A, line 17, OR 1040EZ, line 7 is—		And you are—			
At least	But less than	Single (and 1040EZ filers)	Married filing jointly	Married filing separately	Head of a household
		Your tax is—			
2,700	2,725	335	298	347	307
2,725	2,750	339	301	351	311
2,750	2,775	342	304	354	314
2,775	2,800	346	307	358	318
2,800	2,825	350	309	362	322
2,825	2,850	354	312	366	326
2,850	2,875	357	315	369	329
2,875	2,900	361	318	373	333
2,900	2,925	365	320	377	337
2,925	2,950	369	323	381	341
2,950	2,975	372	326	384	344
2,975	3,000	376	329	388	348
3,000					
3,000	3,050	382	334	394	354
3,050	3,100	389	341	401	361
3,100	3,150	397	349	409	369
3,150	3,200	404	356	416	376
3,200	3,250	412	364	424	384
3,250	3,300	419	371	431	391
3,300	3,350	427	379	439	399
3,350	3,400	434	386	446	406
3,400	3,450	442	394	454	414
3,450	3,500	449	401	461	421
3,500	3,550	457	409	469	429
3,550	3,600	464	416	476	436
3,600	3,650	472	424	484	444
3,650	3,700	479	431	491	451
3,700	3,750	487	439	499	459
3,750	3,800	494	446	506	466
3,800	3,850	502	454	514	474
3,850	3,900	509	461	521	481
3,900	3,950	517	469	529	489
3,950	4,000	524	476	536	496
4,000					
4,000	4,050	532	484	544	504
4,050	4,100	539	491	551	511
4,100	4,150	547	499	559	519
4,150	4,200	554	506	566	526
4,200	4,250	562	514	574	534
4,250	4,300	569	521	581	541
4,300	4,350	577	529	589	549
4,350	4,400	584	536	596	556
4,400	4,450	592	544	604	564
4,450	4,500	599	551	611	571
4,500	4,550	607	559	619	579
4,550	4,600	614	566	626	586
4,600	4,650	622	574	634	594
4,650	4,700	629	581	641	601
4,700	4,750	637	589	649	609
4,750	4,800	644	596	656	616
4,800	4,850	652	604	664	624
4,850	4,900	659	611	671	631
4,900	4,950	667	619	679	639
4,950	5,000	674	626	686	646

Continued on next page

Page 33

Tax Table—*Continued*

If 1040A, line 17, OR 1040EZ, line 7 is—		And you are—			
At least	But less than	Single (and 1040EZ filers)	Married filing jointly	Married filing separately	Head of a household
		Your tax is—			
5,000					
5,000	5,050	682	634	694	654
5,050	5,100	689	641	701	661
5,100	5,150	697	649	709	669
5,150	5,200	704	656	716	676
5,200	5,250	712	664	724	684
5,250	5,300	719	671	731	691
5,300	5,350	727	679	739	699
5,350	5,400	734	686	746	706
5,400	5,450	742	694	754	714
5,450	5,500	749	701	761	721
5,500	5,550	757	709	769	729
5,550	5,600	764	716	776	736
5,600	5,650	772	724	784	744
5,650	5,700	779	731	791	751
5,700	5,750	787	739	799	759
5,750	5,800	794	746	806	766
5,800	5,850	802	754	814	774
5,850	5,900	809	761	821	781
5,900	5,950	817	769	829	789
5,950	6,000	824	776	836	796
6,000					
6,000	6,050	832	784	844	804
6,050	6,100	839	791	851	811
6,100	6,150	847	799	859	819
6,150	6,200	854	806	866	826
6,200	6,250	862	814	874	834
6,250	6,300	869	821	881	841
6,300	6,350	877	829	889	849
6,350	6,400	884	836	896	856
6,400	6,450	892	844	904	864
6,450	6,500	899	851	911	871
6,500	6,550	907	859	919	879
6,550	6,600	914	866	926	886
6,600	6,650	922	874	934	894
6,650	6,700	929	881	941	901
6,700	6,750	937	889	949	909
6,750	6,800	944	896	956	916
6,800	6,850	952	904	964	924
6,850	6,900	959	911	971	931
6,900	6,950	967	919	979	939
6,950	7,000	974	926	986	946
7,000					
7,000	7,050	982	934	994	954
7,050	7,100	989	941	1,001	961
7,100	7,150	997	949	1,009	969
7,150	7,200	1,004	956	1,016	976
7,200	7,250	1,012	964	1,024	984
7,250	7,300	1,019	971	1,031	991
7,300	7,350	1,027	979	1,039	999
7,350	7,400	1,034	986	1,046	1,006
7,400	7,450	1,042	994	1,054	1,014
7,450	7,500	1,049	1,001	1,061	1,021
7,500	7,550	1,057	1,009	1,069	1,029
7,550	7,600	1,064	1,016	1,076	1,036
7,600	7,650	1,072	1,024	1,084	1,044
7,650	7,700	1,079	1,031	1,091	1,051
7,700	7,750	1,087	1,039	1,099	1,059
7,750	7,800	1,094	1,046	1,106	1,066
7,800	7,850	1,102	1,054	1,114	1,074
7,850	7,900	1,109	1,061	1,121	1,081
7,900	7,950	1,117	1,069	1,129	1,089
7,950	8,000	1,124	1,076	1,136	1,096

If 1040A, line 17, OR 1040EZ, line 7 is—		And you are—			
At least	But less than	Single (and 1040EZ filers)	Married filing jointly	Married filing separately	Head of a household
		Your tax is—			
8,000					
8,000	8,050	1,132	1,084	1,144	1,104
8,050	8,100	1,139	1,091	1,151	1,111
8,100	8,150	1,147	1,099	1,159	1,119
8,150	8,200	1,154	1,106	1,166	1,126
8,200	8,250	1,162	1,114	1,174	1,134
8,250	8,300	1,169	1,121	1,181	1,141
8,300	8,350	1,177	1,129	1,189	1,149
8,350	8,400	1,184	1,136	1,196	1,156
8,400	8,450	1,192	1,144	1,204	1,164
8,450	8,500	1,199	1,151	1,211	1,171
8,500	8,550	1,207	1,159	1,219	1,179
8,550	8,600	1,214	1,166	1,226	1,186
8,600	8,650	1,222	1,174	1,234	1,194
8,650	8,700	1,229	1,181	1,241	1,201
8,700	8,750	1,237	1,189	1,249	1,209
8,750	8,800	1,244	1,196	1,256	1,216
8,800	8,850	1,252	1,204	1,264	1,224
8,850	8,900	1,259	1,211	1,271	1,231
8,900	8,950	1,267	1,219	1,279	1,239
8,950	9,000	1,274	1,226	1,286	1,246
9,000					
9,000	9,050	1,282	1,234	1,294	1,254
9,050	9,100	1,289	1,241	1,301	1,261
9,100	9,150	1,297	1,249	1,309	1,269
9,150	9,200	1,304	1,256	1,316	1,276
9,200	9,250	1,312	1,264	1,324	1,284
9,250	9,300	1,319	1,271	1,331	1,291
9,300	9,350	1,327	1,279	1,339	1,299
9,350	9,400	1,334	1,286	1,346	1,306
9,400	9,450	1,342	1,294	1,354	1,314
9,450	9,500	1,349	1,301	1,361	1,321
9,500	9,550	1,357	1,309	1,369	1,329
9,550	9,600	1,364	1,316	1,376	1,336
9,600	9,650	1,372	1,324	1,384	1,344
9,650	9,700	1,379	1,331	1,391	1,351
9,700	9,750	1,387	1,339	1,399	1,359
9,750	9,800	1,394	1,346	1,406	1,366
9,800	9,850	1,402	1,354	1,414	1,374
9,850	9,900	1,409	1,361	1,421	1,381
9,900	9,950	1,417	1,369	1,429	1,389
9,950	10,000	1,424	1,376	1,436	1,396
10,000					
10,000	10,050	1,432	1,384	1,444	1,404
10,050	10,100	1,439	1,391	1,451	1,411
10,100	10,150	1,447	1,399	1,459	1,419
10,150	10,200	1,454	1,406	1,466	1,426
10,200	10,250	1,462	1,414	1,474	1,434
10,250	10,300	1,469	1,421	1,481	1,441
10,300	10,350	1,477	1,429	1,489	1,449
10,350	10,400	1,484	1,436	1,496	1,456
10,400	10,450	1,492	1,444	1,504	1,464
10,450	10,500	1,499	1,451	1,511	1,471
10,500	10,550	1,507	1,459	1,519	1,479
10,550	10,600	1,514	1,466	1,526	1,486
10,600	10,650	1,522	1,474	1,534	1,494
10,650	10,700	1,529	1,481	1,541	1,501
10,700	10,750	1,537	1,489	1,549	1,509
10,750	10,800	1,544	1,496	1,556	1,516
10,800	10,850	1,552	1,504	1,564	1,524
10,850	10,900	1,559	1,511	1,571	1,531
10,900	10,950	1,567	1,519	1,579	1,539
10,950	11,000	1,574	1,526	1,586	1,546

If 1040A, line 17, OR 1040EZ, line 7 is—		And you are—			
At least	But less than	Single (and 1040EZ filers)	Married filing jointly	Married filing separately	Head of a household
		Your tax is—			
11,000					
11,000	11,050	1,582	1,534	1,594	1,554
11,050	11,100	1,589	1,541	1,601	1,561
11,100	11,150	1,597	1,549	1,609	1,569
11,150	11,200	1,604	1,556	1,616	1,576
11,200	11,250	1,612	1,564	1,624	1,584
11,250	11,300	1,619	1,571	1,631	1,591
11,300	11,350	1,627	1,579	1,639	1,599
11,350	11,400	1,634	1,586	1,646	1,606
11,400	11,450	1,642	1,594	1,654	1,614
11,450	11,500	1,649	1,601	1,661	1,621
11,500	11,550	1,657	1,609	1,669	1,629
11,550	11,600	1,664	1,616	1,676	1,636
11,600	11,650	1,672	1,624	1,684	1,644
11,650	11,700	1,679	1,631	1,691	1,651
11,700	11,750	1,687	1,639	1,699	1,659
11,750	11,800	1,694	1,646	1,706	1,666
11,800	11,850	1,702	1,654	1,714	1,674
11,850	11,900	1,709	1,661	1,721	1,681
11,900	11,950	1,717	1,669	1,729	1,689
11,950	12,000	1,724	1,676	1,736	1,696
12,000					
12,000	12,050	1,732	1,684	1,744	1,704
12,050	12,100	1,739	1,691	1,751	1,711
12,100	12,150	1,747	1,699	1,759	1,719
12,150	12,200	1,754	1,706	1,766	1,726
12,200	12,250	1,762	1,714	1,774	1,734
12,250	12,300	1,769	1,721	1,781	1,741
12,300	12,350	1,777	1,729	1,789	1,749
12,350	12,400	1,784	1,736	1,796	1,756
12,400	12,450	1,792	1,744	1,804	1,764
12,450	12,500	1,799	1,751	1,811	1,771
12,500	12,550	1,807	1,759	1,819	1,779
12,550	12,600	1,814	1,766	1,826	1,786
12,600	12,650	1,822	1,774	1,834	1,794
12,650	12,700	1,829	1,781	1,841	1,801
12,700	12,750	1,837	1,789	1,849	1,809
12,750	12,800	1,844	1,796	1,856	1,816
12,800	12,850	1,852	1,804	1,864	1,824
12,850	12,900	1,859	1,811	1,871	1,831
12,900	12,950	1,867	1,819	1,879	1,839
12,950	13,000	1,874	1,826	1,886	1,846
13,000					
13,000	13,050	1,882	1,834	1,894	1,854
13,050	13,100	1,889	1,841	1,901	1,861
13,100	13,150	1,897	1,849	1,909	1,869
13,150	13,200	1,904	1,856	1,916	1,876
13,200	13,250	1,912	1,864	1,924	1,884
13,250	13,300	1,919	1,871	1,931	1,891
13,300	13,350	1,927	1,879	1,939	1,899
13,350	13,400	1,934	1,886	1,946	1,906
13,400	13,450	1,942	1,894	1,954	1,914
13,450	13,500	1,949	1,901	1,961	1,921
13,500	13,550	1,957	1,909	1,969	1,929
13,550	13,600	1,964	1,916	1,976	1,936
13,600	13,650	1,972	1,924	1,984	1,944
13,650	13,700	1,979	1,931	1,991	1,951
13,700	13,750	1,987	1,939	1,999	1,959
13,750	13,800	1,994	1,946	2,006	1,966
13,800	13,850	2,002	1,954	2,014	1,974
13,850	13,900	2,009	1,961	2,021	1,981
13,900	13,950	2,017	1,969	2,029	1,989
13,950	14,000	2,024	1,976	2,036	1,996

Continued on next page

Figure 7-9 Federal Tax Tables (1040EZ and 1040A)

Page 34

Tax Table—Continued

If 1040A, line 17, OR 1040EZ, line 7 is—		And you are—			
At least	But less than	Single (and 1040EZ filers)	Married filing jointly	Married filing separately	Head of a household
		Your tax is—			
14,000					
14,000	14,050	2,032	1,984	2,047	2,004
14,050	14,100	2,039	1,991	2,061	2,011
14,100	14,150	2,047	1,999	2,075	2,019
14,150	14,200	2,054	2,006	2,089	2,026
14,200	14,250	2,062	2,014	2,103	2,034
14,250	14,300	2,069	2,021	2,117	2,041
14,300	14,350	2,077	2,029	2,131	2,049
14,350	14,400	2,084	2,036	2,145	2,056
14,400	14,450	2,092	2,044	2,159	2,064
14,450	14,500	2,099	2,051	2,173	2,071
14,500	14,550	2,107	2,059	2,187	2,079
14,550	14,600	2,114	2,066	2,201	2,086
14,600	14,650	2,122	2,074	2,215	2,094
14,650	14,700	2,129	2,081	2,229	2,101
14,700	14,750	2,137	2,089	2,243	2,109
14,750	14,800	2,144	2,096	2,257	2,116
14,800	14,850	2,152	2,104	2,271	2,124
14,850	14,900	2,159	2,111	2,285	2,131
14,900	14,950	2,167	2,119	2,299	2,139
14,950	15,000	2,174	2,126	2,313	2,146
15,000					
15,000	15,050	2,182	2,134	2,327	2,154
15,050	15,100	2,189	2,141	2,341	2,161
15,100	15,150	2,197	2,149	2,355	2,169
15,150	15,200	2,204	2,156	2,369	2,176
15,200	15,250	2,212	2,164	2,383	2,184
15,250	15,300	2,219	2,171	2,397	2,191
15,300	15,350	2,227	2,179	2,411	2,199
15,350	15,400	2,234	2,186	2,425	2,206
15,400	15,450	2,242	2,194	2,439	2,214
15,450	15,500	2,249	2,201	2,453	2,221
15,500	15,550	2,257	2,209	2,467	2,229
15,550	15,600	2,264	2,216	2,481	2,236
15,600	15,650	2,272	2,224	2,495	2,244
15,650	15,700	2,279	2,231	2,509	2,251
15,700	15,750	2,287	2,239	2,523	2,259
15,750	15,800	2,294	2,246	2,537	2,266
15,800	15,850	2,302	2,254	2,551	2,274
15,850	15,900	2,309	2,261	2,565	2,281
15,900	15,950	2,317	2,269	2,579	2,289
15,950	16,000	2,324	2,276	2,593	2,296
16,000					
16,000	16,050	2,332	2,284	2,607	2,304
16,050	16,100	2,339	2,291	2,621	2,311
16,100	16,150	2,347	2,299	2,635	2,319
16,150	16,200	2,354	2,306	2,649	2,326
16,200	16,250	2,362	2,314	2,663	2,334
16,250	16,300	2,369	2,321	2,677	2,341
16,300	16,350	2,377	2,329	2,691	2,349
16,350	16,400	2,384	2,336	2,705	2,356
16,400	16,450	2,392	2,344	2,719	2,364
16,450	16,500	2,399	2,351	2,733	2,371
16,500	16,550	2,407	2,359	2,747	2,379
16,550	16,600	2,414	2,366	2,761	2,386
16,600	16,650	2,422	2,374	2,775	2,394
16,650	16,700	2,429	2,381	2,789	2,401
16,700	16,750	2,437	2,389	2,803	2,409
16,750	16,800	2,444	2,396	2,817	2,416
16,800	16,850	2,455	2,404	2,831	2,424
16,850	16,900	2,469	2,411	2,845	2,431
16,900	16,950	2,483	2,419	2,859	2,439
16,950	17,000	2,497	2,426	2,873	2,446

If 1040A, line 17, OR 1040EZ, line 7 is—		And you are—			
At least	But less than	Single (and 1040EZ filers)	Married filing jointly	Married filing separately	Head of a household
		Your tax is—			
17,000					
17,000	17,050	2,511	2,434	2,887	2,454
17,050	17,100	2,525	2,441	2,901	2,461
17,100	17,150	2,539	2,449	2,915	2,469
17,150	17,200	2,553	2,456	2,929	2,476
17,200	17,250	2,567	2,464	2,943	2,484
17,250	17,300	2,581	2,471	2,957	2,491
17,300	17,350	2,595	2,479	2,971	2,499
17,350	17,400	2,609	2,486	2,985	2,506
17,400	17,450	2,623	2,494	2,999	2,514
17,450	17,500	2,637	2,501	3,013	2,521
17,500	17,550	2,651	2,509	3,027	2,529
17,550	17,600	2,665	2,516	3,041	2,536
17,600	17,650	2,679	2,524	3,055	2,544
17,650	17,700	2,693	2,531	3,069	2,551
17,700	17,750	2,707	2,539	3,083	2,559
17,750	17,800	2,721	2,546	3,097	2,566
17,800	17,850	2,735	2,554	3,111	2,574
17,850	17,900	2,749	2,561	3,125	2,581
17,900	17,950	2,763	2,569	3,139	2,589
17,950	18,000	2,777	2,576	3,153	2,596
18,000					
18,000	18,050	2,791	2,584	3,167	2,604
18,050	18,100	2,805	2,591	3,181	2,611
18,100	18,150	2,819	2,599	3,195	2,619
18,150	18,200	2,833	2,606	3,209	2,626
18,200	18,250	2,847	2,614	3,223	2,634
18,250	18,300	2,861	2,621	3,237	2,641
18,300	18,350	2,875	2,629	3,251	2,649
18,350	18,400	2,889	2,636	3,265	2,656
18,400	18,450	2,903	2,644	3,279	2,664
18,450	18,500	2,917	2,651	3,293	2,671
18,500	18,550	2,931	2,659	3,307	2,679
18,550	18,600	2,945	2,666	3,321	2,686
18,600	18,650	2,959	2,674	3,335	2,694
18,650	18,700	2,973	2,681	3,349	2,701
18,700	18,750	2,987	2,689	3,363	2,709
18,750	18,800	3,001	2,696	3,377	2,716
18,800	18,850	3,015	2,704	3,391	2,724
18,850	18,900	3,029	2,711	3,405	2,731
18,900	18,950	3,043	2,719	3,419	2,739
18,950	19,000	3,057	2,726	3,433	2,746
19,000					
19,000	19,050	3,071	2,734	3,447	2,754
19,050	19,100	3,085	2,741	3,461	2,761
19,100	19,150	3,099	2,749	3,475	2,769
19,150	19,200	3,113	2,756	3,489	2,776
19,200	19,250	3,127	2,764	3,503	2,784
19,250	19,300	3,141	2,771	3,517	2,791
19,300	19,350	3,155	2,779	3,531	2,799
19,350	19,400	3,169	2,786	3,545	2,806
19,400	19,450	3,183	2,794	3,559	2,814
19,450	19,500	3,197	2,801	3,573	2,821
19,500	19,550	3,211	2,809	3,587	2,829
19,550	19,600	3,225	2,816	3,601	2,836
19,600	19,650	3,239	2,824	3,615	2,844
19,650	19,700	3,253	2,831	3,629	2,851
19,700	19,750	3,267	2,839	3,643	2,859
19,750	19,800	3,281	2,846	3,657	2,866
19,800	19,850	3,295	2,854	3,671	2,874
19,850	19,900	3,309	2,861	3,685	2,881
19,900	19,950	3,323	2,869	3,699	2,889
19,950	20,000	3,337	2,876	3,713	2,896

If 1040A, line 17, OR 1040EZ, line 7 is—		And you are—			
At least	But less than	Single (and 1040EZ filers)	Married filing jointly	Married filing separately	Head of a household
		Your tax is—			
20,000					
20,000	20,050	3,351	2,884	3,727	2,904
20,050	20,100	3,365	2,891	3,741	2,911
20,100	20,150	3,379	2,899	3,755	2,919
20,150	20,200	3,393	2,906	3,769	2,926
20,200	20,250	3,407	2,914	3,783	2,934
20,250	20,300	3,421	2,921	3,797	2,941
20,300	20,350	3,435	2,929	3,811	2,949
20,350	20,400	3,449	2,936	3,825	2,956
20,400	20,450	3,463	2,944	3,839	2,964
20,450	20,500	3,477	2,951	3,853	2,971
20,500	20,550	3,491	2,959	3,867	2,979
20,550	20,600	3,505	2,966	3,881	2,986
20,600	20,650	3,519	2,974	3,895	2,994
20,650	20,700	3,533	2,981	3,909	3,001
20,700	20,750	3,547	2,989	3,923	3,009
20,750	20,800	3,561	2,996	3,937	3,016
20,800	20,850	3,575	3,004	3,951	3,024
20,850	20,900	3,589	3,011	3,965	3,031
20,900	20,950	3,603	3,019	3,979	3,039
20,950	21,000	3,617	3,026	3,993	3,046
21,000					
21,000	21,050	3,631	3,034	4,007	3,054
21,050	21,100	3,645	3,041	4,021	3,061
21,100	21,150	3,659	3,049	4,035	3,069
21,150	21,200	3,673	3,056	4,049	3,076
21,200	21,250	3,687	3,064	4,063	3,084
21,250	21,300	3,701	3,071	4,077	3,091
21,300	21,350	3,715	3,079	4,091	3,099
21,350	21,400	3,729	3,086	4,105	3,106
21,400	21,450	3,743	3,094	4,119	3,114
21,450	21,500	3,757	3,101	4,133	3,121
21,500	21,550	3,771	3,109	4,147	3,129
21,550	21,600	3,785	3,116	4,161	3,136
21,600	21,650	3,799	3,124	4,175	3,144
21,650	21,700	3,813	3,131	4,189	3,151
21,700	21,750	3,827	3,139	4,203	3,159
21,750	21,800	3,841	3,146	4,217	3,166
21,800	21,850	3,855	3,154	4,231	3,174
21,850	21,900	3,869	3,161	4,245	3,181
21,900	21,950	3,883	3,169	4,259	3,189
21,950	22,000	3,897	3,176	4,273	3,196
22,000					
22,000	22,050	3,911	3,184	4,287	3,204
22,050	22,100	3,925	3,191	4,301	3,211
22,100	22,150	3,939	3,199	4,315	3,219
22,150	22,200	3,953	3,206	4,329	3,226
22,200	22,250	3,967	3,214	4,343	3,234
22,250	22,300	3,981	3,221	4,357	3,241
22,300	22,350	3,995	3,229	4,371	3,249
22,350	22,400	4,009	3,236	4,385	3,256
22,400	22,450	4,023	3,244	4,399	3,264
22,450	22,500	4,037	3,251	4,413	3,271
22,500	22,550	4,051	3,259	4,429	3,279
22,550	22,600	4,065	3,266	4,446	3,286
22,600	22,650	4,079	3,274	4,464	3,294
22,650	22,700	4,093	3,281	4,481	3,301
22,700	22,750	4,107	3,289	4,499	3,309
22,750	22,800	4,121	3,296	4,516	3,316
22,800	22,850	4,135	3,304	4,534	3,324
22,850	22,900	4,149	3,311	4,551	3,331
22,900	22,950	4,163	3,319	4,569	3,339
22,950	23,000	4,177	3,326	4,586	3,346

Continued on next page

Page 35

Tax Table—Continued

If 1040A, line 17, OR 1040EZ, line 7 is—		And you are—			
At least	But less than	Single (and 1040EZ filers)	Married filing jointly	Married filing separately	Head of a household
		Your tax is—			
23,000					
23,000	23,050	4,191	3,334	4,604	3,357
23,050	23,100	4,205	3,341	4,621	3,371
23,100	23,150	4,219	3,349	4,639	3,385
23,150	23,200	4,233	3,356	4,656	3,399
23,200	23,250	4,247	3,364	4,674	3,413
23,250	23,300	4,261	3,371	4,691	3,427
23,300	23,350	4,275	3,379	4,709	3,441
23,350	23,400	4,289	3,386	4,726	3,455
23,400	23,450	4,303	3,394	4,744	3,469
23,450	23,500	4,317	3,401	4,761	3,483
23,500	23,550	4,331	3,409	4,779	3,497
23,550	23,600	4,345	3,416	4,796	3,511
23,600	23,650	4,359	3,424	4,814	3,525
23,650	23,700	4,373	3,431	4,831	3,539
23,700	23,750	4,387	3,439	4,849	3,553
23,750	23,800	4,401	3,446	4,866	3,567
23,800	23,850	4,415	3,454	4,884	3,581
23,850	23,900	4,429	3,461	4,901	3,595
23,900	23,950	4,443	3,469	4,919	3,609
23,950	24,000	4,457	3,476	4,936	3,623
24,000					
24,000	24,050	4,471	3,484	4,954	3,637
24,050	24,100	4,485	3,491	4,971	3,651
24,100	24,150	4,499	3,499	4,989	3,665
24,150	24,200	4,513	3,506	5,006	3,679
24,200	24,250	4,527	3,514	5,024	3,693
24,250	24,300	4,541	3,521	5,041	3,707
24,300	24,350	4,555	3,529	5,059	3,721
24,350	24,400	4,569	3,536	5,076	3,735
24,400	24,450	4,583	3,544	5,094	3,749
24,450	24,500	4,597	3,551	5,111	3,763
24,500	24,550	4,611	3,559	5,129	3,777
24,550	24,600	4,625	3,566	5,146	3,791
24,600	24,650	4,639	3,574	5,164	3,805
24,650	24,700	4,653	3,581	5,181	3,819
24,700	24,750	4,667	3,589	5,199	3,833
24,750	24,800	4,681	3,596	5,216	3,847
24,800	24,850	4,695	3,604	5,234	3,861
24,850	24,900	4,709	3,611	5,251	3,875
24,900	24,950	4,723	3,619	5,269	3,889
24,950	25,000	4,737	3,626	5,286	3,903
25,000					
25,000	25,050	4,751	3,634	5,304	3,917
25,050	25,100	4,765	3,641	5,321	3,931
25,100	25,150	4,779	3,649	5,339	3,945
25,150	25,200	4,793	3,656	5,356	3,959
25,200	25,250	4,807	3,664	5,374	3,973
25,250	25,300	4,821	3,671	5,391	3,987
25,300	25,350	4,835	3,679	5,409	4,001
25,350	25,400	4,849	3,686	5,426	4,015
25,400	25,450	4,863	3,694	5,444	4,029
25,450	25,500	4,877	3,701	5,461	4,043
25,500	25,550	4,891	3,709	5,479	4,057
25,550	25,600	4,905	3,716	5,496	4,071
25,600	25,650	4,919	3,724	5,514	4,085
25,650	25,700	4,933	3,731	5,531	4,099
25,700	25,750	4,947	3,739	5,549	4,113
25,750	25,800	4,961	3,746	5,566	4,127
25,800	25,850	4,975	3,754	5,584	4,141
25,850	25,900	4,989	3,761	5,601	4,155
25,900	25,950	5,003	3,769	5,619	4,169
25,950	26,000	5,017	3,776	5,636	4,183

If 1040A, line 17, OR 1040EZ, line 7 is—		And you are—			
At least	But less than	Single (and 1040EZ filers)	Married filing jointly	Married filing separately	Head of a household
		Your tax is—			
26,000					
26,000	26,050	5,031	3,784	5,654	4,197
26,050	26,100	5,045	3,791	5,671	4,211
26,100	26,150	5,059	3,799	5,689	4,225
26,150	26,200	5,073	3,806	5,706	4,239
26,200	26,250	5,087	3,814	5,724	4,253
26,250	26,300	5,101	3,821	5,741	4,267
26,300	26,350	5,115	3,829	5,759	4,281
26,350	26,400	5,129	3,836	5,776	4,295
26,400	26,450	5,143	3,844	5,794	4,309
26,450	26,500	5,157	3,851	5,811	4,323
26,500	26,550	5,171	3,859	5,829	4,337
26,550	26,600	5,185	3,866	5,846	4,351
26,600	26,650	5,199	3,874	5,864	4,365
26,650	26,700	5,213	3,881	5,881	4,379
26,700	26,750	5,227	3,889	5,899	4,393
26,750	26,800	5,241	3,896	5,916	4,407
26,800	26,850	5,255	3,904	5,934	4,421
26,850	26,900	5,269	3,911	5,951	4,435
26,900	26,950	5,283	3,919	5,969	4,449
26,950	27,000	5,297	3,926	5,986	4,463
27,000					
27,000	27,050	5,313	3,934	6,004	4,477
27,050	27,100	5,330	3,941	6,021	4,491
27,100	27,150	5,348	3,949	6,039	4,505
27,150	27,200	5,365	3,956	6,056	4,519
27,200	27,250	5,383	3,964	6,074	4,533
27,250	27,300	5,400	3,971	6,091	4,547
27,300	27,350	5,418	3,979	6,109	4,561
27,350	27,400	5,435	3,986	6,126	4,575
27,400	27,450	5,453	3,994	6,144	4,589
27,450	27,500	5,470	4,001	6,161	4,603
27,500	27,550	5,488	4,009	6,179	4,617
27,550	27,600	5,505	4,016	6,196	4,631
27,600	27,650	5,523	4,024	6,214	4,645
27,650	27,700	5,540	4,031	6,231	4,659
27,700	27,750	5,558	4,039	6,249	4,673
27,750	27,800	5,575	4,046	6,266	4,687
27,800	27,850	5,593	4,054	6,284	4,701
27,850	27,900	5,610	4,061	6,301	4,715
27,900	27,950	5,628	4,069	6,319	4,729
27,950	28,000	5,645	4,076	6,336	4,743
28,000					
28,000	28,050	5,663	4,087	6,354	4,757
28,050	28,100	5,680	4,101	6,371	4,771
28,100	28,150	5,698	4,115	6,389	4,785
28,150	28,200	5,715	4,129	6,406	4,799
28,200	28,250	5,733	4,143	6,424	4,813
28,250	28,300	5,750	4,157	6,441	4,827
28,300	28,350	5,768	4,171	6,459	4,841
28,350	28,400	5,785	4,185	6,476	4,855
28,400	28,450	5,803	4,199	6,494	4,869
28,450	28,500	5,820	4,213	6,511	4,883
28,500	28,550	5,838	4,227	6,529	4,897
28,550	28,600	5,855	4,241	6,546	4,911
28,600	28,650	5,873	4,255	6,564	4,925
28,650	28,700	5,890	4,269	6,581	4,939
28,700	28,750	5,908	4,283	6,599	4,953
28,750	28,800	5,925	4,297	6,616	4,967
28,800	28,850	5,943	4,311	6,634	4,981
28,850	28,900	5,960	4,325	6,651	4,995
28,900	28,950	5,978	4,339	6,669	5,009
28,950	29,000	5,995	4,353	6,686	5,023

If 1040A, line 17, OR 1040EZ, line 7 is—		And you are—			
At least	But less than	Single (and 1040EZ filers)	Married filing jointly	Married filing separately	Head of a household
		Your tax is—			
29,000					
29,000	29,050	6,013	4,367	6,704	5,037
29,050	29,100	6,030	4,381	6,721	5,051
29,100	29,150	6,048	4,395	6,739	5,065
29,150	29,200	6,065	4,409	6,756	5,079
29,200	29,250	6,083	4,423	6,774	5,093
29,250	29,300	6,100	4,437	6,791	5,107
29,300	29,350	6,118	4,451	6,809	5,121
29,350	29,400	6,135	4,465	6,826	5,135
29,400	29,450	6,153	4,479	6,844	5,149
29,450	29,500	6,170	4,493	6,861	5,163
29,500	29,550	6,188	4,507	6,879	5,177
29,550	29,600	6,205	4,521	6,896	5,191
29,600	29,650	6,223	4,535	6,914	5,205
29,650	29,700	6,240	4,549	6,931	5,219
29,700	29,750	6,258	4,563	6,949	5,233
29,750	29,800	6,275	4,577	6,966	5,247
29,800	29,850	6,293	4,591	6,984	5,261
29,850	29,900	6,310	4,605	7,001	5,275
29,900	29,950	6,328	4,619	7,019	5,289
29,950	30,000	6,345	4,633	7,036	5,303
30,000					
30,000	30,050	6,363	4,647	7,054	5,317
30,050	30,100	6,380	4,661	7,071	5,331
30,100	30,150	6,398	4,675	7,089	5,345
30,150	30,200	6,415	4,689	7,106	5,359
30,200	30,250	6,433	4,703	7,124	5,373
30,250	30,300	6,450	4,717	7,141	5,387
30,300	30,350	6,468	4,731	7,159	5,401
30,350	30,400	6,485	4,745	7,176	5,415
30,400	30,450	6,503	4,759	7,194	5,429
30,450	30,500	6,520	4,773	7,211	5,443
30,500	30,550	6,538	4,787	7,229	5,457
30,550	30,600	6,555	4,801	7,246	5,471
30,600	30,650	6,573	4,815	7,264	5,485
30,650	30,700	6,590	4,829	7,281	5,499
30,700	30,750	6,608	4,843	7,299	5,513
30,750	30,800	6,625	4,857	7,316	5,527
30,800	30,850	6,643	4,871	7,334	5,541
30,850	30,900	6,660	4,885	7,351	5,555
30,900	30,950	6,678	4,899	7,369	5,569
30,950	31,000	6,695	4,913	7,386	5,583
31,000					
31,000	31,050	6,713	4,927	7,404	5,597
31,050	31,100	6,730	4,941	7,421	5,611
31,100	31,150	6,748	4,955	7,439	5,625
31,150	31,200	6,765	4,969	7,456	5,639
31,200	31,250	6,783	4,983	7,474	5,653
31,250	31,300	6,800	4,997	7,491	5,667
31,300	31,350	6,818	5,011	7,509	5,681
31,350	31,400	6,835	5,025	7,526	5,695
31,400	31,450	6,853	5,039	7,544	5,709
31,450	31,500	6,870	5,053	7,561	5,723
31,500	31,550	6,888	5,067	7,579	5,737
31,550	31,600	6,905	5,081	7,596	5,751
31,600	31,650	6,923	5,095	7,614	5,765
31,650	31,700	6,940	5,109	7,631	5,779
31,700	31,750	6,958	5,123	7,649	5,793
31,750	31,800	6,975	5,137	7,666	5,807
31,800	31,850	6,993	5,151	7,684	5,821
31,850	31,900	7,010	5,165	7,701	5,835
31,900	31,950	7,028	5,179	7,719	5,849
31,950	32,000	7,045	5,193	7,736	5,863

Continued on next page

Figure 7-9 Federal Tax Tables (1040EZ and 1040A) (continued)

Page 37

Tax Table—Continued

If 1040A, line 17, OR 1040EZ, line 7 is—		And you are—			
At least	But less than	Single (and 1040EZ filers)	Married filing jointly	Married filing separately	Head of a household

(Your tax is—)

Income brackets 41,000 · 42,000 · 43,000 · 44,000 · 45,000 · 46,000 · 47,000 · 48,000 · 49,000

50,000 or over—use Form 1040

Page 36

Tax Table—Continued

If 1040A, line 17, OR 1040EZ, line 7 is—		And you are—			
At least	But less than	Single (and 1040EZ filers)	Married filing jointly	Married filing separately	Head of a household

(Your tax is—)

Income brackets 32,000 · 33,000 · 34,000 · 35,000 · 36,000 · 37,000 · 38,000 · 39,000 · 40,000

Continued on next page

Figure 7-9 Federal Tax Tables (1040EZ and 1040A) (continued)

VOCABULARY

Directions: Can you find the definition for each of the following terms used in Chapter 7?

revenue   dividends
progressive taxes   child support
regressive taxes   alimony
proportional taxes   adjusted gross income
excise taxes   deductions
voluntary compliance   standard deduction
tax evasion   taxable income
exemption   tax liability
gross income

1. An allowance for each person dependent on the taxpayer's income.
2. Money paid to support a former spouse.
3. Expenses that are subtracted from gross income to obtain the amount of taxable income.
4. Money collected by the government through taxes.
5. A system whereby citizens are expected to prepare and file appropriate tax returns.
6. A tax rate that remains constant, regardless of the amount of your income.
7. Internal taxes levied against manufacture, sale, or consumption of a commodity.
8. The amount remaining when deductions have been subtracted from adjusted gross income.
9. A tax rate based on the more income earned, the more tax paid.
10. The actual or total amount of taxes due, based on taxable income, and using the tax tables.
11. A tax rate that decreases in proportion to income increases.
12. Willful failure to pay taxes.
13. An amount you are allowed to deduct, depending on your filing status.
14. All taxable income received during the year (wages, salary, interest, etc.)
15. The amount obtained when allowable expenses are deducted from gross income, (but before the standard deduction and exemptions are subtracted).
16. Money paid to a former spouse for support of dependent children.
17. Money paid to stockholders from the profits of a corporation.

ITEMS FOR DISCUSSION

1. What is the United States government's largest source of revenue?
2. List three types of taxes and define each.
3. List five other taxes besides the three listed in No. 2.
4. List at least five services the government provides for all citizens from taxes collected.
5. When was the first permanent income tax ratified?
6. When was the Internal Revenue Service created?
7. List three services provided by the IRS.
8. Who has the ability to levy taxes on the citizens of the United States?
9. What is meant by a tax system based on voluntary compliance?
10. What can happen if you deliberately do not file your tax return and pay taxes due?
11. List five types of income that are taxable.
12. List five types of income that are not taxable.
13. How is child support different from alimony in terms of taxation?
14. What is meant by a standard deduction? How is it affected if you or your spouse is over 65 or blind?
15. When must you file your tax return? Why?
16. What should you do if you discover an error after you have filed your tax return?
17. Under what circumstances would you file the long Form 1040 tax return?
18. Why should you file your tax return early when you expect a refund?
19. If you check the Yes box for the Presidential Election Campaign Fund on your return, does it increase your taxes by $1? Explain.
20. What are some things you should do when preparing to file your tax return?

APPLICATIONS

1. Bob Smith, single, had $23,022 taxable income last year. Using the tax tables on pages 140-142, how much should he pay in taxes?
2. Marilee West had $15,000 in wages, $233 in interest, and $106 in dividend income. What is her total income on line 10 of Form 1040A? Assuming she has no other additions to or subtractions from income, and that she has only one exemption, what is her tax from the tax tables?

3. Richard Olsen, married filing jointly, has two exemptions. Total income was $33,010 and child care credit was $317 on line 19. What is the tax liability from the tax tables?

4. Martin Newport, single, has total wages of $18,351 and taxable interest income of $300. Using Form 1040EZ, what is his tax liability from the tax tables?

5. David and Marilyn Ackison are married and both work. Their total income before adjustments is $55,301. Marilyn receives alimony from a previous marriage, and they have child care expenses to deduct. Which tax form must they use, and why?

6. Compute the amount of child care credit, assuming two incomes are $13,511 and $15,242, with adjusted gross income (line 13, 1040A) of $26,418. There are two children and total expenses of $5,200.

CASE PROBLEMS AND ACTIVITIES

1. Using Figure 7-7, Form 1040A, and the tax tables given on pages 140-142, compute tax liability for Jim Merrill. Jim's wages were $14,000; he had interest income of $213 and dividends of $54. His filing status is single; he has one exemption and no credits. Taxes withheld from wages are $2,004. Based on this information, how much does Jim owe, or how much is his refund?

2. Using Figure 7-7, Form 1040A, and the tax tables, compute tax liability of Kristy Brooks. Kristy's wages totaled $16,900; interest income $190; dividends $200. She is single, one exemption, and had $2,408 withheld in federal taxes. How much does she owe in taxes, or what is her refund?

3. Using Figure 7-5, Form 1040EZ, prepare a tax return for Manuel Arlos on plain paper. Use the following information:

    Manuel Arlos (333-12-3323)
    55 Valley Street
    San Francisco, CA 94110-3227

    Manuel is a carpenter; he wants $1 to go to the campaign fund. He is single and claims only himself as an exemption. His salary is $18,250, plus interest income of $155. He had $2,530 withheld from paychecks.

4. Using Figure 7-7, Form 1040A, and Figure 7-8 (Schedule 1), prepare a joint return and Schedule 1 for Arden and Bonnie Krauss using plain paper.

    Arden T. and Bonnie M. Krauss
    899-31-0098 488-99-3838
    3000 Park Lane
    Dallas, TX 75220-7242

Arden is an account executive and Bonnie is a marketing specialist. They both want to contribute $1 to the campaign fund. Married, filing jointly.

Arden and Bonnie have two dependent children, Vonnie and Richard. Their social security numbers are 220-38-1839 and 392-83-8388, respectively.

Arden and Bonnie's incomes are $22,880 and $23,040, respectively. They also had interest income of $800 and dividend income of $230, and deductible IRAs of $2,000 each (lines 11a and 11b). They had a total of $7,236 withheld from their wages. (The interest income was as follows: savings at First Interstate Bank, $320; personal loan to B. J. Adams, $210, and time certificate at State Savings, $270.)

For their two children, they paid out $4,321 in child care expenses.

Chapter 8

SAVINGS

•◆•◆•◆•◆•◆•◆•◆•◆•◆•◆•◆•◆•◆•◆

OBJECTIVES

1. Understand the need for and purpose of savings.
2. Explain how money grows and make computations of compounding interest.
3. List institutions where savings accounts and time deposits can be held.
4. Describe savings options and discuss factors to consider in selecting a savings plan.
5. Understand the importance of saving regularly.

WHY YOU SHOULD SAVE

◆◆◆◆◆◆◆◆

The chief reason for saving money is to provide for future needs, both expected and unexpected. When nothing is set aside for these certain-to-happen needs, families experience frustration, financial troubles, and even bankruptcy.

SHORT-TERM NEEDS

Often short-term needs arise that require more money than what a budget normally allows. These needs typically are paid for out of savings. Some

Illustration 8-1
Savings accounts
help people achieve
their needs and
wants.

short-term needs you might encounter include the following:

1. Emergencies — such as unemployment, sickness, accident, or
    death in the family

**Savings provide for
sudden emergencies.**

2. Vacations — short weekend trips and leisure activities
3. Social events — such as weddings, family gatherings, or other
    potentially costly special occasions
4. Major purchases — such as a car, major appliances, or home
    remodeling

LONG-TERM GOALS

Many individuals and families anticipate some major purchases and save to
make those purchases possible. These long-term goals include outlays for
such things as home ownership, children's education, retirement, and
investments.

**Large purchases re-
quire savings plans.**

Home Ownership.   A down payment on a house requires thousands of
dollars. The larger the down payment, the smaller the monthly payments
will be.

Children's Education.   Many couples begin a savings plan when their
children are very young. When it's time for college, the necessary money is
available.

Retirement.   Social security payments probably will not be sufficient to
support most people in their old age. Other plans should be made for
financial security after retirement.

Investment.   To provide a hedge against inflation or make money for future use, people may invest in a business, real estate, insurance, stocks, collectibles, or a number of other alternatives. Because investments are often risky in nature, they should be only *in addition to* regular savings.

Investments should be made only in addition to savings.

FINANCIAL SECURITY

Probably the best reason to save is to ensure that when short-term needs arise adequate money will be available. Another reason to save is to ensure a comfortable retirement. Persons who set aside money each pay period feel secure that money is available if and when it is needed.

You must forgo purchases today to save for tomorrow.

The amount of money you save will vary according to several factors: (a) the amount of your *discretionary income* (what you have left over after the bills are paid); (b) the importance you attach to savings; (c) your anticipated needs and wants; and (d) your willpower, or ability to forgo present spending in order to provide for your future.

HOW YOUR MONEY GROWS

◆◆◆◆◆◆◆◆

Money grows when it is saved and invested. Money deposited in a savings account grows by earning interest. Interest is earned on interest as well as on the beginning amount deposited.

COMPOUNDING INTEREST

The amount of money deposited by the saver is called the **principal**. Money paid by the financial institution to the saver for the use of his or her money is called **interest**. When interest is computed on the sum of the principal plus interest already earned it is **compound interest**. Figure 8-1 illustrates how annual interest is compounded.

Figure 8-1
Compounding Interest Yearly

Year	Beginning Balance	Interest Earned (5%)	Ending Balance
1	$100.00	$5.00	$105.00
2	105.00	5.25	110.25
3	110.25	5.51	115.76

To compound inter-
est, interest is added
to interest.

The more often interest is compounded, the greater the earnings. Figure 8-2 illustrates what happens when five percent interest is compounded quarterly (every three months) and is added to the principal before more interest is calculated. More interest is earned if interest is compounded quarterly than if it is compounded annually.

Figure 8-2
Compounding In-
terest Quarterly

Year	Beginning Balance	First Quarter	Second Quarter	Third Quarter	Fourth Quarter	Ending Balance
1	$100.00	$1.25	$1.27	$1.28	$1.30	$105.10
2	105.10	1.31	1.33	1.35	1.36	110.45
3	110.45	1.38	1.40	1.42	1.43	116.08

True daily interest is computed on each day of deposit. Banks and other financial institutions can rapidly compute the interest compounding daily with computers.

PERCENTAGE RATES

The **nominal rate** of interest is calculated on the principal amount only and does not include compounding. The **true annual percentage rate** is the effective rate you receive when the money is compounded and interest is paid on interest earned. When you see advertisements for interest offered at financial institutions, you often see these two different rates offered, as depicted in Figure 8-3.

The effective rate is
the rate when interest
is compounded.

Figure 8-3
Interest Rates

INTEREST OFFERED

12-month time certificate
Minimum deposit of $500.00

Nominal rate: 6.50%

Effective yield: 7.05%

Some time certificates of deposit allow the interest to accumulate and compound, while others require that interest earned be paid into a passbook account where much lower interest rates are paid. This fact is important to understand before you buy a time certificate of deposit.

WHERE YOU CAN SAVE
◆◆◆◆◆◆◆◆

The main financial institutions found in most cities include commercial banks, savings banks, savings and loan associations, credit unions, and brokerage firms.

COMMERCIAL BANKS

Commercial banks are very convenient.

Many people prefer to keep their checking and savings accounts in the same bank for ease in transferring funds and making deposits and withdrawals. Commercial banks offer much convenience to customers in the form of services that may go with accounts. Services may include automatic cash transfer accounts, bank cards, use of 24-hour teller machines, overdraft protection, and other free services. Ninety-seven percent of banks are insured by the **FDIC** (Federal Deposit Insurance Corporation). Most large commercial banks in states where branch banking is legal have many branches for ease of deposits and withdrawals. Commercial banks may be either nationally chartered or state chartered. Large banks are able to offer more services to customers, but generally, minimum deposits and fees are higher. Rates offered on savings accounts will vary among commercial banks, as well as between commercial banks and savings banks, savings and loan associations, and credit unions.

SAVINGS BANKS

Savings banks are state chartered.

Savings banks are usually referred to as mutual savings banks. There are only about 500 savings banks in roughly a dozen states — mostly throughout New England and the Northeast — but they have nearly $150 billion in assets. Savings banks are state chartered and insured by the FDIC. A major business of savings banks is savings plans and loans on real property, including mortgages and home-improvement loans. Because of deregulation of the banking industry in the early 1980s, savings banks also offer checking accounts and other types of consumer loans and banking services.

SAVINGS AND LOAN ASSOCIATIONS

Slightly better rates are available at savings and loans.

Savings and loan associations are organized primarily to handle savings and lend money: these associations make over 80 percent of all home mortgage loans. Money deposited in savings accounts is loaned to people purchasing homes or making home improvements. Generally, savings and loan associations are able to offer slightly higher interest rates on savings accounts (passbook and certificate) than commercial banks. Eighty percent of all savings and loan associations are insured by the **FSLIC** (Federal Savings and Loan Insurance Corporation), which, like the FDIC, insures individual accounts up to $100,000.

Savings and loan associations offer many of the conveniences and services of commercial banks. NOW accounts and money market accounts are available at savings and loan associations. Some savings and loans offer major credit cards and 24-hour teller machine service. Few, however, have safe-deposit boxes, automatic cash transfers and instant loans. Because savings and loans specialize, they are able to offer higher interest rates than banks. Rates vary among savings and loan associations — customers should shop around before depositing money.

CREDIT UNIONS

Credit unions are growing nationwide.

Credit unions are not-for-profit organizations established by groups of workers in similar occupations who pool their money. Credit unions generally offer higher interest rates on savings and lower interest rates on loans. They are insured through membership in **NCUA** (National Credit Union Administration) so that deposits are insured up to $100,000 in each account. A savings account at a credit union is often called a **share account** because deposits entitle the saver to shares of interest (ownership) in the credit union. Checking accounts (which also pay interest) are called *share draft accounts*, and are very similar to checking accounts, except minimum balances and service charges are usually lower. Credit unions also offer IRA accounts, consumer loans, certificates of deposit, drive-up banking, teller machines, and many other services. Credit unions offer diversified, personalized services (from free tax planning and retirement seminars to membership in the Magic Kingdom Club), and are growing rapidly in most parts of the country.

FINANCIAL NETWORKS

A new concept in financial institutions is the financial network, which is a parent organization that owns diversified types of businesses such as

banking, credit, retail, and investment services. The Sears Financial
Network is an example. Under one major organization, Sears Roebuck
(retail), Allstate (insurance), Coldwell-Banker (real estate), and Dean
Witter-Reynolds (investment) are joined together to provide a variety of
services. The Discover card is the umbrella credit card issued by the Sears
Financial Network and can be used at many other retail establishments and
businesses. Large corporations such as Fred Meyer (grocery chain) offer
their own savings and loan services. Financial networks develop a variety of
products and services to serve the changing financial needs of customers.

*Financial networks
are becoming more
common.*

BROKERAGE FIRMS

Cash management accounts or money market accounts available with
brokerage firms offer less convenience and involve more risk than other
types of accounts, but offer high rates of return to savers. Money you deposit
is invested in your behalf, and you share in the profits earned. Generally,
however, large minimum deposits are required (such as $20,000), and
checkwriting privileges are restricted (minimum of $500). Another
disadvantage of these accounts is that they often are not very liquid. Savers
sometimes find it inconvenient to withdraw money and to make deposits.

Brokerage investment firms do not have insurance on deposits, but they
do offer the advantage of **diversification** — purchasing a variety of
investments to protect against large losses and increase the rate of return.
The investment firm buys different types of securities and investments, from
common stock to government bonds. Consequently, brokerage firms are
able to offer higher interest rates than commercial banks, savings and loan
associations, or credit unions.

*More risk often
means higher
returns.*

SAVINGS OPTIONS

◆◆◆◆◆◆◆◆

Once you have decided to establish a savings program for yourself or your
family, you need to know about the different savings options available to
you. Money that is set aside for future needs can be deposited in a number of
different savings plans. Options include passbook savings accounts,
certificates of deposit, government savings bonds, cash management
accounts, and retirement accounts.

PASSBOOK SAVINGS ACCOUNTS

A passbook savings account has a major advantage of high liquidity.
Liquidity is the quality of being easily converted into cash. A passbook

savings account is said to be liquid because money can be withdrawn at any time without penalty. However, a passbook savings account usually pays the least amount of interest, while it involves taking the least amount of risk for the depositor. Risk is more fully discussed in Chapter 9. Once you have opened a passbook savings account, you are free to make withdrawals and deposits. Some financial institutions charge service fees for making more than a maximum number of withdrawals in a certain period of time. Other institutions charge a monthly fee if your balance falls below a set minimum. Passbook savings account customers often have an automated teller card for making deposits and withdrawals at a teller machine.

> Savings accounts may have minimum balance requirements.

CERTIFICATES OF DEPOSIT

A *certificate of deposit* (CD), or time certificate, represents a sum of money deposited for a set length of time — for example, $500 deposited for six months. A CD is less liquid than a passbook savings account because usually a minimum amount must be deposited for a certain period of time. The longer you can leave your money — three or five years — the higher the rate of interest you will earn. The rate of interest on time certificates is generally higher than on passbook savings accounts, because risk is somewhat higher. (The risk you take is that interest rates will rise while you have your money set aside at a lower rate for a set time.) A certificate of deposit has a set **maturity date** — the day on which you must renew the certificate, cash it in, or purchase a new certificate. If you withdraw your money before the maturity date, you will be penalized by receiving less interest. Some financial institutions offer CDs that allow interest to accumulate to maturity; other financial institutions send you a check for the interest, or deposit the interest in a separate account. The interest earned is placed in a designated account to earn interest at a lower rate than the certificate; that is, you do not receive interest on the interest earned.

> A certificate of deposit is less liquid.

GOVERNMENT SAVINGS BONDS

When you buy a savings bond, you are, in effect, lending money to the United States government. A *Series EE savings bond* is known as a *discount bond* because you buy it for less than its cash-in value. At maturity, you receive the full value of the bond. Series EE bonds mature in approximately ten years at twice their face value. These bonds are market-rate sensitive — the government guarantees a rate of at least 7.5 percent if held to maturity. To earn a higher market rate on the bonds, you must keep them for at least

> U.S. savings bonds are loans to the government.

five years. If you want to cash in the bond, you can do so after just six months, but you will receive no interest. The amount of Series EE bonds that can be bought by any individual investor is limited to $30,000.

A *Series HH savings bond* pays interest semiannually at 7½ annual percent (the government sends a check). The bond is purchased at face value (a $500 bond sells for $500) and is redeemed at face value. Series HH bonds may be redeemed at any time after six months, but mature in ten years. Both EE and HH bonds are exempt from state and local taxes; federal taxes are *deferred* (postponed) until the bonds mature. At maturity, the owner of EE bonds may switch to HH bonds, and the interest and deferred taxes will continue to be deferred.

Savings bonds may be purchased over the counter or by mail at most financial institutions, and the bond certificates should be kept in a safe-deposit box. These bonds are non-negotiable (cannot be transferred to another person). The advantage of the Series EE bond is that interest is not taxed until the bond is cashed. So if you are saving for a child's college education, there is no tax until the child cashes the bond. Your child will probably have a low income when he or she is ready to enter college and will have no tax liability. Bonds are considered very safe; they can be quickly and easily converted to cash; if they are lost, stolen, or destroyed, they can be replaced without cost.

Interest is not taxable until the bonds are cashed.

CASH MANAGEMENT ACCOUNTS

Offered at stock brokerage companies and investment service firms, *cash management accounts*, also called money market accounts, are available for persons wishing to invest their money at higher rates of return, but with less liquidity. The minimum balance in these types of accounts is usually $1,000, $5,000, or $20,000, depending on the account. Interest (often called dividends) is computed monthly, and earnings sometimes are not taxable. A person saves money and makes deposits in this account, and the company invests the money in stocks and bonds. Based on the return earned by the company, a dividend is paid. The dividend is usually much higher than with other savings methods. The investor is given checks, but there are frequently minimum amounts for which the checks can be written and limitations on how often withdrawals can be made.

Risk is a disadvantage.

Cash management accounts are not insured by the FDIC or other government agencies. However, these accounts are considered safe because the securities that are purchased are very stable. Managers of these accounts purchase government bonds and securities issued by the U.S. Treasury. Therefore, the risk of losing your money is low.

RETIREMENT ACCOUNTS

IRAs are tax-deferred savings plans.

An *IRA* (individual retirement account) is a savings plan whereby an individual (or couple) sets aside a certain amount of money (up to a specified maximum) each year for retirement. An IRA is deductible from gross income (if you qualify) and interest earned on the account is tax deferred. You will pay taxes on the IRA (both principal and interest) when you begin withdrawing funds and are probably in a lower tax bracket. When either spouse has an employer retirement plan, an IRA is not deductible if joint income exceeds $50,000 ($25,000 if single). If either spouse has an employer retirement account, but joint income is less than $40,000, both can still deduct IRAs ($2,000 each, or $2,000 for the working spouse and $250 for the nonworking spouse). However, for couples with between $40,000 and $50,000 of income ($25,000 and $35,000 if single) the tax-deductible amount of the IRA is gradually reduced as income rises. For example, a couple with $45,000 of joint income can take one-half the IRA allowable: $1,000 each, or $1,000 for one and $125 for the nonworking spouse. Interest rates paid on IRA accounts vary. You may be able to choose the type of investment your IRA money is placed in — such as fixed rate, stock fund, mutual fund, aggressive fund, balanced fund, and so on. Most financial institutions have IRA accounts available. The disadvantage of an IRA is that you cannot remove any of the money set aside before age 59½ without severe penalty (10 percent, plus the money becomes taxable). This makes the IRA very illiquid as a savings plan.

There are numerous retirement plans available.

Other types of retirement savings plans are also subject to deferred taxes on both amounts deposited and interest and dividends paid during the savings period. Examples are Keogh and Simplified Employee Pension (SEP) plans for self-employed persons, TSAs (tax-sheltered annuities) for state and local government workers and school employees, and 401K plans for employees of for-profit companies. There are maximum amounts that can be set aside annually for each plan, ($9,500 for TSAs, $7,000 for 401K plans, and $30,000 for Keogh plans), and a maximum of 20 percent of gross pay can be deposited. Penalties for early withdrawal may also apply. Savers with long-term goals, such as supplementing retirement income, should give careful consideration to tax-deferred savings plans.

FACTORS IN SELECTING A SAVINGS ACCOUNT

◆◆◆◆◆◆◆◆

There are a number of important factors to consider in selecting a savings account or plan and a savings institution. These factors include (a) safety of principal, (b) liquidity, (c) convenience, (d) interest-earning potential, (e) purpose, (f) tax advantages, and (g) early withdrawal penalties.

SAFETY

Most financial institutions are insured.

You want your money to be safe from loss. Most financial institutions are insured by agencies such as the FDIC (Federal Deposit Insurance Corporation). Accounts protected by this insurance are safe up to $100,000 per account. You should check on the regulations, insurance, and other backing the financial institution of your choice has to be certain of the safety of your deposit. Some deposits are safe because they are invested in government securities; others are considered safe because they are diversified; still others are backed by the assets of the investment company. Remember, of course, that all risk cannot be eliminated. It can, however, be reduced to levels that you can feel comfortable with.

LIQUIDITY

Liquidity, or how quickly you can get your cash when you want it, may be important to you. Some types of deposits may be obtained instantly; others may take weeks or even months to withdraw. Generally, all families need some liquid savings (two or three months net pay) so that small emergencies don't require liquidation of long-term investments.

CONVENIENCE

Most banks have branch offices.

People often choose their financial institutions because of convenience of location and services offered. Interest rates on various savings accounts and certificates may vary only slightly among institutions. Fees charged are often very similar, while minimum deposits required may give preference to a certain type of account. A branch bank located near work or home may be the deciding factor in choosing a financial institution. Automated teller machines and drive-up windows with early, late, or weekend hours increase customer convenience.

Illustration 8-2
People often choose
their financial insti-
tutions because of
convenience of lo-
cation and services
offered.

INTEREST-EARNING POTENTIAL

Your savings should be placed in the institution or account that offers the
highest interest returns. Figure 8-4 is an example of interest rates being paid
on a certain date by a financial institution that advertises in the newspaper.
As you can see from the illustration, interest earned depends both on the
type of financial institution in which you choose to save your money and on
the type of account you open.

PURPOSE

Consider how much
money you can put
away.

Your purpose for saving money may greatly affect your choice of financial
institution or savings plan. Savings for a down payment on a home might
best be placed at the savings and loan association that would someday make
the loan for the home. You would establish credit with that institution and
enhance your opportunities for securing the homeowner financing at a later
date. When you first begin establishing credit, it is wise to have both savings
and checking accounts at the financial institution where you apply for a
VISA or MasterCard.

Figure 8-4
Interest Rates

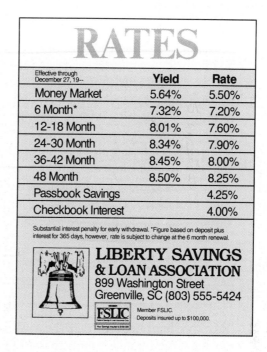

RATES

Effective through December 27, 19--	Yield	Rate
Money Market	5.64%	5.50%
6 Month*	7.32%	7.20%
12-18 Month	8.01%	7.60%
24-30 Month	8.34%	7.90%
36-42 Month	8.45%	8.00%
48 Month	8.50%	8.25%
Passbook Savings		4.25%
Checkbook Interest		4.00%

Substantial interest penalty for early withdrawal. *Figure based on deposit plus interest for 365 days, however, rate is subject to change at the 6 month renewal.

LIBERTY SAVINGS & LOAN ASSOCIATION
899 Washington Street
Greenville, SC (803) 555-5424

FSLIC   Member FSLIC.
Deposits insured up to $100,000.

TAX ADVANTAGES

Some types of savings plans have special tax treatment. Tax-deferred and tax-sheltered plans provide that earnings (interest) are not taxed until withdrawn. Some plans are tax-deductible, which means that you can deduct your contribution to the plan from your taxable income — a big savings when workers are earning higher wages. Other plans are not taxable for state and local taxes, or federal income taxes, or both.

EARLY WITHDRAWAL PENALTIES

Early withdrawal penalties should be considered when you are choosing a savings plan. If you need to withdraw all or some of your money before the maturity or withdrawal date, you may be charged a penalty. Regular passbook accounts have no withdrawal penalties. You may make deposits or withdrawals at your convenience.

Depositors who withdraw time certificates before the maturity date are penalized. Generally, three months' interest is lost on a six-month certificate; six months' interest is lost on time certificates of over six months.

Early withdrawal
penalties can be
substantial.

An IRA or TSA account either partially or fully withdrawn before age 59½ will have an interest loss of six months, plus a 10 percent penalty. In addition, all income previously set aside will become taxable immediately (it had been subtracted from taxable income on tax returns).

Cash management and money market accounts usually do not carry early withdrawal penalties. Money may be withdrawn in full or in part at any time, provided the rules are met.

Beware of restric-
tions on some types
of deposits.

Each type of account at each institution is controlled by different rules. Before you open any account, be sure to read carefully the minimum deposit and withdrawal restrictions, and any other special conditions that may exist (such as being able to borrow money using the account as collateral).

THE IMPORTANCE OF SAVING REGULARLY

◆◆◆◆◆◆◆◆

It is important not only that you save, but also that you save *regularly*. By saving regularly in accounts that accumulate interest and pay interest on interest, you can greatly increase your earnings. Figure 8-5 illustrates the effect of compounding when regular deposits are made to savings. Making or receiving regular payments is an *annuity*.

Figure 8-5
Compounding In-
terest and Making
Additional Deposits

Year	Beginning Balance	Deposits	Interest Earned (5%)	Ending Balance
1	$ 0.00	$100.00	$ 5.00	$105.00
2	105.00	100.00	10.25	215.25
3	215.25	100.00	15.76	331.01
4	331.01	100.00	21.55	452.56

Obviously, no savings plan is effective unless you have the willpower to set aside money — to forgo purchases now in order to provide for them in the future. There are ways to make regular saving easier, however, including payroll deductions, savings clubs, and automatic account deductions.

▬▬▬ AUTOMATIC PAYROLL DEDUCTIONS ▬▬▬

It is often possible to have money withheld from your paycheck and sent directly to your savings plan — an account at the bank, a TSA, or a savings bond. Before any other bills or expenses are paid, you "pay yourself." If the money is set aside before it reaches your checkbook, it is easer to forget about, and you can budget your expenses around the remainder with less difficulty.

Pay yourself first.

SAVINGS CLUBS

Many banks and other institutions offer savings clubs, such as a Christmas Club. You make regular payments into a special account and agree not to withdraw these funds before a specified date. In this way you are forcing yourself to save for some event or need, and when the time comes you know you will have the money. These accounts usually do not have a minimum balance, are temporary accounts, and interest paid on savings clubs may vary substantially among different financial institutions.

AUTOMATIC CHECKING ACCOUNT DEDUCTIONS

Automatic deductions are forced savings plans.

You may authorize an automatic deduction from your checking account each month. In this way you are also forcing yourself to save. You must remember to enter the automatic deduction amount in your checkbook register so that your checkbook will balance each month.

Figure 8-6 illustrates what a person could have saved for retirement, assuming he or she could save $2,000 a year at an average of 12 percent interest a year, beginning at age 20, 25, 30, or 35. You can see the compounding effect of saving. In addition, if the $2,000 a year savings (annuity) were placed in an IRA that would be fully deductible, a substantial tax advantage would also result.

Figure 8-6
Saving for Retirement

Beginning Age	No. of Years Saved	Amount Saved Each Year	Annual Interest Rate	Money at Retirement
20	45	$2,000	12%	$2,716,400
25	40	2,000	12%	1,534,182
30	35	2,000	12%	863,326
35	30	2,000	12%	482,665

VOCABULARY

Directions: Can you find the definition for each of the following terms used in Chapter 8?

10 principal   4 FSLIC
3 interest   6 NCUA
9 compound interest   7 share account
12 nominal rate   8 diversification
11 true annual percentage rate   1 liquidity
5 FDIC   2 maturity date

liquidity 1.   Measure of how easily a deposit can be converted to cash.
maturity date 2.   An ending date on which a certificate or note is due (must be renewed or otherwise dealt with).
interest 3.   Money paid for the use of money.
FSLIC 4.   Insurance company of the federal government that insures your deposit with a savings and loan association.
FDIC 5.   Insurance company of the federal government that insures your deposit with a commercial bank.
NCUA 6.   Insurance company that insures deposits kept at credit unions.
share account 7.   The type of account offered to a saver (regular savings plan) at a credit union.
diversification 8.   A feature of a cash management account whereby the brokerage company buys many different types of investments.
principle 9.   A sum of money in a savings account on which interest accrues.
Compound interest 10.   Interest computed on the sum of the principal plus interest already earned.
true annual percentage rate 11.   The effective yield on a deposit when compounding of interest is considered.
Nominal Rate 12.   The yield on a deposit when compounding does not occur (no interest on interest).

ITEMS FOR DISCUSSION

1. List several short-term needs that you may experience in the next few months or years.
2. List any long-term plans you may have that will require money (savings) in the next five years or more.
3. What four personal factors determine the amount of money you will save?
4. Why does a passbook savings account pay less interest than a certificate of deposit?

5. What are the tax advantages of owning a Series EE savings bond?
6. How is a share account different from a passbook savings account?
7. What type of risk do you take when you save money in a time certificate of deposit?
8. Explain how a cash management account works.
9. What is an IRA? Who can have a fully deductible IRA?
10. What factors should you consider when choosing a financial institution for your savings?
11. Why might people choose to save their money in a commercial bank when they could receive higher interest rates at some other type of financial institution?
12. What is the main purpose of savings and loan associations?
13. How much is an account insured for by the FDIC?
14. What is diversification?
15. List three ways you can force yourself to save every pay period.
16. What types of penalties might you face for early withdrawal of all or part of your savings?
17. List three examples of ways you can save regularly.

APPLICATIONS

1. Write out your savings plans, listing short-term and long-term goals and describe how you plan to achieve them (how much money you will save to meet them).
2. What is discretionary income and what does it have to do with saving?
3. Which of the following is least liquid? Most liquid?

   a. passbook savings account   c. savings bond
   b. certificate of deposit   d. IRA account

4. What happens if you need to withdraw all or part of your time certificate before its maturity date?
5. Why is a Series EE bond called a discount bond?
6. List a significant advantage of saving by purchasing savings bonds.
7. List one disadvantage for each of the following savings plans:

   a. passbook savings account   d. cash management account
   b. certificate of deposit   e. IRA account
   c. savings bond

8. What major advantage is gained by saving at a commercial bank?
9. What major advantages are available for being a part of a retirement plan such as a TSA, Keogh, SEP, or 401K Plan?
10. Why should you join a credit union when you have the opportunity?

11. Is it safe to invest your money with a brokerage firm in a cash management account that is not insured?

CASE PROBLEMS AND ACTIVITIES

1. Compute the interest compounded for Marion Stamps, assuming she deposits $1,000 in a time certificate that compounds interest every six months at the rate of 11½ percent. It is a three-year time certificate. Use these column headings:

Year	Beginning Balance	First-half Interest	Second-half Interest	Total Interest	Ending Balance
1	$1,000	___	___	___	___
2	___	___	___	___	___
3	___	___	___	___	___

2. Bobby Wilson wishes to save $100 a month. His bank computes interest and compounds it monthly. The current rate for a passbook account is 5½ percent. Compute the interest compounded for Bobby. Use this format:

Month	Beginning Balance	Deposit	Total	Interest	Ending Balance
1	___	___	___	___	___
2	___	___	___	___	___
3	___	___	___	___	___
4	___	___	___	___	___
5	___	___	___	___	___
6	___	___	___	___	___
7	___	___	___	___	___
8	___	___	___	___	___
9	___	___	___	___	___
10	___	___	___	___	___
11	___	___	___	___	___
12	___	___	___	___	___

3. Compute the interest compounded quarterly on a deposit of $500 for three years at 12 percent. Use the following column headings:

		INTEREST					
Year	Beginning Balance	First Quarter	Second Quarter	Third Quarter	Fourth Quarter	Total Interest	Ending Balance
1	$500	____	____	____	____	____	____
2	____	____	____	____	____	____	____
3	____	____	____	____	____	____	____

4. Compute your total savings if you keep $1,000 in a passbook savings account at 5¼ percent, compounded quarterly, for two years and if you put $1,000 in a two-year time certificate at 11.89 percent, compounded semiannually. Use these column headings:

PASSBOOK SAVINGS ACCOUNT

		INTEREST					
Year	Beginning Balance	First Quarter	Second Quarter	Third Quarter	Fourth Quarter	Total Interest	Ending Balance
1	$1000	____	____	____	____	____	____
2	____	____	____	____	____	____	____

TIME CERTIFICATE

Year	Beginning Balance	First-half Interest	Second-half Interest	Total Interest	Ending Balance
1	____	____	____	____	____
2	____	____	____	____	____

5. Suppose you need to have the money from the time certificate in Problem 4 before the two years are up. What is the penalty for withdrawing all or part of your passbook savings account?

Chapter 9

INVESTING FOR THE FUTURE

◆◆◆◆◆◆◆◆◆◆◆◆◆◆◆◆◆◆◆◆◆◆◆◆◆

OBJECTIVES

1. Understand investment essentials, including the need for and purpose of investments, and risks involved in investing.
2. Outline effective investment strategies and practices, including how to find and interpret investment information.
3. Discuss the securities investment market, including major auction exchanges and over-the-counter markets for buying and selling securities.
4. List and compare investment options available.

INVESTMENT ESSENTIALS

◆◆◆◆◆◆◆◆

Good investments protect income.

Investment is the outlay of money in the hope of realizing a profit. Money that is invested is above and beyond the cash needed for short-term plans and temporary needs. As shown in Figure 9-1, investment is reserved for "permanent" rather than "put-and-take" savings. Initial investments are conservative (cautious). Once a safe cushion of investment is established, more risky (and potentially profitable) investments can be made.

Figure 9-1
Essentials of Invest-
ing

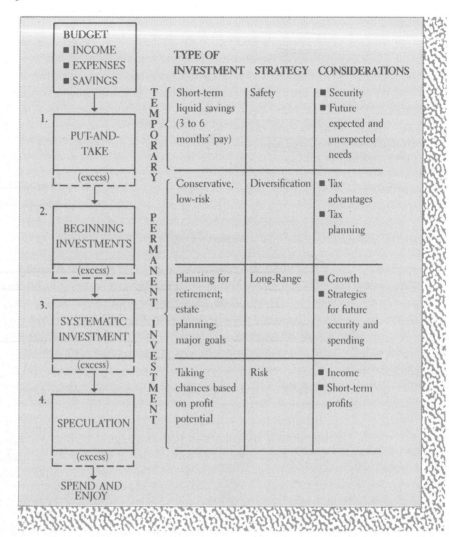

Money that is *saved* each month first goes into a "put-and-take" account. Savings are *put* first, expenses are paid, and you *take* money to pay for short-term goals and temporary needs. For example, you may need money to fix the car, pay for an emergency trip, or buy new tires. The put-and-take account is *temporary* because it is money set aside temporarily for short-term security. Many financial advisors recommend that you have three to six months' net pay set aside for this type of need. Then, should an emergency arise you won't be dipping into permanent, long-term investments to pay for temporary, short-term needs.

As you accumulate your put-and-take account, eventually you will have more than you need. As we learned in the previous chapter on savings, liquid savings options pay lower interest than illiquid options. You want to have enough in the put-and-take (liquid) account to meet those short-term

Temporary savings
are for short-term
needs.

needs. When you reach a comfort level, the excess then should be put into investments that will earn more return. Beginning investments should be conservative and low risk and should take tax strategies into account. For example, two-wage earner families can benefit from investment plans that are tax deductible, tax deferred, or nontaxable. Beginning investments are *permanent* because they should be maintained for future long-term needs, goals, and plans. The maximum returns (interest and dividends) will be realized when you can set aside your money and "forget about it" for a number of years.

> Permanent investments are for long-term plans and goals.

Once you have accumulated a comfortable amount in beginning investments, the excess then can be used for systematic investment, which is a permanent savings for retirement and estate planning. This type of investment centers on growth and future security.

After you reach the comfort zone in systematic investment, the final step is speculation. Taking greater risk also provides the opportunity to make fast, large profits. With an emphasis on income and short-term profit maximization, these excess funds are used for speculating (taking chances). Profits can be used to spend and enjoy because they are not a part of present or future security. Those who "play" in this category know only too well that "if you can't afford to lose it, you can't afford to invest it."

> Speculation is very risky.

REASONS FOR INVESTING

Investing is an important part of personal financial management because it provides effective use of money that is set aside for future use. There are five basic reasons to invest money: (a) to provide supplemental income, (b) to make profits, (c) to provide a hedge against inflation, (d) to minimize tax burdens now and in the future, and (e) to provide income for retirement.

Inflation is the increased cost of living. A hedge against inflation is a way to make your money earn more than the rate of inflation. For example, if the annual inflation rate is 8 percent, you want to invest your money to make more than 8 percent. A savings account would pay 5 to 6 percent. Therefore, a regular savings account would be worth less to you because it would represent less purchasing power.

> Investments protect you from the effects of inflation.

At retirement, people need to have more income than social security payments will provide. Investments provide retirement income for security when earning power is diminished, and the desire to earn money through employment is low.

RISK

Investing involves risk. The more risk you are willing to take, the more profits you can make. **Risk** is the uncertainty as to whether economic loss will be incurred. Types of risk include speculative risk; short-term and long-term risk; market, company, and industry risk; inflation and interest rate risk; and political risk.

Speculative Risk.   Speculative risk involves taking actions (such as investing in a particular stock) that could produce either a loss or a gain, depending on factors that you cannot control but which you attempt to predict.

There are many types of risk.

Short-Term and Long-Term Risk.   Short-term risk is generally lower than long-term risk because you can analyze and predict much more easily what will happen in a week, month, or year than you can in ten or twenty years.

Market, Company, and Industry Risk.   Market risk affects many types of investments at once. Market risk is caused by business declines, important national or world events, or interest rates. Company or industry risk is produced by events that affect only one company or industry. For example, if you invest in the candy industry or a candy manufacturer and the nationwide trend is toward dieting or avoidance of sugar, your investment will be affected.

Consumer buying trends can affect investment potential.

Inflation and Interest Rate Risk.   Increased prices and rising interest rates, which make your existing investments worth less because they are "locked in" at lower rates of interest, create inflation and interest rate risk. For example, if you own a bond that pays 8 percent, and interest rates are increasing to above 10 percent or inflation is rising at 10 percent or more a year, your investment is worth less.

Political Risk.   Government actions that affect business profits are the basis of political risk. Taxes and regulations (such as environmental controls) can make some investments less attractive.

INVESTMENT STRATEGIES

A wise investment is one that results in the greatest financial gain available for your money; a poor investment is one that results in financial loss. Investing wisely is a difficult and time-consuming task. The suggestions that follow, however, may make this task easier for you.

CRITERIA FOR CHOOSING AN INVESTMENT

Some investments rise in value at a rate higher than inflation; some do not. Some investments provide retirement income that is tax sheltered; some do not. Some investments provide for increases in value that do not show up as

Some investments serve as tax shelters.

taxable income for many years; others do not. The ideal investment would fulfill *all* of these criteria:

1. Complete safety from loss
2. High liquidity
3. High interest return
4. Growth in value that exceeds inflation rate
5. Reasonable (low) purchase price or initial cost

Obviously, you may not find all of these elements in any single investment. However, all of your investments should fulfill as many of these criteria as possible. The more elements fulfilled, the more desirable the investment.

WISE INVESTMENT PRACTICES

People commonly make one or more serious mistakes in their investment practices. Some mistakes are minor and can be corrected easily; others will cause serious financial damage. If you wish to avoid investment disaster, follow the wise investment practices described below.

Mistakes cause financial damage.

Define Your Financial Goals. In Chapter 5, you were introduced to the importance of setting financial goals. If these goals are not clearly defined, you will not know which investments can best serve to meet them.

Go Slowly. Before making investment decisions, gather enough information to make a wise decision. Don't rush into something on impulse or because it "sounds good" on the surface. It takes time to obtain the needed information, analyze it, and make a sound choice.

Follow Through. Putting off plans and delaying action will doom your financial goals. If a goal is important, it should be worked on *now*, not put off until some never-to-come future day. A common mistake is keeping too much money in the "put-and-take" account rather than taking advantage of higher rates of return.

Keep Good Records. In order to monitor progress toward meeting your future needs and goals, you need to keep good financial records. Your personal inventory and net worth statement, lists of insurance policies and investments, balances and locations of bank accounts, contents and location of your safe-deposit box, etc., are essential pieces of information. Unless you know where you have been and where you are, it is difficult to plan where you are going.

Personal records must be complete.

Seek Good Investment Advice. Don't be afraid to ask questions. Many people think they can make wise investments without seeking and paying for advice from an expert. In the long run, uninformed investments may prove

Illustration 9-1
Trained professionals can help you make wise investment decisions.

to be expensive, because poor investments can cost a great deal in lost profits. In general, it is wise to seek competent advice from a trained professional before making any investment decision.

Keep Investment Knowledge Current.   You should be aware of what is new in the financial market, what is or is not a good investment, when to sell, and when to buy. The economy is a major consideration in making investment decisions, and you need to understand how it works and what various economic indicators mean to you. Although you should seek advice before making a major investment move, it is your responsibility to know when to ask questions and to make any final decisions about the handling of your investments. Making a thorough analysis of economic trends — past, present, and future — and carefully planning and following through on your financial goals will help you to make wise investment choices.

Keep yourself informed about the financial market.

SOURCES OF FINANCIAL INFORMATION

Sources of financial information include six main areas: (1) newspapers, (2) financial services, (3) financial magazines, (4) stockbrokers, (5) investment counselors, and (6) annual reports of corporations.

Newspapers.   Financial pages of local newspapers are the most widely available source of financial data, so you should learn how to read and understand the data reported. Reading these pages daily will help you keep track of what is going on in the financial markets and obtain the information needed to make wise decisions. In addition, *The Wall Street Journal* is a daily publication that provides detailed coverage of financial information

Newspapers are a timely source of financial information.

needed for wise investing. *Barron's* is a weekly newspaper that also provides charts of trends, financial news items, and technical analysis of financial data.

The most widely reported and followed financial index is the *Dow Jones Industrial Index*. Often called the Dow, it is an index of the price movements of 30 major industrial corporate bonds listed on the New York Stock Exchange. Separate Dow indexes are maintained for transportation and public utility stocks. The *New York Stock Exchange (NYSE) Index* includes every stock traded on the New York Stock Exchange.

Financial Services.   Raw data is information that has not been analyzed or interpreted. Main sources of raw data are *Moody's Industrial Manual* and *Standard and Poor's Register*. These publications are found in public libraries and brokerage firms. They contain precise historical summaries of financial income and balance sheets. Many investors subscribe to investment services that mail weekly investment letters which report the latest financial data and happenings. You are free to make your own analysis of what the information means to you.

Financial Magazines.   There are a number of popular weekly and monthly magazines that provide personal financial investment information. Most of them interpret financial data and give opinions and recommendations. Popular weekly magazines include *BusinessWeek*, *Forbes*, and *Fortune*; monthly magazines include *Money*, *Nation's Business*, and *The Economist*.

There is a wide variety of financial magazines available.

Stockbrokers.   A **broker** does the buying and selling of stocks on the exchange. Stockbrokers provide clients with analyses and opinions based on their expertise and judgment. Nevertheless, you cannot expect a broker to pick winners for you. Almost all full-line brokers provide monthly market letters that advise the purchase and sale of certain stocks and bonds.

Investment Counselors.   Professional investment planners and advisors are trained to give intelligent overall investment advice, based on your goals, age, net worth, occupation, investment experience, life-style, family responsibilities, and other factors. You will be asked to fill out a confidential information packet showing assets, liabilities, net worth, income, and budget, as well as your financial goals. The investment planner usually receives a fee for services rendered, although some planners receive fees when investment products (such as stocks, bonds, or life policies) are sold. Many people hesitate to use planners and advisors because they are embarrassed about the small amount of money they have to invest. However, investment counselors are available for most investment levels.

Investment counselors help you pick investments.

Annual Reports.   The **annual report** of a corporation provides information to evaluate that corporation as an investment. The annual report gives the financial history of the company, comparisons of data for several years, a description of products and services, an assessment of the company's future growth plans and prospects, news of lawsuits against the company, news about competitors and their positions in the industry, and other information. You can receive copies of annual reports by writing to large companies, or you can review them in school and public libraries.

Some people are well informed and know what they want to buy and sell on the stock market. For these people, there is a service available called *discount brokerage.* Discount brokers buy and sell stocks for individuals for a reduced fee. The fee can be half as much as the one ordinarily charged by a full-service stockbroker who gives competent investment advice. But the discount broker provides no service other than to buy and sell stock for the customer. Large banks and savings and loan associations now have discount brokers to perform this service for customers. In most cases, you will be required to have an account at that bank so that money can be transferred from your account to pay for any stocks and bonds you purchase. For an annual fee, the bank will also keep a brokerage account for you, keep your stock certificates in the bank, and send you monthly or quarterly statements of value (showing the current value of your securities). A phone call to the discount broker is all that is needed to buy or sell stocks and bonds.

Discount brokers charge lower fees for buying and selling stocks.

THE SECURITIES INVESTMENT MARKET
◆◆◆◆◆◆◆◆

The securities investment market is where you buy and sell securities — stocks and bonds — either through an auction process or through a dealer. The market is described as a bull (rising) or bear (falling) securities market.

STOCK MARKETS

✗ Example

Stock market is a general term that describes the securities market — the place where supply and demand for investment alternatives meet. Stocks of larger companies are listed with a specific *stock exchange,* where stocks and bonds are bought and sold. The largest organized stock exchange in the United States is the New York Stock Exchange. The smaller American Stock Exchange is also in New York City. Ten other regional exchanges are located throughout the country.

There are many stock exchanges in this country.

The New York Stock Exchange is in a big building at the corner of Wall and Broad Streets in New York City. The trading floor (where stocks are bought and sold) is about two-thirds the size of a football field. Around the edge of the trading floor are teletype booths that are open at both ends, with room inside for a dozen or more brokers. Only brokers who are members of the exchange may buy and sell stocks on the exchange.

Spaced at regular intervals around the trading floor are trading posts, which are horseshoe-shaped counters, each occupying about 100 square feet on the floor. Behind each counter are a dozen or more specialists and employees of the exchange. All buying and selling is done around trading posts. About 90 different stocks are assigned to each post. Placards above each counter show which stocks are sold in each section, the last price of that stock, and whether that price represents an increase or a decrease from the previous price.

> Stock exchanges are central places for buying and selling.

Orders received at a brokerage firm are phoned or teletyped (sent by computer) to that firm's booth at the exchange. A message is printed out and is given to the floor broker to carry out. When the transaction is completed, the clerks for the brokers who bought and sold the stock report back to their respective home offices. The buyer and seller can then be advised that the transaction has been concluded and can be told the final price. The stock market is a form of *auction market* where buyers and sellers are brought together. Stock brokers earn commissions when stocks are bought and sold. Stocks listed with the exchange may be traded only during official trading hours — 10 a.m. to 4 p.m., New York Time, Monday through Friday (except holidays).

OVER-THE-COUNTER EXCHANGES

> Unlisted securities are considered more risky.

Stocks not listed with an exchange are called *unlisted securities*. Individual brokers working directly with the corporation issuing stock may purchase and sell unlisted securities. An individual may buy and sell unlisted securities with another individual. When securities are bought and sold through brokers, but not through a stock exchange, the transaction is called an *over-the-counter (OTC) exchange*. This market is a form of *dealer market* (as opposed to auction) because an ask price is matched to a bid price. Here dealers make money because they own the stocks and make profits through differences in what they paid for the stock and what they sell it for, rather than by commissions. Government and municipal bonds are traded over the counter. Generally, unlisted securities are those small companies well known locally but not nationally. Because prices for unlisted securities are not set by auctioning at a large exchange and their value is more difficult to determine, they are considered more risky.

BULL AND BEAR MARKETS

A *bull market* is a rising market characterized by rising prices, rising stock volume, increasing new issues, and a general feeling of investor optimism. A *bear market* is one in which prices are falling, the outlook is bleak, and buyers stand on the sidelines with funds committed to falling prices. Bears are pessimists. Bull markets (rising) typically take a long time to develop before they reach their peak. Bear markets are usually short and savage. The average bull market is often three to four times as long as a bear market. Bears have to time purchases to buy stock when the price is at its lowest.

Bulls and bears are stock market terms for optimism and pessimism.

INVESTMENT OPTIONS

◆◆◆◆◆◆◆◆

A number of relatively safe investments that provide fixed income or have other safety features are discussed first. Then investments that involve greater risk, but also provide greater returns, are considered. All of these investments could be included in your **portfolio**, which is a list of investments and securities owned.

A portfolio is a list of investments and securities.

FIXED-INCOME AND LOW-RISK
INVESTMENTS

These investments include treasury bills, notes, and bonds; notes and debentures; municipal and corporate bonds; preferred stock; and investment companies (closed-end funds and mutual funds). Many conservative investors believe these investments provide the best return for the *risk averse* investor who is not willing (psychologically) to take large risks.

Many conservative investors are risk averse.

Treasury Bills, Notes, and Bonds. *U.S. Treasury bills* are government debt sold at a discount, and available in denominations of $10,000; then in increments of $5,000. A Treasury bill is usually a three-month, six-month, or one-year obligation, auctioned weekly and monthly. Rates for Treasury bills are often used as the basis for rates paid on CDs, IRAs, money market funds, and so on.

Example

U.S. Treasury notes are government obligations that mature in less than ten years and bear interest-bearing coupons. *U.S. Treasury bonds* are government obligations with ten-year maturities or longer.

Treasury bills, notes, and bonds are safe, but because they involve longer commitments of time and larger sums of investment money, they are often not considered by small individual investors. They are tax free for state and local taxes, like all U.S. government debt.

Treasury obligations are safe but involve large sums of money.

Corporate Notes and Debentures. A **corporate note** is an investment wherein money is loaned to a corporation or other business and a note, or written promise to repay the loan plus interest, is received in exchange as evidence of the debt. A corporate note may be *secured*, which means payment is guaranteed by a pledge of property or other assets. If your note is not repaid, you can then claim the property pledged and sell it. An unsecured note, called a **debenture**, is an investment made on the creditworthiness of the corporation as a whole. Because the companies and corporations that borrow your money have good credit ratings and the purposes for borrowing the money are good, notes and debentures are generally considered safe investments.

Interest rates and maturity dates for notes are determined at the time of purchase. You know how much you will receive on your investment and when you will receive it. Notes and debentures can be short-term (six months or less) or long-term (over a year), and interest earned is generally taxable. *Commercial paper* (sometimes called "corporate IOUs") is short-term lending and borrowing of funds wherein a corporation with excess funds makes short-term loans. Banks are not involved and interest rates vary according to market conditions. For the lender the rate is higher than could be received for depositing it at a bank; the borrower pays lower interest rates than would be charged at a bank. Like debentures, this type of loan is unsecured.

Municipal and Corporate Bonds. Municipal bonds are issued by a government division, such as a city or county, and are guaranteed by the property owners within the tax district (see Chapter 7). Before bonds are issued, they must be approved by voters. Municipal bonds have a major advantage: you pay no federal income tax on interest earned. Because they are tax free, municipal bonds will have lower rates than corporate bonds.

Corporate bonds may be of five types. *Secured bonds* are guaranteed by a pledge of property or other assets. A **bond indenture** is written proof of the debt; the bonds are secured by the pledge of corporate assets. *Unsecured bonds* are issued on the general credit of a corporation, and they do not involve a pledge of property. *Registered bonds* are those for which the corporation keeps a record of bonds and names of their owners; a change in ownership requires a change of records. *Coupon bonds* have individual coupons attached for each interest payment. The coupons are in the form of a check payable to the bearer, or anyone who presents them to the bank for payment on the date of the coupon (usually semiannually). *Zero-coupon bonds* have no coupons attached and do not pay interest. They are sold at a discount (less than face value) and profits are made by holding the bond until maturity. Bonds are issued in various denominations — from $1,000 to $10,000 or more. Bonds are considered safe, long-term investments. You know when you purchase the bond exactly how much will be earned and when you will receive it. Bonds can be sold before maturity dates, but this will result in lower yields.

Junk bonds are issued when a corporation wants to borrow money quickly, such as for a take-over attempt. They are risky because they are unsecured, and interest rates are high. If the take-over attempt fails, you can lose your investment.

Commercial paper is short-term borrowing.

A bond indenture is a secured debt.

Junk bonds are a risky, unsecured investment.

Preferred Stock. Stock on which dividends are paid first and whose holders are paid first (after bond holders) in the event of company liquidation is called **preferred stock**. There are four classes of preferred stock. *Cumulative* stock is the most common type of preferred stock. Dividends not paid the year before because there were no profits must be paid the next year before common stock dividends are paid. *Noncumulative* stock provides that dividends not paid in previous years will not be made up when there is a profit to be distributed. *Participating* stock means that preferred stockholders are paid a set dividend, common stockholders then receive a share of the profits, and any additional profits are then shared by preferred and common stockholders. In other words, preferred stockholders participate in profits with common stockholders. *Nonparticipating* stockholders receive only the predetermined dividend, regardless of profits.

A cumulative, participating preferred stock is a more expensive stock to purchase, but a very safe investment with a solid rate of return and possible bonus of additional dividends. Dividends not paid one year would be made up when profits allowed, and any excess profits (after common stockholders are paid) would be shared. Preferred stock is typically much more expensive than common stock because it has a higher, set return on investment that involves little risk. Corporations must pay dividends to preferred stockholders before they pay common stockholders.

Investment Funds. Investment companies sell shares of stock in various investment funds (such as common stock funds, bond funds, and precious metal funds) to accumulate money to invest for the benefit of shareholders. Funds of many shareholders are combined to buy different securities for the portfolio. The market value of each investor's share is called the *net asset value (NAV)* per share. For example, if the company has $5,000,000 in net assets and 500,000 outstanding shares, the NAV per share is $10.

Investment companies offering investment funds provide the advantages of diversification (spreading the risk), professional management, and other services such as automatic reinvestment of dividends, acceptance of small investments, and periodic withdrawals.

Investment companies sell two major types of investment funds — closed-end and open-end. A **closed-end fund** has a fixed number of shares to be issued and sold. The shares are bought and sold on a stock exchange or over-the-counter market.

A **mutual fund** is an **open-end fund** that continuously receives new funds from investors by issuing new stocks. The fund will grow as large as the number of shares that can be sold. The purchase price of the mutual fund is equal to current net asset value (NAV). Each business day the mutual fund offers to redeem (buy back) shares from existing shareholders at current net asset value.

Shares in closed-end or open-end funds are sold through brokerage firms that charge a commission, or through their own sales staffs who sell directly

There are many types of preferred stock.

Investment funds are designed for special purposes.

Example

Mutual funds are ideal for small investors.

to investors. (To avoid a commission, you can reinvest dividend checks.) A commission paid to buy mutual funds is called a *load*. Some funds, called *no-load funds*, sell shares directly to investors by mail and do not charge a fee to buy or sell. In financial papers, the difference between the "bid" and "ask" price is the sales charge, or load. For no-load funds, the bid and ask price are the same.

A *money market fund* concentrates on high-quality, short-term, marketable, interest-bearing debt securities such as certificates of deposit, commercial paper, and Treasury bills. *Tax-exempt money market funds* invest in short-term, good-quality municipal bonds. *Growth funds* invest in quality common stocks of companies expected to grow at a more rapid rate than the economy as a whole. *Balanced funds* have portfolios that invest about 30 percent in bonds and the remainder in stocks — a more conservative approach. *Specialty funds* provide concentration of funds in one industry or investment concept. *Income funds* provide maximum dividends in the short run and are more speculative. Mutual funds cater to the small investor by selling shares in convenient installments, such as monthly payments of under $100.

There are many types of mutual funds.

VARIABLE-INCOME AND ILLIQUID INVESTMENTS

Illiquid investments are not easily converted to cash. High-risk investments are not easily sold, and the market to sell them is small. Variable-income investments include common stocks, real estate, precious metals and gems, commodities, collectibles, and business ventures.

Common Stocks.   Corporate stocks may be in the form of preferred stock, discussed earlier, or common stock. **Common stock** is a security representing a share in the ownership of a company. Common stockholders share in the profits of a corporation, elect a board of directors, vote in stockholders' meetings, and take the greatest investment risk. Common stock does not carry a fixed dividend as does preferred stock. Dividends are based on corporate profits: the better the company does, the more common stockholders stand to make. Directors of the corporation declare a dividend out of the profits of the corporation, and common stockholders receive a dividend for each share of common stock owned.

Real Estate.   To purchase **real estate** is to purchase land and anything attached to it. The largest single real estate investment most people make during their lives is the purchase of their home.

While real estate is generally considered illiquid, buying your own home is regarded as a safe investment. Homes are purchased by making a *down payment*, which in most cases is 10 percent or more of the purchase price of

An illiquid investment is not easily converted to cash.

Real estate is considered an illiquid investment.

Illustration 9-2
The largest single investment most people make is the purchase of their home.

the home, and financing the balance with a mortgage or trust deed. If you buy a home costing $60,000, your down payment would be about $6,000 or more. You would pay the rest in monthly payments for the next 30 years. At 12 percent interest, your payments would be about $690 a month. The cost of owning your own home is discussed in Chapter 19.

There are many types of real estate.

Some people buy real estate rentals, such as single-family homes, duplexes, triplexes, fourplexes, apartment buildings, and commercial (business) buildings. Ownership of these assets requires real estate investment skill in choosing good values. In addition, more cash down payments and more cash outflows for repairs and maintenance may be required. Real estate investments provide tax advantages for people with large incomes because they can write off costs of repairs, maintenance, property taxes, and depreciation. To pay these expenses, however, they must collect enough in rent from tenants and keep the rental units occupied.

Precious Metals and Gems. Gold, silver, and platinum are examples of **precious metals** — tangible, beautiful, desirable substances of great value. Precious metals are said to be the best hedge against inflation; however, in times of low inflation, values of precious metals are also low.

Purchasing and storing precious metals can be inconvenient.

The price of gold fluctuates with world economic conditions. The reason for this fluctuation is that gold is rare, yet a basis for money, which is always of value and universally acceptable. Figure 9-2 shows how gold and silver prices have fluctuated since 1967.

Precious metals earn no interest or dividends for their owners. The profit is realized when they are sold. Gold and silver may be purchased in coins, medallions, jewelry, and bullion. You can also hold gold indirectly by investing in gold-mining stocks or in mutual funds specializing in these stocks. Storing and safekeeping precious metals presents a problem because of their bulk. Gold and silver can also be purchased in the form of a

Figure 9-2
Gold and Silver
Prices

Date	Gold (troy oz.)	Silver (troy oz.)
6/1/67	$ 35.00	$ 1.80
6/1/80	850.00	32.00
6/1/83	437.50	11.80
6/1/87	475.25	6.75

certificate that states how much gold or silver bullion is being held in storage. However, for banks to hold it in storage, a minimum investment of $1,000, a commission of 4 percent, and storage fees are usually required.

Gems are natural precious stones such as diamonds, rubies, sapphires, and emeralds. Diamond prices are high and are subject to drastic change. Prices have fluctuated rapidly in the last 20 years. A flawless, Grade D one-carat diamond purchased for $1,900 in 1971 would have sold for $50,000 in 1980, dropped to $17,500 in 1983, and then rose to $25,000 in 1987. Likewise, rubies, sapphires, and emeralds increase in value as interest and inflation rates rise, but when economic conditions are more favorable, precious stones (like precious metals) lose their investment value.

Precious metals and gems have their greatest value as jewelry. Stones that are one carat or more are rare and are much more valuable than smaller stones. *Semiprecious stones,* such as garnets, spinels, and opals, often are a good investment. A one-carat semiprecious stone might cost between $1,000 and $2,000. Cultured pearls, however, are a poor choice for the average investor. The demand for pearl jewelry has increased over the past decade, but so has the supply of the most popular sizes of pearls. Consequently, only perfectly round black or rose pearls of a certain diameter are considered rare enough to be considered good investments — and these pearls are much too expensive for the average investor to consider.

The biggest disadvantage of investing in metals and gems is, of course, that the market to sell them is often unpredictable. If you are eager to sell, you may face a loss. When purchasing metals and gems for investment, be aware of the markup. When buying from a jewelry store, the profit to the store is 50 to 100 percent of the actual value, so you should get several quotes and wait for sales before buying.

Commodities. **Commodities,** such as livestock, crops, or copper, are quantities of goods or interests in tangible assets. You can purchase the commodity itself or what is called a *futures contract* — a contract to buy or sell a commodity on a specified date at a specified price. You could, for example, contract to buy a certain commodity at what you consider its lowest price. You would buy on credit, putting up 8 to 10 percent of the value of the contract. You would then attempt to sell the contract for a higher price before the delivery date of the commodity. Thus you buy on

Semiprecious stones are a poor investment for inexperienced investors.

paper without ever having to take possession of the goods. Enormous profits can be made.

Speculation in commodities is very risky; more people lose money than make money. You can lose your investment if prices drop or if you are unable to sell (such as the crop rots in storage). Timing is the crucial ingredient of effective investment in futures — knowing when to buy, how long to hold, and when to sell. Investment in commodities should be limited to those with excess money, financial wisdom, and the ability to take a big risk.

Commodities are considered very risky.

Collectibles. *Collectibles* are valuable or rare items, from antiques and coins to comic books and art pieces. They are valuable because they are old, no longer made, unusual, irreplaceable, or of historic importance.

Coins are the most commonly collected items. Coins that are silver (rather than an alloy) are worth more than 20 times their face value. For example, a fifty-cent piece dated before 1964 contained almost pure silver and is worth about $10, depending on its year and condition.

Coins are the most common collectible.

People like to collect favorite items, from ornaments to memorabilia, and hope someday that their collection will be valuable. An advantage to collectibles is that you can start small and buy in small quantities. Unfortunately, they are very illiquid, because a ready buyer for your collection may be difficult to find. The trick is to collect wisely by purchasing only the highest quality of anything you are fond of collecting. Over the years (and generations) the collection gains in value.

Business Ventures. Many a quick and tidy profit has been made by a person or group who invests in a *business venture* — the creation of a business to sell a specific idea, product, or service. The business venture is a risky type of investment. If the idea, product, or service catches on, it will be very profitable; but if it fails it means a large financial loss. Pet rocks were a popular fad for a short time and their original manufacturers and sellers made large, quick profits before the market declined and disappeared. In general, the best business ventures are those that offer a service that is unique, valued, or needed but is not otherwise available.

Business ventures are risky because there is no proven record.

VOCABULARY

Directions: Can you find the definition for each of the following terms used in Chapter 9?

12 investment	*17* portfolio
1 inflation	*4* corporate note
13 risk	*15* debenture
3 broker	*16* bond indenture
14 annual report	*5* preferred stock
8 stock market	closed-end fund

6 mutual (open-end) fund   11 precious metals
7 common stock   10 gems
9 real estate   8 commodities

1. The increased cost of living.
2. Livestock, crops, or copper — quantities of goods or interests in assets.
3. A person who buys and sells stocks and bonds on the exchange.
4. The written promise of a corporation to pay a debt.
5. Stock for which dividends are paid first but which confers no voting rights on the holder.
6. An investment fund that continuously issues new stock.
7. A type of stock that represents a share of ownership in a company.
8. The place where supply and demand for investment alternatives meet for auction purposes.
9. Property such as land and buildings.
10. Natural precious stones, including diamonds, rubies, and sapphires.
11. Gold, silver, and platinum — tangible substances of great value.
12. Outlay of money in the hope of realizing a profit.
13. Uncertainty as to whether economic loss will be incurred.
14. A document that gives the financial history of a corporation and is a good information source for evaluating an investment.
15. An unsecured corporate note.
16. A written proof of debt, secured by pledge of corporate assets.
17. A list of investments and securities owned by an individual or an investment fund.
18. An investment fund with a fixed number of shares outstanding.

ITEMS FOR DISCUSSION

1. How are temporary savings different from permanent money set aside for investments?
2. What is speculation?
3. List the five basic reasons for investing.
4. What is inflation? How has inflation affected you?
5. What are the five types of risk?
6. List the characteristics of the ideal investment.
7. List six wise investment practices.
8. What are six main sources of financial information?
9. List five financial magazines.
10. How can you obtain a copy of a corporation's annual report to stockholders?

11. What is *the Dow*?
12. What is the difference between an *auction market* and a *dealer market*?
13. What is a risk averse investor?
14. How is a debenture different from a bond indenture?
15. List five types of corporate bonds.
16. Why is a mutual fund considered an *open-end* fund?
17. List ten investment alternatives.
18. Give examples of precious metals.
19. Give examples of gems.
20. What are commodities?
21. How do the maturity dates for Treasury bills, notes, and bonds differ?

APPLICATIONS

1. Explain the type of investments you might choose in the beginning investments stage.
2. What types of investment would you consider to be pure speculation — where greatest profits (and losses) can be made?
3. List your top five choices of investment alternatives and give an advantage and disadvantage of each.
4. Assume that you have $5,000 to invest (permanently) as you wish. Describe your investment choices and reasons for choosing those investments.
5. Select five stocks listed in the financial section of your newspaper and list the stock exchange closing prices for five days. The illustration in Case No. 1 explains how to read the columns.
6. From a current edition of *The Wall Street Journal*, list the 30 "blue-chip stocks" that currently make up the Dow Jones Industrial Index.
7. Check in a current issue of *BusinessWeek* or *The Wall Street Journal* and report the current market prices for:

   a. gold (per troy ounce)
   b. silver (per troy ounce)
   c. copper

   Check these prices in one week. Record the new prices and changes for each.

CASE PROBLEMS AND ACTIVITIES

1. The financial section of your newspaper generally has a listing of the closing prices of the daily stock market. The daily newspaper reports

the weekday closing prices; the weekend newspaper reports a summary of the week's trading activities. The following represents the columns of information you will find in the financial section of your newspaper:

New York Stock Exchange Prices

* *
* Prices are posted at 2 p.m. E.S.T. today   *
* * * * * * * * * * * * * * * * * * * *

New York (AP) — national prices

Stock		PE	SALES	LAST	CHG.
	— A—A —				
AAR	.33	15	1	11⅜	− ⅛
ACF	2.76	7	20	36⅛	− 1
AMF	1.36	7	9	18⅞	+ ⅜
ARA		12	4	28½	+ 1
ASA	2		12	133⅝	− ¼

On this partial listing, there are five columns of stock listings. Beginning at the left of each column and proceeding to the right, there are five important columns: (a) stock name, (b) price-earnings (PE) ratio, (c) sales (in hundreds), (d) last price (closing price), and (e) change. Names of companies are abbreviated and listed alphabetically. The PE ratio is determined by dividing the current price of the stock by the earnings (dividends) for the past 12 months. Sales indicates the number of shares sold during the day in hundreds. The column headed *last* lists the last or closing price for the day. Changes from the previous day's closing price are shown in the final column. Both stock prices and changes are listed in fractions. Dividends (if any) are listed between the stock name and the PE columns. Dividends are those paid during the last year.

In the sample, look at the first stock listed: AAR. It is down about 12.5 cents in the day's trading (as shown by -⅛). Closing price was 11⅜ or $11.375 a share. One hundred shares were sold that day. The price-earnings ratio is 15 (the price is 15 times last year's earnings). A dividend is paid, but only 33 cents for every $10 of stock owned, which is considered low.

Clip a similar column from your local newspaper and list the following information for five stocks:

a. Price-earnings ratio
b. Sales in hundreds that day

     c. Dividend paid (if any)
     d. Last (closing) price
     e. Net change

2. Using the financial section of your daily newspaper (or *The Wall Street Journal*), keep track of the progress of five different stocks for five consecutive days. List for each stock the closing price and net change for each day. On a piece of paper, prepare a form that looks like this to record your information:

NAME OF STOCK	CLOSING PRICE					NET CHANGE				
	DAY 1	2	3	4	5	DAY 1	2	3	4	5
1.										
2.										
3.										
4.										
5.										

3. Your friend Marjorie Blankenship has asked for your advice. She has just $500 in savings, and no other money except her checking account. She wants to start building for her future. She's 18 now and plans to go to college next year.

Chapter 10

RISK MANAGEMENT AND INSURANCE

OBJECTIVES

1. Understand and define risk management principles and insurance terminology.
2. Explain the purpose and types of life insurance coverage.
3. List the coverages available through private and group health insurance policies.
4. Explain the types of coverage provided by automobile insurance.
5. Explain the major provisions of property insurance.

PRINCIPLES OF RISK MANAGEMENT AND INSURANCE

Risk management is the management of personal risks to improve the likelihood of protecting assets and income against loss. As discussed in the previous chapter, risk can never be eliminated. But by using a risk management approach, you can lower risks and manage them with a level of confidence that is both economically sound and financially rewarding. Risk management is a three-step process: identifying risks, assessing risks, and handling risks.

Risk management is a three-step process.

IDENTIFYING RISKS

Consider the risks you take on when you buy a home or drive a new car. When you own a home, you have risks of fire, smoke damage, flood, theft, personal injury to guests, glass breakage, vandalism, lightning damage, and so on. Each type of ownership and income represents risks to be identified.

ASSESSING RISKS

After you have identified your risks, assess the seriousness of each one. Some risks are immediate and of high priority. Others are limited or less likely and would have less serious consequences.

HANDLING RISKS

Handling risk doesn't always mean buying insurance.

Handling risk does not mean you buy insurance to cover every potential loss you might incur. In risk management, you may choose to insure against, avoid, reduce, or assume risk. The flowchart in Figure 10-1 represents the risk management process.

Insuring against risk will be the subject of the rest of this chapter. Once you have decided to insure against risk of loss, get at least three quotes from reputable insurers. You will be guided by the family budget as you search for insurance companies that are sound and give you good advice on options and prices. Consider options and compare coverages and prices. Read and understand policies — what is included and excluded — before signing and paying premiums. Know how to file claims. Periodically review your insurance program and compare it with your family's changing needs.

Avoid acts that you consider too risky.

Avoiding risk means avoiding situations that involve risk. Instead of buying a house, you may decide to rent; you may avoid skiing and other dangerous sports; you may avoid gambling — in other words, you avoid acts that you consider too risky.

Reducing hazards means taking measures to lessen the frequency and severity of losses that may occur. This usually reduces the cost of insurance for the part you choose to insure. For example, you may put studded snow tires on your car; you may install sprinklers or fire alarms in your home; you may limit your gambling money to a set amount you can afford to lose.

Figure 10-1
Risk Management
Process

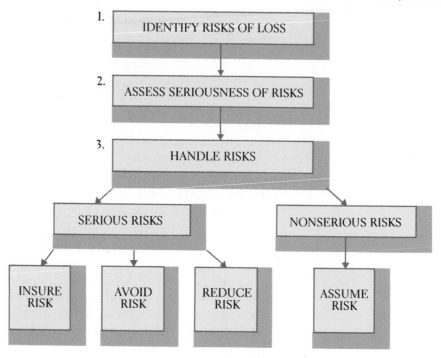

Assuming risk means self-insuring or paying for losses personally and setting aside a certain amount of money for that purpose. This strategy may be used when insurance is expensive or unavailable, or when the probability of loss is too low to justify paying a high insurance premium. **Probability** is the chance that a given event that causes loss will occur.

Self-insure when probability is low.

INSURANCE TERMINOLOGY
◆◆◆◆◆◆◆◆

To understand insurance, you must understand the basic vocabulary. Here are some typical words that relate to insurance:

1. *Actuarial table* — a table of premium rates based on ages and life expectancies
2. *Actuary* — one who calculates insurance and annuity premiums, reserves, and dividends; a specialist on insurance statistics
3. *Agent* — a trained professional acting for the insurance company in negotiating, servicing, or writing a policy
4. *Beneficiary* — a person named on an insurance policy to receive the benefits (proceeds) of the policy
5. *Benefits* — sums of money to be paid for specific types of losses under the terms of an insurance policy

6. *Cash value* — the amount of money payable to a policyholder upon discontinuation of a life insurance policy

7. *Claim* — a demand for payment for a loss under the terms of an insurance policy

8. *Coverage* — protection provided by the terms of an insurance policy

9. *Deductible* — a specified amount subtracted from covered losses; the insurance company pays only the amount in excess of the amounts subtracted

10. *Exclusions* — circumstances or losses that are not covered under the terms of an insurance policy

11. *Face amount* — the death benefit of a life insurance policy

12. *Grace period* — the period following the due date of an unpaid premium during which the policy is still in effect (usually 30 days)

13. *Insurable interest* — a condition required of the insured in nearly all insurance contracts, wherein the insured must be in a position to sustain a financial loss if the event insured against occurs

14. *Insurance* — a cooperative system of sharing risk of financial loss

15. *Insured* — the person, partnership, or corporation protected against loss (not always the owner of the policy)

16. *Loss* — an unexpected reduction or disappearance of an economic value; the basis for a valid claim for repayment under the terms of an insurance policy

17. *Peril* — an event whose occurrence can cause a loss

18. *Premium* — the sum of money the policyholder agrees to pay to an insurance company periodically (monthly, quarterly, annually, or semi-annually) for an insurance policy

19. *Proof of loss* — the written verification of the amount of a loss that must be provided by the insured to the insurance company before a claim can be settled

20. *Risk* — the chance of a loss

21. *Standard policy* — a contract form that has been adopted by many insurance companies, approved by state insurance departments, or prescribed by law (modifications are made to suit needs of the individual)

22. *Unearned premium* — the portion of the original premium that has not been earned by the insurance company and is returned to the policyholder when a policy is canceled

LIFE INSURANCE

◆◆◆◆◆◆◆◆

Families need life insurance because the spouse and children depend on income from the wage earner. A family that has no life insurance protection

Insurance   protects
the survivors.

may have to change its life-style drastically when its primary wage earner
dies — even to the point of moving from its home and giving up many
conveniences. **Life insurance** protects a family from the financial loss that
might otherwise result when a primary wage earner dies.

FINANCIAL NEEDS FOR LIFE
INSURANCE

Life insurance needs are often hard to measure. One approach to determine
the importance of life insurance coverage is to consider the financial needs
that will exist for the family after the death of a primary wage earner. These
needs typically include funds for last expenses, funds to support dependents,
money to maintain a home, and funds for ongoing monthly expenses.

The primary wage
earner will leave
many expenses.

Funds for Last Expenses.   Death-related costs to be paid include
medical bills from a last or prolonged illness, funeral expenses, and burial
costs. Funeral expenses of more than $5000 are common. (Some people
choose to assume risk via prepaid funeral costs and arrangements. This saves
loved ones the necessity of making decisions at an emotional time and
ensures that wishes will be carried out as intended. It also "locks in" the
price.)

Funds to Support Dependents.   If the head of household dies, his or
her dependents will still need income. In the case of small children, much
insurance is needed to provide support for many years until they are able to
support themselves. Insurance coverage of $100,000 or more on the life of
each wage earner is common.

Money to Maintain a Home.   Mortgage payments on the family home
must continue each month. Otherwise, the remaining family members will
be forced to sell the home and lower the family's living standard in order to
reduce housing payments. (Some people buy mortgage insurance to pay off
the balance of the mortgage in the event of the death or permanent disability
of the wage earner.)

Maintaining the fam-
ily home is a major
expense.

Funds for Ongoing Monthly Expenses.   Outstanding debts must be
paid. Food, clothing, education, utilities, and other fixed and variable
expenses continue.

TERM LIFE INSURANCE

One type of life insurance, often labeled "temporary insurance," is **term life
insurance**, which protects you for a set period of time — five, ten, or twenty
years, or until you reach a certain age. Term insurance is death protection

Illustration 10-1
Families need life
insurance because
they depend on in-
come from the pri-
mary wage earner.

Term life insurance is
temporary insurance.

for a number of years only. There is no savings or cash value from a term life
policy. For this reason, term insurance is the least expensive of all types of
life insurance.

When a term life insurance policy is written, the insured names a
beneficiary to receive the benefits of the policy if the insured dies during the
term of the policy. The insured then pays the premiums, which are based on
approximate life expectancy as computed by an actuary. Premiums vary
with the age of the insured and the amount of the coverage. At age 25, for
example, a person can purchase $100,000 of term insurance for about $150
a year. At age 35, the same insurance will cost closer to $200 a year. By age
50, the premium will be around $400 a year. Most term policies end at age
70, when premiums are about $1,000 or more a year.

Decreasing Term.   Decreasing term life insurance policies are those in
which the coverage value decreases each year while the premium remains
the same. A 20-year decreasing term policy decreases in value each year

There is no value at
the end of a term
policy.

until the value reaches zero at the end of 20 years. If the insured dies during
the first year of the policy, it pays $100,000. If the insured dies during the
second year, death benefits decrease to $95,000. The value of the policy
decreases proportionately each year.

Level Term.   Level term life insurance (also called renewable term) is
renewable yearly, every five years, or every ten years. Evidence of
insurability is not required for renewal. When a level term policy is
renewed, premiums go up while the face value of the policy remains the

Premiums go up on
level term policies.

same. A policy for $100,000 might have premiums of $150 the first year,
$175 the fifth year, $200 the tenth year, and so on. The premiums increase
because as you get older the risk is greater to the insurance company.

Term insurance policies can have additional features, such as optional
conversion to a whole life policy, or automatic renewal. These additional

features, however, raise the premiums. Also, at a certain age, such as 55 or 60, a term policy cannot be renewed. Therefore term insurance is temporary protection for the wage earner while the family needs ongoing income.

WHOLE LIFE INSURANCE

Another type of major life insurance is **whole life insurance**, which pays the face amount to the beneficiaries on the death of the insured. Whole life insurance is considered "permanent insurance" because it builds cash value and can remain in force after premiums end. The policyholder can buy a straight life or limited-payment life contract.

Whole life policies represent permanent insurance.

Straight Life.   A type of whole life policy on which premiums are paid throughout life and the face value is paid at death is called **straight life insurance**. When a policyholder stops making payments (premiums), she or he may choose to receive (a) a cash settlement of a guaranteed amount (less than face value), (b) income for a period of time, (c) full insurance protection for a period of time, or (d) continued protection at a reduced amount.

Limited-Payment Life.   **Limited-payment life insurance** is a type of whole life insurance on which premiums are higher because the payment period is limited to a specific number of years, such as 20 years, or until age 65. At the end of the established payment period, the policy is considered paid up.

Both types of whole life insurance build cash value. Money can be borrowed from the insurance company at low interest rates against policies carrying a cash value. The loan does not have to be repaid, but the loan amount is deducted from the face value of the insurance policy.

UNIVERSAL LIFE

Universal life insurance is a life policy that combines term insurance with a savings plan. It has some tax advantages provided by the Tax Reform Act of 1986. With universal life, the policyholder pays a monthly or yearly payment (or a lump sum payment) that first pays the premium for the term insurance. The balance accumulates interest. The policyholder can borrow from this cash value, but the amount borrowed is considered to be "principal" rather than "interest" and therefore is not taxable. As money is borrowed, the face value of life insurance decreases under level term universal life. An increasing term universal life policy allows added cash value to increase the face value of the death benefits.

Universal life policies have tax advantages to policyholders.

Most insurance companies pay a guaranteed interest rate that is fairly competitive. Interest earned on the cash value of the policy is not taxed until all principal is first withdrawn. (If you take the cash value as an added death benefit, the interest earned is not taxed.) You can start withdrawing the cash balance as it accumulates. However, you cannot withdraw it all for a five- or ten-year period, depending on the policy.

In addition, the policyholder has access to the cash value and unlike the IRA, 403(b) and 401(k) plans, can withdraw funds without penalty or taxation. Universal life provides a savings plan in combination with life insurance for the policyholder who cannot beat the interest rate offered, or who wants a safe place to accumulate cash. Insurance rates are usually higher for the term insurance than when it is purchased as a term policy.

Universal life is a savings plan combined with term insurance.

PURCHASING LIFE INSURANCE

When purchasing life insurance, keep in mind that life insurance contracts are based on the assumption that the insured is of average health and physical condition for his or her age. A person with a serious health problem, such as a heart condition, may be uninsurable (unable to get insurance). Life insurance premiums are low for young people because their death risk is low.

When you have group life insurance through your employer, you are not the owner of the policy; therefore, when you terminate employment you may not be able to convert the policy to an individual policy. At the time you leave employment, you also may not be insurable or able to get your own policy.

Because of discrimination laws, unisex premiums will be coming.

Females generally have higher life expectancies than males and their premiums may be lower. However, antidiscrimination laws may require that unisex premiums be charged. In addition, life insurance companies likely will raise all premium levels to compensate for the risk of acquired immune deficiency syndrome (AIDS) death claims. Insurance companies make profits by "sharing the risk" or collecting premiums from many people while paying death benefits to only a small number in a given year.

HEALTH INSURANCE

◆◆◆◆◆◆◆◆

Health care expenditures have risen more rapidly than inflation in the last 20 years. Between 1970 and 1980, health care costs rose by more than 259 percent. In the 1980s, every man, woman, and child spent more than $1,000 per year in medical care. Much of this expense has been covered by health insurance companies.

Several factors are responsible for the continued increase in costs of medical care. Advances in technology and new disease treatments result in a continuous need for expensive equipment and specially trained, highly paid personnel. The high cost of medical schooling, the shortage of medical doctors, the increasing malpractice insurance premiums, and the rising cost of overhead and office operations are also factors that contribute to the increase in medical expenses paid by the public.

Health insurance is a plan for sharing the risk of financial loss due to accident or illness — of avoiding financial disaster in the event of large medical bills. Over 70 percent of all health insurance is issued in the form of *group health insurance* plans. Group plans provide coverage for employees or other large groups of people; all those insured have the same coverage and pay a set rate for insurance. Pooling of resources results in greater coverage for lower premiums on group policies than could be obtained through individual polices. An *HMO (Health Maintenance Organization)* is a group plan whereby medical services are contracted. Individuals must go to a chosen hospital or clinic for medical services. Rather than choosing your own doctor, you go to a provider of service who is a member of the plan. An HMO plan generally provides for health maintenance costs such as physical examinations. The patient pays little or no deductible, but monthly premiums (paid by employer, employee, or both) are generally higher. *Individual health insurance* plans are expensive because only a single person or household is insured under one policy. There is no pooling or grouping of financial resources to allow lowering of premiums. Most states require that Blue Cross or Blue Shield be available for purchase by people who do not have group policies.

MEDICARE AND MEDICAID PROGRAMS

For persons over age 65, the federal government has a medical and hospital insurance program under social security called *Medicare*. A monthly premium is charged for each type of coverage (medical and hospital). Medicare hospital insurance covers hospitals and nursing home facilities. Hospital insurance pays for all covered hospital services from the first through the sixtieth day in each benefit period, except for a deductible amount (over $300). After that, covered services are paid partially.

For a monthly charge, social security recipients may add benefits to help pay costs of doctors' fees, office calls, and other medical services not covered by Medicare. For the elderly, group or individual health insurance policies supplement Medicare and offer additional coverage for retired persons. The supplemental or added coverage usually pays the deductible that Medicare will not pay, plus other expenses not covered fully by Medicare. Aged persons receive benefits under this supplementary program only if they sign up for the program and pay the monthly premium. The plan pays for 80 percent of doctors' visits, health services, and tests, as well as physical therapy and outpatient services.

Another government program, called *Medicaid*, is provided for indigent persons, regardless of age, who do not qualify for Medicare. Medicaid benefits are paid through welfare offices and are designed for those persons who cannot pay their regular medical expenses. There is no deductible. Those who qualify to receive welfare payments generally qualify to receive Medicaid as well for medical care.

Medicaid is for those who can't pay medical expenses.

TYPES OF HEALTH INSURANCE COVERAGE

Health insurance coverage usually contains a "package" of coverages such as hospital and surgical, medical expense, major medical, disability income, and dental, which are explained next. Because each health insurance plan is unique, insurance coverages and plans for employees vary from employer to employer.

Hospital and Surgical Insurance. Hospital and surgical insurance benefits pay for all or part of hospital bills, surgeons' fees, and expenses connected with in-hospital services such as anesthesia, laboratory work, X-rays, drugs, and other care items. Usually a maximum dollar amount is allowed for each day a patient is in the hospital, for a maximum number of days. The greater the number of days and the larger amount per day, the higher the premiums. Group policies generally pay 100 percent of these medical costs.

Most hospital bills have full coverage (no deductible).

Medical Expense Insurance. Medical expense insurance pays for doctors' fees for office visits and routine services other than those connected with hospital care. Most policies have a deductible. Typically, in a group policy, the deductible is the first $150 per person, or $450 maximum per family. After the deductible is met (paid by the insured) the insurance company begins paying 80 percent of qualifying medical expenses.

Major Medical Insurance. Major medical insurance applies to both hospitalization and medical services and may be purchased as a separate policy. Most major medical policies have high limits — $250,000 to $1,000,000. Major medical insurance provides the coverage necessary to protect from financial ruin as a result of a prolonged hospitalization or medical care. For example, being hospitalized for a month or longer could cost $50,000 or more, depending on services provided.

Major medical protects against catastrophic illness or injury.

Disability Income Insurance. Disability income insurance helps to replace income of a wage earner who can't work for a prolonged period of time because of illness or injury. Benefits are for a maximum number of days at a maximum amount a day. Most policies have a waiting period of a week to 90 days before benefits begin; the longer the waiting period, the lower the premium. The maximum benefit is usually no more than 50 to 75 percent of an individual's regular earnings.

Dental Insurance.   Dental insurance covers such expenses as repair of damage to teeth, examinations, fillings, extractions, inlays, bridgework, dentures, oral surgery, and root canal work. Most dental insurance policies have a deductible, in addition to restrictions on the types of dental work covered and maximum amounts payable (usually 80 percent of dental bills). Orthodontic work (correction of irregularities with braces) is rarely covered, or if it is covered, a set maximum amount is paid. The high cost of individual dental policies makes group policies most feasible.

Dental insurance has many exclusions.

▮ MINI-MEDICAL COVERAGE ▮

For households with two wage earners, *mini-medical* (mini-med) coverage is usually chosen by one spouse. Because you cannot collect twice for the same medical expense, you need one primary policy which pays 80 percent. The mini-med policy pays the deductible plus the other 20 percent.

A single person or a family should have adequate health insurance coverage so that unforeseen medical and dental expenses do not cause financial ruin. Although a form of national health insurance may be legislated in the United States at some future time so that all citizens have coverage (as in Canada), it is more likely that the individual family will continue to determine its own health insurance needs and provide for them.

National health insurance has been proposed many times.

AUTOMOBILE INSURANCE
◆◆◆◆◆◆◆◆

In most states, automobile insurance is required for operation of a motor vehicle. Automobile insurance provides protection to owners and operators of motor vehicles. It covers costs of damage to a motor vehicle, its owner, and any passengers. It also covers cost of repairs to other vehicles and medical expenses of occupants in other vehicles with which you are involved in an accident.

Automobile insurance is expensive. Premium rates are based on (a) driving record; (b) driver's education and training; (c) model, style, and age of car; (d) age and sex of driver; (e) location (city, county) of driver and car; (f) distances driven; (g) purpose of driving (such as work); and (h) age and sex of other regular or part-time drivers. The driving record includes number and

Automobile insurance rates are based on many variables.

type of tickets (infractions) received and accident record. Arrests for driving under the influence, speeding, or driving without a valid license are also a part of the driving record. Except for vintage models, the older the car, the less insurance required, because the car is worth less. New and expensive cars cost more to insure because they are worth more. Sports cars are more expensive to insure than family cars. Young single drivers pay more for insurance than those over 25 and married; male drivers pay more than females. Certain locations are considered more hazardous because of narrow roads, country roads, number of licensed drivers in the area, and area accident rate. The farther you drive on a regular basis (such as work), the higher the premiums. Who will be driving, primarily and occasionally, will also be a factor in determining cost. Adding a teenage driver to a policy will increase premiums.

Young drivers pay more for automobile insurance.

There are five basic types of automobile insurance. These include liability, collision, comprehensive, personal injury protection, and uninsured motorist. All five types of insurance purchased in one policy is known as *full coverage.*

LIABILITY COVERAGE

Liability coverage is required in most states. Liability protects the insured against claims for personal injury or damage to another person or their property. However, the insured receives nothing for his or her losses. Payments under liability coverage are only for injuries and damages caused to others.

Liability insurance is required in most states.

Liability insurance coverage is described using a series of figures, such as 100/300/50. The figures mean the insurance will pay up to $100,000 for injury to one person, $300,000 total for all persons, and $50,000 for property damage. Premiums charged for liability insurance vary according to amounts of coverage.

COLLISION COVERAGE

Most policies provide **collision coverage** — coverage of the insured's own car in the event of an accident. Most collision insurance has a deductible: the policyholder pays the first $100 or $500 (or amount specified by the policy) for repairs, and the insurance company pays the rest. Because many minor traffic accidents involve damage that costs less than many deductibles, it is wise to have a deductible and pay lower premiums. In other words, paying the first $250 for each accident would be less expensive than having no deductible and paying higher insurance premiums.

No-fault insurance laws provide for the repair or replacement of your car by your insurance company, regardless of who is at fault at the scene of the accident. Payment for repairs is made by each insurance company to its own client. Repairs are made and paid for; then the insurance companies settle the costs later, based on which driver is at fault.

COMPREHENSIVE COVERAGE

Comprehensive coverage covers damage to your car from events other than collision or upset. Events other than collision include fire, theft, tornado, hail, water, falling objects, acts of God, accidental acts of man, and acts of vandalism. If your car is scratched while parked in a parking lot, or it receives a broken window or dent from a flying rock, your insurance will pay for costs of repairs. There is usually no deductible.

PERSONAL INJURY PROTECTION

Commonly known as medical coverage, **personal injury protection** (PIP) pays for medical, hospital, and funeral costs of the insured and his or her family and passengers, regardless of fault. If the insured is injured as a pedestrian, automobile insurance personal injury protection will pay the medical costs.

UNINSURED MOTORIST COVERAGE

Uninsured motorist coverage protects you in the event you sustain loss because of the acts of an uninsured motorist. This coverage pays you as if it represented the other driver — it pays for car rental, medical, and other costs. Your insurance company then recovers this amount from the uninsured driver. Most states have *financial responsibility laws* that require motorists who do not have insurance to file statements proving they are able to take financial responsibility for their actions. Uninsured motorist coverage also protects you as a pedestrian when hit by a car that is uninsured.

In many states, proof of insurance is required in order to obtain a current vehicle registration. Liability insurance (to protect others in the event of your negligence) is minimum. Most lenders who finance the purchase of cars require full coverage. Figure 10-2 shows a comparison of coverages for automobile insurance.

Figure 10-2
Automobile Insurance

AUTOMOBILE INSURANCE		
	WHO IS PROTECTED:	
	Policyholder	Other Persons
Liability insurance:		
Personal injuries	No	Yes
Property damage	No	Yes
Collision coverage:		
Damage to insured vehicle	Yes	No
No-fault provision	Yes	No
Comprehensive coverage:		
Damage to insured vehicle	Yes	No
Personal injury protection:		
Bodily injury	Yes	Yes
Uninsured motorist coverage	Yes	Yes
Medical payments	Yes	Yes
Pedestrian coverage	Yes	No

PROPERTY INSURANCE

◆◆◆◆◆◆◆◆

When you rent an apartment or buy a home, you need property insurance to protect your personal possessions. You will need property insurance on the structure if you own the property. An apartment or house landlord can insure the building but cannot insure personal possessions of tenants. Therefore, tenants must insure the contents of their apartment or rented house.

The basic types of property insurance are fire insurance, loss or theft insurance, liability insurance, and homeowners insurance.

Tenants must insure the contents of their apartments.

FIRE INSURANCE

More than a billion dollars is lost each year because of fires that destroy buildings and their contents. **Fire insurance** will reimburse you for fire

Illustration 10-2
Property insurance
protects your home
against damage and
loss.

damage to your home and possessions. Generally, insurance for contents is half the value of the building. If the building is insured for $50,000, the contents would be covered for $25,000. Fire insurance protects against damage caused by fire and lightning, as well as smoke and water damage resulting from the fire.

Overinsuring will cost money in unneeded premiums.

Overinsuring property (buying more insurance than the amount necessary to cover the value) is unwise because the insurance company will pay only the true value. If a home valued at $40,000 with contents of $20,000 is totally destroyed, the insurance company will pay no more than $60,000, even if the owner carries $75,000 insurance. Carrying extra insurance only causes higher premiums. The lot or land will not burn; only the part of the structure that will burn or can be destroyed needs to be insured.

You can add extra provisions to a basic policy.

For a small additional premium, the property owner can extend coverage or add an endorsement for loss caused by windstorm, hail, riot, civil commotion, vehicles and aircraft, smoke, explosion, and other causes. This is called *extended coverage* to a basic policy. Instead of adding separate coverages, the homeowner may wish to purchase a package homeowners policy, which contains all the coverages mentioned.

LOSS OR THEFT INSURANCE

Loss or theft insurance coverage applies to personal property, whether it is at home or with you. Valuables are insured in the event of burglary, robbery, or damage. A *personal property floater* may also be purchased to protect certain specified items of property (such as jewelry or a camera). Under a floater policy, property is protected without regard to its location at the time of loss or damage. Rates are reasonable. For example, a camera worth $500 can be insured for about $12 a year.

LIABILITY INSURANCE

Property liability insurance protects the owner against legal claims by persons injured while on the insured's property. For instance, if a guest in your home slips and falls, you may be held liable for medical expenses for a broken leg. This coverage is part of a homeowners policy.

All homeowners and landlords should carry liability insurance, because they are responsible for acts occurring on their property, even acts involving uninvited persons. If you own a dog, you are responsible for acts of the dog. If the dog bites someone, your liability insurance covers expenses of treating the injury. Except in the case of an attractive nuisance, a homeowner will not be held liable for damages when someone trespasses on private property, unless a trap was set with the intent to harm the trespasser.

An *attractive nuisance* is a dangerous place, condition, or object that is particularly attractive to children. A swimming pool is an example. If a child sneaks into a private pool, without permission, and is hurt, the homeowner will be held liable for damages and injuries. This is true even if steps had been taken to prevent entry into the pool.

HOMEOWNERS INSURANCE

Homeowners insurance combines fire, loss and theft, and liability coverage into one comprehensive policy. Generally, homeowners policies provide coverage at a lower cost than if coverages were purchased separately. A minimum liability for most homeowners policies is $25,000, with $100,000 being a more common limit. Homeowners policies cover home and personal property at or away from home.

Many insurance companies offer property insurance in a homeowners menu format, as shown in Figure 10-3.

In addition to a flat dollar deductible (usually $50 to $500) applicable to any one loss, homeowners policies contain a **coinsurance** clause that requires you to carry coverage equal to or exceeding 80 percent of the replacement cost of your home. If you do not meet this requirement, you will receive less than full replacement cost. For example, suppose your house has an estimated value (replacement cost) of $100,000. The coinsurance requirement means you must insure for $80,000. But suppose

Figure 10-3
Homeowners Poli-
cies

HO-1	Basic Coverage	Fire, lightning, windstorm, hail, explosion, riot, civil commotion, aircraft, nonowned vehicles, smoke, vandalism, malicious mischief, theft, and glass breakage. Limits apply, such as $500 or 5 percent of policy value, whichever is less.
HO-2	Broad Form	Broader list of perils; broader definitions; still has restrictions and limits, such as fire from fireplaces is excluded; limit of $1000 or 10 percent of policy value, whichever is less.
HO-3	Special Form	All-risk coverage on dwelling itself; a loss not specifically excluded (such as flood) is covered.
HO-4	Renters	Insuring personal property on a broad-form basis with advantages of homeowners policy (such as special coverage in event of flood or water damage).
HO-5	Comprehensive	Most comprehensive policy available; dwelling and contents are covered on all-risk basis.
HO-6	Condominium Owners	HO-4 coverage for condominium owners (wording is adjusted to fit legal status of condominium owner).
HO-7	Older Homes	Meets special needs of owners of older buildings that have been remodeled and would have high replacement costs (actual cash value basis rather than replacement cost basis).

instead you insure for only $60,000. If you would then suffer a $40,000 loss, you would collect only 60/80 (75 percent) of the loss ($30,000).

VOCABULARY

Directions: Can you find the definition for each of the following terms used in Chapter 10?

risk management
probability
life insurance
term life insurance
decreasing term life insur-
    ance

level term life insurance
whole life insurance
straight life insurance
limited-payment life insur-
    ance
universal life insurance

health insurance	personal injury protection (PIP)
liability coverage	uninsured motorist coverage
collision coverage	fire insurance
no-fault insurance	homeowners insurance
comprehensive coverage	coinsurance

1. A type of auto insurance that eliminates the need to establish fault before payment is made to cover damages.

2. A plan of sharing the risk of financial loss due to illness or injury requiring medical treatment.

3. Life insurance that is considered permanent insurance because it builds cash value and can remain in force after premiums end.

4. Life insurance that pays face value to beneficiaries only if the insured dies during the term of the policy, while premiums are being paid.

5. A plan of sharing the risk of financial loss that might otherwise result when a primary wage earner dies.

6. A policy that combines fire, loss and theft, and liability coverage into one policy.

7. The chance that a given event that causes loss will occur.

8. Management of personal risks to improve the likelihood of protecting assets and income against loss.

9. Life insurance coverage where the coverage value decreases each year while the premium remains the same.

10. Life insurance that is renewable and premiums go up while the face value of the policy remains the same.

11. A type of whole life policy on which premiums are paid throughout life and the face value is paid at death.

12. A type of whole life policy on which premiums are paid over a specific number of years, and then is considered paid up.

13. Automobile insurance that covers the insured against claims for injury or damage to another person or their property.

14. Automobile insurance that covers the insured's own car in the event of an accident.

15. A policy that combines a savings plan with term life insurance and provides certain tax advantages for borrowing from the cash value.

16. Automobile insurance that covers damage to your car from events other than collision or upset.

17. Commonly known as medical coverage for automobile insurance.

18. Automobile insurance coverage that protects you in the event you sustain a loss because of the acts of a motorist who has no automobile insurance.

19. A policy clause that requires you to carry coverage equal to or exceeding 80 percent of the replacement cost.

20. Insurance that will reimburse you for fire damage to your home and possessions.

ITEMS FOR DISCUSSION

1. List the three steps in risk management.
2. What are four things you can do about risk?
3. Why do families need life insurance?
4. What are some of the financial needs to be considered following the death of the primary wage earner?
5. What are three main types of life insurance?
6. Why has the cost of health insurance risen so drastically in the last several years?
7. Who is eligible to receive Medicare? Medicaid?
8. List five major types of health insurance coverage.
9. What is mini-med?
10. What type of automobile insurance coverage is required in most states? Who is protected under this type of insurance?
11. On what factors are the insurance premiums for automobile insurance based?
12. List the five types of automobile insurance coverage.
13. Explain the concept of *no-fault automobile insurance.*
14. Why do renters need property insurance?
15. List the four major types of property insurance.
16. What type of policy protects a valuable item of personal property regardless of its location at the time of loss?

APPLICATIONS

1. What are your life insurance needs at this time in your life? What are the life insurance needs of your family?
2. Assume that you are married and have two small children. You and your spouse are both working. What type of insurance should you have? How much?
3. Why do families need health insurance or major medical insurance coverage? Cut an article from a newspaper about an event (injury or illness) that would require health insurance for protection of the family.
4. What type of automobile insurance is required in your state? How does your state ensure that this requirement is met?
5. Does your state have no-fault insurance laws? Explain the provisions.

6. Why should you not have more fire insurance coverage on your home than the home and its contents are actually worth?

7. Why should you not have less insurance coverage than the replacement value of your home?

8. Why is it necessary for homeowners to have some type of liability insurance?

CASE PROBLEMS AND ACTIVITIES

1. Cathy Pierce, a friend of yours, is thinking about putting an in-ground swimming pool in her back yard. Explain to her the dangers of having a pool and the type of insurance coverage needed.

2. A local department store delivers a couch to your home and your dog bites the delivery person, who demands that you pay the medical bills. You had a sign warning "Beware of Dog" posted on your front door. What responsibilities do you have, and what type of insurance coverage do you need?

3. Interview an employee who has a group health insurance plan. Discuss what types of expenses are covered, what deductibles are applied, how much of the premium is paid by the employer and how much by the employee, and what the maximum benefits are. Also ask if an HMO is available, and if so, why it was chosen or not chosen.

4. Call a private health insurance carrier (company) such as Blue Cross or Blue Shield, and ask for information about an individual major medical policy. What types of coverage are available and what are the premiums for individuals?

5. Identify the risks of (a) a single person, (b) a married couple, and (c) a married couple with dependent children. Assess each risk as serious or nonserious. Beside each risk, indicate how to handle it: insure, avoid, reduce, or assume.

6. Your house is insured for $120,000. The replacement value is $100,000 plus a lot worth $15,000 and a foundation worth $5,000. Your house burns and is a total loss. How much will you recover for the structure?

7. You have a coinsurance clause on the same house worth $100,000, but you have insurance of $70,000. A fire causes $18,000 damage. How much will you recover from the insurance policy?

UNIT THREE CREDIT

UNIT OBJECTIVES

After studying the chapters in this third unit that describe credit and plans for using credit in terms of present and future needs and income, the student will be able to:

1 ■ Describe the history of credit, define basic credit vocabulary, and list advantages and disadvantages of credit, kinds of credit, and sources of credit.

2 ■ Explain the concept of creditworthiness as it relates to credit records, credit ratings, credit reports, and credit laws.

3 ■ Compute the costs of credit and discuss methods of reducing credit costs and responsibilities of consumer credit.

4 ■ List major causes of bankruptcy, understand the advantages and disadvantages of bankruptcy, discuss bankruptcy laws and their purpose, and understand how to solve credit problems.

Chapter 11

CREDIT IN AMERICA

◆◆◆◆◆◆◆◆◆◆◆◆◆◆◆◆◆◆◆◆◆◆◆◆◆◆◆◆◆◆

OBJECTIVES

1. Describe the history of credit in America and define credit vocabulary.
2. List advantages and disadvantages of the use of credit by the American consumer.
3. List and describe the kinds of credit available to the American consumer.
4. Describe and compare sources of credit in the American economy.

HISTORY OF CREDIT

◆◆◆◆◆◆◆◆◆

Most purchases are made on credit.

When you borrow money or use a charge account to pay for purchases, you are taking advantage of the most commonly used method of purchase in the United States: credit. **Credit** is the privilege of buying something now, with the agreement to pay for it later, or borrowing money with the promise to pay it back later. For the privilege of charging purchases or accepting a loan, you will usually pay an interest or finance charge. It is estimated that over 80 percent of all purchases made in the United States are made through the use of credit.

The need for credit arose in the United States when the country grew from a bartering and trading society to a currency exchange economy. Most historians attribute this transition to the time of the Industrial Revolution. For the first time, items were manufactured for sale on a wide scale — no longer did everyone produce everything they needed themselves.

Americans began to be dependent on one another. Instead of each family being wholly self-supporting, growing its own food and providing its own clothing and shelter, family heads began to work for others to earn wages. Soon the need developed for sources of credit to help families meet their financial needs. Consumer credit had begun.

Lack of self-support created a need for credit.

One of the earliest forms of credit was the account at the local mercantile or general store. The wage earner or farmer would pick up supplies and put the amount due "on account." Accounts would accumulate for a month, for a season, or even for a year. When a paycheck was received or a crop was harvested, the account would be paid in full, and the charging process would begin again. Interest was rarely charged. But only those customers who were well known to and trusted by the business owner were offered credit.

Banks loaned farmers lump sums of money as large as $500 at the start of the planting season to put in crops. The loans were repaid after the harvest. This type of credit was very expensive, however. In the 1800s, bank interest rates were very high, and loans were generally made only in emergency situations. Most people, including bankers, knew very little about credit and how it worked. Consequently, bankers and others making loans charged high interest rates and were very reluctant to loan large sums of money.

The first loans were expensive.

EARLY 1900s

Since 1900 rates have dropped.

Since 1900, interest rates have dropped. The decrease is mainly a result of a new awareness and understanding of the advantages — especially the financial rewards — of loaning money. The United States was changing from an agricultural economy, where the main occupation was farming, to an industrial economy of laborers and manufacturing. Lending institutions began to ask for security on loans (the pledging of property and income); consequently, they became more willing to make loans.

As the use of credit expanded, individual purchasing power also expanded. Because more people were willing and able to buy more goods and services, the American economy grew at a healthy pace. Conveniences as well as necessities were purchased with the help of credit, and the standard of living of the average American rose. Businesses and consumers benefited from credit. New jobs were created, and the economy grew until World War I, which created significant debt. The war debt was paid off, however, and the United States entered the 1920s in a secure position with credit stronger than ever.

THE NEXT 65 YEARS

Between 1920 and 1970, buying on credit became the American way of life. No longer was credit saved for emergencies. Many different forms of credit developed to meet changing consumer needs and wants.

When the stock market crashed in 1929, many Americans lost their savings. Banks went bankrupt, and loans were defaulted because jobs were lost. It took almost a decade to restore confidence in credit and investments. But recovery was followed by war again, and World War II proved costly. The federal government went heavily into debt and was no longer able to balance its budget. However, consumer credit continued to grow and flourish. Interest rates were low through the 40s, 50s and 60s, and inflation rates were stable and under 10 percent.

The 1970s brought unusually rapid economic growth, overuse of credit, worldwide dependence on oil, and high inflation rates. The 1970s closed with double-digit inflation. Interest rates were so high that many people could not afford to buy new homes or cars even with the use of credit.

From 1981 through 1985, the U.S. had a recession that cost many jobs and saw a rapid decline in the use of credit. The recovery that followed was slow and painful. Credit was often seen as an enemy as record numbers of bankruptcies occurred and hundreds of financial institutions failed. Some areas of the country suffered more than others — areas dependent on one industry, such as automobiles or timber — and lost the most jobs and confidence in credit.

CREDIT TODAY

As a result of the Tax Reform Bill of 1986, deducting interest paid on credit purchases (other than home mortgages) on income tax returns was phased out. (The phase out of deductibility began in 1987 at 65 percent; 40 percent in 1988; 20 percent in 1989; and 10 percent in 1991.) Nevertheless, lenders are willing to make loans to consumers considered high risk — those who have poor credit records or little capital or resources to ensure their ability to repay debt. Credit cards are easy to obtain for most consumers who have earning ability and the desire to use credit.

CREDIT LEGISLATION

The 1970s brought the first powerful consumer credit protection legislation. No longer was "buyer beware" the rule in credit transactions. Laws were enacted to protect consumers from fraudulent practices. Both government and private agencies were formed to assist consumers with their rights and responsibilities.

Consumer protection interests grew in the 1970s.

The late 1970s brought a new occupation — credit counseling. Credit counselors advise others on how to use credit wisely, pay bills, and get out of trouble with credit; when to seek legal advice; and how to avoid damaging their credit ratings.

The 1980s saw a new wave of credit assistance in the form of certified financial planning. Planners assist consumers who have overextended themselves to the point of insolvency, by setting up payment plans with creditors and getting the customer back on his or her feet again. In addition, financial planners offer such services as banking and investment advice, assistance in budgeting and planning, and selection of insurance and investment alternatives. Fees charged vary with the ability to pay.

Financial planners assist with credit problems.

CREDIT VOCABULARY
◆◆◆◆◆◆◆◆

To understand credit fully, you must understand certain terms. These words are commonly used to describe credit, its availability, and its cost.

1. *Balance due* — the amount that remains due on a loan, including both principal and interest
2. *Billing (closing) date* — the last date of the month that any purchase you made with your credit card or any payment made on your account is recorded in the account
3. *Borrower* — the person who borrows money and uses another form of credit (When you charge something, you are, in effect, borrowing.)
4. *Capital* — the property you possess that is worth more than your debts (one of the requirements for credit)
5. *Collateral* — personal property (bonds, stocks, automobiles, livestock, proceeds from an insurance policy) pledged to a lender to secure a loan
6. *Creditor* — person to whom one owes money or goods
7. *Due date* — the date on or before which payment is due (typically 25 to 30 days after the billing date)
8. *Finance charge* (handling charge) — the interest or money charged the borrower for the use of credit
9. *Installment contract* — a written agreement to make regular payments on a specific purchase
10. *Prorate* — divide, as to divide the interest or handling charge, proportionately over a period of time

11. *Secured loan* — a loan wherein the borrower pledges property or other assets to assure the creditor of repayment

12. *Service charge* (carrying charge) — the amount charged to borrowers (customers) by merchants or banks for servicing an account or loan.

ADVANTAGES OF CREDIT
◆◆◆◆◆◆◆◆

The wise consumer can gain many advantages from the use of credit. Used correctly, credit can greatly expand a family's purchasing potential and raise its standard of living in many ways.

Credit is handy for emergencies.

Credit can, for example, provide emergency funds — a sudden need for cash can be solved by a credit card or a **line of credit,** which is a pre-established amount that can be borrowed on demand. To establish a line of credit, you fill out the application at your bank and an amount is approved based on your income and financial position that enable you to repay a loan. Using a line of credit, money is always available should you need it.

Budgeting and increased buying power can be achieved through the use of credit. Major purchases may be paid for over a period of time, and establishing a good credit record by the early and wise use of credit makes future use of credit for major purchases easier.

Credit is convenient and easy to use.

Credit is convenient. Credit customers often get better service because they can withhold payment until a problem is resolved. Regular charge customers receive advance notices of sales and special offers not available to the general public, such as deferred billing. **Deferred billing** is a service to charge customers whereby charged purchases are not billed to the customer until several months later, and no finance charge accrues. For example, merchandise purchased in October is not billed to the customer until January and no payment is due until February.

The proof of purchase provided by a charge slip is usually more descriptive than a cash register receipt and helps in making adjustments when merchandise is returned. Finally, shopping is safer with the use of credit. Carrying a credit card or store charge card makes for faster shopping and is safer than carrying large sums of cash.

DISADVANTAGES OF CREDIT
◆◆◆◆◆◆◆◆

There are also disadvantages associated with the use of credit. For instance, credit purchases may cost more than cash purchases. Gasoline is an example

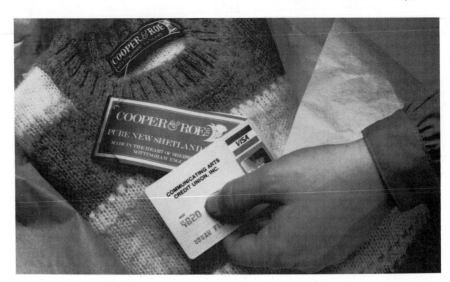

Illustration 11-1
Credit is conve-
nient to use.

of an item that often costs more — five cents or more per gallon — when purchased on credit. In addition, an item purchased on credit and paid in monthly installments costs more than the ticket price when interest is added.

Credit can be expensive.

An interest rate of 18 percent a year is 1½ percent a month. On a $100 purchase, the interest would be $1.50 a month. The larger the purchase and the longer the period of time taken to pay the balance due, the greater the interest charges.

Using credit reduces the amount of comparative shopping. Many consumers shop only in stores where they have credit. Comparing prices and quality at several different stores can save money.

Credit ties up future income.

Future income is tied up when credit is used. Buying something that will require payments for several years reduces funds available for items that may be needed in the months to come. This situation can put a strain on the budget that may be discouraging.

Buying on credit can lead to overspending. People get into trouble with credit when they buy more than they can pay back comfortably. At the end of the month, when the bills come in, they realize how much they have really spent.

A bad credit rating can make it very difficult to get credit when you need it in the future. The use of computers makes it very difficult to escape previous acts of poor judgment and get a fresh start with credit.

Credit is a privilege, not a right.

These disadvantages can be avoided by the wise use of credit. Consumers who start out slowly and plan their credit purchases can avoid credit problems. Credit is a privilege that must be earned and responsibly maintained — it is not a right. Use this privilege wisely and you will find credit to be a good friend.

KINDS OF CREDIT

◆◆◆◆◆◆◆◆

There are many different credit opportunities to explore. An awareness of the kinds of credit available and the sources of credit will help you to make wise choices when you make credit purchases. Most credit purchases or uses can be divided into these major categories: charge and other credit card accounts, layaway plans, installment purchase agreements, and service credit.

CHARGE AND OTHER CREDIT CARD ACCOUNTS

Charge and other credit card accounts are open-ended forms of credit. **Open-ended credit** is credit wherein the lender places a limit on how much a qualifying customer can borrow during a given period. The borrower usually has a choice of repaying the entire balance within 30 days or repaying over a number of months or years.

Regular Credit Accounts. A regular credit account (open account) provides credit for an open period, usually 30 days. Normally, full payment is expected at the end of each period, and no interest is charged. If full payment is not made, however, a finance charge is added. A charge plate (plastic card) is provided to identify customers with valid accounts. Clothing and other items are charged to the account. When the card is lost or stolen, a new account number and new card are issued.

Full payment is expected on open accounts.

Charge Cards. American Express and Diner's Club are examples of charge cards. On all but travel-related charges (such as airline tickets), the balance charged must be paid in full when the bill is received. There is no credit extended beyond the billing cycle. These cards are widely accepted nationwide and overseas, usually have high or no limits, and provide instant purchasing power.

Other Credit Card Accounts. Bank credit cards such as VISA or MasterCard, oil company credit cards, financial network cards, and entertainment and travel cards operate on the same basis as the regular credit account. The bank or other creditor charges your account for purchases made during the month and bills you at the end of the month. Usually you do not pay a finance charge if you pay the total bill each month. However, a finance charge will be added if you pay only a portion of the unpaid balance

Bank credit cards operate like regular credit accounts.

and allow your account to accumulate. There is a maximum credit amount, which is adjusted periodically, and an annual fee may be charged for use of the credit card.

LAYAWAY PLANS

Many retail businesses offer **layaway** plans whereby merchandise is held in your name; you make regular payments and claim the merchandise when it has been paid for in full. Most merchants require 25 percent or more down payment, with regular payments to be made monthly or twice monthly. A service fee, ranging from $1 to 5 percent of the purchase price, is usually charged. A coat purchased for $100 on layaway, for instance, might require a deposit of $26 (25 percent plus a $1 fee). Then three monthly payments of $25 each would pay off the balance, and you would receive the coat. You would receive a receipt when the coat is selected and as regular payments are posted to the account.

If you change your mind about a layaway purchase, a portion of the payments already made may be forfeited. The merchant has provided a service — credit and storage of the merchandise — and is entitled to payment for that service.

Layaways provide credit for a service.

Because layaway account terms vary among merchants, it is wise to compare service fees, down payment requirements, and penalties. The advantage of layaway credit is that payment can be made over a period of time. Layaway credit is available to most customers whether or not they have any other form of credit with a particular merchant.

INSTALLMENT PURCHASE AGREEMENTS

Installment purchase agreements, also called **installment loans**, are contracts defining the repayment of the purchase price plus finance charges in equal regular payments (installments). For example, if an item with a purchase price of $800 is bought on a two-year payment plan with a 15 percent annual finance charge, the total installment price is $1040 ($800 plus $240 interest). Regular monthly payments of $43.34 ($1040 divided by 24) include both principal and interest. More purchases cannot be added to an installment purchase agreement, although another agreement can be drawn up, requiring separate, additional payments.

Installment payments include principal and interest.

Some businesses carry their own financing, and monthly payments are made directly to them. Some businesses sell their contracts to finance companies and customers make payments to the finance companies. Other businesses require that customers get outside financing for installment purchases. Such financing may be obtained from a bank, credit union, or finance company. By requiring the customer to borrow money to cover the purchase, the merchant is assured of immediate payment in full. Installment payments are then made to the lender.

Installment purchase agreements generally are used for large purchases such as automobiles, appliances, furniture, or large cash loans. A signed contract is evidence of the loan. The purchased items serve as *collateral* and will be repossessed if the agreed upon payments are not made. In the case of an automobile or mobile home, the lender retains the title until the full purchase price is paid. Such large purchases often require the signing of a promissory note. As a consumer, it is your responsibility to read and understand any contract or note before signing it.

Large purchases often require a promissory note.

SERVICE CREDIT

Almost everyone uses some type of **service credit** by having a service performed and paying for it later. Your telephone and utility services are furnished a month in advance, then you are billed. Many businesses — including doctors, lawyers, dentists, hospitals, dry cleaners, repair shops, and others — extend service credit. Terms are set by individual businesses. Some of these creditors do not charge interest on unpaid account balances, but they do expect that regular payments will be made until the bill is paid in full. Others, such as utility and telephone companies, expect payment in full within a time limit; however, they usually offer a budget plan as well, which allows you to average bills to get lower monthly payments. Service credit accounts are usually offered by businesses whose services are considered necessary to the average consumer.

Service credit is available when needed.

SOURCES OF CREDIT
◆◆◆◆◆◆◆◆

There are many sources of consumer credit. Some of the major sources are retail stores, commercial banks, credit unions, finance companies, pawnshops, and private lenders.

RETAIL STORES

Retail stores include department stores, drug stores, clothing stores, hardware stores, and all types of service businesses. Retailers purchase from wholesalers, who purchase from manufacturers and producers. Consumers buy directly from the retailers.

Retail stores take advantage of credit because customers like to shop where they have credit established. Many retail stores offer their own accounts, and also accept bank credit cards and other well-known charge cards. Credit customers receive discounts and other privileges not offered to cash customers.

Many retail stores have several credit plans.

COMMERCIAL BANKS AND CREDIT UNIONS

Commercial banks and credit unions make loans to individuals and companies based on collateral, capital, and credit records. Interest rates vary with location or financial institution and according to what is being purchased. Good reasons for a loan, such as the need to purchase a car or home or the desire to take a vacation, are required. Banks generally charge the maximum loan rates allowed by law. Regular bank customers who have established credit are able to get loans more easily than noncustomers. Loans are also available through credit card advances.

Banks require good reasons for loans.

Credit unions make loans available to their members only. Interest rates are generally lower than those charged by banks because credit unions are non-profit and are organized for the benefit of members. Credit unions are more willing to make loans because the members who are borrowing also have a stake in the success of the credit union.

FINANCE COMPANIES

Often called *small loan companies,* **finance companies** usually charge high rates of interest for use of their money. The reason for the high rates is that finance companies are willing to take risks that banks and credit unions will not take. In many cases, people who are turned down by banks and credit unions can get loans at small loan companies. Finance companies are second only to banks in the volume of credit extended.

Finance companies take more risk than banks.

There are two types of finance companies. A **consumer finance company** is a general-purpose company that extends mostly consumer loans to customers buying consumer durables. Well-known companies include Household Finance, AVCO, and Beneficial Finance. The second type of company is the manufacturer-related **sales finance company** that makes loans through authorized representatives. For example, General Motors Acceptance Corporation (GMAC) finances General Motors automobile dealers and their customers. Both types of finance companies borrow money from banks and lend it to consumers at higher rates.

Small loan companies take more risk than banks. Therefore, they must be more careful to protect their loans. When payment is not received when due, an officer calls the customer for an explanation. Constant contact is kept to make sure payments are made as agreed. Phone calls, letters, and personal visits are to be expected if the customer deviates even slightly from the agreed upon payment schedule. High interest rates are also another form of protection for the small loan company.

Finance companies lend relatively small amounts of money repayable on the installment basis. These companies are regulated by states under the Uniform Small-Loan Law, which permits fairly high interest rates to cover the costs of making many small loans. Typically, the law permits loans up to $5,000 and allows interest rates up to 42 percent a year. The growth of finance companies is the result of efforts to eliminate **loan sharks** — unlicensed lenders who charge very high and usually illegal interest rates. Nevertheless, it is difficult to eliminate such practices that take advantage of the poorest members of society who can least afford to pay.

Usury laws set the maximum interest rates that may be charged. In states where usury laws exist, finance companies charge the maximum. Where no usury laws exist, finance companies charge as much as the customer is willing to pay. When an emergency or other extreme need arises, consumers often feel forced to pay these higher rates of interest to get the money they need.

> Finance companies watch repayment patterns closely.

> Usury laws protect consumers from high rates of interest.

PAWNSHOPS

A **pawnshop** is a legal business where loans are made against the value of specific personal possessions. Merchandise that is readily salable, such as guns, cameras, jewelry, radios, TVs, and coins, is usually acceptable. The customer brings in an item of value to be examined and appraised. A loan made against the property is considerably less than the appraised value of the item. Some pawnshops give only 10 to 25 percent of the value of the article; most give no more than 50 or 60 percent. For example, if you have a ring appraised at $500, you will probably be loaned between $50 and $250. You will be given a receipt for the ring and a certain length of time — from two weeks to six months — to redeem the ring by paying back the loan plus interest. If you do not pay back the loan and claim the ring, it will be sold. Merchandise taken in a pawnshop is considered collateral for the loan because it is something of value that may be sold if you fail to pay off the loan. Prices charged for the used merchandise in a pawnshop are generally lower than actual value. Sometimes you can find a bargain, and the pawnbroker still makes a profit.

> Pawnshops make loans based on appraised value.

Illustration 11-2
Pawnbrokers sell
items left as collat-
eral if they are not
redeemed prompt-
ly.

PRIVATE LENDERS

The most common source of cash loans is the private lender. Private lenders include an individual's parents, other relatives, friends, etc. Interest may or may not be charged on loans made by private lenders.

OTHER SOURCES OF CONSUMER CREDIT

Your life insurance policy may have loan value.

Life insurance policies can be used as an alternate source of consumer credit. As a whole life or universal life policy builds cash value, the policyholder can borrow at low rates of interest against his or her policy. The loan does not have to be repaid, but interest will be charged, and the amount of the loan will reduce the face value of the life insurance policy.

If you have a certificate of deposit with a bank, credit union, or savings and loan association, you can borrow money against the certificate. The certificate is used as collateral, and the interest rate charged is usually only 2 to 5 percent above the interest rate you are receiving on the certificate. If you cash in the certificate, you incur interest penalties; but if you borrow money using the certificate as collateral, you are charged only a moderate rate of interest on the loan, and the certificate retains its full value.

VOCABULARY

Directions: Can you find the definition for each of the following terms used in Chapter 11?

credit   retail stores
line of credit   finance companies
deferred billing   consumer finance company
open-ended credit   sales finance company
layaway   loan sharks
installment loans   usury laws
service credit   pawnshop

1. A plan whereby merchandise is set aside in a customer's name until it is paid for.
2. Paying at a future date for the present use of money, goods, or services.
3. Having a service performed and paying for it at a later date.
4. Businesses offering goods and services to consumers, including department stores, drug stores, clothing stores, and so on.
5. Laws setting maximum interest rates that may be charged.
6. A legal business where loans are made based on the value of merchandise pledged as collateral.
7. A pre-established amount that can be borrowed on demand.
8. A service to credit customers whereby purchases are not billed for several months.
9. Unlicensed lenders who charge elevated and illegal rates of interest.
10. Small loan companies that charge high but legal rates of interest.
11. Credit whereby you can add purchases up to a set credit limit.
12. Closed-ended credit using a contract that defines payment of purchase price plus finance charge.
13. A general-purpose finance company that extends mostly consumer loans.
14. A manufacturer-related company that makes loans through authorized representatives.

ITEMS FOR DISCUSSION

1. What is credit?
2. What is collateral?
3. When credit first began in this country, did loans have high interest rates?

4.   When credit began, why were bankers and merchants reluctant to loan money and give credit?
5.   How has credit affected the American economy?
6.   What kinds of jobs are created by credit?
7.   List four advantages of using credit.
8.   List four disadvantages of using credit.
9.   What are three major kinds of credit?
10.   How is open-ended credit different from installment (closed-ended) credit?
11.   Explain how layaway credit operates. Why is it a good way to begin to establish credit?
12.   Give three or four examples of service credit.
13.   How are consumer finance companies different from sales finance companies?
14.   List the five major sources of credit for consumers.
15.   Why do retail stores accept VISA, MasterCard, or Discover Card in addition to their own credit cards?
16.   Why do credit unions offer lower interest rates on loans than do commercial banks?
17.   Why do finance companies charge higher rates of interest on their loans than do commercial banks?
18.   Explain how a pawnshop works.

APPLICATIONS

1.   Give an example of a situation in which you would use collateral when making a purchase on credit.
2.   How does your family make use of credit? Do you think credit use in your family is a good thing or a bad thing? What advantages of credit do you use?
3.   List retail stores in your area that:

      a. extend credit by accepting store credit cards.
      b. accept VISA, MasterCard, Discover, or other major credit cards.
      c. offer installment credit.

4.   List several businesses in your area that offer layaway plans. Choose one such plan and list the following:

      a. Name of store
      b. Amount of down payment required
      c. Layaway fee
      d. Penalty for failure to complete payments
      e. Maximum amount of merchandise that may be purchased on layaway
      f. Frequency of and amount of payments needed

5. List five sources of service credit that most families use. Of these sources, do any charge a fee or interest if full payment is not made?
6. List four commercial banks and credit unions in your area. Write down their addresses and telephone numbers.
7. List four finance companies in your area, together with addresses and telephone numbers. (Hint: The Yellow Pages of your telephone book will list them by subject, such as under the heading "Finance.")
8. List pawnshops in your area; include addresses and telephone numbers.
9. Does your state have usury laws? You can find out by consulting your library (the current *World Almanac & Book of Facts*). List some of the finance rates that states allow, including your state and neighboring states.

CASE PROBLEMS AND ACTIVITIES

1. Friends of your grandparents have never used credit. Having lived through the Great Depression, when they lost their life savings, they have never trusted others enough to pay for anything except with cash. What types of problems can result from not using credit? What would be your advice to them, knowing that they have a good income from investments and have no need to buy on credit?
2. Interview three or four adults about credit. Ask them the following questions. Prepare a short report.

    a. How do you feel about the use of credit in America?
    b. Do you use credit cards, such as store or bank credit cards?
    c. Do you think the rates of interest charged by stores and banks on unpaid balances are reasonable?
    d. What rate of interest is charged by some creditors?
    e. How would you advise a young person just starting out about credit?

3. Do you feel that the advantages of using credit outweigh the disadvantages? Write a paper in paragraph form, either defending the use of credit or explaining why it should be avoided.
4. A friend of yours wishes to buy a new car. She has one picked out at a local dealer, but she has only enough money to make a down payment. She asks your advice about where she can finance the balance of her loan for $6,000. What will you tell her?
5. Your cousin Bill needs $100 immediately. He has a hunting rifle worth at least $800 and wants to take it to a pawnshop. Explain to him how much he can borrow against the rifle, and what will happen with pawnshop credit.

Chapter 12

CREDIT RECORDS, REPORTS, AND LAWS

♦♦♦♦♦♦♦♦♦♦♦♦♦♦♦♦♦♦♦♦♦♦♦♦♦

OBJECTIVES

1. Understand the importance of credit records and summarize how and why records are compiled.
2. List the six Cs of credit, discuss the information contained in credit records, and explain reasons for and rights of consumers in credit denial.
3. Describe credit ratings and a point system for determining creditworthiness.
4. Outline the contents of a credit report.
5. Discuss the provisions of the major credit laws.

CREDIT RECORDS
♦♦♦♦♦♦♦♦

In determining your creditworthiness, a creditor will ask about past credit performance: Were bills paid on time? Were bills paid off as agreed? How much total credit was given? What is the credit that appears to be outstanding at this time? Your credit history, the complete record of your credit performance, will provide answers to these questions and thus help the creditor gauge your ability to pay back new debts.

CREDIT FILE

Every person who uses credit has a credit file. The **credit file** is a summary of a person's credit history. Each time credit is used and reported, information on the transaction will appear in the credit file.

Maintaining credit files is a big business. A company that operates for profit in the business of accumulating, storing, and distributing credit information is a **credit bureau**. There are an estimated 2,500 credit bureaus in the United States, supplying 125 to 150 million credit reports a year. TRW Credit Data, a major credit bureau, reports having files on 40 million consumers and supplying 15 million credit reports a year to 26,000 creditors.

Some credit bureaus still keep records in handwritten form and post new information by hand as it is received. Most larger bureaus, however, use *databases*, which are computerized, organized collections of related data, to search and retrieve a record for potential creditors. Each credit record in the database file is given a record number and contains a set of information similar to other credit records in the file. Information is stored on a local level, and when you purchase through national companies or mail-order houses, you also establish a file with national bureaus. You may have a file in three or more places, depending on the sources and types of credit used.

Most people have credit files.

Modern methods of storage make credit information readily available.

HOW INFORMATION IS GATHERED

Credit bureaus gather information from creditors, called **subscribers**. A subscriber pays dues or an annual fee to the credit bureau; each subscriber supplies information about its accounts — names, addresses, credit balances, how payments are being handled, and so forth. Credit bureaus also gather information from many other sources. Articles about consumers found in local newspapers are clipped and added to files. Public records are searched for information to add to a consumer's file. When someone applies for credit from a subscriber, a credit report showing all accumulated data on the applicant is requested by the subscriber. Information in the credit report is then used as the basis for granting or denying credit. Because the credit report shows the credit history of an applicant, risks to a creditor in granting credit are lowered when that creditor makes use of credit reports.

Businesses support the credit bureaus.

TYPES OF INFORMATION KEPT

Any public information becomes a part of your credit record. For example, if you fail to pay your property taxes, file bankruptcy, file for a divorce, or apply for a marriage license, this information will appear in your credit file. Birth announcements published in newspapers, job promotions, lawsuits, and other visible activities are recorded. When you fill out a credit application, information requested such as occupation, length of employment, spouse's name and occupation, residence, length of occupancy, number of children and other dependents, and so forth, is sent to the credit bureau by the subscriber. Your social security number is often used as the key piece of information to locate you and keep you differentiated from others. Facts supplied in this way can give future creditors enough information to make a wise decision about granting or denying credit to you.

> All public information may be included in credit files.

FACTORS IN DETERMINING CREDITWORTHINESS

♦♦♦♦♦♦♦♦

Before potential creditors will grant credit to you, they must determine whether you are a good risk — whether you are creditworthy. If you meet certain standards that creditors believe are important, you will usually qualify for the credit you desire.

THE SIX Cs OF CREDIT

A person who is considered a good credit risk usually meets six basic qualifications. These qualifications include character, capacity, capital, conditions, collateral, and common sense.

> Your qualifications determine your credit rating.

Character.   A person with a good **character** is one who willingly and responsibly lives up to agreements. One distinctive sign of a good character is a responsible attitude toward paying bills and meeting obligations on time.

Capacity.   The ability to repay a loan or make payments on merchandise with present income is known as **capacity**. Creditors want to make certain that you will have enough money left over each month after other fixed expenses have been met to pay your credit debts.

Capital.   Property and other assets that total more than debts are known as *capital*. In other words, when you add up all that you own (assets) and subtract all that you owe (liabilities), the difference (net worth or capital) should be sufficient to ensure payment of another debt.

Conditions.   All other existing debts, stability of employment, personal factors, and other factors that might affect a person's ability to meet financial obligations are important **conditions** to be considered. For example, a person who has moved six times during the past year might not be

> Stability is important to your credit rating.

considered a good risk because of living conditions that indicate some type of problem.

Collateral.   Property or possessions that can be mortgaged or used as security for payment of a debt are known as *collateral*. If a debt is not paid as agreed, the collateral is repossessed and sold to pay the debt.

Common Sense.   A person's ability to make wise decisions is often referred to as **common sense**. A loan officer or credit manager would determine that you have good common sense based on how you answer questions (orally or in writing). Good decisions are reflected in answers such as reasons for leaving employment, number and types of credit cards and balances outstanding, or references listed on an application.

> Your ability to handle credit shows in your decisions.

If a credit applicant meets all six of the above qualifications, he or she is considered worthy of credit. The applicant has shown a willingness and ability to pay bills in an acceptable and responsible manner.

CREDIT RECORDS AND CREDITWORTHINESS

Your credit record will reveal to a potential creditor whether you have the character, capacity, capital, conditions, collateral, and common sense necessary to gain access to additional credit. Information in your file concerning your income, payment record, employment record, and various personal factors will affect the potential creditor's decision.

Income.   On an application for credit, you will be asked how much your gross or net pay is each pay period. Part-time employees who earn only a few hundred dollars a month generally will not qualify for credit without a cosigner. Unless you can show that your expenses are so low that you have enough money left over to pay extra bills adequately, part-time jobs are not enough. Many credit card companies, such as American Express and VISA, require an annual income of $12,000 to $15,000 or more before they will grant credit to an applicant. Income other than regular pay, such as interest income, child support or alimony, spouse's income, or dividend income, may be listed. It is wise not to apply for credit until you are earning enough income or have enough personal wealth to afford the payments.

> Part-time workers may not qualify for credit.

Payment Record.   Your payment record is a list of your previous credit accounts and how you paid off those debts. Based on your payment record, the credit bureau will assign you a credit rating (credit ratings will be discussed later in this chapter). If you have paid your bills on time, your credit rating will be favorable. Consequently, potential creditors will be more likely to grant you additional credit, based on the character, capacity, and common sense you have exhibited through your responsibility in paying your bills.

> Paying your bills responsibly will result in more credit.

Employment Record.   Many creditors require a credit applicant to have worked steadily at one job for at least six months or longer before they will extend credit. If your work history shows that you switch jobs several times a year, you will not be considered a good risk. Creditors will assume that at some future time you may be unemployed and unable to make your credit payments. You are considered stable in your employment if you have worked for a number of years for one company, or in one particular job. The longer you work consistently, the better your stability rating.

Personal Factors.   Personal factors that are often considered by creditors include such things as occupation, geographic area, type of residence (renting or owning), age or age group, bank affiliations (types of accounts), and purpose for the credit (a good reason).

DENIAL OF CREDIT

There are many legitimate reasons for which an applicant may be denied credit. Some reasons used for denying credit, however, are considered discriminatory. **Discrimination** is the act of making a difference in treatment or favor on a basis other than individual merit. The Equal Credit Opportunity Act of 1975 was designed to prevent such discrimination in judgments of creditworthiness. The act provides that:

1. Credit may not be denied solely because you are a woman, single, married, divorced, separated, or widowed.
2. Credit may not be denied specifically because of religion, national origin, race, color, or age (except as age may affect your ability to perform, or your ability to enter into contracts; i.e., minors cannot be held liable for their contracts because they are not considered competent parties).
3. Credit may not be denied because you receive public assistance (welfare), unemployment, social security, or retirement benefits.
4. Credit applications may be oral or written. However, a creditor is prohibited from asking certain questions either orally or in writing.
5. A creditor may not discourage you, in writing or orally, from applying for credit for any reason prohibited by the act (such as being divorced).

In addition to these prohibitions, the act states that creditors must notify you of any action taken on your credit application within 30 days of submittal. If you are denied credit, the denial must be in writing and must list a specific reason for the denial. After a denial of credit, the creditor must keep for 25 months all information used to determine the denial and any written complaint from you regarding the denial. You have the right to appeal, and the creditor must give you the name and address of the state or federal agency that enforces laws for his or her type of business (there are numerous agencies).

You can appeal if credit is denied.

It is lawful and proper for creditors, in determining your creditworthiness, to ask you for the following personal information: name; age (provided it is not used as the basis for denying credit); source and amount of income; number of dependents, their ages, and other obligations to them; obligations to pay alimony, child support, or other such payments; permanent residence and immigration status; a list of assets; place and length of employment; history of employment; outstanding debts and accounts; telephone number (or whether you have a telephone); whether you rent or own your home; length of residence at present address; residence history; and savings and checking accounts in your name. A creditor may ask you about marital status only if you are making a joint application or if your spouse will be an authorized user. If you reside in a community property state, where income and debts incurred during a marriage are shared equally by both parties, marital status is important. (Community property states are Arizona, California, Idaho, Louisiana, Nevada, New Mexico, Texas, and Washington.) In any case, a creditor may ask only whether you are married, unmarried, or separated.

Community property states have different credit laws.

The Equal Credit Opportunity Act is a federal law. Many states also have similar laws; these laws vary widely from state to state and are changing rapidly. Many state laws are stricter than federal laws.

CREDIT RATINGS

◆◆◆◆◆◆◆◆

Many different systems are used nationwide in rating consumers' creditworthiness. In a **point system**, you are given points for employment, amount of income, length of residence, type of residence, etc. If your points total a certain number, you are given credit. But if you don't have enough points, then your personal factors don't total enough to warrant the risk of extending credit to you.

A point system may be used to determine creditworthiness.

A rating system, which is fairly well accepted by many creditors, rates consumers according to how well they pay back money borrowed or pay off amounts charged. Consumers may earn ratings such as excellent, good, fair, or poor.

To earn an **excellent credit rating**, sometimes called an A *rating*, a customer must pay bills before the due date. If a payment is due on the fifth of the month, it must be received *before* the fifth. An excellent rating also means that the customer is well established (has used credit successfully for many years), has not missed any payments, and has made larger payments than the minimum amount required (paying off debts early).

To earn a **good credit rating**, which is designated a *B rating*, a customer must pay bills on the due date or within a five-day grace period. That is, if the payment is due on the first of the month, it must be received by the fifth but no later than the tenth of the month. (When a bill is paid within 10 days of its due date, this is considered an automatic grace period.) A good customer pays around the due date, but never outside the grace period, and does not miss any payments.

It is important to pay your bills on time.

A **fair credit rating** is earned by a customer who usually pays all bills within the grace period, but occasionally takes longer. Late charges are sometimes necessary, but normally no reminder is needed. This person is often described as slow in paying, but fairly dependable.

A person with a **poor credit rating** is usually denied credit because payments are not regular — months are often missed in making payments, and frequent reminders must be sent. In many cases, this person has failed entirely to pay back a debt, has filed bankruptcy, or has otherwise shown that he or she is not a good credit risk.

In establishing a rating for a consumer, many credit bureaus ask their subscribers to rate their own customers. Based on other information gathered, such as total credit outstanding, job stability, and other personal factors, a composite rating is determined. Some credit bureaus merely supply credit files (names of customers, account balances, and payment records) to their subscribers and allow the subscribers to make their own rating decisions. Because different credit bureaus use different systems of compiling information and ratings, you should check in your local area to be familiar with the system used for your credit file.

Ratings are often determined by creditors.

CREITT REPORTS

◆◆◆◆◆◆◆◆

A **credit report** is a written report issued by a credit bureau. This report contains relevant information about a person's creditworthiness. A separate file is kept for each person, although spouses are listed on each report. Reports are usually in the form of a computer printout, called an *automated credit file*. Each report is divided into sections such as Identification, Summary of Information, Public Records and Other Information, Inquiries, and Trade.

Credit reports contain several types of information.

IDENTIFICATION

The *Identification* section is the first part of the report, and it identifies the subject. Included is such information as full name of consumer, spouse's

Illustration 12-1
A credit report summarizes a person's creditworthiness.

name, how long the file has been active, last file activity date, present address, previous addresses, any nicknames, marital status, number of dependents, date of birth, social security number, and social security number of spouse.

Following the personal information is employment information, which includes dates and types of employment; salary; spouse's employment, dates, and salary; and other household income sources.

SUMMARY OF INFORMATION

The *Summary of Information* section may show total (composite) credit rating points, if a point system is used; newest and oldest reporting dates; and whether public records or foreign (out-of-area) information is included. This section may also show the number of active accounts the consumer has and the credit ranges of those accounts, plus any statements added to the file by the consumer.

Active credit accounts are part of your record.

PUBLIC RECORDS AND OTHER INFORMATION

The *Public Records and Other Information* section contains information such as filing for bankruptcy — court and case number, liabilities, assets, exemptions; and how filed (individual, joint, or business). Also in this section is information about loan repayment or default and balance owing. Any other court proceedings against the consumer with regard to debt payment are reported in this section (including such things as alimony and child support).

INQUIRIES

The *Inquiries* section shows the number of inquiries made by subscribers to the credit bureau within the last six months. The inquiries are listed by name, number, and date of inquiry.

TRADE

The *Trade* section shows the consumer's present credit status. Companies reporting credit information and the dates of their reports are listed. Dates accounts were opened, credit limits, amounts of monthly payments, number of years or months paying or left to pay, balances owing, and any amounts past due are listed here. Account types (joint or individual) and account numbers, number of months the accounts were late, and previous high balances are also shown. Any out-of-area (foreign) information would be reported in this section, along with the reporting bureau, in-file date, and date given to local bureau.

Types of accounts are listed and rated.

All information included on the credit report is written in abbreviated form. A listing of key words and abbreviations is necessary for understanding information included on the report. Files are updated continuously and information stays in the file for seven years. In bankruptcy cases, information stays in the file for ten years.

Certain uses of credit reports are lawful.

Credit reports legally may be requested for investigations of credit applications, employment applications, and insurance matters. Anyone making unauthorized use of a credit report is liable for a $5,000 fine and/or one year in jail. You may see your own credit report, in person, for a small fee usually under $20.

CREDIT LAWS
◆◆◆◆◆◆◆◆

A number of credit laws have been enacted for consumer protection purposes and to provide assistance to consumers using credit. Several of these laws are summarized in the following paragraphs.

FAIR CREDIT REPORTING ACT

If you are denied credit based on a credit bureau report, inaccurate information in your file may be the cause of the denial. Under the Fair Credit Reporting Act, you have a right to know what is in your file and who has seen your file. A listing of requests made for your file for credit purposes in the last six months, and for employment purposes in the last two years, must be available to you. You may see your credit file at no charge within 30 days of a credit denial. A small fee may be charged in the event you want to see your file at any other time for any reason. You have the right to have inaccurate information investigated, corrected, and deleted from your file and have a new report furnished to creditors. Or, if the information is essentially correct, you can write your own statement giving your side of the story. Your statement will be added to the file.

> You can see your file for a small fee.

FAIR CREDIT BILLING ACT

Under the Fair Credit Billing Act, creditors must resolve billing errors within a specified period of time. A *statement* is an itemized bill showing charges, credits, and payments posted to your account during a billing period. Suppose your monthly statement shows purchases you did not make, or that you were charged for items you returned. Perhaps you are billed for merchandise you ordered but have not received. Creditors are required to have a written policy for correction of such errors. Figure 12-1 is an error policy.

> Write immediately when you discover an error.

If you believe there is an error on your bill, you should act immediately. Do not write on the bill that has been sent to you. On a separate piece of paper, write a letter explaining what you believe the problem to be. Write clearly and give a complete explanation of why you believe there is an error. Be specific about the amount in dispute, when you noticed the error, and any details relevant to the disputed amount. For example, you might say:

> I have just received my December bill. I noticed today that there is a charge dated November 24 for Wyatt's Department Store in Calooga, Wisconsin, in the amount of $42. I have never shopped at Wyatt's, and I have never been to Calooga, Wisconsin. I have not lost my credit card, nor have I authorized anyone else to use it. Therefore, I would appreciate your looking into this matter at your earliest convenience.

Your complaint must be in writing and mailed within 60 days after you receive the statement. The error or amount disputed must be dealt with by the company in a reasonable manner and within a reasonable period of time. The creditor must acknowledge your complaint within 30 days.

Within 90 days after receipt of your letter, the creditor must either correct the error or show why the bill is correct. Customers are still liable for amounts not disputed while the error dispute is being settled.

Figure 12-1 is an example of one company's written policy for handling billing errors.

You are responsible for amounts not in dispute.

Figure 12-1
Error Policy

IN CASE OF ERRORS OR INQUIRIES ABOUT YOUR BILL:

The Fair Credit Billing Act requires prompt resolution of errors. To preserve your rights, follow these steps:

1. Do not write on the bill. On a separate piece of paper write a description as shown below. A telephone call will not preserve your rights.
    a. Your name and account number.
    b. Description of the error and your explanation of why you believe there is an error. Send copies of any receipts or supporting evidence you may have; do not send originals.
    c. The dollar amount of the suspected error.
    d. Other information that might be helpful in resolving the disputed amount.
2. Mail your letter as soon as possible. It must reach us within 60 days after you receive your bill.
3. We will acknowledge your letter within 30 days. Within 90 days of receiving your letter, we will correct the error or explain why we believe the bill is correct.
4. You will receive no collection letters or collection action regarding the amount in dispute; nor will it be reported to any credit bureau or collection agency.
5. You are still responsible for all other items on the bill and for the balance less the disputed amount.
6. You will not be charged a finance charge against the disputed amount, unless it is determined that there is not an error in the bill. In this event, you will be given the normal 25 days to pay your bill from the date the bill is determined to be correct.

EQUAL CREDIT OPPORTUNITY ACT

Discrimination on the basis of sex or marital status in granting or denying credit is prohibited under the Equal Credit Opportunity Act (see also pages 226-227). According to the U.S. Department of Labor, Bureau of Labor Statistics:

Illustration 12-2
If you believe there is an error in your bill, report it at once.

More women are in the labor force.

1. Women make up over 44 percent of the labor force.
2. Sixty percent of all women between ages 18 and 64 are in the labor force.
3. Thirty-two percent of mothers with children under three are working.
4. Forty percent of all working women are single, divorced, or separated and qualify for head-of-household status.
5. The employment life expectancy of a single woman is 45 years — two years longer than a man's.
6. More single young women between the ages of 18 and 24 are entering the labor force than ever before, pursuing careers that will be continued regardless of marriage and childbearing.

As a result of the Equal Credit Opportunity Act, new accounts must reflect the fact that both husband and wife are responsible for payment. In this way, both spouses establish their own credit histories. Existing accounts should be changed to assure that the wife, as well as the husband, is being given credit for the payment record.

FAIR DEBT COLLECTION PRACTICES ACT

The Fair Debt Collection Practices Act was designed to eliminate abusive collection practices by debt collectors. A **debt collector** is a person or company hired by a creditor to collect the balance due on an account. The

Debt collectors' actions are limited.

fee charged by the debt collector is often half of the amount collected. The use of threats, obscenities, and false and misleading statements to intimidate the consumer into paying when there is a legitimate reason for nonpayment, such as an error, is prohibited. Time and frequency of collection practices, such as telephone calls and contacts at place of employment, are restricted. Debt collectors are required to verify the accuracy of a bill and give the consumer the opportunity to clarify and dispute the bill.

CONSUMER CREDIT PROTECTION ACT

You must be informed of credit charges.

The Consumer Credit Protection Act of 1968, known as the Truth in Lending Act, requires that consumers be fully informed about the cost of a credit purchase before an agreement is signed. Regulation Z of this act provides that the creditor (lender) must disclose all of these facts, in writing, to a debtor (borrower):

1. Cash price
2. Down payment and/or trade-in price
3. Amount financed
4. Insurance costs, filing costs, and other miscellaneous added costs of any kind
5. Finance charge
6. Annual percentage rate of the finance charge
7. Deferred payment price
8. Amount(s) and date(s) of payment
9. Description of security interest (item being purchased)
10. Method of computing unearned finance charge (in case of early payoff)
11. Any other information that may be applicable or necessary

In addition, Regulation Z requires a grace period of three business days in which the purchaser can change his or her mind about a purchase. The Truth in Lending Act also limits your liability to $50 after your credit card is reported lost or stolen. There is no liability at all if the card is reported lost prior to its fraudulent use.

VOCABULARY

Directions: Can you find the definition for each of the following terms used in Chapter 12?

credit history   discrimination
credit file   point system
credit bureau   excellent credit rating
subscribers   good credit rating
character   fair credit rating
capacity   poor credit rating
conditions   credit report
common sense   debt collector

1. Members of a credit bureau who pay fees or dues to the bureau in exchange for credit information collected and compiled into reports.
2. A person or company who is hired by a creditor to collect the balance due on an account that has not been paid by a customer.
3. A summary of a person's credit history that is kept at a credit bureau and from which a credit report is made.
4. A rating based on payment of bills on the due date or within a few days (but never outside the grace period).
5. A business that accumulates, stores, and distributes credit information to members.
6. A rating given a person who pays during the grace period, but occasionally takes longer, incurring some late charges.
7. A type of rating used by credit bureaus in determining a person's general creditworthiness.
8. A responsible attitude toward paying bills and meeting obligations on time.
9. Existing debts, stability of employment, and personal factors which determine a person's ability to meet financial obligations.
10. A written statement about a person's creditworthiness, issued by a credit bureau, which summarizes credit history, present indebtedness, public records, and other information available.
11. Ability to repay a loan or make payments out of present income.
12. Past credit performance in paying debts, amount of credit outstanding, and creditworthiness based on facts of previous credit experience.
13. A rating earned when bills are paid before due dates and extra effort is shown in paying debts.
14. A person's ability to make wise decisions.
15. A rating likely to harm chances for further credit because it shows that past payments were irregular and that frequent problems arose in the credit accounts.
16. The act of making a difference in treatment or favor on a basis other than individual merit.

ITEMS FOR DISCUSSION

1. What does a credit bureau do to earn money? Who pays for its services?
2. What is the advantage for businesses of becoming members (subscribers) of credit bureaus?
3. What types of public records become a part of your credit record?
4. Why is it important to pay your bills when they are due, rather than a few days late?
5. Why do creditors care about how long you have worked at your present job and about how many jobs you have had?
6. List personal factors that are often considered by creditors.
7. What are the Six Cs of Credit?
8. What types of discrimination are unlawful when considering personal factors in granting or denying credit?
9. What types of personal information can lawfully be asked of credit applicants?
10. What is the name of the federal law enacted in 1975 to protect consumers from unlawful discrimination in credit?
11. How long are bankruptcy records kept in a credit file? How long are other records kept on file?
12. What is the possible penalty for unauthorized use of a credit report?
13. Do you have a right to see your own credit file? Explain.
14. What should you do if you are denied credit based on your credit file? What can you do if information in your credit file is basically correct, but damaging to you as is?
15. What is the purpose of the Fair Credit Reporting Act?
16. What should you do if there is an error on your statement from a creditor?
17. What is the purpose of the Truth in Lending Act?

APPLICATIONS

1. Go to a local credit bureau and see what type of system is being used for locating, storing, and using credit information. Write a one-page report describing the process. Be sure to include the credit rating system used and explain how customers are rated and by whom (the creditor or the credit bureau). Before visiting the credit bureau, prepare a list of questions to ask and call first to make an appointment.
2. You have filled out an application for credit at a local department store. The store has notified you that they cannot give you credit

because you have a poor credit rating. What are your rights, and what are some things you should do? You really have no bad payment records, and you have paid previous debts as agreed. Suppose there is an error; what responsibilities to you does the credit bureau have?

3. What types of personal information are likely to appear in the identification section of a credit report? Where would a credit bureau get this information?

4. Describe what you must do if you believe a statement you receive from a creditor contains an error. Describe the process for error correction, including your responsibilities and time limits and the responsibilities and time limits of your creditor.

5. What kinds of credit do you think you will be using in five years? How will you establish a good credit rating?

CASE PROBLEMS AND ACTIVITIES

1. Obtain a credit application from a local merchant or national credit card company. On a separate piece of paper, list each question on the form in a column on the left. To the right of the column of questions, make another column. Indicate beside each question whether it is a(n) (a) personal question, (b) payment record question, (c) employment stability question, or (d) income question.

2. You have just received your monthly VISA bill. There is a charge on your bill of $42, but you have a receipt showing the amount should have been $24. The purchase was made at a local clothing store (you supply the name and address) one month ago. Write a letter to the bank that issued the VISA (choose a local bank) and explain the error.

3. Obtain a written error policy supplied by a local or national credit card company or other creditor. Compare it to Figure 12-1 and state how it is different (if at all) or how it is similar.

Chapter 13

COST OF CREDIT

◆◆◆◆◆◆◆◆◆◆◆◆◆◆◆◆◆◆◆◆◆◆◆◆◆◆

OBJECTIVES

1. Describe the responsibilities accompanying credit use.
2. Have a working knowledge of the terminology of loans and credit costs, and understand why credit costs money.
3. Understand and compute simple interest.
4. Compare methods of computing finance charges.
5. Describe how credit costs can be reduced and avoided.

RESPONSIBILITIES OF CONSUMER CREDIT

◆◆◆◆◆◆◆◆

Credit must be used wisely and carefully. Failure to do so can result in having credit limited, or in some cases, withdrawn. For this reason, credit users must understand their responsibilities to their creditors and to themselves, and creditors must understand their responsibilities to credit users.

USERS' RESPONSIBILITIES TO CREDITORS

All credit users have the responsibility to limit spending to amounts that can be repaid according to the terms of their credit agreements. By signing a credit agreement, the consumer agrees to make all payments promptly, on or before the due date.

In addition, the credit user has a responsibility to read and understand the terms of all agreements signed, including finance charges, what to do in case of error, how to return items, and any other provisions of the agreement. The consumer must contact the creditor or merchant immediately when there is a problem with a bill or merchandise is discovered to be defective. In an emergency situation, when a payment cannot be made, the consumer must contact the creditor to make arrangements for payment at a later date.

You make many agreements to use credit.

USERS' RESPONSIBILITIES TO SELF

Credit users' most important responsibility is to themselves: they are responsible for using credit wisely. This responsibility includes checking out businesses and companies before making credit purchases. Better Business Bureaus and Chambers of Commerce have information about businesses and complaints that have been filed against them.

Be responsible when using credit.

Another important aspect of the credit user's responsibility is to do comparative shopping. A wise buyer does not make a purchase the first time an item is inspected, nor does the buyer limit his or her shopping to one store because that store offers credit. Before making a major purchase, the wise buyer comparison shops and thinks about it for at least 24 hours.

To use credit privileges wisely, the consumer should be familiar with billing cycles, annual percentage rates, and any added charges related to each credit account. Credit users should understand state and local laws regarding the use of credit. Finally, the credit user must have the right attitude about borrowing and using credit. This means entering into each transaction in good faith and with full expectation of meeting the obligations and upholding a good credit reputation.

Enter into transactions in good faith.

CREDITORS' RESPONSIBILITIES TO CREDIT USERS

Creditors, including banks, retail stores, finance companies, credit unions, and private individuals, also have responsibilities when extending credit to individuals and businesses. Some of these responsibilities include:

1. Assisting the consumer in making wise purchases by clearly representing goods and services, with all their advantages and disadvantages.
2. Informing customers about all rules, regulations, charges, fees, and interest rates.
3. Cooperating with established credit reporting agencies, making credit records available to the consumer, and promptly discussing and clearing mistakes in records when they occur.
4. Establishing and carrying out sound lending and credit extension policies that do not overburden or deceive customers. (Setting reasonable guidelines and standards for credit helps to prevent more credit from being extended to customers who cannot afford it.)
5. Establishing and maintaining fair and reasonable credit charges and methods of contacting customers who fail to meet their obligations, assisting whenever possible with payment schedules and other means for solving credit problems.

Creditors have well-designed credit policies.

JOINT RESPONSIBILITIES — CREDIT CARD FRAUD

Both creditors and credit users have a responsibility to prevent credit card fraud. The most common type of fraud is the illegal use of a lost or stolen card. While the credit card holder's liability is limited to $50, the merchant is not protected from losses. Consequently, merchandise prices must be raised to cover such losses.

It is your responsibility to protect your credit cards from loss. Carry only the cards you need. Keep a list of credit and charge cards and their numbers in a safe place. Notify issuers immediately when a loss occurs. Keep a copy of all sales receipts. Put your cards in your wallet immediately after completing a credit purchase. Sign newly issued cards immediately and completely destroy (cut) expired cards.

Protect your credit cards from loss.

Use your credit or charge cards carefully. Giving credit card numbers over the telephone or sending them through the mail increases the risk of fraudulent use. Know the creditor before you purchase with a credit card.

Merchants should check credit cards against lists of lost or stolen cards, run cards through their authorization machine for large purchases, and ask for identification when accepting credit cards. New cards should be sent to customers by registered mail (not forwarded to a new address). When creditors promptly prosecute persons who use a lost or stolen credit card, fraudulent practices are discouraged.

Expect to have your credit card number checked.

Illustration 13-1
Merchants should
take steps to verify
credit card pur-
chases.

CREDIT CAN BE EXPENSIVE
◆◆◆◆◆◆◆◆

To fully understand and appreciate the use of credit in your daily life, it is important to be aware of the total cost of credit. Total cost, annual percentage rate, monthly payments, and all information available should be clear before a decision is made to enter into a credit agreement.

VOCABULARY OF CREDIT COSTS

Before you borrow money or purchase goods or services for payment at a future date, you need to know the meaning of the terms that will appear most frequently in credit agreements. Understanding the meaning of these terms before entering into a credit agreement can help you avoid problems later.

Special credit terms are widely used.

1. **Add-on interest** — interest that is added to the principal; equal payments that include both principal and interest are made each month
2. **Annual percentage rate** — the true annual rate of interest
3. **Deferred payment price** — the total amount, including principal and interest, that will be paid under a credit agreement
4. **Discount interest** — interest that is subtracted from principal, but full principal is loaned (for instance, on a $1,000 note at 10% interest, you would receive $900 but pay back $1,000 — interest is deducted at the beginning)

5. **Full disclosure** — to reveal to a purchaser (borrower), in complete detail, every possible charge or cost involved in the granting of credit
6. **Interest** — the amount paid for the use of credit
7. **Principal** — the total amount that is financed or borrowed and on which interest is computed

███   WHY CREDIT COSTS SO MUCH   ███

How much you will pay for the use of credit is determined by several factors. When each factor is considered carefully, the best possible credit agreement can be reached. These important factors include the following:

The cost of credit varies with the conditions.

1. Source of credit
2. Total amount of money borrowed
3. Length of time for which money is borrowed
4. Ability of the borrower to repay the loan
5. Type of credit selected
6. Collateral or security offered
7. Costs other than finance charges (such as delivery charges)
8. Method used to compute interest
9. Current rate of interest
10. Amount of money the lender has available to loan, and business and economic conditions that affect the lender's willingness to loan money

As stated in Chapter 11, the source of credit is important; some financial institutions and lenders are able to offer lower rates of interest and better credit plans than others. The more money you borrow, and the longer you take to pay it back, the more interest you will pay. Your ability to repay the loan also affects the total cost of the loan. The greater your ability to repay and, consequently, the less risk to the lender, the better the rate of interest you will be charged. The type of credit selected — whether a charge account, a bank loan, or a bank credit card — will vary according to the amount and rate of interest and repayment plans available. (Some require that you pay 2 percent of the balance each month; others require 25 percent — for example, 2 percent of a $1000 balance is $20 per month, while 25 percent is $250.) The more secure your collateral, the lower the rate of interest you will have to pay. Real estate and real property are often considered the most solid collateral; personal property, such as automobiles, and income are often considered less reliable. Additional costs that may be involved with credit include service or delivery fees, title or license fees, filing fees for security documents such as mortgages, liens, appraisal,

Consider how long you need to pay off a debt.

Collateral will help you get a better interest rate.

inspection, or credit check fees, and so on. Total cost, including principal, interest, and any other expenses involved in the purchase, is known as the *deferred payment price.*

To get an accurate picture of the total cost of credit, add up all the costs. Then subtract the original purchase price (or cash price) of the item. The difference is the dollar cost of credit.

$$\begin{array}{ll} \text{TOTAL PRICE} & \text{(including all finance charges)} \\ -\ \text{CASH PRICE} & \text{(what you would pay if you paid} \\ \hline \text{COST OF CREDIT} & \text{in full, in cash, at the time of purchase)} \end{array}$$

The current rate of interest is often affected by the **prime rate**, which is the rate of interest lenders offer to their best commercial (business) customers. Private individuals pay more than prime rate because the risk is greater to the lender.

The **discount rate** is the rate of interest that banks are charged to borrow money from the Federal Reserve System. The prime rate is usually at least three percentage points above the discount rate, a difference that allows banks to make a reasonable profit on loans. Therefore, when the discount rate is 8 percent, the prime rate is about 11 percent, and consumers can expect to pay about 14 percent for consumer loans.

When business conditions and interest rates call for tight lending policies, consumer loans become more expensive and difficult to obtain.

Individual loans are riskier than business loans.

COMPUTING THE COST OF CREDIT
◆◆◆◆◆◆◆◆

Easy computations can be made to determine the cost of credit, using the formula for simple interest, or the formula for calculating the total installment interest. The cost of a regular charge account can be calculated using the previous balance method, the adjusted balance method, or the average daily balance method.

There are several methods for computing the cost of credit.

SIMPLE INTEREST

Simple interest is computed on the principal only. The result is the total amount to be paid to the lender, usually in equal monthly payments for a set length of time. The formula for computing simple interest is:

$$\text{Interest (I)} = \text{Principal (P)} \times \text{Rate (R)} \times \text{Time (T)}$$

Principal.   The amount borrowed, or original amount of debt, is called the *principal.* When you ask for a loan, the principal is the amount loaned to you, before interest is added (add-on interest) or subtracted (discount interest). For example, if you borrow $5,000 to buy a car, that $5,000 is the principal, or amount of the loan.

Rate.   The interest **rate** is expressed as a percentage. The higher the rate, the less desirable the loan for the consumer.

Time.   The length of **time** the borrower will take to repay a loan is expressed as a fraction of a year — 12 months, 52 weeks, or 360 days (in most business transactions, the standard practice is to use 360 as the number of days in a year for computing simple interest). For example, if a loan is taken for six months, the time is expressed as ½. If money is borrowed for three months, the time would be expressed as ¼. When a loan is for a certain number of days, such as 90, time would be expressed as 90/360, or ¼.

A simple interest problem is shown in Figure 13-1. In this problem, a person has borrowed $500 and will pay interest at the rate of 12 percent a year. The loan will be paid back in four months.

Figure 13-1
Simple Interest

$$I = P \times R \times T$$

I = ?
P = $500
R = 12%
T = 4 months

To multiply by a percent, first change it to a decimal: drop the percent sign, then move the decimal point two places to the left.

$$
\begin{aligned}
I &= 500 \times .12 \times 4/12 \\
&= 500 \times .12 \times 1/3 \\
&= 60 \ \times .3333 \\
&= \$20
\end{aligned}
$$

(Four months is 4/12 or 1/3 of a year.)

The simple interest formula can also be used to find principal, rate, or time when any one of these factors is unknown. For example, in Figure 13-2, the rate of interest is 18 percent, and the loan was repaid in 18 months. What was the principal?

Figure 13-2
Simple Interest
(Principal)

$$I = P \times R \times T$$

I = $26
P = ?
R = 18%
T = 18 months

$$
\begin{aligned}
26 &= P \times .18 \times 18/12 \\
&= P \times .18 \times 3/2 \ (1.50) \\
&= P \times .27
\end{aligned}
$$

$$
\begin{aligned}
P &= 26 \div .27 \\
&= \$96.30
\end{aligned}
$$

(or change the formula to read:

$$P = \frac{I}{R \times T}$$

$$= \frac{\$26}{.18 \times 1.50}$$

$$= \frac{\$26}{.27}$$

$$= \$96.30)$$

To find the missing rate, the formula may be used again. See Figure 13-3 for an illustration.

Figure 13-3
Simple Interest
(Rate)

$$I = P \times R \times T \qquad \text{(or change the formula to read:}$$

$$I = \$18$$
$$P = \$300$$
$$R = ?$$
$$T = 240 \text{ days}$$

$$R = \frac{I}{P \times T}$$

$$18 = 300 \times R \times 240/360$$
$$= 300 \times 2/3 \times R$$
$$= 200 \times R$$

$$= \frac{18}{300 \times 2/3}$$

$$= \frac{18}{200}$$

$$R = 18 \div 200$$
$$= .09 \text{ or } 9\%$$

$$= .09 \text{ or } 9\%)$$

As shown in Figures 13-2 and 13-3, you can either plug the numbers into the existing formula, or rearrange the formula. Either way, you can find the unknown amount by simple mathematics.

INSTALLMENT INTEREST

As you have just learned, simple interest is calculated on the basis of one year at a time. However, lenders may charge a monthly interest rate on unpaid balances. On installment loans, charge accounts, and credit card accounts, interest may be charged only on the amount that is unpaid at the end of each month. When you borrow money from a bank, the amount of interest is added to the principal amount. This total, or installment, price is also part of the deferred payment price.

Interest is often charged on the un-paid balance.

The down payment is often called a *deposit*, or amount given as security to ensure that other payments will be made. When you buy a car, the car you traded in is often considered the down payment because the older car is worth money. The down payment is part of the deferred payment price because it is part of the total amount needed to purchase the good or service desired. Many merchants require that a down payment be at least 10 percent or more of the purchase price.

The rate of interest charged on installment contracts is the *annual percentage rate* (APR). By law, installment contracts must reveal the finance charge, the amount financed, and the annual percentage rate. The formula for calculating the annual percentage rate is presented in the Appendix.

The annual percent-
age rate must be
revealed.

In Figure 13-4, the annual percentage rate is computed on an installment purchase in which a down payment was made. The total number of payments is multiplied by the amount of each payment to determine how much, in addition to the down payment, will be paid for the merchandise. Each payment includes principal and interest. The deferred payment price is the total of all the payments added to the amount of the down payment. When the cash price is subtracted from the deferred payment price, the difference is the amount of the finance charge. When the amount of the finance charge is divided by the cash price, the result is the annual percentage rate.

Figure 13-4
Annual Percentage
Rate

The Kramers are buying a new sofa. The cash price is $800. The installment terms are $100 down and the balance in 12 monthly payments of $66 each.

1.	Down payment..................	$100
	+ Payments (12 × 66)............	+ 792
	= Installment price................	$892
2.	− Cash price.........................	−$800
3.	= Finance charge..................	$ 92
4.	APR (divide finance charge by cash price: 92 ÷ 800 = APR).............	11.5%

INTEREST ON REGULAR CHARGE ACCOUNTS

The cost of using an open credit account varies with the method a merchant uses to compute the finance charge. Merchants use the method that will bring the highest amount of interest. Interest is usually calculated by computer and is based on the monthly billing cycle. Purchases made up to the closing date are included in the monthly bill. Finance charges are computed on the unpaid balance after the billing date. Merchants may calculate finance charges on revolving charge accounts using the previous balance method, the adjusted balance method, or the average daily balance method.

Merchants   choose
methods of comput-
ing interest that are
most   advantageous
to them.

Previous Balance Method.   When the **previous balance method** is used, the finance charge is added to the previous balance. Then the payment made during the last billing period is subtracted to determine the new balance in the account. Figure 13-5 shows how a $500 balance at 18 percent interest (1 ½ percent per month) would be computed using the previous balance method.

Figure 13-5
Previous Balance
Method

Beginning BALANCE	+	FINANCE CHARGE	=	Adjusted BALANCE	−	PAYMENT Amount	=	NEW BALANCE
$500.00		$ 7.50		$507.50		$50.00		$457.50
457.50		6.86		464.36		50.00		414.36
414.36		6.22		420.58		50.00		370.58
		$20.58						

To compute the finance charge, the balance is multiplied by .015 (18 percent divided by 12). The finance charge is then added to the balance before the payment is subtracted to determine the new account balance. **Adjusted Balance Method.** When the **adjusted balance method** is used, the monthly payment is subtracted from the balance due before the finance charge is computed. As you can see in Figure 13-6, using $500 at 18 percent with $50 payments, the finance charge is less than when the previous balance method is used.

Figure 13-6
Adjusted Balance
Method

BALANCE	−	PAYMENT	=	BALANCE	+	FINANCE CHARGE	=	NEW BALANCE
$500.00		$50.00		$450.00		$ 6.75		$456.75
456.75		50.00		406.75		6.10		412.85
412.85		50.00		362.85		5.44		368.29
						$18.29		

Average Daily Balance Method. Many large department stores and creditors use the **average daily balance method** of computing finance charges. The finance charge is based on the average outstanding balance during the period. This average daily balance is computed by adding together all daily balances and dividing by the number of days in the period (usually 25 or 30). Payments made during the billing cycle are used in figuring the average daily balance, as of the date received. Because payments made during the period reduce the average daily balance, the finance charge using this method is often less than when the previous balance method is used. The minimum finance charge is 50 cents to $1 if the account is not paid in full, regardless of the amount of the balance.

When an installment agreement or loan is paid off before it is actually due, the result is unearned interest. If you agree to an installment loan that will take two years to pay off, but you pay it off in less than two years, you will pay less total interest. Therefore, the sooner you pay off a loan, the more you save in interest charges. Various methods of calculation are used to determine how much interest is saved. Two methods, the Rule of 78 and the U.S. Rule, are presented in the Appendix.

Unearned interest means less interest paid.

AVOIDING UNNECESSARY CREDIT COSTS

◆◆◆◆◆◆◆◆

Credit can be very advantageous to the consumer when it is used wisely. Most credit costs can be avoided or minimized if the following guidelines are followed:

Unused credit can work against you.

1. Accept only the amount of credit that you need. Although having credit available when you need it may seem comforting, unused credit can count against you. **Unused credit** is the amount of credit above what you owe that you could charge, to a maximum amount (credit limit). For example, if the maximum credit limit on your VISA is $1,000 and you owe $200, your unused credit is $800. Other creditors may be reluctant to loan money to you because you could at any time charge the other $800, thereby reducing your ability to pay back another debt. Potential creditors, then, may view you as a bad risk because of your unused credit. Unused credit accounts are also temptations for you to use more credit than you need.

2. Keep credit spending steady when your income increases. Instead of spending or tying up that increase in income, put it into savings or invest it. This way you can avoid the trap of being totally dependent on your income. Other costs of living will rise also; therefore, that increase in pay should not be spent so readily. It is wiser to reduce existing debt or save the additional income for future use.

3. Keep credit cards to a minimum. Most credit counselors recommend carrying only two or three credit cards. The more credit cards you have, the more temptation you have to buy. A bank credit card is often good at many places, eliminating the need for having several individual accounts.

4. Pay cash for purchases under $25. If you make yourself pay cash for small purchases, you won't be surprised with a big bill at the end of

Illustration 13-2
Paying cash for
small purchases
guards against the
overuse of credit.

Pay for small purchases with cash.

the month. Paying cash will help you realize the importance of a purchase; consequently, you will buy less and only when you really need an item.

5. Understand the cost of credit. You should compute for yourself the total cost, payment, length of time you will make payments, total finance charges, and so on, for all credit purchases, if this information is not provided in writing. Study the figures carefully and consider how this commitment of income might affect your budget in the months to come.

6. Shop for loans. The type and source of your loan will make a big difference in cost. The costs from three different sources should be compared. Decisions to make major purchases should be planned carefully — never made on the spur of the moment. Don't sit and figure costs in a lender's office — go home, figure all costs, and consider the purchase carefully without the presence of third persons.

Major credit purchases should be planned carefully.

7. Use credit to beat inflation. With the help of credit, you can often purchase needed items on sale that you would not purchase if cash were your only payment option. In this way, you can avoid price increases and save dollars.

8. Let the money you save by using credit work for you. When you purchase on credit, rather than spending cash, you can put your cash into savings or investments that will earn interest or dividends. Many people find it very difficult to save any money at all. But by putting aside some money in this way, you not only provide funds for later use, but you also earn more money to help pay for the cost of the credit.

9. Time your credit purchases carefully. By purchasing after the closing date of your billing cycle, you can delay your payment for two months rather than one month. Your repayment time is usually 25 to 30 days. You can extend your time to repay to 60 days, interest free, if your timing is right. Know the closing dates and billing cycles for all your credit accounts and use them to your advantage.

10. Use service credit to the best advantage. Don't pay bills that will be covered by insurance. If your medical or dental insurance will pay for 80 percent or more of a claim, do not pay your share until the insurance company has been billed and has paid its portion. In this way you will have full use of your money and will not overpay a bill and have to wait for a refund. Hospitals, doctors, and others often take weeks or months to refund overpayments. Service credit, which is available to most consumers, should be used wisely.

11. Keep track of all interest paid on credit purchases. Interest paid may be partially deductible on your tax return; knowing how much you are paying helps you to avoid excessive amounts of interest.

Through credit, you can have use of your money longer.

VOCABULARY

Directions: Can you find the definition for each of the following terms used in Chapter 13?

add-on interest	simple interest
annual percentage rate	rate
deferred payment price	time
full disclosure	previous balance method
interest	adjusted balance method
principal	average daily balance method
prime rate	unused credit
discount rate	

1. The total amount borrowed, on which interest is charged.
2. The total amount, including principal, interest, and down payment, that will be paid for merchandise in an installment purchase agreement.
3. The amount of credit available, above what you owe, up to your maximum credit limit.
4. A short and easy method of computing interest on short-term loans that have no down payment.
5. To reveal to a borrower in complete detail every possible charge or cost involved in the granting of credit.
6. An installment plan whereby interest is added to principal, then equal payments of principal and interest are made monthly until

the balance is paid in full.

7. The true annual rate of interest.
8. The dollar cost of credit.
9. Stated as a percentage that represents interest.
10. Written as a fraction of a year and used to compute interest charged in payment of a loan.
11. A method of computing finance charges whereby the interest is first added to the amount due, then the amount of payment is subtracted to get the new balance.
12. A method of computing finance charges whereby the monthly payment is first subtracted from the balance, then the finance charge is computed and added to get the new balance.
13. A method of computing finance charges that is based on the average of balances during the month.
14. The rate of interest bank lenders offer to their best commercial (business) customers.
15. The rate of interest banks are charged to borrow money from the Federal Reserve System.

ITEMS FOR DISCUSSION

1. How is a loan with add-on interest different from a loan that has discount interest? Which is probably better, and why?
2. Describe how the cost of credit is determined.
3. List ten factors that affect the cost or rate of interest a customer will have to pay to get a loan.
4. What is the prime rate?
5. List ten things you can do to avoid unnecessary credit costs.
6. What is meant by "timing your purchases to your advantage"?
7. What is the formula for computing simple interest?
8. Why is the down payment added to the total amount of payments made to determine the deferred payment (installment) price?
9. What is included in the deferred payment price?
10. How can unused credit work against you when you are applying for a new loan?
11. What is meant by the word *time* used in computing simple interest?
12. What is your liability and responsibility if your credit card is lost or stolen?
13. What kinds of things can you do to protect yourself from losing your credit cards and having large purchases made with your credit cards?
14. What kinds of things can merchants do to protect themselves from losses due to fraudulent credit card use?

APPLICATIONS

1. Using the formula for simple interest (I = PRT), solve the following problems, rounding to the nearest penny.

   a. I = ?
      P = $500
      R = 18 percent
      T = 6 months

   b. I = ?
      P = $1,000
      R = 13.5 percent
      T = 8 months

   c. I = ?
      P = $108
      R = 21.6 percent
      T = 3 months

   d. I = ?
      P = $89.50
      R = 16 percent
      T = 9 months

2. The following simple interest problems have different elements missing. Either change the formula to find the missing element, or insert the given elements into the formula and solve as shown in this chapter.

   Round to the nearest penny. Use the formula I = PRT.

   a. I = $8
      P = ?
      R = 12 percent
      T = 60 days (60/360)

   b. I = $54
      P = ?
      R = 18 percent
      T = 18 months (18/12)

   c. I = $510
      P = $2,100
      R = ?
      T = 2 years (24/12)

   d. I = $36
      P = $108
      R = ?
      T = 18 months (18/12)

3. Using the procedure illustrated in Figure 13-4, determine the annual percentage rates for the following problems:

   a. The purchase price of an item requiring a down payment of $60, with the balance to be paid in 12 equal payments of $60 each. The cash price is $700.
   b. The purchase price of an item that has a down payment of $100 and 24 equal payments of $90. The cash price is $2,000.
   c. The cash price of an item is $200. The down payment is $20, and 10 equal payments of $22 each are to be made.
   d. The cash price of an item is $895. With $95 down, the balance is payable in 15 payments of $60 each.

4. The previous balance method of computing interest is determined by first calculating interest, then subtracting the monthly payment to

determine the new balance. Complete the following chart, using a calculator and rounding to the nearest penny. The interest rate is 12 percent. What is the total interest paid?

BALANCE	+	FINANCE CHARGE	=	BALANCE	−	PAYMENT	=	NEW BALANCE
$100		————		————		$20.00		————
————		————		————		20.00		————
————		————		————		20.00		————

Total Interest ————

5. With the adjusted balance method of computing interest, the monthly payment is subtracted before interest is calculated. The amount of interest is then added to obtain the new balance. Complete the following chart, using a calculator and rounding to the nearest penny. The interest rate is 18 percent. What is the total interest paid?

BALANCE	−	PAYMENT	=	BALANCE	+	FINANCE CHARGE	=	NEW BALANCE
$500		$50.00		————		————		————
————		50.00		————		————		————
————		50.00		————		————		————

Total Interest ————

CASE PROBLEMS AND ACTIVITIES

1. Your friend Marty is unable to determine whether he is getting a good deal on a loan of $100 for 6 months when he pays back $114. What is the simple interest rate he is paying? (Use I = PRT)
2. You are considering buying a piano. The cash price of the piano is $600. The company selling the piano is willing to sell it to you for $50 down and 12 equal payments of $50. What is the installment price? What is the amount of interest?
3. If you were to purchase a major appliance and pay for it this year, borrowing $800 at 18 percent for 8 months, how much total interest would you pay?
4. What is the annual percentage rate when you buy a car that would sell for $8,000 cash by trading in your used car for a down payment of $2,000 and paying the balance at $195 a month for 36 months?

Chapter 14

BANKRUPTCY

◆◆◆◆◆◆◆◆◆◆◆◆◆◆◆◆◆◆◆◆◆◆◆◆◆

OBJECTIVES

1. List and explain the different methods of solving credit problems.
2. Outline bankruptcy laws, including exempted items, types of income excluded, and bankruptcy options.
3. List the major causes of bankruptcy.
4. Describe the advantages and disadvantages of declaring bankruptcy.
5. Understand the bankruptcy petition form.

SOLVING CREDIT PROBLEMS

◆◆◆◆◆◆◆◆

One of the major disadvantages of credit is that it can lead to overspending. When credit is not budgeted wisely, credit problems can arise. In this chapter, some ways of dealing with credit-related problems are described.

Credit problems do not happen suddenly. They usually arise after months and years of poor planning, impulse buying, and careless budgeting. If a credit problem is detected early enough, the cure is simple and easy. However, it is best to plan to use your credit wisely from the beginning, so that credit does not become a major problem.

Credit problems don't happen suddenly.

Illustration 14-1
Credit problems
usually arise only
after long periods of
credit misuse.

THE 20/10 RULE

The 20/10 Rule ap-
plies to credit pur-
chases.

Credit counselors often suggest use of the **20/10 Rule** to people beginning to use credit: Never borrow more each year than 20 percent of your *yearly* take-home pay, and never agree to *monthly* payments that are more than 10 percent of your monthly take-home. The 20/10 Rule applies to credit purchases other than for housing; that is, it applies to charge account purchases. By keeping your take-home pay free from set or fixed payments, you have more control over your finances.

For example, suppose that you and your spouse have yearly take-home pay of $21,000 (monthly take-home pay of $1,750). Your credit borrowing should not exceed a total of $4,200 (20 percent of yearly take-home pay), and your monthly credit payments should not be more than $175. By following the 20/10 Rule, you avoid tying up future income with large credit-related debts. Thus, you maintain control of your finances. You can make reasonable house and car payments; pay insurance, utilities, and other necessary fixed expenses; and still have money left over for entertainment, clothing, and miscellaneous purchases.

NOT-FOR-PROFIT CREDIT COUNSELING

When you get into serious problems with credit, you can seek advice and counseling from one of many private or government-sponsored counseling services. Small fees are charged, usually according to your ability to pay. A counselor will help you set up a good budget and show you how to make your income do the most for you. The credit plan is voluntary; you are under no legal obligation to use or to continue to use the plan. You cannot get loans from a credit counseling service, but you can get good advice for finding a workable plan for your situation. You can learn about credit counselors by calling county or city offices and asking for consumer credit counseling services. Some churches and private foundations provide similar services. Private agencies and groups that assist in credit counseling are also listed in the Yellow Pages of your telephone book.

Fees are based on your ability to pay.

COMMERCIAL DEBT-ADJUSTMENT FIRMS

There are numerous companies operating for profit that charge a fee to help you get out of credit trouble. Services provided and fees charged vary widely, and any fee charged will increase the debt you owe. Often you will be asked to turn over your checkbook, paychecks, and bills to the debt-adjustment company. A credit advisor will contact your creditors to work out repayment plans and will make payments for you. Generally services include a five-step plan. The debt-adjustment advisor will

1. Contact creditors and arrange for payments that can be made from your earnings.
2. Take your paycheck and checkbook, then make debt payments and give you an allowance until all bills have been paid off and you can be trusted to take over again. This can take two years or more if you are in deep trouble.
3. Counsel you so that you understand how you got so far into debt and how to avoid doing so again in the future.
4. Work with you to create a workable budget that you can live with. Credit cards are taken away and given back slowly as the advisor becomes certain that you understand how to use them wisely.
5. Supervise your budget and help you make any needed changes or adjustments.

It may take two years to clear up a credit problem.

When you are desperate and cannot seem to control your purchases, you should seek professional credit counseling. You may not like the strictness or discipline involved, but the valuable training can help you avoid getting too deeply into debt again. Debt-adjustment companies, like credit counseling services, are listed in your Yellow Pages and in business directories.

Consult the Yellow Pages or business directories.

LEGAL RECOURSE

When credit problems arise that cannot be solved by your own actions or through assistance, the final step for relief is bankruptcy. When you are **bankrupt** you are unable to meet your bills. Bankruptcy is a legal process whereby you are declared legally *insolvent* — having insufficient income and assets to pay your debts (liabilities). Bankruptcy is processed through a federal court. All your assets, income, and property are controlled by the court. You are permitted some allowances, and the rest is divided among your creditors. The bankruptcy procedure allows you to start over by ridding you of most of your debts. In many cases, your creditors receive only a percentage of what you owe them. But as we shall see later in this chapter, there is much more to bankruptcy than meets the eye. A decision to declare bankruptcy is not an easy one, but one that involves the careful weighing of many considerations.

Creditors receive a proportional share.

THE BANKRUPTCY LAWS AND THEIR PURPOSE

◆◆◆◆◆◆◆◆

Bankruptcy laws have operated in this country for many years. Their purpose has been to rescue debtors from hopeless situations and allow them to start over again. Bankruptcy can be launched once total unsecured debts total $5,000 or more. Bankruptcy laws treat two general classes of debt: secured and unsecured. In *secured* debt, the debtor has pledged specific assets as collateral for payment. If the debt is not paid, the creditor can repossess the asset that has been pledged. For **unsecured debt**, no specific asset is pledged, but all of the debtor's resources are considered in a bankruptcy action. In recent years, bankruptcy laws have been revised to make it easier for individuals to declare bankruptcy. However, many pitfalls still remain.

There are two basic types of bankruptcy: voluntary and involuntary. **Involuntary bankruptcy** occurs when creditors file a petition with the court, asking the court to declare you bankrupt. The court makes a determination as to whether or not you should be so declared. If the court agrees with your creditors, it takes over your property and other assets and pays off your debts proportionally. Involuntary bankruptcy does not occur very often because most creditors prefer to be repaid in full over a period of time rather than settle only for a portion of your remaining assets.

The court takes over your property.

Voluntary bankruptcy, the most common kind, occurs when you file a petition with a federal court asking to be declared bankrupt. After notice of your pending bankruptcy is given in local newspapers and by letters to your creditors, creditors may file claims. The court collects your assets, sells your property as needed, and distributes the proceeds equitably among your creditors. A **proportional share** is a percentage based on total debt. For example, let us say that your total debt is $15,000 and your total assets are $5,000. You owe one creditor $1,500. The proportional share owed this creditor is 10 percent of your assets, or $500. The remainder of that debt is **discharged** — the balance of the debt is no longer owed after the bankruptcy. Be aware, however, that some debts, such as taxes, child support, and alimony, continue after bankruptcy.

Taxes and family obligations remain.

■ BANKRUPTCY REFORM ACT OF 1978 ■

The federal bankruptcy code was revised by Congress in 1978, and more liberal rules took effect in October, 1979. The new act was considered a sign of the times; anticipation of the recession and economic woes of the 1980s made the revision necessary. Many businesses and creditors complain that the bankruptcy code requires them to tighten credit because it is too easy for people to give up their debts rather than accept responsibility for them. On the other hand, bankruptcy still casts a black shadow over an individual's credit record. Further revisions of the bankruptcy laws are under consideration.

Bankruptcy casts a dark shadow on your credit record.

For businesses, **Chapter 11 bankruptcy** provides that existing management retains control of a business unless a trustee is appointed by the court. The main purpose of Chapter 11 bankruptcy is to reorganize the debt structure of a business and not to liquidate the company. A court can impose a reorganization plan over objections of creditors if it is deemed to be fair and in the best interests of those involved.

For individuals, there are two basic ways to file bankruptcy: Chapter 7 and Chapter 13.

■ CHAPTER 7 BANKRUPTCY ■

Commonly called a straight bankruptcy proceeding, **Chapter 7 bankruptcy** wipes out most, but not all, debts. Some debts must still be paid, including child support, alimony, income taxes and penalties, student loans, and court-ordered damages due to malicious (intentional) acts. Once declared bankrupt, an individual cannot file for straight bankruptcy again for six years.

To get debts discharged, debtors must give up all their property except for certain exempted items. An **exempted item** is an item of value or a

Exempted items allow a debtor to start over.

possession that the debtor is allowed to keep because it is considered necessary for survival. Federal laws allow the following items to be exempted:

1. $7,500 equity in a home
2. $1,200 interest in a motor vehicle
3. Items worth up to $200 each under the categories of household goods and furnishings, appliances, clothing and personal items, animals, crops, and musical instruments
4. $500 in jewelry
5. $750 in tools or books required for work
6. Proceeds from life insurance policies, unemployment insurance income, pension income, and veterans benefits

Eighteen states allow a choice.

Thirty-two states require a debtor to use a state exempted item schedule rather than a federal schedule. The remaining 18 states allow a choice of either federal or state exempted item schedules. Some state exempted item schedules are more generous than the federal list.

Bankruptcy causes tighter credit rules.

New legislation is periodically introduced to tighten up the code revisions of 1978. Many businesses and creditors are afraid of the liberal bankruptcy code and desire legislation that gives more rights to creditors while making bankruptcy less desirable for debtors. The only precaution creditors can take is careful screening of applicants and higher requirements of income, employment, and credit stability.

CHAPTER 13 BANKRUPTCY

An alternative proceeding that avoids much of the stigma of straight bankruptcy is **Chapter 13 bankruptcy**, which allows creditors to get some of their money back. Debtors keep all their property and work out a compulsory, court-enforced plan to repay a portion of the debts over a period of time, usually three years. Under Chapter 13, often referred to as the wage earner's plan, some debts are totally discharged, but family obligations still remain for child support and alimony.

Chapter 13 bankruptcy may seem more equitable and better for the debtor in terms of reestablishing credit. However, the blemish on the debtor's credit record caused by any form of bankruptcy is hard to overcome for a number of years.

LEGAL ADVICE

A person considering bankruptcy should seek good legal advice. In most states it is possible to file for bankruptcy without an attorney. But the law is complicated, and a good bankruptcy attorney can tell you which of your assets will be protected and which exempted items you can claim. The attorney can also assist you in deciding which bankruptcy plan will work best to help you solve your credit problems. Attorney's fees for handling bankruptcies can range from $150 to $1,500, depending on the case, but good legal advice can save you that much and more.

You need an attorney.

REAFFIRMATION OF DEBTS

Creditors may ask debtors to agree to pay their debts after bankruptcy is completed. This agreement is called **reaffirmation**. Reaffirmation requires a court hearing, and the debtor is given 30 days to change his or her mind about making a promise to repay. A creditor is prohibited from harassing the debtor to reaffirm after the court proceedings are over.

Reaffirmation requires a court hearing.

While there is little incentive for debtors to reaffirm debts, an honest and sincere person might want to choose one debt over another and try to pay back some of what he or she is not legally obligated to pay.

MAJOR CAUSES OF BANKRUPTCY

Bankruptcy is a last-resort solution to credit problems. The most common reasons for claiming bankruptcy are catastrophic injury or illness, business failure, emotional spending, and failure to budget and plan.

CATASTROPHIC INJURY OR ILLNESS

Medical care costs a great deal. Insurance policies have dollar limits for major illnesses. The single largest cause of bankruptcy is large medical bills beyond the amount insurance covers. For example, a person hospitalized for six months to a year could easily owe $100,000 a month for medical care, drugs, room charges, and other fees. If there is no insurance, that person's savings can be wiped out in the first month. Often, the only way to escape this type of debt is through bankruptcy.

A major illness can wipe out your savings.

BUSINESS FAILURE

Every year thousands of small businesses fail. People invest their life savings and more to start a business. Unfortunately, for a number of reasons, from

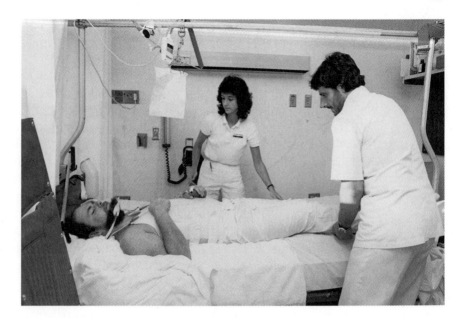

Illustration 14-2
The single largest
cause of bankruptcy
is large medical bills
beyond the amount
insurance covers.

ruinous economic conditions to poor financial planning, many small
businesses do not make it beyond the first year. Other small business owners
borrow more money and go further into debt in order to keep afloat until
times get better. Owning and operating a small business can be very risky.
Success depends on a great deal of luck — in addition to good financial
plans, knowledge of the product or service, favorable business location, and
good economic conditions.

**Small businesses are
very risky.**

EMOTIONAL SPENDING

Emotional rather than rational reasons for buying lead many consumers to
eventual bankruptcy. Purchases in excess of what can be afforded, income
increases eaten up by inflation and soaring expenditures, money spent to
impress others rather than for planned purchases — all result in
overextension of credit. **Overextension** occurs when purchases exceed what
can be handled comfortably with present income. Usually overextension is
temporary and not a serious problem. A job loss, a business failure, or some
other disaster, however, can put sudden and great pressure on an already
weak financial structure. Then, before the deficiency can be corrected, debt
rises beyond the debtor's capability to pay it off. In most cases there is very
little to show for the thousands of dollars spent unwisely — nothing that can
be sold to pay off debt. Extensive travel, long vacations, or extravagant
parties and entertainment are expensive pleasures that have no resale value.

**It is easy to slip
deeper into debt.**

FAILURE TO BUDGET AND PLAN

Most people who go bankrupt for none of the preceding reasons fall into another category: people who have no goals or plans. They neither have nor follow a budget. Many do not know how to set up or keep a budget and are not willing to ask for help or advice in solving their credit problems.

Bankruptcy is not limited to any class of people.

Bankruptcy is not a condition limited to poor people. Many classes of people find themselves in trouble with credit. Poor planning can occur at any income level in any financial circumstance. At whatever financial level a person may be, spending and charging must be kept in proportion to income. While preventing or preparing for a major illness may not be possible, most other causes of bankruptcy can be avoided by careful planning and forming of decisions based on good financial judgment, advice, and goals.

ADVANTAGES OF BANKRUPTCY
◆◆◆◆◆◆◆◆◆

For those who are beyond the point of no return, bankruptcy offers a solution to credit problems. While this solution is not without a price, bankruptcy does offer a number of advantages.

DEBTS ARE ERASED

Bankruptcy gives a fresh start.

Straight bankruptcy offers a fresh start. Overwhelming bills can be reduced or eliminated, and the debtor can start over. With good financial planning and counseling, future credit problems can be avoided, and the bankruptcy will have taught many valuable lessons.

EXEMPTED ITEMS ARE ALLOWED

While the majority of assets must be given up in order to erase debts under straight bankruptcy, certain amounts and types of properties are not taken. With these exempted items, a new start is possible. When a husband and wife file joint bankruptcy, the cushion for a new start becomes even softer because the dollar amounts for exempted items are doubled.

CERTAIN INCOMES ARE UNAFFECTED

Certain types of income are not included.

Bankruptcy will not affect certain types of income a debtor may have, such as social security; veterans benefits; unemployment compensation; alimony; child support; disability payments; and payments from pension, profit-sharing, and annuity plans. These sources of income need not be considered, even in a Chapter 13 bankruptcy, in which a compulsory payment plan is established.

THE COST IS SMALL

Attorneys' fees and court costs in bankruptcy are relatively small in comparison to the amount of financial relief provided. When total debts reach such a level that income cannot stretch to pay them off, the relief is considerable in comparison to the costs involved. On the first visit to an attorney's office, a debtor will be given total cost estimates and information about the options available in bankruptcy proceedings.

DISADVANTAGES OF BANKRUPTCY

Bankruptcy is a last resort.

While bankruptcy offers several advantages to the debtor, there is a price to be paid. Bankruptcy should be considered a last resort, and then only after a thorough investigation of the consequences of bankruptcy and of all the available alternatives. Some of the consequences of bankruptcy are discussed in the following paragraphs.

CREDIT IS DAMAGED

Despite the more liberal bankruptcy regulations, a bankruptcy judgment still casts a heavy cloud over an individual's credit record. The judgment cannot be wiped off credit records for ten years. Bankruptcy is a notice to creditors and others that, at one time, the debtor was not able to meet his or her responsibilities. Depending on the circumstances that caused the bankruptcy, mistrust in personal and business affairs may result and continue well beyond the ten years.

PROPERTY IS LOST

A bankrupt (person who becomes insolvent) does not necessarily get to keep exempt items unless they are owned free and clear. When something is owned **free and clear**, no debt of any kind is owed against it.

Consider this example. Assume that you own a house worth $40,000 that has a mortgage of $25,000 against it. Your equity is $15,000. While the bankruptcy code allows you to keep the first $7,500 of equity in your home, you may be required to sell the home. You will be allowed $7,500 and the other $7,500 must be used to pay off creditors.

If you own a car valued at $3,000 and you owe $1,800 against it, your equity is $1,200. Since this amount equals the allowance for a car, you will not have to sell the car. However, if you have a car valued at $8,000 with a loan of $5,000, your equity is $3,000. You are allowed only $1,200 equity, the legal limit. In this case you will probably have to sell the car and use all proceeds over $1,200 to help pay off your creditors.

SOME OBLIGATIONS REMAIN

Regardless of the type of bankruptcy selected, all debt is not erased. Certain obligations, such as child support, must be paid in full. Other debts also remain: income taxes and penalties, student loans, court-ordered damages in connection with intentional acts of mischief, and other debts at the discretion of the bankruptcy court.

SOME DEBTS CAN BE REAFFIRMED

If a lender can prove that there was any type of false representation on the bankrupt's part in connection with a debt, the debt will not be discharged. In other cases, creditors may ask debtors to reaffirm a debt — to promise to pay it back even though it was discharged. By reaffirming old debts, the bankrupt does not get the fresh clean start that is probably needed.

COSIGNERS MUST PAY

A cosigner can be held responsible for guarantee of a debt after the borrower has been declared bankrupt. A cosigner does not have to pay if the debtor has chosen a Chapter 13 bankruptcy, however, because creditors receive an equitable share of the debtor's assets and must accept this share as full payment.

BANKRUPTCY PETITIONS

◆◆◆◆◆◆◆◆

Forms for filing bankruptcy are complicated and lengthy. The first form that is filed in a bankruptcy proceeding is the bankruptcy petition. An example of a bankruptcy petition prepared and submitted by an attorney is shown in Figure 14-1. Numerous other forms requiring specific information and declarations are required to complete the bankruptcy procedure.

Figure 14-1
Bankruptcy Petition

IN THE FEDERAL BANKRUPTCY COURT FOR THE <u>Eastern</u> DISTRICT OF <u>Kentucky</u>

IN THE CASE OF _____)   DEBTOR'S PETITION FOR BANKRUPTCY
)
<u>Matthew Franklin</u> _____)   Chapter 7
)
_____ , Debtor,)
)
_____)   Case No. 89- <u>202</u> ____
)

Petitioner, herein called debtor, appears before the Court and alleges as follows:

1. Petitioner's address is <u>513 Main Street, Biggs, KY 43721-0132</u> , and the above court has jurisdiction over this matter.

2. Petitioner has resided in this federal district for the last 180 days, or six months, prior to the filing of this petition.

3. Petitioner is entitled to the benefits of the bankruptcy laws of the United States, and files this petition as a voluntary debtor, seeking relief under Chapter 7 of the United States Bankruptcy Code.

WHEREFORE, petitioner prays for relief according to the provisions of said bankruptcy Chapter 7, and files herewith all supplemental information necessary for the court to make said determination of voluntary bankruptcy.

Patricia Van Schaik
Attorney for Petitioner

<u>5101 Third Street</u>
Address of Attorney

<u>Cincinnati, OH 45201-6735</u>

ATTESTATION:

I, <u>Matthew Franklin</u> _____ , petitioner (debtor) named in the foregoing petition, do hereby certify that I have read the foregoing petition and its documents attached thereto, and they are true and correct.

Matthew Franklin
Petitioner

STATE OF <u>Kentucky</u> _____)
) ss.
County of <u>Pike</u> _____)

On <u>May 3</u> _____ 19 -- , the petitioner, <u>Matthew Franklin</u> _____ , did appear before me and acknowledge that s/he did sign the foregoing petition of his/~~her~~ own free will.

Geoffrey Combs
Notary Public for <u>Kentucky</u> _____ (state)

My Commission Expires: <u>March 14, 19--</u>

VOCABULARY

Directions: Can you find the definition for each of the following terms used in Chapter 14?

20/10 Rule
bankrupt
unsecured debt
involuntary bankruptcy
voluntary bankruptcy
proportional share
discharged

Chapter 11 bankruptcy
Chapter 7 bankruptcy
exempted item
Chapter 13 bankruptcy
reaffirmation
overextension
free and clear

1. Legally insolvent — not capable of paying bills.
2. A plan designed to prevent credit problems, which allows 20 percent of yearly take-home pay or 10 percent of monthly take-home pay to be used for paying off charge account debts.
3. A percentage of the bankrupt's total assets received by a creditor, based on how much is owed that creditor, in proportion to the bankrupt's total debts.
4. A type of bankruptcy in which creditors file a petition with the court asking the court to declare the debtor bankrupt.
5. A type of bankruptcy in which the debtor files a petition with the court asking to be declared bankrupt.
6. A value or possession in which the debtor is allowed to retain a certain equity because that item is considered necessary to the debtor's fresh start.
7. A type of bankruptcy proceeding known as straight bankruptcy.
8. A type of bankruptcy that is often called the wage earner's plan.
9. Agreement to pay back a debt to a creditor after the debtor has been declared bankrupt and the debt has been discharged.
10. The use of more credit than can be paid back comfortably with income.
11. A debt that has been excused by the court and, by judgment of bankruptcy, no longer has to be paid by the debtor.
12. A phrase that describes an item having no debt, loan, or other credit outstanding against it.
13. A debt for which no specific asset is pledged, but all of the debtor's resources are considered.
14. A type of bankruptcy for businesses that attempts to reorganize the debt structure of the business but not to liquidate the company.

ITEMS FOR DISCUSSION

1. List the four commonly used plans for solving and preventing credit problems.
2. Explain the 20/10 Rule.
3. Where can you find out about the not-for-profit credit counseling services in your area?
4. What is the purpose of bankruptcy?
5. What are the two types of bankruptcy (one is initiated by creditors, the other by debtors)?
6. Which types of family obligations are not discharged by bankruptcy?
7. List six exempted items under Chapter 7 bankruptcy. Are the exempted item amounts for these items doubled for married persons?
8. Once declared bankrupt, how long before you can again file straight bankruptcy? How long does a bankruptcy judgment remain on your credit records?
9. How does Chapter 13 bankruptcy differ from Chapter 7?
10. Why is it a good idea to seek advice from an attorney before filing for bankruptcy?
11. How long does a debtor have to change his or her mind about reaffirmation of a debt?
12. List the four most common reasons for claiming bankruptcy.
13. List four advantages and five disadvantages of filing bankruptcy.
14. Which types of income are not subject to bankruptcy?
15. Why do creditors object to liberal bankruptcy laws?
16. On the bankruptcy petition (Figure 14-1), identify the following:

    a. Who is the petitioner (debtor)?
    b. Is this a petition for straight bankruptcy or the wage earner's plan?
    c. What is the address of the petitioner?
    d. Who signed the petition?
    e. Who signed the attestation (verification that the petition is true)?
    f. Is this petition filed as voluntary or involuntary bankruptcy?

APPLICATIONS

1. Read the classified section of your newspaper every day for one week, checking for bankruptcy notices. Cut all you can find from the legal

notices section and answer these questions:

   a. How many total bankruptcies were filed in a seven-day period?

   b. How many of the bankruptcies were joint bankruptcies (husband and wife)?

   c. What is the lowest amount of debt claimed?

   d. What is the highest amount of debt claimed?

   e. How many of those filing represented themselves? How many used an attorney?

   f. What was the lowest amount of property claimed as exempt?

   g. What was the highest amount of property claimed as exempt?

2. Search through the Yellow Pages of a telephone book and through business directories and make a list of the following:

   a. Not-for-profit credit counseling services

   b. Commercial debt-adjustment firms

   c. Attorneys specializing in bankruptcy

   d. Classes or other credit counseling services provided in the community, either for a fee or free.

3. Look up the original Bankruptcy Act in a reference book and write a report covering the following:

   a. Provisions of the law (in outline form)

   b. Exempted items allowed and types of income excluded

   c. Procedures or steps involved in filing bankruptcy

4. Look up the Bankruptcy Reform Act of 1978 and answer these questions:

   a. How has the law changed to help consumers?

   b. What are the new provisions not found in the old bankruptcy laws regarding exempted items and excluded income?

5. Does the state in which you live require you to use a state exempted item schedule rather than the federal schedule?

6. Is it possible in your area to file bankruptcy without the aid of an attorney? What is the procedure for filing a bankruptcy, with or without an attorney? (You can find out by calling your local legal aid society or by asking at a courthouse.)

CASE PROBLEMS AND ACTIVITIES

1. Jack and Marcene Churchwell are considering bankruptcy. They have the following assets. How much (total) will they be allowed in exempted items?

   a. $18,000 equity in home
   b. $5,000 interest in motor vehicle
   c. $500 in household goods and furnishings, $2,000 in appliances,
      $1,000 in personal items and clothing, and $2,000 in musical
      instruments
   d. $5,000 in jewelry

2. M. J. Majesky has filed for bankruptcy and has the following debts.
   After the bankruptcy, which debts will remain?

   a. $500 owed to a chiropractor
   b. $300 owed in child support
   c. $870 owed in student loans
   d. $1,200 owed in back taxes
   e. $530 owed to a department store
   f. $650 owed to an automobile repair shop
   g. $950 owed to a jewelry store

3. Jeffrey Luther has the following assets. What amounts would be
   considered exempted items?

   a. $3,500 equity in a home
   b. $3,000 interest in a motor vehicle
   c. $150 in household furnishings
   d. $300 in appliances
   e. $150 in personal items
   f. $300 in a pet parrot
   g. $1,500 in musical instruments
   h. $300 in jewelry
   i. $600 in tools
   j. $15,000 life insurance proceeds
   k. $300 a month in unemployment insurance benefits

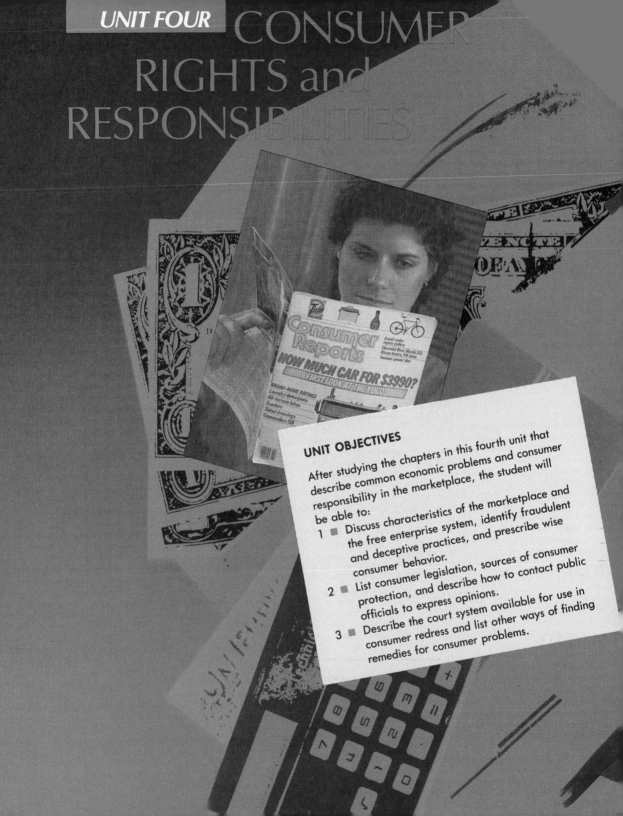

CONSUMER
RIGHTS and
RESPONSIBILITIES

UNIT OBJECTIVES

After studying the chapters in this fourth unit that describe common economic problems and consumer responsibility in the marketplace, the student will be able to:

1 ■ Discuss characteristics of the marketplace and the free enterprise system, identify fraudulent and deceptive practices, and prescribe wise consumer behavior.

2 ■ List consumer legislation, sources of consumer protection, and describe how to contact public officials to express opinions.

3 ■ Describe the court system available for use in consumer redress and list other ways of finding remedies for consumer problems.

Chapter 15

ROLE OF THE CONSUMER IN THE MARKETPLACE

◆◆◆◆◆◆◆◆◆◆◆◆◆◆◆◆◆◆◆◆◆◆◆◆◆◆◆

OBJECTIVES

1. Understand the basic characteristics of the marketplace.
2. List and describe the three basic components of a free enterprise system.
3. Describe deceptive practices used to defraud consumers and explain how consumers can protect themselves.
4. Explain wise buying practices and consumer rights and responsibilities when making purchases and resolving problems.

CHARACTERISTICS OF THE MARKETPLACE

◆◆◆◆◆◆◆◆

All countries operate by means of some type of economic system. When citizens understand their roles in the marketplace, they benefit themselves and the total economic system as well.

We live in a free enterprise system.

The United States economy is a free enterprise system. The basic characteristics of free enterprise and how this system affects personal financial management are explored briefly in this chapter. In Unit Six, "Microeconomics and You," the free enterprise system is discussed in detail.

MIXED ECONOMY

In the United States we have a **mixed economy**, which means that both producers and consumers are active and vital parts of the system. **Producers** are citizens and businesses that make products and services available for others to purchase. **Consumers** are citizens and businesses that purchase and use the goods and services produced for sale. Everyone is a consumer; that is, everyone must consume at least some goods and services produced by others in order to live. Many consumers are also producers; that is, they provide goods and services for others to consume.

Everyone is a consumer.

SUPPLY AND DEMAND

Supply and demand are the key factors that determine what product or service is produced, in what quantity it is produced, and at what price it is sold. **Supply** is the quantity of goods and services that producers are willing and able to manufacture. **Demand** is the willingness and ability of consumers to purchase goods and services at certain prices.

Generally if consumers demand a product (are willing and able to buy it at a certain price), producers will make it. The system works like this: Increased demand pushes up the price of the product. The high price brings large profits to the producers. High profits attract more producers and often cause current producers to make more of the product, increasing the supply. More supply pushes the price back down. The principle is simple — the more scarce an item is, the more expensive it becomes. The supply and demand process continues indefinitely until the market for the product attains equilibrium.

As supply increases, price decreases.

CONSUMER POWER

Consumers have the ultimate power in a supply and demand economy; indeed, consumers determine what is produced and at what price. When consumers purchase a good or service, they are casting dollar votes for continued production of that good or service. If consumers refuse to buy a

Consumers have the ultimate power.

good or service, the price will drop. If the product or service still does not sell, it will no longer be produced. Producers will only supply those goods and services that people want and are able to buy. Thus, in our free enterprise system, consumers actually exercise the power to determine what will be produced and at what price. There are, of course, exceptions to this rule, as in any economy; but generally the consumer plays a vital role in the marketplace through decisions to purchase or not to purchase goods and services.

CREATING DEMAND

Producers also have power in a supply and demand economy because they can employ various techniques to affect consumer buying decisions. Advertising is perhaps the method most commonly used to induce consumers to want products. **Advertising** is the communication of product information through mass media to the consumer for the purpose of increasing the demand for a good or service. It can be informative and give important facts about quality goods and services. Sometimes, however, advertising can be false and misleading and, unfortunately, damaging to the consumer's personal financial situation. In order to manage your personal finances successfully, you must learn to understand the role of advertising in our economic system and become a careful consumer.

Advertising creates demand.

BALANCE IN A FREE ENTERPRISE SYSTEM

◆◆◆◆◆◆◆◆

Three basic components are necessary for a free enterprise economy to function smoothly. Competition, income distribution, and informed consumers work together to balance this type of economic system. If one of these components is missing or is not functioning properly, the system begins to fail. We see inflation, high prices when supply is high, and other by-products of an inefficient economy.

COMPETITION

In order for prices to be based on supply and demand, competition is necessary. **Competition** occurs when there is more than one producer or supplier of a good or service. All producers must compete with each other to sell the same or similar products. When there is only one producer or

Illustration 15-1
Competition occurs
when there is more
than one producer
or supplier of a good
or service.

supplier, a *monopoly* exists, and low-quality goods and services and high prices often result. When many producers compete to sell a product to the consumer, high-quality goods and services and low prices usually result.

It is not enough, however, for competition simply to exist. To be truly effective in maintaining the supply and demand system, competition must also be pure — without price fixing or other controls. **Price fixing** occurs when producers who are supposed to be competitors conspire to set the same prices on the same goods or services. There is no real competition because prices have been predetermined, or fixed. Price fixing violates the principles of a free enterprise system, and it is illegal. Producers found guilty of price fixing are subject to fines and imprisonment.

**Price fixing elimi-
nates competition.**

INCOME DISTRIBUTION

In a free market society, all consumers must have purchasing power. To have **purchasing power** is to have money with which to buy goods and services. In our country, most all persons have purchasing power through income distribution; for instance, workers have income from their jobs.

**All persons have pur-
chasing power.**

Those persons who cannot work may receive **transfer payments** from the government — money collected from employers and workers, which is then distributed to those who do not work. Transfer payments may be "in kind" or "in cash." Food stamps and housing assistance are "in kind" benefits. Social security payments, veterans benefits, welfare and child assistance programs, and disability payments are examples of payments "in cash."

Children and minors have purchasing power through their parents. Basically, in this country, all persons have the ability to purchase goods and services. Income distribution gives balance to a marketplace in which it is necessary for *all* citizens (not just a privileged few) to participate.

 Consumers must be informed.

INFORMED CONSUMERS

The final component of a free enterprise system is informed consumers who know their rights and responsibilities in the marketplace. When consumers make wise decisions, the system works to weed out inferior products and keep prices at acceptable levels. When consumers do not act in a responsible manner, prices increase. The free enterprise triangle gains strength when each of the three parts works to its fullest potential. When one component breaks down, the others go out of control. Figure 15-1 illustrates the balance of basic components in a free enterprise system.

Figure 15-1
Free Enterprise
System

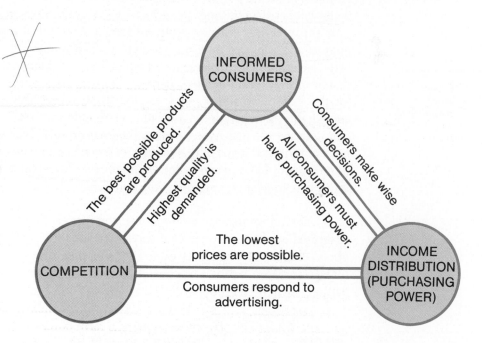

FRAUDULENT AND DECEPTIVE MARKETING PRACTICES

The marketplace is full of deceptive and misleading ways for suppliers to increase demand for a product — ways to induce consumers to buy goods and services of inferior quality, or things they do not really need or want.

The marketplace can be deceptive.

Described in the following pages are a number of commonly reported fraudulent and deceptive marketing practices that all consumers should be aware of in order to protect themselves and their finances. In many cases, little can be done once the consumer has been duped into making a purchase. Dishonest sellers quickly disappear or deny wrongdoing. Therefore, consumers must educate themselves to recognize a potential fraud before they become a victim. Prevention is still the best safeguard against financial misfortune.

BAIT AND SWITCH

Consumers are baited by spectacular bargains.

The **bait and switch** technique is an insincere offer by a merchant who baits the buyer into the store by advertising an exciting bargain. When the customer arrives to purchase the advertised product, however, the merchant then switches the customer's interest to a more expensive product that will yield the merchant a higher profit. In some cases the bait is a poor-quality product and is placed next to high-quality merchandise. The poor-quality bait is advertised to be of better quality than it is, giving the customer the idea that he or she is really getting a bargain. In other cases, when customers ask for the bait merchandise, they are told that it has been sold, but that comparable merchandise is available — for more money. Sometimes a crafty salesperson may try to convince the customer that he or she really does not want the bait item, but rather a similar product of better quality — for more money. The bait and switch technique is a clever plan to get customers into a store to sell them more expensive merchandise than they had planned to buy.

The baited item is switched to a more expensive model.

A wise consumer knows products and prices. When a product is advertised at a special price, the consumer knows its quality and regular price. Product knowledge is gained by shopping around before making major purchases. In this way, consumers can protect themselves against the bait and switch technique.

REFERRAL SALES

A **referral sale** means that the seller promises a money rebate, prize, or discount if the buyer can provide names of friends and acquaintances who are prospective customers. Such promises are illegal when actual payment of the rebate, prize, or discount is not made. Delaying payment pending a sale, presentation, or other event is also illegal.

In any event, referral sales techniques provide the seller with names, addresses, and telephone numbers of prospects. People on the referral list are expected to purchase the product because their friend gave the seller their names. Persons who volunteer the names and addresses of friends cannot expect appreciation from the friends who are later harassed by companies or organizations to purchase merchandise they do not want in order to help others win a prize or receive a discount or rebate. Consumers should resist providing sellers with the names and addresses of their friends and acquaintances. The end of a friendship is a high price to pay for a discount.

Do not give names and addresses of friends.

FAKE SALES

Probably the most common of all consumer frauds is the **fake sale**. A merchant advertises a big sale, but items are at regular price, or the price tags are disguised to show a price reduction when there actually is none. Often prices are increased just prior to the sale, and price tags are altered to show the so-called markdowns. The only way consumers can protect themselves from fake sales is to know products and prices and to plan purchases. Just because a flashy sign shouts "SUPER SAVINGS" does not mean that there are price reductions. Advertising campaigns, newspaper ads, and window signs may announce a big sale. Only a wise consumer is able to distinguish a real bargain from a fake sale.

Super savings may be no savings at all.

LO-BALLING

Many repair businesses engage in the deceptive practice of lo-balling. **Lo-balling** is advertising a repair service at an unusually low price to lure customers, then attempting to persuade consumers that additional services are needed. For example, when an appliance or implement is dismantled, other "necessary" repairs are discovered. The consumer is offered a special or regular rate for the additional repairs, and if the offer is refused, an extra fee is charged for reassembly.

Additional "needed repairs" are found.

Another form of lo-balling is applying pressure, either bluntly or subtly, to convince an automobile owner that additional work is necessary for the safe maintenance of his or her car. For example, a repair shop may offer a special on brake relining. But when the brakes are inspected, several other "necessary" repairs are discovered. The customer may wind up with a front-end alignment, wheel balancing, or other repairs that are not really as urgent as the car owner is led to believe.

Consumers can protect themselves against this type of lo-balling by stipulating that they want no repairs other than those agreed upon. Any repair other than the one specified must be authorized by the consumer *after* the repair shop has informed the consumer of the additional cost. Consumers should not pay for unauthorized work. Before having additional work done, the consumer should get a second opinion. The matter should be discussed with a spouse, a friend in the business, or someone who can offer an expert opinion. Consumers should indicate that no extra services or repairs beyond those advertised will be paid for without prior consent.

Another defense against lo-balling is to deal with merchants you know or who are recommended to you by friends or relatives who have received good service. Check around with people who have had similar work done — ask neighbors, coworkers, and others. Check the reputations of businesses before you deal with them. In other words, ask questions and know what you need to have done before you take in your car or appliance for repairs.

PYRAMID SALES

Multilevel sales, called **pyramid sales**, are selling schemes, illegal in many states, in which sellers are promised a lot of money quickly and with little effort for selling a product. A cash investment of some kind is usually required. The pyramid consists of managers or dealers at the top and a lot of middle and lower workers arranging parties, recruiting new salespersons, and selling products to friends and acquaintances. Having a lot of people selling products to their friends allows a manager to make big profits with little effort. However, the consumer finds it very difficult to make a profit or recover the initial cash investment because friends are unwilling to buy the product or service.

Pyramid sales are often begun with a meeting in which a fast-talking and enthusiastic person convinces a group of people that they can make a fortune. They cannot lose; everyone can make it big! Unfortunately the product is often not of high quality or even comparable quality to the same or similar products sold through regular retail outlets. In a relatively short time, there is neither profit nor sales because people will not buy the product more than once. Only persons at the top of the pyramid can expect to win. The remainder, those persons at the bottom of the pyramid, are expected to continue mushrooming sales at an increasing pace. Increasing sales is not possible because the market becomes saturated, and sellers run out of friends who will buy the product.

The best defense against pyramid sales schemes is to remember that you cannot expect to make big profits without hard work. If it sounds too good to be true, it probably is. Before committing to such a plan, think it over for a

---

Get a second opinion.

Pyramid sales mean selling to your friends.

No way to lose — or is there?

week or two — and investigate the plan. Talk to others who have purchased such merchandise; check with local consumer protection agencies; think it through. Ask yourself: Who will buy this product? Do I want to sell this to my friends and relatives? How much will I have to invest to get started? What happens if it doesn't work out? How much can I afford to lose?

PIGEON DROP

The term **pigeon drop** refers to any method used by experienced con artists to convince vulnerable people to invest in phony deposits, swampland real estate, or other swindles. People are said to be vulnerable when they are open to attack and easy to convince or persuade.

Vulnerable people fall for swindles.

The pigeon is the unsuspecting consumer. People who have few defenses or little knowledge of such scams, but do have a source of money, are most often chosen. For example, older people on fixed incomes become the targets of fast-talking "financial experts." Older people may be asked to deposit their savings in an investment fund. These funds are then to be loaned out at high interest rates. Monthly payments are promised the pigeon for the use of his or her money. In some cases the pigeon is dropped (defrauded) immediately, and the trusted adviser disappears with the money. In other cases the swindler maintains an outwardly healthy business and pays dividends to the pigeon until it is no longer advantageous to do so. Then the swindler disappears with the investments. By maintaining a supposedly legitimate business for a period of time, the swindler can gain additional victims — friends eager to get in on the deal at the recommendation of the original pigeon. New victims are also dropped.

They disappear with the investments.

The best protection against this type of swindle is the local Better Business Bureau. The Bureau is equipped to investigate questionable schemes, so-called investment experts, and unsound business firms. Consumers should insist upon credentials, annual financial reports, and proof of past dealings. Trust in and trade with only ethical and established firms. Deposit your money in banks and savings and loan associations that are insured by the government.

Deal with a reputable business.

FRAUDULENT REPRESENTATION

Telephone or door-to-door sales made by persons who claim to represent well-known and reputable companies is a recent new type of swindle. Consumers buy products or services, then learn that they have been sold rebuilt, stolen, or inferior merchandise with the reputable name on it. In some cases the product or service purchased is worthless or unusable. One such scam is the sale of discount coupons to be used in numerous restaurants and businesses. The coupons sound like a wise purchase because for a very reasonable price the buyer can save hundreds of dollars. But when the buyer presents the coupons for a discount or free merchandise, she or he discovers that the merchant has not authorized the coupon.

The name may be fraudulent.

Before buying a service or product from someone claiming to represent a major company, it is smart to check with the company. One phone call can save a lot of money. Don't feel compelled to buy a product when it is demonstrated. The local Better Business Bureau is informed of questionable practices reported on the same salespeople.

HEALTH AND MEDICAL PRODUCT FRAUDS

A common type of swindle involves deceptive advertising for expensive "miracle" pills, creams, and devices to enhance the consumer's health and beauty. Advertisements promise that these products can do everything, from causing hair to grow on a bald head to causing a person to lose ten pounds a week. The advertisements are designed to appeal to the typical consumer's desire to be healthy and attractive with little or no effort. Usually deceptive health and medical advertisements carry endorsements and pictures of people who have found success using the product. Magazines, newspapers, and flashy tabloids often carry these advertisements. The manufacturers ask that you mail a sum of money to a post office address to receive one of the miracle devices or a quantity of pills or cream. Many times the money is accepted, but the product is not mailed to the consumer. If any product is received, in most cases it is totally ineffective. Pills, creams, and similar products, when analyzed, may actually be sugar or an over-the-counter medication readily available for a much lower price in local stores.

Ads claiming amazing results should be questioned.

"Miracle" products often are totally ineffective.

THE RESPONSIBLE CONSUMER

◆◆◆◆◆◆◆◆

Knowing of the existence of various deceptive marketing tactics is the first step toward consumer responsibility. To keep our economic system running efficiently and to manage your personal finances successfully, you also need to learn how to protect yourself from becoming the victim of these fraudulent and deceptive practices. Prevention is the best protection; after you have been swindled, it is difficult to undo the financial damage you have suffered. In order to protect yourself, you must identify deceptive practices, use safeguards when buying, understand your rights and responsibilities, and seek redress when necessary.

IDENTIFY DECEPTIVE PRACTICES

When any of the following claims are made, they should serve as warnings of possible deception. These warning signals include claims or offers made through advertising and by salespersons; for example,

1. Something can be obtained for free.
2. You will receive a free gift for an early reply.
3. You or your home has been specially selected.
4. High earnings can be made with no experience or little effort.
5. An advertising survey or questionnaire is being taken.
6. A no-obligation demonstration is offered.
7. You must decide immediately or lose the golden opportunity.
8. An incredibly low price is offered for a high-quality product.

Something for nothing usually has a price.

USE SAFEGUARDS WHEN BUYING

The following list includes several recommendations to help you make wise buying decisions:

1. Be aware of regular or "list" prices of common items. Terms often used in advertising, such as *manufacturer's list price* and *suggested retail price*, and phrases such as "comparable value," "very important value," or "value $40, you pay only $35," attract your attention, but prices actually may not be reduced.
2. Shop at several stores. Comparative shopping is comparing quality, price, and guarantees for the same products at several different stores.
3. Understand sale terminology. *Sale* means that certain goods are offered at certain prices, but not necessarily at reduced prices. *Clearance* means that the merchant wants to clear out all the advertised merchandise, but not necessarily at a reduced price. *Liquidation* means that the merchant wants to sell immediately to turn the inventory into cash; again, prices may not be reduced.
4. Avoid impulse buying. Follow a list.
5. Do not make major purchases during periods of emotional stress — at the end of a crisis, during a time of loneliness or frustration, or at

List prices are the usual prices.

any time when your judgment is impaired.

Avoid buying during times of stress.

6. Compute unit prices. **Unit pricing** is the determination of the cost per unit of items sold in quantity. The selling price is reduced to the lowest unit price. For example, to compare the price of a 15-ounce box with the price of a 24-ounce box, divide the price of each box by the number of ounces in each box. The result is the price per ounce of each box. The lowest unit price for products of comparable quality is the best buy. Figure 15-2 shows unit price computations.

Figure 15-2
Unit Pricing

Which is the better buy?

A. 24 ounces for $2.59 or 15 ounces for $1.89?

$2.59 ÷ 24 = 10.8 cents per ounce
$1.89 ÷ 15 = 12.6 cents per ounce

B. 3/89 cents or 6/$1.99?

$ .89 ÷ 3 = 29.7 cents each
$1.99 ÷ 6 = 33.2 cents each

To determine unit pricing, divide the price by the number of ounces or units. This gives you a price per unit to compare to another price per unit.

7. Read labels. Know ingredients.
8. Check containers and packages carefully to see that they have not been opened or damaged. Report any suspicious packaging defaults to the store manager.
9. Read and understand contracts and agreements before signing.
10. Check the total cost of an item, including delivery charges, finance charges, and other add-on costs.
11. Ask for references from representatives of companies to be sure they really do represent the company. Call the company to check.
12. Patronize businesses that have good reputations and those at which you are a well-known customer.
13. Check the validity of certifications and endorsements. Use your local Better Business Bureau.
14. Always wait at least 24 hours before making a major purchase. Be sure the purchase is not made on impulse and that you were not coerced into wanting the item.

Ask questions to understand your rights.

UNDERSTAND YOUR RIGHTS AND RESPONSIBILITIES

Consumers who take precautions avoid many errors and later problems with their agreements and purchases. You are responsible for seeking

Illustration 15-2
It is important to read and understand contracts and agreements before signing.

Know your responsibilities as a consumer.

information and advice to become knowledgeable of products and services before you buy. To protect yourself, you should observe the following practices:

1. Be familiar with sources of information on goods and services, such as *Consumer Reports* and local agencies.
2. Read warranties and guarantees; ask questions so that you can fully understand performance claims. Get written guarantees and warranties whenever possible.
3. Read and understand care instructions before using a product.
4. Analyze advertisements about products before buying.
5. Insist upon enforcement of consumer protection laws — know how to get consumer redress.
6. Inform appropriate consumer protection agencies of fraudulent and unsafe performances of products and services. Do not hesitate to make your dissatisfactions known so that others may be helped, and the product or service improved.
7. Suggest, support, and be aware of consumer legislation.
8. Report wants, likes, and dislikes as well as suggested improvements and complaints to dealers and manufacturers.

State your likes and dislikes.

SEEK REDRESS

When you have a complaint or need to solve a problem about a product or service, you have several consumer redress alternatives. **Consumer redress** is getting the action needed to resolve a problem with a product or service. Here are some suggestions for filing a complaint and obtaining adjustments for problems.

Complain first in writing to the person or company selling the product. Be specific about the problem. Produce evidence of the problem. Retain all warranties, sales slips, receipts, etc. Send photocopies of necessary information to explain and support your position. Be firm; say that you are dissatisfied and explain why. Indicate the type of adjustment desired — refund, repair, replacement, or other action.

Use the firm approach.

If the seller refuses to make an adjustment, then write to the manufacturer or distributor and state your complaint. Indicate that you previously wrote to the original seller of the product. Be specific. Enclose a copy of your letter of complaint to the company that sold you the product or service. Send photocopies of evidence, such as sales slips, warranties, receipts, or anything else that will help you support your position. Be firm and again state the type of adjustment you want. Specify a reasonable time limit to resolve the problem.

Give a time limit to resolve the problem.

If the desired adjustment is still not made, file a complaint with the appropriate government agency for consumer protection. There may be more than one private or public agency to assist you in solving the problem.

Seek legal recourse when advisable. For claims of less than $1,000, small-claims court offers a much faster and less expensive process. Some states may have different dollar limits for small-claims, but still have very effective small-claims court procedures. Because attorneys are not required for filing in a small-claims court, costs are lower. All that is required is payment of a small filing fee and appearance on the assigned court date. Small-claims courts are discussed in detail in Chapter 17.

In some cases, you may receive a judgment in your favor if a supplier has violated the federal Consumer Protection Act or a state law. You could be awarded attorneys' fees, court costs, minimum damages of $200, and punitive damages. An attorney could advise you of your chances of such a judgment. Class action suits filed on behalf of a number of consumers who have the same complaint generally take many years to settle.

VOCABULARY

Directions: Can you find the definition for each of the following terms used in Chapter 15?

mixed economy	advertising
producers	competition
consumers	price fixing
supply	purchasing power
demand	transfer payments

bait and switch	pyramid sales
referral sale	pigeon drop
fake sale	unit pricing
lo-balling	consumer redress

1. The action needed for a consumer to resolve a problem with a product or service.
2. Reducing the cost of a product to the per-unit price so it can be compared to prices of other sizes or products.
3. Deceptive marketing practice whereby consumers are supposed to get others to sell to their friends.
4. A fraudulent practice whereby con artists convince people to invest in phony deals.
5. Advertising certain repairs at unusually low prices, then urging additional repairs and more costs upon the consumer.
6. An advertised "big sale" that really offers merchandise at regular prices.
7. A deceptive practice whereby the seller promises money, prizes, or discounts if the buyer provides names of friends.
8. A technique in which an item is offered for sale, but customers are urged to buy a similar item at a higher price.
9. Money given to citizens that was collected from other citizens.
10. Having money with which to buy goods and services.
11. Occurs when more than one producer or supplier of a good or service exists, and each tries to get the majority of consumers to buy its product.
12. A method of communicating information to the consumer to sell goods and services.
13. Willingness and ability of consumers to purchase goods and services at certain prices.
14. The quantity of goods and services that producers are willing and able to manufacture.
15. An economic system in which both producers and consumers play an active and vital role.
16. Citizens and businesses that purchase and use goods and services.
17. Citizens and businesses that make products and services available for others to purchase.
18. Occurs when producers get together and set prices, eliminating competition.

ITEMS FOR DISCUSSION

1. Explain what is meant by this statement: Everyone is a consumer.

2. As the supply of a product increases, what happens to the price?

3. How do consumers have the power to determine what is produced and at what price?

4. What are the three basic components that provide balance in a free enterprise system?

5. How can the consumer be protected from bait and switch tactics?

6. What can you do to prevent lo-balling?

7. Con artists prey on vulnerable people. What is meant by the term vulnerable?

8. List five warning signals that alert consumers to the possibility of deceptive marketing practices.

9. What are some safeguards to use when buying products and services?

10. List four ways that you, as a responsible consumer, can protect yourself in the marketplace.

11. What procedures should you follow to seek a solution to a problem with a product or service?

12. Why should you consider a small-claims court to resolve a consumer complaint?

APPLICATIONS

1. What is the purpose of advertising?

2. Watch one hour of television in the early evening (between 7 and 8 p.m. is best) and record the number and types of commercials. What do the advertisements tell you about goods and services? Make a chart on a piece of paper, listing each commercial and describing it as shown in the following example:

TIME OF COMMERCIAL	PRODUCT ADVERTISED	LENGTH OF COMMERCIAL	PRODUCT INFORMATION FEATURED
7 p.m.	Toothpaste (NewBrite)	30 seconds	New flavor; old also available

3. There are three basic components that create balance in a free enterprise system: competition, income distribution (purchasing power), and informed consumers. What happens when competition is missing? purchasing power? informed consumers?

4. Search through magazines, newspapers, and other sources for advertisements offering the following:

a. Something for nothing

b. Bonus for early reply

c. Offers of gifts and prizes

d. Other deceptive practices

Collect the advertisements and bring them to class.

CASE PROBLEMS AND ACTIVITIES

1. Compute the following unit prices (lowest units to compare values):

    a. 3/98 cents

    b. 4/$1.00

    c. 24 oz./$1.98

    d. 2 lbs./$2.19

    e. 3 lbs. 6 oz. /$6.99

    f. 6/89 cents

    g. 3/$1.49

2. Copy the ingredients from the labels of the following products:

    a. Pain pills

    b. Breakfast cereal

    c. Liquid cleaning product

    d. Poisonous substance

    Are there any warnings on any of the above labels? What types of precautions are suggested?

3. Copy the words written on a warranty or guarantee for a household product that your family has purchased. What does the manufacturer agree to do? What exceptions are stated? What actions does the manufacturer state it will not agree to do?

4. Read through a copy of *Consumer Reports* in your library and answer the following questions:

    a. Who publishes the magazine?

    b. Who advertises in the magazine?

    c. In one issue, how many different types of products are tested and compared for quality?

    d. Write a short (one paragraph) summary of an article that interested you (from the issue of *Consumer Reports* that you read).

5. Assume that you bought a new hair dryer at a local department store last week. Write a letter of complaint because the hair dryer makes a strange rattling noise. Give factual information concerning the dryer and request a refund or other adjustment.

Chapter 16

CONSUMER PROTECTION

••••••••••••••••••••••••••

OBJECTIVES

1. Describe the provisions of the Consumer Bill of Rights.
2. Describe the provisions of significant federal consumer legislation.
3. Identify national sources of consumer information and assistance.
4. List and describe state and local agencies and private organizations that provide consumer assistance and information.
5. Explain how to contact public officials to express opinions.

SIGNIFICANT FEDERAL CONSUMER LEGISLATION

••••••••••

For many years the consumer's position in the marketplace was characterized by the phrase "buyer beware"; in other words, the consumer was given little assistance or protection against fraudulent practices. Since 1960, however, a number of major consumer-protection laws have been passed. One of the most important steps in the direction of consumer protection was the adoption of the Consumer Bill of Rights. The Consumer

Consumer rights are outlined in the Consumer Bill of Rights.

Bill of Rights was proposed by President Kennedy during his 1962 State of the Union Address, and later expanded by Presidents Nixon and Ford. It includes the following:

1. The right to safety — protection against products that are hazardous to life or health.
2. The right to be informed — protection against fraudulent, deceitful, or grossly misleading practices and assurance of receiving facts necessary to make informed choices.
3. The right to choose — access to a variety of quality products and services offered at competitive prices.
4. The right to be heard — assurance of representation of consumer interests in formulating government policy and of fair and prompt treatment in enforcement of the laws.
5. The right to redress or remedy — assurance that buyers have ways to register their dissatisfaction and to have complaints heard.
6. The right to consumer education — assurance that consumers have necessary assistance to plan and use their resources to their maximum potential.

Specific laws have been passed to ensure that consumers get quality products and services for their hard-earned dollars. The most significant consumer laws enacted by Congress are described in the following pages.

FOOD, DRUG, AND COSMETIC ACT OF 1938

The FDA enforces the Food, Drug, and Cosmetic Act of 1938.

The Food, Drug, and Cosmetic Act of 1938 requires that foods be safe, pure, and wholesome; that drugs and medical devices be safe and effective; and that cosmetics be safe. The law also provides that these products be truthfully labeled. The weight or volume of the contents and name and address of the manufacturer must be on the label. The use of containers that are misleading because of size, thickness, or false bottoms is prohibited.

WOOL PRODUCTS LABELING ACT OF 1940

Wool products must have proper labels.

Amended in 1965, the Wool Products Labeling Act of 1940 requires proper labeling of the amount and kind of wool contained in all products made of wool, except carpeting and upholstery. Percentages of new, reused, or reprocessed wool and other fibers, care of the product, and the identity of the manufacturer must be shown on the labels of products containing 5 percent or more wool.

FLAMMABLE FABRICS ACT OF 1953

Amended in 1967, the Flammable Fabrics Act enabled the Consumer Product Safety Commission to set flammability standards for clothing, children's sleepwear, carpets, rugs, and mattresses. Interstate commerce of all wearing apparel made of easily ignited material is prohibited. The flammability standard for children's sleepwear requires that the garment will not catch fire when exposed to a match or small fire. The flame retardant finish must last for 50 washings and dryings. Proper care instructions to protect sleepwear from agents or treatments known to cause deterioration of the flame retardant finish must be on all labels.

Children's clothing must be flame resistant.

KEFAUVER-HARRIS DRUG AMENDMENT OF 1962

As a result of the Kefauver-Harris Drug Amendment of 1962, drug manufacturers are required to file notices of all new drugs, which must be tested for safety and effectiveness before being sold to consumers. This amendment also provides for the manufacture and sale of generic drugs. **Generic** is a term used for a product having the same qualities or contents as a well-known brand-name product. A generic drug is often less expensive than a brand-name drug because it carries no trademark registration. National brand names are usually more expensive than generic products because of the added costs of advertising and marketing.

Brand names are more expensive than generic products.

NATIONAL TRAFFIC AND MOTOR VEHICLE SAFETY ACT OF 1966

The National Traffic and Motor Vehicle Safety Act of 1966 established national safety standards for automobiles and for new and used tires. The National Highway Traffic Safety Administration of the Department of Transportation is charged with supporting and enforcing provisions of the act. Increasing public awareness of the need for safety devices, testing for safety, and inspecting vehicles for proper safety equipment are also responsibilities of the National Highway Traffic Safety Administration.

HAZARDOUS SUBSTANCES LABELING ACT OF 1960; CHILD PROTECTION AND TOY SAFETY ACT OF 1969

Labels must warn of potential dangers.

The Hazardous Substances Labeling Act, passed in 1960, requires that warning labels appear on all household products that are potentially dangerous to the consumer. As a further precaution against unfortunate accidents, the Child Protection and Toy Safety Act was passed in 1969, banning from interstate commerce those household products that are so dangerous that warning labels do not provide sufficient safeguards. This act also bans the sale of toys and children's articles containing hazardous substances and those that pose electrical, mechanical, or thermal dangers. Under either law, these products can be inspected and removed from the marketplace. In most cases, hazardous products are recalled. A **recall** is a procedure whereby the manufacturer stops production of a product and refunds the purchase price of items already sold. Sometimes a recalled product can be repaired so that it is no longer hazardous; it can then be returned to the consumer.

PERMANENT CARE LABELING RULE

Read the label to know what care is needed for a garment.

Effective since 1972, the care labeling rule specifies that clothing and fabrics must be labeled permanently with laundering and care instructions. Labels must give instructions sufficient to maintain a garment's original character. By carefully reading the labels on garments you purchase, you can estimate how much time or money will be required to maintain the garment. Care labels must stay attached and be easy to read for the life of the garment.

SOURCES OF CONSUMER PROTECTION

♦♦♦♦♦♦♦♦

When you need assistance with a consumer problem, you may not be sure where to look. There are numerous sources available to you. Your first choice may not be the right one, but by asking, you will be referred to the appropriate agency of the federal or state government, or to a specific private organization. The following descriptions of consumer protection agencies might help you select the appropriate source of information.

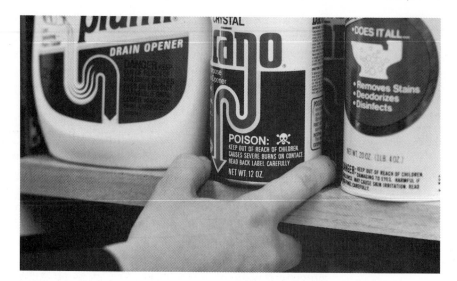

Illustration 16-1
Warning labels
must appear on all
potentially danger-
ous household
products.

FEDERAL CONSUMER AGENCIES

Numerous government agencies on the federal level provide information of
interest to consumers. Some of these agencies handle consumer
complaints, and others direct complaints to agencies or sources that address
consumer issues. Some well-known federal agencies are described in the
following paragraphs.

Some agencies han-
dle complaints;
others do not.

Department of Agriculture. Within the Department of Agriculture,
there are a number of agencies that exist to meet various consumer needs.
The **Agricultural Marketing Service** inspects food to ensure wholesomeness
and truthful labeling, develops official grade standards, and provides grading
services. For example, eggs must meet specific standards to be classified as
extra large, jumbo, large, medium, or small. The *Food and Nutrition
Service* provides food assistance programs, such as the food stamp and school
lunch programs, and information on diets, nutrition, and menu
preparation. The *Cooperative Extension Services* provides consumer
education materials (pamphlets and booklets) on such topics as budgeting,
money management, food preparation and storage, gardening, credit
counseling, and many more. Most of the materials are free.

Assistance is provid-
ed for school lunch
programs.

Department of Commerce. The **National Bureau of Standards** is an
agency within the Department of Commerce that sets measurement,
product, and safety standards. All food packages must indicate whether the
weight shown includes the packaging or is a **net weight** — the weight of the
product without the container or package.

Department of Health and Human Services. Two of the many
agencies within the Department of Health and Human Services are the

Food and Drug Administration and the Office of Consumer Affairs. **The Food and Drug Administration (FDA)** is charged with enforcing laws and regulations preventing distribution of mislabeled foods, drugs, cosmetics, and medical devices. The FDA requires testing and approval of all new drugs; conducts testing of new and existing products for health and safety standards; provides standards and guidelines for poisonous substances; controls the standards for identification, quality, and fill of food containers; establishes guidelines for labels and proper identification of product contents, ingredients, nutrients, and directions for use; investigates complaints; conducts research; and issues reports, guidelines, and warnings about substances its researchers find to be dangerous or potentially hazardous to health.

All new drugs are tested before they enter the market-place.

The **Office of Consumer Affairs** represents consumer interests in federal agency proceedings, develops consumer information materials, and assists other agencies in responding to consumer complaints. Specific consumer complaints received by the Office of Consumer Affairs are referred to the appropriate government and private agencies for further assistance.

Federal Communications Commission.   The **Federal Communications Commission (FCC)** regulates radio and television broadcasting and interstate telephone and telegraph companies. In addition, the FCC establishes communications standards for and controls the quality of transmissions from radio stations, television networks, cable television networks, CB (citizens band) and ham radios, and any other transmissions through public airspace. What can or cannot be said or done over the air is regulated by the FCC. An advertisement may be discontinued or modified if the FCC determines that it is false or misleading.

Telephone and tele-graph lines are con-trolled by the FCC.

Federal Trade Commission.   The **Federal Trade Commission (FTC)** is concerned with protecting consumers from unfair methods of competition, false or deceptive advertising, deceptive product labeling, inaccurate or obsolete information on credit reports, and concealment of the true cost of credit. Anyone can file a complaint with the FTC by sending a letter, accompanied by as much supporting evidence as possible.

Anyone can file a complaint by sending a letter.

United States Postal Service.   The United States Postal Service operates the **Postal Inspection Service** to deal with the consumer problems pertaining to illegal use of the mails. The Postal Inspection Service enforces postal laws, protecting consumers from dangerous articles, contraband, fraud, and pornography. Through its Consumer Protection Program, the Postal Inspection Service resolves unsatisfactory mail-order transactions, even in cases where no fraud has occurred.

Federal Aviation Administration.   The Federal Aviation Administration (FAA) is an agency of the U.S. Department of Transportation. It controls air traffic and certifies aircraft, airports, pilots, and other personnel. The FAA writes and enforces air safety regulations and air traffic procedures. Consumer protection and rights while flying on domestic aircraft are provided through the **Civil Aeronautics Board (CAB)**, which keeps track of complaints, inspects aircraft, investigates accidents, and enforces safety regulations. Airline passengers have rights enforced by the CAB, such as the right to a non-smoking seat. Any person requesting a non-smoking seat must be accommodated. All airlines now have the requirement of no smoking on flights of less than two hours, a requirement that is mandated through the CAB.

Federal Bureau of Investigation. The **Federal Bureau of Investigation (FBI)** is the chief investigating branch of the United States Department of Justice. The FBI investigates federal crimes such as bank robbery and kidnapping. It also collects evidence in lawsuits involving the federal government, and collects intelligence (information) about individuals or groups that are believed to be dangers to national security. FBI investigators are called *special agents*. The FBI director is appointed by the President with approval of the Senate.

The FBI investigates federal crimes.

STATE AND LOCAL AGENCIES

Most states have a consumer protection agency, or the state attorney general may handle consumer affairs. Other consumer leagues and public interest research groups are also active in many states. These groups may publish newsletters, pamphlets, brochures, and handbooks on current consumer issues. A handbook published in many states addresses landlord/tenant rights and responsibilities.

There are numerous consumer research groups.

On the local level, consumers may have access to legal aid societies, newspaper and broadcast action reporters, or consumer representatives on local utility or licensing boards. Independent consumer groups focusing on specific issues, such as food prices, may operate on the local level as well.

The **Better Business Bureau (BBB)** functions on both state and local levels. The BBB has no legal authority, but serves as a clearinghouse of information about local businesses. Complaints against local businesses may be filed with the BBB. The merchant is given an opportunity to respond to the complaint. If the merchant does not respond to the complaint, the Better Business Bureau may advise the consumer to seek another form of redress. Information regarding the nature of complaints filed against local merchants is available upon request.

The Better Business Bureau is a clearinghouse of information.

PRIVATE ORGANIZATIONS

Private organizations help by giving consumers advice on the purchase of various products and the performance that can be expected from these products. Two such organizations are Consumers' Research, Inc., and Consumers Union of the United States, Inc. A not-for-profit organization, Consumers' Research conducts extensive testing for quality and performance. Results of these tests are published in *Consumers Research Magazine* along with ratings given the products tested. Also a not-for-profit organization, Consumers Union has the largest consumer testing facility in the world. Through its monthly magazine, *Consumer Reports*, Consumers Union gives test results and product ratings. To assure that all ratings are unbiased, all products tested are purchased by Consumers Union. No advertising is accepted, and no free products are accepted for testing from manufacturers. *Consumer Reports* also prints articles dealing with insurance, credit, and other items of consumer interest. An annual report of items previously published in *Consumer Reports* is also published by Consumers Union.

Products are tested and ratings are published.

Another private organization providing assistance in protecting consumer rights is the **Major Appliance Consumer Action Panel (MACAP)**. MACAP is comprised of representatives of the home appliance industry and provides assistance in resolving or minimizing consumer problems in the purchase and use of home appliances.

Consumers may also seek the support of a **consumer advocate** — one who promotes or protects the causes or interests of consumers. Ralph Nader is the most well-known consumer advocate. When Ralph Nader finds, through research and investigation, that an injustice or dangerous condition exists, he pursues it in behalf of all consumers. Ralph Nader may file lawsuits against companies or organizations to force them to meet safety standards, correct inequitable situations, or properly inform consumers of dangers in the use of their products.

A consumer advocate helps to protect consumers in the marketplace.

Many other consumer groups are active in helping consumers find solutions to problems in the marketplace. Names and addresses of these groups may be obtained from sources such as Better Business Bureaus, the Consumers Federation of America, and the Consumer Information Center in Pueblo, Colorado. Information about other agencies and their purposes, consumer rights and responsibilities, and sources of consumer assistance, both governmental and nongovernmental, is available in most public libraries.

STATE AND FEDERAL NUMBERS
◆◆◆◆◆◆◆◆

Many states have toll-free numbers to call for assistance.

Many consumers are unaware of complaint-handling resources available through their own state governments. Each of the 34 states listed in Figure 16-1 maintains a toll-free 800 number for consumers to make inquiries or register complaints. Some offices handle complaints on almost any subject;

Illustration 16-2
Ralph Nader is the
most well-known
consumer advocate.

others specify their area of interest. Hours of operation are listed for local time zones. Figure 16-1 is a list prepared by the U.S. Government and available free of charge from the Consumer Information Center, Pueblo, Colorado.

For information and help with your questions about the federal government, use the toll-free information numbers given in Figure 16-2. These numbers will allow you to contact the nearest Federal Information Center (part of the U.S. General Services Administration). You can contact a center toll free if you live in any of the cities listed in Figure 16-2, or in a state with an 800 number shown.

CONTACTING THOSE WHO REPRESENT YOU
◆◆◆◆◆◆◆◆

National elected officials include the president and the vice president of the United States, serving four-year terms; United States senators, serving six-year terms; and the members of the United States House of Representatives, serving two-year terms. Governors of states usually are elected to four-year terms. Other state elected officials include the secretary of state, state treasurer, and state attorney general; superintendent of public instruction; labor commissioner; and state senators and representatives.

Each court (federal, state, and local) has at least one judge, and several clerks of the court assist in filing and information gathering. County elected officials include the county administrator, district attorney, sheriff, and tax assessor, plus a number of commissioners. Other elected local officials include the mayor, city council members, and city manager. These officials are available at county and city office buildings and meet regularly or are available to the public by appointment. The phone book lists various officials separately by state and by county, with each department listed alphabetically.

If you desire to communicate with an elected official, there are several ways to do so:

1. *In Person.* Appointments can be made during regular office hours as well as at meetings of government bodies, which are generally open to the public (except for executive sessions). There are opportunities to speak at almost all hearings.

Figure 16-1
State Consumer
Toll-Free Numbers

ALABAMA (Montgomery) Hours: 8:00-5:00 1 800 392-5658 In state only. Advice given over the phone. Complaints must be submitted in writing for action.	**ILLINOIS** (cont.) 1 800 252-8980 In state only. Handles complaints and inquiries on used car problems. 1 800 252-8903 In state only. Handles complaints and inquiries on public aid fraud.
ARIZONA (Phoenix) Hours: 8:00-5:00 1 800 352-8431 In state only. Handles complaints concerning possible fraud.	**INDIANA** (Indianapolis) Hours: 8:15-4:45 1 800 382-5516 In state only. Handles general consumer complaints and inquiries.
ARKANSAS (Little Rock) Hours: 8:00-5:00 1 800 482-8982 In state only. Handles complaints concerning possible fraud or false advertising and will answer general inquiries.	**KANSAS** (Topeka) Hours: 8:00-5:00 1 800 432-2310 In state only. Handles general complaints and inquiries.
CALIFORNIA (Sacramento) Hours: 8:00-5:00 1 800 952-5210 In state only. Handles complaints concerning auto repair jobs. 1 800 952-5567 In state only. Information regarding solar energy uses/insulation. Hours: 9:00-12:00; 1:00-4:00 1 800 952-5225 In state only. Takes general complaints.	**KENTUCKY** (Frankfort) Hours: 8:30-5:00 1 800 432-9257 In state only. Advice given over the phone. Will send complaint forms or refer. **LOUISIANA** (Baton Rouge) Hours: 8:30-5:00 1 800 272-9868 In state only. Handles general complaints and inquiries.
COLORADO (Denver) Hours: 8:00-5:00 1 800 332-2071 In state only. Handles complaints concerning possible price fixing or other antitrust matters.	**MASSACHUSETTS** (Boston) Hours: 9:00-5:00 1 800 632-8026 In state only. Handles energy related complaints and concerns. 1 800 392-6066 In state only. Handles public utility complaints and inquiries.
CONNECTICUT (Hartford) Hours: 8:30-4:30 1 800 842-2649 In state only. Handles all types of complaints and inquiries.	**MICHIGAN** (Lansing) Hours: 8:30-5:00 1 800 292-4204 (Bureau of Automotive Regulation) In state only. Handles auto complaints. 1 800 292-5943 (Commissioner of Insurance) In state only. Handles insurance related complaints. 1 800 292-9555 (Public Service Commission) In state only. Handles utility related complaints.
FLORIDA (Tallahassee) Hours: 7:45-4:30 (recording after hours) 1 800 342-2176 In state only. Handles most types of complaints and inquiries.	
GEORGIA (Atlanta) Hours: 8:00-5:00 1 800 282-4900 In state only. Handles general complaints and inquiries.	**MISSISSIPPI** (Jackson) Hours: 8:00-5:00 1 800 222-7622 (Governor's Hotline) In state only. Consumer complaints are referred.
ILLINOIS (Chicago) Hours: 8:30-5:00 1 800 252-8972 In state only. Handles complaints and inquiries related to state tax, senior citizens relief tax and other matters.	**MISSOURI** (Jefferson City) Hours: 8:15-4:45 1 800 392-8222 In state only. Handles complaints involving fraud and misrepresentation in the sale of goods.

Public officials are
available for ap-
pointments, tele-
phone calls, and
correspondence.

2. *By Phone.* Brief calls at reasonable hours are generally effective. Your state may have a Wide Area Telecommunications Service (WATS) line, which enables citizens to call elected officials toll free. You can leave a message, and your call will be returned. When calling Washington, D.C., remember time zone differences.

3. *By Wire.* Personal Opinion Messages may be sent to the president, vice president, U.S. senators and representatives, your governor, and the state legislators. The cost is $3.50 for 20 words, excluding your name and address, unless there are additional signatures. You can call 1-800-648-4100 to place a message.

4. *By Letter.* An effective letter written to the appropriate representative states clearly the purpose of the letter; identifies a bill by proper name

Figure 16-1
(continued)

MONTANA (Helena) Hours: 8:00-5:00 (answering service after hours) 1 800 332-2272 In state only. Refers complaints and inquiries to the proper state office.	**OHIO** (Columbus) Hours: 8:00-5:00 (recording after hours) 1 800 282-0515 In state only. Handles general complaints and inquiries.
NEVADA (Carson City) Hours: 8:00-5:00 1 800 992-0900 In state only. Operator connects consumer with state agencies. Consumer must know which agency to request.	**OKLAHOMA** (Oklahoma City) Hours: 8:00-5:00 1 800 522-8555 (Capitol Straight Line) In state only. Handles general complaints and inquiries.
NEW HAMPSHIRE (Concord) Hours: 8:00-4:00 1 800 852-3456 (Governor's Office of Citizens Services) In state only. Handles complaints and inquiries concerning energy. 1 800 852-3311 (State Council on Aging) In state only. Information about and for the elderly.	**OREGON** (Portland) Hours: 8:00-5:00 1 800 452-7813 In state only. Will link caller to appropriate state agency.
	SOUTH CAROLINA (Columbia) Hours: 8:00-5:00 1 800 992-1594 In state only. Handles general complaints and inquiries.
NEW JERSEY (Trenton) Hours: 9:00-5:00 (recording after hours) 1 800 792-8600 In state only. Refers complaints and inquiries to the proper agency.	**SOUTH DAKOTA** (Pierre) Hours: 8:00-5:00 1 800 592-1865 In state only. Tie line. Must ask for specific division.
NEW YORK (Albany) Hours: 7:30-4:30 1 800 342-3736 In state only. Handles consumer inquiries on all types of insurance coverage. Hours: 9:00-5:00 1 800 522-8707 In state only. Refers consumer inquiries on utilities to the proper public service/utility. Hours: 7:30-4:30 1 800 342-3823 In state only. Handles complaints concerning auto repairs performed within the last 90 days. Hours: 9:00-4:00 1 800 342-3722 (recording after hours) In state only. Answers inquiries about energy programs, conservation and regulations.	**TENNESSEE** (Nashville) Hours: 8:00-4:30 1 800 342-8385 In state only. Handles general complaints and inquiries. **VERMONT** (Montpelier) Hours: 8:00-4:30 1 800 642-5149 In state only. Handles general complaints and inquiries. **VIRGINIA** (Richmond) Hours: 8:30-5:00 1 800 552-9963 In state only. Handles general complaints and inquiries.
NORTH CAROLINA (Raleigh) Hours: 8:00-5:00 1 800 662-7777 In state only. Receives inquiries about insurance coverage.	**WASHINGTON** (Seattle) Hours: 1:00-5:00 1 800 552-0700 In state only. Will mail out complaint forms or make referrals.
NORTH DAKOTA (Bismark) Hours: 8:00-5:00 1 800 472-2600 In state only. Investigates allegations of consumer fraud. Hours: 8:00-5:00 1 800 472-2927 In state only. Handles general consumer complaints.	**WISCONSIN** (Madison) Hours: 8:00-4:45 1 800 362-3020 In state only. Handles general complaints and inquiries.

You can write to elected officials.

and number; refers to only one issue; and arrives while the issue is current. Give reasons for your position and avoid emotionalism. Ask for specific relief — what you want the elected official to do.

In almost all cases, your contact will be answered by an elected official. Telephone calls are generally returned within one or two working days. Letters are answered within a week or two.

Figure 16-2
Federal Toll-Free
Information Numbers

ALABAMA
Birmingham 205 322-8591
Mobile 205 438-1421
ALASKA
Anchorage 907 271-3650
ARIZONA
Phoenix 602 261-3313
Tucson 602 622-1511
ARKANSAS
Little Rock 501 378-6177
CALIFORNIA
Los Angeles 213 688-3800
Sacramento 916 440-3344
San Diego 714 293-6030
San Francisco 415 556-6600
San Jose 408 275-7422
Santa Ana 714 836 2386
COLORADO
Colorado Springs 303 471-9491
Denver 303 837-3602
Pueblo 303 544-9523
CONNECTICUT
Hartford 203 527-2617
New Haven 203 624-4720
FLORIDA
Fort Lauderdale 305 522-8531
Jacksonville 904 354-4756
Miami 305 350-4155
Orlando 305 422-1800
St. Petersburg 813 893-3495
Tampa 813 229-7911
West Palm Beach 305 833-7566
Northern Florida 1 800 282-8556
  (Sarasota, Manatee, Polk, Osceola, Orange, Seminole,
  and Volusia counties and north)
Southern Florida 1 800 432-6668
  (Charlotte, DeSoto, Hardee, Highlands, Okeechobee,
  Indian River and Brevard counties and south)
GEORGIA
Atlanta 404 221-6891
HAWAII
Honolulu 808 546-8620
ILLINOIS
Chicago 312 353-4242
INDIANA
Gary/Hammond 219 883-4110
Indianapolis 317 269-7373
IOWA
Des Moines 515 284-4448
Other locations 1 800 532-1556
KANSAS
Topeka 913 295-2866
Other locations 1 800 432-2934
KENTUCKY
Louisville 502 582-6261
LOUISIANA
New Orleans 504 589-6696
MARYLAND
Baltimore 301 962-4980
MASSACHUSETTS
Boston 617 223-7121
MICHIGAN
Detroit 313 226-7016
Grand Rapids 616 451-2628

MINNESOTA
Minneapolis 612 349-5333
MISSOURI
Kansas City 816 374-2466
St. Louis 314 425-4106
Other locations within area code 314 1 800 392-7711
Other locations within area codes 816 & 417 1 800 892-5808
NEBRASKA
Omaha 402 221-3353
Other locations 1 800 642-8383
NEW JERSEY
Newark 201 645-3600
Paterson/Passaic 201 523-0717
Trenton 609 396-4400
NEW MEXICO
Albu-querque 505 766-3091
Santa Fe 505 983-7743
NEW YORK
Albany 518 463-4421
Buffalo 716 846-4010
New York 212 264-4464
Rochester 716 546-5075
Syracuse 315 476-8545
NORTH CAROLINA
Charlotte 704 376-3600
OHIO
Akron 216 375-5638
Cincinnati 513 684-2801
Cleveland 216 522-4040
Columbus 614 221-1014
Dayton 513 223-7377
Toledo 419 241-3223
OKLAHOMA
Oklahoma City 405 231-4868
Tulsa 918 584-4193
OREGON
Portland 503 221-2222
PENNSYLVANIA
Allentown/Bethlehem 215 821-7785
Philadelphia 215 597-7042
Pittsburgh 412 644-3456
Scranton 717 346-7081
RHODE ISLAND
Providence 401 331-5565
TENNESSEE
Chattanooga 615 265-8231
Memphis 901 521-3285
Nashville 615 242-5056
TEXAS
Austin 512 472-5494
Dallas 214 767-8585
Fort Worth 817 334-3624
Houston 713 226-5711
San Antonio 512 224-4471
UTAH
Ogden 801 399-1347
Salt Lake City 801 524-5353
VIRGINIA
Newport News 804 244-0480
Norfolk 804 441-3101
Richmond 804 643-4928
Roanoke 703 982-8591
WASHINGTON
Seattle 206 442-0570
Tacoma 206 383-5230
WISCONSIN
Milwaukee 414 271-2273

VOCABULARY

Directions: Can you find the definition for each of the following terms used in Chapter 16?

generic
recall
Agricultural Marketing Service
National Bureau of Standards
net weight
Food and Drug Administration
  (FDA)
Office of Consumer Affairs
Federal Communications
  Commission (FCC)

Federal Trade Commission
  (FTC)
Postal Inspection Service
Civil Aeronautics Board (CAB)
Federal Bureau of Investiga-
  tion (FBI)
Better Business Bureau (BBB)
Major Appliance Consumer
  Action Panel (MACAP)
consumer advocate

1. The administrative agency that regulates radio and television broadcasting and interstate telephone and telegraph companies.
2. A local and state agency with no legal authority that is a clearinghouse of information about local businesses.
3. A general term used for a product having the same qualities or contents as a well-known brand name.
4. The procedure whereby a manufacturer stops production and refunds the purchase price of items already sold.
5. The weight of a product without the container or package.
6. An agency that inspects food to ensure wholesomeness and truthful labeling.
7. This group represents consumer interests in federal agency proceedings, develops consumer information materials, and assists with consumer complaints.
8. An agency that sets measurement, product, and safety standards for food packages.
9. An agency concerned with protecting consumers from unfair methods of competition, false or deceptive advertising, and other deceptive practices.
10. An agency charged with enforcing laws and regulations preventing distribution of mislabeled foods, drugs, cosmetics, and medical devices.
11. A division of the U.S. Postal Service that deals with consumer problems pertaining to illegal use of the mails.
12. One who promotes or seeks to protect the causes or interests of consumers.
13. A group comprised of representatives of the home appliance

industry, which provides assistance in resolving and minimizing consumer problems in the purchase and use of home appliances.

14. An agency of the U.S. Justice Department which investigates crimes and collects evidence for federal lawsuits.

15. An agency of the U.S. Department of Transportation which investigates complaints, inspects aircraft, and enforces safety regulations.

ITEMS FOR DISCUSSION

1. What consumer protection action was proposed by President Kennedy in 1962?

2. List the six major items in the Consumer Bill of Rights.

3. What was the purpose of the Food, Drug, and Cosmetic Act of 1938?

4. How long must a flame retardant finish last in children's sleepwear, as provided by the Flammable Fabrics Act of 1953?

5. Who tests all new drugs that are produced for sale in the marketplace?

6. What are the functions of the National Highway Safety Administration?

7. What was the major purpose of the care labeling rule (1972)?

8. Which two major agencies are within the Department of Health and Human Services?

9. What types of communications, in addition to radio and television broadcasting, are controlled by the FCC?

10. What types of crimes are investigated by the FBI? Give an example.

11. If you have a complaint about airline service, whom should you contact?

12. What do the letters BBB stand for?

13. List and describe the four ways to communicate with an elected official.

APPLICATIONS

1. Why are consumers encouraged to ask for generic products rather than brand-name products?

2. Does your state have a toll-free number to call for consumer inquiries or to register complaints? If so, what types of assistance are available?

3. What is the federal toll-free information number nearest you?

4. In your state, who holds each of the following elected offices?

    a. Governor
    b. Secretary of state
    c. State treasurer
    d. Attorney general
    e. Superintendent of public instruction
    f. Labor commissioner
    g. State senators for your district
    h. State representatives for your district

5. For your city and county, list the names of the following elected officials:

    a. Sheriff
    b. District attorney
    c. Mayor
    d. City council members
    e. City manager
    f. Tax assessor

CASE PROBLEMS AND ACTIVITIES

1. Select any garment from your closet. Read the care label and write down its entire message.
2. Cut the labels from three or four food products, such as soup, cereal, snacks, and processed foods. List the different types of information — such as quantity per serving, ingredients, and vitamin and mineral content — you find on the label. Are there ingredients you do not recognize? Is the nutritional value what you expected?
3. List your state and local sources of consumer assistance, such as the consumer protection, private, and governmental agencies that could assist you with a consumer complaint.
4. Consult the last annual report of *Consumer Reports*. Summarize three articles in this paperback book that are of interest to you.
5. Your local library contains much information about consumer problems and assistance. Visit the library and list in outline form what types of information are available for consumers who need information.
6. Attend a public hearing on a local issue — land use, zoning, etc. — and write a report on who was present, what was discussed, and the conclusion reached. Hearings are held in city hall or county buildings and are open to the public for testimony and input.

Chapter 17

LEGAL PROTECTION

◆◆◆◆◆◆◆◆◆◆◆◆◆◆◆◆◆◆◆◆◆◆◆◆◆

OBJECTIVES

1. Describe the organization of the legal system in the United States at federal, state, and local levels.
2. Explain the procedures involved from the time a complaint is filed until a judgment is entered by a court.
3. Define remedies available to consumers — from self-help through negotiating, to filing a lawsuit and seeking government assistance.

THE LEGAL SYSTEM
◆◆◆◆◆◆◆◆◆

Certain courts have power to hear certain types of cases.

At the base of our legal system are the courts. A **court** is a tribunal established by government to hear and decide matters properly brought before it, to give redress to the injured or enforce punishment against wrongdoers, and to prevent wrongs. Each court is empowered to decide certain types or classes of cases. This power is called **jurisdiction**, which is the legal right and authority of the court to hear and decide a case. A court may have original or appellate jurisdiction, or both. The court of original jurisdiction is the trial court. A **trial court** has the authority to hear a dispute when it is first brought into court. A court having appellate jurisdiction is the appellate court. An **appellate court** has the authority to review the judgment of a lower court.

Courts are also classified in terms of the nature of their jurisdiction. A **civil court** has the authority to hear disputes involving the violation of the private legal rights of individuals. Disputes between private citizens, private groups, companies, and corporations are heard in civil courts. In addition, both disputes against a branch of the government (local, state, or federal) and consumer complaints are heard in civil courts. A **criminal court** is for the trial of crimes regarded as violations of certain duties to society and disturbances of public peace and order. The government, representing all the people, prosecutes the alleged wrongdoer. Appeals can be made by the losing party in civil or criminal matters, if it appears that an error or injustice has been committed.

The government represents the people in criminal cases.

COURT PERSONNEL

The assistance of many people is required for the efficient operation of our federal and state court systems. Included are persons in the direct employ of the courts, officers of the court, and sometimes a jury.

Judge.   The judge is the presiding officer in the court and is either elected or appointed. Attorneys are usually selected by the parties in the dispute, but are sometimes selected by the judge, to present the issue in the case to the court.

The judge is the presiding officer.

Clerk.   The duties of the clerk of the court are to enter cases on the court calendar; to keep an accurate record of the proceedings; to accept, label, and provide safekeeping for all items of evidence; to administer the oath to witnesses and jurors; and sometimes to approve bail bonds and compute the costs involved.

Reporter.   The court reporter keeps a word-by-word record of the trial, usually through the use of a special recording machine. These trial records are available to each of the attorneys and are necessary for appeals.

Bailiff.   Deputy sheriffs serve as sergeants at arms during court proceedings. Bailiffs maintain order in the courtroom at the instruction of the judge.

Jury.   The **jury** is a body of citizens sworn by a court to hear the facts submitted during a trial and to render a verdict. A trial jury consists of not more than twelve persons. A juror must be over age 21 and under age 70, a resident of the county, and able to see and hear. Jurors are chosen from a list of local citizens — usually from tax or voter rolls.

Jurors are selected from lists of local citizens.

FEDERAL COURTS SYSTEM

The bases of federal jurisdiction are the United States Constitution and the laws enacted by Congress. The federal courts hear only matters that concern

Illustration 17-1
The jury hears the facts submitted during a trial and renders a verdict.

the nation as a whole — matters pertaining to constitutional rights, civil rights, interstate commerce, patents and copyrights, internal revenue, currency, and foreign relations. Other areas, such as crimes, contracts, and divorces, are left to the states in which the acts are committed. The federal courts may hear matters between citizens of two different states, but only if the dispute involves $10,000 or more.

United States Supreme Court. The Supreme Court is the top court of the federal court system and is located in Washington, D.C. The Supreme Court is the only federal court expressly established by the Constitution. Appeals from federal appellate courts and from state supreme courts that pertain to federal issues are heard by the Supreme Court. The Supreme Court chooses which cases it will hear. The Court sets its own **docket**, or schedule of cases, dates, and times for issues to be heard. Only cases of the greatest importance and national consequence are accepted. Thousands of actions are appealed every year; but the Supreme Court accepts only about 125 for consideration. There are nine Supreme Court justices, including a chief justice, who are appointed to their positions for life. No federal judge may be dismissed or impeached for any reason other than gross misconduct.

The U.S. Supreme Court chooses cases it will hear.

Courts of Appeal. The United States, including the District of Columbia, is divided into twelve judicial circuits. Each of the circuits has a court of appeals. Each appellate court has from five to nine judges, who review final decisions of the district courts. The decisions of the courts of appeal are final in most cases.

District Courts. The United States is divided into ninety federal districts, with a court assigned to each. Each district covers a state or a portion of a state. Consequently, some states may be home to more than one federal district court, while other states contain none (these states are part of a federal district whose court is in a different state). Each district court is a

There are 90 federal courts.

trial court, also divided into civil or criminal divisions. District courts are
staffed by judges who hear cases individually, not as a panel.

Special Federal Courts.   Additional special courts have been established
by Congress to hear only cases of a special nature. These special federal
courts include the Court of Claims, Customs Court, Court of International
Trade, Tax Court, Court of Military Appeals, and the territorial courts.

STATE COURTS SYSTEM

The greatest share of legal matters is handled in state court systems. This is
not only because state systems outnumber the federal system by 50 to 1, but
also because there are limits placed on the federal system by the
Constitution. The Tenth Amendment to the United States Constitution
grants each state the sovereign power to enact and enforce state laws. A
state's laws are contained in its constitution and enacted by its own
legislature. These laws are binding upon the citizens of a state and must not
violate the U.S. Constitution. Each state has the power to run its own court
system to decide issues that involve state laws. Each state establishes its own
set of court procedures, determines court names, divides areas of
responsibility among the various courts, and sets limits of authority among
the state courts.

State Supreme Court.   In most states the highest court is the state
supreme court, sometimes called the Court of Final Appeal. Ordinarily, the
state supreme court has appellate jurisdiction. The decision of a state
supreme court is final, except in cases involving the federal Constitution,
laws, and treaties. In many states, there are appellate courts and one
supreme court.

District and Circuit Courts.   General trial courts, often called state
district courts, circuit courts, or superior courts, decide matters beyond local
courts. These courts hear civil cases involving large sums of money,
criminal matters with major penalties, and cases that are appealed from
local courts whose decisions are questionable. Judges at this level are usually
appointed by the state governor, although some may be elected for terms of
four to six years. Decisions from district courts may be reviewed by the
highest state court.

County and City Courts.   The lowest state court levels are found at the
city or county level. These courts may also be called municipal or justice
courts. Courts at this level have authority limited by geographic boundaries.
Civil and criminal cases are heard at the local level. However, civil cases
must be for small amounts only. In some states, the maximum amount in
dispute in a civil case is $500. At the local level, disputes usually are heard
and decided by judges, not by juries. In very small areas, a judge may be

---

A state's laws are found in its constitution.

Cases may be appealed to higher courts.

Many disputes are heard by judges.

called a justice of the peace, who is an appointed, part-time official. Justices of the peace in other areas are elected officials. Special courts at the local level may be called police courts, traffic courts, small-claims courts, and justice-of-the-peace courts.

COURT PROCEDURE

The filing of a lawsuit involves many steps, costs, and outcomes. You will need an attorney who will advise you of your chances of winning your case, laws pertaining to your case, and what you need to do to prepare for trial. The services of a competent attorney will cost from $50 to $100 an hour, or more in some areas. Some attorneys will work on a contingency fee basis, which means they receive fees only if you win the case. Your state bar association can supply names of attorneys who specialize in the area of your complaint. Your attorney will appear in court on your behalf and represent your interests. In all states there is a **Statute of Limitations**, which restricts the length of time in which court action may be taken on various complaints. For example, in many states personal injury lawsuits must be filed within two years from the date of the injury. A lawsuit filed after the two-year limit will be dismissed.

You have a time limit within which to file.

Generally, a lawsuit involves the following steps: a complaint is filed; the defendant is served; the defendant appears; the case is tried; a judgment is entered; and costs are awarded.

Plaintiff Files Complaint.   The person filing the complaint is known as the **plaintiff**. The plaintiff sees an attorney and discusses the facts of the case. The attorney considers the matter, conducts extensive research on similar cases, and advises the client of the prospect of winning the lawsuit. If the client (plaintiff) wishes to pursue the matter, the attorney draws up the necessary papers, which the plaintiff signs. Action is begun by filing the complaint with the clerk of the appropriate court. A filing fee of $75 to $200 is usually required. Generally, the complaint consists of a description of the acts complained of by the plaintiff and a request for relief.

A filing fee is required if you wish to appear in court.

Defendant Is Served.   A certified copy of the complaint is served upon the defendant named in the lawsuit. The **defendant** is the person against whom the plaintiff is making a complaint. The local sheriff's department or a private service company may be used to serve the defendant. Usually, several days are required to serve the defendant, who must be presented with the papers personally. A reasonable time in which to appear (file a response to the complaint) is then allowed the defendant. Ten days are allowed if the defendant is served in the same county; if in the same state, 30 days; outside the state, 60 days or more. The defendant must decide whether to default — not answer and automatically lose — or answer the complaint. If the defendant does not answer, the plaintiff will receive the requested relief by default judgment.

The defendant must first obtain the services of an attorney and discuss the case. Then the defendant's attorney prepares and files the answer. A counterclaim asserting the plaintiff's guilt, and therefore liability in the matter, could be filed by the defendant. A **counterclaim** states that the defendant believes the plaintiff to be at fault and demands damages as a result of the plaintiff's actions. At this point, the defendant may also file a motion to dismiss (called a *demurrer*), which states that even if the plaintiff's complaint is true, the plaintiff is still not entitled to any relief. The defendant may also allege that there is insufficient evidence, improper jurisdiction, or other legal reasons why the matter should not be set for trial.

Defendant Appears.   After the defendant's attorney has filed an answer with the appropriate court, a date is set for the trial. The trial date is set several months before the matter can be heard. During the time before trial, much work must be done by the plaintiff and defendant, and by their attorneys. Attorneys gather information, talk to witnesses, prepare legal arguments, take depositions, hire investigators, examine reports, and negotiate with the opposing party. **Depositions** are written, sworn statements of witnesses taken before court appearances in order to preserve the memory of the issues. Many cases are settled before going to trial because both parties realize the risk involved in a trial. If a settlement can be reached, a formal agreement is signed, and the case is dropped.

Trial Takes Place.   All defendants are entitled to request a jury trial in state courts. For a jury trial, several days may be necessary to question and choose a panel of jurors. Attorneys are careful to eliminate anyone who appears prejudiced, knows any person who will be present at the trial, or who for any reason might not be able to reach an unbiased decision. Once the jury is seated, the trial begins.

The plaintiff's case is presented first. Any evidence and witnesses to support the case are included in the presentation. The defendant then presents evidence and witnesses in defense against the plaintiff's allegations. Then the attorneys for both sides make closing arguments and the jury deliberates. A decision is reached and announced to the court by the foreman (chosen leader) of the jury.

Judgment Is Entered and Costs Are Awarded.   Based on the decision of the jury or the judge, a judgment is entered. A **judgment** is an obligation or debt created by the decree (decision) of a court. The losing party has a limited time in which to appeal. A case heard in a state district court may be appealed to a circuit court. After the circuit court, the case may go to the state appeals court, and then to the state supreme court. Any matters involving national interests may be appealed to the United States Supreme Court, which may or may not choose to hear the issue.

Sidebar notes:

Attorneys prepare papers to file in court.

Written statements are taken to preserve memory of an event.

You can ask for a jury trial.

Costs awarded to the winning party include the cost of filing papers with the court, the cost of having the sheriff or other officers of the court take official action, fees paid to witnesses, jury fees, and the cost of printing the record of the trial. Sometimes a reasonable attorney's fee may be awarded.

In addition to monetary damages, the plaintiff may seek what is known as equitable relief. **Equitable relief** is a legal action that allows a previous order to be rescinded, requires a situation to be restored to its previous state, or provides for the performance of a specific act. For example, you could ask the judge to allow you to withdraw from a legal contract. A judge may, in some situations, deny monetary damages to a plaintiff if the defendant will restore certain items to their rightful owner — the plaintiff. Equitable relief is often granted when a monetary judgment would not adequately serve to compensate an innocent or damaged party for injuries caused by the actions of the defendant. An action or restraint from action (equitable relief) may be more appropriate than monetary damages.

FINDING A REMEDY

If you are a victim of a consumer problem, you may want to review the courses of action available to you. Alternatives for redress are self-help, small-claims court, a private or class action lawsuit, or assistance from a government or private agency to stop the objectionable practices and help you recover your money.

SELF-HELP

After you have carefully analyzed the problem and believe you are entitled to some type of relief, you can proceed to seek redress. Negotiating and withholding payment are two self-help techniques you may find effective. Negotiating.   A negotiated settlement is one voluntarily entered into by both sides. The buyer must be willing to give up some things in return for the seller's changing his or her position. In most cases, when consumers complain and want some type of settlement, the seller is willing to discuss the issues to reach some type of agreement so that the goodwill of the customer can be maintained. Negotiating is a process that requires tact and precision. You must know the problem, what you want done about it, and what you are willing to do to make a settlement. Negative emotions and statements will not facilitate an agreement.

A customer who has purchased a product that is faulty or otherwise unsatisfactory should seek an agreeable remedy with the merchant before pursuing legal remedies. Once the merchant is alienated from (unfriendly toward) the customer because of the customer's actions, the possibility of a negotiated settlement is reduced. Negotiated settlements are often much less expensive and easier to achieve than seeking legal relief. It is essential that the consumer follow up immediately after the damage has occurred. A long wait before seeking a remedy can sometimes result in no relief for damages.

Legal action is more expensive than other alternatives.

When two parties in a dispute cannot reach an agreement, arbitration may be used. The arbitrator is usually chosen by both parties, and both parties agree to accept the decision of the arbitrator. In some cases a panel is chosen — one arbitrator representing each party, and the two arbitrators choosing a third panel member. Arbitration services are expensive, but much less expensive than court action.

There are many alternatives to settling disputes in the courts. The Yellow Pages of your telephone book has listings for mediation and arbitration services. In addition, Figure 17-1 lists sources of information and assistance that you can contact by writing or calling.

Withholding Payment. As a consumer you have rights when there is a credit dispute. You must put your complaint in writing and explain clearly the reason why you are withholding payment on the disputed amount. The seller is compelled to respond to your complaint and has time limits in which to resolve the matter. You should pay all other amounts due as agreed. Do not withhold payment on amounts not in question, as this will weaken your position. Your credit cannot be damaged if you follow the proper procedures for questioning credit charges.

Pay amounts not in dispute.

When merchandise is purchased with credit, you have more leverage than if you pay cash, because the merchant is motivated to get payment for the merchandise that is already in your possession. Again, diplomacy is required.

SMALL-CLAIMS COURT

If the amount is relatively small, you might consider small-claims court. The matter will be heard quickly, but the decision is final. Fees are small. You must represent yourself — no attorneys are allowed — and there is no jury. The matter is decided by a judge. A request for a jury would remove the matter to a district or circuit court. Most states have a maximum amount of $500 to $1,000 in damages that can be recovered in a small-claims court.

Attorneys are not allowed in small-claims court.

Small-claims courts are usually easy to use. An instruction sheet that explains how to file a small claim is available at your county courthouse. You must know the name and address of the person with whom you have a problem. You must know the amount in controversy and make a short statement of why you are entitled to the money.

Figure 17-1
Sources of Assistance

Arbitration	The American Arbitration Association (headquarters) 140 W. 51st Street New York, NY 10020
	Call: 212-484-4000
	Has offices in 25 cities (see your local telephone book).
Bar Referral	The American Bar Association can give the name and address of the nearest dispute resolution center. Write:
	American Bar Association's Special Committee on Alternative Dispute Resolution 1800 M Street NW Washington, D.C. 20036
	Call: 202-331-2258
	You will receive a list of 200 centers for $10.
Business Disputes	For free publications for businesses on saving money on legal disputes through use of a panel of dispute resolvers, write:
	Center for Public Resources 680 Fifth Avenue New York, NY 10019
	Call: 202-541-9830
Divorce Mediation	Divorce Mediation Research Project 1720 Emerson Street Denver, CO 80218
	Send $10 to receive a partial list of mediators who specialize in divorce.
	Endispute Suite 803 11 Dupont Circle NW Washington, D.C. 20036
	Call: 202-232-5368
	Offices also in Chicago, Los Angeles, and San Francisco.
	West Coast affiliate: Judicial Arbitration & Mediation Service P.O. Box 10333 Santa Ana, CA 92711
	Call: 714-972-1616
Lawyer Tips	For tips on dealing with lawyers, write: HALT Americans for Legal Reform Suite 309 201 Massachusetts Avenue NE Washington, D.C. 20002
	Call: 202-546-4258

Once your claim is filed, a copy of it is served upon the defendant. The defendant has ten days to appear. If the defendant contests the claim, a hearing date is set. The hearing lasts about a half hour. The plaintiff presents his or her side of the case; the defendant presents his or her side. You may bring in written statements or evidence, as well as witnesses. You should summarize your position on one page and present it to the judge.

No record is made of the small-claims court hearing. It cannot be appealed — the judge's decision is final. The benefit of taking your dispute to small-claims court is the saving of money. You pay no attorney fees. Court filing fees are small — $5 to $20 is common. The case is heard in a few weeks at most, giving you speedy relief. If the defendant does not appear, you win by default. The judge proclaims a judgment and the losing party is required to pay damages.

It is important in a small-claims court hearing that you be organized, calm, and specific about your complaint. If you are asking for $500 in damages, you must be prepared to show why you deserve that sum. The judge will ask questions of the plaintiff and defendant. Usually the judge will make an immediate decision, or will take a 15-minute break and return with the decision.

Many people are experts at appearing in small-claims court. Collection agencies, for example, appear often in small-claims court and know exactly what will happen. If it is your first appearance, you may be nervous and unable to explain your position. Therefore, it is important to prepare yourself by outlining what you will say, gathering evidence you want to present, and summarizing your position. You may read your statement and give a copy to the judge.

Under the Unlawful Trade Practices Act, a person who purchases goods or services and suffers a loss of money or property as a result of the willful practices performed by another person may bring an action to recover actual damages or $200, whichever is greater. In other words, if you bought a piece of merchandise valued at $15 that caused you great harm, and it was the willful act of the seller to sell you that defective merchandise, you can collect $200 rather than the value of the merchandise. You, the buyer, must prove loss. For example, if the $15 item exploded and caused you to break your glasses and see the doctor to be treated for burns, then you have actual loss.

The Truth in Lending Act provides that if the lender willfully fails to disclose required information, the buyer is entitled to actual damages sustained, or twice the finance charge under the contract, but not less than $100 or more than $1,000.

In any small-claims action, the plaintiff must prove that the defendant's act was willful — in other words, that the defendant intended to defraud and knowingly and willingly proceeded to do so. The plaintiff must also prove that a loss was sustained as a result of the defendant's willful actions.

No permanent record is kept.

Willful acts by sellers can cost $200 in damages.

You must prove the acts were intentional.

PRIVATE OR CLASS ACTION

You may wish to consider filing a private lawsuit. If others are similarly affected, a class action lawsuit may be appropriate. In either event, lawsuits can be very costly and take several years to resolve. Be sure you are willing to take the risk and invest the time to resolve the matter in court.

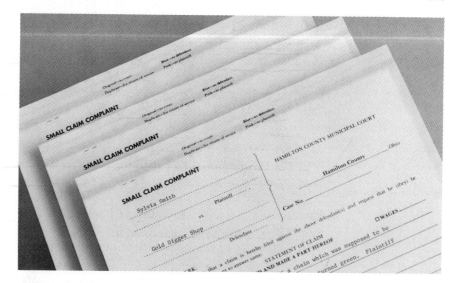

Illustration 17-2
Small-claims courts
are used to resolve
disputes involving
small amounts of
money.

A private lawsuit is filed to resolve a dispute between an individual (or a business) and others. The lawsuit is called a civil case and is resolved by compromise or formal court trial. Many lawsuits are settled between parties before going to trial.

When more than one person is damaged because of the acts of another, a class action lawsuit may be filed. In this case, a person sues another in behalf of himself or herself and all others who may have been affected by the defendant's actions in the same way.

In a class action, the maximum recovery allowed against creditors is $100,000 or 1 percent of the net worth of the creditor, whichever is less. Consumers suing creditors through class action are not given the double recovery or minimum $100 damages that are normally awarded in private lawsuits. In a class action suit, there could be a million consumers represented; setting a limit on damages awarded prevents an unreasonable recovery amount.

Maximum recovery protects from an unreasonable penalty.

In a class action, the size of the attorneys' fees ordered by the court (the losing party pays the attorneys' fees for the winner) and the court costs are at the discretion of the judge. For example, if the creditor loses the suit, the judge considers the size of damages awarded, frequency of complaints and severity of damages, the failure of the creditor to meet his or her responsibilities to the public, the resources of the creditor, and the number of persons adversely affected by the creditor's actions.

Anyone can file a lawsuit.

Anyone can file a lawsuit. The advantages and disadvantages of filing a lawsuit should be weighed carefully before you decide. Because of the courts' busy schedules, you may wait from one to three years after you have filed the complaint to appear in court. After a court renders a decision, the losing party may file an appeal. You cannot collect a judgment until the appeal is resolved. Therefore, it could be many years before you actually receive any monetary benefits from a lawsuit.

One can never be sure of winning a lawsuit. There may be unknown facts or conditions that will affect the outcome of the action. Therefore, you should enter a lawsuit only if you can afford to lose the money you invest in it, and only if you believe there is much more involved than the money you stand to gain.

Consumer groups help you if your rights are violated.

In some cases, you can convince a consumer protection group to file a lawsuit in your behalf. For example, the American Civil Liberties Union (ACLU) files lawsuits to protect the rights of masses of citizens. The ACLU collects money from donations to pay the fees and costs involved. Many individuals cannot afford to pursue legal remedies without the help of such groups, because of the cost involved.

GOVERNMENTAL ASSISTANCE

Government agencies will give information and assist with a complaint.

In addition to the sources of consumer assistance listed in Chapter 16, you may wish to seek help from a government agency to help stop objectionable practices and get your money back. In many cases, the cost to you is small, while the benefit to all consumers is great. Government agencies that have information and can assist you with a consumer complaint include the following:

AUTOMOBILES

National Highway Traffic Safety Administration

COLLECTION, CREDIT

State Consumer Protection Division (at your state capitol)

DRUGS/FOODS

Food and Drug Administration

HOUSEHOLD

Consumer Product Safety Commission

INVESTMENT FRAUD

Federal Trade Commission
Securities and Exchange Commission

MEDICAL/DENTAL

State Board of Medical Examiners

State Department of Commerce
State Board of Dental Examiners
State Health Division
State Board of Pharmacy

MEDICARE

Social Security Administration

MISREPRESENTATION/FRAUD

State Consumer Protection Division
Local District Attorney
Local or State Better Business Bureau

TRANSPORTATION

Interstate Commerce Commission

WARRANTIES

Federal Trade Commission

VOCABULARY

Directions: Can you find the definition for each of the following terms used in Chapter 17?

court	Statute of Limitations
jurisdiction	plaintiff
trial court	defendant
appellate court	counterclaim
civil court	depositions
criminal court	judgment
jury	equitable relief
docket	

1. A legal action that allows a previous order to be rescinded, restoration of a previous state, or the performance of a specific act.
2. A tribunal to hear and settle matters brought before it.
3. A tribunal for the trial of crimes regarded as violations of duties to society.
4. A tribunal having authority to hear disputes involving private individuals.
5. The legal right and authority to hear and decide a case.
6. A body of citizens sworn by a court to hear issues of fact and render a verdict.
7. A schedule of cases, dates, and times of issues to be heard by the court.
8. The original court that hears a dispute first brought into court.
9. The person who files a complaint and brings an issue before a court.
10. A tribunal having authority to review the judgment of a lower court.
11. A law that controls the length of time in which a court action must be taken or else the grievance must be forgotten.
12. The person against whom a complaint is made.
13. Written, sworn statements of witnesses, records of which are used in court at a later date.
14. An assertion by a defendant that the plaintiff is at fault.
15. An obligation or debt created by the decree (decision) of the court.

ITEMS FOR DISCUSSION

1. Describe what types of matters are heard before these courts:

    a. Trial court
    b. Appellate court

c. Civil court

d. Criminal court

2. List and briefly describe the officers of the court.

3. On what bases is the federal court system operating?

4. What is the top court of the federal court system?

5. How many districts are there for federal district courts in the United States?

6. List several courts that are considered special federal courts.

7. What is the top court in the state court system?

8. What are the lowest state courts? Give two examples.

9. List the six steps that occur when a court action is filed and carried through trial to a decision of a judge or jury.

APPLICATIONS

1. Why are small-claims courts easy to use and, in some cases, more advantageous?

2. A lawsuit is filed by the plaintiff. Explain what happens until a judgment is entered for the plaintiff.

3. A case that involves a dispute in a city is filed with the circuit court of a county in the same state. When the case is heard in a trial court, where can the case be appealed?

4. As a store customer, you are dissatisfied with a product purchased. Explain the self-help remedies and actions to consider in resolving the dispute.

5. List six government agencies that have information and can assist you in a consumer complaint. What type of complaint is each agency responsible for?

CASE PROBLEMS AND ACTIVITIES

1. Name the present justices of the U.S. Supreme Court, with their terms of office. Put a star by the name of the chief justice.

2. Spend a half day at a local county courthouse. Make arrangements to observe a case being tried. You will not be allowed to leave the room until the court adjourns, nor will you be allowed to enter while court is in session. You may observe a civil or criminal matter. Write a report on what you observe.

3. Visit your local law library located at the county courthouse or at a law school if there is one in your area. List five types of references available. Look up the Statute of Limitations for filing lawsuits in

your state and tell how long you have to file actions in the following situations:

a. Wrongful death or injury
b. Real property infringement
c. Civil action where you are the injured party of a contract

Also in your law library, you will find books that summarize cases tried and decided in your state. Find a case that interests you and summarize the issues of the case, the court's decision, and your reactions.

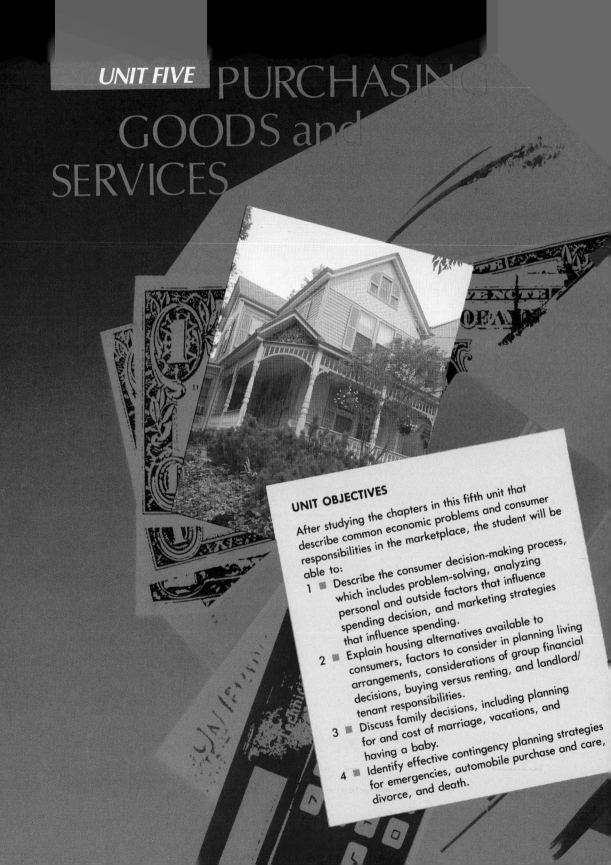

UNIT OBJECTIVES

After studying the chapters in this fifth unit that describe common economic problems and consumer responsibilities in the marketplace, the student will be able to:

1 ■ Describe the consumer decision-making process, which includes problem-solving, analyzing personal and outside factors that influence spending decision, and marketing strategies that influence spending.

2 ■ Explain housing alternatives available to consumers, factors to consider in planning living arrangements, considerations of group financial decisions, buying versus renting, and landlord/ tenant responsibilities.

3 ■ Discuss family decisions, including planning for and cost of marriage, vacations, and having a baby.

4 ■ Identify effective contingency planning strategies for emergencies, automobile purchase and care, divorce, and death.

Chapter 18

CONSUMER DECISION MAKING

◆◆◆◆◆◆◆◆◆◆◆◆◆◆◆◆◆◆◆◆◆◆◆◆◆

OBJECTIVES

1. Demonstrate an understanding of the decision-making process by applying it to a real or hypothetical problem.
2. List and describe personal factors that influence consumer decision making.
3. List and describe outside factors that influence spending decisions.
4. Analyze and compare marketing strategies used to induce consumer spending.

THE CONSUMER DECISION-MAKING PROCESS

◆◆◆◆◆◆◆◆

Decisions should be carefully planned.

Buying decisions play an important role in your efforts to manage your personal finances. Good decisions can save you money; bad decisions can be expensive. For this reason, your decision to purchase a product or service should always be based on careful consideration of available information and alternatives. The five-step consumer decision-making process presented in this chapter is a logical plan to use in solving problems caused by wants, needs, and goals. By following this process, you can make wise and economical buying decisions.

DEFINE THE PROBLEM

First, you must define
the problem.

The first step in the consumer decision-making process is simple: **define the problem** — state the problem (the need or want to be satisfied) in a short, concise sentence. When your want or need has been pinpointed, you can proceed to the goal of satisfying the need or want in a way that fits your financial resources. For example, you and your roommate have just moved into an apartment complex that offers no laundry facilities. Your problem is that you want and need clean clothes; your goal is to find a way to satisfy this need in an economical fashion. The problem, when solved, will achieve your goal of finding laundry facilities and will satisfy the need for clean clothes in a way that will give you the most value for the money you spend. This first step in the consumer decision-making process is an important one, because you make decisions concerning the purchase of products and services at the problem level of satisfying needs and wants.

OBTAIN ACCURATE INFORMATION

List all possible solutions to the problem.

Once you have determined the problem, you must then gather information relating to your problem. To **obtain accurate information**, list all alternative solutions to the problem and the cost of each. In the laundry problem example, there are three possible solutions:

1. Use a laundromat.
2. Buy a new washer and dryer.
3. Buy a used washer and dryer.

In order to make a wise decision about your problem of obtaining clean clothes, you will need to know what products and services are available and how much it will cost you to use or purchase them. For instance, you will need to know where laundry facilities are located. The cost of use will include the price for each washer and dryer load, mileage for driving to and from the laundry, and the time involved. For the possible purchase of new appliances, you will need to list desired equipment features and then visit various appliance stores, department stores, and discount stores to compare prices. At each location, you should list the brands available, features available, costs, and warranties. The classified ads are a good source for used washers and dryers.

Comparison shopping provides alternatives.

Whenever possible, keep a written record of the information you collect on choices of products and services. By doing so, you can compare alternatives and costs more easily. Figure 18-1 shows information collected for comparison in the laundry problem.

Figure 18-1
Information for
Comparison

COST COMPARISON

	Per Month	Per Year
Option 1: Use a Laundromat		
Time: about 4 to 6 hours each weekend spent at laundromat	20 hrs.	250 hrs.
Gasoline: 6 miles round trip, once each weekend, 52/year	$ 3.00	$ 36.00
Washer, 75 cents each load, 6 loads each weekend	18.00	216.00
Dryer, 50 cents each load, 6 loads each weekend	12.00	144.00
	$33.00	$396.00

Option 2: Buy New Machines		
Average quality machines, on sale (washer/dryer)	$600.00	one-time cost
Monthly payments (2 years to pay off, 13 percent interest)	$26.63	$319.56

Costs of repair, upkeep, service contract, etc. are additional.
There is no time expense, because other things can be done while machines are running.
Machines should last 5 to 10 years.

Option 3: Buy Used Machines		
Average quality used washer/dryer at garage sale	$300.00	one-time cost
Monthly payments (usually have to pay cash; borrow money from bank for 1 year at 13 percent interest)	$28.25	$339.00

Costs of repair and upkeep are additional.
Machines should last 3 to 5 years.

Illustration 18-1
If you need clean
clothes, you must
decide how to sat-
isfy that need.

COMPARE ALTERNATIVES

The third step is to **compare alternatives** — examine good and bad points for
each possible solution. When comparing total costs, consider time and
convenience factors as well as dollar amounts. In some cases, convenience
may be more important than cost, as long as the cost is reasonable. Using the
previous example, you may decide that the convenience of having a washer
and dryer in your apartment is worth the extra dollar cost. You may also
decide to buy a new washer and dryer, even though the cost will be greater,
because you prefer to avoid the expense of possible repairs. Purchasing used
rather than new appliances is riskier because previous owners may or may
not have cared for and maintained the appliances properly.

Convenience may be
more important than
cost.

On the other hand, if your housing situation is temporary, and you and
your roommate plan to share the apartment for less than a year, going to the
nearest laundromat and dividing the expenses may be the best choice. These
are just a few of the factors you must consider in this step of the consumer
decision-making process.

Consider how long
you will live in the
apartment.

SELECT AN ALTERNATIVE

The fourth step is to **select an alternative** — make your decision. If you
follow the steps outlined in the preceding paragraphs, the decision you make
will be based on a careful analysis of the problem, thorough information

gathering, and analysis of that information. In our example, the decision is to determine whether to use a laundromat or to buy a washer and dryer. The cost is the price you will pay for what you decide to do. All choices have prices, because to choose one thing is not to choose another. The wise decision in this or in any situation is the one that is within your budget and that gives you the most value for your money.

You should be satisfied with your decision.

TAKE ACTION

After you have selected the best alternative, you must **take action** — carry out your decision and satisfy your need. Because you have made a thorough analysis of information necessary to solve your problem, you can be sure that you have made a wise decision.

PERSONAL FACTORS THAT INFLUENCE SPENDING DECISIONS

♦♦♦♦♦♦♦♦

There are many personal factors that influence consumer spending decisions. **Personal factors** are those influences in a person's or family's life that determine spending patterns, preferences, and choices. Some persons and families may be influenced greatly by one or more of the following factors: personal resources; position in life; customs, background, and religion; and values and goals.

PERSONAL RESOURCES

Your personal resources affect your choices.

Your **personal resources** include your time, money, energy, skills and abilities, and available credit. The greater the quantity and the higher the quality of any one of these factors, the greater your purchasing power. Generally speaking, the more resources available to you, the greater your earning potential and the greater your buying capacity.

POSITION IN LIFE

Your position in life includes such factors as age, marital status, sex, employment status, and life-style. At different times in your life, your needs and wants are different. Within each of life's stages, your spending patterns will also vary. Spending patterns of single people are different from those of married couples and families. Spending patterns at age 40 are different from those at age 30. Right now your spending patterns are probably different from those of your parents, and your parents' patterns differ from your grandparents' because of age differences alone. If you have been working for 20 years, your spending patterns are different from the person who just started working three months ago.

CUSTOMS, BACKGROUND, AND RELIGION

A **custom** is a long-established practice that may be considered an unwritten law. Families may be dedicated to traditions that have been followed for generations. This is particularly true of religious groups or cultures in which strict rules and practices are followed. Persons in these religious or cultural groups may observe special holidays and occasions that are not observed nationally. The buying patterns of these groups are greatly influenced by the values and priorities in their lives. In many cases, custom overshadows all other buying preferences.

Customs can be strong motivating influences.

VALUES AND GOALS

Values, which lie at the base of all our purchasing decisions, are slow to change. Goals change often. You accomplish goals and move on to others. Your total value system may change as your goals in life are met, or not met. Individual and family values and goals are expressed through choices of entertainment, literature, sports, luxuries, and so on. These choices are reflected in decisions to purchase goods and services, use of time and energy, and attitudes toward possessions and their accumulation.

Values are expressed through choices.

OUTSIDE FACTORS THAT INFLUENCE SPENDING DECISIONS

◆◆◆◆◆◆◆◆

To understand how the world in which you live plays a role in your decision-making process, you must consider the following: the economy, technological advances, the environment, and social pressures.

THE ECONOMY

The **economy** is the system or structure of economic life in a country. This term describes the financial well-being of the nation as measured by economists. As you will learn in Unit 6, the general condition of the economy affects every one of us, and we react to it accordingly. For example, in a period of high inflation, when prices are rising rapidly, people tend to buy more and save less. Prices rise so rapidly that money purchases less each day. There is little incentive to save because the rate of interest on savings is much less than the rate of inflation, and to save money is to lose money. When the rate of inflation is low, the economy is slow, and interest rates are high. When interest rates on automobile loans are high, fewer people are able to buy new cars. Consequently, older cars are kept longer. In these times, people save more and buy less (or buy less expensive items) because they do not want to pay high rates of interest on purchases, but they do want to *be* paid high interest rates on their savings accounts.

Inflation causes loss of purchasing power.

TECHNOLOGICAL ADVANCES

You may be fascinated or even obsessed with new electronic games. Or you may be interested in the world's first water-powered automobile. Perhaps you want to add a new solar heating device to your home to make it more energy efficient. In America, a high value is placed on new technological advances. Many people want to have the newest, most convenient, modern, and interesting gadgets. As new goods and services are created to increase our level of comfort and standard of living, we willingly purchase them. These types of purchases, whether large or small, are important to the emotional well-being of the consumer who needs to have the latest gimmick to feel a part of what is going on in the world.

Faster, better ways of doing things are important to us.

THE ENVIRONMENT

Concern for the environment can affect consumer buying decisions to a great extent. The physical environment and quality of life are concerns today. Our natural resources are scarce and are disappearing rapidly. Air quality, of vital importance to our health and well-being, is an issue individuals and the government spend much time and money discussing. In addition, millions of dollars are spent each year to help preserve the natural beauty, landscape, waterways, wildlife, and other natural resources of our

Conservation is a high priority in America.

country. Citizens involve themselves with home projects, community activities, and statewide programs to beautify and preserve, recycle, and protect existing resources and environment. Thus, this interest in the environment affects consumers' actions and also their product preferences because products purchased must be ecologically safe and biodegradable (or otherwise recyclable) to meet present and future environmental standards.

SOCIAL PRESSURES

Social pressures often induce consumers to buy goods and services beyond their real wants and needs. People can be influenced to make purchases by their friends, relatives, and coworkers. The media (radio, television, newspapers) also act as sources of social pressure for consumers. Through advertising, the media convince consumers to buy goods and services designed to keep them young, good looking, healthy, and appealing to the opposite sex. America is a country obsessed with youth, beauty, physical fitness, and material comforts. We are easily enticed into buying merchandise we do not need — status symbols, such as a second car or designer clothes that are beyond our budget, rather than necessities. The list is endless. Understanding how outside factors such as the economy, technological advances, the environment, and social pressures influence our spending patterns can help us to make wise consumer decisions.

Advertising appeals to hidden fears and desires.

MARKETING STRATEGIES THAT INFLUENCE SPENDING DECISIONS

◆◆◆◆◆◆◆◆

Marketing strategies are designed to sell products.

Numerous marketing strategies lure us into stores to buy goods and services. Many of these strategies are subtle, and we are often unaware of their impact on our buying patterns. Some frequently used marketing strategies explained in this chapter are advertising, pricing, sales, and promotional techniques.

ADVERTISING

The primary goal of all advertising is to create within the consumer the desire to purchase a product or service. Some advertising is false and misleading; other advertising is informational and valuable.

A variety of media is available for advertising — billboards, television, radio, newspapers, magazines, leaflets, balloons, and T-shirts — each carefully intended to reach specific consumer groups. Advertising agencies create colorful and attractive campaigns: They compose jingles and catchy tunes, develop slogans and trademarks, design colorful logos, and choose mascots to identify their products. There are three basic types of advertising: product, company, and industry.

Product Advertising. Advertising to convince consumers to buy a specific good or service is called **product advertising**. The name of the advertised product is repeated several times during radio and television commercials. Testimonials from people who have used the product, giveaways, promotional gimmicks, and other clever and catchy methods are used to persuade consumers to purchase products and services. Advertisements are carefully planned to appeal to specific types of consumers. A **target audience** is a specific consumer group to which the advertisements for a product are directed. Research has revealed specific characteristics of people who will probably be interested in a given product or service. Day of the week, time of day, and type of program are taken into consideration by television advertisers. All these factors are important when trying to reach a target audience. Products advertised during football games differ from products advertised during daytime television because the target audiences are different.

Advertising is directed to a target audience.

Company Advertising. Advertising to promote the image of a store, company, or retail chain is known as **company advertising**. Usually price is not a consideration, and specific products are not mentioned. Emphasis is placed on the quality of the products or services the company sells, warranties or guarantees offered, or social and environmental concerns of the company. In a store advertisement, you may hear or read about the company's friendly employees, its wide selection of products or services, or its claim that you can find everything you want in one place. These advertisements are designed to prompt a favorable attitude toward the company so that you develop a loyalty to the store and will not shop anywhere else. Company advertisements may be accompanied by catchy slogans and tunes, happy cartoons, or pleasant scenes to which products of this company make a contribution.

Companies advertise to promote a good image.

Industry Advertising. Advertising to promote a general product group, without regard to where these products are purchased, is called **industry advertising**. For example, the dairy industry emphasizes the nutritional value of milk and other natural dairy products. Consequently, the whole dairy industry benefits when people drink more milk and eat more dairy products. Oil industry advertisements stress concern about energy conservation, environmental protection, and the search for new alternative forms of fuels. The automobile industry gives safe-driving tips and reasons

Industry advertising is general and many retailers benefit.

Illustration 18-2
Advertisers want to
convince you to buy
their product or
service.

for buying American-made cars. General health and safety advertisements
are often presented in industry advertising campaigns, such as the Smokey
the Bear fire safety commercials and the stop-smoking ads.

PRICING

The price of merchandise depends on several factors. Supply and demand
determine what will be produced and what the general price range will be.
The cost of raw materials and labor, competitive pressures, and the seller's
need to make a reasonable profit are some of the factors that determine the
price of a product. But there is more to pricing than adding up the
production costs and including a profit. Retailers understand the
psychological aspects of selling goods and services and use pricing devices to
persuade consumers to buy. For example, if buyers believe they are getting a
bargain, or are paying a lower price, they are more inclined to buy a product
or service. **Odd-number pricing** is the practice of putting odd numbers on
price tags — 98 or 99 cents instead of $1.00. Because the price is under a
dollar, it appears to be a bargain. By paying $5.98 instead of $6.00, the
customer is happy to have found a good buy; the retailer is happy to have
made a profitable sale.

There are psycholog-
ical aspects of selling
products.

Discounts or low unit prices are often available for buying in large sizes or
quantities. However, you cannot assume that because you are buying the
large economy size you are actually paying less per ounce than if you bought
a small size. Compare unit prices on all sizes.

SALES

Stores advertise end-of-month sales, anniversary sales, clearance sales, inventory sales, holiday sales, preseason sales, and so on. Merchandise may be marked down substantially, slightly, or not at all. In order to be sure that you are actually saving money by buying sale items, you must do comparative shopping and know the usual prices. When an advertisement states that everything in the store is marked down, check carefully for items that only appear to be marked down in price.

Know product prices when shopping sales.

A **loss leader** is an item of merchandise marked down to an unusually low price, sometimes below the store's actual cost. The store may actually lose money on every sale of this item because the cost of producing the item is higher than the retail price. However, the loss leader is used to get customers into the store to buy other products as well. Sales on other items are expected to make up for the loss sustained on the loss leader. There is nothing illegal or unethical about a loss leader as long as the product advertised is available to the customer on demand. A customer who buys only loss leaders and super sale items is called a **cherry picker**. Retailers rely on customers to buy other products to make up for the loss caused by sales of the loss leader. Consequently, cherry pickers are not highly favored by retailers.

Loss leaders are used to draw you in to buy other things, too.

PROMOTIONAL TECHNIQUES

In order to get customers into stores, retailers may use one or more promotional techniques: displays, contests and games, trading stamps, coupons, packaging, and sampling.

Displays.   Retail stores often use window displays, special racks of new items, or sampling promotions to entice customers. Products are arranged attractively, and the promotion may carry a theme centered around the nearest holiday — Halloween, Thanksgiving, Christmas, Valentine's Day, Mother's Day, Father's Day, or the Fourth of July. Color schemes, decorations, music, and special effects often set off the products being offered to appeal to consumers' ego needs.

Contests and Games.   Grocery stores, department stores, fast food restaurants, and other retail stores that depend on repeat customers often use contests and games to bring customers back. Individual product packages, such as cereal boxes, may contain game cards. The possibility of winning something or getting something for nothing appeals to many people. Large and small prizes are offered with the intention of getting customers to come back and buy more so that they can get more game cards, have more chances to win, and receive some of the minor prizes. Careful reading of the rules on

Contests and games lure in new customers and keep old ones interested.

the reverse side of the game card or other token reveals the customer's chances of winning. Usually, the chances of winning a major prize are small.

Trading Stamps. The trading stamp is a promotional gimmick that is still popular in some parts of the country. Some stores give trading stamps based on the total dollar amount of individual purchases. These stamps are collected and redeemed for prizes, reduced prices on special purchases, or other types of rewards. This type of promotion is designed to maintain customer loyalty — the more times customers shop in the same store, the more stamps they can collect. Many customers think that they are getting more for their money or are getting something for nothing when they receive trading stamps. Video rental stores and record stores often give stamps. When a book of stamps is filled, a customer may receive one free movie rental or a free record album. *Marble Slab*

Coupons. Manufacturer coupons offer cents off on specifically described products from a specific manufacturer and may be redeemed wherever the product is sold. Store coupons offer discounts on specific products, usually for a short period of time, and only at a specific store. Manufacturer and store coupons may be inside a package, on the outside of the package, in newspapers or magazines, or on a store shelf. Coupons may not be redeemed for cash, but may be used to take cents off on the price of the product promoted on the coupon. The effect of the coupon is to lower the price of the product in an attempt to lure customers to choose that product or the store offering the bargain over its competitors. Stores that accept manufacturer coupons return the coupons to the manufacturer for a refund in the amount given to the customer. Figure 18-2 shows coupons issued by a manufacturer and a store.

In addition to manufacturer and store coupons for specific products, some stores offer *double coupons* that double the value of a manufacturer's coupon, up to a maximum of $1.00 per coupon. This gives the customer incentive to buy the product from that store, but allows the customer to choose which coupon to double. For example, if you have three coupons for 10 cents, 25 cents, and 50 cents, you'd choose to double the 50-cent coupon and save a dollar. Double coupons are usually found in newspaper inserts and in-store advertising brochures, and are used extensively in some parts of the country.

Packaging. Packages are designed to appeal to the eye with the necessary information correctly and attractively arranged. Distinctively designed packages are used to attract the customer's attention away from competitive products. Company logos, brightly colored designs, pictures of people promoting or using the product, and other attention getters may appear on product boxes. Special features are emphasized, such as sugar free, no cholesterol, fortified with eight vitamins and minerals, new and improved, and safe for children. Manufacturers know that the package or container

Trading stamps are still popular in some areas.

Coupons offer discounts on merchandise.

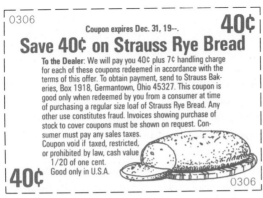

Figure 18-2A   Manufacturer Coupon   Figure 18-2B   Store Coupon

must be attractive because it plays such an important role in inducing purchases. Size and shape of packages are significant. Containers that appear to hold more of the product and containers that are reusable as storage devices also attract consumers. Often, a game or prize inside the box is also shown on the outside, or coupons are contained inside the package or on the package. A cents-off price means that the price on the package is reduced by a discount amount usually shown in big letters.

Sampling.   Many companies use direct advertising of their products through sampling. Small sample-size free packages of a product may be sent directly to households. Sometimes company representatives may give out samples, free drinks, or tastes of products in selected stores, in shopping centers, or on street corners. Usually when a new product is first introduced into the marketplace, sampling allows potential customers to try the new product. Some companies advertise in magazines and newspapers, with offers for free samples by mail. All you have to do is fill out the coupon with your name and address and mail it in. In addition to a sample of the product, you may receive a coupon to be used on future purchases of the new product.

VOCABULARY

Directions: Can you find the definition for each of the following terms used in Chapter 18?

define the problem	economy
obtain accurate information	product advertising
compare alternatives	target audience
select an alternative	company advertising
take action	industry advertising
personal factors	odd-number pricing
personal resources	loss leader
custom	cherry picker

1. To state what specific want or need must be satisfied.
2. A customer who buys only loss leaders and super sale items.
3. An item of merchandise marked down to a very low price, often below actual cost.
4. The practice of putting uneven price numbers on merchandise to make the price appear low.
5. Factors present in one's life that influence spending patterns.
6. Time, money, energy, skills, abilities, and credit — the more you have, the more you can spend.
7. A long-established practice that is the same as an unwritten law.
8. A system or structure of life in a country that describes its financial well-being.
9. Advertising that attempts to convince you to buy a certain good or service.
10. Technique used to promote and maintain customer loyalty.
11. A specific consumer group.
12. A type of promotion that attempts to sell a general product group, without regard to where it is purchased.
13. The final step in the consumer decision-making process.
14. The fourth step in consumer decision making, whereby you make the decision.
15. The second step in consumer decision making, whereby you gather data relating to the problem.
16. The third step in consumer decision making, whereby you examine the good and bad points for each possible solution.

ITEMS FOR DISCUSSION

1. List the five steps in the consumer decision-making process. Briefly describe each.
2. What are some personal factors that influence a person's or a family's spending patterns?
3. What are some outside factors that determine a person's or family's spending patterns?
4. List six different advertising media. Which one(s) do you see most frequently?
5. What is a target audience?
6. What is odd-number pricing? Is it used frequently in the advertising that you see most often?
7. Why don't retailers like to see cherry pickers?
8. On what theme do promotional displays often center?
9. What types of businesses often offer contests and games to attract customers?

10. What types of trading stamps are available in your community?
11. What is a store coupon?
12. What is a manufacturer coupon?

APPLICATIONS

1. Using the steps in the consumer decision-making process, make a decision that will satisfy your need for a piano.
2. How do your spending patterns differ from those of your parents? What things do you buy that your parents also purchase? Can you trace any of these purchases to strong family custom, background, or religion?
3. How are you or the members of your family affected when interest rates are very high? Do you benefit, or are you hurt? How? Can you think of anyone who is affected in an opposite way from you? Why is this so?
4. What community-centered and national environmental concerns do you have? What can you do as a single concerned citizen to help preserve the quality of the environment?
5. Spend an evening viewing television or listening to the radio. List the jingles, tunes, key words, phrases, and slogans used in each commercial. How many commercials can you automatically sing along with?

CASE PROBLEMS AND ACTIVITIES

1. Watch a television program for one hour any time during the day. Determine the target audience (teenagers, children, homemakers, sports fans, families, adults only) of the program. Pay close attention to all commercials shown during the hour. Write your answers to the following questions on a separate piece of paper.

   a. List all the commercials. Categorize them as either product, company, or industry advertising. (Public service advertisements and political campaigns are industry advertisements.)
   b. Rate each commercial as good, fair, or poor, depending upon how well it is directed to the television program's target audience.
   c. Rate each commercial according to tastefulness (either good taste or poor taste). Do you find it offensive, degrading, insulting? Explain why you liked or disliked the commercial.

2. Bring to class an advertisement insert from a newspaper. It should be from a department store, local discount store, or grocery store. Write

your answers to these questions on a separate piece of paper:

a. How many advertisements show odd-number pricing?
b. How many individual advertisements mention how much money will be saved or what the regular price is?
c. Are there any coupons or references to coupons?
d. Are trading stamps, games, or special incentives mentioned in the advertisement?
e. Is the advertisement insert attractively arranged?
f. Is the insert in color or black and white?
g. Rate the advertisement insert as to quality, attractiveness, and readability.
h. Do you see any loss leaders or super buys?

Attach the advertisement insert to your paper. On the insert, write comments next to items to identify them as examples of loss leaders, odd-number pricing, etc.

3. Describe a store display built around the theme of the most recent major holiday. Describe such things as colors used, products displayed, product arrangement, and location in the store. Were there any actual price reductions?

4. List any stores in your area that use one or more of the following promotional techniques. Beside each store name, describe the specific techniques used.

a. Contests and games   d. Sampling
b. Trading stamps   e. Other
c. Coupons

Chapter 19

HOUSING

◆◆◆◆◆◆◆◆◆◆◆◆◆◆◆◆◆◆◆◆◆◆◆◆◆◆

OBJECTIVES

1. Describe the various housing alternatives and potential living arrangements.
2. List the advantages and disadvantages of renting a residence, complete a rental application, and understand a lease and an inventory.
3. Discuss landlord/tenant responsibilities, including inventory and condition report and appropriate notices.
4. Discuss considerations of home ownership (positive and negative) and describe the process of buying a home.
5. List moving costs and installation charges that arise from physical change of residence.

HOUSING ALTERNATIVES

◆◆◆◆◆◆◆◆

Housing choices depend on needs.

Most people spend half or more of their time at their place of residence. For this reason, it is important to give careful thought and planning to selecting the best housing alternative at a given period in your life. Making wise housing decisions will provide you with comfort, convenience, affordability, and utility. Alternatives for housing discussed in this chapter include dormitories, apartments, duplexes, condominiums, and houses.

DORMITORIES

Many college students prefer to live in a dormitory on campus. Dormitories provide a convenient location, plus eating facilities, with the meals included in the cost. Although individual rooms are small, with limited space for a bed, study area, and closet, the cost per school term may be less than for other available private housing. Major advantages to on-campus housing include closeness to classes and campus activities, access to campus resources such as library and health center, security, and a feeling of being a part of the campus life. On the other hand, students pay a flat fee and do not have the opportunity to budget their resources. For example, meals are paid for whether or not they are eaten.

APARTMENTS

An apartment is typically the preferred choice for the first residence away from the parents' home. The amount of rent paid for an apartment is based on the size of the apartment and facilities provided. The larger the apartment and the more facilities provided, the higher the rent.

Efficiency apartments provide the least amount of living space, but are also the least expensive. In an efficiency (sometimes called a *studio*) apartment, there is only one large room serving as the kitchen, living room, and bedroom. Larger apartments with separate living and dining areas are available in a variety of floor plans, including two-story models, called *townhouses*.

Efficiency apartments are usually less expensive.

Apartments are usually located in multiunit buildings in which the number of units may be as few as two or as many as several hundred. Facilities provided may include a laundry room, storage area, swimming pool, tennis courts, and clubhouse. In addition, all or part of the utilities may be included in the rent payment.

Apartments provide the greatest amount of independence and flexibility but also require responsibility and good judgment. Most apartment buildings have rules that make close living more enjoyable for all: no pets, no music or noise after 11 p.m., restricted hours for use of facilities, and so on.

DUPLEXES

A duplex is a two-family house. Usually both halves of the house are exactly the same, but there are separate entrances for each. Generally located in

Duplexes offer more
privacy than apart-
ments.

quiet residential areas, duplexes offer more space than apartments. Duplexes also offer more privacy, with only one close neighbor, and may include a garage or carport, private laundry facilities, and other privileges and responsibilities similar to a house. For example, a tenant at an apartment is not expected to perform maintenance activities; a duplex tenant may be expected to mow the grass and maintain the landscaping.

CONDOMINIUMS

A condominium is an individually owned unit in a multiunit structure. The condominium owner, upon purchase of a unit, becomes a member of the homeowners' association, which is responsible for the property management. A monthly fee is paid by each owner to cover the cost of maintaining the common areas and the outside portion of the units. The individual owners are responsible for maintaining the interior of the units. Common areas may include a variety of athletic and recreational facilities. Condominium ownership is very similar to home ownership (deductibility of interest and private property rights) but with shared responsibility for common areas shared and enjoyed by all owners.

HOUSES

A house is a single-family detached home. Both rental costs and purchase prices of houses vary with size, facilities, and location.

LIVING ARRANGEMENTS
◆◆◆◆◆◆◆◆

Make living decisions
before leaving home.

Major decisions to determine your living arrangements must be reached before moving out on your own. With whom to live, where to live, what to take, when to move — all are considerations that must be given careful thought.

WITH WHOM TO LIVE

Choosing a roommate is sometimes a difficult task. Is there someone, or ones, among your friends and acquaintances with whom you would enjoy living? Be sure you are compatible with your potential roommate(s) before you move in together. Discuss possible areas of disagreement that may cause trouble if not settled in advance. Some questions that should be answered before making a commitment to share living quarters include these:

1. Do you smoke or drink? How do you feel about others who do?
2. Do you like a clean living area at all times, or are you easygoing and casual about your environment?
3. Do you have steady employment or another source of income to ensure that you can be depended on to pay your share of the common expenses?
4. What are some of your goals? Do you want to continue your education, work full-time, travel, etc.?
5. What are your leisure activities? What activities can you share with your roommate(s)?
6. What type of transportation do you and your roommate(s) have? What is the approximate cost? Will you share expenses? If so, how will you divide them?

Share your feelings with potential roommates.

You might want to consider having more than one roommate. The more personalities involved, however, the more difficult it becomes to have problem-free relationships. Matching similar personality types will increase the chances for a successful living arrangement.

The more you know about each potential roommate, the better you will be able to get along and work out problems. It is a good idea to get to know each person before moving in together. Spend time together at school, after school, in the evenings, and on weekends participating in group activities. In this way, you can see what interests you have in common, how each of you interacts with the other(s) and in groups, and what personality traits are strongest. It is not necessary that roommates be completely alike in order to get along. However, they do need to be aware of, and be able to accept, each other's qualities and traits.

Get to know your roommate(s) well before moving in.

WHERE TO LIVE

The decision of where to live will depend largely on finances. For students attending college and choosing on-campus housing, many of the decisions discussed in this chapter will be predetermined. Off-campus housing involves more planning and careful consideration. Those who will not attend college or who choose an off-campus residence must begin their housing plan with a solid financial analysis: What is a realistic amount to pay for rent or mortgage payments? You must determine how much you can

Off-campus housing needs careful planning.

Illustration 19-1
To live together harmoniously, roommates need to like and accept each other.

comfortably pay. Then you can begin shopping for the best housing plan to meet your needs. Some costs to consider when deciding where to live include the following:

1. Deposits and fees to rent or purchase a residence. A **deposit** is a pledge or down payment.
2. Deposits for and average monthly costs of utilities. A **utility** is a service such as light, power, or water provided by a public utility company.
3. Length of time you plan to live in the residence.
4. Distance from place of work or school.
5. Distance from laundry, shopping facilities, and other frequently used services.
6. Costs of maintenance you are expected to perform.

Car and gasoline expenses are a big consideration.

Most financial experts advise allotting between 15 and 30 percent of your total budget for housing. At first, you may need a roommate to share costs. Later, you may be able financially to carry the burden of living alone.

WHAT TO TAKE

If you are buying a home, you will need to plan to furnish it completely yourself. Rental residences, however, come furnished or unfurnished. **Furnished** means that the basic furnishings are provided — bed and dresser; sofa, chairs, and lamps; dining table and chairs; and essential appliances. An **unfurnished** rental residence may or may not include basic kitchen

You will pay lower rent by providing your own furniture.

appliances such as stove and refrigerator. Usually the fewer the items furnished, the lower the rent. If you have enough items or can acquire the essentials for an unfurnished residence, the savings in rent payments can be considerable.

Home furnishings can be purchased or rented. Purchase and rental payments should be carefully compared before any decision is made. Renting furnishings can be very expensive. Many furniture rental companies offer a lease option. With a **lease option**, each rent payment applies toward the purchase. Your option may be for a specified period of time, at the end of which you will have paid for the furniture entirely. An alternative is that at the end of the one-year rental period, you have the option to buy the furniture at a price reduced by a part of each rental payment made during that year.

Basic household and personal items necessary for setting up housekeeping include the following:

Make a list of needed items for living independently.

1. Towels, sheets, tablecloths, and cleaning cloths
2. Cleaning supplies (including mops, brooms, buckets, vacuum cleaner, detergent, and cleansers)
3. Personal items (including shampoo, cosmetics, soap, lotions, medicines, and other personal hygiene items)
4. Clothing, shoes, and other apparel
5. Dishes, silverware, pots, pans
6. Lamps, clothes hangers, clocks, radio, television, plants, and other decorations.

Carpeting is usually provided. But you may need to supply such items as throw rugs, draperies, a shower curtain, and mirrors. Some of these items may be contributed by the roommate(s); some may be purchased jointly. A list of things to be purchased jointly should be made before moving. Each

Some expenses are shared with roommate(s).

roommate should have available his or her share of the expenses prior to making the purchases. If some things are purchased jointly and one of you decides to move, you must then divide the purchases. At the time of purchase, each person should agree to take some items and give up other items. To avoid arguments later, keep a written record of these agreements.

WHEN TO MOVE

The timing of your move can be an important factor in its initial success or failure. At least six months before you actually plan to move, you should begin making preparations. Others who have experienced a similar move can be of great help to you with advice and contributions of household items.

At the time you are ready to move from your present home, you should make these preparations:

1. Set aside money in savings to cover cleaning deposits, first and last months' rent, fees, and initial expenses and purchases. In most cases $500 or more may be necessary. If you have a pet, an additional deposit or fee may be charged. Most *deposits* are refundable, if you meet your obligations. *Fees* are not refundable.

2. Have a steady and reliable source of income with which you can pay the obligations you agree to pay, such as rental agreements, utility bills, and shared expenses.

3. Accumulate what you need to have in order to live independently, such as clothing, towels, sheets and other bed items, small appliances, and dishes. You may have been accumulating these things through the years. If so, you will have to purchase few items when you move.

4. Discuss with your roommate(s) all options, requirements, expenses, and other concerns. Decide if you are prepared financially and emotionally to meet the challenges. Be aware of each other's strengths and weaknesses and decide if you are willing to make changes to meet each other's needs.

5. Plan the move with your career goals in mind. If it is your goal to finish college, then your plan should work in harmony with that goal and help you to achieve it. For example, if you are planning to go to college in September and live on campus, it would probably not be wise to go out on your own for the three summer months. The expenses would be too high, and you would be better off saving your money to help meet college expenses. Your goals and those of your roommate(s) should be discussed in detail.

6. Make arrangements for transporting furnishings.

A good way to organize your preparations is to make a needs inventory, such as the one shown in Figure 19-1. You and your roommate(s) will decide what will be needed and check off each item when it is acquired or accomplished.

GROUP FINANCIAL DECISIONS

All roommates will have a responsibility to meet the obligations they agree upon. Rent is an example of a joint obligation; each person must pay his or her share so that the total rent is paid on time. Utilities probably will be shared equally, as will garbage service, cable TV, monthly telephone charges, and group activity expenses. Long-distance telephone calls should

---

(margin notes)

You need to be able to pay your rent on time.

A well-planned move can save you unnecessary expense and effort.

Plan to pay your share of joint expenses.

Figure 19-1
Needs Inventory

	What Is Needed	Date Needed	Cost	Date Completed
1.	Dishes/towels	Oct. 1	$100	_____
2.	First and last months' rent	Oct. 1	700	_____
3.	Cleaning deposit	Oct. 1	100	_____
4.	Car (one to share)	Sept. 1	100/mth.	_____
5.	Radio/television	Oct. 1	300	_____
6.	Job for roommate	Aug. 1	– –	_____
7.	Household budget	Sept. 1	– –	_____
8.	Discussion with roommate(s)	June 1	– –	_____
9.	Discussion with parents	June 1	– –	_____

be paid for individually. But expenses such as gasoline or groceries might be divided according to percentage of use. Laundry services usually are an individual expense.

Group budgeting allows for the careful allocation of expenses, so that each person pays his or her share. The budget should be prepared and put into writing following a good discussion. Figure 19-2 is an example of a group budget.

Figure 19-2
Group Budget

EXPENSE	MONTHLY COST	COST PER ROOMMATE		
		ROBIN	HELEN	ARLENE
Rent	$300	$100	$100	$100
Utilities (avg.)	60	20	20	20
Gasoline	60	30	20	10
Groceries	150	50	50	50
Household supplies	12	4	4	4
	$582	$204	$194	$184

A method of paying these expenses is for each person to have a separate account for individual expenses, and for the group to have a joint account from which shared expenses are paid. Each person is required to deposit a certain amount into the joint account by the first of each month. Then checks are written from the joint account to pay for rent, utilities, and other

A joint account can be used to pay some expenses.

expenses incurred throughout the month. Individual expenses are paid individually.

Any plan for taking care of expenses should be agreed upon by all roommates so that everyone is satisfied. Each will know how group expenses will be paid and how individual expenses will be paid.

RENTING YOUR RESIDENCE

◆◆◆◆◆◆◆◆

Renting may cause some inconveniences.

A **tenant** is one who rents or leases from a landlord. A **landlord** is the owner of the property that is rented or leased to another person. The variety of rental housing provided by landlords emphasizes the advantages of renting. The lack of many conveniences and facilities provided by landlords, however, adds to the disadvantages of renting your residence.

ADVANTAGES OF RENTING

Rental living is the most popular choice among singles and young married couples. Renting provides a number of advantages, such as mobility, convenience, social life, and lower living expenses.

Mobility.   Many single persons prefer to rent because of the ease and speed with which they can move when a good job opportunity comes along. One of the advantages of renting is that the living arrangement need not be permanent. If you plan to work or go to school for only a few months, renting a residence for that short period is wise.

Convenience.   Many landlords provide a number of conveniences for their tenants. For example, some rental properties have laundry facilities in each unit; others have laundry facilities located in a central area for all tenants. Extra storage space may also be provided. Recreational facilities are

Many apartments have recreational facilities.

available on many rental properties. Finally, many apartment or condominium complexes are conveniently located near major shopping areas, downtown areas, or important industrial and professional business centers.

Social Life.   Apartments located in multiunit buildings of any size offer the opportunity to meet others and socialize on an informal basis. You are not isolated, without neighbors and other people nearby, when living in a rental complex. In addition, recreational facilities at many large complexes

Socializing is easier in a multiunit building.

provide numerous opportunities to socialize regularly.

Lower Living Expenses.   Apartments usually are less expensive to rent than houses. But the most important factor in lowering individual living expenses is provided by sharing expenses with roommates.

DISADVANTAGES OF RENTING

Anyone who has lived in apartments or other rental properties can list numerous disadvantages. Noise, lack of privacy, small quarters, lack of storage space, and lack of parking space are frequently mentioned disadvantages of renting.

Noise.   Those who live in apartments, duplexes, or condominiums share common walls with neighbors above, below, or beside them. Consequently, music, conversations, and other activities of neighbors can be overheard. Late hours or unusual habits of neighbors can be very irritating.

Close living creates noise problems.

Lack of Privacy.   Because conversations and other activities can be overheard through common walls, tenants often feel that their neighbors know too much about their private lives. Problems associated with shared facilities — laundry, recreation, etc. — also become annoying to some tenants after a time.

Small Quarters.   The typical apartment is smaller than some other housing alternatives. Five hundred to 1,000 square feet of living space is average for an apartment. A house may have 1,200 or more square feet of living space.

Lack of Storage Area.   The small size of many apartments means that less cabinet and closet space is available. Also, few rental properties offer more than a small amount of additional storage space for rarely used items.

You may not have all the storage space you need.

Lack of Parking Space.   Many rental properties do not provide garages or off-street parking. Tenants' automobiles are subjected to the hazards of the weather and those associated with parking on busy streets. In complexes that provide parking lots, visitor parking is often very limited.

RENTAL APPLICATION

Whenever you rent a residence, you may be expected to fill out an application. The purpose of the application is to allow the landlord to check out your employment (income), previous rental experience, credit rating, and so on. This type of checking is done to assure the landlord that you are a good risk — that you pay your bills and will be a good tenant. A landlord may deny rental because of past rental experience, employment record, and credit rating. Rental may not be denied, however, solely on the basis of race, religion, national origin, sex, or marital status. Some states have passed laws to prohibit denial of rental to tenants with small children. Figure 19-3 is an example of a rental application.

Landlords often check references.

Figure 19-3
Rental Application

Rental Application

Name _____ Date _____

Address _____ Phone _____

Name(s) of other person(s) to be living here _____

_____

Previous Address _____

_____ How Long? _____

Employer _____ Phone _____

Address _____ How Long? _____

Bank _____ Savings _____ Checking _____

Credit References

Name _____ Address _____

Name _____ Address _____

LEASES AND MONTH-TO-MONTH TENANCY AGREEMENTS

A lease is a written
contract.

Basically there are two types of agreements used when renting: leases, sometimes called *rental agreements*; and month-to-month tenancy agreements. A **lease** is a written agreement to rent certain property at a certain price for a specified time period. You may sign a lease for six months, one year, two years, or any period agreed upon. Rent will not be raised until the lease expires. But if you decide to move before the lease expires, you are still responsible for the remaining rent payments. At least 30 days prior to the end of your lease, the landlord should inform you of the rent increase. If you do not wish to stay longer than the time of your lease, you must notify the landlord in writing at least 30 days prior to departure. See Figure 19-4.

A **month-to-month tenancy agreement** is an agreement, oral or written, to rent certain property at a set price on a month-to-month basis; that is, with 30 days' notice, a tenant may move out and not be held responsible for additional rent payments. The ease of moving in and out is an advantage. But, because the time length of the agreement is not specified, the rent may be raised at any time. You can also be asked to leave at any time.

A lease and a month-to-month tenancy agreement will include provisions for deposits and their return, termination of rental, rent

Figure 19-4
Lease

RESIDENTIAL LEASE AGREEMENT
AND SECURITY DEPOSIT RECEIPT

THIS INDENTURE, made this ___29th___ day of ___October___ , 19⁻⁻ , between

___Brendan Martin___ , hereinafter designated the Lessor

or Landlord, and ___Teresa Thomas___ , hereinafter designated the Lessee,

WITNESSETH: That the said Lessor/Landlord does by these presents lease and demise the residence

situated at ___614 Dundas Street___ in ___Cincinnati___ City,

___Hamilton___ County, ___Ohio___ State,

of which the real estate is described as follows:

614 Dundas Street, Cincinnati, Ohio,

upon the following terms and conditions:

1. **Term:** The premises are leased for a term of ___one (1)___ years, commencing the ___1st___ day of ___November___ , 19⁻⁻ , and terminating the ___30th___ day of ___November___ , 19⁻⁻ .

2. **Rent:** The Lessee shall pay rent in the amount of $ ___400.00___ per month for the above premises on the ___1st___ day of each month in advance to Landlord.

3. **Utilities:** Lessee shall pay for service and utilities supplied to the premises, except ___None___ which will be furnished by Landlord.

4. **Sublet:** The Lessee agrees not to sublet said premises nor assign this agreement nor any part thereof without the prior written consent of Landlord.

5. **Inspection of Premises:** Lessee agrees that he has made inspection of the premises and accepts the condition of the premises in its present state, and that there are no repairs, changes, or modifications to said premises to be made by the Landlord other than as listed herein.

6. **Lessee Agrees:**
(1) To keep said premises in a clean and sanitary condition;
(2) To properly dispose of rubbish, garbage and waste in a clean and sanitary manner at reasonable and regular intervals and to assume all costs of extermination and fumigation for infestation caused by Lessee;
(3) To properly use and operate all electrical, gas, heating, plumbing facilities, fixtures and appliances;
(4) To not intentionally or negligently destroy, deface, damage, impair or remove any part of the premises, their appurtenances, facilities, equipment, furniture, furnishings, and appliances, nor to permit any member of his family, invitee, licensee or other person acting under his control to do so;
(5) Not to permit a nuisance or common waste.

7. **Maintenance of Premises:** Lessee agrees to mow and water the grass and lawn, and keep the grass, lawn, flowers and shrubbery thereon in good order and condition, and to keep the sidewalk surrounding said premises free and clear of all obstructions; to replace in a neat and workmanlike manner all glass and doors broken during occupancy thereof; to use due precaution against freezing of water or waste pipes and stoppage of same in and about said premises and that in case water or waste pipes are frozen or become clogged by reason of neglect of Lessee, the Lessee shall repair the same at his own expense as well as all damage caused thereby.

8. **Alterations:** Lessee agrees not to make alterations or do or cause to be done any painting or wallpapering to said premises without the prior written consent of Landlord.

9. **Use of Premises:** Lessee shall not use said premises for any purpose other than that of a residence and shall not use said premises or any part thereof for any illegal purpose. Lessee agrees to conform to municipal, county and state codes, statutes, ordinances and regulations concerning the use and occupation of said premises.

10. **Pets and Animals:** Lessee shall not maintain any pets or animals upon the premises without the prior written consent of Landlord.

11. **Access:** Landlord shall have the right to place and maintain "for rent" signs in a conspicuous place on said premises for thirty days prior to the vacation of said premises. Landlord reserves the right of access to the premises for the purpose of
(a) Inspection;
(b) Repairs, alterations or improvements;
(c) To supply services; or
(d) To exhibit or display the premises to prospective or actual purchasers, mortgagees, tenants, workmen, or contractors.
Access shall be at reasonable times except in case of emergency or abandonment.

12. **Surrender of Premises:** In the event of default in payment of any installation of rent or at the expiration of said term of this lease, Lessee will quit and surrender the said premises to Landlord.

13. **Security Deposit:** The Lessee has deposited the sum of $ ___400.00___ , receipt of which is hereby acknowledged, which sum shall be deposited by Landlord in a trust account with ___Citizens___ bank; savings and loan association or licensed escrow, ___Cincinnati___ branch, whose address is ___201 Main Street, Cincinnati, Ohio___

All or a portion of such deposit may be retained by Landlord and a refund of any portion of such deposit is conditioned as follows:
(1) Lessee shall fully perform obligations hereunder and those pursuant to Chapter 207, Laws of 1973, 1st Ex Session or as may be subsequently amended;
(2) Lessee shall occupy said premises for ___one (1)___ months or longer from date hereof;
(3) Lessee shall clean and restore said residence and return the same to Landlord in its initial condition, except for reasonable wear and tear, upon the termination of this tenancy and vacation of apartment;
(4) Lessee shall have remedied or repaired any damage to apartment premises;
(5) Lessee shall surrender to Landlord the keys to premises;
Any refund from security deposit, as by itemized statement shown to be due to Lessee, shall be returned to Lessee within fourteen (14) days after termination of this tenancy and vacation of the premises.

IN WITNESS WHEREOF, the Lessee has hereunto set his hand and seal the day and year first above written.

/s/ Brendan Martin   /s/ Teresa Thomas

_____   _____
LANDLORD   LESSEE
610¹ Dundas Street

_____
Cincinnati, Ohio

ADDRESS

(Acknowledgment)

Source: *Real Estate Principles & Practices,* Maurice A. Unger and George R. Karvel, Seventh Ed., South-Western Publishing Co., 1983.

payments, tenant and landlord responsibilities, and various other matters. If you do not understand any part of the lease or agreement, ask the landlord about it. If the answer is not satisfactory, get a legal interpretation or refuse to sign the agreement. Both a lease and a month-to-month tenancy agreement are legally binding documents when you have placed your signature on them. Therefore, it is very important that you fully understand the lease or agreement before signing it.

Understand the lease before you sign it.

INVENTORY

If you reside in a rental property, you are expected to leave the property as you found it. Normal wear and tear is expected and accepted. However, anything broken or misplaced is not acceptable. Therefore, to assure that you are not accused of such acts as breaking, damaging, or taking furnishings, take an inventory of the premises at the time you move in. The inventory should list and describe the conditions of the property. Note such things as broken windows, missing window screens, holes in walls, torn carpeting, plumbing problems, and appliance damage or problems. This inventory should be taken with the landlord, and a copy made for each of you. When you move out, you and your landlord should once again take an inventory. Figure 19-5 shows an inventory and condition report that can be used in a variety of rental situations.

Take an inventory when you move in.

LANDLORD/TENANT RESPONSIBILITIES
◆◆◆◆◆◆◆◆

Although most states have passed landlord/tenant laws, there are no national laws. However, landlord/tenant laws for residential rental units generally include similarly worded landlord and tenant obligations.

LANDLORD OBLIGATIONS

Housing laws in most states require that landlords provide a dwelling place that is habitable (livable) at all times. A dwelling place is considered habitable if the following conditions are met:

Landlords have responsibilities to tenants.

1. The exterior (including roof, walls, doors, and windows) is weatherproof and waterproof.
2. Floors, walls, ceilings, stairs, and railings are in good repair.

Figure 19-5
Inventory and Con-
dition Report

INVENTORY AND CONDITION REPORT

Use this report to record the contents and condition of your unit when you move in and before moving out. If you mark anything as being either dirty or damaged, describe it fully on an additional sheet. Use the blank before each item to indicate how many there are. Ask the landlord to sign your copy.

LIVING ROOM		Dirty Yes* No	Damaged Yes* No			Dirty Yes* No	Damaged Yes* No
___ Couch	1	☐ ☐	☐ ☐	___ Oven racks	43	☐ ☐	☐ ☐
___ Chair	2	☐ ☐	☐ ☐	___ Broiler pan	44	☐ ☐	☐ ☐
___ End table	3	☐ ☐	☐ ☐	___ Working refrigerator	45	☐ ☐	☐ ☐
___ Easy chair	4	☐ ☐	☐ ☐	___ Ice trays	46	☐ ☐	☐ ☐
___ Floor lamp	5	☐ ☐	☐ ☐	___ Working sink	47	☐ ☐	☐ ☐
___ Table lamp	6	☐ ☐	☐ ☐	___ Working garbage disposal	48	☐ ☐	☐ ☐
___ Coffee table	7	☐ ☐	☐ ☐	___ Counter tops	49	☐ ☐	☐ ☐
___ Light fixture	8	☐ ☐	☐ ☐	___ Range hood with working fan	50	☐ ☐	☐ ☐
___ Rug or carpet	9	☐ ☐	☐ ☐	___ Working dishwasher	51	☐ ☐	☐ ☐
___ Floor	10	☐ ☐	☐ ☐	___ Hot and cold running water	52	☐ ☐	☐ ☐
___ Walls	11	☐ ☐	☐ ☐	___ Drawers	53	☐ ☐	☐ ☐
___ Ceiling	12	☐ ☐	☐ ☐	___ Dinette table	54	☐ ☐	☐ ☐
				___ Dinette chairs	55	☐ ☐	☐ ☐
BEDROOM				___ Light fixture	56	☐ ☐	☐ ☐
___ Bed frame(s)	13	☐ ☐	☐ ☐	___ Floor	57	☐ ☐	☐ ☐
___ Headboard(s)	14	☐ ☐	☐ ☐	___ Walls	58	☐ ☐	☐ ☐
___ Mattress	15	☐ ☐	☐ ☐	___ Ceiling	59	☐ ☐	☐ ☐
___ Mattress cover	16	☐ ☐	☐ ☐				
___ Bed springs	17	☐ ☐	☐ ☐	BATHROOM			
___ Dresser	18	☐ ☐	☐ ☐	___ Towel racks	60	☐ ☐	☐ ☐
___ Nightstand	19	☐ ☐	☐ ☐	___ Tissue holder	61	☐ ☐	☐ ☐
___ Drapes or curtains	20	☐ ☐	☐ ☐	___ Mirror	62	☐ ☐	☐ ☐
___ Mirror	21	☐ ☐	☐ ☐	___ Medicine cabinet	63	☐ ☐	☐ ☐
___ Light fixture	22	☐ ☐	☐ ☐	___ Counter top	64	☐ ☐	☐ ☐
___ Rug or carpet	23	☐ ☐	☐ ☐	___ Working sink	65	☐ ☐	☐ ☐
___ Floor	24	☐ ☐	☐ ☐	___ Working tub	66	☐ ☐	☐ ☐
___ Walls	25	☐ ☐	☐ ☐	___ Working shower	67	☐ ☐	☐ ☐
___ Ceiling	26	☐ ☐	☐ ☐	___ Working toilet	68	☐ ☐	☐ ☐
				___ Toilet seat	69	☐ ☐	☐ ☐
BEDROOM				___ Shower curtain	70	☐ ☐	☐ ☐
___ Bed frame(s)	27	☐ ☐	☐ ☐	___ Cabinet	71	☐ ☐	☐ ☐
___ Headboard(s)	28	☐ ☐	☐ ☐	___ Light fixture	72	☐ ☐	☐ ☐
___ Mattress	29	☐ ☐	☐ ☐	___ Hot and cold running water	73	☐ ☐	☐ ☐
___ Mattress cover	30	☐ ☐	☐ ☐	___ Floor	74	☐ ☐	☐ ☐
___ Bed springs	31	☐ ☐	☐ ☐	___ Walls	75	☐ ☐	☐ ☐
___ Dresser	32	☐ ☐	☐ ☐	___ Ceiling	76	☐ ☐	☐ ☐
___ Nightstand	33	☐ ☐	☐ ☐				
___ Drapes or curtains	34	☐ ☐	☐ ☐	MISCELLANEOUS			
___ Mirror	35	☐ ☐	☐ ☐	___ Door key	77	☐ ☐	☐ ☐
___ Light fixture	36	☐ ☐	☐ ☐	___ Windows	78	☐ ☐	☐ ☐
___ Rug or carpet	37	☐ ☐	☐ ☐	___ Window screens	79	☐ ☐	☐ ☐
___ Floor	38	☐ ☐	☐ ☐	___ Mailbox	80	☐ ☐	☐ ☐
___ Walls	39	☐ ☐	☐ ☐	___ Mailbox key	81	☐ ☐	☐ ☐
___ Ceiling	40	☐ ☐	☐ ☐	___ Thermostat	82	☐ ☐	☐ ☐
				___ Other	83	☐ ☐	☐ ☐
KITCHEN				___	84	☐ ☐	☐ ☐
___ Working stove	41	☐ ☐	☐ ☐	Do all the windows work?			
___ Working oven	42	☐ ☐	☐ ☐	Does the heat work properly?			

_____   _____
Tenant   Landlord

_____   _____
Witness   Date

_____
Date   * Describe fully on an additional sheet.

Source: Oregon Student Public Interest Research Group (OSPIRG)

3. Elevators, halls, and stairwells meet fire and safety regulations. (Smoke detectors are required in each unit in most states. Tenants are responsible for testing the alarms, replacing batteries, and reporting any defects.)

4. Adequate locks are provided for all outside doors, working latches are provided for all windows, and exits meet fire and safety regulations.

5. Plumbing facilities comply with local and state laws and are in good working condition.

6. Water supply provided is adequate.

Illustration 19-2
Before you move in, inventory the condition of the rental property.

Safety standards must be met in rental units.

7. Lighting, wiring, heating, air conditioning, and appliances are in good condition and comply with local and state building and safety codes.

8. Buildings and grounds are clean and sanitary; garbage receptacles are adequate. (Tenants may be responsible for garbage removal charges.)

TENANT OBLIGATIONS

Tenant obligations usually are stated specifically in the lease or month-to-month agreement. If tenant obligations are not stated, the following obligations and responsibilities are implied:

1. To read, understand, and abide by the terms of any lease or month-to-month agreement signed.

2. To pay the rent on or before the due date. Failure to make a rent payment as stated in the lease or rental agreement may result in late fees, termination of the lease or agreement, or eviction. Through **eviction**, a landlord may legally demand that a tenant move from the premises.

You must give notice of your intent to vacate.

3. To give 30 to 60 days' notice of intent to move. This notice will prevent the forfeiture of deposits and allow the landlord time to rent the unit before you move. See Figure 19-6.

4. To keep the premises in good, clean condition and to prevent unnecessary wear and tear or damage to the unit.

Figure 19-6
Notice to Landlord

Date _____

Dear _____ :
        Landlord's Name

I will vacate the premises located at _____
Apt. _____ , on _____ . This letter constitutes
30 days' notice as required in my lease.

Attached is a copy of the Inventory and Condition Report that I completed when I moved in. You will note the items for which I am not responsible. I believe the premises will be left in the condition in which they were found, with these exceptions:

for which I know I am responsible. Other than those listed, I know of no other damages to the premises, and I believe I am entitled to a refund of $ _____ of my original deposit of $ _____ , made when I moved in.

My new address will be _____
_____

Please mail my deposit check to the address within 30 days of vacancy.

                    Yours truly,

                    _____
                    Tenant(s) Name(s)

Figure 19-6
Notice to Landlord

Use landlord's property with care and consideration.

5. To use a dwelling unit only for the purposes for which it is intended. For example, you should treat appliances and other furnishings in a reasonable manner. If the landlord pays for any or all utilities, use them in a reasonable manner. If a washer and dryer are provided in individual living units, commercial usage is prohibited.
6. To allow the landlord access to the living unit to make repairs or improvements.
7. To obey the rules of the apartment complex or other community living area covering such things as quiet hours, use of recreational facilities, use of laundry facilities, and parking regulations.

BUYING YOUR RESIDENCE
◆◆◆◆◆◆◆◆

Many people reach a point in their lives when they must decide whether to buy a house or continue to rent. Because the purchase of a home is probably the most important and most expensive decision people make, the advantages and disadvantages should be weighed carefully. Although many single people own their own homes, marriage and family usually create the greatest needs for home ownership. To provide more space and room for expansion, hobbies, and recreation for children are often the reasons given for buying a home. Most financial experts advise that house purchase price should be no more than two and a half times your gross income.

Home ownership provides financial advantages.

ADVANTAGES OF HOME OWNERSHIP

Some of the more important advantages that home ownership provides are the savings in taxes, an increase in equity with each payment, and increased privacy and personal freedom. Home ownership likewise provides a sense of security, permanence, and belonging to a neighborhood or city. The personal values that cause a desire for home ownership are hard to describe, but nevertheless they are important factors in the decision to buy a home.

Tax Savings.   Interest paid on your mortgage and real estate property taxes are deductible from state and federal income taxes. The effect of these deductions is to lower the cost of home ownership. Renters cannot deduct any part of their rent payments from their income taxes.

Equity Increases.   **Equity** is the difference between the appraised value of your home and what you owe on your home. For example, if you purchase a home valued at $75,000 with a mortgage of $50,000, your equity is $25,000. With each mortgage payment, you decrease the amount of debt but increase the amount of equity. When you sell the home for more than you paid for it, you will make money because you will have the amount of your equity and a profit returned to you.

Privacy and Personal Freedom.   Home ownership offers privacy and personal freedom not available to renters. In your own home you make all the decisions and have free use of all facilities. Owning a home also provides a feeling of security and independence. Knowing that the roof over your head is yours to do with as you wish and when you wish can be very satisfying. With home ownership comes the freedom to have pets, a backyard to work and play in, and, possibly, space to plant a garden.

Privacy is very important to some people.

DISADVANTAGES OF HOME OWNERSHIP

Most of the disadvantages of home ownership relate to cost. In addition to a monthly mortgage payment, other costs generally not found in renting are necessary for homeowners. Some of the costs involved are the down payment, mortgage, closing, property taxes, insurance, utilities, and maintenance and repairs.

Down Payment.

Most conventional (not government backed) loans require a 10 to 30 percent down payment. For example, if you are purchasing a home for $50,000, you will need $5,000 (10 percent) to $15,000 (30 percent) for the down payment. For many singles and young married couples, saving enough money for the down payment takes a number of years.

Mortgage.

The balance of the purchase price, after the down payment, is usually borrowed from a bank or other financial institution. You will sign a note, which is secured by a 20- to 30-year mortgage. The larger your down payment, the lower your monthly mortgage payments. Property taxes and insurance premiums are often included in the mortgage payments.

Closing.

Closing costs may add another $1,000 to $5,000 to the purchase of your home. The purchaser usually pays for a title search to have the abstract on the property updated. The abstract is a summary of all previous transactions involving the property you wish to buy. Additional costs that the purchaser may pay are for a personal credit report, loan fees, assumption fees (to assume someone else's mortgage loan), closing fees, recording fees, tax and interest prorations, and fire insurance.

Property Taxes.

Homeowners pay property taxes based on the market value of their home. The market value is the highest price a property will bring in a competitive and open market. The local taxing authority determines a taxable value for your home that is close to the market value. A tax rate is determined based on a county budget. If the property tax rate is $24 a thousand, and you own a $50,000 home, you will pay 50 times $24, or $1,200 a year, in property taxes. The total amount of property taxes paid annually is deductible on your income tax return.

Insurance.

A homeowner must have insurance covering the structure as well as the contents. A more detailed explanation of homeowners insurance is presented in Chapter 10.

Utilities.

Because most homes are larger than apartments or other rental units, the utility bills are also usually larger. The homeowner pays for all utilities and garbage services, whereas a renter may pay for some but not all of these items. In addition, when any repairs are needed to water or sewer lines, the homeowner is fully responsible for the costs involved.

Maintenance and Repairs.

Maintenance and repairs, inside and outside the home, are the responsibility of the owner. These include such responsibilities as painting, mowing, trimming, landscaping, fertilizing, pulling weeds, and spraying for insects. Roofs are generally good for 15 to 25 years. If you have purchased an existing (not new) home, you may have to replace the roof after only a few years. The amount of insulation necessary to keep the house warm in winter and cool in summer may need to be increased.

THE PROCESS OF BUYING YOUR HOME

Searching for your home can take several months.

If after you consider carefully all the costs involved, you decide to own a house, you begin the process of purchasing a home. This process can take many weeks or even months. Generally, the procedure can be summarized as in the following paragraphs.

Selection. In order to find the house you want to buy, you will need to see many houses. You can look by yourself or work with a real estate salesperson, who is trained to know the market, help you find the right home, and assist you in the purchase, financing, and closing. There is no charge to you, the purchaser, for these services. Either way, you will visit many homes listed with the real estate agency, advertised for sale in the newspaper, or that you drive past and want to see. In the newspaper classified ads, homes are listed by area of town or geographic location. Some are for sale by the owner; others are listed with real estate offices.

Real estate offices that belong to a multiple listing service offer a valuable service to homeowners: wide exposure to persons in the business of selling homes. Most metropolitan, urban, and suburban areas have many real estate sales offices located within their boundaries. When these real estate offices form an organization called a **multiple listing service**, all listings from each office are combined into one book. All salespeople within that geographic area have access to all real estate listings and can sell any one of them to a buyer. Thus, when you list your house for sale with one real estate salesperson, you really have all the salespeople in the area working for you. The person who lists your house receives half of the sales commission; the person who sells your house receives the other half. The cost to you is the same, yet your exposure to the sales market is much greater.

All salespeople have access to multiple listings.

Persons seeking to buy a home in a specific area also have greater exposure to available homes because they can see many listings in all parts of the city. The cost to the buyer is the same; real estate commissions are included in the sale price of a home. Most multiple listing books come out twice a month. Homes are listed according to location and value. The less expensive homes are listed first in each section.

After you have viewed many homes in the area you prefer, you may decide you want to buy one of them. Before you can take possession of the house, however, you must complete the formal buying process, which may take several weeks or months.

Earnest Money Offer. To let the seller (owner) know you want to buy his or her home, you sign an agreement called an **earnest money offer**. It is a formal, written offer to buy the home. The offer explains the terms of the purchase — the down payment; the mortgage you will assume or get on your own; when you will pay what is due, take possession, and close the deal. This agreement is called an earnest money offer because with it you will pay a certain amount of money — the earnest money, usually $1,000 to $5,000, depending on the selling price — to show the seller that you are serious and that the home can be removed from the market. If you fail to meet the terms of the agreement, you will have damaged the seller because the house was held off the market for awhile and could not be sold to anyone else. Therefore, you may forfeit your earnest money to the seller if you do not buy the home according to the agreement. One way to avoid losing your money is to write into the offer that the sale is contingent on obtaining financing and passing all inspections.

Protect yourself from losing an earnest money offer.

When the seller accepts your offer exactly as it is stated, this is called an **acceptance**. You may withdraw your offer at any time until the seller accepts it. If any conditions of the offer are changed, the seller makes what is known as a **counteroffer**. You have the choice of accepting or rejecting the counteroffer. For example, the seller may want a different date of possession or a larger cash down payment.

You can withdraw an offer before it is accepted.

Escrow.   After both parties have reached an agreement, a neutral third party is chosen to prepare the transaction for closing. A written agreement authorizing a neutral third party to hold the deed until the conditions of a transaction for the purchase of a home are fulfilled is known as **escrow**. The deed is the written document which conveys ownership of real property. The escrow agent accepts the earnest money offer and the amount of money paid, which is kept in a trust account. Then the escrow agent orders a title search, which lists all the facts about the property being purchased: name(s) of title owner(s), liens against the property, easements and assessments, property taxes, and so forth. Loan papers are ordered from lending institutions, and all necessary papers are prepared. If any problems arise, the buyer and seller are notified. For example, some deeds may carry restrictions which limit the kind of building that can be erected and the use of the property. Inspections, such as termite examinations, are carried out. Credit reports are ordered. Proper prorations are computed, and closing documents are prepared.

Problems sometimes arise during the escrow process.

Closing.   When the escrow process is completed, the seller and buyer are notified of a closing date. The buyer brings in the amount of money needed and signs necessary papers. Then the seller signs necessary papers. The escrow agent records necessary papers for transfer of title and pays the money to the seller. Finally, the buyer can take possession of the property. The buyer of the house gets papers, such as title insurance policy and mortgage release, held in escrow until the last mortgage payment is made. Until then, the buyer holds only the mortgage papers.

The buyer takes possession after closing.

LIENS

Because of the permanence (immovability) of real estate, it is good security for a loan, debt, or judgment. A *lien* is a hold or claim that one person has on the property of another person to secure payment of a debt. In addition to property tax liens (by government), there are three types of liens placed against real property: mortgage liens, judgment liens, and mechanic's liens.

1. A *mortgage lien* is a pledge of property by its owner to secure repayment of a debt. In contrast to a property tax lien imposed by law, a mortgage lien is created by the property owner. If the mortgage is not repaid, the creditor can foreclose and sell the pledged property.

2. A *judgment lien* arises from a lawsuit for which money damages are awarded by the judge or jury. The law permits a hold against property of the debtor until the judgment is paid. The judgment remains attached to the property until the debt is paid, and the creditor can force the sale of the property to pay the debt.

3. A *mechanic's lien* gives anyone who has furnished labor or materials for the improvement of property the right to place a lien against that property; a sale of the property can be forced to recover the money owed. To be entitled to a mechanic's lien, the work or materials must have been provided under a contract with the property owner. The legal theory behind mechanic's lien rights is that labor and materials enhance the value of the property, and the property should be security for payment. The mechanic's lien must be filed within a set period of time (60 to 120 days after work completion) and expires in a year or two (depending on state law). Unfortunately, if the property owner pays the contractor, but the contractor fails to pay a subcontractor for labor or materials, the mechanic's lien can force double payment by the owner.

MAKING THE MOVE
◆◆◆◆◆◆◆◆

Several costs are involved in the actual, physical change of your residence. Two costs you will need to be prepared for are moving costs and installation charges.

MOVING COSTS

Moving costs may involve time and money in careful packing, storing, transporting, loading and unloading, and unpacking. The distance you move is an important factor. The greater the distance you move, the greater the expenditure of time, energy, and money. A move across town is much less expensive and time-consuming than a cross-country move. If you have your own automobile, the problem is eased somewhat. Still, careful

The greater the distance, the higher the cost.

planning and packing are essential to be sure you move the items that you really need and will use.

In order to move, you may need to rent a truck or trailer; borrow a van or pickup; have friends or family help; or send some items by mail, freight, bus, or other available carrier. You may also decide to store some items because you have no immediate need for them, and because they would take up valuable space.

If you rent a truck or trailer, you may find a local rental agency that will rent one that you can leave in the city to which you are moving. One-way truck and trailer rental fees are based on a flat rate, plus mileage and gasoline. The rates vary and should be compared to get the best price. A typical rate is $100 a day, plus 20 cents a mile and gasoline. Some one-way rental agencies will not accept cash in payment of a rental. They require a credit card number or may charge you a deposit of $300 or more, which will be refunded when you return the truck to the designated location.

Rental rates vary.

Trucks, vans, pickups, and trailers may also be rented for local moves. The charges are similar, except that you will not pay as much per mile because you will not drive as far.

Of course, if you hire a moving company to move your possessions to your new residence, the charges will be considerably more because you will pay for labor as well. By renting a truck, pickup, van, or trailer and using your own labor for loading, driving, and unloading, you save money. But you also accept the responsibility involved in using the equipment of others.

INSTALLATION CHARGES

As a new occupant of a house or rental unit, you will pay some installation charges. Although fees vary with the type and location of the residence, there are usually charges for installation of a telephone and cable TV, and for turning on the electricity and other utilities. To obtain these services, most of which are essential, you may be required to show your ability to meet your financial obligations. Many utility companies charge a deposit, which is refundable after a year or two, when you have proved your ability to pay your bills.

Hook-up charges can be costly.

Other companies, such as the telephone company, charge a one-time fee that is not refundable. You may be charged a fee of $60 to $100, depending on your city, to have a telephone installed. The installation charge is added to your first bill. Then monthly service rates vary according to the type and number of phones you choose, kinds of services selected, and other factors. Many people buy their telephones to avoid paying monthly telephone rental fees. You will pay more to have an **unlisted telephone number**. If your telephone number is unlisted, it is not listed in the telephone directory and cannot be obtained through directory assistance. An unlisted number assures privacy and prevents many unwanted calls.

Monthly service charges rise as options increase.

VOCABULARY

Directions: Can you find the definition for each of the following terms used in Chapter 19?

deposit	eviction
utility	equity
furnished	abstract
unfurnished	market value
lease option	multiple listing service
tenant	earnest money offer
landlord	acceptance
lease	counteroffer
month-to-month tenancy	escrow
agreement	unlisted telephone number

1. A landlord's legal remedy for removing someone from a rental unit.
2. A condition of a rental unit when nothing is provided — no chairs, tables, beds, etc.
3. A service, such as light, power, water, or gas, that is provided by public companies or corporations.
4. The difference between the value of your home and what you owe on your home.
5. A pledge or a down payment.
6. An agreement whereby each rent payment applies toward the purchase of an item.
7. A rental unit with living room furniture, bed, table, and chairs provided by the landlord.
8. One who rents or leases from a landlord.
9. A summary of all previous transactions involving a certain property.
10. The highest price a property will bring in a competitive and open market.
11. When the seller accepts a buyer's offer exactly as it is stated.
12. A telephone number that is not listed in the telephone directory and cannot be obtained through directory assistance.
13. The owner of the property rented or leased to another person.
14. A written agreement to rent property at a certain price for a specified time period.
15. A change by the seller of any conditions of the original offer.
16. A written agreement letting the seller know that you want to buy the house.
17. A written agreement to rent certain property at a set price on a month-to-month basis.

18. A written agreement whereby a neutral third party prepares the real estate transaction for closing.

19. A real estate service whereby homes for sale are listed in a book issued to a real estate agent.

ITEMS FOR DISCUSSION

1. How soon before a move should you begin making plans?
2. List four advantages of renting a residence.
3. List four disadvantages of renting a residence.
4. What is the difference between a furnished and an unfurnished residence?
5. How does a condominium differ from an apartment?
6. What is the purpose of a rental application?
7. How does a lease differ from a month-to-month tenancy agreement?
8. Why should you complete and have a landlord sign an inventory when you move into a rental unit?
9. List five tenant obligations when renting.
10. List six conditions a landlord must meet in order to make rental property habitable.
11. What are some advantages of owning your home?
12. What would be the typical down payment on a $50,000 home?
13. What is the market value of a home?
14. What is a lien?
15. How is a judgment lien different from a mortgage lien?

APPLICATIONS

1. Ask two persons each of the questions below. Based on the answers, determine if the three of you would be a compatible living group.

   a. Do you smoke or drink? How do you feel about persons who do?
   b. Are you a clean, fussy housekeeper or easygoing, casual, and relaxed about your surroundings? How often do you clean?
   c. Do you work steadily, part-time or full-time? How would you pay your share of the rent and other shared expenses?
   d. What are some of your goals regarding college, your job, or recreation?
   e. What do you like to do in your spare time? What are your group activities? your individual activities?
   f. What type of transportation do you have or plan to have? What are the costs involved? Which costs will be shared?

2. What have you accumulated that you would want to take with you to a new residence? (Examples: radio, television, towels, furniture, cleaning items, dishes.)

3. What basics would you have to buy to live independently?

4. Make a list of things you should do before moving out on your own.

5. In order to move your possessions from your present home to a new residence, what types of transportation are available to you? What is the best and least expensive for you?

CASE PROBLEMS AND ACTIVITIES

1. Prepare a report comparing the rental prices and availability of apartments, duplexes, condominiums, and houses in your area. To compare prices, living conditions must be comparable; you must compare two-bedroom unfurnished apartments to two-bedroom unfurnished duplexes, and so forth. Also note how many are available in each category at the present time, the high and low prices, and the average rental prices.

2. Study the listings of homes for sale in the classified ads of your newspaper. Answer these questions:

   a. What is the lowest sale price you can find?
   b. Describe the house with the lowest sale price.
   c. What is the highest sale price you can find?
   d. Describe the house with the highest sale price.
   e. How many houses are for sale in one day's newspaper ads? What is the name and date of the newspaper?
   f. How many homes are listed for sale by the owner?
   g. Describe the house that you would choose to own; include size, price, features, and location.

3. Using the community resources in your area, find out the hookup or installation deposits and fees for the following services:

   a. Telephone   c. Cable TV
   b. Electricity   d. Water or garbage services

   Are any of these fees partially or fully refundable? If so, under what conditions?

4. Find out the monthly rates for the following telephone services in your area:

   a. Standard phone   f. Call Forwarding
   b. Touch-Tone service   g. Call Waiting
   c. Conference call   h. Unlisted telephone number
   d. Speaker phone   i. Additional phone jack installed
   e. Private line

Chapter 20

FAMILY DECISIONS

◆◆◆◆◆◆◆◆◆◆◆◆◆◆◆◆◆◆◆◆◆◆◆◆◆

OBJECTIVES

1. Describe the steps, costs, and planning involved in getting married.
2. Discuss the decisions, goals, and responsibilities in making family living decisions.
3. Outline the steps needed in planning a successful vacation.
4. Discuss the planning and costs involved in having a baby.

MARRIAGE

◆◆◆◆◆◆◆◆

Marriage is an important decision.

An important decision usually made in the early adult years is about the family. Will you get married in the near future? Will you and your spouse both work? What are your desires about raising children? What are some joint family goals you want to plan? When you decide to begin your own family, these decisions need careful consideration.

Couples planning a life together will make a number of decisions and choices. When planning for their marriage, a couple will discuss in detail the engagement, premarital counseling, ceremony costs and plans, and the honeymoon.

ENGAGEMENT

When two people decide to be married, they become engaged. If an engagement ring is chosen, it is worn on the third finger of the left hand of the prospective bride. The choice of style, size, and kind of stone and setting will determine the price of the engagement ring, which may range from a few hundred to a few thousand dollars or more. Jewelers generally counsel that it is wise to invest approximately two months' income in the engagement ring. Some couples prefer matching wedding bands, in which case an engagement ring often is not worn.

An engagement period of six months to a year is customary in this country. Once the engagement is announced, careful planning of the many steps to ensure a smooth and memorable wedding begins.

PREMARITAL COUNSELING

In order to have a wedding in some churches, counseling sessions are often required. The couple meets with a member of the clergy or other counselor, together and separately, to discuss issues that will be vital to the success of the marriage and later family life. There may be a predetermined number of sessions, or the number of sessions may vary according to how well prepared for marriage the counselor or cleric thinks the couple is. Topics most often discussed include money and budgeting, the meaning of the marriage commitment, in-laws and other potential problems, and religious aspects of marriage that are unique to each faith and each house of worship. The counseling sessions should be planned early, well before final preparations are being made for the wedding.

Premarital counseling often answers important questions.

CEREMONY COSTS AND PLANS

Planning for the wedding ceremony should begin at least six months in advance. Figure 20-1 is a bride's budget worksheet, which shows the many preparations to consider. This worksheet should be completed in rough draft form as the wedding planning progresses. The cost of each item will vary according to style, quantity, and preferences. As costs begin to add up, the bride and groom may decide to eliminate, expand, or reduce some of the expenses involved.

Guest lists are prepared by the bride and groom and by each set of parents; these lists are then combined. Guests may include relatives and friends of the couple. The number of guests being invited and the size of the wedding

Guest lists are prepared by the bride and groom.

Figure 20-1
Bride's Budget
Worksheet

ENGAGEMENT PARTY	BRIDESMAIDS' LUNCHEON	RECEPTION
Invitations............$_____	Invitations and	Hall rental............$_____
Food..................._____	place cards.........$_____	Decorations..........._____
Beverages.........._____	Food..................._____	Music................._____
Music................._____	Beverages.........._____	Food..................._____
Rental fees........._____	Rental fees........._____	Beverages.........._____
Decorations........._____	Decorations........._____	Wedding cake........._____
Professional	Professional	Favors................._____
services........._____	services........._____	Professional
Gratuities........._____	*Gratuities........._____	services........._____
		*Gratuities........._____
Total.................$_____	Total.................$_____	
		Total.................$_____

STATIONERY	PHOTOGRAPHS	OTHER
Invitations............$_____	Engagement	Bridal consultant
Announcements......._____	portrait.............$_____	fees................$_____
At-home cards........._____	Wedding	Accommodations
Personal	portrait............._____	for out-of-town
stationery.........._____	Formal photos........._____	attendants........._____
Stamps................._____	Reprints............._____	*Security guard........._____
		Sound recording
Total.................$_____	Total.................$_____	of ceremony......._____
		*Insurance for

CLOTHING	WEDDING CEREMONY	
		wedding gifts......._____
Wedding dress........$_____	Sanctuary rental.......$_____	Bride's
Headpiece/veil........._____	Music................._____	blood test
Shoes................._____	Decorations........._____	(if required)........._____
Accessories........._____	Flowers for	Groom's ring........._____
Personal	attendants........._____	Gift for groom........._____
trousseau.........._____	Aisle runner........._____	Gift for
	Transportation	attendants........._____
Total.................$_____	to/from ceremony..._____	Special effects........._____
	*Gratuities........._____	Other fees........._____
* Denotes expenses usually shared by both families	Miscellaneous........._____	_____
		_____
	Total.................$_____	
		Total.................$_____

GRAND TOTAL...$_____

party will determine the number of invitations needed, size of the church, cost of the reception, and so forth. The **wedding party** consists of the persons who are active participants in the wedding ceremony: the bride and groom, best man, maid or matron of honor, bridesmaids, ushers, flower girl, and so on.

In the past, almost all wedding expenses were paid by the bride's family. This custom is changing. Now, the groom's family usually pays some of the expenses — such as rehearsal dinner or reception — or splits the expenses with the bride's family. Generally, however, the following expenses belong solely to the groom:

Wedding costs can be shared.

1. Bride's ring(s)
2. Marriage license
3. Wedding gift for the bride

4.   Gifts for the best man, groomsmen, and ring bearer
5.   The bride's bouquet and going away corsage, corsages for mothers and grandmothers, and boutonnieres for the men in the wedding party
6.   Cleric's or judge's fee
7.   Bachelor dinner (unless given and paid for by the best man)
8.   Lodging (if necessary) for out-of-town groomsmen
9.   Groom's special clothing, including clothing for rehearsal dinner, wedding, and honeymoon
10. Delivery of wedding presents to new home
11. Honeymoon costs (which may be shared equally between bride and groom if the bride is working)

The planning of the wedding is usually done jointly by the bride and groom, with much consideration given to cost. The size of the wedding, the time of day, the location, and the formality of the bride's dress are what determine the style of the wedding. A **formal wedding** may be held in the daytime or in the evening, and all guests and participants wear formal attire (which, for evening, includes long gowns and tuxedos). A **semiformal wedding** usually is held during the afternoon or early evening, with less formal wear required of guests. While the wedding party may still dress as formally or informally as they choose, guests generally wear suits and dresses normally chosen for special occasions. An **informal wedding** may be held outside, in a church, or almost anywhere. No special clothing is required for the wedding party or for the guests.

Other types of wedding ceremonies are preferred by some couples. A civil ceremony is performed by a public official, such as a judge or justice of the peace. This type of ceremony is quick, inexpensive, and requires the presence of two witnesses in most states.

HONEYMOON

Most honeymoons are out of town.

Immediately following the wedding reception, the newly married couple usually takes a honeymoon trip. Most couples plan a trip out of town. Resort areas and places that provide different types of entertainment are popular. A honeymoon may last from several days to several weeks, and cost as much as several thousand dollars. A couple generally plans the honeymoon together, carefully considering preferences and costs involved. Honeymoons may be inexpensive automobile trips, elaborate cruises, or flights to exotic islands. The length and type of honeymoon will depend on time available, cost, and desires of the couple. More elaborate plans usually involve using travel agencies and other sources of travel information. Travel options are discussed thoroughly in the vacations section of this chapter.

FAMILY LIVING DECISIONS

◆◆◆◆◆◆◆◆

Families must set goals for the future, too.

When two people unite in marriage, they form a new family unit. Thereafter, decisions are made by the couple, based on each person's needs and wants, and joint needs for the future. Ideally, joint decisions regarding family goals, the family budget, and division of responsibilities must be open to discussion at all times.

FAMILY GOALS

Budgeting will help goals become a reality.

Just as individuals make plans and goals, the family unit must examine needs and priorities and set goals for the future. Plans for major purchases, vacations, leisure activities, hobbies, club and group memberships, and special events should be thoroughly discussed.

The couple must look also at short-term goals, such as where to live; whether both partners will work; what major purchases to make this year and next; and what activities the couple will participate in, jointly and separately.

Intermediate goals include what will happen in the next five or ten years: whether children are wanted; where the couple will live, geographically; when to purchase a home; and the employment outlook and stability for each spouse.

More than half of all American wives choose to work or must work, even after children are born. Two incomes allow couples to purchase more goods and services because they have more disposable income; they can afford higher housing payments and qualify for more credit. The career goals of each spouse should be discussed, understood, and agreed upon by the couple. How long the wife will work, when and if the couple wants children, when the wife will return to work, if the husband will take leave from work for child care — all are important decisions.

Some couples may need to live on one income temporarily while the other spouse finishes education, training, or job preparation. Because it takes five to ten years to become financially secure, many couples choose to work longer before having children. Other couples choose to keep two incomes and not have children.

Long-term goals include plans for children's education (savings and investments), special events, retirement, and vacations for leisure time.

Illustration 20-1
More than half
of all American
women choose to
work or must work,
even after children
are born.

To define each of the above types of goals is a time-consuming but necessary activity. This activity is important because it serves to outline the family's future expectations so that plans can be made to meet them.

FAMILY BUDGET

Financial security
helps marriages.

A family budget should allow for savings and investments to meet future goals. Joint decisions are often complicated and difficult to reach because there are more variables to consider. Nevertheless, family budgeting is an essential part of a successful marriage. Financial security is an important element in a successful relationship. And financial security can be attained by careful planning and budgeting.

Financial plans ensure that mutual goals will be met. The family budget makes provisions for short-term, intermediate, and long-term goals. A two-income family is able to set aside extra money for expected and unexpected events.

Working couples
look for tax shelters.

There are tax advantages to be considered in financial planning. For married couples, the total tax on combined earnings is lower. With planning, a couple can avoid taxes while setting aside money for future needs. A **tax shelter** is a legal method of avoiding paying taxes on present earnings. Couples whose combined incomes total $40,000 or more a year often seek tax shelters to avoid paying large amounts of taxes.

A **tax-deferred annuity** is a contract wherein you agree to set aside a certain amount of money each month and defer paying taxes on the earnings until a later date. The advantage of a tax-deferred annuity is that when you retire you will be earning less, and your total tax payments will be less.

DIVIDING RESPONSIBILITIES

Two-income families will probably have different divisions of duties than one-income families. Because both spouses work, household responsibilities need to be divided appropriately so that each spouse bears an equal share of the burden. In addition to household chores and duties, the couple also needs to divide other responsibilities. For example, individual and joint checking accounts may be desirable. If there is only one checking account, it makes balancing the account much easier when only one person writes checks on that account. But who will carry the checkbook and be responsible for paying the bills? Many couples choose to have individual checking accounts, where each spouse is responsible for part of the income and part of the bills. For example, the wife may choose to pay utilities, groceries and household expenses, and the car payment. The husband may choose to pay the rent or house payment, entertainment, insurance, and miscellaneous expenses. Then each spouse is responsible for balancing his or her checking account each month and meeting his or her part of the budget.

Household responsibilities differ for working couples.

Separate accounts are often desirable for working couples.

Perhaps one spouse is in charge of collecting, storing, and retrieving tax information for the preparation of tax returns. The other spouse might be responsible for making vacation arrangements, reservations, and itineraries. By dividing and sharing the responsibilities of the household, goals can be achieved in an orderly manner with each spouse contributing equally.

VACATIONS
◆◆◆◆◆◆◆◆

Vacations are an important part of our lives. Planned vacations maximize the time available for fun and enjoyment. Vacation decisions include determining the kind of vacation, making plans and reservations, at-home preparations, and covering last-minute details.

KIND OF VACATION

The type of vacation determines other plans.

The first decision is to determine the kind of vacation you want: relaxation, excitement, travel, adventure, special events, visiting relatives, or a combination of these. The vacation plans for any type of vacation also depend on how much time you have, including travel time, and how much money you will have to spend.

idea to use an automatic timer for lights so that they come on in the evening and go off a few hours later. It is often recommended to leave soft music playing on the radio. All doors and windows should be locked securely, and curtains and drapes closed. It is a good idea to ask a neighboring family to keep an eye on things, and let them know when you are leaving and returning. It is also common to alert the local police so that they can drive by your home once in a while to check for intruders while you are gone.

LAST-MINUTE DETAILS

Careful packing of clothing and supplies is necessary. Make a list of things you will need, including cameras, special clothing, shoes, and personal items. Take only what you need, in the smallest possible containers. Be sure to pack enough clothing to last the entire vacation without laundering (unless it is a very long vacation). Any rented equipment should be obtained as early as is convenient without incurring additional cost. All bottles and other containers should be closed tightly to avoid leakage. Do not forget any prescriptions or other medications frequently needed.

You may wish to take major credit cards. However, leave at home in a safe place all those cards you do not need. Take enough cash to pay those expenses that require cash only; others can be charged on a bank card or paid for by traveler's checks. Traveler's checks may be purchased at any bank or other financial institution in denominations of $10, $20, $50, etc. The smaller denominations are usually easier to cash. You will usually pay a small fee to buy traveler's checks, depending on the dollar amount. If traveler's checks are lost or stolen, they will be replaced if you produce the list of check numbers. Always keep the list separate from the checks.

Traveler's checks can be replaced if lost or stolen.

Reservations may need to be confirmed because flights are often canceled or changed. You should check at least 24 hours in advance to be sure your flight is confirmed. You may choose to use a **travel agency**, which is an authorized agent for all airlines to issue tickets and make reservations and confirmations in your behalf. There is no fee for the services of a travel agent. Because travel agents do not work for any specific airline, they can find flight connections that will result in less waiting time between flights, lower air fares, and better departure times. Sometimes, however, you may need to change planes more often to get a lower rate or better flight time.

There is no charge for use of a travel agency's services.

Plan to arrive at the airport at least an hour before your flight's departure time. This gives you time to check in, get a seat assignment, and go through the appropriate steps for boarding. Often, flights are **overbooked**, which means that the airline has sold tickets for more seats than are available. Airline ticket agents sometimes do this because many people book more than one reservation and do not show up for the less-preferred flight. Should

Arrive early to avoid being a victim of overbooking.

Illustration 20-2
Travel agents can
help make planning
your vacation eas-
ier.

you be a victim of overbooking, the airline will offer from $100 to $300 to
any passengers willing to take a later flight. The money will help pay for your
vacation, but you will also be thrown off your itinerary. By arriving ready to
check in, you can avoid an overbooking problem. If you travel frequently,
you may be eligible for discount flights or special bonuses through airlines'
frequent flyer plans. These plans are usually based on air miles traveled; you
are given credit for miles each time you take a regular flight aboard an
airline. In most cases, there is no charge to participate in the plan.

Be sure that all appliances are turned off before you leave home. As a
precaution, do not use any appliances the morning of your departure. In the
excitement of preparing to leave, you could easily forget to turn off or unplug
them. A last check before leaving will reassure you that nothing has been left
on. Leave a copy of your itinerary with a neighbor or friend in case of
emergency.

HAVING A BABY
◆◆◆◆◆◆◆◆

Having a baby may be one of the family's decisions. Some of the costs to be
considered are prenatal expenses, delivery costs, and first-year needs.

PRENATAL EXPENSES

A **prenatal expense** is a cost that is incurred before the baby is born. After
pregnancy is first discovered, there are many initial expenses that continue
until the birth of the baby.

Prenatal Medical Care.   During the first trimester (three months) of pregnancy, visits to the doctor occur about once a month. Routine blood tests and special vitamins for proper nourishment of the baby are usually required.

In most cases, the doctor will expect payment for services to begin immediately. Even when the patient has insurance, most medical offices expect the patient to make regular payments, because insurance companies do not pay their share of costs until after the baby is delivered. These costs are usually a package deal that includes doctor visits and delivery fees. For example, a doctor may charge a flat fee of $950. Charges for blood tests, laboratory services, special tests or extra services, or hospital charges are not included in the doctor's fee. Many women prefer to go to an obstetrician during pregnancy. An **obstetrician** is a doctor who specializes in delivering babies.

During the next six months of pregnancy, doctor visits will become more frequent. During the last month, doctor visits are weekly, hospital arrangements are made, and the delivery is planned for a set date.

Maternity Clothing.   The expectant mother will need special clothes. After the third or fourth month, everyday clothes become tight and are no longer comfortable. Specially designed maternity clothes allow for expansion and comfort. Usually, five or six changes of clothing are desirable. The maternity wardrobe will include tops and slacks, a dress or two, special underclothing and nylons, and comfortable shoes.

Furniture and Supplies.   Before the baby arrives in the home, some essential pieces of furniture must be acquired. Furniture used the most during the first few months includes a crib, dresser, and dressing table. In the baby's crib are blankets and sheets, a mobile, and bumper guards to protect the baby from the crib rails. Within a short time, parents will also need to provide additional furniture, such as a high chair, playpen, walker, and stroller. A car seat is required by law in many states. All of these items are relatively expensive, and purchases should be planned well in advance of the time they will be needed.

The baby will also need diapers and personal care products. If a diaper service is not used, several dozen cloth or disposable diapers are needed, as well as baby bottles, powder, lotion, and other items that parents may choose or doctors may recommend. Many babies are fed a milk formula until six months of age or older. The formula may be liquid in cans or bottles, or a powder mixture. All of these things need to be ready and waiting when the baby comes home from the hospital.

DELIVERY COSTS

In addition to the doctor's charge for delivery, other costs at delivery include anesthesia or any type of pain reliever. Additional doctors necessary during delivery and the pediatrician will also submit their charges for payment. A **pediatrician** is a doctor who specializes in the care and treatment of diseases of small children. Immediately upon delivery, the pediatrician takes the baby to be checked, weighed, and prepared for the nursery. The pediatrician will then remain the child's physician for approximately twelve years.

Many costs at delivery are in addition to the package deal.

The usual hospital stay for a normal delivery is one or two days. A Caesarean (surgical) delivery usually requires a hospital stay of three to five days. While they are in the hospital, there is a daily charge for both mother and child. In addition, all services rendered carry a charge.

FIRST-YEAR NEEDS

The new family member has many needs, and many new expenses are incurred during the first year. Some of these needs are food, postnatal visits, clothing, personal care supplies, toys, and babysitters.

Food.   In a few months, the baby will begin eating cereals, baby foods (strained fruits and vegetables), and soft solids. Special vitamins and fluoride are often prescribed for the teeth that the child will begin cutting around six months of age.

A baby needs special care in feeding the first year.

Postnatal Visits.   The baby will need to be examined by a pediatrician regularly during the first two years. These visits are called **well-baby visits**. The baby is not ill, but the doctor checks for proper growth and gives necessary immunizations. Because there is no illness, insurance coverage usually does not provide benefits for these visits or the immunizations. These visits usually occur at four months, six months, one year, one and one-half years, and again before the child starts school. Shots and pills are administered to protect the baby from diphtheria, polio, measles, tetanus, whooping cough, and other childhood diseases that could be very harmful to a small baby.

Well-baby visits are not covered by insurance.

Clothing.   Baby and toddler clothing is expensive. The baby grows rapidly and clothes are soon too small. First year clothing requirements for babies include underclothes, socks, shoes, sleepers, pants and shirts, jackets and coats, hats, and gloves. Many different changes of clothing are usually needed.

Babies soon outgrow their clothes.

Personal Care Supplies.   Personal products specifically for the baby — diaper rash creams, powders, shampoos and soaps, baby aspirin and other over-the-counter medicines, thermometers, and special prescriptions — are necessary during the first year. Care should be taken to keep these products out of reach of a crawling baby or toddler.

Toys.   As the child grows physically, it has the need to explore the world and learn about its shapes, colors, and parts. Toys and gadgets aid in the development of coordination and stimulate mental growth. Crib toys, such

Toys stimulate a child's mental development.

as mobiles, aid the development of visual acuity and hand and finger dexterity. Many parents also provide tub toys, teddy bears, teething rings, building blocks, and an assortment of other carefully selected products that are safe and suited to the age of the child.

Babysitters.   The baby cannot go everywhere with the parents. Careful selection of a competent and trustworthy babysitter to care for the baby properly when the parents are absent is essential. Babysitting fees vary, but are usually under minimum wage.

Babysitters should be carefully selected.

VOCABULARY

Directions: Can you find the definition for each of the following terms used in Chapter 20?

wedding party	reservation
formal wedding	travel agency
semiformal wedding	overbooked
informal wedding	prenatal expense
tax shelter	obstetrician
tax-deferred annuity	pediatrician
itinerary	well-baby visits

1. A legal way to avoid paying taxes on present earnings.
2. A contractual savings program wherein taxes are postponed until payments are received at retirement.
3. An advance commitment whereby a traveler is assured of a plane seat or a motel room.
4. A cost incurred before a baby is born.
5. Doctor visits that are not covered by insurance because the baby is not ill.
6. A doctor who specializes in the treatment of medical needs and diseases of small children.
7. Persons who participate in the wedding ceremony: bride and groom, best man, maid of honor, bridesmaids, ushers, flower girl, ring bearer, candle lighters, etc.
8. A type of wedding in which everyone, including guests, wears formal attire.
9. A type of wedding in which only the wedding party is dressed formally.
10. A type of wedding that is usually held outdoors and has no special clothing requirements for wedding party or guests.
11. A detailed list of events, times, and places planned for a trip or vacation.
12. An agent who is authorized to write and sell airline tickets.

13. The result when an airline sells more tickets for a flight than it has seats available.

14. A doctor who specializes in delivering babies.

ITEMS FOR DISCUSSION

1. What is the purpose of premarital counseling?
2. How long before the wedding should a couple begin making preparations?
3. List some responsibilities (expenses) that are traditionally accepted by the bride and her family.
4. List some responsibilities (expenses) that are traditionally accepted by the groom and his family.
5. Who is included in the wedding party?
6. What is the difference between a formal wedding and a semiformal wedding?
7. What are some advantages and disadvantages experienced by couples who work for several years before having children?
8. What types of vacation options are available?
9. What types of things are listed on a vacation itinerary?
10. How soon should you make hotel reservations before taking a vacation trip?
11. List some preparations that you need to make before leaving on vacation. Include those preparations designed to keep people from realizing that you are gone.
12. What is the purpose of using traveler's checks instead of carrying cash?
13. How much does a travel agency charge a customer for making reservations and issuing airline tickets?
14. List three prenatal expenses.
15. What are some of the costs involved in child delivery?
16. List some expenses that will be incurred by a couple during the first year of a child's life.

APPLICATIONS

1. Describe a wedding that you have attended in the last year or two (include wedding party, dress, flowers, reception, etc.).
2. Describe the wedding you would choose for yourself, including setting, type of ceremony, wedding party, total cost, number of guests, honeymoon plans, etc.
3. Why do working couples need to find tax shelters and annuities?

4. How does a family's budget differ from an individual's budget?

5. Design a three-day itinerary for a plane trip to a resort area within about a thousand miles of where you live. Include all necessary information.

CASE PROBLEMS AND ACTIVITIES

1. Write a report describing different engagement ring options:

   a. Diamond solitaire with matching bands. Compare costs of different size diamonds.

   b. Gold and silver bands. Compare quality, width, and costs.

   c. Costs of stones other than diamonds: rubies, emeralds, sapphires. Compare different sizes of each.

   d. Financing plans available to young couples.

2. Tom Nielsen and Teresa Kimball will be married in a month. Both are working and plan to work at least five years before having children. They have asked for your opinion on how household duties should be divided because both of them work eight hours a day, five days a week. Devise a plan for dividing duties and responsibilities; include checkbook balancing and financial planning.

3. You and a friend have decided to take a trip. Based on the following three hypothetical cases, describe the kinds of trips you would take and list all of the costs that would be involved in each.

   a. You each have $75 to contribute and could get away for a three- or four-day weekend. You have one automobile that does not need maintenance or repairs.

   b. You each have $500 to spend and could get away for three to five days.

   c. You each have $1,500 to spend and could be away for ten days.

Chapter 21

CONTINGENCY PLANNING

◆◆◆◆◆◆◆◆◆◆◆◆◆◆◆◆◆◆◆◆◆◆◆◆◆

OBJECTIVES

1. Identify emergency situations that can be prevented and list safety precautions.
2. Explain what is involved in automobile purchase and maintenance.
3. Define the costs and steps of divorce.
4. Discuss why a person needs a will and identify the costs involved in death.

EMERGENCIES

◆◆◆◆◆◆◆◆

Misfortune strikes everybody. Although it may not be possible to avoid certain emergency situations, others can be minimized as far as damages suffered. Emergency situations can be divided into these general categories: household accidents, vehicular accidents, work-related injuries, and other accidents and injuries.

HOUSEHOLD ACCIDENTS

Thousands of injuries occur each year in the home, many of them serious. Household injuries can be avoided, however, through the use of certain commonsense preventative measures.

The kitchen, with cupboards, shelves, drawers and storage areas, food, and appliances, is an especially attractive area for small children. Cleansers, detergents, and other products that are **toxic** (poisonous) can cause serious injury or death. Cooking ingredients should be placed in high cupboards, out of the reach of small children. Poisonous products should always be stored in their original containers: a soda bottle should not be used to store cleaning fluid. Any product containing a questionable substance should be stored away from food. The kitchen is a good place to display emergency information about what to do and whom to call in case of poisoning, choking, drowning, electric shock, bleeding cuts, fractures, burns, shock, and head injuries. A complete first aid kit (with instructions on use) should be handy at all times. (See Figure 21-1.)

Poisonous substances should be kept out of reach.

The bathroom is a potentially **lethal** — deadly — play area for small children. The toilet lid should always be kept down when a toddler or infant is in the house. If a small child falls headfirst into the toilet, he or she can

Keep a first aid kit handy at all times.

WHAT TO DO IN CASE OF:

BLEEDING CUTS

The first concern is to stop the bleeding. Use gauze or a clean cloth; apply pressure directly to the wound. Once the bleeding has stopped, clean the wound, using *hydrogen peroxide.* Wash the entire area with soap and water; bandage.

Call a doctor if:
1. Blood is spurting.
2. You cannot stop the bleeding with direct pressure.
3. There is a deep puncture wound.
4. There is glass or another substance in the wound.
5. There is a large and gaping wound.

FRACTURES

Broken bones always require medical attention. Do not try to realign a fractured limb. Splint the arm or leg in order to transport the victim without jarring the injury. If you suspect a broken neck or back, do not move the victim; call an ambulance immediately.

HEAD INJURIES

Hard blows to the head can cause internal bleeding.

Call a doctor if:
1. The person loses consciousness at the time of the accident.
2. A child is confused or disoriented, or is drowsy and hard to arouse.
3. There is vomiting.
4. There is bleeding from the nose or ears.

SHOCK

Serious injury, bleeding, or severe blow can cause shock. The victim will look very pale, with cold clammy skin. The pulse will be weak and rapid. This is serious; call an ambulance or get the person to the hospital immediately. Keep the person warm, lying flat with legs elevated.

BURNS

Soak the burned area in cold water for 30 minutes or so. This will cool the burn, prevent further damage, and diminish the pain and swelling. Do not use ointments or oils. If the burn is severe, however, do not apply anything. Do not remove clothing if it is sticking to the burn. Transport the victim to a hospital immediately.

NOSEBLEED

Twist small pieces of cotton into shapes to be inserted into nostrils. Pinch the nose firmly and hold for several minutes. Remove the cotton when the bleeding stops. Have the person lie down. Call a doctor if bleeding has not stopped after 20 minutes.

CHOKING

If the victim is a child, hold him or her upside down across the knees and give blows to the back between the shoulder blades. On an adult, use the Heimlich maneuver: Approach from behind. Make a fist with one hand, thumb side against the victim's abdomen, below the rib cage. Press into the victim's abdomen with a quick upward motion. Repeat if choking continues. You must force air around the lodged object. Try artificial respiration until help arrives.

DROWNING

Mouth-to-mouth resuscitation must be started immediately. Because of water swallowed, vomiting often follows. Push against the victim's stomach to get water out. Get air into the victim's lungs. Seek medical help immediately. Water in the lungs can result in pneumonia.

ELECTRIC SHOCK

Do not touch the victim until the source of power is removed. Turn off the current; give mouth-to-mouth resuscitation. Call for medical help.

POISONING

Call the nearest poison control center immediately, or take the victim to the emergency room of the nearest hospital. You can make the person vomit or you can neutralize the substance in the stomach. Corrosive poisons burn the mouth and inner parts; do not induce vomiting.

Figure 21-1   Emergency Information

drown in the small amount of water it contains. Children should never be left unattended while bathing, swimming, or otherwise in or near water. Appliances such as hair dryers should be unplugged and kept away from sinks and tubs. Personal care items should be kept out of reach of children.

Because of lack of space, many families store items not frequently used in attics, garages, high cupboards, and basements. Retrieval of stored items can be dangerous. Ladders should be placed firmly with a second person holding the legs for support. Falling is a common household accident that can be avoided with care and thought.

Weapons, including guns and knives, should be locked away with ammunition locked in a separate place. Tools and power devices stored in garages and work areas should be kept out of reach of children. Chemicals, fertilizers, oil, gasoline, and other such products should be stored securely, following rules of storage safety for combustible and flammable products. Fire hazards are created by cleaning rags, papers, and cluttered possessions. Unused refrigerators or other storage containers should have the doors removed so that children cannot become trapped in them.

Weapons should be locked away securely.

VEHICULAR ACCIDENTS

The National Highway Traffic Safety Commission estimates that every person will be involved in at least one automobile accident during their lifetime, on the average. The commission also estimates that one in three persons will be involved in a major accident that will send them to the hospital for treatment. The leading cause of death of persons under age 35 is the automobile accident, which can injure, cripple, or kill without warning. Careful driving, seat belt use, and proper car maintenance all help reduce risks. Tires need to be maintained at the correct pressure and replaced when the tread becomes too thin for driving safely. The engine should be serviced regularly, the belts and hoses inspected, and the water and fluid levels (brakes, transmission, battery) checked. Most serious accidents happen after dark and within 25 miles of home. **Defensive driving** is watching for the bad driving decisions of others and involves tactics such as slowing down, yielding right-of-way, maintaining safe distances between cars (one car length for every 10 mph), and using headlights on two-way roads and whenever visibility is impaired.

Tire pressure is important to mileage and safety.

WORK-RELATED INJURIES

Each year there are injuries and illnesses that are employment related. Many work-related injuries are caused by carelessness and employee error.

Illustration 21-1
Children should
never be left unat-
tended in or near
water.

Others are caused by unsafe working conditions. High levels of chemicals or toxins in the air, noise that damages hearing after a number of years, or fumes that damage lung tissue are examples of unsafe working conditions. On-the-job injuries can be reduced by carefully observing safety rules, wearing proper clothing or other protective equipment, and being constantly aware of possible dangers. The nature of the work can cause symptoms to develop many years later. For instance, black lung is developed by coal miners after years of working in the mines with insufficient oxygen. Noxious gases and fumes circulate in the air while the workers are digging. Persons who work with radioactive substances and agents known to cause cancer may not develop cancer until several years later. Some instances of radiation exposure do not result in incurable cancer for as long as 20 years. Yet the cancer can be traced back to the direct exposure or risk taken in the past. Developing an awareness of the types of potential hazards of an occupation should be a priority for today's worker.

OTHER ACCIDENTS

Other types of accidents and injuries also occur daily. Most are the result of some human error or mechanical failure. Examples include drownings, plane and train accidents, injuries due to extreme weather conditions, and bicycle mishaps. Broken bones, torn ligaments, and other injuries occur when people participate in sports and athletic activities.

You can prepare for emergencies.

While you cannot prevent injuries and accidents entirely, you can prepare yourself in several ways to survive them: (a) insure against the risk of loss, (b) reduce the risk of loss, or (c) avoid the circumstance that could lead to loss. For example, you may be considering a ski trip to the mountains. Risks include icy roads that may cause automobile damage and personal injury, and skiing accidents. Health insurance can protect against personal injury losses; automobile insurance can protect against car damage losses; taking chains and preparing your vehicle for snow and ice can reduce driving risks; and not taking the risk at all will prevent any loss.

AUTOMOBILE PURCHASE AND CARE

Expenses of automobile ownership only begin with the purchase. One must also consider the contingency costs of maintenance and the possibility of loss due to vehicle theft.

BUYING A CAR

Whether you want a new or used car, as a wise consumer you should shop around, compare prices, and take your time in selecting such a major purchase. Before looking, make a list of features that are important to you, such as power steering, power brakes, automatic transmission, or air conditioning. While such features can be added later, it is more convenient to buy the car equipped. Stick to your list and know what you want. Test drive many different cars and ask questions. A new-car price **markup** includes any additions to the basic price of a delivered car. Additional preparations for sale, such as undercoating, paint touch-ups, and the dealer profit, are included in the markup. Markups usually begin at about 10 percent of the basic car price and go as high as customers will pay. Several sources are available to consumers for determining the dealer's cost and suggested retail prices for new cars and factory-installed optional equipment. One source for new car prices is a paperback book called *Edmund's New Car Prices*. Another source is *Consumer Reports* magazine.

When you buy a new car, you can pay cash for the car or trade in your old car as a down payment. A **trade-in** is an older vehicle of some type used to reduce the price of the new car by the amount of money the dealer will give you on your old vehicle. Because the dealer will try to make a profit from the sale of your old car, you should try to get as much for your old car as possible. Sometimes you can advertise and sell your old car and get more for it than a dealer would give you on a trade-in. When you are not trading in an old car that the dealer may have to repair before reselling, the dealer will usually offer a lower price on the new car.

Before selling or trading your old car, find out what a realistic selling price is for your car. Used car values are listed in the **NADA** (National

Added features increase your car's value.

A trade-in will reduce the price of a new car.

Automobile Dealers Association) **Blue Book**, which lists a low book value for a basic car for six years. Additional features of your car, such as automatic transmission, power steering, air conditioning, and low mileage, will add to its value. When these features are added, your car is said to meet high book value. The **high book value** of a used car includes the low book value plus the value of its added features. Know the book values for your used car as well as for any used car you plan to purchase to assure that you pay or receive a realistic price.

Probably the most important thing to remember in purchasing a car is patience. A car is a large purchase that deserves the time and attention of a careful choice. Avoid high-pressure sales tactics. Take your time in making the decision, because a car purchase will result in monthly payments for three or four years.

There are approximately 25,150 franchised new car dealers in the United States. The U.S. Better Business Bureau reports that less than 10 percent of complaints about car purchases are against new car dealers. The National Automobile Dealers Association issues a code of ethics for its members — the franchised new car dealers. If you feel you have been treated unfairly by a new or used car dealer, you can complain to the growing network of Automotive Consumer Action Programs (called AUTOCAPs). There are more than 40 AUTOCAPs in the U.S. that mediate disputes between consumers and car dealers. AUTOCAP panels include dealers and nondealers, state and local consumer protection agency members, and representatives from district attorneys' offices. The local automobile dealers association listed in the Yellow Pages of the telephone book can give you the address of the nearest AUTOCAP.

New car dealers have a code of ethics.

AUTOMOBILE MAINTENANCE

The monthly car payment is only the beginning of the cost of owning a car. Your budget must include a monthly provision for regular car maintenance and repairs. While the car is new — for the first 12,000 miles or whatever is covered by a warranty — you may be relieved of some maintenance and repair costs. But the car will still need regular servicing, such as oil changes, which include a new oil filter and lubrication. Oil changes and lubrications are recommended every 3,000 to 5,000 miles or every three months. Engine tune-ups are needed every 12,000 to 20,000 miles or once a year. Checking and replacement of belts and hoses, wiper blades, fuses, lights, and tires are needed regularly. Occasionally, a major repair is needed. For example, a water pump may need replacing, brakes may become worn after a few years, and other repairs under the car and in the engine may be needed. Mufflers may need replacement or repair, wheels may need to be balanced, and front-end alignments are needed regularly, too.

Many costly repairs can be avoided or minimized by careful driving habits and regular maintenance. Caution is needed when having your car repaired, however. An estimated $125 a year for each car in the United States is spent on unnecessary repairs. A vast majority of auto repair shops do not charge for labor by the clock hour. They charge for the amount of time allowed for a repair in a flat-rate manual. Flat-rate manuals allow no time for road tests after repairs are made. Therefore, the mechanic has incentive to do the job as quickly as possible and to sell extra parts. Choose your repair shop carefully. An authorized automobile dealership is not always the best choice for servicing and making repairs on your car. Check with the Better Business Bureau about service and repair shops in your area. Ask for recommendations from friends and neighbors. When you find a shop to service your car, become a steady customer. The more you know about your own car, the more protection you have against repair fraud. Read the manual that came with your car and ask questions.

Maintenance costs also include protecting your car's paint. Keep the car clean and have a good coat of wax on it. Use a cleaning compound to remove tar and scratches and then apply wax at least once a year. If your car is parked outside during all kinds of weather, the paint has less protection and can **oxidize** — permanently lose its shine due to exposure to weather and sun.

CAR THEFT

Nearly a million motor vehicles are stolen each year in the United States. About a third are never recovered. While theft is covered under comprehensive automobile insurance, the insurance company only pays the value of the car at the time of the theft — not the price you paid for it.

Expensive automobile models (those costing $12,000 or more) are the main targets for car theft. Some cars are stolen for parts, or only parts are stolen, because manufacturers do not stock all the parts needed for older, used cars. Let's look at some ways you can protect yourself against automobile theft.

Shopping centers are popular places for car thieves. Make sure your car is locked and parked in a well-lighted area, as close to stores and traffic as possible. Less than 45 seconds are required to enter a car, cross the distributor wires, and start it. Approximately 40 percent of stolen cars are taken by tow trucks in broad daylight. A tow truck without a name on it, or with a name not listed in local telephone books, signals something is wrong.

Persons living in highly populated urban areas are most often car theft victims. Professional car thieves cannot be stopped, but they can be slowed down. The best protection against theft is an ignition-kill system, which

Repair shops use flat-rate manuals.

Cars need frequent washing and waxing.

Expensive cars are stolen most often.

You can slow down car thieves.

Illustration 21-2
When you find a
mechanic you trust,
become a steady
customer.

interrupts the voltage needed to start a car. A second switch must be turned on with a second key before the car will start. An ignition-kill system costs about $60 installed. A factory-installed system can also ward off thieves. One of the best precautions against theft of older used cars is the removal of the standard door lock buttons and installation of tapered buttons. Tapered lock buttons are very difficult to pull up with any type of device inserted through the doors or windows. New cars usually have horizontal locks that are more difficult to unlock.

Remove tape decks at night.

Never leave packages, purses, or other valuables in plain sight in the car. Keep these items in the trunk or well covered. Also, home-installed tape systems and speakers are easily removed by thieves. If your car is parked outside at night, these valuables should be removed.

DIVORCE
◆◆◆◆◆◆◆◆

In all but a few states, a divorce is now called a **dissolution of marriage**, which means that irreconcilable differences have led to the breakdown of the marriage. Furthermore, one partner does not have to prove fault by the other partner to be granted a divorce. If one partner wants the marriage to be dissolved, it can be done. The only time fault is considered is when the issue of child custody arises.

COST OF DIVORCE

Expenses involved in divorce are high. Attorneys' fees (one attorney for each party), court costs and filing fees, child support and alimony, division of

Divorce expenses are
high.

property, and settlement costs may be included. The more issues there are to settle, the higher the attorneys' fees will be. When child custody is an issue and a court hearing is necessary, the fees are even higher. Often parties can agree outside of court and enter into a property settlement agreement. The **property settlement agreement** is a document specifying the division of property and assets agreed to by both parties and entered into court for the judge's approval. The more that can be settled outside of court, the less divorce proceedings cost.

In most cases, the parent who is granted custody of the children will receive child support from the other parent. The amount of child support is based on the income and ability of the parties, on the assumption that both parties are responsible for supporting the children to the best of their abilities. Alimony is awarded in some cases when one spouse has been dependent on the other for a number of years and has little means of self-support. Most alimony awards are for a limited number of years, or may be based upon a former spouse completing education or training for employment. Child support and alimony are at the discretion of the judge and become binding on the parties under the divorce decree. Amounts of child support and alimony can only be modified by another court order.

Child support is at
the judge's discre-
tion.

STEPS IN DIVORCE

Dissolving a marriage is often a lengthy and unpleasant matter. Usually the papers are not actually filed until the couple has been separated for some time and it appears to be in everyone's best interest to pursue a legal dissolution of marriage. One party goes to an attorney, and the attorney prepares the documents, which are filed with the court. The other party is served with copies of the papers, called Petition for Dissolution of Marriage, and given a short time to appear (file papers) if there is a disagreement with the proposals set forth in the petition. The petition sets forth how the first party proposes to divide property and award custody, amounts desired for child support, visitation rights, and so on. If the second party fails to appear (defaults) then the first party is awarded whatever is asked in the petition. In most cases, the second party does appear and a court date is set to decide the issues that cannot be settled between the parties. Often it takes many months, even a year or more, for the case to be heard in court. Consequently, a temporary hearing will be held to establish temporary custody, child support, visitation rights of the noncustodial parent, and other matters. Many of the temporary provisions tend to become permanent. That is, often both parties agree in writing to property settlement and other matters prior to the court date. When the judge approves the agreement, it is entered as part of the **decree**, which is a final

A default is a failure
to appear in court.

statement of the dissolution decisions. A decree is final and binding on both parties until modified by the court.

A decree is final and binding on all parties.

If the parties cannot agree on a settlement, the case then goes to court. There is no jury in divorce cases. Both parties testify and present their cases. Witnesses may be called in the issue of child custody to determine which parent would be the better custodial parent. The judge's decision is based entirely on the best benefit for the child or children of the marriage. All other matters — property, alimony, amount of child support, visitation rights — are also decided in court. The court hearing may last several days. Once the decree is entered, a waiting period of 60 to 90 days before either party may remarry is usually imposed.

DEATH
♦♦♦♦♦♦♦♦

Aging and death are parts of living and need planning and attention. Preparations are not only for those who are about to die; they should be considered by all responsible adults.

WRITING A WILL

Many people do not understand the need for a will. A will expresses a person's wishes for disposal of property after his or her death. A will only passes title to property that does not otherwise pass. For example, if you own a car jointly with another person, on your death the car will go to that other person. The car need not be mentioned in the will. A **testator** is the person who makes a will. If you die not having a will, but own property that will not automatically pass to another person, you are said to be **intestate**, and the state in which you live will determine to whom your property will go. In most states, if you die without a will and are married, your property will go to your spouse. If you have a spouse and children, the spouse will get half and the children will divide the other half. Each state has its laws about how property and money will be divided. If you want things to be otherwise, you need a will.

You need a will if you have children or property.

Anyone who has reached the age of majority (18 years of age in most states) and is of sound mind can make a valid will. Couples with children need to have a will in order to name guardians to provide care for their children in the event of their deaths. Anyone previously married needs a will to be sure property will be divided as he or she wishes.

A **simple will** is a short one- or two-page document that lists spouse and children and provides how each shall inherit. Most wills are prepared by

A simple will is inex-
pensive.

attorneys. Simple wills for a husband and wife take a short time to prepare and usually cost less than $150. A will must be witnessed by two persons not mentioned in the will. Witnesses must be 18 or older, not related, and able to attest to the mental competency of the person making a will at the time the will is written. An example of a simple will is shown in Figure 21-2.

A **holographic will** is one written in a person's own handwriting. A handwritten will is legally valid in nineteen states and should be witnessed just as one typed and prepared by a lawyer. Because a handwritten will is often easier to contest (question), a typed will is recommended.

Figure 21-2
Last Will and
Testament

LAST WILL AND TESTAMENT OF ANTHONY JOHN HINTON

I, Anthony John Hinton, of the City of Dayton and State of Ohio, do make, publish, and declare this to be my Last Will and Testament in manner following:

FIRST: I direct that all my just debts, funeral expenses, and the cost of administering my estate be paid by my executrix hereinafter named.

SECOND: I give, devise, and bequeath to my beloved daughter, Carol Hinton Campbell, now residing in Englewood, New Jersey, that certain piece of real estate, with all improvements thereon, situated in the same city and at the corner of Hudson Avenue and Tenafly Road.

THIRD: All the remainder and residue of my property, real, personal, and mixed, I give to my beloved wife, Kimberly Sue Hinton, executrix of this, my Last Will and Testament, and I direct that she not be required to give bond or security for the performance of her duties as such.

LASTLY: I hereby revoke any and all former wills by me made.

IN WITNESS WHEREOF, I have hereunto set my hand this tenth day of October, in the year nineteen hundred --.

Anthony John Hinton
Anthony John Hinton

We, the undersigned, certify that the foregoing instrument was, on the date thereof, signed and declared by Anthony John Hinton as his Last Will and Testament, in the presence of us who, in his presence and in the presence of each other, have, at his request, hereunto signed our names as witnesses of the execution thereof, this tenth day of October, 19--; and we hereby certify that we believe the said Anthony John Hinton to be of sound mind and memory.

                                                         251 Wonderly Avenue
William Schoenborn ___ residing at Dayton, Ohio 45419-2521

                                                         3024 James Hill Road
Samuel Ucirre ___ residing at Kettering, Ohio 45429-2454

                                                         423 Goldengate Drive
Irene Vasilkova ___ residing at Centerville, Ohio 45459-2459

A **trust will** is a very complicated will, most always prepared by a lawyer. A trust is many pages long and lists specific provisions for holding property, assets, and money for minor children or others. A *trustee* is named to manage the money, and all duties and powers are described. The trustee may be a bank, a financial institution, or a person. The testator lists all persons who may have a claim to his or her estate, specifies all bequests of property to other persons, and lists any specific needs and how they shall be fulfilled.

A trustee acts in behalf of the testator.

In any will, all *issue* (children) must be mentioned, whether or not they shall inherit money or property. When a child is left out, a question arises as to the intent of the testator. Children not born when a will is drawn are presumed to inherit along with other children. Because of the complexities of inheritance laws and taxes, it is advisable for all couples with children and assets to consult a lawyer to draw up wills to dispose of their property as they wish.

Wills should be kept in a safe-deposit box, with a copy of the will and location of important documents listed in the home. Less than 25 percent of all people are prepared for death. This preparation involves writing a will, leaving burial instructions, listing the location of important papers and all accounts, and making specific bequests of personal property.

SURVIVORS' BENEFITS

Surviving spouse and children are usually provided with some kind of death benefits. Life insurance benefits are not taxable to the recipients. Benefits from a life insurance policy can be obtained by mailing a copy of the death certificate, the original life insurance policy, and a claim form to the life insurance company. Social security pays a one-time lump-sum benefit of about $255 to help cover funeral expenses. The social security benefit is paid to the estate of any person who was collecting social security retirement benefits or who was eligible to collect benefits. If this benefit is not received soon after death, it must be applied for. The Veterans Administration pays another stipend to survivors of veterans. The benefit may include a grave marker, funeral services, and cash of $400 or more, depending on type and length of service and branch of armed forces. Children of veterans may also be entitled to scholarships and educational grant benefits. Many employer pension plans pay lump-sum or monthly benefits to widows and families. Employer-paid benefits may not be automatic, and the widow(er) may have to apply to receive these benefits. Survivors need to check thoroughly to see what policies, retirement plans, and other benefits have accrued through the years.

Survivors are entitled to benefits but may have to apply for them.

LAST EXPENSES

Final expenses require planning.

The costs involved when a person dies can range from a few hundred dollars to several thousand dollars. These expenses include final medical and hospital charges, funeral expenses and casket, and burial. By preparing instructions and making provisions for these costs in advance, you spare survivors the emotional decision-making process that may be capitalized on by others. Survivors who are grieving the loss of a loved one often are unprepared to make the many decisions involved in planning a funeral and burial. At such an emotional time, a family may incur elaborate final expenses that they or the estate cannot afford.

Cremation is less expensive than burial.

Cremation is a process of reducing a body to ashes in a high-temperature oven. The ashes are placed in an urn that is presented to the family or placed in a vault. Cremation is a less-expensive alternative to burial, but there are special requirements. When a body is not cremated within a certain time span, usually two days, it must be embalmed or otherwise prepared for burial. These costs must be paid even though cremation is later chosen.

Funeral services, which usually last a half hour, may be performed in a church or in a funeral home. The cost can be as much as $1,500, which includes embalming, preparations, music, printed remembrances, and newspaper notices. All decisions about these matters must be made in a relatively short period of time.

A prepaid funeral plan saves survivors emotional stress.

Many funeral homes have prearranged plans available at guaranteed costs. Money for the funeral is placed into an account that is insured by the FDIC or FSLIC and earns interest. Although the money is for the funeral, it can be withdrawn in an emergency. Written instructions will save the family from overspending at the time of death, save emotional and financial distress, and assure the family that the type and cost of the funeral is as desired by the loved one.

Typical funeral home charges include moving the body (to funeral home, to cemetery); embalming and preparation; casket; use of facilities; funeral director's and staff fees; hearse; family limousine; pallbearers' car; flower car; escort to cemetery; obituary (newspaper death notice); notice in newspaper; printed memorial folders, memorial book, and thank-you cards; death certificate; and all necessary permits. The cost of a burial plot and marker are additional expenses.

VOCABULARY

Directions: Can you find the definition for each of the following terms used in Chapter 21?

toxic	defensive driving
lethal	markup

trade-in	decree
NADA Blue Book	testator
high book value	intestate
oxidize	simple will
dissolution of marriage	holographic will
property settlement agreement	trust will

1. Watching for poor driving by others to avoid accidents.
2. An old car used as a down payment to purchase a new vehicle.
3. Dangerous and potentially deadly.
4. Value resulting when value of added features is added to the low book value of an automobile.
5. Permanent loss of shine to a car's paint because of exposure to sun and weather.
6. A substance that is poisonous and causes illness or death if swallowed.
7. A form of divorce that provides that a marriage can be ended without proving fault.
8. Additions to the base price of an automobile, such as delivery costs, undercoating, and dealer profit.
9. A written agreement by husband and wife to dispose of and divide the assets of a marriage.
10. A handbook for car dealers and financial institutions that lists values of used cars for six years.
11. A final statement that settles all issues of a dissolution of marriage and is binding on the parties.
12. A long and complicated will that makes guardianship or trustee provisions.
13. To die without making a will.
14. A will that is handwritten.
15. One who makes and signs a will before two witnesses.
16. A short, one- or two-page will listing bequests by a testator.

ITEMS FOR DISCUSSION

1. What are some precautions to take in the kitchen to protect small children and toddlers from injury and accident?
2. How can you reduce the risk of automobile accident injuries?
3. What are three ways to be prepared for injuries and accidents?
4. What are some things to remember before making an automobile purchase?
5. To whom can you complain if you feel you have been treated unfairly by an automobile dealer?
6. What types of regular maintenance are needed on an automobile?

7. Why does an automobile need to be washed and waxed regularly?
8. List several ways you can help prevent your car from being stolen.
9. What are some of the costs involved in getting a divorce?
10. What is meant by the term *intestate*?
11. Where should a will be kept? What about copies?
12. What types of survivors' benefits are available when a person dies?
13. What is cremation?

APPLICATIONS

1. Make a list of potentially dangerous areas in your home. What can be done to make them safer?
2. Identify some work hazards for the occupations listed below. What can workers or the employer do to reduce some of these hazards?

   a. Mine worker
   b. School teacher
   c. Construction worker
   d. Dentist
   e. Barber

3. Make a list of features that are very important to you to have in an automobile. Describe what your ideal car would look like, inside and out.
4. Interview someone who has owned the same car for three consecutive years. Within a three-year period of time, what types of repairs and maintenance were required on the vehicle? List them, together with the cost of each.
5. What property or money do you own that is not jointly held with someone else? To whom would you like to see your property go at your death? Make a list of what you have and to whom you would like to make bequests.

CASE PROBLEMS AND ACTIVITIES

1. From library sources, locate the following information:

   a. Number of traffic deaths in your state last year
   b. Whether this figure represents an increase or a decrease over the previous year
   c. Number of victims not using a safety belt

2. Have you or someone you know been involved in an accident or injury? Describe the injury or accident — how it happened, injuries

sustained, and how it could have been prevented or injuries reduced.

3. A friend comes to you for advice about buying a car. What advice will you give to aid the person in making a good choice and getting the most for his or her money?

4. Determine the NADA Blue Book value for a used automobile that you might be interested in purchasing. What things will add to the low book value? What is the range (low book value to high book value)? Check a library source, such as *Edmund's New Car Prices*, and find the dealer's cost of several new cars. List them, together with the cost of added features you would like to have on a car (air conditioning, power windows, etc.).

5. What types of divorce/dissolution laws are in effect in your state? Are they no-fault or fault laws? What are the waiting periods? Describe the procedures for dissolution.

6. Write a simple will for yourself, listing your property and to whom you want it to go. Date the will and have two witnesses sign it. If you are 18, is your will valid?

7. In your area, what would be the approximate total cost of a funeral? Visit a funeral home or get information through research about the costs and services provided.

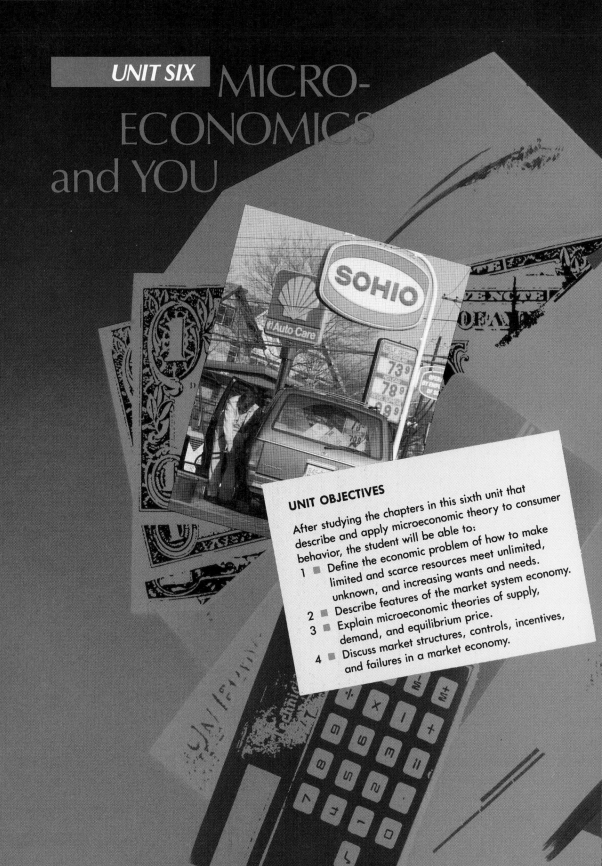

UNIT SIX MICRO-ECONOMICS and YOU

UNIT OBJECTIVES

After studying the chapters in this sixth unit that describe and apply microeconomic theory to consumer behavior, the student will be able to:

1 ■ Define the economic problem of how to make limited and scarce resources meet unlimited, unknown, and increasing wants and needs.

2 ■ Describe features of the market system economy.

3 ■ Explain microeconomic theories of supply, demand, and equilibrium price.

4 ■ Discuss market structures, controls, incentives, and failures in a market economy.

WHAT IS ECONOMICS?

HUMAN WANTS:	PROBLEM OF SCARCITY	RESOURCES:
■ Unlimited ■ Can be satisfied in different ways		■ Limited ■ Can be used in different ways

CHOICES MUST BE MADE

CREATES NEED FOR
ECONOMIC SYSTEM

ECONOMIC SYSTEM MUST
MAKE DECISIONS:

WHAT WILL BE PRODUCED?	FOR WHOM?	HOW? (WHAT RESOURCES WILL BE USED?)	AT WHAT COST?

IN ORDER
TO MAKE BEST
USE OF:

NATURAL RESOURCES	HUMAN RESOURCES	CAPITAL
■ Land and all resources not provided by man ■ Some cannot be replaced	■ Quantity of labor force ■ Quality of labor force ■ Productivity (quality of human effort)	■ Tools, machines, factories ■ Investment capital from savings of business and individuals

Chapter 22

THE ECONOMIC PROBLEM

◆◆◆◆◆◆◆◆◆◆◆◆◆◆◆◆◆◆◆◆◆◆◆◆◆

OBJECTIVES

1. Identify personal and societal benefits of understanding basic economic principles.
2. Explain the basic economic problem of scarcity and choice.
3. List and define the four factors of production and list the payoff for each factor.
4. Define the five economic goals of the U.S. economy.

WHY STUDY ECONOMICS?

◆◆◆◆◆◆◆◆

Economics is the study of how individuals, families, organizations, and societies make and carry out their choices — how they use their resources to achieve their goals. In the study of economics, we learn how the marketplace affects those choices, and how those choices are modified by tradition, values, government, and the political process. When we study economics, we study human behavior — in producing, exchanging, and consuming goods and services that satisfy needs and wants. We will study a vast array of topics, from making individual choices that maximize satisfaction to labor disputes, debt, inflation, unemployment, and international trade.

No one can escape the principles of economics — the study of scarcity. Society's needs and wants are always increasing, and there is no way our existing resources can possibly meet all of our present needs and wants, nor the continuing and unknown needs and wants of the future. As a result, consumers must choose which needs and wants to fulfill and how best to fulfill them. We study economics to learn how to make wise and responsible choices, for the good of society and for our own good. We study economics to learn how to solve *the economic problem*: how to make wise choices so that scarce, diminishing, and limited resources can best cover growing, unknown, and unlimited wants and needs.

Well-informed consumers know basic economics.

BENEFITS TO SOCIETY

An informed citizen has an understanding of economics.

Consumers who are well informed and knowledgeable about economics make wise decisions that determine the courses of their own lives and contribute to the destiny of their country's economic future. By giving you a better understanding of the world in which you live, economics can help you be a more productive, responsible, and effective citizen who is a part of the positive changes in society. One major function of an informed citizen — voting — depends on a good understanding of important economic issues.

Consumers who are knowledgeable about economics can help to conserve the country's resources. Wise economic decisions facilitate the use of resources to their maximum potential (conservation), while unwise choices lead to waste and mismanagement of scarce resources, to the detriment of society as a whole. Because natural, human, and human-made resources are limited in supply and quality, consumers have a responsibility to future generations to make good decisions now.

PERSONAL BENEFITS

Understanding economics is a personal benefit.

The study of economics is of practical value in our daily lives, both personally and professionally. Knowledge of economics can aid in making good decisions that will allow us to enjoy effective, productive, and rewarding lives. For instance, a citizen who understands such concepts as inflation and unemployment (their causes and cures) is better able to survive during periods of inflation or recession. In studying economics, we learn not only how and why such things happen, but also how to deal with such problems and bring about solutions.

Many people find careers in economics. Big businesses, labor unions, and government offices hire economists, economic counselors, and advisers. Every successful business relies on dependable interpretation of economic indicators. Although economic knowledge may not specifically teach you how to make more money, it can give you insight into ways to make your money do more for you, and make you better equipped to exist in a world that can be threatening, unsympathetic, and uncertain.

SCARCITY AND CHOICE
◆◆◆◆◆◆◆◆

An economic system is designed to make allocation decisions.

Human wants and needs exceed society's ability to satisfy them. All societies are faced with the problem of scarcity. Because of scarcity, we study the choices available to satisfy unlimited wants with limited resources. This allocation problem is solved by selecting an economic system that will answer the three basic types of questions:

1. Decision Question: What and how much will be produced?
2. Production Question: How should production take place (what resources will be allocated, at what cost)?
3. Distribution Question: How will the production be distributed among the population?

Limited resources means that any individual, family, business, or country has only so many goods and services available to it. *Unlimited needs* means that any individual, family, business, or country has increasing needs and wants that are continually changing and growing and will never be fully satisfied.

BASIC NEEDS

Basic needs must be met first.

Basic survival needs include (a) food and water, (b) shelter, and (c) clothing. **Basic needs** are those ingredients necessary for maintaining physical life. Some authors would add safety and security to this list, because until these needs are met, there is little necessity to seek life-fulfilling needs.

LIFE-FULFILLING NEEDS

Life-improving or fulfilling needs and wants include the following:

1. Food, clothing, and shelter beyond what is necessary for biological survival.

2. Medical care to improve the quality and length of life.
3. Education to achieve personal goals, both social and economic.
4. Travel, vacations, and recreation to improve personal enjoyment of life.
5. Gadgetry or extra items that make life more fun and give it extra excitement, challenge, or meaning.

You may have decided that many of the life-improving needs and wants are necessary for your happiness. But you must admit, they are not absolutely necessary for your physical survival — you have simply become used to them, and therefore expect to have them.

Two important concepts can be inferred: (a) material wants and needs are virtually unlimited, and (b) economic resources to meet those wants and needs are limited (scarce). Humanity's material desires for goods and services cannot be satisfied; we always want more than we can have. It can safely be said that at any point in time, society has unfulfilled wants and needs — biological needs plus life-fulfilling needs that may be socially oriented or involve learned responses (cars, vacations, luxuries).

Our needs and wants are unlimited.

INDIVIDUAL NEEDS AND WANTS

What each of us decides we need and want depends on individually unique factors. These vary among societies, and include personal style, income, education, security level, and leisure time.

Personal Style. Each person has his or her own set of values and personal preferences. Personal taste may be formal or informal, flashy or subdued, dominating or easygoing. Based on personal tastes and values, we make choices that fulfill our perceived wants and needs.

Our choices are based on our tastes and styles.

Income. What a person is able to earn and spend will influence greatly the type of consumer choices made. The more disposable income — money left over after expenses are paid — the higher the quality and quantity of your selections. Whether or not a person can afford to buy goods and services to fulfill wants and needs will affect his or her satisfaction or dissatisfaction with employment, personal life, goals, and other personal factors.

Education. **Formal education** is knowledge gained through attending formal institutions of learning. The end result is a diploma or degree, which is evidence that the recipient has accomplished a certain educational goal and has met the standards required for graduation. The level of education achieved will influence a person's needs and wants and methods of fulfilling them because it will affect income. See Figure 22-1.

Education increases your earning capacity.

Security Level. A person acts and reacts in accordance with the degree of safety, security, and peace enjoyed. These factors include personal safety as

Figure 22-1
Education and In-
come

Average Monthly Salary by Educational Level

High School Dropout.. $ 693/month
High School Graduate....................................... 1045/month
Undergraduate Degree..................................... 1910/month
Professional Degree.. 3871/month

Source: U.S. Bureau of the Census (1988)

well as personal freedoms and fears for life, liberty, and property. Security from physical harm — whether from civil conflicts or robbery and property damage — influences our perceptions and, therefore, our needs and wants. Job security is another important factor. If you feel secure and satisfied in your employment, your choices will be different from those you would make if you felt threatened or dissatisfied.

Leisure time needs careful planning.

Leisure Time. Individual needs and wants are often satisfied in our choices of pleasure and recreational activities. The average workweek, which was 44 hours in 1960, is 38 today, according to the U.S. Department of Labor Statistics. This shorter workweek gives us more leisure time. Wise choices in this area can make life rewarding and satisfying; wasting and making poor use of leisure time often leads to frustration, loneliness, and depression.

COLLECTIVE VALUES

Collective values are those things important to society as a whole. All citizens share in their costs and in their benefits. The society in which you live influences your values, goals, and choices because it demands from citizens and provides for citizens legal protection, employment, progress, quality environment, and public services.

Legal and personal rights are important to society.

Legal Protection. One of the first needs of the individual that is met by society is preservation of legal and personal rights, and protection from others who would deny those rights. Law enforcement is the result of society's value of protection for citizens and property. Laws are passed to protect freedoms and rights guaranteed by the Constitution or by local, state, and federal governments.

Employment. Society as a whole expects that its able members will be productive; employment is an acceptable measure of productivity. Most people who are able will work during their lifetimes because work is necessary to survive in society.

Illustration 22-1
The wise use of leisure time can make life more rewarding and satisfying.

Progress.   The relative state of the country in which you live — its technological advances and their importance to your fellow citizens — will affect your personal goals. Our society is technologically advanced and places a high value on positive innovations. **Innovations** are new ideas, methods, or devices that bring about changes. Positive innovations, such as more efficient equipment or machinery, timesaving devices, or new solutions to old problems, bring about progress. Because society encourages us to be innovative, many citizens seek higher education and academic achievement to enhance their positions in society.

High value is placed on progress and innovation.

Quality Environment.   Natural resources are of great value and concern to society as a whole because they are very limited, and some cannot be replaced. Because of our priority of preserving a quality environment for ourselves and future generations, we concentrate on activities such as land-use planning, preserving natural beauty and wildlife, and establishing air pollution standards. Environmental quality is of great importance to society as a whole, and individuals respond to this concern by acting and purchasing accordingly.

Quality of environment is a collective value.

Public Services.   Our country is organized to be "of the people, by the people, and for the people." In our highly advanced system made up of people performing services for people, with money contributed (through taxes) by the people, high value is placed on providing services for all citizens — from police protection to public parks. Services, such as roads and highways, are provided for all citizens, regardless of how much citizens are able to contribute to society. Most citizens have come to expect public goods and services automatically — as a right rather than a privilege. What is often forgotten or ignored is that these goods and services are provided because of taxation of productive workers, and that no one can be excluded from receiving their benefits.

FACTORS OF PRODUCTION

◆◆◆◆◆◆◆◆

Factors of production are necessary for producing goods and services to meet consumer wants and needs. The quantity and quality of these factors determines a country's productive capacity. Effective use of factors of production strengthens a country's ability to meet the needs and wants of its own citizens and of others in the world. There are four factors of production: land, labor, capital, and ownership (entrepreneurship) risk.

A nation's productivity depends on the factors of production.

LAND

Land is the factor of production that represents resources that are fixed or nonrenewable. Land includes water, climate, minerals, quantity of soil, and quality of soil. Natural resources exist or do not exist in a given geographic area. **Rent** is the payoff or price paid for the use of the land. We can use up natural resources, but only limited circumstances allow replacement of what has been used. Reforestation is one example of replacing a resource that has been used. Once a resource such as oil is used up, however, there is no way to remake it. Consequently, alternative sources of energy are necessary. Land, a factor of production, is scarce and valuable because it exists in limited quantities and qualities and cannot be replaced.

Land is our most limited productive resource.

LABOR

Labor is the human factor of production. The labor force is the human resource available within a country to work and produce the necessary goods and services, and constitutes all persons ages 16 to 70 who are regularly employed for 35 hours or more a week (not including temporary or part-time employment). Persons under age 16 are not considered a part of the labor force because they are required to attend school until age 16.

The labor force directly affects a country's productivity. When the labor force changes in quantity or quality, productivity changes proportionately. For example, in the U.S., women are entering the labor force in large numbers. Most women work outside the home at some time during their lives. There are more than 3 million women business owners and sole

The quantity and quality of the labor force determines its productivity.

proprietors. In 1941, less than 30 percent of all American women worked outside the home. Today more than half of all American women work outside the home, and according to Bureau of Labor statistics, that number is increasing.

The quality of the work force is affected by the level of education attained. An increased standard of living is directly related to a higher educational level. Education, from the standpoint of labor productivity, is for the benefit of all, not just those currently receiving an education.

Another factor affecting the quality of the work force is the general health of the nation. Whether or not national health insurance is the solution, all persons need good medical care and services. The reason is clear: when people feel well, they do better work.

Motivation can make a great deal of difference in productivity, too. Factors that motivate workers include rate of pay, working conditions, performance incentives, and fair labor agreements. In a "work ethic" society such as ours, productive employment is considered a positive goal.

Payment for the labor force is in the form of wages. **Wages** are total compensation for employment and include gross pay, insurance, sick pay, fringe benefits, and all other types of direct and indirect compensation. Wage level acts as an indication to the employee of his or her worth and value to the employer in terms of quality and quantity of work performed. A wage increase is the greatest incentive for higher productivity.

CAPITAL

Capital is the factor of production that represents the durable, but depreciable, input in the production process. Capital represents human made, rather than natural, resources. Machines, tools, roads, factories, equipment, trucks, and buildings are capital. Capital is not money but tangible assets that are used to produce goods and services. The payoff or price paid for capital is called **interest**.

Money is a *measure* of the productivity of capital. Money is NOT capital. In order to produce goods and services, all factors of production are necessary. The United States has a great capacity for generating capital (machinery, factories, tools) and the knowledge to use them effectively.

OWNERSHIP RISK

Ownership risk is the factor of production that represents management, innovation, and risk-taking. *Entrepreneurs* are owners or persons who are

Illustration 22-2
Profit is the reward
entrepreneurs re-
ceive for taking the
risk of ownership.

Entrepreneurs take
the risk of ownership.

taking the risk of loss for owning the land, investing in capital equipment, and hiring labor. The return for ownership is **profit**. If a profit is made, the owner knows he or she has an effective combination of productive resources. The profit is the excess income received from the sale of a product or service over the cost of the land, labor, and capital used to make the product or provide the service. In other words, the sale price less the cost of production equals profit. Profit is the compensation to the owner for the risk that has been taken.

ECONOMIC GOALS

◆◆◆◆◆◆◆◆

The U.S. economy
has economic goals.

The people of any economic system choose a set of economic goals that are compatible with their personal and collective values, needs, and wants. The U.S. economy has directed itself toward a set of economic goals that include economic freedom, economic growth, economic stability and security, economic efficiency, and economic equity.

ECONOMIC FREEDOM

Economic freedom is the right of individuals to make their own economic decisions — where to live, where to work, how to spend their income — so long as they stay within the law. Economic freedom is guaranteed by the U.S. Constitution and is considered important by our society.

ECONOMIC GROWTH

Growth is needed for future opportunities.

Economic growth is the condition of a rising standard of living for the individual and a greater output of goods and services for the economy as a whole. Without growth, there is little opportunity for youth and others to freely enter the labor force. Growth provides incentive for workers, businesses, and government to enjoy increased satisfaction of individual and societal wants and needs.

ECONOMIC STABILITY AND SECURITY

Economic stability and security provide the people a high level of employment without high inflation, and at the same time allow those who are unable to provide for themselves (either temporarily or permanently) some means of survival and enjoyment of life. Overall stability and security provide the basis for optimism and quality of life within a country. Without it, there is fear of loss of employment, loss of earning ability, and loss of ability to have food, clothing, and shelter.

ECONOMIC EFFICIENCY

Scarce resources must be allocated wisely.

Economic efficiency is the result of the best possible use of an economy's scarce resources — avoidance of waste, conservation and wise allocation, alternate uses, and innovations that preserve the quality of life as technological advances allow more needs and wants to be met.

ECONOMIC EQUITY

Economic equity is the ingredient of fairness (as viewed by society) in the process of allocating resources to meet needs and wants of individuals, families, businesses, and society as a whole. As we will see in later chapters, because of economic equity — the perception of fairness — many economic forces will be controlled which otherwise would be allowed to be self-determinate (allowed to make any choices they wish) in our economy.

VOCABULARY

Directions: Can you find the definition for each of the following terms used in Chapter 22?

economics   capital
basic needs   interest
formal education   ownership risk
collective values   profit
innovations   economic freedom
factors of production   economic growth
land   economic stability and security
rent   economic efficiency
labor   economic equity
wages

1. The excess amount earned by the owner (entrepreneur) over the cost of production.
2. The payoff (price paid) for capital (a factor of production).
3. Knowledge gained through attending formal institutions of learning, such as colleges and universities.
4. The study of human efforts to solve the problem of making scarce resources meet the unlimited needs and wants of society.
5. Ingredients necessary for maintaining physical life.
6. Things that are important to society as a whole; all citizens share in their benefit and their cost.
7. New ideas, methods, or devices that bring about change.
8. A factor of production that is the human work force necessary to work and produce within a country.
9. The factor of production necessary to produce other goods and services, such as tools, factories, roads, and buildings.
10. The payoff (price) for land (factor of production).
11. The return or payoff to those who make up the labor force (factor of production).
12. The factor of production that represents management, innovation, and risk-taking.
13. The right of individuals to make their own economic decisions.
14. The economic goal of providing employment without high inflation so that individuals and families can provide for themselves.
15. Ingredients necessary to produce goods and services.
16. A factor of production that is provided by nature, such as water, climate, and soil.
17. The goal of having a rising standard of living for the individual and a greater output of goods and services for the economy.
18. The economic goal of fairness, as viewed by society, in allocating resources to meet needs and wants.
19. The goal of best possible utilization of scarce resources.

ITEMS FOR DISCUSSION

1. What are the basic needs for survival?
2. List five life-improving wants and needs.
3. How many of the life-improving needs/wants are met in your life?
4. How does level of income relate to amount of education attained?
5. Why are natural resources expensive and valuable?
6. List the factors of production.
7. Who takes the risk and makes the decisions about what and how much is to be produced?
8. List the five economic goals of the U.S. economy.

APPLICATIONS

1. Why is it important for everyone to have a good basic understanding of economics?
2. List the life-fulfilling and improving needs and wants that you have now and expect to have in the future. Prioritize them, placing a numeral 1 by the very important wants and a 5 by your least important wants. How do you expect that each of these needs will be met in your life (by self, parents, government, others)?
3. Explain what your achieved level of education has to do with the amount of and types of wants and needs you will have and will be able to meet.
4. As a citizen, what types of societal values do you consider important? List them and prioritize them, giving very important values a 1 and least important values a 5. How are these societal values provided?
5. What types of things are being done in your community and state to preserve natural resources, land use, and air quality?
6. What types of public goods and services do you expect to receive as a citizen? Are most of these taken for granted? How are these goods and services provided for all?
7. Most countries that are in deep poverty lack one major productive resource — capital. How can American business owners assist these countries? (Send them money? Food? Help them to be productive?)
8. Explain how the quality of a labor force can be improved or adversely affected.
9. Explain the importance of profits to the owner who is taking the risk.

10. Explain your understanding of each of these economic goals:

a. economic freedom   d. economic efficiency
b. economic growth   e. economic equity
c. economic stability and security

CASE PROBLEMS AND ACTIVITIES

1. Amy does not understand the need to study economics. Can you give her a definition of economics, and explain both personal and societal benefits of studying economic principles?

2. Innovations are highly valued in our society. Interview a person who lived through the 1960s and 1970s. Ask them what things they now have, enjoy, and consider "essential" that were not in existence before or during the 60s and 70s. In the alternative, do you know someone such as a grandparent, who lived through the 30s, 40s, or 50s and can identify many inventions of those years?

3. A farmer sells fresh corn in a vegetable stand at the side of the road. To sell what was planted, raised, and harvested, farm labor was hired during the summer growing months. In addition, farm equipment and tools, sprinklers, and fertilizers were purchased. Yearly, the farmer plants crops, and when there is a good crop and expenses are low, the farmer makes a good profit. But when expenses of production are too high, labor costs too much, or bad weather causes a poor or small crop, the farmer is likely to lose money. Identify the factors of production the farmer uses.

4. Describe a recent money-making project at your school or in your community. List the factors of production that went into the project, and list the payoff for each resource used. Who makes the decisions regarding whether or not to do the money-making projects? What is the basis (how is this decision reached) of going ahead with, or deciding not to have, a certain project?

5. An underdeveloped country is unable to meet its citizens' needs for food, clothing, and shelter. Yet this country has a vast untapped potential for economic prosperity because of its underground copper and uranium fields. How could the United States help this underdeveloped country to feed its citizens? Choose one of these options (or make up your own) and explain why you think it would be the best way to help the underdeveloped country.

a. send them food
b. give them money
c. help them build capital equipment and teach them how to use it
d. install mining operations, take out the minerals, and pay the country for it.

Chapter 23

THE MARKET SYSTEM

◆◆◆◆◆◆◆◆◆◆◆◆◆◆◆◆◆◆◆◆◆◆◆◆◆

OBJECTIVES

1. Discuss optimizing, economizing, and external factors that affect individual choices.
2. Compare and contrast societal decision making in traditional, command, and market economies.
3. List and define the characteristics of a market economy.
4. Describe factors that enhance, limit, and control choices in a market economy.

INDIVIDUAL ECONOMIC CHOICES

◆◆◆◆◆◆◆◆

We all make choices in our daily lives. Most of these choices are dependent on our ability to earn and the wants and needs we have as individuals and as families. Individuals make choices based on needs to optimize and economize. External factors affect choices of both individuals and society.

OPTIMIZING

The procedure of **optimizing** is getting the most from all available resources — spreading the resources to cover as many needs as possible. Optimizing does not attempt to limit or do away with needs, but tries to cover all needs as well as possible. A family that optimizes divides its income into categories of a budget and determines how the total income shall be best allocated to meet as many needs and wants as possible. If at the end of the year some money is left over in one area, it can be used to increase or offset another need or desired purchase. But all areas are initially provided for so that the family makes maximum use of its money.

Optimizing is spreading resources as far as possible.

ECONOMIZING

The procedure of **economizing** is saving and eliminating uses to make a product or resource last as long as possible. The family that economizes begins each month with a budget and spends as little as possible, cutting corners whenever possible. Living on a day-to-day basis, the family spends money only when necessary. Less expensive alternatives are continually being sought to eliminate any possible waste. Money is stretched and saved so that it will go as far as possible. Money not spent is set aside for future needs. Economizing is cutting back and saving whenever possible.

Economizing is saving and eliminating uses.

EXTERNAL FACTORS

Just as individuals make choices in their lives, groups of people and societies must make decisions for the benefit of all. Individual decisions must take into consideration any societal choices that may limit or affect the desirability of the decision. Some of these limitations and considerations are laws, customs, and expectations.

Laws.   **Laws** are rules of conduct accepted by people and enforced to protect people. Environmental protection laws have been passed in our country to protect the air, water, and quality of environment for all citizens, present and future. Factories must meet standards established for clean air. Automobiles are made with devices to limit the pollutant content of exhaust. As individual citizens, we must consider what is acceptable to society when making our choices.

Laws set standards for the benefit of all.

Customs.   Many customs are so much a part of our lives that we may not realize they are not written laws. For example, it is customary in our country to sit down in a restaurant, order a meal and eat it, then pay for it. In many other countries, you must pay for the meal before you can eat it. Customs affect many of our purchasing decisions and choices. Holidays are the customary times for families to gather for celebrations, large dinners, and reunions.

Illustration 23-1
Many families econ-
omize by compar-
ing prices and shop-
ping wisely.

Expectations.   We are affected by our own self-expectations, those that friends and loved ones in our lives have for us, and those that are valued by society. For instance, our society places a high value on education and expects that those capable of doing so will graduate from high school and pursue further educational opportunities. Parents and friends likewise expect that each of us will use our abilities to their fullest. As a result, we create expectations for ourselves that are the basis of our goals and values. Many expectations are unstated and subtle; others are very obvious and apparent in our daily lives.

We are affected by
others' expectations.

SOCIETAL ECONOMIC DECISIONS
◆◆◆◆◆◆◆◆

A society as a whole must answer the basic economic questions of production and distribution. Economic systems differ according to who makes the basic economic decisions of what will be produced, for whom, and at what price. There are three economic systems in the world, and we will define each system as if it were a pure model. In reality, all systems are not pure, but contain ingredients of more than one system. But for purposes of understanding how economic decisions are made, we will define traditional, command, and market economies in their pure forms.

Societal decisions
depend on the eco-
nomic system.

TRADITIONAL ECONOMY

In a **traditional economy**, the rules of custom and habit are decided by following long-established values and beliefs. The problems of choice, production, and distribution are solved almost exclusively through rules and priorities set by past generations. This kind of system has a clearly defined role for every individual in the society. The choices made in traditional societies are static with very few changes over long periods of time. An example of such a system is the caste system of India or a tribal society of Africa or the Middle East. Some elements of tradition exist in all types of societies.

COMMAND ECONOMY

A command system contains few individual freedoms.

In a **command economy**, the basic economic decisions are made through a central governmental authority, usually the dominant political party. Under such a system, the government role can be of an extreme totalitarian nature or a more democratic form. In a command economy, the central authority owns the productive resources and directs their allocation according to its own set of established priorities. The production of capital goods usually is given a higher priority than consumer goods and services. Examples of the command economy can be found in the Soviet Union, China, Yugoslavia, and most other communist countries. **Communism** is a political theory that does not recognize private property ownership. In communist societies, the government controls economic activity, including individual rights and spending, as well as the means of production. Citizens purchase whatever the government makes available.

MARKET ECONOMY

A market economy is based on capitalism, or private ownership of productive resources.

In a **market economy**, the basic needs and wants are fulfilled by allowing the marketplace to make the choices. The society is based on free enterprise, or **capitalism**, where most productive resources and decisions are made by private individuals and businesses. Or the economy can be based on a great deal of government, or **socialism**, where the government has a substantial influence on the productive decisions. Examples of socialistic countries are Canada and Sweden, where the government plays a significant role in decision making and allocation of resources. In socialist societies, many services are provided to all citizens. Through government, people have security. There is also private enterprise that cooperates with the government to provide goods and services. Generally, taxes are high to deliver extensive government services, such as health care, for everyone.

There are no pure economic systems — all are combinations.

It should be noted that there is no pure system — capitalism contains some elements of socialism and communism. Likewise, socialism contains

Illustration 23-2
In command econ-
omies such as
China's, economic
decisions are made
by the government.

some elements of free choice. Both communism and capitalism contain ingredients of tradition.

MARKET ECONOMY CHARACTERISTICS

♦♦♦♦♦♦♦♦

According to economists, the United States uses a market economy system, which is characterized by private property ownership, self-interest behavior, consumer sovereignty, competition, and limited government involvement. Our market economy is often called *capitalism*, *free enterprise*, and *democracy*. All of these terms are used interchangeably for a market economy but are not equally descriptive of the actual type of exchange that takes place in the marketplace.

PRIVATE PROPERTY OWNERSHIP

Ownership of private
property is a key
ingredient.

Individuals have the right to buy, sell, and own property, including land and natural resources, houses, tools, machinery, and equipment. We own and exchange private property, which is a means of production. Without ownership of private property, a market economy could not exist.

The concept of private property ownership is often called *capitalism*. In a free enterprise economic system, private individuals and groups — not governments — control the factors of production. While there is government participation, as seen in Chapter 28, the government does not play the major role in controlling what is produced and consumed. For the most part, consumers decide what will be produced by their dollar votes.

The market system based on supply and demand will determine price, provided the necessary ingredients are present — competition, informed consumers, and self-interest behavior.

In our market economy, each person is entitled to ownership and control of his or her productive capacity — including property owned, tools of production, investment capital, and ownership risks. The rewards (profits) are earned by those who make the best decisions and wisest choices in the allocation of scarce and valuable resources into production possibilities.

SELF-INTEREST BEHAVIOR

Each person owning his or her share of the resources will act with his or her own best interests in mind. This is an important element of the market economy. Each person will desire to make the most of the resources available to him or her for the purpose of making the largest possible profit. The **profit motive** (the desire to maximize income while minimizing expenditures) is quite evident throughout our country's history. The automobile would not have been produced and sold if the producers were not interested in making a profit; the clothing you wear and the food you eat are the result of the profit anticipated by the producers who made the decision to produce these goods.

Profit motive allows the best possible utilization of resources.

Not only businesses exhibit the self-interest motive. Workers and consumers must also function with their own best interests in mind to make the market economy most efficient. While producers are expecting to sell their products for the highest profit, consumers are also looking for the best possible product for the least amount of money. Workers are seeking the highest paying jobs with the best working conditions and benefits. Everybody within the market economy must pursue his or her own best interests: this is what makes the system operate most effectively. If workers did not care how much they got paid, if pay level were controlled by government, if producers did not care what kind of product they produced because there was no profit incentive, then resources would cease to be used wisely with the best production decisions.

Some people contend that self-interest behavior is selfish and wasteful. But there is no better motive for maximum efficiency and productivity than self-interest. Self-interest is the best possible incentive to conserve and make wise decisions — when you do your best and make the best decisions, then the profit is higher.

Wise decisions result in higher profits.

CONSUMER SOVEREIGNTY

Consumer sovereignty is the power or ability of consumers to affect what is being produced and consumed. The consumer will ultimately decide what will be produced and how resources will be allocated. If, for example, consumers demand a certain product and reject another (do not buy it), the profit motive will dictate that the product that will continue to be produced is the one the consumer prefers to buy.

Consumers have power in a market economy because they freely choose what they will buy. Although their decisions are based on external controls, such as laws, customs, and expectations, these factors are taken into consideration before products are made. As we shall see later, producers discover first and make decisions as to what is likely to be a good selling product long before it is actually produced.

As a consumer, you vote with your dollars on whether a product should or should not be made. Every time you purchase a product, you are casting a vote for that product at that purchase price. Each dollar you spend represents your choices for production.

> As a consumer, you vote for products with dollars you spend.

COMPETITION

The fourth vital factor essential to the proper functioning of a market economy is competition. Competition is vital because it ensures that producers will produce at the cheapest price possible what is demanded by consumers. If one producer will not supply the product demanded at an attractive price, other producers (competitors) will, and the competitors' products will be purchased. Whenever a new product or industry comes into being and big profits are generated, new producers freely enter the market and begin producing the product. This competition forces prices down because all producers are trying to get the consumer's support for their products.

> Competition is the regulating factor in a market economy.

Competition also plays an important part in the allocation of scarce resources. Producers will seek to use available resources efficiently in order to keep prices down. This way they can sell the most and make the most profit from their limited quantity of resources.

LIMITED GOVERNMENT INVOLVEMENT

In a market economy, government involvement and interference in the production and consumption of goods and services must be very limited. Our country is not a pure market economy, where there is no government involvement. The term *mixed economy* is often used interchangeably with the term *market economy* because we do have an active government that produces, consumes, and also controls production and consumption within the society to some extent. In a market economy, some controls must exist to prevent outrageous or selfish activities from damaging a majority of the citizens of the country.

There is government involvement in a market economy.

When the activities of private ownership, self-interest behavior, consumer sovereignty, and competition mix with a modest amount of government participation, a circular flow of economic activity results in consistent and steady productivity. Figure 23-1 shows a circular flow diagram to illustrate how all the elements of the market economy interact to make it efficient.

Figure 23-1
Circular Flow Diagram

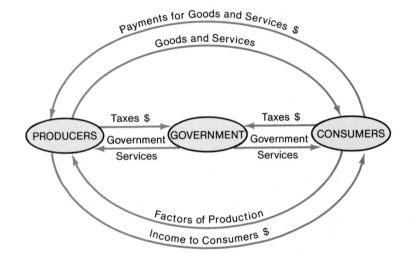

Consumers are purchasers of goods and services and suppliers of factors of production. Producers are purchasers of factors of production and suppliers of goods and services. The monetary flow that accompanies the flow of goods and services to consumers is called *payments for goods and services*. The monetary flow from producers to consumers is called *income*. Government taxes consumers and producers and provides services for both.

The circular flow describes interactions of consumers, producers, and government in a market economy.

In a market economy, competition transforms self-interest behavior into socially desirable ends. Competition limits the self-interest of businesses to ensure that they do not have the power to promote their own interests at the expense of public interests. Consumers direct the market system; self-interest behavior motivates the people to act; and competition regulates their behavior.

Competition benefits everyone.

Competition benefits everyone in a market economy because (a) it encourages producers to increase production in those areas where consumer demand is strong, (b) it keeps prices low as producers compete for consumers' dollar votes, and (c) it forces producers to improve the quality of their products, thereby achieving the most efficient allocation of economic resources.

FACTORS AFFECTING CHOICES IN A MARKET ECONOMY
◆◆◆◆◆◆◆◆

A market economy must consider many factors that will help in effective economic decision making. Factors to consider include trade-offs and opportunity costs, specialization and interdependence, and external controls.

TRADE-OFFS AND OPPORTUNITY COSTS

Whenever a decision or choice is made, something is gained and something is lost (not chosen). An **opportunity cost** is something that you must give up to get something else you also want. Usually, it is not a direct monetary cost. For example, you may be part of a group that will decide what to do with 100 acres of land. The land could be used for parks and recreation, or it could be used for timber harvesting. By choosing one option, you are giving up part or all of the other option, forgoing one opportunity for another.

A **trade-off** is what you get when you choose one option over another. When scarce resources are used for a particular purpose, the opportunity cost may be less than another choice. What you do receive, the trade-off, must be weighed carefully and be more valued than the choice given up.

Economists use a graph commonly called a *production possibilities curve* to illustrate the choices and combinations possible when decisions are made about scarce resources. A **production possibilities curve** plots combinations of two goods that can be produced with a given level of resources and technology. Figure 23-2 is a production possibilities curve that shows the possible combinations of lumber production and recreational park area on a 100-acre tract of land.

Within a production possibilities curve, we can see the concepts of scarcity (limited resources), choice, opportunity cost, and trade-off. In Figure 23-2, when all 100 acres are used for parks, there is no land left to use for timber production. The 100 acres represents a scarce and limited resource. A choice is required to make wise use of limited resources. When all 100 acres are used for timber production, a total of one million board-feet of timber can be produced. The decision, then, is to choose what number of acres will be used for timber and what number of acres will be used for parks.

When a trade-off is chosen, an opportunity cost is incurred.

Possibilities for production are found in the production possibilities curve.

Figure 23-2
Production Possibi-
lities Curve

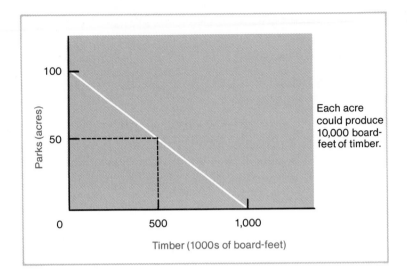

We can see from the graph that as the amount of parkland increases, the amount of timber production decreases. The opportunity cost is the value of the parkland or timberland forfeited, while the trade-off is the timberland or parkland gained.

In the example, 50 acres could be used for parks, and 50 acres could be used for timber production. Fifty acres would produce 500,000 board-feet of timber. Timber is in limited supply; yet, natural wilderness areas and parks are also scarce and valuable. A choice must be made because there is not enough land to allow unlimited timber production and also provide for all the parks and wilderness areas we want. Individuals and societies must make choices that trade off one potential benefit in return for another.

To produce all of one product eliminates production of others.

SPECIALIZATION AND INTERDEPENDENCE

Taking advantage of greater efficiency will release some productive resources for other uses. Society is able to increase its output of goods and services while using fewer resources because of **specialization** — concentrating efforts in one area to gain maximum efficiency. For example, workers are more productive as a result of performing repetitive tasks or using special abilities. Mechanization is the use of capital goods to increase productivity of labor. Specialization allows each factor of production to yield its greatest possible amount of society's wants. **Comparative advantage** is the principle that the greatest gain in total output will occur if each society specializes in producing those goods and services that can be produced with

Comparative advantage allows the greatest total gain in output.

the greatest efficiency and buys goods (imports) that could be produced only at great cost.

Increased specialization, mechanization, and comparative advantage lead to **interdependence** — a condition wherein each person or unit depends on others to do what each can do best. The individual and family depend on the whole economic system for the goods and services they consume. As a result, economic lives become complex and comfortable. No person, household, community, city, or state can claim self-sufficiency; rather, each is in part specialized in activities where they have greatest advantage. Through trade and interdependence, all economic units can have their economic wants satisfied.

EXTERNAL CONTROLS

To make economic decisions, the producers in a market economy must consider the following controls:

Entrepreneurs must also consider external controls in decision-making.

1. Laws that may prohibit and dictate production or nonproduction, quantities, qualities, or other decision factors
2. Customs that judge some things as necessary and others as luxuries
3. Government restrictions, controls, guidelines, or standards
4. Amount, quality, and cost of available resources
5. Company goals and plans as well as profitability requirements to generate the highest possible profit
6. Economic concerns and stability of the nation, including interest rates and loan costs, times of peace or conflict, and issues of importance to all citizens

Failure to consider one of these important items may cost a company in the salability of a product (profits). Therefore, all of these considerations must be weighed carefully by the producer before a decision is made.

TIME AND SPACE

Time is a significant consideration when making production decisions.

Time refers to the crucial timing of production so that a product or service is available for consumption when it is desired by the consumer. Time has three significant characteristics that affect production decisions:

1. Once time has been invested, it cannot be recaptured. Time is money; once it has been used (spent), it is gone.

2. Time cannot be stored.
3. Time is limited in quantity and therefore is very valuable in terms of production.

Time is an important part of the production decision. Once a decision has been made and time is invested, then the decision has incurred a cost that cannot be recovered. That is, it is too late to make a change. Perhaps the most important decisions made in a society relate to time because it is the one element that is unchanging in relation to other conditions.

Space is the physical attribute of production that is concerned with dimensional, geographic, and measurable commitments of productive resources. Space is also very limited in quantity and must be considered in the following arenas:

> Space is physical measurement of factors that must be considered in production.

1. Amount of living or producing space that is available to the citizen or to the business
2. Population of the area in which production is being considered (Is it large enough to pay the costs of production? Will enough be purchased to make production worthwhile?)
3. Distances to be traveled in the process of production or distribution

The producer in a market economy must decide issues that involve the wise use of available space in relation to cost, projected profit, storage, and many other areas of concern. Space, like time, is expensive in terms of production, and is a significant component in the market system.

VOCABULARY

Directions: Can you find the definition for each of the following terms used in Chapter 23?

optimizing	consumer sovereignty
economizing	opportunity cost
laws	trade-off
traditional economy	production possibilities curve
command economy	specialization
communism	comparative advantage
market economy	interdependence
capitalism	time
socialism	space
profit motive	

1. An economy where rules of custom and habit decide problems of choice, production, and distribution.

2. Something that you must give up to get something else that you also want.

3. An economy in which basic economic decisions are made by a central government authority.

4. The power and ability of consumers to affect what will be produced and consumed in a market economy.

5. A political theory that does not recognize private property ownership rights.

6. Rules of conduct established and enforced for the benefit of all citizens.

7. Getting the most from all available resources; spreading the resources to all possible areas of use.

8. Saving and eliminating uses to make a product or resource last as long as possible.

9. To choose one option over another.

10. A system characterized by private ownership, self-interest behavior, consumer power, competition, and limited government involvement.

11. A graph to illustrate choices and combinations when decisions are being made about the use of scarce resources.

12. An economy where productive decisions are made by private individuals and businesses.

13. An economy that is based on private ownership of resources and a great deal of government influence on production decisions.

14. The desire to maximize income while minimizing expenditures.

15. Concentrating efforts in one area to gain maximum efficiency (not trying to produce everything you consume).

16. The principle that the greatest gain in total output will occur if each society produces those goods and services that can be produced most efficiently, and buys the rest.

17. A condition wherein each person or unit depends on others.

18. The ingredient of production wherein a service is made available for consumption when it is desired.

19. The physical attribute of production that is concerned with dimensional, geographic, and measurable use of productive resources.

ITEMS FOR DISCUSSION

1. What is optimizing? Economizing?
2. What are external factors that affect consumer buying choices?
3. What is the difference between a law and a custom?
4. How are economic decisions made in a traditional economy? A command economy? A market economy?

5. How is socialism different from capitalism?
6. What are the five major characteristics of a market economy?
7. What is self-interest behavior?
8. How do consumers have the ultimate power of deciding what will or will not be produced?
9. What is the role of competition in a market economy?
10. How much is government involved in a market economy?
11. What is an opportunity cost? A trade-off? Explain how all choices involve both of these.
12. What is shown by the production possibilities curve?
13. What are some external controls that affect what is produced in a market economy?
14. What are three characteristics of time?
15. What are three factors to consider in the production consideration of space?

APPLICATIONS

1. What are your self-expectations in terms of education and career for the next five years? What are your parents' expectations for you? How do you feel your decisions for those five years are affected by others around you, including subtle societal expectations?
2. What is meant by private property ownership in an free enterprise system?
3. Explain how the self-interest behavior of wanting a profit results in higher quality goods and services at the lowest possible prices.
4. Why is it important for consumers to cast their dollar votes wisely?
5. What is the natural result in a market economy when someone finds a unique way to produce a product that is in high demand by consumers for a high profit?
6. Explain how the circular flow diagram operates.
7. Explain the concepts of specialization, comparative advantage, and interdependence and how they relate to maximum utilization of resources.
8. Explain why time is such an important consideration in production decisions. Can you cite an example of how timing has affected a decision you have made?

CASE PROBLEMS AND ACTIVITIES

1. As student body treasurer, you have been given the responsibility of allocating student body funds this school year. There are sixteen

groups and clubs that are requesting funds. You have only $1,000. The junior class has asked for more money than other groups because of special needs, such as financing the prom. Explain how the $1,000 could best meet needs — by economizing or by optimizing.

2. You and a friend have just invented a new fuel additive that will increase gasoline or diesel efficiency and will allow an automobile to go from zero to eighty miles an hour in eight seconds. With your product, the average car can get fifty miles a gallon. What types of laws, customs, and expectations can you expect to run into when pursuing the production of this new invention?

3. Abdul is a very bright student, and had good grades in high school. He has wanted to be a teacher for a long time; his parents have encouraged him to go to college. Abdul owns a car and has a part-time job at the cannery. His employer has offered him a promotion to shift manager and says Abdul could be plant manager in five to ten years. After carefully considering the choices, Abdul has decided to quit his job and go to college. What was his opportunity cost? What were his trade-offs?

4. You have worked all summer to save $500 for clothes for school. School starts in four weeks. Your brother comes to you and has an emergency. He needs parts for his motorcycle that cost $300. He does not know when he can pay you back. Will you loan him the money? Identify your opportunity costs and your trade-offs.

5. Mrs. Schwartz owns a bakery. Mr. Dimitri owns a bakery three blocks away. Mrs. Schwartz just discovered a unique way to make bagels that are very tasty and twice as big as Mr. Dimitri's bagels. She sells them for 50 cents each, including cream cheese. Her business is booming. Then Mr. Dimitri discovers a similar method and starts selling his giant bagels for 45 cents. Mrs. Schwartz's business drops. Mrs. Schwartz lowers her price to 39 cents and business booms again. Explain the concept of competition as illustrated in this case. How did self-interest behavior bring prices down?

Chapter 24

THE MARKET IN OPERATION

◆◆◆◆◆◆◆◆◆◆◆◆◆◆◆◆◆◆◆◆◆◆◆◆◆

OBJECTIVES

1. Define market demand and explain how elasticity affects demand in a market economy.
2. Define market supply and construct schedules and curves to illustrate the microeconomic principles of supply and demand.
3. Describe equilibrium price, the functions of price, and the advantages and disadvantages of a price system.
4. Explain the role of government in a market economy.

The price system of a market economy is based on the interaction of demand and supply. The shape of the total demand for a good or service will incorporate individuals' demands, households' demands, and companies' demands as consumers and producers — everyone who is part of the market individually, and all consumers collectively — come together in any marketplace to buy or sell goods or services. To arrive at the total supply of any product that will be available, all the individual quantities supplied at each price are added together. The higher the price, the more that will be produced.

The marketplace consists of all buyers and sellers.

MARKET DEMAND

◆◆◆◆◆◆◆◆

Demand on an individual level is what a person is willing and able to purchase at various prices during a given period of time. Demand is not a fixed number, but rather a schedule. As shown in Figure 24-1, demand goes up as price goes down. For example, at 25 cents each, you may be willing to buy 15 candy bars a week. But at $1 each, you aren't willing to buy any.

Figure 24-1
Demand Schedule
for Candy Bars

Price	Quantity Demanded
$1.00	0
.75	3
.55	7
.40	10
.25	15

Factors that affect demand include income, individual tastes, cost of credit, and the general economic climate. The **demand schedule** for a good or service is the quantities demanded at various prices. Suppose that a toy manufacturer is considering making and selling kites to a certain geographic area. Based on market research, its demand schedule is shown in Figure 24-2.

Figure 24-2
Demand Schedule
for Kites

Price	Quantity Demanded
$4	100
3	200
2	300
1	400

At a price of $4 each, 100 kites would be demanded; but at a price of $1 each, consumers would want to buy 400 kites. A demand schedule is shown graphically in a demand curve. A **demand curve** illustrates the relationship between price and quantity demanded. A demand curve slopes downward to the right because at the higher price, fewer units are sold. Figure 24-3 shows the demand curve for kites.

Figure 24-3
Demand Curve for
Kites

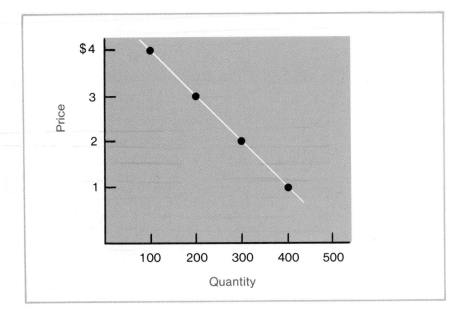

The **law of demand** states that consumers will buy more at lower prices
than at higher prices, if everything else is constant. That is, quantity
demanded of a good or service has an inverse relationship to its price.
    A major consideration must be the *elasticity of demand*. **Elasticity** is the
measure of responsiveness of quantity demanded to changes in price.
Elasticity of demand is the way in which a change in price affects the
quantity demanded. There are three types of elasticity: a product can be
elastic, unitary elastic, or inelastic.

**There are three types
of elasticity.**

ELASTIC *= equal to/greater % of price decrease*

Demand for a product is **elastic** when a decrease in price results in a greater
increase in demand. For example, if you drop the price of a candy bar by 10
percent, the demand for candy bars will increase by more than 10 percent.
Products that tend to be highly elastic are consumer goods such as food and
clothing.

UNITARY ELASTIC *= no gain*

Demand for a product is called **unitary elastic** when a decrease in price
results in an increase in demand that only offsets the price reduction; in
other words, there is no gain. For example, if price is dropped 10 percent,

Illustration 24-1 Demand for items such as food and clothing tend to be highly elastic.

there is a 10 percent increase in sales such that profits are not increased. (If you can sell 100 candy bars at 50 cents each, you earn $50. By reducing the price to 45 cents each, you now sell 110, or $49.50. The result is no gain.)

INELASTIC =no response

When there is no response in quantity demanded to changes in price, demand is **inelastic**. When demand for a product is inelastic, price has little effect on quantity demanded. Demand for surgery is considered inelastic — even if the cost of a gallbladder operation is low, you will not rush out and have one. However, if you need gallbladder surgery, you will probably have it done, regardless of cost.

Good substitutes make products more elastic.

The most important consideration separating elastic from inelastic demand is the availability of good substitutes. If an acceptable substitute is available for a good or service, then consumers will turn to the substitute when the price goes up. For example, if candy bars cost too much, consumers may choose other snack foods instead.

MARKET SUPPLY

◆◆◆◆◆◆◆◆

Supply is not a fixed number but a schedule of prices and quantities.

Supply is the quantity of a product or service that a producer is willing and able to offer for sale at a given price and time, or at a particular place. A producer is willing to produce quantities according to prices that will be received. Supply is not a fixed number, but rather a schedule. For example, let's assume that we are a small toy manufacturer, and we make and sell kites. Our **supply schedule** is a list of quantities we will provide at certain prices, as shown in Figure 24-4.

Figure 24-4
Supply   Schedule
for Kites

Price	Quantity Supplied
$4	400
3	300
2	200
1	100

At $4 we are willing to supply all the kites that are demanded. But at a price of $1, we will make something else because we cannot cover our costs of production. Producers must consider more than just what people want — there are four factors to consider: price of the product, price of the factors of production, level of technology, and expectations.

Producers must consider more than just what people want.

PRICE OF THE PRODUCT

The lower the price, the smaller the quantity of a product supplied. At higher prices, producers are willing to produce more because profits are higher.

PRICE OF THE FACTORS OF PRODUCTION

As production costs rise, the total price of the final product also rises. As price rises, demand decreases. Therefore, producers want to keep the price as low as possible while still making a reasonable profit. As the cost of the factors of production increases, the incentive to make products decreases because the profit decreases.

LEVEL OF TECHNOLOGY

Because new and creative ideas are important, producers like to introduce new and stimulating products into the marketplace. New technology, inventions, and improvements on old ways of doing things are in great demand. Because it is slower to change than demand, supply is very sensitive to the needs of society. The higher the level of technology, the quicker the supply can be altered to meet the new demands of consumers. Improved technology brings better products at lower prices.

New technology and improvements are in high demand.

EXPECTATIONS

Our society expects to have variety of choice in purchases.

We as a society are spoiled. We expect to have a multitude of products in a variety of colors, sizes, and shapes. We expect the marketplace to satisfy our wants and needs instantly. That is, when something new is found, we want to have it and benefit from it immediately. We invest millions of dollars in research each year; we expect results.

There are hundreds of different models of cars and trucks sold in the U.S. each year. If you want a subcompact, you can choose from over 120 different types. You can shop for light bulbs at a store that sells thousands of types of light bulbs. There are several hundred brands of cigarettes from which to choose.

The supply curve slopes upward to the right.

A **supply curve** illustrates the quantity that will be supplied at various prices. The supply curve slopes upward to the right because as the price increases, the supply increases. Figure 24-5 shows the supply curve for kites from the supply schedule on page 426.

The **law of supply** states that the higher the price, the greater the quantity that will be produced or supplied, if everything else is constant. The quantity supplied of a good has a positive relationship to price.

Figure 24-5
Supply Curve for
Kites

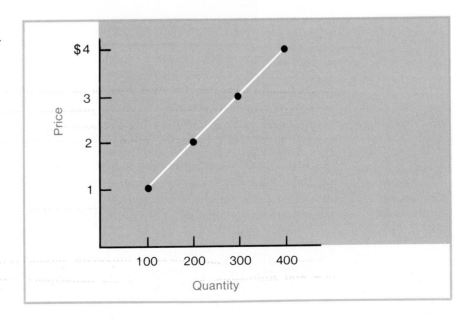

EQUILIBRIUM PRICE

◆◆◆◆◆◆◆◆

Product prices are determined by the interaction of demand and supply in the marketplace. The price of a product set by the competitive interaction of demand and supply is the **equilibrium price**. It is the point at which the demand curve intersects the supply curve. Figure 24-6 shows the intersection of demand and supply curves for kites. The equilibrium price for the kite is $2.50. At that price, the producer could sell about 250. If the price is higher, fewer kites will be sold. If the price is lower, more kites could be sold.

Figure 24-6
Equilibrium   Price
for Kites

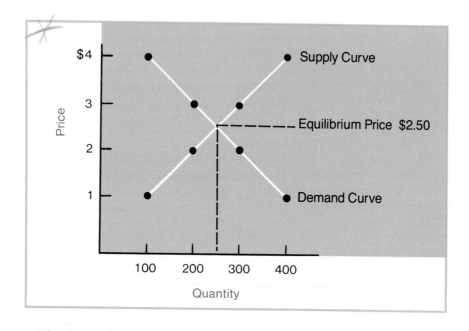

The demand curve changes quickly. One day consumers may want to have a certain product. The next day a government study may reveal a potential health hazard posed by that product, and the product will be unsalable. The supply curve, however, is slow to change. When consumers indicate a desire to buy goods and services, those products may not be instantly produced. Before producers can begin production of a good or service, they must do considerable work and research. A **market study**, which researches the profit potential of a new product or service, is done to determine how much genuine demand there is for a new product. Costs of production are calculated; a potential profit is determined. Often a product

While demand
changes rapidly,
supply is slower
to change.

is made in a limited quantity and _test marketed_. This means that the product is sold for consumer use only in a limited geographic area. If the product does well in the test market, it will be produced for sale to a larger population.

Because there is a great deal of work and expense involved in preparing to produce a product, the supply curve is slow to change. Costs of production can be extensive. Therefore, the producer must carefully calculate the price to determine if a reasonable profit can be made. If the price is too high, consumers will not buy the product. Demand and supply curves are used in market research to determine the quantity of a product that will sell at a given price. When the equilibrium price is determined, the producer must decide if the profit margin is large enough to justify the expense of production. Costs of production that go into a good or service include land, labor, capital, advertising, overhead, and taxes. The price of a good or service will include the costs of production, transportation, distribution, advertising, and profit.

Demand and supply are tools of the marketplace to determine what should and should not be produced.

FUNCTIONS OF PRICE

Price performs three important functions in the marketplace: resource allocation, product rationing, and income distribution. **Resource allocation** determines which resources are given higher price tags. Those resources with higher values (higher profit potential) will be pulled to higher priced uses. For example, land can be used to grow corn or wheat. If the farmer (entrepreneur) can make more profit growing corn, the land will be used to grow corn rather than wheat.

Profit potential determines what will be produced.

Product rationing determines who will and will not purchase products. Products are rationed by price because consumers who are willing and able to pay the price of a certain good or service will purchase that product. Those consumers who are unable or unwilling to pay the price of a good or service will not be users of that good or service.

Income distribution determines the value of a product and the value or price of the factors of production necessary to produce that product. These prices of the factors determine the income to the household units who own the resources. Income will be discussed in a later chapter.

ADVANTAGES OF THE PRICE SYSTEM

The price system that is the basis for a free enterprise economy has the following advantages:

1. *The consumer is the primary director of the economy.* The consumer is the decision maker, not as an individual, but as a group. Society is a group that collectively signals its wants and needs and guides and controls the productive efforts through the market mechanism.

2. *The self-interest motive keeps all factors in balance.* Consumers seek satisfaction in the purchase of goods and services. Producers seek to produce those with the highest return on investment (profit). Because both groups are working for their own best interests, they keep each other in balance and continually weigh decisions of need and want, desirability, and profitability.

3. *The market system is free to operate with little government interference, assistance, or controls.* Through the free market system, those who do the best job of satisfying consumers are rewarded with large profits. Those who produce inferior products suffer large losses. The government allows businesses to freely enter and leave the marketplace — to start business and go out of business at the appropriate times. Those who do the best planning make the largest profits. Those who fail to meet the needs and demands of the marketplace go out of business, to be replaced by others who more fully meet needs and wants.

DISADVANTAGES OF THE PRICE SYSTEM

Because the price system is based on freedom of choice and self-interest behavior, it also has some disadvantages:

1. *Producers do not necessarily produce what is most needed in our society.* They may decide to allocate scarce resources to the production of something that brings them more profit but that is of less functional value to society. When profit is the motive, producers will pursue their own best interests first.

2. *People do not always make the best decisions for their own good.* People are not always rational; they may perceive their own needs differently from the way in which government or business might see them. People are not always predictable. A producer may foresee a demand for a particular product, but consumers may, for one reason or another, reject the product.

3. *Mistakes can be costly.* The production of goods and services requires the consumption of resources and the production of by-products and waste products. These may be environmentally unsafe or unhealthy. As a whole, society pays for the mistakes of

Illustration 24-2
Society pays for industry mistakes that cause unhealthy environmental conditions.

industry and the inefficiencies that result in contamination of air and water and reduced quality of life. Many years are often required to make appropriate changes in industrial equipment to make waste products satisfactory to the environment. Likewise, errors and miscalculations in products themselves may result in hazards for consumers.

ROLE OF GOVERNMENT

Our discussion would be incomplete without an explanation of the role of government in a market economy. In a pure market economy, consumers are in total control. In a mixed market economy, decisions of what, how, how much, and for whom are not left entirely to the market; there is some government intervention.

Government has many roles in a market economy.

Government has several important roles in a market economy, all of which vitally affect the decisions that are made. Government controls production of some goods and services, such as our national defense, system of justice, and highway systems. In this light, we can say that government is a producer. Government hires many employees to carry out the functions and directives of the people. To do this, government purchases goods and services and is therefore a consumer.

The government produces public goods and services that have three unique characteristics that make them unlikely prospects for production by private business:

1. All persons receive the benefits, either directly or indirectly, from government services.

2. No one can be excluded from receiving the benefits, either directly or indirectly, from government services.

3. There is no way to adequately place a price tag on the value, and therefore the price, of government services. Nor is there any way to determine who will be charged for the cost of producing public goods and services. For example, weather warning systems, clean air standards, public campgrounds, fire and police protection, and streets and highways are all maintained by government. Everyone receives benefits and everyone is entitled to use the services. Everyone also shares in paying for the services through taxation.

The government also regulates and controls certain aspects of the marketplace, ranging from labeling requirements of the FDA to minimum wage laws. All of these regulations and controls are made law by Congress in the best interest of a majority of the citizens and are necessary regulations and controls within the marketplace.

Government's most significant activity is that of taxation and income redistribution. The government taxes businesses and individuals based on income. It redistributes collected funds to others through social security, welfare, and unemployment compensation payments. These government activities affect what and how much will be produced, how it will be produced, and how it will be distributed among the citizens of the country. Left alone, the marketplace most likely would not care for the nonproductive members of society; consequently, government takes over the role of caretaker. Government involvement is apparent in subsidies and legislative priorities.

SUBSIDIES

The government contributes money to, or subsidizes, programs or agencies that deal with selected problems. **Subsidies** are partial and temporary payments to help relieve financial burdens. They are based on need and are in the best interests of society as a whole. Veteran's programs, business assistance plans, school lunches, and natural disaster loans are all examples of government subsidies or subsidized programs. Subsidies are also made directly to individuals and businesses from time to time when a clear and specific need is demonstrated.

LEGISLATIVE PRIORITIES

The final distribution of revenue is by decision of the U.S. Congress, which meets annually to determine the distribution priorities. Congress creates programs according to the needs apparent in our country and others. It designs a federal budget and spending program to meet the country's needs, as designated by the president and committees in the House and Senate. Programs such as JTPA (Job Training Partnership Act), WIN (Work Incentive Program), and school lunch program assistance are examples of federally subsidized programs legislated by Congress.

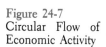

Congress determines many priorities that must be met to care for all citizens.

GOVERNMENT AND THE CIRCULAR FLOW

Government is the center of the circular flow of economic activity, as shown in Figure 24-7. This figure illustrates how government serves the needs of households and businesses by linking together spending and resources. The **product market** is the composite (total) of all the individual markets in which buyers and sellers interact to exchange goods and services. Anytime a buyer and seller get together to buy and sell, a market exists. All these markets put together are called the *product market*; it includes business transactions, household purchases, and government activities.

The product market consists of the buying and selling of goods in the marketplace.

The **resource market** is the composite of all productive resources in which economic resources are purchased and used. It includes all labor hired, all

Figure 24-7
Circular Flow of
Economic Activity

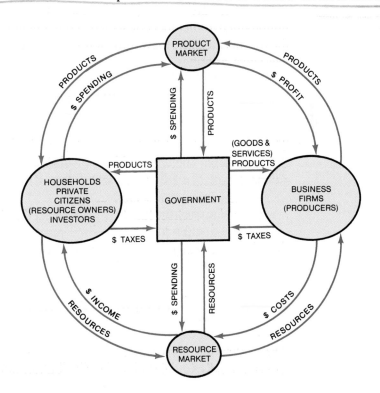

natural resources consumed or used in production, all investment in capital equipment, and all innovations for producing new and existing goods and services.

The circular flow of economic activity illustrates the interdependence of the ingredients of a market economy. Government taxes income of businesses and individuals. It purchases goods and services from businesses and individuals (labor). Government produces and consumes products; it buys and sells resources through its controls. Consumers, represented by households, private individuals, and investors, participate actively by purchasing and selling goods and services in the product market; resources are consumed and sold through the resource market. In other words, individuals own the resources and are able to sell them to others for consumption. Businesses likewise purchase and sell resources and make and sell products using the resources.

Government is a producer and a consumer.

VOCABULARY

Directions: Can you find the definition for each of the following terms used in Chapter 24?

demand	supply curve
demand schedule	law of supply
demand curve	equilibrium price
law of demand	market study
elasticity	resource allocation
elastic	product rationing
unitary elastic	income distribution
inelastic	subsidies
supply	product market
supply schedule	resource market

1. Partial and temporary payments to help relieve financial burdens.
2. Type of elasticity where a decrease in price is exactly offset by an increase in demand.
3. Type of elasticity where there is no response in quantity demanded to changes in price.
4. The willingness and ability of consumers to buy goods and services at various prices.
5. Consumers buy more at lower prices than at higher prices, if everything else is the same (the lower the price, the higher the demand).
6. A graphic representation of the relationship between price and quantity demanded.
7. A list of quantities of a good or service demanded at various prices.

8. A measure of the responsiveness of quantity demanded to changes in price.
9. Demand where a decrease in price results in a greater increase in demand.
10. The quantity of a product or service that a producer is willing and able to offer for sale at a given price and at a given time and place.
11. The price set by the competitive interaction of demand and supply.
12. A list of quantities that will be provided (produced for sale) at certain prices.
13. The composite of all individual markets where buyers and sellers interact.
14. The composite of all productive resources in which resources are purchased and used to make goods and services.
15. A graphic illustration of the quantities that will be supplied at various prices.
16. The higher the price, the greater the quantity that will be produced for sale, everything else being constant.
17. A study of the potential profit that can be made by producing and selling a product or service.
18. The function of price that determines which resources are given higher price tags.
19. The function of price that determines who will and who will not purchase products.
20. The function of price that determines the value of a product and of the factors of production.

ITEMS FOR DISCUSSION

1. What is the relationship between demand for a product and its price?
2. List some factors that affect demand.
3. Why does a demand curve slope downward and to the right?
4. What is elasticity of demand? Why is it important?
5. What is the relationship between supply for a product and its price?
6. What factors are considered in the decision of whether or not to produce a good or service?
7. Why does the supply curve slope upward and to the right?
8. What is a market study? Why is it important?
9. What are the functions of price in the marketplace?
10. List three advantages of the price system. List three disadvantages.
11. What are three roles of government in a market economy?
12. List three characteristics of government produced goods and services.

13. How does government fit into the circular flow of economic activity?
14. How is the product market different from the resource market?

APPLICATIONS

1. Demand and supply for a product are shown in the following demand and supply schedules. Construct a demand curve, a supply curve, and show the equilibrium price and quantity.

Demand Schedule		Supply Schedule	
Quantity	Price	Quantity	Price
3	$1.00	25	$1.00
5	.75	20	.75
9	.60	15	.60
15	.45	8	.50
20	.30	3	.45

2. Which of these products would likely be (a) elastic, (b) unitary elastic, (c) inelastic? Explain why.

coffee   clothing
school supplies   tonsillectomy
microwave ovens   jewelry
laundry detergent   snack foods
dental exam   tetanus shot
milk   taxi fare
gasoline   soft drinks

3. What new products have you tried in the last year or two? Did any of these products prove to be unsuccessful and have disappeared from the marketplace?
4. Explain why demand changes more rapidly than supply.
5. Can you think of products or services that you would like to see produced and made available to consumers which are not being produced today? What do you suppose is the reason these products are not being produced?
6. What public goods and services do you and your family use daily?
7. What is meant by "the government redistributes funds"?
8. How is government a producer? a consumer?

CASE PROBLEMS AND ACTIVITIES

1. A local merchant sees that the market for 26-inch, 10-speed bicycles is this: at $150 the merchant is able to sell 10 bicycles a week; at $125

the merchant can sell 20 bicycles a week. The lower the price, the more bicycles the merchant will sell.

a. From the information given below, construct a demand curve:

If price is:	Consumers would buy:
$150	10/week
125	20/week
100	30/week
90	40/week
80	50/week

b. Construct a supply curve on the same chart as the demand curve. The bicycle merchant can produce and offer for sale the following:

If price is:	Producer willing to sell:
$150	50/week
125	40/week
100	30/week
90	20/week
80	10/week

What is the approximate equilibrium price? At this price, how many bicycles will be sold?

2. A market survey shows that high school students are interested in buying calculators for use in school and personal work. The results of the study are as follows:

At a price of:	Students would buy:
$ 5.00	950/month
7.50	750/month
10.00	500/month
15.00	250/month
20.00	0/month

After computing costs of production and a reasonable profit margin, producers of calculators are willing to produce the calculators as follows:

At a price of:	Producers willing to sell:
$25.00	1,000/month
20.00	800/month
15.00	600/month
10.00	450/month
5.00	100/month

a. Draw a demand curve and a supply curve on the same graph. What is the approximate equilibrium price?

b. At this price, how many calculators will be sold?

3. You and your friend have decided to attend an auction. There are a wide variety of items being sold, but those items bringing the highest price include an old violin, a piece of costume jewelry worn by Michael Jackson, and a handmade quilt. Explain how the three functions of price operate to determine (a) who will and will not purchase the items, (b) the price tags of the three items, and (c) the value of the products (factors of production).

4. Explain how it is possible that your economic decisions have an effect on others; how are you affected by decisions made by others? First, assume that you are a consumer working for a big corporation. Then, assume that you are a big corporation making and selling sewing machines. How does interdependence operate in the circular flow of economic activity to influence all citizens in a market economy?

5. You and your family are planning a vacation next summer. You will travel by automobile to a nearby state and visit a national park. List the government services, controls, and benefits you will receive as travelers in this country.

Chapter 25

THE MARKETPLACE AND YOU

◆◆◆◆◆◆◆◆◆◆◆◆◆◆◆◆◆◆◆◆◆◆◆◆◆

OBJECTIVES

1. Describe the four market structures of pure competition, pure monopoly, monopolistic competition, and oligopoly.
2. Discuss market controls.
3. Define price controls and how they affect supply and demand in a market economy.
4. Explain economic incentives and how they affect the consumer in the marketplace.
5. List the reasons for failure in our economic system.

MARKET STRUCTURES

◆◆◆◆◆◆◆◆

Four market structures create and affect competition: pure competition, pure monopoly, monopolistic competition, and oligopoly. Within a market economy, all four market structures are present and contribute to production decisions.

PURE COMPETITION

When a marketplace is characterized by **pure competition**, there are a large number of buyers and sellers all interacting at the same time within the marketplace. The firms produce a homogeneous product, and there is free entry and exit of these firms to and from the industry. *Homogeneous products* are basically the same as other products produced by each firm in the industry; buyers have no preference for the product of one seller over another.

Pure competition allows the lowest prices.

The large number of sellers means that no single seller's production can affect price. Similarly, the large number of buyers prevents any individual buyer from affecting the price in any noticeable way. No single purchaser has any significant market power. **Market power** is the ability of firms or buyers to influence price. Large numbers of buyers and sellers ensure that no one buyer or seller affects price.

PURE MONOPOLY

When a marketplace is characterized by **pure monopoly**, there is only one producer of a particular good or service, and there are no substitutes available for that product. Therefore, large numbers of consumers have no choice but to buy the product or do without it. Until recently, many geographic areas were serviced by only one telephone system. In almost every city or town, there is only one seller of electricity. If consumers in these areas wanted telephone or electrical service, they had no choice but to use the only supplier available for each.

Some industries lend themselves entirely to monopoly.

When a monopoly exists, governmental regulations are often present to prevent practices that are not in the best interest of consumers. When government regulates a monopoly, the controlling company must request permission to raise rates or fees. The controlling company does not have the authority to make production decisions as does a private company in an industry not characterized as a monopoly.

MONOPOLISTIC COMPETITION

Monopolistic competition exists where there are many sellers of products that are not exactly the same but very similar. The products are *differentiated* — there is a difference in the product of one firm when compared to others. The differences may be actual physical differences, or they may be superficial or imaginary. In addition, the differences may be in function, quality or brand, trademark, or package.

Heterogeneous products compete based on style, quality, and uniqueness.

The automobile industry is a good example of monopolistic competition. Each of the major automobile producers is a giant corporation that produces a uniquely different product. The automobile manufacturers do not compete strongly with each other on price. But the auto manufacturers do try to differentiate between their products on style, mileage estimates, fuel

Illustration 25-1
The American automobile industry is characterized by monopolistic competition.

efficiency, status, price discounts, rebates, or warranties. Monopolistic competition is monitored by the government and by consumer groups to ensure that price fixing and other unfair trade practices do not occur.

OLIGOPOLY

The market situation characterized by very few firms is an **oligopoly**. Because of their small number, firms recognize their mutual interdependence. As a result, a firm will forecast or expect a certain response from its rivals to any price or production decision that it makes. An oligopoly is similar to a monopoly, except that there is more than one producer in the marketplace. An oligopoly, like a monopoly, offers little choice of style or quality, yet there are many different brands from which to choose.

> An oligopoly has more than one producer.

An example of an oligopoly is the automobile tire industry. While there are only a few large producers of automobile tires, each producer offers a large number of choices of tires that are similar to those produced by all other tire producers. Oligopolies become frequent as a society becomes more specialized and makes more efficient use of resources.

> Oligopolies become more common as a society becomes more specialized and efficient.

Although oligopoly means higher prices than pure competition, it also means lower prices than when a monopoly exists.

MARKET CONTROLS
◆◆◆◆◆◆◆◆

Within a market economy, antitrust laws seek to control, limit, and define acceptable market structure practices such as mergers, acquisitions, and takeovers. Antitrust laws were enacted to preserve free enterprise as much as possible.

ANTITRUST LAWS

Antitrust laws limit the growth and use of monopoly power. The government enforces these laws to protect consumers from such practices as price fixing and creating monopoly-like business situations which would otherwise be competitive. The Interstate Commerce Act of 1887 was the first antitrust act passed to limit the monopoly powers of railroads. In 1890, the Sherman Antitrust Act was written into law to prohibit businesses from trying to monopolize any market, either by joining together or by collusion (agreeing to control prices in the marketplace). These acts were not strictly enforced, however, and many industrial giants emerged (Standard Oil and American Tobacco are examples). The U.S. Supreme Court forced such giants to split up. In 1914 two new laws were passed — the Clayton Antitrust Act and the Federal Trade Commission Act — to strengthen the government's position against monopoly. These laws still stand today to preserve the market system.

Antitrust laws are still valid and enforced today.

MERGERS, ACQUISITIONS, AND TAKEOVERS

In the 1980s, mergers, acquisitions, and takeovers became common to prevent financial collapse of businesses from retail chains to banks. In a **merger** (joining of two companies), a weak company's assets are combined with a stronger company's assets, both becoming more financially sound. An **acquisition** occurs when one company buys out or acquires another company to strengthen its financial position or to diversify (take on new and different products). A **takeover**, which may be friendly or hostile, is the purchasing of massive shares of stock of a corporation in order to win a seat on the board of directors and control the corporation. These three acts make the marketplace more monopolistic than freely competitive and are subject to antitrust laws.

Mergers, acquisitions, and takeovers reduce free competition.

ARTIFICIAL PRICE CONTROLS

In a market economy, demand and supply are usually balanced by price. Price serves to allocate resources — as the value of a given resource is in one use more than another, those resources will be pulled to the higher priced use. Price serves to ration — those individuals who cannot pay the equilibrium price are rationed out of the market. A high level of competition among producers of a product will permit the supply and demand conditions in the market to set the price. Because the price mechanism alone may cause hardship to either producers or consumers, there are price controls that are enacted through legislative priorities and enforced by government agencies. Two examples are price ceilings and price floors.

Price controls are enacted and enforced by the government.

PRICE CEILING

A **price ceiling** is a maximum price set by government that is below the market equilibrium price. A price ceiling set below the equilibrium price prohibits the market from clearing out all supplies of the product. The quantity that consumers wish to purchase at the ceiling price is greater than the quantity suppliers are willing to supply at this price. The result is a shortage. A **shortage** occurs when the quantity that consumers wish to purchase at some price exceeds the quantity suppliers wish to supply. The shortage is created by the ceiling and can only occur on a lasting basis when a ceiling is in effect.

A price ceiling will create a shortage of a product.

Figure 25-1 illustrates the concept of a price ceiling. The price ceiling is set at $1.75. The equilibrium price, however, is $2.50. At a price of $1.75, producers are willing to produce only 1,000 units; but consumers want to purchase about 1,500 units. The shortage is 500 units.

Figure 25-1
Price Ceiling

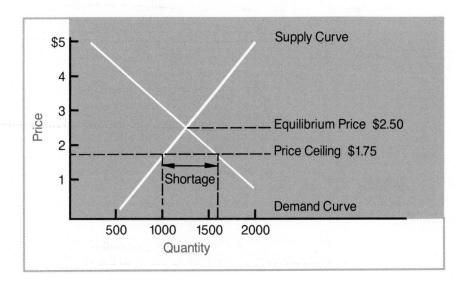

PRICE FLOOR

A **price floor** is a minimum price set by government that is above the equilibrium price. A price floor set above the equilibrium price prohibits the market from clearing. The quantity that suppliers offer for sale at the floor price is greater than the quantity consumers wish to purchase at this price. The result is a surplus. A **surplus** occurs when the quantity that suppliers wish to supply at some price exceeds the quantity that consumers wish to purchase. The surplus is created by the price floor and can only occur on a lasting basis when a price floor is in effect. Minimum wage is a price floor in the labor market.

A price floor will create a surplus of a product.

Figure 25-2 illustrates the concept of a price floor using minimum wage. The equilibrium wage is $2.50 an hour. However, government has set the minimum wage at $3.75 an hour. At $3.75 an hour, almost 2,000 workers are willing to go to work. However, at $3.75 an hour, businesses are willing to employ only 850 or 900 workers. The result is a surplus of 1,100 or more workers. At the equilibrium wage, 1,400 workers would be employed.

Minimum wage laws are price floors that create surplus (unemployment).

Figure 25-2
Price Floor

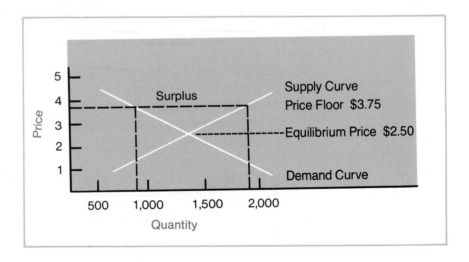

Government exerts controls such as price ceilings and floors to protect businesses, workers, and consumers as needed. Without some price floors, large producers would be able to undercut prices and put small producers out of business. Minimum wage laws were written to protect workers from unfair wage levels. Rent control is an example of a price ceiling intended to protect consumers from exorbitant rent payments. Unfortunately, at a price less than the market clearing price, there will be a shortage of rental units. The number of rental units available will be less than the number of people looking for them. Because there are a number of people waiting to rent each apartment, the landlord can be selective in choosing tenants. Prospective

Shortages cause problems for poorer people.

tenants who are young or old, or who have children or pets, may be excluded because there are numerous other people who want to rent the apartments.

ECONOMIC INCENTIVES
◆◆◆◆◆◆◆◆

The marketplace is also affected by a number of economic incentives that are present among consumers of goods and services. These incentives, or reasons for purchasing some products while forsaking others, include utility, marginalism and sunken cost, optimizing and economizing, conservation, and maximization behavior.

UTILITY

Utility is a measure of satisfaction.

Utility is the satisfaction that an individual receives from consuming a good or service. A consumer will demand any product if she or he feels that the product will give the desired return or satisfaction. Total utility is the total amount of satisfaction you receive. As we shall see in the following section, as you consume more of a good or service, your *total* satisfaction will increase, but at a decreasing rate (the subsequent items consumed will provide less satisfaction than the previous items).

MARGINALISM AND SUNKEN COST

Marginal, in economic terms, means added or extra. It refers to the added value or benefit — the effect of buying or selling one more item. Individually, consumers make marginal decisions daily. When shopping for groceries, you decide how many bananas, oranges, or cans of soup to purchase. You try to come up with the right combination so that you do not run out before the next shopping day. You also do not want to waste any groceries or allow any to spoil because you bought too many.

Marginal utility is added satisfaction received.

Marginal utility is the added satisfaction (utility) that is received when an additional unit is consumed. The more units that are purchased, the less added or marginal satisfaction each gives. For example, if you purchase five candy bars and begin to eat them, each additional candy bar consumed will be less enjoyable than the previous candy bar. If you eat all five candy bars at the same time, you may find that the fifth candy bar is the least enjoyable and is perhaps even unpleasant to consume.

Marginalism is a technique used to analyze problems in which the results of small changes in quantity are examined. At 10 cents a pound, oranges are very inexpensive. You know you are getting a good deal if you purchase 25 pounds of oranges for only $2.50. But you also have to consider whether you can consume 25 pounds of oranges before they spoil. If 20 pounds of oranges go to waste, then any oranges you purchase above the 5 pounds you are certain to consume are said to be "marginal." You must weigh the added benefit of getting 20 pounds of extra oranges against the added cost — $2.00 worth of merchandise that might spoil.

Marginal thinking is comparing added costs to added benefits.

Producers also make marginal decisions. They must decide whether to produce additional units of output and how many extra workers to hire. If a producer believes that the added benefit (increased profits) would pay for the extra costs (salary of additional workers), then he or she will choose to increase production. Producers must know where the break-even point is, and all points above that are marginal. Will the added revenue exceed added costs incurred by hiring one more worker or producing one more unit? The break-even point is called *equilibrium* — the point at which there is very little risk.

The study of marginalism is called *marginal analysis.* An economist might describe the concept in the following way: Don't look at the whole; examine the parts. For each additional product produced over the base (equilibrium) quantity, minimize the production costs to get the most return for the amount spent. At each point beyond equilibrium, you must compare added benefits to added costs. Remember that marginal cost is *additional* cost, not total cost. Every time you take a new step — make or buy one more item — you must be better off than before you took that step.

Marginalism is crucial beyond the point of equilibrium.

The **sunken cost** is the amount already spent, the amount it costs to reach equilibrium. Once money has been spent or invested, there is nothing you can do about it. But you must decide if you want to spend or invest more. For example, a person spends $1,000 for a car. This $1,000 is the sunken cost. After a short time, he or she discovers that the car now needs new brakes. For $75, the car will run safely again. Marginal analysis is used to decide whether the added cost ($75) will return to the owner enough added miles of service. The $1,000 is already spent (sunken) and is not a consideration. If adding another $75 to the car will give sufficient return, then it is a good investment. If the car needs a lot of other work, too, spending more money on it might be wasted because it would not increase the value of the car, nor would it give enough added use to the car.

Sunken costs are not considered in marginal analysis.

CONSERVATION

Conservation will protect the quality of life for future generations.

The wise use of scarce resources is known as **conservation**. Careful choices made after examining all possible uses of scarce resources will ensure that resources are conserved and used wisely. For example, because land is limited in quantity and quality for producing certain foods, the soil most conducive to producing fruits should be used for that purpose.

To accomplish conservation, we have several options: decrease wants and needs; develop alternative resources; improve the quality of existing resources; and make better use of existing resources.

1. *Decrease Wants and Needs.* Individually and collectively, we can make an effort to reduce consumption. Decreasing wants and needs affects our standard of living and often involves sacrificing and choosing alternatives that are not pleasing or desirable. In order to take the city bus rather than drive to work, it may be necessary to get up an hour earlier in the morning or walk a few extra blocks.

2. *Develop Alternative Resources.* In some cases it is not possible to increase our supply of resources: we are limited in quantity and quality of land, water, climate, etc. We can, however, attempt to develop alternative resources. For instance, we can use solar power or coal rather than electricity and oil for heating, or an electric car to replace the gasoline driven car.

3. *Improve the Quality of Existing Resources.* We can increase output by improving the quality of existing resources. To improve the quality of the nation's labor force, we can better educate our citizens, increase safety and working conditions, and provide medical care for all citizens. To save fuel, we can make cars more fuel efficient and less damaging to the environment at the same time.

4. *Make Better Use of Existing Resources.* Like decreasing wants and needs, decisions involving better use of resources are not always popular. Using fertilizers, pesticides, and other chemicals can enhance the productivity of the land. Using plastic instead of metal on automobiles may conserve the metal but result in a product that is not as safe. Recycling is a method of making existing resources go further.

> New and better ways of doing things will save scarce resources.

MAXIMIZATION BEHAVIOR

The motivational dimension of the market is based on two basic assumptions: (a) consumers attempt to maximize their well-being (utility), and (b) businesses seek to make the largest possible profit. To make the largest profit, businesses seek to produce at the lowest possible cost. By lowering costs, a larger profit is made. To lower costs, businesses seek the following:

> Profit maximization serves to lower costs for all.

1. More efficient techniques of production
2. Less expensive combinations of factors to produce the product
3. A more efficient level or size of production

When a business can produce a product more efficiently than its competitors, the firm makes greater profits. Competition results when other businesses find ways to cut costs and thereby lower prices. *Normal profit* is the minimum return or payment necessary to maintain a business — pay its costs of operation and a reasonable profit above that to continue in business. *Extra profits* are above normal profits; they are excess revenues that make it possible to expand, pay large dividends to stockholders, and achieve increased production.

FAILURES IN OUR ECONOMIC SYSTEM

◆◆◆◆◆◆◆◆

Our economic system is very complex, yet very efficient. It does not give preference to any product, good or service, producer, or consumer. You may wonder why it is, then, that so many small businesses, and a few large ones, fail each year. Failure occurs because the market is unsympathetic to those who do not produce what consumers want, at the appropriate price, the most efficiently. Few exceptions exist. The market system is therefore not characterized as moral or immoral, but rather as **amoral**, which means it doesn't care — the marketplace exists on the survival of the fittest.

The marketplace is neither sympathetic (moral) nor cruel (immoral).

Generally, when a business has failed to meet the demands of the consumer, it will go out of business. These are the basic reasons why some businesses fail:

1. *Lack of Information.* The business owners did not forecast the market that existed for their product. In some cases, consumers were not adequately informed of the availability or characteristics of the product.
2. *Resource Immobility.* The resources needed for the product are too expensive to move or cannot be utilized efficiently enough to produce a product that is competitive in price.
3. *Competition.* There are too many similar products being produced by other producers; the market is already saturated.
4. *Unstable Market.* During times of economic recession, inflation, or other unstable periods such as high unemployment, consumer buying habits may be unsatisfactory. This could cause a product otherwise in demand to be replaced by a cheaper product.
5. *Government Intervention.* Because of government controls, taxation, or regulations, a business might be prevented from producing or distributing an otherwise profitable product.
6. *Poor Management and Planning.* Making a business profitable requires a lot of financial planning and expertise.

By understanding and applying basic economic concepts such as supply, demand, equilibrium, utility, and others, businesses can avoid many of the problems that can lead to failure in the marketplace.

VOCABULARY

Directions: Can you find the definition for each of the following terms used in Chapter 25?

pure competition	shortage
market power	price floor
pure monopoly	surplus
monopolistic competition	utility
oligopoly	marginal utility
antitrust laws	marginalism
merger	sunken cost
acquisition	conservation
takeover	amoral
price ceiling	

1. A market structure characterized by only a few sellers and a homogeneous product.
2. A characteristic which means the marketplace does not care.
3. The wise use of scarce resources.
4. The maximum price that can be charged for a product, good, or service.
5. The ability of firms or buyers to affect price.
6. A market structure characterized by many sellers of products that are not exactly the same but very similar.
7. A term to describe satisfaction per unit consumed.
8. A large number of buyers and sellers interacting at the same time in the marketplace. The firms produce a homogeneous product.
9. The minimum price set for goods and services.
10. The joining together of two companies to make a weak one stronger, thus making both more financially sound.
11. The added satisfaction received when an additional unit is consumed.
12. The procedure in which one company buys out or acquires another company in order to diversify and strengthen position.
13. A friendly or hostile purchase of stock in order to control a corporation.
14. Controls enacted and enforced by government to limit the growth and use of monopoly power.

15. The result when the quantity that consumers wish to purchase at some price exceeds the quantity suppliers wish to supply.
16. A technique to analyze problems in which the results of small changes in quantity are examined.
17. The result when the quantity that suppliers wish to supply at some price exceeds the quantity that consumers wish to purchase.
18. An amount already spent; the amount it costs to reach equilibrium.
19. A condition wherein the marketplace is characterized by only one producer of a good or service, with no substitutes available.

ITEMS FOR DISCUSSION

1. Explain the four market structures that exist within our market price system.
2. Give two examples of antitrust laws.
3. What is the result when a price ceiling is set for a good or service?
4. What is the result when a price floor is set for a good or service?
5. As a consumer, what is utility?
6. What is marginalism?
7. Define conservation.
8. List four ways to accomplish conservation.
9. List four reasons why businesses fail in a market economy.

APPLICATIONS

1. List several businesses in your area that fit into each of these market structures:

   a. Pure competition   c. Monopolistic competition
   b. Pure monopoly   d. Oligopoly

2. Explain the difference between homogeneous and differentiated products.
3. Is there a business in your local area that has failed in the last year? Why do you think the business did not succeed?
4. Explain utility and marginal utility with an example (using a consumer's interests).
5. Explain utility and marginal utility with an example (using a producer's interests).
6. Explain sunken cost, using a consumer example.
7. Explain sunken cost, using a producer example.
8. List an example of each of the four conservation options to solve the economic problem of water shortage.

CASE PROBLEMS AND ACTIVITIES

1. A local merchant sees that the market for video cassettes is this: at $15 the merchant is able to sell 100 cassettes a week; at $12.50 the merchant can sell 200 cassettes a week. The lower the price, the more cassettes the merchant will sell.

   a. From the information given below, construct a demand curve:

If price is:	Consumers would buy:
$15.00	100/week
12.50	200/week
9.00	300/week
7.50	400/week
5.00	500/week

   b. Now construct a supply curve on the same chart as the demand curve. The merchant can produce and offer for sale the following:

If price is:	Producers willing to sell:
$15.00	600/week
12.50	400/week
9.00	200/week
7.50	150/week
5.00	75/week

   What is the approximate equilibrium price? At this price, how many cassettes would be sold?

   c. The government decides that cassettes must be made available to all citizens and therefore sets a price ceiling at $8. On the same graph, insert the price ceiling and label the result (surplus or shortage).

   d. The government decides that manufacturers of cassettes need to be protected from price wars and therefore sets a price floor of $12.50 for the cassettes. On the same graph, insert the price floor and label the result (surplus or shortage).

2. Has there been a major corporate merger, acquisition, or takeover in your city or state recently? Do a research project wherein you identify the names of the companies, dates, reasons given for the action, and effects of the action on the local economy (such as jobs lost).

3. Conduct an action research project as follows: First, choose a snack food that you really enjoy and give it a rating. For example, you may

love to eat watermelon. A four-ounce serving will give you 100 "utils" of satisfaction. Divide a watermelon into four-ounce servings. Eat the first serving and record the utils you received. Eat a second serving and record the utils. Continue until your utils cease to increase and begin to decrease. You will find that your satisfaction (utility) will increase at a decreasing rate (cumulative). Eventually, it will stop increasing and start bringing negative satisfaction. Report the results of your experiment in a paragraph. Construct a chart to show your utils received with each serving, such as this:

Serving No.	Number of Utils	Cumulative
1	100	100
2	90	190
3	60	250
4	30	280
5	0	280
6	-30	250

4. Linda and Bert purchased a refrigerator last month for $100 (a real bargain). Unfortunately, the thermostat had to be replaced last week at a cost of $25. When they fixed it, they expected the refrigerator to last for several more years. Then the compressor went out. The estimated cost is $75. Explain to Linda and Bert the economic concepts of sunken cost and marginalism.

5. Frank Zibrenski serves on the City Council. The air quality in the city has steadily deteriorated over the last 15 years, but this year the air quality has slipped below environmental air quality standards. The area has heavy traffic, heavy industrialization, and heavy wood stove use during the year, all of which is causing concern about the health of the citizens in the area. Make suggestions to Frank about ways of improving the air quality and preserving the quality for years to come.

6. Do a library research project into business failures. (Consult the Business Periodicals Index.) Find a magazine article about a business that has failed in the last few years and find out (a) why it failed, (b) how long it had been in business, and (c) what impact was felt in the local area by its going out of business. In the alternative, find an article about a new business that has been very successful and find out (a) why it has succeeded, (b) how long it has been in business, and (c) what impact is felt in the local and state economy because of its presence.

MACRO-ECONOMICS and the U.S. ECONOMY

UNIT OBJECTIVES

After studying the chapters in this seventh unit that describe and apply macroeconomic theory to the economy of the United States, the student will be able to:

1. ■ Explain macroeconomic theory in the areas of aggregate supply and demand, investment and growth, measures of economic growth, and list sources of economic information and analysis.

2. ■ Define monetary policy and discuss money, the Federal Reserve System, and implementation and impact of monetary policy in the U.S. economy.

3. ■ Define fiscal policy and discuss the role of government, the purpose of fiscal policy, the national debt, and explain major economic theories that operate in the U.S. economy.

Chapter 26

THE SYSTEM AS A WHOLE

◆◆◆◆◆◆◆◆◆◆◆◆◆◆◆◆◆◆◆◆◆◆◆◆◆

OBJECTIVES

1. Describe the economic system as a whole and define the macroeconomic concepts of aggregate supply, aggregate demand, and types of inflation.
2. Explain how the economy grows through savings and investment.
3. Discuss the different measures of economic growth — GNP, CPI, PPI, and the Index of Leading Economic Indicators.
4. List and describe sources of economic information, national income and product accounts, and economic forecasting.

THE ECONOMIC SYSTEM AS A WHOLE

◆◆◆◆◆◆◆◆◆

Economic decisions are based on macroeconomics.

Macroeconomics is the study of how the economy as a whole functions. Macroeconomics is concerned with policy issues such as output of the economy, employment, capacity to produce, capacity to spend, and economic growth and stability. When information on all these topics is put together and studied, economic decisions can be made that will result in a healthy economy. We have studied supply and demand on the individual level. Now we will study supply and demand as they relate to the *aggregate*, or collective, level.

AGGREGATE SUPPLY

The total amount of goods and services available to purchasers is the **aggregate supply**. Aggregate supply depends upon productive capacity, which is fixed at any given moment in time. Productive capacity depends on land, labor, capital, entrepreneurship, and technology, as well as how rapidly an industry is able to move forward into new and unknown paths. Thus, the aggregate supply curve is slow to change because decisions to increase or decrease productive capacity involve many risks and large capital investments. There are several ways to change productive capacity in a nation:

Aggregate supply is slow to change.

1. Change the size and quality of the labor force.
2. Change the quantity and quality of capital used in the production of goods and services.
3. Discover new resources, replenish diminishing resources, and create new types of products that replace demand for scarce and irreplaceable resources.
4. Make new technological advances that improve the quality of life (but not at the expense of using all scarce resources).

Productive capacity is fixed at a moment in time.

Productive capacity, fixed at a moment in time, can grow over time. Improvement of the education or skill level of workers would substantially affect the nation's capacity to produce.

AGGREGATE DEMAND

The total demand of all consumers for all goods and services produced in an economy is **aggregate demand**. *Consumption* includes all purchases by individuals, households, businesses, and government. When aggregate demand falls short of what the economy is producing (aggregate supply), the result is *recession,* or a slowing down of the economy usually for a short period of time of a year of two. (Some recessions last longer, particularly in some parts of the country that do not recover as rapidly.)

Imbalance in macroeconomics leads to other economic events.

When aggregate demand is greater than aggregate supply, at a full-employment level, the result is inflation. The goal of a market economy is to balance the forces of aggregate demand and aggregate supply. When aggregate demand and aggregate supply get out of balance, other economic events occur. A *depression* is a serious, prolonged period of high unemployment, low output, and low income in the economy. In our study of macroeconomics, we will look at some of these occurrences, how to control them, and how to prevent them.

The condition of full employment exists when all persons who are able and willing to work are able to find employment. Some unemployment always exists because (a) inadequate training or education makes some people unemployable; (b) depressed areas of the country often lack industries; (c) discrimination in hiring may occur; (d) industries are replaced by newer technologies and ideas (technological unemployment); (e) some people are between jobs, causing temporary unemployment (frictional unemployment); (f) the structure of the economy changes, making some products — and jobs —obsolete (structural unemployment); and (g) workers are needed only at certain times of the year (seasonal unemployment). Some workers will learn new skills, others will not. During periods of normal, healthy economic growth, unemployment rates are generally less than 6 percent. A "natural rate" of unemployment tends to settle between 4 and 6 percent. During the Great Depression (1929-1941), however, the unemployment rate was over 25 percent.

Aggregate demand can be affected by the following:

A healthy unemploy-
ment rate is around 6
percent.

1. Government taxation, which takes away spending power of individuals and businesses
2. Government spending, which stimulates spending power of individuals and businesses
3. A change in the amount of money available caused by changes in credit and interest rates
4. National or societal expectations, priorities, and emphases during a given period of time

INFLATION

The interaction of aggregate demand and aggregate supply influences the level of prices, of output, and of employment. Thus, changes in aggregate demand or aggregate supply have dramatic effects. For example, inflation can enter the picture. There are three basic types of inflation: demand-pull inflation, cost-push inflation, and real cost inflation.

There are three types
of inflation to deal
with.

Demand-pull inflation is a rise in the general level of prices caused by excessive aggregate demand in relation to aggregate supply. Buyers are, in effect, bidding up prices, or demanding more than the supply is providing. In other words, when you go into a store, you buy whatever product you are seeking. You do not look for the best buy and compare prices, but purchase what you want without considering cost. Because consumers demand more goods and services than are being produced, those in existence are "bidded up." Merchants who have such products are able to raise the prices because they know supplies are limited and therefore consumers will pay the higher prices.

Cost-push inflation is a rise in the general level of prices that is caused by increased costs of making and selling goods. The costs rise, but the quality and quantity of goods does not increase. For example, wages increase for workers, but productivity remains unchanged. Therefore, the cost of the item being produced increases, while more or better units are not being produced to compensate for increased price.

> Cost-push inflation does not improve the quality or quantity of production.

Real cost inflation occurs when costs of the factors of production increase. For example, natural resources may become more valuable and therefore cost more. As supplies of natural resources continue to diminish, their value increases, and the real costs of producing goods and services cannot be controlled.

The result of inflation often is a spiral. As prices increase, workers need raises to pay for the increased cost of living. But increased wages create higher production costs, which result in higher prices. Unfortunately, when the inflation spiral begins, most workers' wages tend not to keep pace with the increasing cost of living.

ECONOMIC GROWTH THROUGH SAVINGS AND INVESTMENT

◆◆◆◆◆◆◆◆

> Savings and investment make growth possible.

At the base of growth and productivity are savings and investment. An increase in capital contributes both to increased production and increased productivity.

SAVINGS

Saving occurs when individuals and businesses do not consume all of their current income. Saving affects the growth and productivity of the whole economy and can have both positive and negative aspects. Many consumers do not want to postpone current spending in order to have buying power at a later time.

> Savings must be reinvested to help increase productivity.

On a nationwide scale, savings is a leakage from the flow of productivity when it is not invested by banks. When money is saved, not spent, it is not available to businesses for reinvestment in capital equipment, inventories, or wages. When consumers choose to save and buy fewer goods and services, production slows down, and eventually higher prices result. Saving does not result in lower production and higher prices, however, if the money you save is reinvested by the bank or savings and loan where you deposit your money. In this case, when you save, you are indirectly investing in capital along with many other depositors who save money.

The housing industry is one of the first to suffer during times of high interest rates. Most people must buy their homes on credit and finance them over 25 or 30 years. Construction loans, which are temporary loans given to builders to make houses, have higher rates than ordinary loans. But when rates are very high, most builders cannot afford to get the loans because of the risk of being unable to sell the home when it is finished.

Propensity to Consume.   **Propensity to consume** is the proportion of income that will be spent for consumer goods and services. In the United States, consumers spend 93 to 94 percent of their disposable income. Economists often refer to this propensity to consume as the *consumption function,* because people's consumption (spending for consumer goods) is a function of (is determined by) the size of their incomes.

Consumer spending reflects people's expectations. If people are concerned about their economic future, they will usually spend less. Business spending is determined by expected return. Individuals and businesses purchase three types of goods and services: durables, nondurables, and services.

1. **Durable goods**, like automobiles, refrigerators, and furniture, are goods expected to last for many years. Durable goods often require servicing and upkeep, and large initial investments.
2. **Nondurable goods**, such as groceries, clothing, and supplies, are goods that will be used up in a relatively short time and require replacement.
3. **Services,** such as haircuts, repairs, and medical care, are performed by individuals and companies and contain no measurable quantity once performed.

Propensity to Save.   **Propensity to save** is the proportion of income that will be saved for future purchases. When propensity to spend is 94 percent, propensity to save is 6 percent. When savings is invested, it increases the circular flow of economic activity (see Figure 24-7) and results in economic growth.

INVESTMENT

Investment occurs when money is used to increase the productive capacity of industry by developing new technology and building new capital equipment, buildings, factories, roads, or tools. Money invested by savers directly, through the banks in which they put their savings, and through other economic institutions, can be an important part of economic growth.

Government policies and actions also have effects on investment and productivity. Government generally wants more productivity and growth; therefore, it increases its investment in education, transportation, and research. Other government actions and programs, such as taxation, welfare

---

Construction loans are temporary loans.

Goods and services are classified as durable, nondurable, and service.

programs, and price ceilings, restrict and control growth. These policies adversely affect saving and investment and prevent the most efficient use of resources.

Economic Institutions.   There are four formal economic institutions in our society: (a) households, the largest source of spending and saving; (b) corporations and businesses; (c) banks, credit unions, and savings and loan associations; and (d) labor unions, pension funds, life insurance trusts and other groups of people who gather for strength and power. Each of these institutions acts both as consumer and producer. Each citizen is involved in one or more of these economic institutions.

Economic institutions are both consumers and producers.

Productivity.   **Productivity** is the output per unit of input, or the amount of return that is received when factors of production are used to produce goods and services. Figure 26-1 illustrates the flow of saving and investment and the productivity that results from the interaction of the economic institutions with government.

Figure 26-1
Productivity

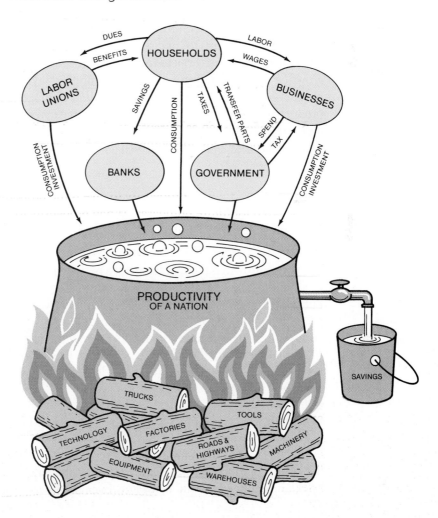

When saving is invested, productivity increases. But when saving is taken out and not reinvested, productivity decreases, leading to unemployment. Savings decrease the output of a nation when not reinvested into capital equipment. In Figure 26-1, the small bucket at the side represents savings that are not reinvested. The nation as a whole does not benefit; productivity is actually slowed down because that money is taken out of circulation.

The logs in the figure (fuel for the fire) represent capital equipment — investment in the tools of production whereby more goods and services can be produced, transported, and sold in the marketplace. The fire represents the national economy — a continually active, growing, and measurable output of goods and services. Within the pot are consumers, producers, businesses, and government, all interacting and producing goods and services that are consumed, taxed, invested in, and benefited from by individuals, businesses, and government. Without the fire, the pot slows down its boiling. When the fire (economy) cools, the results can be unemployment, inflation, recession, and depression.

In order for an economy to continue to grow and achieve higher productivity, and thus for its citizens to have higher standards of living, more and better goods and services must be produced. The first step in economic growth is saving. The second step is directing the savings accumulated to the production of capital goods that are needed to make the labor force more productive and to realize the efficiencies of mass production, specialization, division of labor, and comparative advantage. Consumers have, over the past two decades, consistently saved about 6 to 7 percent of their disposable income each year.

Our economy is fueled by capital equipment.

Economic principles describe a nation's efficiency.

MEASURES OF ECONOMIC GROWTH

◆◆◆◆◆◆◆◆

Economic growth is the increase over a period of time of the total output and production of an entire economy as a unit. Economic growth is desirable, but growing too fast means inflation. Growing too slowly results in unemployment. Growth must be controlled and planned to provide an equilibrium or balance of healthy growth, low inflation, and low unemployment. Real economic growth is determined after inflation has been taken into consideration. Let us look at a few ways of measuring real economic growth.

Economic growth needs to be steady, planned, and slow.

GROSS NATIONAL PRODUCT

The **Gross National Product** (GNP) is the total value of all final goods and services produced in an economy over a given period of time. GNP measures the dollar value of the performance of an economic system. It is not a measure of quality of life or happiness, nor does it measure illegal activities that produce income. There are also omissions and duplications in a measurement of this scope. Everything that has a price tag and goes through the marketplace is counted in the GNP. Intermediate goods, such as the materials used in production, are not counted into the GNP. To count intermediate materials would be to count their value twice and would overstate the value of our total national output. Government contributions are included at their cost rather than market value: for example, police protection is valued at total cost.

GNP has deficiencies in its measurement.

If the GNP goes up 3 percent annually, the economy is experiencing a normal, steady growth. Population increases have been about 1.8 percent a year, including births and immigrations. Therefore, if we experience a 3 percent rise in GNP we know that productivity is increasing at a faster rate than population is increasing.

A 3 percent growth in GNP is considered healthy.

When government stimulates the economy by giving consumers more money to spend through a new jobs bill, increased transfer payments, or an immediate tax cut, consumers buy more. Added spending increases aggregate demand. Producers are able to hire more workers to meet the increase in demand. New wages create more purchasing power, and the effect continues to multiply and stimulate growth in the economy. This is called a *multiplier effect*. A **multiplier effect** is the concept that any change in policy affects total demand and total income by an amount larger than the amount of the change in policy. The multiplier effect is reflected in a high GNP.

CONSUMER PRICE INDEX

The **Consumer Price Index** (CPI) is an index showing changes in the average price of a basket of goods purchased by consumers. A market basket is a selection of goods and services that is studied for price increases. The selection is composed of products that people buy for day-to-day living. The quantity and quality of these items is kept unchanged between major revisions so that only price changes are compared. Prices listed in the CPI are based on an index in relation to the base year of 1967. Index points indicate how much prices have risen above the 1967 level. Most items were re-indexed in 1982-84 to keep the CPI meaningful in terms of what people purchased.

The CPI consists of items people buy every day.

Figure 26-2 is an excerpt from the CPI which shows a summary of all items, including food, housing, and household items. All items, as a whole, are indexed at 346.7 in January of 1988. This means prices have risen 246.7 points because the base year, 1967, is indexed at 100.

(1982-84 = 100, unless otherwise indicated)

Series	Annual average 1986	Annual average 1987	1987 Feb.	Mar.	Apr.	May	June	July	Aug.	Sept.	Oct.	Nov.	Dec.	1988 Jan.	Feb.
CONSUMER PRICE INDEX FOR ALL URBAN CONSUMERS:															
All items	109.6	113.6	111.6	112.1	112.7	113.1	113.5	113.8	114.4	115.0	115.3	115.4	115.4	115.7	116.0
All items (1967 = 100)	328.4	340.4	334.4	335.9	337.7	338.7	340.1	340.8	342.7	344.4	345.3	345.8	345.7	346.7	347.4
Food and beverages	109.1	113.5	112.5	112.5	112.8	113.3	113.8	113.7	113.8	114.2	114.3	114.3	114.8	115.7	115.8
Food	109.0	113.5	112.5	112.5	112.8	113.3	113.8	113.7	113.8	114.1	114.3	114.2	114.7	115.7	115.7
Food at home	107.3	111.9	111.2	110.9	111.3	112.0	112.6	112.1	112.1	112.4	112.4	112.1	112.8	114.1	113.9
Cereals and bakery products	110.9	114.8	113.3	113.4	114.3	114.6	114.7	115.2	115.3	115.4	115.6	116.2	116.8	118.1	118.7
Meats, poultry, fish, and eggs	104.5	110.5	108.8	108.9	108.6	109.6	110.4	111.4	111.9	112.7	112.0	111.2	110.3	111.0	110.6
Dairy products	103.3	105.9	105.9	105.4	105.3	105.7	105.5	105.3	105.7	106.4	106.9	106.9	106.7	107.4	107.3
Fruits and vegetables	109.4	119.1	118.3	117.4	120.1	121.8	124.1	119.6	117.4	117.4	117.8	117.4	123.4	126.4	124.7
Other foods at home	109.4	110.5	111.3	110.8	110.6	110.5	110.2	110.0	110.4	110.3	110.6	110.2	110.0	111.3	111.8
Sugar and sweets	109.0	111.0	110.3	110.7	110.7	110.8	111.2	111.1	111.3	111.6	111.6	111.4	111.0	112.2	112.2
Fats and oils	106.5	108.1	107.4	109.0	108.0	108.5	107.8	108.4	108.3	107.8	107.4	108.0	107.7	108.5	109.5
Nonalcoholic beverages	110.4	107.5	111.3	109.8	108.5	108.0	106.8	105.9	105.9	105.8	106.7	105.0	104.8	106.9	107.7
Other prepared foods	109.2	113.8	112.9	112.6	113.3	113.4	113.7	114.1	114.8	114.6	114.7	115.1	115.0	115.9	116.1
Food away from home	112.5	117.0	115.5	115.9	116.1	116.4	116.8	117.2	117.5	118.0	118.3	118.6	118.9	119.3	119.7
Alcoholic beverages	111.1	114.1	112.8	112.9	113.3	113.6	114.0	114.4	114.7	114.9	115.2	115.4	115.4	115.8	116.8
Housing	110.9	114.2	112.4	112.8	113.2	113.6	114.3	114.7	115.4	115.6	115.5	115.5	115.6	116.2	116.6
Shelter	115.8	121.3	119.0	119.6	120.2	120.5	120.8	121.3	122.2	122.5	123.2	123.4	123.7	124.6	125.0
Renters' costs (12/82 = 100)	121.9	128.1	125.8	126.4	127.1	127.3	127.9	129.3	130.1	129.8	129.4	129.2	129.1	130.8	131.3
Rent, residential	118.3	123.1	121.7	121.8	122.0	122.3	122.3	123.0	123.8	124.4	124.8	124.8	125.6	126.0	126.3
Other renters' costs	118.6	127.4	122.8	125.0	127.1	127.1	129.1	132.8	133.3	130.5	127.7	126.7	124.1	129.4	130.4
Homeowners' costs (12/82 = 100)	119.4	124.8	122.5	123.0	123.6	124.0	124.2	124.4	125.4	126.0	127.1	127.4	128.0	128.5	129.0
Owners' equivalent rent (12/82 = 100)	119.4	124.8	122.5	123.0	123.6	124.1	124.2	124.4	125.4	126.0	127.2	127.5	128.0	128.6	129.0
Household insurance (12/82 = 100)	119.2	124.0	122.0	122.2	122.4	123.0	123.6	124.5	125.1	125.5	125.8	125.9	126.2	126.9	127.1
Maintenance and repairs	107.9	111.8	110.2	110.7	110.3	110.2	111.1	113.2	112.9	112.7	112.8	113.5	113.3	113.7	114.3
Maintenance and repair services	111.2	114.8	112.5	113.4	112.8	112.3	113.7	116.8	116.5	116.3	116.4	116.9	116.6	117.4	117.9
Maintenance and repair commodities	103.7	107.8	107.2	107.1	107.2	107.5	107.8	108.4	108.2	107.8	108.1	108.9	109.1	108.7	109.5
Fuel and other utilities	104.1	103.0	101.4	101.5	101.3	102.2	104.9	105.0	105.9	105.5	103.2	102.4	102.0	102.4	102.8
Fuels	99.2	97.3	95.3	95.2	94.7	96.1	100.8	100.4	101.4	101.0	96.9	95.5	95.1	95.6	96.0
Fuel oil, coal, and bottled gas	77.6	77.9	77.9	77.5	77.5	77.1	77.2	77.1	77.8	77.6	78.5	80.3	80.5	80.8	80.9
Gas (piped) and electricity	105.7	103.8	101.5	101.5	100.8	102.5	108.1	107.6	108.7	108.2	103.3	101.4	100.9	101.5	101.9
Other utilities and public services	117.9	120.1	119.1	119.3	119.7	119.8	119.4	120.5	121.1	120.8	121.2	121.3	120.9	121.3	121.8
Household furnishings and operations	105.2	107.1	106.5	106.8	107.2	107.1	107.1	107.2	107.3	107.5	107.4	107.4	107.3	107.5	107.7
Housefurnishings	102.2	103.6	103.3	103.6	104.0	103.5	103.5	103.6	103.8	103.9	103.6	103.6	103.3	103.5	103.7
Housekeeping supplies	108.2	111.5	110.1	110.9	111.1	111.7	111.9	111.7	111.5	111.8	112.3	112.4	112.5	113.1	113.2
Housekeeping services	108.5	110.6	109.8	109.9	110.3	110.6	110.5	110.8	110.9	111.0	111.2	111.2	111.4	111.5	111.6

Figure 26-2   Consumer Price Index   Source: *Monthly Labor Review*, April, 1988, page 98.

The CPI covers two groups of the population: (a) All Urban Consumers and (b) Urban Wage Earners and Clerical Workers. In addition to wage earners and clerical workers, the All Urban Consumers group includes professional, managerial, technical, self-employed, and short-term workers, plus the unemployed, retirees, and others not in the labor force. Data are collected from more than 24,000 retail establishments and 24,000 tenants in 85 urban areas across the country.

The CPI has weaknesses. It only measures regular shelf prices. It does not measure prices for military or for farmers. Things you might buy may not be listed in the index. Included in the CPI are such items as the single family home. If you already own your home or do not buy a home, the CPI numbers will reflect a higher-than-reality housing price increase for you. New technology may have put many items in your market basket not included in that index of items. If the CPI shows a 12 percent increase in the general index, your actual personal cost is probably closer to 9 percent because you will not buy all the goods and services listed. The CPI is a widely used index. For example, social security payments are increased on the basis of CPI figures. Like GNP, the CPI does not measure *quality* of life.

The CPI measures regular shelf prices.

Illustration 26-1
Social security ben-
efits increase on the
basis of the Con-
sumer Price Index.

PRODUCER PRICE INDEX

The PPI measures price changes in commodities being produced for sale.

The **Producer Price Index** (PPI) is an index showing changes in the average price of goods that are of particular interest to producers. It measures average changes in prices by producers of commodities in all stages of processing. The samples used for calculations contain about 2,800 commodities and 10,000 quotations a month. These samples represent the movement of prices from all commodities produced in manufacturing, agriculture, forestry, fishing, mining, gas and electricity, and public utilities sectors. The Producer Price Index is also found in the *Monthly Labor Review*.

INDEX OF LEADING ECONOMIC INDICATORS

The government uses a composite rating of the economy to make economic forecasts.

The **Index of Leading Economic Indicators** is the government's gauge of future economic activity. Based on all its reports and information gathered, the government makes a composite rating. When the rating shows a 1.2 percent increase for one month, that is over 12 percent annual growth. When this is translated into a GNP figure, it is likely to equal about 3 percent, which is a steady, healthy economic growth. The composite rating is affected by all possible areas of input — interest rates; foreign trade; the strength of the dollar at home and overseas; inflation and credit; and the actions of the Federal Reserve System, the president, and Congress.

ECONOMIC INFORMATION AND ITS USES
◆◆◆◆◆◆◆◆

Economic data (facts and figures) and information (data that is organized to be useful) is monitored, analyzed, reported, and used by government agencies, Congress, the president, the Federal Reserve System, economists, and others who make decisions — private and public — in this country. In this section, we will examine major sources of data and information, how data is organized to be useful (income and product accounts), and how that information is used in our economy.

SOURCES OF ECONOMIC INFORMATION

There are many reliable, current sources of economic information that contain raw data, charts and graphs, trends, articles, and analyses of economic information. Some of the most commonly used sources include the *Monthly Labor Review* (MLR), *Economic Indicators*, *Survey of Current Business* (SCB), *Business Conditions Digest* (BCD), *The Economist* (magazine), *The Wall Street Journal* (newspaper), and the *Federal Reserve Bulletin*. The MLR, SCB, BCD, and *Economic Indicators* are all monthly publications of the U.S. government.

There are many sources of economic data and information.

NATIONAL INCOME AND PRODUCT ACCOUNTS

National income is the total income received (rent, wages, interest, and profits). The income account is shared among the owners of the factors of production that helped produce the product. **National product** is the output that is produced by the factors of production. National income and product accounts must be the same — each dollar paid for new output is a dollar received by someone as new income. These accounts, used extensively by all sources and analysts of economic information, are more than simple indicators of national product and national income. The accounts show how much of the national income people actually get to keep, and how much they spend for consumer goods. All income, production, and spending in this country are accounted for. National income and product account tables are found in the SCB, BCD, and *Economic Indicators*.

Income and product accounts chart income and output of the economy.

ECONOMIC FORECASTING

Projections of Gross National Product, employment, and inflation are useful to economic planners and businesspeople who must make long-term decisions. **Economic forecasting** is the prediction of future economic conditions based on current information, past information, economic policies, and trends that are shown in economic statistics. Analyzing economic statistics allows more accurate planning for large investments such as construction of new factories. Government, economists, advisors, financial institutions, and others must decide when certain adjustments are needed in the economy, such as raising interest rates, cutting taxes, or creating economic incentives.

VOCABULARY

Directions: Can you find the definition for each of the following terms used in Chapter 26?

macroeconomics	productivity
aggregate supply	Gross National Product
aggregate demand	multiplier effect
demand-pull inflation	Consumer Price Index
cost-push inflation	Producer Price Index
real cost inflation	Index of Leading Economic
propensity to consume	Indicators
durable goods	national income
nondurable goods	national product
services	economic forecasting
propensity to save	

1. The portion of income that will be spent for consumer goods and services.
2. The result of buyers bidding up prices or demanding more than is being supplied.
3. A rise in the general level of prices that is caused by increased costs of making and selling goods.
4. The concept that any change in policy affects total demand and total income by an amount larger than the amount of the change in policy.
5. The portion of income that will be saved for future purchases.
6. Goods that are expected to last for many years.
7. Output per unit of input (amount of return received for factors that are used in production).
8. The result of an increase in the costs of the factors of production.

9. The total demand of all consumers for all goods and services produced in an economy.
10. An index showing changes in the average price of a basket of goods purchased by consumers.
11. The total value of all final goods and services produced in an economy over a given period of time.
12. The government's composite gauge of future economic activity.
13. The total amount of goods and services available to purchasers.
14. The study of how the economy as a whole functions.
15. An index showing changes in the average price of goods that are of particular interest to producers.
16. The total income received by the owners of the factors of production.
17. The total output produced by factors of production (equal to total income received for their production).
18. Goods that will be used up in a relatively short period of time and require replacement.
19. Consumption that is performed by individuals and businesses and contains no measurable quantity that can be inventoried.
20. Projecting future economic conditions, based on past conditions, current conditions, and trends shown by economic statistics.

ITEMS FOR DISCUSSION

1. How can productive capacity within a nation be changed?
2. What can affect aggregate demand?
3. List and define the three types of inflation.
4. What are the four formal economic institutions in the U.S.?
5. Give examples of durable goods, nondurable goods, and services you and your family consume.
6. List four ways of measuring economic growth that are used in this country.
7. List three weaknesses of the CPI.
8. What Department of Labor periodical contains the current CPI and PPI?
9. List six sources of economic statistics, analyses, and forecasts.
10. What are national income and product accounts?
11. What is economic forecasting?

APPLICATIONS

1. Why is productive capacity fixed at a given point in time?

2. What happens when aggregate demand is greater than aggregate supply?
3. Why will we never experience full employment?
4. How can saving hurt the productive capacity of a nation?
5. How can investment have both positive and negative effects on the economy?
6. How can government affect a nation's productivity?
7. What happens when economic growth is too fast? Too slow?
8. Explain the multiplier effect of a tax cut.
9. Why do businesses and governments make economic forecasts?
10. When you receive additional money because of raises, tax cuts, or a decreased cost of living, you can either spend it or save it. If you choose to save the money, how are you responsible for capital investment?

CASE PROBLEMS AND ACTIVITIES

1. Collect information from different years on the average annual income of different occupational groups in the country that are of interest to you. This can be found in the *Monthly Labor Review*, a magazine published by the U.S. Department of Labor. Write a brief summary of the type of information that can be found in this publication.

2. Find one of these sources in a library and report the types of information and data it contains.

   a. *Economic Indicators*
   b. *Survey of Current Business*
   c. *Business Conditions Digest*
   d. *The Economist*
   e. *The Federal Reserve Bulletin*

3. Using one or more of the same sources as No. 2 above, write a summary of an economic forecast being made (such as projected unemployment, recession, higher interest rates, or inflation) in 200 words or less. Do you agree with the forecast? Why or why not?

Chapter 27

MONETARY POLICY

◆◆◆◆◆◆◆◆◆◆◆◆◆◆◆◆◆◆◆◆◆◆◆◆◆◆◆

OBJECTIVES

1. Explain the history, forms, and making of money.
2. Describe the Federal Reserve System, including its history, structure, and purposes.
3. List and define the four controls exercised through monetary policy.
4. Explain the impact of monetary policy in the economy.

HISTORY AND FORMS OF MONEY

◆◆◆◆◆◆◆◆

Modern societies need efficient methods of exchange.

We know that money is not a productive resource. **Money** is anything that is acceptable in exchange for goods and services. In order for something to be useful as money, five requirements must be met. Money can take any form as long as it is accepted as (a) a medium of exchange, (b) a unit of account, (c) store of wealth, (d) easily divisible, and (e) difficult to counterfeit.

A *medium of exchange* is something commonly accepted in exchange for goods and services or as payment for a loan. Coins, currency, checks, money orders, or credit cards are mediums of exchange. A *unit of account* refers to how an economy's prices are expressed (such as dollars and cents). We use dollars to express price, hours to express time, and miles to express distance. A *store of wealth* is a characteristic of money which means that it does not diminish in value with use or time. Other stores of value or wealth

Illustration 27-1
Money has taken many forms throughout history.

Money should be easily divisible and difficult to counterfeit.

include gold, jewels, paintings, real estate, stocks, and bonds. In other words, people can save money (or other stores of wealth) and then use it to make purchases in the future. Money that is *easily divisible* can be traded in exact amounts. When you purchase a candy bar for 55 cents, the merchant takes your dollar bill and returns 45 cents to you.

The concept of money began with barter and commodity money, then progressed to metal coins and tokens (metallic money) and the making of currency (paper money), followed by checks, credit (plastic money), money orders and travelers checks, and electronic funds transfers.

BARTER

Barter was the first form of exchange of goods and services.

Barter is the exchange of goods and services between persons or units, without involving the use of money. Both persons or units have a need for the items they wish to obtain in trade. A toolmaker trades a stone axe to a hunter in exchange for an animal skin. The toolmaker's family uses the skin to make a winter coat, while the hunter's family uses the axe to cut wood for fires for cooking and heating. Barter, however, isn't always that simple. The toolmaker may not need the skin, but may trade for it anyway, and then trade the skin for a sack of wheat. Used in this way, the skin becomes a *medium of exchange* — if it is readily accepted for something of value.

The first true form of money was *commodity money*. Commodity money is a medium of exchange because commodities are used as money. Commodities used as money must keep their exchange or market value until they can be traded again. Fresh meat or eggs would not be a good form of exchange because they would spoil. Animals are not a good form of commodity money because they could get sick or die and are costly to keep, difficult to transport, and not divisible.

An exchange rate defines the market value of each commodity being exchanged.

Seashells were a common commodity money in societies with sufficient food, clothing, and shelter. The shells serve as a luxury, decoration, or symbol of wealth or status. Societies establish an "exchange rate" to define the value of each commodity. With an exchange rate, the commodity is stable in value. For example:

1 animal skin = 1 stone axe
1 sack of wheat = 1 stone axe or 1 animal skin
1 pound of flint = 2 blocks of salt and 3 sacks of wheat

Such exchange rates are based on needs and scarcity and vary in geographic areas. Bartering was the first form of exchange in our country because when the first settlers arrived from other parts of the world, there were no coins or other more convenient forms of exchange. But soon, commodity money became more common than bartering and set the foundation for the money supply we have today.

COINS AND CURRENCY

Coins and currency represent money in one form. These are easily exchanged for goods and services. The value of coins and currency is readily understood in terms of price. *Metallic money* is a special type of commodity money in which some metal, such as gold, silver, or copper, is used because it is readily recognized or understood to have value as a metal.

Coins, however, have two major faults. They are not convenient to carry in large amounts, and the supply is limited to the amount of metal available. At first, the money supply depended on silver and gold supplies rather than on society's need for food and clothing. Because of these two reasons, coins soon gave way to currency, or paper money. Paper money first began in China in the 7th Century A.D. Europeans did not adopt paper money until the 1600s when they developed bank notes. In the American colonies, money was scarce; colonists were forbidden to make their own coins. As a result, colonists used any foreign coins they could get — English shillings, Spanish dollars, French and Dutch coins all circulated. While paper money was issued in the U.S. at the time of its independence, it wasn't until the 1860s that *paper money* was readily accepted in the form of national bank notes that were backed by U.S. government bonds. National bank notes were the nation's chief currency.

Marco Polo discovered Chinese paper money long before it was used in Europe.

Nations create their money supply through their own banking systems. *Full-bodied money* is money in which the intrinsic value of the material content is equal to the monetary value (face value). For example, a $10 gold piece was worth $10 as money and was worth $10 as gold. You could use the $10 gold Eagle to buy $10 worth of groceries or you could sell it for $10 in the gold market.

A country is on the **gold standard** when it will redeem any of its money for gold and when it agrees to buy and sell gold at a fixed price. The ability to redeem money for gold ties the country's currency to that of other countries also following the gold standard. The U.S. used a gold standard from 1900 to 1917, 1919 to 1933, and a modified gold standard was adopted in 1934 (Gold Reserve Act). The government stopped minting gold coins, and persons could no longer hold gold money, except rare coins. In the 1960s, pure coins were no longer made; in 1971, the U.S. stopped buying and selling gold at a fixed price and dropped the modified gold standard created in 1934.

We are no longer on a gold standard.

Today the value of money is based on faith — faith in the U.S. economy, the U.S. government, and each other. For example, when you accept a dollar bill or a coin, you know its value is not in gold, silver, precious metal, or gold backing. But you believe that you can exchange it at will and others will accept it as you have. Today, the value of money is also based on purchasing power, or the ability to buy goods in domestic (U.S.) and foreign markets. The purchasing power of the dollar rises and falls with inflation rates — as inflation increases, purchasing power of the dollar decreases.

Most of our money supply today is in bank deposits, credit, and other cash substitutes.

About one-thirtyfifth of our total money supply is in coins; another one-fifth is in currency; the balance is in demand deposits, credit, and other cash substitutes.

CHECKS

Checks (demand deposits) are used to make most financial transactions and are the most popular form of money. With automatic check deposit, it is common today for workers to receive and spend large sums of money without handling more than small amounts of cash and currency.

CREDIT AND OTHER CASH SUBSTITUTES

Most people use many forms of credit and carry small amounts of cash. While on vacations and trips, most travelers carry some cash, credit cards, and travelers checks. For the minority of people who do not maintain checking accounts, money orders are available to avoid sending cash by mail. Money can be wired through Western Union and other telex services. And most people have used *electronic funds transfers* (ETFs) to move money from one account to another electronically (using the telephone or automated teller machines). With ETF, no checks or currency need exchange hands. Futurists proclaim that we will one day live in an electronic paperless society where encoding will replace the physical handling of money.

Electronic funds transfers involve no use of checks or currency.

THE MAKING OF MONEY

Under federal law, only the Department of the Treasury and the Federal Reserve System issue U.S. currency. The Treasury issues all coins and paper money known as *United States Notes* (in $100 denomination only); the Federal Reserve issues paper money called *Federal Reserve Notes*.

Coins come in six denominations (values): penny (1 cent), nickel (5 cents), dime (10 cents), quarter (25 cents), half dollar (50 cents), and dollar ($1). All coins are made of *alloys* — mixtures of metals. Pennies are copper-coated zinc alloyed with less than 3 percent copper. Nickels are a mixture of copper and nickel. Dimes, quarters, half dollars and dollars are made of three layers of metal sealed together. The core is pure copper, and the outer layers are an alloy of copper and nickel. Mints in Denver and Philadelphia make all coins for general circulation. Prior to 1963, coins were silver and were worth their face value in metal as well as a medium of exchange. Likewise, currency is not backed by gold or silver, but merely on faith in the United States economy. Currency in the United States includes $1, $2, $5, $10, $20, $50, and $100 bills. The $500, $1,000, $5,000, and $10,000 bills were removed from circulation in 1969.

Counterfeiting is the unlawful production of imitations of money. It is not legal to photocopy or otherwise attempt to reproduce money to make it look real. Counterfeiting is a serious federal crime that results in fines from $5,000 to $10,000 and mandatory imprisonment in a federal prison for 5 to 15 years.

Coins come in six denominations for easy divisibility.

Counterfeiting is a serious federal crime.

THE FEDERAL RESERVE SYSTEM

◆◆◆◆◆◆◆◆

The central banking system in the United States is called the **Federal Reserve System (the Fed)**. The Federal Reserve System plays a key role in balancing the U.S. economy and it is important to understand its history, structure, and purposes.

HISTORY AND STRUCTURE

The Fed supervises banking and controls the nation's money supply.

The Fed was created by Congress during President Wilson's term of office in 1913 to provide an "elastic currency" and more effective supervision of banking. Without a central banking system, there were no standards, controls, or supervision of banking practices. The Fed has many responsibilities, such as maintaining central banking functions and designing and implementing effective monetary policy. The Fed is a **quasi-governmental agency**, which means it is essentially governmental in nature, although it operates as a private, not-for-profit business to serve the banking industry. The system was set up by Congress as an "independent agency" to keep an eye on the nation's money supply. Congress could pass a law to restrict, change, or even abolish the Fed at any time.

The chairman of the Federal Reserve System is appointed by the President of the United States to serve a four-year term. The seven members of the Fed's Board of Governors are appointed by the president with approval of Congress to serve 14-year terms. There are 12 Federal Reserve Banks and 25 branches, with approximately 5,000 member banks across the United States. Nearly 80 percent of the nation's demand deposits are in those 5,000 banks, which represent about 40 percent of the total number of banks in the nation. The 12 Federal Reserve Banks are located in San Francisco, Minneapolis, Kansas City, Dallas, Chicago, St. Louis, Cleveland, Atlanta, Boston, New York, Philadelphia, and Richmond, Virginia. The head offices of the Fed are in Washington, D.C.

> The chairman of the Fed and members of its Board of Governors are appointed by the president.

PURPOSES OF THE FED

Through the banking system, the Fed operates to control money. The actions of the Federal Reserve System to influence money supply growth, credit conditions, and level of interest rates, are called **monetary policy**. The purpose of monetary policy is to balance the economy to prevent inflation and unemployment, recession, and other adverse economic conditions. The sum of bank reserves and currency held by banks in their vaults and by the public is known as the **monetary base** because it represents a basic resource, or raw material, for creating money.

The Fed also performs the central banking functions of the United States:

> Monetary policy seeks to prevent adverse economic conditions.

1. Serves as a banker for the commercial banks — holds their deposits and lends money to them.
2. Supplies currency to the banks who then supply them to the public.
3. Helps in the "clearing and collection" of checks — checks deposited in one bank and drawn on another bank.
4. Serves as fiscal agent for the federal government — holds deposits for the U.S. Treasury, aids in buying and selling government bonds and other securities, aids in the collection of taxes.
5. Supervises, examines, and regulates activities of member commercial banks.
6. Plays an important role in foreign exchange transactions.

> The Fed has six central banking functions in addition to monetary policy.

IMPLEMENTING MONETARY POLICY
◆◆◆◆◆◆◆◆

The Fed can influence money supply, credit, and interest rates by bank reserve requirements, lowering or raising interest rates, controlling open-market transactions, and establishing direct controls.

RESERVE REQUIREMENTS

The **reserve requirement** is the percentage of each deposit that a bank must keep in reserve (not lend to others). The reserve requirement is usually approximately 20 percent of all deposits held by banks. The Fed raises and lowers the requirement to meet economic needs. By raising the rate, the Fed slows down the economy because there is less money to borrow, and consequently consumers cannot buy as much. When a bank opens new accounts because of the increased demand deposits, it is able to lend its **excess reserves** — the amount that exceeds the reserve requirement. (If banks must keep 20 percent, they can lend 80 percent of new deposits.)

> The reserve requirement ensures that consumers can get their money on demand.

INTEREST RATE ADJUSTMENTS

The discount rate is the rate of interest that the Fed charges its member banks to borrow money. As the discount rate rises, the prime rate (charged to the most creditworthy customers) also rises, and long-term and short-term rates charged to consumers rise as well. To raise the discount rate is to tighten the money supply and discourage spending through the use of credit.

> When the discount rate goes up, all interest rates go up.

OPEN-MARKET TRANSACTIONS

The Fed owns a large portion of the national debt. The **national debt** (or federal debt) is the amount of government bonds and other securities that have been sold by the U.S. government to private individuals, businesses, and the Fed to pay for government obligations. Bonds constitute government debts. When government bonds are purchased or sold, interest rates are affected. When the Fed buys more bonds, the government has more money to circulate and distribute. But when the Fed sells bonds, money is taken away from the government and out of the hands of the people, tightening the money supply. When a government deficit is

> When the Fed sells bonds, the government must pay the Fed to buy them back.

accompanied by monetary policy of buying government bonds, we say the Fed *monetizes the debt*. Monetization of the federal debt has the same impact on the economy as printing dollar bills to finance an excess of government payments over tax collections.

DIRECT CONTROLS

The Fed can change the amounts of down payments needed for bank loans, as well as lengths of loans, repayment amounts, and rates of interest. It can limit the use of credit cards and allow fees to be added. Requirements to obtain bank credit cards can be tightened by the Fed to slow down the use of credit. Higher monthly payments on credit card balances also slow credit use. Charging annual fees and placing tighter controls on who can have credit cards, using income and length of employment as guidelines, also reduce spending, lower inflation, and curb demand. Figure 27-1 is a review of monetary policy and how it works.

> **Making credit more expensive and tougher to get will reduce consumer spending.**

Figure 27-1
Monetary Policy

The Fed controls the supply and cost of money to stimulate or shrink the economy.

The major purpose of the Fed is to control spending and inflation.

The Fed works within the banking system to expand or shrink the purchasing power of individuals and businesses with interest rates and credit.

Federal Reserve Board has power to:

1. Set reserve requirements

2. Set discount rate

3. Control open-market operations

4. Establish direct controls

These policies are effective when interest rates are very high but do not hit the economy with the same impact in that some businesses and individuals rely more heavily on credit (e.g., housing industry and small businesses).

IMPACT OF MONETARY POLICY

Monetary policy is effective in speeding up and slowing down the economy — speeding up an economic recovery or slowing down a recession — through the expansion and contraction of the money supply. We will see how it works through the deposit multiplier, credit expansion, inflation and unemployment, and economic stability.

DEPOSIT MULTIPLIER

The **deposit multiplier** is the result of a change in the money balances because of a change in the reserve requirement in the banking system. A new deposit in the banking system (created because reserve requirements are lowered) permits a multiple expansion of the money supply, or the deposit multiplier, to take place. Any new reserves that enter into the banking system permit a major expansion of demand deposits, and thereby, the money supply. The deposit multiplier formula is shown below.

$$\text{DEPOSIT MULTIPLIER} = \frac{1}{\text{Reserve Requirement}}$$

To see how the formula works, let's assume that a deposit of $1,000 is made and the reserve requirement is 20 percent. When we divide 1 by .20, the deposit multiplier is 5. This means that the $1,000 that was deposited will result in a total of $5,000 being added to the money supply ($1,000 × 5).

Here's how it works. Assume that Customer A borrows $1,000. The reserve requirement is 20 percent. Therefore, the excess reserves are 80 percent. Of the new deposit of $1,000 into Customer A's account, the bank can lend $800 to Customer B. Of Customer B's account of $800, the bank can lend 80 percent, or $640, to Customer C, and so on. Thus, one initial loan of $1,000 can result in a total deposit multiplier of $5,000 ($1,000 divided by .2).

Actually, the money expansion process goes from bank to bank. But total money supply within the economy is increased by the amount of the deposit multiplier. When a new demand deposit is created this way, it is called a **primary deposit**, or high-powered money, because it creates more money supply than its own deposit amount.

CREDIT EXPANSION

Because of consumers' propensity to consume, when credit is made more convenient, less expensive, and more desirable, we can be sure that spending will increase. The Fed is able to increase (or decrease) spending and thereby speed up (or slow down) the economy as a whole through the judicious exercise of these controls. A change in credit controls will have an unequal impact on businesses and households. Economic activities that are heavily dependent on credit (such as housing) are especially affected.

INFLATION AND UNEMPLOYMENT

Inflation and unemployment are economic public enemies. Inflation robs workers of spending power. Those on fixed incomes are unable to maintain standards of living. When inflation (rising prices) goes too high, too fast, people stop buying. When businesses are unable to sell their inventories, they begin laying off workers and canceling factory orders, which leads to even higher unemployment. Eventually, as supply increases and demand decreases, prices fall, and people are able to buy more.

Monetary policy encourages people to spend less when it raises the discount rate (making it more expensive to borrow), tightens credit standards, imposes credit card fees, raises minimum monthly payments on accounts, or raises reserve requirements (making loans harder to get).

Monetary policy is also used to encourage people to spend more. As people spend more, store inventories decrease and businesses purchase more goods from factories which then hire more workers. This is called the **business cycle** — the recurrent (one after the other) speeding up and slowing down of the economy.

Monetary policy attempts to soften the impact of business cycles.

Monetary policy seeks to lessen the effects of inflation and unemployment to prevent recession and depression. Widespread unemployment has many tragic and unpleasant results, both economically and socially. Labor is wasted; people are unhappy and frustrated. Crime increases. Factories are sitting idle, depreciating, becoming obsolete. Productive resources waste away. If some action isn't taken to bring about economic recovery (speeding up the economy), the result can be prolonged depression.

By encouraging spending, making more money available to consumers and producers, and lending money to the government to spend — accomplished by lowering reserve requirements, lowering interest rates, and buying government bonds — the Fed is able to speed up the economy (lower unemployment). When the Fed believes that the economy is moving too fast and will lead to inflation, it tightens the money supply, raises interest rates, and sells government bonds, thus slowing the economy.

The Fed slows inflation by tightening the money supply.

ECONOMIC STABILITY

The purpose of any economic policy is *economic stabilization* — slow but steady economic growth, characterized by low inflation and low unemployment. The Fed works closely with the president to monitor the economic climate in this country. If economic analysis predicts a period of inflation, the Fed takes action to slow down the economy — usually by raising interest rates. If economic analysis predicts a period of high unemployment or recession, the Fed takes action to speed up the economy

The Fed reduces unemployment by expanding the money supply.

and encourage spending — usually by lowering interest rates. The Fed uses one or more of its four controls to bring about the desired results.

How effective is monetary policy? After several decades of experience, results show monetary policy has been effective at times, ineffective at other times. Not only does the Fed have to know *when* to tighten or loosen the money supply, it must know *how much*. Reactions to monetary policy are not always predictable — we may not even notice a small increase in interest rates, or business may ignore a small decrease. Monetary policy is very important in a complex market economy, but it isn't the only approach to economic stabilization.

VOCABULARY

Directions: Can you find the definition for each of the following terms used in Chapter 27?

money   monetary base
barter   reserve requirement
gold standard   excess reserves
counterfeiting   national debt
Federal Reserve System   deposit multiplier
quasi-governmental agency   primary deposit
monetary policy   business cycle

1.   The redemption of money for gold and purchasing and selling gold at fixed exchange rates.
2.   Essentially governmental in nature, set up by Congress to act as an independent agency of the government.
3.   Recurrent speeding up and slowing down of the economy.
4.   Anything acceptable in exchange for goods and services.
5.   The amount of government bonds and other securities that have been sold to pay for government obligations.
6.   Amount that banks can lend to customers.
7.   Exchange of goods and services without use of money.
8.   Unlawful production of imitations of money.
9.   The central banking system in the United States (a quasi-governmental agency).
10. Actions of the Fed to control inflation and unemployment.
11. The sum of the bank reserves and currency held by banks and by the public.
12. The percentage of each deposit that a bank must keep (not lend to others).
13. Multiple expansion in the money supply caused by a new deposit in the banking system.
14. A new demand deposit, often called *high-powered money*.

ITEMS FOR DISCUSSION

1. What are five requirements for something to be useful as money?
2. How is barter different from commodity money?
3. What was the first form of exchange in our country?
4. What are two major faults of coins?
5. Other than coins and currency, list five forms of money commonly used today.
6. Who has the legal responsibility for making money in the U.S.?
7. What is an alloy?
8. What is our currency based on?
9. When and by whom was the Fed created?
10. What is meant by "quasi-governmental" agency?
11. Where are the head offices of the Fed?
12. List six banking functions of the Fed.
13. List the four ways the Fed influences money supply, credit, and interest rates (monetary policy).
14. What is meant by "tight money" policy?
15. How does a change in credit controls have a unequal impact on businesses and households?
16. What are some negative effects of unemployment?

APPLICATIONS

1. Have you ever traded a thing of value for something else of value (without using money)? List the items you traded and what you received in return.
2. Commodity money must have a defined exchange value. List things of value that you own and the values they would have for purposes of exchange.
3. Whose image is found on the following coins and currency?

    a. penny
    b. nickel
    c. dime
    d. quarter
    e. half dollar
    f. dollar
    g. dollar bill

    h. two dollar bill
    i. five dollar bill
    j. ten dollar bill
    k. twenty dollar bill
    l. fifty dollar bill
    m. hundred dollar bill

4. Explain how lowering the reserve requirement expands the money supply.

5. Explain how raising interest rates tightens the money supply.
6. Explain how buying and selling U.S. bonds (by the Fed) expands and tightens the money supply.
7. Explain the deposit multiplier, assuming a new primary deposit is made.
8. Why is inflation a public enemy?
9. How does the Fed attempt to accomplish economic stabilization?

CASE PROBLEMS AND ACTIVITIES

1. Your friend William has a gold watch, Jane has a collection of comic books, and Midori has an electric guitar. They all want new scuba gear. Explain to them the concept of commodity money.
2. Divide the class into groups. Within each group, find out how much (percentage) money owned is in the form of (a) cash (coin and currency), (b) demand deposits, and (c) credit and other cash substitutes.
3. Who is the current chairman of the Federal Reserve System? Which president appointed the chairman?
4. Using the *Statistical Abstract of the United States,* the *Survey of Current Business, The Economist, The Federal Reserve Bulletin,* or some other current economic periodical, what is the current monetary policy being implemented by the Fed?
5. A new primary deposit of $10,000 is made because of a business loan. What is the deposit multiplier (i.e., how much will the $10,000 result in totally) assuming a reserve requirement of 21 percent?
6. Is our country presently believed to be expecting a recession, expansion, slow growth, high or low inflation, high or low unemployment? Write a short report outlining economic conditions. List your sources of information.

Chapter 28

FISCAL POLICY AND ECONOMIC THEORIES

◆◆◆◆◆◆◆◆◆◆◆◆◆◆◆◆◆◆◆◆◆◆◆◆

OBJECTIVES

1. Explain the role of government in terms of the budget of the United States, the deficit, and government spending.
2. Discuss automatic and discretionary fiscal policy.
3. Describe how fiscal policy controls inflation, unemployment, and economic stability and growth.
4. Explain major macroeconomic theories.

Fiscal policy is adjusting government expenditures and taxes to stabilize the economy, provide for slow and steady growth, and overcome inflation and unemployment. The basis of fiscal policy is the federal budget, which is prepared by the president and approved by Congress.

THE ROLE OF GOVERNMENT

◆◆◆◆◆◆◆◆

Government distributes revenues to individuals and businesses.

The federal government is a large purchaser and provider of goods and services. To pay for these expenditures, the government receives revenue from taxation. Money that is received by government is distributed to individuals, businesses, subsidies, and legislative priorities through the budgeting process. When revenues fall short of expenditures, a deficit results. Government spending is a major component of American output (GNP) and is the basis of economic theories.

THE BUDGET OF THE UNITED STATES

Almost all government expenditures require approval through the budgeting process before the *line items* (specific budget requests, such as an education grant or a highway project) can be legally contracted for purchase. The federal government budgets on a **fiscal year** — an accounting period of 12 months — which begins October 1 and ends September 30 of the next year. The steps in the budgeting process are as follows:

1. Various agencies compile spending requests. Spending requests are made, based on previously authorized programs or suggestions made by administrators, the president, or others. These requests are compiled in February, one year prior to the year in which the fiscal year will begin.

2. The president compiles the agency requests. The requests are modified by the president's Office of Management and Budget (OMB) to fit the direction the president may choose. This process lasts until fall of the year before the budget year.

3. The president proposes the budget to Congress. The budget is printed and available by January 15 of the year in which the fiscal year will start. Copies are available in libraries; newspapers and business periodicals analyze and report the major highlights of the budget.

4. The House and Senate work on the budget and approve it. Various legislative and appropriation (budget) committees hold hearings, consider new spending ideas, and add modifications to the budget. The Ways and Means Committee (in the House) and the Senate Finance Committee report the budgetary impacts of these committees' decisions to the Budget Committee by May 15. The Budget Committee sends its *first budget resolution*, which sets tentative revenue and expenditure targets. The Budget Committee bases recommendations on reports based on the current service estimate and political considerations. The **current service estimate** is the expenditure required to meet the ongoing and previously authorized programs for the fiscal year in question without any change in service level except for legislation already on the books. By May 15, both houses are supposed to pass the first budget resolution and resolve differences. Debate and compromise follow, and by

The budgeting process begins over a year before the actual fiscal year.

The Budget Committee prepares the budget resolutions that list projected spending and revenues.

September 25, both houses are expected to pass a second budget resolution.

5. The president can modify the budget as approved. While the president cannot change expenditures authorized by resolution, the president can veto bills that authorize tax changes or new spending programs.

The budget provides information about the spending programs proposed by the budget; this *unified budget* is on a cash basis — without concern for whether the outlays match up with income. In addition, the government prints a special analysis of the budget document, printed as a companion to the unified budget document. The February issue of the *Survey of Current Business* also contains an analysis of the proposed budget.

The budget of the United States is a thick document.

THE DEFICIT

A **deficit** occurs when expenditures by government are greater than total revenues collected by the government. As a result, the budget must be balanced by borrowing and/or creating money (monetizing the debt). A budget deficit adds to the *national debt* (amount owed by the government). Each year's deficit adds to that debt.

Ownership of the federal debt is constantly changing.

1. Who owns the national debt? Each year the government must pay billions in interest to holders of U.S. bonds. Who owns these bonds? The Federal Reserve System owns about 10 percent, and interest it receives is returned to the Treasury. Commercial banks, private individuals, state and local governments, government agencies, pension funds, and foreign investors hold U.S. securities. Ownership of U.S. bonds is changing all the time. The *Federal Reserve Bulletin* publishes current statistics on ownership of the debt. The interest payments on the debt amount to transfers of money from taxpayers to the holders of these government securities. A large debt requires large interest payment. One kind of spending government cannot cut is interest on the government debt, which is the major problem. We are said to have "mortgaged our future" because interest on the debt will have to be paid before expenditures for social programs, legislative priorities, subsidies, transfer payments, or other needed expenditures of government.

2. What's wrong with debt? Most economists agree that the type of debt is a problem. With **productive debt**, money is spent in such a way that the debt will be paid out of the earnings from the investment (such as equipment, factories, or machinery) used to produce goods for sale. But with **consumption debt**, there is no source of funds to

The national debt is a form of consumption debt.

pay off the debt, and other sources of income must be used to pay interest and the principal. With productive debt (loans to business), the loan will be paid off because it will have purchased something that will generate income. With consumption debt (loans to government), there are no means to repay the debt.

GOVERNMENT SPENDING

All levels of government spend money.

Government's role in a market economy is not clearly defined in terms of how much government is needed, how much government should cost, and how much government is responsible for providing. Our two-party political system is in constant debate about government's role. Taxation and income distribution is the main function of government. Closely related to fiscal policy is government spending. All levels of government — federal, state, and local — spend money. They buy goods (consumer goods and capital goods), including school buildings, highways, teacher services, space shuttles, and services of the armed forces. **Government spending** consists of the purchases of domestic goods and services by all government units. Government spending has a substantial effect on the economy because of its sheer size in billions of dollars a year.

FISCAL POLICY

◆◆◆◆◆◆◆◆

There are two types of fiscal policy, or actions taken by the government, to control inflation and unemployment and to stabilize the growth of the economy: automatic fiscal policy and discretionary fiscal policy.

AUTOMATIC FISCAL POLICY

Automatic fiscal policy is effective in stabilizing the economy.

Automatic fiscal policy refers to the built-in spending programs that are already in place and act to stabilize spending power and distribute economic wealth within the economy. Some examples of built-in spending programs are revenue sharing projects; federal grants to schools, cities, counties and states; disaster relief funds; and other programs set up periodically by the legislature or president to be used during times of need. **Automatic stabilizers** are immediate benefits that prevent consumers from losing purchasing power or being unable to survive. Examples of automatic stabilizers are progressive taxes, transfer payments, and subsidies and relief programs.

Progressive Taxes.   A progressive tax system increases the tax burden as individuals and businesses earn more, thereby taxing more heavily those

Illustration 28-1
Government spending supports hundreds of projects, such as our country's space program.

who can afford it. Those who earn income below the poverty level pay no taxes and usually receive some form of payment from the government. A *negative income tax* is a government program for paying out money to people whose incomes are below a certain level — a concept often discussed, but used only in the form of transfer payments.

Transfer Payments.   A transfer payment is a one-way payment whereby nothing is received in return from the recipient. Transfer payments from the government may be in cash (social security, welfare, unemployment) or in kind (food stamps, rent subsidy). Payments "in kind" are made on behalf of the individual or allow the individual to procure certain goods and services. Transfer payments assure all citizens the ability of purchasing food, clothing, and shelter.

Transfer payments preserve the purchasing power of individuals.

Subsidies and Relief Programs.   Government often subsidizes crops and products so that farmers can compete in mature markets and where market prices would not permit reasonable profits. This type of "guarantee" protects certain groups (such as farmers) from unfair competition or allows them to produce commodities (like milk and cheese) that would not be profitable without government subsidizing. Relief programs include disaster funds, whereby money is available to individuals and businesses when certain economic events occur. An example is a low interest government loan for farmers or property owners when a drought or natural disaster is declared. These types of payments ensure stability and are ready to be accessed when needed (no act of Congress is necessary).

Disaster loans are available when governors officially declare disaster areas.

DISCRETIONARY FISCAL POLICY

Discretionary fiscal policy refers to acts of Congress and government in response to economic conditions. There are four major tools of discretionary fiscal policy: taxation, government spending, investment tax credits, and wage and price controls.

Taxation.   Through increasing or decreasing taxes, the government is able to put more or less money into the hands of the people and businesses. Raising or lowering taxes requires approval of Congress and the President of the United States.

Government Spending.   The government purchases goods and services, as well as financing legislative priorities, social programs, grants, revenue sharing, urban renewal, work projects, aid to cities, highway construction and maintenance, and many other federally funded programs. When the government spends money, people are hired, and money is spent in the economy, encouraging individuals to spend more.

Investment Tax Credits.   Government encourages businesses (producers) to`spend more money through **investment tax credit**, a tax write-off or credit for undertaking investment spending. Investment spending is the purchase of capital goods — equipment, factories, and tools of production. By giving businesses a tax incentive to invest in new plant equipment and production, the government stimulates employment and output. Those who gain new jobs also have added purchasing power, which further stimulates the economy.

Wage and Price Controls.   The government, through executive order, can control — freeze — wages and prices to slow down inflation. During the early 1970s, President Nixon imposed wage and price controls. Employers were not allowed to give raises, and retailers were not allowed to raise prices. The controls were somewhat effective in the short run. But after a few months, more and more exceptions were allowed so that many prices were rising, yet wages remained frozen. Consequently, many workers lost purchasing power. Wage and price controls, particularly freezes, are considered radical acts and are not viewed favorably by many people, especially workers.

The chief objectives of fiscal policy are to control recession and inflation. The economy is said to be in *recession* when production (output) has declined for two or more quarters (six months), when there is rising and widespread unemployment because of decreased spending and production, and when the profits of businesses and the purchasing power of consumers are diminished.

A **depression** is a severe recession where production has declined for a year or more, unemployment is above 10 percent nationally, and the economy is in a state of panic — people are afraid to buy, businesses are afraid to invest — and things come to a standstill. During the Great Depression (1929-1939) many people lost everything they had, including their homes, because they were unable to get work and pay their bills. Real national income (true purchasing power) dropped by over 50 percent.

Government spending expands the economy.

Wage and price freezes are not popular among consumers.

A depression is a serious economic condition that requires drastic action.

A recession occurs when people stop buying — when demand is greatly reduced. Because purchases are down, production is cut back and employees are dismissed. We have had a number of recessions in the past two decades. The reason none of them became a depression is that fiscal policy and monetary policy have lessened the effects and severity of each recession and brought about recovery. Figure 28-1 summarizes the purpose, basis, and tools of fiscal policy.

Most recessions are reversed by fiscal and monetary policy.

Figure 28-1
Fiscal Policy

Government controls to stimulate or shrink the economy.

Major purpose is to control recession and inflation.

Basis is the federal budget.

Balances revenues and expenses; by manipulating these, government can control or counteract the economic forces.

Automatic fiscal policy:

Progressive taxes

Transfer payments (unemployment, social security, welfare payments)

Subsidies and relief programs

Discretionary fiscal policy:

Taxation (increase or decrease)

Government spending

Investment credits

Wage and price controls

IMPACT OF FISCAL POLICY

Fiscal policy is enacted through government and serves to control inflation and unemployment, and to provide economic stability. Because fiscal policy operates through government, a time lag diminishes its effects. The fiscal policy *time lag* is the period of time between the need for fiscal policy action and when the results of that action are felt. For example, it is determined that high unemployment requires a tax cut. The tax cut is proposed by the president and discussed in Congress, hearings and recommendations are made, a compromise is drawn, and the president signs the bill. Then several months later, the bill takes effect. A tax cut proposed in January may not actually be seen in paychecks until the following January. The time lag reduces the effectiveness of fiscal policy.

Fiscal policy is accompanied by a time lag because of the time required for an act of Congress.

■■■■   CONTROLLING INFLATION   ■■■■

Fiscal policy actions to reduce inflation might include increasing taxes (to reduce spending), cutting government spending, or wage and price controls. Consumers prefer to cut government spending rather than increase taxes. Politics becomes an issue of fiscal policy as well. During election years, tax increases are not likely because voters will reject the candidate and political party that proposes them.

Tax increases are not likely during national election years.

Fiscal policy is effective in controlling demand-pull inflation but more careful analysis is needed for cost-push inflation. The theory of **rational expectations** provides that when consumers and businesses expect the government to enact some program to control inflation (and with fiscal policy there's plenty of warning — a year or more), they take action to protect themselves. In other words, they maximize their own positions in light of the "rationally expected" effects of government policy. Because people rationally expect to be harmed if they respond to government policy, they do not do what the government wants and expects them to do. For example, if a tax cut is announced, consumers rationally expect that the government wants and expects them to spend the extra money. Under this theory, consumers intentionally do not spend the extra money in ways that will help the economy.

People expecting certain fiscal policy actions will not respond as predicted.

■■■■   CONTROLLING UNEMPLOYMENT   ■■■■

Unemployment and recessions occur as the economy slows down. Economic indicators reveal trends and project economic events. Automatic fiscal policy lessens the effects of unemployment and recession but usually is not enough to change it. If we are willing to take enough fiscal policy action — cutting taxes, increasing government spending, hiring people on government projects, buying up surplus outputs, and so on — we are certain to overcome a recession. But each time we take such action, we risk the danger of *overkill* — if we stimulate the economy too much, it will lead to inflation. Or if we cut inflation too much (slow down the economy), it can lead to unemployment and recession.

Slowing the economy too much (reducing inflation) can lead to higher unemployment.

Therefore, when some serious economic problem exists, fiscal policy is often called upon for the remedy. When fiscal policy to slow the economy is too strong, it can choke off economic expansion too soon. This is called **fiscal drag** — to bring expansion to a halt rather than just slow it down. Then the opposite fiscal policy is needed to eliminate the fiscal drag and expand the economy again. To control unemployment and recession, massive spending programs are used. The effect of massive spending programs is to unbalance the federal budget on purpose! In other words, such a program will increase the budget deficit and increase the national debt in order to get things moving again — with the hope that added revenues will generate enough added taxes to offset the deficit.

ECONOMIC STABILITY AND GROWTH

Discretionary fiscal policy is rarely used to fine tune the economy. To maintain just the right level of spending, employment, output, and income, fiscal policy attempts to adjust its automatic stabilizers to be certain that all citizens are protected. Once again, fiscal policy involves a time lag that reduces its effectiveness because people can anticipate and preplan. For example, if the progressive tax structure is altered to eliminate some tax deductions for the wealthy, they find other ways to hide the income.

> People look for ways to escape from automatic fiscal policy.

Expectations play an important role in macroeconomic policy. The *self-fulfilling prophecy* provides that whatever people expect to happen will happen because their expectations will *cause* it to happen. Presidents give speeches to influence the mood of the nation because they know that a healthy economy (spending and income stream) depends on optimism and positive expectations. Fiscal policy is ineffective without people's confidence; building optimism is a subtle part of fiscal policy.

ECONOMIC THEORIES
♦♦♦♦♦♦♦♦

Use of monetary or fiscal policy, or some combination, is based upon economic theory. In this section, the economic theories that are the basis for economic policies and decisions are introduced.

ADAM SMITH — CLASSICAL ECONOMICS

Known as the "Father of Economics," Adam Smith (1723-1790) wrote his book *Wealth of Nations* in 1776. His key line is said to be that "self-interest as a motive is the propelling force within a market economy." His book marks the beginning of modern economics.

> Adam Smith founded "classical" economics.

Smith believed that competition causes efficiency in production. Those who are not productive are eliminated (survival of the fittest). He concluded that a competitive price system is in the best interests of the economy; that individuals and producers seeking to further their own self- interests will be guided by an *invisible hand* to promote public and social interest. The invisible hand is free competition — absence of government influence and control. This theory is often called the *classical theory of economics*.

Smith is the original conservative of economics. Followers of Smith believe that the economy will self-regulate and needs no interference from government. Followers of Adam Smith advocate reduced government, growth through private investment (business), and use of monetary policy (higher interest rates) to reduce spending and inflation.

JOHN MAYNARD KEYNES — GOVERNMENT HAS RESPONSIBILITY

Keynes believed in the need for fiscal policy.

An English economist, John Keynes (1883-1946) believed fiscal policy is necessary to balance the economy. A writer and economist, Keynes lived in Cambridge and published his book *Treatise on Money* in 1930. He disputed Adam Smith's model of classical economics and asserted that fiscal policy is needed to assure full employment; that the marketplace needs government control.

Keynes believed that the market system would find its equilibrium with as many workers employed as possible. He attacked monetary policy, saying money supply was an artificial stimulation that would only cause more inflation and more unemployment. In 1936, Keynes introduced a new explanation for the level of employment in capitalistic countries. **Demand-side economics** is concerned with total spending (aggregate demand) in the economy, and how government actions can adjust this spending flow to achieve full employment and stable prices. Keynes believed that pure competition does not contain the mechanisms capable of guaranteeing full employment. Capitalism cannot be depended on to run itself; unemployment and inflation result when saving and investment are too low. The answer, according to Keynes, is fiscal policy — the role of government to get the economy stimulated and growing with full employment.

Demand-side economics relies on government actions to adjust the spending flow.

JOHN KENNETH GALBRAITH — USE GOVERNMENT SPARINGLY

Stagflation occurred between 1980 and 1982 — high inflation and high unemployment.

John Galbraith (1908-) is an economist, educator, author, political activist, and diplomat. Born in Canada, he became a U.S. citizen in 1937. Galbraith supports the use of government interventions with moderation. He argues that **stagflation** — rapid inflation and high rates of unemployment at the same time — should not occur in a market economy. In *The Affluent Society* (1958), Galbraith wrote that the American economy needs more public goods and services such as highways and education. Galbraith advocates fiscal policy such as wage and price controls to eliminate stagflation, but less government intervention in the natural wheels that turn the economy.

MILTON FRIEDMAN — A MONETARIST

Milton Friedman (1912-) was born in New York City and received a Ph.D. from Columbia University. He taught economics at the University of Chicago from 1946 to 1977. A monetarist who fears the ever-increasing power of government, Mr. Friedman is also known as a "free enterprise economist" and believes that a free market economy will adjust itself if left alone. Friedman argues against government intervention. According to Friedman, only monetary policy can speed up the economy or slow it down. By controlling the money supply, people will buy less or more. According to Friedman, "only people learn" — government does not learn from its mistakes. Therefore, we need less government.

Friedman believes in monetary policy because government does not learn from its mistakes.

SUPPLY-SIDE ECONOMICS — REAGANOMICS

The basic idea of **supply-side economics** is this: to slow inflation and unemployment, we need more output — more *supply* of products in the marketplace. To increase the total (aggregate) supply, we can increase worker productivity and increase business investment in capital goods and services. Supply-side economics proposes tax cuts to stimulate productivity. If businesses then decide to invest in high technology equipment, worker productivity will increase. This increased productivity will provide more output (supply) and reduce inflation. Unfortunately, when taxes are cut, a government deficit results. To finance the debt, supply-side economics says that productivity will increase output so much that there will be increased total tax revenues.

Supply-side economics relies on increased worker productivity and investment spending.

The *Laffer Curve* illustrates the basic idea that as tax rates go up, productivity is discouraged, and vice versa. So, according to Arthur Laffer, at some point, a tax rate increase will reduce productivity so much that it will result in a tax revenue decrease. When tax rates are high, how do we get more revenue and increase productivity? Cut taxes. Figure 28-2 shows the Laffer Curve.

The Laffer Curve illustrates the relationship between tax rates and tax revenues.

As tax rates increase (moving up the Y axis), government revenues increase. But as tax rates keep going up, revenues go up less and less (point b) until a maximum point is reached (point c), after which tax revenues decline (point d). There aren't any numbers on the axes because nobody knows where they should be. President Reagan adopted supply-side economics and the Laffer Curve as his basic economic platform, and the term *Reaganomics* was born.

Ronald Reagan's supply-side economics became known as Reaganomics.

Which economic theories are right? The answer is the ones that work. Unfortunately, all of them work some of the time. Economists have argued

Figure 28-2
The Laffer Curve

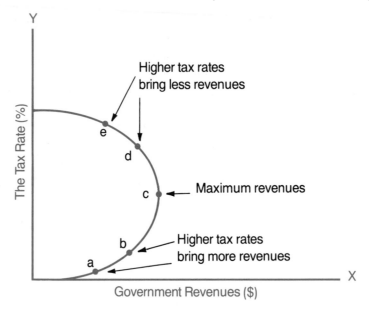

the virtues and weaknesses of all economic theories ever since the theories were proposed. It is each citizen's right and responsibility to make economic decisions based on his or her choice of economic theories and policies.

VOCABULARY

Directions: Can you find the definition for each of the following terms used in Chapter 28?

fiscal policy	discretionary fiscal policy
fiscal year	investment tax credit
current service estimate	depression
deficit	rational expectations
productive debt	fiscal drag
consumption debt	demand-side economics
government spending	stagflation
automatic fiscal policy	supply-side economics
automatic stabilizers	

1. An economic theory based on aggregate supply increasing worker productivity to stimulate growth.
2. The theory that provides that when consumers and businesses expect some fiscal policy, they take action to protect themselves.
3. Adjusting government spending and taxes to stabilize the economy and overcome inflation and unemployment.
4. Debt where money is spent so that the debt will be paid from earnings of that investment.

5. Immediate benefits, already in place, to prevent consumers from losing purchasing power.
6. Acts of Congress and government in response to economic conditions.
7. A tax write-off or credit to encourage businesses to increase investment spending.
8. Bringing an expansion to a halt rather than slowing it down because fiscal policy is too strong.
9. Rising inflation together with high rates of unemployment occurring at the same time.
10. A federal government accounting period that begins October 1 and lasts 12 months.
11. The expenditure required to meet ongoing and previously authorized programs by Congress.
12. A condition whereby expenditures by government are greater than revenues collected by government.
13. Debt generated where there is no source of funds to pay the debt.
14. Purchases by government of domestic goods and services.
15. Built-in spending programs already in place that act to stabilize spending power and distribute wealth.
16. A severe recession whereby production has declined for a year or more, unemployment is very high, and the economy is in a state of panic.
17. An economic theory concerned with aggregate demand and how government actions stabilize the economy.

ITEMS FOR DISCUSSION

1. What is the basis of fiscal policy? Explain how the government is involved in the budgeting process.
2. What is the fiscal year of the U.S. government?
3. In what publication can you find an analysis of the proposed budget of the United States?
4. Who prepares the budget of the United States?
5. Who owns the national debt?
6. What are three examples of automatic stabilizers? Define each.
7. What are four tools of discretionary fiscal policy? Describe each.
8. How is a recession different from a depression?
9. Explain how automatic and discretionary fiscal policies operate to prevent a depression.
10. What is the effect of a fiscal time lag?
11. Who is the "Father of Economics?"
12. Who first introduced the concept of "demand-side economics?"

13. Explain the following theories of classical economics, demand-side economics, supply-side economics, and Reaganomics.

APPLICATIONS

1. Explain the U.S. budgeting procedure.
2. Explain how productive debt is different from consumption debt.
3. How does a progressive tax system operate as an automatic stabilizer?
4. Explain how an investment tax credit stimulates economic growth.
5. Why do people dislike wage and price controls?
6. What can be done (using fiscal policy) to (a) bring down inflation, and (b) to bring down unemployment?
7. How does politics enter into fiscal policy?
8. How can the president assist fiscal policy in the area of expectations? Listen to a speech given by the president and list topics covered that influence the mood of the nation.
9. What is the invisible hand described by Adam Smith? Explain how it works in a market economy.
10. Explain how supply-side economics is different from demand-side economics. Which do you prefer? Why?

CASE PROBLEMS AND ACTIVITIES

1. Draw the Laffer Curve and explain the economic theory behind it.
2. From a current issue of the *Federal Reserve Bulletin*, find out who owns the national debt and what percentage is owned by each group or type of investor (such as individuals, businesses, banks, and foreign investors).
3. In the last year or two, what types of emergency loans, subsidies, disaster relief programs, and other forms of government programs have been used in this country? (Hint: Use the *Guide to Business Periodicals* and also look under economics.)
4. Economists, the president, the Fed, and Congress are often slow to act and very cautious when implementing action to slow down or speed up the economy. Explain their fear of overkill.
5. Your friend does not understand why a president or Congress would choose fiscal policy or monetary policy to stabilize (fine tune) the economy. Explain to your friend each of the following theories that are often used as the basis of such decisions:

   a. classical economics   c. stagflation
   b. demand-side economics   d. monetarist
      (Keynesian)   e. supply-side economics

THE WORLD ECONOMY

UNIT OBJECTIVES

After studying the chapters in this eighth unit that discuss world economic problems and theory, the student will be able to:

1. ■ Discuss world economic conditions and theories, including reasons for international trade, measurement of trade, process of international trade, and problems of international trade.

2. ■ Discuss world economic problems including progress, pollution, population, urbanization, poverty, and discrimination.

Chapter 29

INTERNATIONAL ECONOMICS

◆◆◆◆◆◆◆◆◆◆◆◆◆◆◆◆◆◆◆◆◆◆◆◆◆

OBJECTIVES

1. Explain why international trade is economically sound.
2. Explain how international economics is measured.
3. Describe the process of international trade, including the exchange rate and the international monetary system.
4. Discuss problems created by international trade, including competitiveness and productivity, national defense, protectionism, and trade restrictions.

International economics is the study of economics in the world economy. It attempts to explain why and how trade takes place between nations. The answer to the why question is often called the *theory of international trade*, while the answer to the how question is often called *international trade finance*. We will cover the why first and then the how, and conclude with problems of international trade.

REASONS FOR INTERNATIONAL TRADE
◆◆◆◆◆◆◆◆

We are said to be moving toward a "world economy" where there is a free flow of goods and services among nations to conserve worldwide resources and meet as many wants and needs as possible. Economically speaking, there are three main reasons for international trade: comparative advantage, absolute advantage, and mass production.

COMPARATIVE ADVANTAGE

Comparative advantage applies to nations as well as local regions.

The primary reason why nations trade is explained by the concept of *comparative advantage* — the principle that the greatest gain in total output will occur if each society specializes in producing those goods and services that can be produced with greatest efficiency and buys (imports) goods that could be produced only at great cost.

ABSOLUTE ADVANTAGE

Climate, land, and people are the deciding factors in absolute advantage.

Another reason for international trade is the concept of **absolute advantage**. This concept states that nations produce and trade the products in which they are naturally superior (more productive) than other nations due to climate, availability of natural resources, or innate ability of its people. Absolute advantage explains why the U.S. imports coffee, cocoa, tea, coconuts, bananas, and other commodities that either cannot be produced here or can be produced only at great expense. In contrast, nations that do produce coffee, for example, are able to do so with little effort and expense. The climate, land, and people are able to produce coffee beans so efficiently that it is an absolute advantage for them to do so. For the U.S. to produce coffee, the comparison might look like Figure 29-1.

Figure 29-1
Absolute Advantage

PRODUCT	COUNTRY	WORKHOURS TO PRODUCE
Coffee	Brazil	1.5 hours/ton
	USA	30.5 hours/ton
Potatoes	Brazil	15 hours/ton
	USA	30 minutes/ton

Illustration 29-1
The absolute ad-
vantage concept
states that nations
produce and trade
the goods in which
they are naturally
superior.

In 1817, David Ricardo (1772-1823), a 19th century economist, stock broker, and millionaire, became well known for his *labor theory of value,* which held that the value of a commodity is determined by the amount of labor needed in its production. He was a strong proponent of economic freedom through free trade and competition. His theory of *productivity ratios* is shown in Figure 29-2. Keep in mind, the year is 1817. The concept behind Ricardo's productivity ratios still applies today, however. Ricardo listed items produced in those days and compared the time spent in the production of each. From his analysis, we can see that in the mid-1800s, America would have been wise to produce and export food and cotton but import clothing and machine parts. Productivity ratios clearly show the mutual profitability of countries being *interdependent* — producing and exporting some goods while importing others.

Productivity ratios are the basis of absolute advantage today.

Figure 29-2
Labor Theory of Value (Productivity Ratios)

PRODUCT	IN AMERICA	IN EUROPE
1 bushel of corn	1 day labor	3 days labor
1 cotton dress	2 days labor	1 day labor
1 piece of equipment used in production of silk	8 days labor	2 days labor
1 cotton bale ready for processing	1 day labor	3 days labor

MASS PRODUCTION

A third reason for international trade is mass production. **Mass production** is the use of machinery and capital goods to make mass quantities of goods available for consumption. Because of advanced technology and capital equipment, costs decrease as output expands. Equipment set to produce a commodity, such as silicon chips, at its optimum production will produce the cheapest product. Let's say that a factory can produce 800 expansion cards per day. If all it produces is 500, the cost per card is higher because fixed costs must be spread over fewer units. See Figure 29-3.

Mass production makes it easy to export products.

Figure 29-3
Unit Cost Comparison

| | COSTS OF PRODUCTION | | PER DAY | PER UNIT |
TOTAL OUTPUT	Wages	Raw Materials	TOTAL COST	COST
800	$80/day	$5/unit	$4,080	$5.10
500	$80/day	$5/unit	2,580	5.16

Fixed costs of production remain constant regardless of production. Rent, salaries, taxes, depreciation, and insurance are usually fixed costs in the short run. In other words, regardless of how many units produced, the rent is the same. **Variable costs of production** go up and down in direct proportion to production. For each unit produced, raw materials that go into the product are used. If units are not produced, materials are not used. Therefore, as you produce more, your costs go up in direct proportion.

In addition to fixed and variable costs, there are some **semi-variable** (or semi-fixed) **costs of production**; part of the cost is fixed and part is variable. Repair and maintenance, janitorial costs, and utilities are examples. A set amount is required regardless of how much is produced; as production goes up beyond that point, costs increase in proportion to production. The following graph, Figure 29-4, illustrates fixed, variable, and semi-variable costs.

Costs are fixed, variable, or semi-variable.

Figure 29-4
Costs of Production

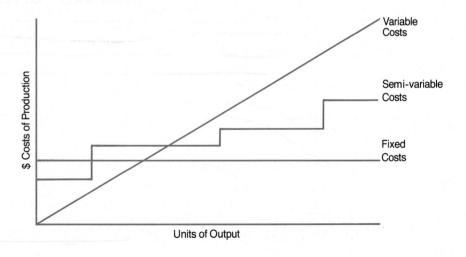

$ Costs of Production

Variable Costs

Semi-variable Costs

Fixed Costs

Units of Output

Large countries, such as the United States or the Soviet Union, with diversified resources, favorable climate, and adequate labor force, are less dependent upon international trade than small nations. Nevertheless, large countries fare better economically — that is, they conserve scarce resources more efficiently — with international trade than without it. Every country depends on international trade to supply some of its material goods and to sell some of its raw materials or manufactured products. All countries must make two important decisions — which products to produce for export, considering comparative advantage, absolute advantage, and mass production — and which products to import.

Scarce resources are conserved through world specialization and trade.

MEASUREMENTS IN INTERNATIONAL ECONOMICS

◆◆◆◆◆◆◆◆

Economic integration is the elimination of restrictions to the flows of products and factors of production between nations. The benefits can be great because the combined production possibilities of two countries is far greater than one alone. The newly integrated economic unit, however, may run into costs of interdependence created by free trade. In this section, we will learn the effects of world trade in terms of dollars spent and received, through the balances of trade and payments.

Economic integration also creates problems and costs.

BALANCE OF TRADE

In terms of volume, a country's most important foreign economic transactions are **importing** — the purchasing of commodities from foreign countries — and **exporting** — the selling of commodities to foreign countries. The difference between a country's exports and imports is usually called the **balance of trade**. If exports are larger than imports, the country has a *trade surplus* and is in a favorable economic position. When imports are larger than exports, the country has a *trade deficit*, which is an unfavorable economic position.

A trade deficit is harmful when it continues very long.

BALANCE OF PAYMENTS

The balance of trade constitutes a portion of the country's total international economic transactions. These transactions also include the sale of services, securities (stocks and bonds), spending by tourists, foreign aid, investment in plants and equipment by corporations, and transactions among consumers of one country and businesses of another. All these transactions are entered

Foreign spending by all citizens is important.

into a country's **balance of payments**, which is a listing of all foreign transactions among a country's residents and the rest of the world. A surplus in the balance of payments exists when there is a larger inflow of money into the country as compared to the outflow of money. A deficit in the balance of payments results from a larger outflow of money as compared to the inflow of money.

A country can have a surplus in its balance of trade and show a deficit in the balance of payments. In 1970 and 1975 the U.S. showed a positive trade balance; but by 1980, the balance was negative. When the *net flows* (export minus import payments) are added together, we obtain the **current account balance**. The current account balance is maintained each year, with monthly tabulations of monies spent and received that reveal deficit or surplus status. From the monthly and yearly balances, economists are able to make projections and analyze trends.

The current account balance is a barometer gauge for policies and decisions.

In 1980, although we had a negative balance of trade, the current account balance was positive. Unfortunately, in 1988 the current account balance reached nearly $40 billion (negative). Balance of payments and the current account balance help policymakers consider all money flows into and out of a country.

THE PROCESS OF INTERNATIONAL TRADE

◆◆◆◆◆◆◆◆

America has been involved with trade since her beginning.

International trade began with Columbus's arrival in 1492 and his discovery of plants and foods to help feed Europe — corn, sweet potatoes, peppers, allspice, plantains, and pineapples. In 1608, the first usable shipment of American goods was sent to Europe — a cargo of pitch, tar, soap, and glass. America continued to trade throughout the Industrial Revolution, and was a leading exporter of manufactured goods (clothing, leather goods, wool, and cotton) through the 1800s and into the 1900s.

International trade has become an important part of our economy, and the world economy. International trade finance is based on the exchange rate and the international monetary system.

THE EXCHANGE RATE

The exchange rate measures the value of currency in world markets.

The value (price) of a country's currency in terms of other currencies is referred to as the **exchange rate**. The rate is determined by the supply and demand for a particular currency. The *supply* of a currency is determined by the outflow of money from a country (imports) and the *demand* for the currency by other countries (exports). Therefore, if a country has a persistent deficit in its balance of payments (the outflow of money is larger than the inflow of money), its currency exchange rate will decline. This is what is meant by a "weak dollar" as opposed to a "strong dollar." With a weak dollar, the value of currency (in terms of other currencies) will decline, thereby causing that country's imports to be more expensive for its residents and its exports to be cheaper for its trading partners. Over a period of time, a weak dollar will stimulate exports and curtail imports, thereby improving a deficit in the balance of payments.

A strong dollar reduces exports.

■ INTERNATIONAL MONETARY SYSTEM ■

The determination of exchange rates is important because the exchange rate determines a country's trading position with the rest of the world. The purpose of the international monetary system is to set exchange rates.

Following World War II, there were *fixed exchange rates*, usually referred to as the Bretton Woods System or the Gold Exchange System. This system had exchange rates fixed to the dollar, and the dollar had a fixed value in terms of gold. Exchange rates were changed by international agreement only when balance of payment problems arose. However, as the U.S. balance of payments position worsened over the years, other countries had to absorb excess dollars to maintain the exchange rate.

Fixed exchange rates failed because of the U.S. balance of payments deficit.

In 1971 the U.S. discontinued its dollars-for-gold policy. This decision and the continuing deficit in U.S. balance of payments resulted in the collapse of the Bretton Woods System in 1973. Today, a *mixed system of flexible and fixed exchange rates* dominates the world. Under this system, the forces of the market — supply and demand — determine the relationship between currencies. There is little interference to guarantee stability in foreign exchange rates. Figure 29-5 shows foreign exchange rates that were in effect in August, 1988.

Figure 29-5
Major Foreign
Exchange Rates

Currency Name	Foreign Currency in U.S. Dollars	U.S. Dollar in Foreign Currency
Australia (dollar)	.8055	1.2430
Britain (pound)	1.7125	.5845
Canada (dollar)	.8316	1.2070
France (franc)	.1581	6.3150
Greece (drachma)	.0066	150.2000
Hong Kong (dollar)	.1281	7.8056
Israel (shekel)	.6160	1.6367
Italy (lira)	.000723	1382.2500
Japan (yen)	.007536	132.9500
Mexico (peso)^z	.000437	2290.0000
West Germany (mark)	.5336	1.8737

^{z}floating rate

International monetary relations between nations are monitored by the **International Monetary Fund** (IMF), which was established after World War II by the free nations of the world. Today the IMF helps nations correct balance of payment problems without interfering with the flow of trade. This correction is done by extending credit to deficit countries and forcing surplus countries to bear some of the burdens of adjustment.

The IMF seeks to prevent interruption of trade flows.

PROBLEMS OF INTERNATIONAL TRADE

Most economists agree — free trade benefits all people of the world because scarce resources worldwide are conserved and allocated wisely. Nevertheless, there are numerous arguments for restrictions of trade and controls in international economics. In a world economy, we are all in this together, and we are all responsible for our actions and decisions. But will everyone act as responsible citizens? Will fairness be observed? Will weaker members be given opportunities to survive? In this section, we will examine the reasons and consequences of imposing trade restrictions and controlling international trade.

Free trade depends on everyone's doing his or her part.

COMPETITIVENESS AND PRODUCTIVITY

The U.S. trade deficit has brought about a need for *economic competitiveness* — being able to produce a quality product at the lowest possible price so that products can compete globally. Because wage levels and the cost of living are higher in the United States, prices for finished goods are usually higher. But higher prices means that our products are not salable. Countries that can produce products cheaper get the sale. How can the U.S. increase its economic competitiveness and still maintain its standard of living? Economists point to the need for increased *productivity* — more output per unit of input. Because of the high cost of labor (wages) in the United States, increasing productivity (output) is difficult to achieve. While manufacturing productivity is increasing (3.5 percent in 1988), our competitors have increased productivity as well, and real cost inflation wipes out our gains.

Productivity is usually blamed for lack of competitiveness.

Results of declining productivity are widespread. American manufacturers are not only losing the export battle in foreign markets (goods too expensive to sell overseas), they are also losing shares in the **domestic market** — purchases of goods and services by American consumers. Almost 30 percent of all new cars sold in the U.S. are imports (compared to 15 percent in 1970); jewelry, 48 percent (compared to 4 percent in 1970); TV sets, 62

Americans are buying more foreign goods in the U.S.

percent (up from 35 percent); and household furniture, 18 percent (up from 3 percent in 1970). In all arenas, American manufacturers are losing their share of the domestic market, and with it, millions of jobs for Americans.

NATIONAL DEFENSE

During periods of war and conflict, international trade is severely interrupted. It is possible for a country to be cut off from strategic supplies. For example, a country that depends on another to supply its weapons parts would be politically unable to take actions that might result in disrupting the supply of that product. If a country were to hurt trade relations with another for some reason, that country might find its national defense at risk.

National defense may be jeopardized when nations depend on others for many products.

The United States has many allies that depend on us to enhance their economic and defense needs. Without our military bases and foreign aid, their national defense and economic stability would be weakened. Likewise, the U.S. is dependent on others through free trade. We import much of the oil that is consumed. If one of our major suppliers of oil (such as Saudi Arabia) were unable or unwilling to supply that oil, our national defense could be at risk.

PROTECTIONISM

Protectionism is an obstacle to free trade. An example of protectionism is the infant industry argument. An **infant industry** is a beginning or young industry that cannot compete against already-established corporate giants that could easily underprice and run it out of business. The infant industry argument contends that if an industry is protected in its early years of development, when it is unable to compete on the world market, it will be saved in the long term because the production experience it gains will ultimately make it competitive in the world market. The argument also contends that unless an industry is protected against world competition long enough to get established, the country will never know whether it has a comparative advantage in that product. Opponents of protectionism argue that imposing such restrictions only aggravates the trade deficit problem by boosting prices of imports and triggering trade wars — measures of retaliation by foreign competitors.

Protectionism seeks to give infant industries a chance to survive.

TRADE RESTRICTIONS

There are several ways to restrict or control trade and international economics. By restricting trade, a country can correct a deficit in its balance of payments. It could impose a **tariff**, which is a tax or "duty" assessed against imported products, which thereby increases the price of imported products. Unfortunately, when one country imposes tariffs against another country's products, the second country is likely to retaliate and institute tariffs as well, thus negating many of the effects.

A country could also set a **trade quota**, which is a physical restriction on the number of units of a particular product allowed to enter the country. Once again, the affected country could install retaliatory quotas and undermine the effects.

A more severe restriction is a **trade embargo**, whereby government prohibits the sale or trade of goods for foreign money or goods. The U.S. has used trade embargoes in the past (such as the Russian grain embargo in December, 1979) to punish countries for unacceptable or unhumanitarian acts. President Carter issued the embargo to punish Russia for invading Afghanistan. (In addition, the U.S. boycotted the 1980 Moscow Olympics as a protest.) Failure of domestic companies to comply with an embargo can result in a fine, imprisonment in a federal prison, or both.

The world community, through cooperation under the General Agreement of Tariffs and Trade (GATT), generally discourages and reduces trade restrictions. Countries with balance of payments deficits are encouraged to find alternative policies.

A tariff is a method of reducing trade.

An embargo is a severe restriction of trade.

VOCABULARY

Directions: Can you find the definition for each of the following terms used in Chapter 29?

absolute advantage	balance of payments
mass production	current account balance
fixed costs of production	exchange rate
variable costs of production	International Monetary Fund
semi-variable costs of produc-	(IMF)
tion	domestic market
economic integration	infant industry
importing	tariff
exporting	trade quota
balance of trade	trade embargo

1. Use of machinery and capital equipment to make large quantities of goods available for consumption.
2. Costs that go up or down in direct proportion to production.
3. Costs that are partially fixed and partially variable.
4. Purchasing of commodities from foreign countries.
5. The difference between a country's exports and a country's imports.
6. The value of a country's currency in terms of other currencies.

7. Purchases by American consumers.
8. A tax or duty assessed against imported goods that serves to increase the price of imported goods.
9. The theory that nations should trade products (produce) in which they are superior to other nations.
10. Costs that remain constant regardless of production, such as rent and salaries.
11. The elimination of restrictions to the flows of products and factors of production among nations.
12. The selling of commodities to foreign countries.
13. A listing of all foreign transactions among a country's citizens and the rest of the world.
14. The figure obtained when net cash flows (export minus import payments) are added together.
15. An organization established to monitor international monetary relations between nations.
16. A young industry that cannot compete against already-established corporate giants.
17. A physical restriction on the number of units of a particular product allowed to enter a country.
18. A government-enforced prohibition of international trade.

ITEMS FOR DISCUSSION

1. What is comparative advantage?
2. Give an example of a fixed cost of production. A variable cost. A semi-variable cost.
3. Are small countries or large countries more dependent on international trade?
4. What is a trade surplus? A trade deficit?
5. What effect do trade deficits have on jobs in this country?
6. How is balance of payments different from balance of trade?
7. Is our current account balance positive or negative?
8. When did our country begin the process of international trade?
9. How is the supply of currency determined? Demand of currency?
10. What is meant by a "weak dollar?"
11. What is the purpose of the IMF?
12. What is economic competitiveness?
13. What is productivity?
14. What effect do tariffs and trade quotas have on prices of imported goods?
15. What is GATT?

APPLICATIONS

1. List and explain three reasons why nations trade with other nations.
2. Explain the concept of *productivity ratios*.
3. Explain how fixed costs result in increased cost per unit when production is below capacity.
4. Why is a trade deficit a negative consequence of international trade?
5. What are the effects of a balance of payments deficit?
6. International trade finance is based on what two major components?
7. How is the exchange rate determined?
8. List and explain three reasons why free trade does not work well in today's world economy.
9. How does the national debt affect productivity (capital investment)?
10. Explain how infant industries are protected by trade restrictions (protectionism).
11. What can happen when a tariff or trade quota is imposed by one country against the products of another country?

CASE PROBLEMS AND ACTIVITIES

1. List products that the United States has absolute advantage in producing for export. List products that the United States should import because they would be too expensive to produce.
2. What is the current U.S. balance of trade (dollar amount, favorable or unfavorable)? What is the current U.S. current account balance (dollar amount, favorable or unfavorable)?
3. Using Figure 29-5, compute the following: You have $500 to spend on a trip. You convert your dollars to foreign currency when entering a foreign country. How much money would you have in (a) pounds, (b) francs, (c) liras, (d) Canadian dollars, and (e) Mexican pesos?
4. Find an article in a current periodical (*BusinessWeek, Time, Fortune, The Economist,* or others) that defends or attacks the concept of protectionism of infant industries. Summarize the argument in 200 words or less. List your source and date of information.
5. Find an article in a current periodical that discusses trade restrictions of tariffs and trade quotas between the United States and Japan. Summarize the article in 200 words or less. List your source and date of information.

Chapter 30

WORLD ECONOMIC PROBLEMS

◆◆◆◆◆◆◆◆◆◆◆◆◆◆◆◆◆◆◆◆◆◆◆◆◆◆

OBJECTIVES

1. Discuss the benefits, costs, and problems that result from progress.
2. Define types of pollution and describe methods of controlling and cleaning up pollution from the environment.
3. Explain the world population problem and population trends and discuss proposed solutions.
4. Discuss poverty, causes of poverty, and steps in overcoming poverty.

PROGRESS
◆◆◆◆◆◆◆◆

Progress is moving forward to a higher, better, and more advanced stage. Since around 1900, progress has moved us from an agricultural society to an information society. Notable inventions and discoveries of the last hundred years or so have included electricity, automobiles, airplanes, television, penicillin, polio vaccine, transistors, microwaves, radar, computers, artificial intelligence, and laser technology. In every sector of life, from giving childbirth to maintaining national defense, we are irrevocably committed to the newest technology, techniques, and training. Progress has

Progress has added to the quality of life.

provided numerous benefits to society. Americans as well as many other citizens around the world have enjoyed the benefits of progress.

BENEFITS OF PROGRESS

Some countries have benefited more from progress than others.

Industrialized nations have benefited the most from progress. **First World nations** are those free world, industrialized countries that enjoy great economic advantage from specialization, interdependence, and free trade among economic partners. Examples are the United States, Great Britain, France, Japan, West Germany, Italy, Canada, and Australia. **Second World nations** are communist nations that enjoy relative economic growth through limited trade and interdependence. The USSR, East Germany, Yugoslavia, Red China, and Romania are examples. **Third World nations** are those underdeveloped or undeveloped nations that have received little benefit from modern medicine, conveniences, technology, or automation. Many of these nations are still in the pre-agricultural stage of economic development and are often characterized as primitive. Examples are New Guinea and remote tribal areas of South America and Africa.

Major benefits of progress are increased standards of living, longer and more productive lives, better medical care, more and better recreational facilities and choices, less physically strenuous work for most, shorter work weeks, higher quality products and more of them, and many choices in the marketplace including color, design, and features.

COSTS OF PROGRESS

Costs of progress are both monetary and social. Even though some nations have benefited more than others from progress, all must pay part of the costs. Major costs of progress include cleaning up the environment (air, water, and land), replacing and conserving remaining resources, and eliminating the poverty that has resulted from the inequitable distribution of the benefits of progress. These are *opportunity costs* because we have given up much to enjoy the rewards of progress. For example, to have modern transportation systems, we have given up land that could have been used for crops and forfeited clean air. To have more, better, and faster cars we are using up a nonrenewable resource — oil. To have products that bring income for some, we are giving up air and water quality.

Progress has its price.

Each year, American industry spends over $5 billion to reduce industrial wastes. But it isn't enough, and doesn't begin to pay for the social damages already inflicted. Many of us will pay the costs in terms of forfeited health and well being, physical discomfort, and diminished opportunities — social costs for us and for future generations. Social costs of poverty are high because poverty is self-perpetuating, difficult and time-consuming to eliminate, and because poverty results in additional social costs such as increased crime and disease.

PROBLEMS OF PROGRESS

Major problems created by progress are pollution which reduces the quality of our environment, increased population which places a strain on already scarce and diminishing resources, and rapid growth without careful planning to provide for equitable distribution of wealth and benefits to all members of society.

Blaming others does not solve the problems.

Societies have always faced problems but two points seem certain. First, it does little good to blame others for the problems — the rich people, the landowners, the labor unions, big business, or the government. We are all a part of the *ecosystem* — the world community functioning in relation to its environment. We all contribute to the problems of progress because we purchase the goods and services and enjoy the time-saving devices and luxuries, and we can all be a part of the solution. Second, there are no quick remedies. Most of the problems of progress have been building for three and four generations. Some have become a part of our lives, and it takes many years to solve them. For example, the "American love affair with the automobile" began in the 1950s and 60s when bigger and faster cars were demanded and enjoyed. The automobile became an idol as Americans became two- and three-car households. Gas economy was not important, nor was air quality — cars burned leaded gas at the rate of 10 miles per gallon. It wasn't until the gas shortages of the 1970s that we focused on smaller cars, more fuel conservation, and pollution control devices for cars.

POLLUTION
◆◆◆◆◆◆◆◆

Pollution will destroy the quality of life.

Pollution is the contamination of the environment with human-made wastes, making it impure and unclean. Pollution is an environmental crisis worldwide as the oceans fill up with chemicals and destroy a vital link in the food chain; as over 150 million tons of garbage are discarded each year; as more than 100 million tons of carbon monoxide are released into the air each year; and as other pollutants such as fluorocarbons, hydrocarbons, sulphur oxides, and nitrogen oxides add millions of tons yearly and threaten to destroy the ozone layer. The *ozone layer* is the upper atmosphere that protects us from the ultraviolet rays of the sun and keeps the temperature on the earth's surface inhabitable. The *greenhouse effect* is a term used by scientists to describe what is happening to the earth's surface as a result of destroying ("burning holes in") the ozone layer — a gradual heating of the climate and diminished protection from the sun's harmful rays.

TYPES OF POLLUTION

All pollution results from either final consumption activities or from production. If it results from final consumption activities, it is called **final pollution** because the final consumers are the ones *directly* responsible. If pollution results from production activities of manufacturers, it is called **derived pollution** because consumers are *indirectly* responsible. (The pollution is derived from the knowledge that consumers will buy the product that is being produced.)

CONTROLLING POLLUTION

All industrial activity requires some form of environmental destruction and some form of waste disposal. Environmental protection and waste disposal have become more than afterthoughts of progress. Today, environmental protection and waste disposal have become parts of every productive activity — cleaning up is a part of the job. All pollution cannot be eliminated if we are to have progress. Yet, how much pollution should be allowed? While zero pollution isn't possible, there are a number of approaches to controlling pollution: through the political process, government controls, and self-regulation.

Taking care of pollution is a part of the job.

The Political Process.   Pollution in the environment is called an **externality** because it is "external" to the market; that is, it is a by-product of production and of marketplace supply and demand. Through the political process, there are three possible ways to control pollution:

The political process provides several options to reduce pollution.

1. Businesses can be charged fees (dumping rights) for the use of the environment. The fees are used to clean up the mess created by production.
2. Businesses can be given tax incentives to clean up production processes. Then policing is necessary to ensure that it occurs.
3. Businesses can be subsidized or given direct payments to install and operate pollution control equipment.

The first two choices are said to *internalize the environmental externalities* because the cost is passed along to those who buy the product. The third choice passes along the cost to the general public. Most economists do not favor the third approach because consumers buy products for less than the true social cost, which is socially wasteful.

Government Controls.   The government, through the Environmental Protection Agency, sets standards and timelines that must be met for reducing and eliminating pollutants. When standards are not met, fines are imposed. Often businesses are granted extensions of time to "come up to standards." Sometimes standards are lowered because they are considered too costly. Many economists and environmentalists argue that government controls aren't fair. Firms that can clean up their pollution at relatively low costs are placed in the same situation as firms that must clean pollution up at high costs, thereby giving them an advantage.

Government controls are often viewed as unfair.

Self-Regulation.   Social responsibility means that all of us must redefine progress into terms of environmental quality first and output as the by-product of production and consumption. Awareness of pollutants and individual efforts of citizens, business, and government will slow down the pollution problem. Voluntary self-regulation is effective and important at all levels of production and consumption. For example, recycling tin cans reduces garbage disposal and alleviates diminishing disposal site capacity. Using waste by-products to make other products rather than dumping them preserves the quality of water. Recycling paper not only saves on garbage disposal but also allows better use of timber resources.

Self-regulation would help slow the problem of pollution.

CLEANING UP POLLUTION

The financial cost of "total clean up" of pollution isn't acceptable. Figure 30-1 illustrates the increasing cost of cleaning up wastes. The cleaner the waste becomes, the more expensive it is to clean it up.

Figure 30-1
Increasing Cost of
Cleaning Up Waste

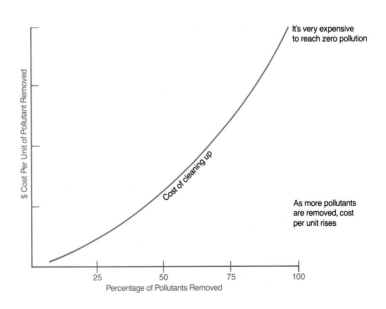

Liquid effluent is the dumping of industrial sewage into rivers and streams. There are three stages in the clean-up process. *Primary treatment* removes large particles from the sewage itself. Primary treatment is not very expensive and eliminates a lot of pollutants. *Secondary treatment* costs much more. It involves adding expensive equipment to remove fewer pollutants per dollar spent. The final stage is *final removal* of pollutants from water and land after the waste has been dumped. This is the most expensive stage and involves massive equipment, the latest technology, and time to remove offensive materials and restore the environment.

Final removal of wastes is extremely expensive.

The same stages apply to air pollution. The cleaner the discharge being omitted from factories, wood stoves/fireplaces, and automobiles becomes, the more expensive it is to clean the air even more. Like damage to water and land, sometimes air damage cannot be "undone." Once the ozone layer is destroyed, it cannot be repaired — at least not with our present technology.

The economic concept of an optimum social level of pollution (dumping pollutants into the ecosystem) is shown in Figure 30-2. **Social costs of pollution** refer to what is lost — examples include quality of life, diminished resources, reduced options for future production and enjoyment, health and comfort, and future medical problems for masses of people. **Social costs of cleaning up pollution** refer to forgone opportunities for goods and services that could have been developed or purchased with money spent instead on restoring the environment but not resulting in progress, enjoyment, or production. Society must minimize the social cost of pollution. According to this model, when the social cost of cleaning up the pollution becomes greater than the social cost of the pollution itself, then it's time to stop cleaning up.

Figure 30-2
Optimum Level of
Pollution

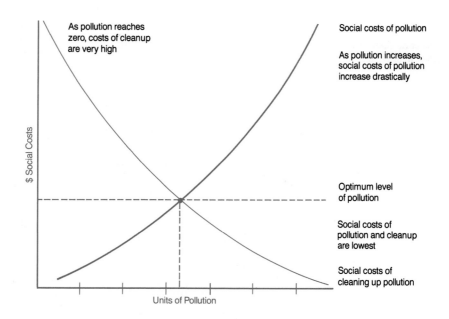

As pollution reaches zero, costs of cleanup are very high

Social costs of pollution

As pollution increases, social costs of pollution increase drastically

$ Social Costs

Optimum level of pollution

Social costs of pollution and cleanup are lowest

Social costs of cleaning up pollution

Units of Pollution

POPULATION

◆◆◆◆◆◆◆◆

Increasing population adds to the pollution problem. World population growth has slowed in recent years but still remains a threat because it is a sensitive issue not easily or quickly resolved.

Progress has not only enhanced the quality and enjoyment of life, it has also increased life expectancy for people of all ages. In 1900 there were 1.5 billion people on earth; by 1960 it was 3 billion; by the year 2000, conservative projections show it will easily reach 6 billion. In other words, three fourths of the current total population (nearly 4.5 billion) will be added this century! It has been said that of all the people who have ever been alive on earth since the beginning of time, half of them are alive today. Population trends, such as better and longer lives, are creating major concerns and adding new dimensions to world economic problems.

World population trends cause economic concerns.

POPULATION TRENDS

The masses of people are scattered worldwide. The largest country in terms of population is India, followed by China. Wherever they are, masses of people are moving to cities to find food, work, and opportunity. More than half the people in the world today are in their teens or younger. In such countries, these teens are already having more babies. In China, the number of children under ten is greater than the total population of the United States.

The United States is characterized by the "graying of America." For the first time ever, we have more people over age 40 than we have teenagers. The baby boomers born between 1948-1962 are middle aged and the young professionals are having fewer, if any, children. The U.S. population is experiencing slow but steady population growth — increasing by 6 to 7 percent every ten years. Few countries are experiencing **zero population growth**, which means that for as many babies born and immigrants entering a country, an equal number dies or leaves the country. Zero population growth has been discussed as a worldwide economic goal to preserve the quality of life for present and future generations. However, population growth is very difficult to control.

U.S. population shows a graying of America.

CONTROLLING POPULATION

Social values, ethical considerations, religious beliefs, and lack of awareness of the potentially harmful results of overpopulation are often cited as obstacles to organized efforts to control population. Three approaches to population control are cooperative action, decisive action, and political process.

Cooperative Action.   Under a system of **cooperative action**, citizens cooperate with the government to promote desired population growth. Through representative government and direct participation, citizens agree to various measures such as prescribing birth control pills and limiting the number of children. Some countries, such as France, have encouraged citizens to have more children and have provided financial incentives to do so. These cooperative efforts are possible in advanced societies where citizens understand the significance of population control to preserve the quality of life for themselves and future generations.

Decisive Action.   Under **decisive action**, the government sets quotas and regulates population growth through economic and civil penalties. In 1976, India announced that a person's rights, privileges, and government benefits would be removed if they had a third child. Government employment also would be denied. In the 1980s, mainland China began a population control plan in major cities which allowed families only one child each. Such drastic measures may help some countries, but they don't reach remote rural areas where many of the problems begin. Therefore, while population control is theoretically possible through technological advances, the socio-cultural problems (attitudes and fears) that prevent implementation are difficult to overcome.

Political Process.   *Political process* is a plan whereby governments provide assistance and incentives to encourage and plan population growth. The international community must work together to develop rationale and convince all people of the significance of population control. The political process can then direct resources toward that objective in a global effort to assure quality of life for all.

In the meantime, while methods of population control are being developed and understood, there are millions of children who go to sleep hungry every night. Many will die of malnutrition and disease because of inadequate food, clothing, and medical care. Overpopulation leads to another major world problem — poverty.

POVERTY
◆◆◆◆◆◆◆◆

Poverty is the condition of having insufficient money to live comfortably with adequate food, clothing, shelter, and medical care. A person is said to be *indigent* when he or she is unable to care for himself or herself through lack of financial means or ownership of material possessions. The **poverty level** is a level of family income below which one is classified as "poor"

There are many obstacles to population control.

Decisive action is often drastic and harsh.

The political process requires global efforts.

Illustration 30-1
Even in America,
poverty is a serious
social and eco-
nomic problem.

according to government standards. It has been estimated that at least one in
ten people over 65 in the U.S. lives in poverty. Many live in the South and
work in agriculture. Poverty occurs four times as often among non-whites as
among whites. While the poverty rate among minorities is high, nearly
two-thirds of all poor people are white. In 1988, an estimated 13.5 percent of
the U.S. population was below the poverty level of $11,611 for a family of
four. Worldwide, an estimated 50 percent of the people are considered poor.

**Those in poverty
have many common
characteristics.**

PROFILES OF POVERTY

Who are the poor? Where are they? In the United States, the most frequent
profile of poverty is the fatherless household where there are small children.
Other examples include families living on seasonal employment or working
at part-time and minimum wage jobs, and a large number of people
depending on one or two low-wage earners. Some are elderly who are living
on what they can get from relatives, savings, and government assistance
programs.

Worldwide, the poor are found in large cities, underdeveloped countries,
and remote regions of jungles and arid lands. Most are uneducated,
unneeded by their governments, and unable to understand modern world
economics or systems. They live by traditional customs and laws of survival,
and they are unable to help themselves out of poverty.

Urbanization is the process of becoming a part of inner-city life. Many
poor people are concentrated in inner-city housing developments of large
cities. These urban areas have no job opportunities or training. Crime and
overcrowding characterize impoverished slums. As masses of poor migrate
to city centers, those who can escape to suburbs, leaving the inner city
unable to counteract the spread of poverty. Social scientists refer to this

**Urbanization of pov-
erty makes the prob-
lem worse.**

inner-city problem as the *urbanization of poverty*. Here, poverty-stricken people suffer from lack of medical care and foods to stay healthy. The poor have more diseases and die younger than more privileged people. Slum buildings contain inadequate heat and plumbing. Unskilled jobs provide no opportunity for advancement. Financial, medical, and emotional problems result. The poor have little economic and political influence.

CAUSES OF POVERTY

An important cause of poverty is the *existence* of poverty: poverty causes poverty! Studies show that many children born into low-income families remain poor all their lives. These children acquire their parents' feelings of helplessness and hopelessness. Malnutrition stunts a child's growth — physically and mentally — thus diminishing educational opportunities. Public schools rely on local property taxes, yet low-income communities do not generate tax money for quality educational programs. In addition, such children often receive little encouragement from parents to do well. This *culture of poverty* emphasizes luck rather than setting and achieving goals. The culture has a tendency toward violence and causes more poverty as environment, education, and life experiences all point toward poverty as a way of life.

Poverty is a cause of poverty.

Poverty among children is caused by factors including location and environmental deficiencies, inadequate education and training, poor medical and nutritional care — all related to lack of financial resources. Poverty among adults can be traced to poverty as children, illness which causes unemployability, illiteracy, inability to speak English, and lack of opportunities for training and education programs.

OVERCOMING POVERTY

There are two approaches to eliminating poverty. The first is to lessen the discomforts of poverty and the second is to cure poverty. While the first is only temporary, it solves social problems (such as reducing crime) and assists those for whom there is no cure — those who are too young, too old, too unhealthy, or otherwise unable to overcome poverty on their own.

Lessening the Discomfort of Poverty. Income redistribution is used to lessen the effects of poverty. Government transfer payments include social security, unemployment compensation, and welfare benefits. Welfare includes Aid to Families with Dependent Children (AFDC) and Medicaid. In 1974 a federal program called Supplemental Security Income (SSI) began to provide assistance to aged, blind, and disabled people; more than 3 million people are covered by this program. Other welfare programs include

Lessening the discomfort of poverty is only temporary, not a cure.

day care centers, emergency support programs, food stamps, and school lunch programs. In addition to government efforts, it should be noted that religious organizations and private charities also provide assistance to those suffering from poverty.

Curing Poverty.   To overcome poverty permanently — a long and difficult task at best — poor people must become productive and lift themselves out of poverty to become self-sufficient. Education, vocational training, and special services are often cited as keys to solving poverty. Project Head Start, which provides pre-schooling to prepare culturally deprived children for school, has been a successful program. JPTA (Job Partnership Training Act) is a job training program for economically deprived young people. Many schools have begun reading and literacy programs and have added courses such as English as a Second Language. Educational television programs such as Sesame Street and Electric Company (which began in the 1964 War on Poverty) keep in mind youngsters from poor families. Special services include neighborhood information and help centers, legal aid for the poor, minority entrepreneurship programs, job development activities, and volunteer counseling.

Urban renewal — the use of federal, state and local money to enhance urban areas through improved housing, sanitation, businesses, culture, and urban environment — is a long-range plan to improve the nation's urban areas. In recent years, urban renewal projects have encouraged the urbanization of middle class, white and blue collar workers — many have returned to city centers to reclaim areas abandoned to poverty, thus bringing a new optimistic flavor and quality of life to urban America.

The worldwide poverty problem is more difficult to solve. Millions lack sufficient job skills to grow crops and feed themselves. Within a short time it is not possible to take such people from an underdeveloped agricultural economy to an electronic society. Providing food and shelter lessens the effects of change. Education and training is a slow process of teaching people how to care for themselves — a process requiring international effort, commitment, and time.

> Many government programs seek to cure poverty in the long run.

> Reclaiming city centers is a long-term solution to poverty.

VOCABULARY

Directions: Can you find the definition for each of the following terms used in Chapter 30?

First World nations	liquid effluent
Second World nations	social costs of pollution
Third World nations	social costs of cleaning up
pollution	pollution
final pollution	zero population growth
derived pollution	cooperative action
externality	decisive action

poverty   urbanization
poverty level

1. Countries often described as primitive and undeveloped.
2. Communist countries that enjoy relative economic gains through limited trade and interdependence.
3. Pollution that results from consumption activities.
4. Pollution that results from production activities.
5. The dumping of industrial sewage wastes into rivers and streams.
6. A system whereby citizens work with government to promote desired population growth.
7. A system whereby the government sets quotas and regulates population growth.
8. An income minimum below which a family is classified as "poor" according to government standards.
9. The process of becoming a part of inner-city life.
10. Free world, industrialized nations that enjoy the greatest economic advantages.
11. Contamination of the environment with human-made wastes.
12. A condition that is a by-product rather than a desired result of production.
13. Lost quality of life, diminished resources, and reduced options for future production and enjoyment.
14. Forgone opportunities for products and services that could have been developed with money spent to restore the environment.
15. A condition whereby the number of people dying and leaving the country is the same as the number of people born or becoming new citizens of the country.
16. A condition of having insufficient economic resources to care for oneself.

ITEMS FOR DISCUSSION

1. How does progress create problems?
2. List major benefits of progress in the world economy.
3. List some of the costs of progress in the world economy.
4. What are three major problems that have resulted along with progress?
5. What is the ozone layer and why is it important?
6. List and define two types of pollution.
7. List three approaches to controlling pollution.
8. What three actions can be taken through the political process to control pollution?

9. Explain what is meant by "the cost of total clean up of pollution isn't acceptable."
10. What are the three stages in the clean-up process? Which is the most expensive and why?
11. What is the "optimum level of pollution?"
12. What are three approaches to controlling population?
13. What are some causes of poverty?
14. What are the two approaches to working on poverty?
15. List some government-sponsored programs designed to eliminate poverty.

APPLICATIONS

1. List ways that you and your family have benefited from progress. Can you also list problems that have resulted because of progress?
2. Why do Third World nations not enjoy the major benefits of progress?
3. Have you observed pollution in the air or water in your community? List the pollutants created by individuals and businesses in your community.
4. Why is it that consumers are ultimately responsible for all pollution?
5. Why can't all pollution be removed and none ever allowed again?
6. Why is the population explosion a worldwide problem?
7. Why do poor people move into major cities?
8. Why is controlling population difficult to accomplish?
9. What is wrong with the urbanization of poverty?
10. How can poverty cause poverty?
11. Why should we lessen the discomfort of poverty rather than just take steps to cure it?

CASE PROBLEMS AND ACTIVITIES

1. Using an almanac, list the fastest growing cities in the U.S. in terms of population. Also list the populations of the largest cities and countries of the world and their population growth rates.
2. Do a research project on the nation of India or China and write a one-page summary of population trends and major economic problems of the country.
3. Write a report on poverty in America, using three sources (almanac, encyclopedia, current periodical) to give a clear picture of the problem, current opinion, and facts.
4. How would you solve poverty in the United States and worldwide?

APPENDIX

●●●●●●●●●●●●●●●●●●●●●●●●●●●●●●●●●

ANNUAL PERCENTAGE RATE FORMULA
●●●●●●●●

The simplified methods of computing interest (finance charges) shown in Chapter 13 are adequate for most comparison purposes. The formula shown here is used in colleges and advanced courses in personal finance and economics to illustrate an effective method of computing installment interest. The annual percentage rate (APR) formula is used when there is a down payment, payments to be made on the principal that include interest, and agreements requiring more than one regular payment.

By completing this relatively complicated formula, the annual percentage rate can be determined fairly accurately. Other methods exist, but this formula always proves to be accurate within tenths of a percent. The annual percentage rate is expressed first as a decimal, carried to the fourth decimal place. Then it is changed to a percent by moving the decimal point two places to the right and rounding to tenths — 9.8 percent from .0981. The formula is as follows:

$$R = \frac{2mI}{P(n+1)}$$

Where

R = the annual percentage rate
2 = a constant (always used)
m = the method of payment ($m = 12$ if monthly payments are made, $m = 4$ if quarterly payments are made, and $m = 1$ if annual payments are made.)
I = the dollar amount of interest
P = the principal (total amount borrowed — not including the down payment)
n = the total number of payments
1 = a constant

An examination of the important parts of this formula is essential in order to make it work properly.

DOWN PAYMENT

The down payment must be subtracted from the purchase price because interest will not be charged on the amount that is paid in the beginning. Most merchants require the down payment to be 10 percent or more of the purchase price. Then the purchaser will have an incentive to keep making the payments and not lose the down payment.

NUMBER OF PAYMENTS

The actual number of payments to be made under the agreement is entered and added before any multiplication is done. For instance, if you were to multiply the principal by 36 and then add 1, you would have a much different answer than if you multiplied the principal by 37.

CASE PROBLEMS

Let us do a case problem to see how this formula works. Assume that a person buys a car for $6,000, making a $400 down payment. The buyer will make 36 equal monthly payments of $170, as illustrated in Figure A-1.

Figure A-1
Annual Percentage
Rate Examples

ANNUAL PERCENTAGE RATE

$$R = \frac{2mI}{P(n+1)}$$

$$R = \frac{2(12)I}{P(36+1)}$$

$$R = \frac{2(12)520}{5,600(37)}$$

$$R = \frac{24(520)}{207,200}$$

$$R = \frac{12,480}{207,200}$$

$$R = .0602$$

$$R = 6\%$$

I is found by multiplying the total number of monthly payments by the amount of each payment:

$$36 \times \$170 = \$6,120$$

Then subtract the principal from that amount:

$$\$6,120 - \$5,600 = \$520$$

P is found by subtracting the down payment from the purchase price:

$$\$6,000 - \$400 = \$5,600$$

Remember to do what is in the parentheses first (i.e., add 36 and 1 before multiplying).

Use of a calculator will greatly speed these computations.

To make this formula work best, you need to fill in each missing item and then follow through mathematically. Let us work through another example, as illustrated in Figure A-2. In this case the purchase price is $1,200, with a down payment of $200 and 12 equal monthly payments of $90.

Figure A-2
Annual Percentage
Rate Examples

ANNUAL PERCENTAGE RATE

$$R = \frac{2mI}{P(n+1)}$$

$$R = \frac{2(12)I}{P(12+1)}$$

$$R = \frac{24(80)}{1,000(13)}$$

$$R = \frac{1,920}{13,000}$$

$$R = .1477$$

$$R = 14.8\%$$

P is found by subtracting the down payment from purchase price:

$$\$1,200 - \$200 = \$1,000$$

I is found by multiplying the total number of payments by the amount of each payment:

$$\$90 \times 12 = \$1,080$$

Then subtract the principal from that amount:

$$\$1,080 - \$1,000 = \$80$$

When using a calculator, carry out your answer to the fourth decimal place. Then round to a tenth of a percent.

Problems using the annual percentage rate formula are in the Appendix of MANAGING YOUR PERSONAL FINANCES, Student Activities, 2d Edition, accompanying this textbook.

RULE OF 78
◆◆◆◆◆◆◆◆

The Rule of 78 is a method of computing the amount of interest the consumer will save by paying a debt early. The interest refund schedule is based on the number 78, which is the total of the digits for each month of the first year $(12 + 11 + 10 + 9 + 8 + 7 + 6 + 5 + 4 + 3 + 2 + 1 = 78)$. The first month, representing the first monthly payment, has 12 as a factor. Therefore, if you pay off a 12-month loan after you make the first payment, you pay 12/78 of the total interest. The rest of the interest is unearned and, therefore, saved and refunded to you. If you pay the loan off after the third month, you add 12 (first month) + 11 (second month) + 10 (third month) for a total of 33. You will pay 33/78 of the total interest. This calculation is done by dividing 33 by 78 (.4231). The total amount of interest due (example: $30) is multiplied by .4231 to get the amount of interest paid after 3 months ($30 × .4231 = $12.69). The amount of interest paid ($12.69) is then subtracted from the total amount of interest due ($30) to determine how much interest is saved by paying off the loan early ($30 − $12.69 = $17.31). Figure A-3 shows the amounts of interest saved when one-year loans are paid off early.

RULE OF 78

Length of Loan	Total Interest	Date of Early Payment	Interest Paid	Interest Saved
1 year	$300.00	After 4th month	(42/78) $161.54	(36/78) $138.46
1 year	$150.00	After 8th month	(68/78) $130.77	(10/78) $19.23
1 year	$100.00	After 1st month	(12/78) $15.38	(66/78) $84.62

When a loan is extended for more than one year, a new base is used. For example, the base for 2 years is $24 + 23 + 22 + \ldots + 3 + 2 + 1 = 300$. The base for three years begins at 36 and totals 666; the base for 4 years begins at 48 and totals 1,176. A 3-year loan paid off after 3 months is 105/666 interest paid. The method of calculating the amount of interest paid on a loan of more than one year is like that of a single-year loan, the first month of the loan having the highest factor. If you pay off a 2-year loan after the first month, for example, you pay 24/300 of the interest and save the remainder.

Figure A-4 shows examples of the Rule of 78 when calculated on loans of longer than 1 year. The amount of interest already paid on the 2-year loan is computed by adding together $24 + 23$, which is 47. Then 47/300 is the percentage of interest already paid. Multiply 47/300 by $240 to get the dollar amount of interest paid, $37.61. The rest of the interest ($240 − $37.61) is unearned and refunded to you ($202.39).

Not all businesses use the Rule of 78 plan of refunding unearned interest, but each business will outline and explain in the loan agreement the system used. On most revolving accounts, the interest merely stops when the entire balance is paid off. No unearned interest is accumulated because it is computed on the new balance each month. However, a plan for refunding unearned interest is needed on installment accounts because the regular monthly payments include both principal and interest and are calculated to pay off the loan after a set number of months.

RULE OF 78
(for loans of longer than one year)

Length of Loan	Total Interest	Date of Early Payment	Interest Paid	Interest Saved
2 years (300)	$240.00	After 2d month	(47/300) $37.61	(253/300) $202.39
3 years (666)	$168.00	After 4th month	(138/666) $34.81	(528/666) $133.19
4 years (1,176)	$818.00	After 11th month	(473/1,176) $329.01	(703/1,176) $488.99

Problems using the Rule of 78 are in the Appendix of MANAGING YOUR PERSONAL FINANCES, Student Activities, 2d Edition, accompanying this textbook.

U.S. RULE
◆◆◆◆◆◆◆◆

The U.S. Rule, like the Rule of 78, is a method of calculating unearned interest. The difference is that many people make larger payments or lump sum additional payments, rather than paying the entire remaining balance at once. The U.S. Rule shows how a borrower is given credit for payments that are made before maturity of a loan. Businesses use the U.S. Rule to determine how much credit will be given for extra payments.

CASE: Mary owes $1,000 and has signed a 90-day, interest-bearing note at 12 percent. After 30 days, she pays $200. After 50 days (20 additional days), she pays $200 more.

STEP:	CALCULATIONS:
1. Calculate interest due from the date of the loan to the date of the partial payment.	1. $1,000 \times .12 \times \dfrac{30}{360} = $10 interest (Multiply by 30 and divide by 360, or use 4 decimal places — 1/12 = .0833)
2. Apply the partial payment to cover interest due for the 30 days.	2. $200 partial payment − 10 interest $190 principal part of payment

3. Subtract the principal part of the payment from the loan balance. This is the adjusted loan balance.

3. $1,000 loan balance
   − 190 principal part of payment
   $ 810 adjusted loan balance

Mary pays an additional $200 after 20 more days.

4. On the next partial payment, first calculate interest on the adjusted loan balance.

4. $810 × .12 × $\frac{20}{360}$ = $5.40 interest
   (or use 4 decimal places — .0556)

5. Apply the partial payment to cover interest due for the 20 days.

5. $200.00 partial payment
   −   5.40 interest
   $194.60 principal

6. Subtract the principal part of the payment from the loan balance. This is the new adjusted loan balance.

6. $810.00 adjusted loan balance
   −194.60 principal
   $615.40 adjusted loan balance

40 days are remaining on the note. (90 − 30 − 20)

7. At maturity of the loan, the interest is calculated from the date of the last partial payment.

7. $615.40 × .12 × $\frac{40}{360}$ = $8.20 int.
   (or use .1111)

   $615.40 adjusted loan balance
   + 8.20 interest on last 40 days
   $623.60 new adjusted loan balance

Problems using the U.S. Rule are in the Appendix of MANAGING YOUR PERSONAL FINANCES, Student Activities, 2d Edition, accompanying this textbook.

GLOSSARY

◆◆◆◆◆◆◆◆◆◆◆◆◆◆◆◆◆◆◆◆◆◆◆◆◆◆◆◆

absolute advantage. The economic concept of producing products in which a country is naturally superior to other nations due to climate, natural resources, or ability of the labor force.

abstract. A summary of all previous transactions involving a piece of property.

acceptance. When a seller agrees to an offer exactly as stated.

acquisition. One company buys another company to strengthen its financial position or to diversify.

actuarial table. A table of premium rates based on ages and life expectancies.

actuary. One who calculates insurance and annuity premiums; a specialist on insurance statistics.

add-on interest. Interest added to the principal; equal payments that include principal and interest are made each month.

adjusted balance method. Method of computing finance charges in which the monthly payment is subtracted from the balance due before the finance charge is computed.

adjusted gross income. Gross income minus allowable adjustments.

administrative agency. A group established by Congress and authorized by the executive branch of government to enforce administrative laws.

ad valorem tax. A tax based on the value of a possession (e.g., property tax).

advertising. The communication of product information through mass media to the consumer for the purpose of increasing the demand for a good or service.

agent. A trained professional acting for an insurance company in negotiating, servicing, or writing a policy.

aggregate demand. The total demand of all consumers for all goods and services produced in an economy.

aggregate supply. The total amount of goods and services available to purchasers.

Agricultural Marketing Service. A federal agency that inspects food to ensure wholesomeness and truthful labeling, develops official grade standards, and provides grading services.

alimony. Money paid to support a former spouse.

allowance. A person who is dependent on your income for support.

amoral. A characteristic of the marketplace based on survival of the fittest.

annual percentage rate. The rate of interest charged on installment contracts.

annual report. Information provided by a corporation, which gives financial history, data, product description, future plans, and so on.

antitrust laws. Laws to protect consumers from price fixing and monopolies.

appellate court. A court that has the authority to review the judgment of a lower court.

aptitude. A natural physical or mental ability that permits a person to perform certain tasks well.

arbitration. A process whereby a decision is made by a neutral third party.

audit. The examination of tax records by the Internal Revenue Service.

automatic fiscal policy. Built-in government spending programs that stabilize spending power and distribute economic wealth.

automatic stabilizers. Immediate benefits that prevent consumers from losing purchasing power or being unable to survive.

average daily balance method. A method of computing finance charges based on the average outstanding balance during a given period.

bait and switch. An insincere offer by a merchant who attracts the buyer into the store by advertising an exciting bargain, then switches the customer's interest to a more expensive product.

balance due. The total amount that remains due on a loan, including both principal and interest.

balance of payments. A listing of all foreign transactions among a country's residents and the rest of the world.

balance of trade. The difference between imports and exports.

bankrupt. Legally insolvent — not capable of paying bills.

barter. The exchange of goods and services without the use of money.

basic needs. Those ingredients necessary for maintaining human life.

beneficiary. A person named on an insurance policy to receive the benefits of the policy.

benefits. Sums of money to be paid for specific types of losses under the terms of an insurance policy.

Better Business Bureau (BBB). On state and local levels, a clearinghouse of information about local businesses.

billing (closing) date. The last date of the month that any purchases or payments made are recorded in a charge account.

blank endorsement. The signature of the payee written on the back of the check exactly as it appears on the front of the check.

bond indenture. A written proof of a secured bond debt.

borrower. The person who borrows money or uses another form of credit.

brokers. Members of a stock exchange who do the buying and selling of stocks that are listed with the exchange.

budget. An organized plan of matching income and expenses.

business cycle. The recurrent speeding up and slowing down of the economy.

cafeteria-style. Insurance programs whereby employees are allowed to choose desired coverages.

canceled checks. Checks the bank has processed.

capacity. The ability to repay a loan from present income.

capital. Property possessed that is worth more than debts owed; a factor of production representing equipment, machines, and other durable but depreciable inputs to the production process.

capitalism. An economic system wherein productive resources and decisions are made by individuals and businesses.

carrying charge. *See* service charge.

cashier's check. A check written by a bank on its own funds.

cash value. The amount of money payable to the policyholder upon discontinuation of a life insurance policy.

certified check. A personal check that the bank guarantees to be good.

Chapter 7 bankruptcy. A straight bankruptcy proceeding that wipes out most, but not all, debts.

Chapter 11 bankruptcy. A proceeding for businesses to reorganize their debt structure.

Chapter 13 bankruptcy. The wage earner's plan of bankruptcy, wherein debtors keep all of their property and repay a portion of their debts over a period of time under a court-enforced plan.

character. A trait of creditworthiness indicating a responsible attitude toward paying debts.

checkbook register. A record of deposits to and withdrawals from a checking account.

checking account. A banking service wherein money is deposited into an account, and checks are written to withdraw money as needed.

cherry picker. A customer who buys only loss leaders and super sale items.

child support. Money paid to a former spouse for support of dependent children.

Civil Aeronautics Board (CAB). Agency that provides consumer protection and rights for passengers on domestic aircraft.

civil court. A court that has the authority to hear disputes involving the violation of the private rights of individuals.

claim. A demand for payment for loss under the terms of an insurance policy.

closed-end fund. An investment fund with a fixed number of shares to be issued and sold.

coinsurance. A policy clause that requires you to carry coverage equal to or exceeding 80 percent of the replacement cost.

collateral. Personal property pledged to a lender to secure a loan.

collective bargaining. The process of negotiating the terms of employment for union members.

collective values. Those things important to society as a whole.

collision coverage. Coverage of the insured's own car in the event of an accident.

command economy. An economic system wherein basic economic decisions are made through a central authority.

commodities. Quantities of goods or interests in tangible assets.

common sense. Ability to make wise decisions.

common stock. A security representing a share in the ownership of a company.

communism. A political theory that does not recognize private property ownership.

company advertising. Advertising to promote the image of a store, company, or retail chain.

compare alternatives. The third step in problem solving wherein good and bad choices are examined for possible solutions.

comparative advantage. The principle that the greatest gain in total output will occur if each country or state specializes in producing those goods and services that can be produced with the greatest efficiency and imports goods that could be produced only at great cost.

competition. A situation wherein there exists more than one producer or supplier of a good or service.

complimentary close. Sincerely yours or other appropriate phrase that courteously ends a letter.

compound interest. Interest computed on the sum of the principal plus interest already earned.

comprehensive coverage. Insurance that covers damage to your car from events other than collision or upset.

conditions. Existing debts, employment stability, and other circumstances that affect a person's ability to meet financial obligations.

conservation. The wise use of scarce resources.

consideration. Something of value that each party to a contract must receive.

consumer advocate. One who promotes and protects consumer interests.

consumer finance company. A general-purpose company that extends mostly consumer loans to customers buying consumer durables.

Consumer Price Index (CPI). An index showing changes in the average price of a basket of goods purchased by consumers.

consumer redress. The resolution of a problem with a product or service.

consumers. Citizens and businesses that purchase and use the goods and services produced for sale.

consumer sovereignty. The power or ability of consumers to affect what is being produced and consumed.

consumption debt. A debt that has no source of funds to pay it off, requiring other sources of income to be used.

contact. A relative, friend, person you have worked for, or anyone who may be able to provide inside information on job openings.

contract. A legally enforceable agreement between two or more parties to do or not to do something.

cooperative action. A system whereby citizens cooperate with government to promote desired population growth.

corporate note. The written promise of a corporation to repay loans it has accepted from private citizens.

cosigner. A person with an acceptable credit rating who promises in writing to repay a promissory note if the maker fails to do so.

cost-push inflation. A rise in the general level of prices, caused by increased costs of production.

counterclaim. A statement asserting the defendant's belief that the plaintiff is at fault and demanding damages as a result of the plaintiff's actions.

counterfeiting. Unlawful production of imitations of money.

counteroffer. A new offer made in response to an original offer.

court. A tribunal established by the government to decide matters properly brought before it, to give redress to the injured or enforce punishment against wrongdoers, and to prevent wrongs.

coverage. Protection provided by the terms of an insurance policy.

credit. What you use when you buy something now and agree to pay for it later, or borrow money and promise to pay it back later.

credit bureau. A company that operates for profit in the business of accumulating, storing, and distributing credit information.

credit file. A summary of a person's credit history.

credit history. The complete record of your credit performance.

creditor. Any person to whom one owes money or goods.

credit report. A written report issued by a credit bureau that contains relevant information about a person's creditworthiness.

criminal court. A court for the trial of crimes regarded as violations of duties to society and disturbances of public peace and order.

current account balance. Net cash flows (export minus import payments).

current service estimate. An expenditure required to meet ongoing and previously authorized programs.

custom. A long-established practice that may be considered an unwritten law.

databases. Computerized, organized collections of related data.

debenture. An unsecured corporate note.

debt collector. A person or company hired by a creditor to collect the balance due on an account.

decisive action. Intervention through which government sets quotas and regulates population growth.

decreasing term. A type of insurance policy for which the coverage value decreases each year while the premium remains the same.

decree. A final statement of the dissolution of a marriage.

deductible. A specified amount subtracted from covered losses. The insurance company pays only the amount in excess of the amount subtracted.

deductions. Amounts subtracted from gross pay; expenses the law allows the taxpayer to subtract from gross income.

defendant. The person against whom the plaintiff is making a complaint.

defensive driving. Watching for the bad driving decisions of others.

deferred billing. A service to charge customers whereby charged purchases are not billed to the customer until a later date.

deferred payment price. The total amount, including principal and interest, that will be paid under a credit agreement.

deficit. Spending by the government of more money than it collects.

define the problem. The first step in problem solving.

demand. The willingness and ability of consumers to purchase goods and services at certain prices.

demand curve. A graph that illustrates the relationship between price and quantity demanded.

demand schedule. Quantities demanded at various prices.

demand-side economics. An economic theory concerned with total spending and the use of government actions (fiscal policy) to adjust the spending flow.

demand deposit. An account wherein you can demand portions of your deposited funds at will.

demand-pull inflation. A rise in the general level of prices caused by too high a level of aggregate demand in relation to aggregate supply.

deposit. A pledge or down payment.

depositions. Written, sworn statements of witnesses taken before court appearances in order to preserve the memory of the issues.

deposit multiplier. The result of a change in money supply because of a change in the reserve requirement.

depression. A severe recession wherein production declines for a prolonged time, unemployment is high, and the economy is in a state of panic.

derived pollution. Pollution resulting from production (consumers are indirectly responsible).

discharged. A debt that is no longer owed after declaration of bankruptcy.

discount brokerage. A service through which individuals can buy and sell stocks for a reduced fee.

discount interest. Interest that is deducted from the loan principal at the beginning of the loan.

discount rate. The rate of interest that banks are charged to borrow money from the Federal Reserve System.

discretionary fiscal policy. Acts of Congress and government in response to economic conditions.

discrimination. The act of making a difference in treatment or favor on a basis other than individual merit.

disposable income. The money you have to spend as you wish after taxes, social security, and other required and optional deductions have been withheld from your gross pay.

dissolution of marriage. Divorce.

diversification. The practice of purchasing a variety of investments to protect against large losses and increase the rate of return.

dividends. Monies paid to stockholders from the profits of a corporation.

docket. The schedule of cases, dates, and times for issues to be heard in a particular court.

domestic market. Purchases by Americans of goods that are made in America.

drafts. Checks.

drawer. The depositor to a checking account.

due date. The date on or before which a credit payment is due.

durable goods. Goods expected to last many years, such as automobiles.

earnest money offer. A formal, written offer to buy a home.

economic efficiency. The best possible use of scarce resources.

economic equity. Fairness in the process of allocating resources to meet needs.

economic forecasting. Prediction of future economic conditions.

economic freedom. The right of individuals to make their own economic decisions.

economic growth. A rising standard of living (individually) and a greater output of goods and services (economy as a whole).

economic integration. The elimination of restrictions to the flow of products and factors of production between nations.

economic stability and security. A high level of employment without high inflation, allowing all people to survive and enjoy life.

economics. The study of society's attempts to fill unlimited needs and wants with scarce resources.

economizing. Saving and eliminating uses to stretch the life of a product or resource.

economy. The system or structure of economic life in a country.

elastic. Demand where a decrease in price results in a greater increase in demand.

elasticity. The measure of responsiveness of quantity demanded or quantity supplied to changes in price and other factors.

elasticity of demand. The way in which a change in price affects the quantity demanded.

endorse. To sign a check across the left end of the back so that the check may be cashed.

equilibrium price. The price of a product set by the competitive interaction of demand and supply.

equitable relief. A legal action that allows a previous order to be rescinded, requires a situation to be restored to its previous state, or provides for the performance of a specific act.

equity. The difference between the appraised value of a property and the debt owed on the property.

escrow. The process whereby a neutral third party holds the deed and works through the details of a transaction for the purchase of a property.

eviction. A landlord's legal demand that a tenant move from the premises.

excellent credit rating. A credit rating earned by paying all bills before their due dates.

excess reserves. The amount that exceeds the reserve requirement.

exchange rate. The value of a country's currency in terms of other currencies.

excise taxes. Taxes levied against the manufacture, sale, or consumption of a commodity.

exclusion. A part of income that is not, by special exception, taxable; a circumstance or loss that is not covered under the terms of an insurance policy.

exempted item. An item of value or a possession that a bankrupt is allowed to retain a certain equity in because it is considered necessary for survival.

exemption. An allowance a taxpayer claims for each person dependent on the taxpayer's income.

exempt status. A claim that allows you to have no federal income tax withheld from your paycheck.

expense account. A company account that allows employees to charge expenses.

expenses. Money you will need for day-to-day purchases.

exporting. The selling of commodities to foreign countries.

externality. A by-product of production and market-place supply and demand.

face amount. The death benefit of a life insurance policy.

factors of production. Land, labor, capital, and entrepreneurship—the components necessary for producing goods and services to meet consumer wants and needs.

fair credit rating. A rating earned by a customer who usually pays all bills within the grace period, but occasionally takes longer.

fake sale. A situation wherein a merchant advertises a big sale, but items are at regular prices, or the price tags are disguised to show a price reduction when there actually is none.

Federal Bureau of Investigation (FBI). The chief investigating branch of the U.S. Department of Justice.

Federal Communications Commission (FCC). A government agency that regulates radio and television broadcasting and interstate telephone and telegraph companies.

Federal Deposit Insurance Corporation (FDIC). A company that insures bank deposits.

Federal Reserve System. The central banking system in the United States.

Federal Savings and Loan Insurance Corporation (FSLIC). A company that insures deposits in savings and loans.

Federal Trade Commission (FTC). A government agency concerned with protecting consumers from unfair methods of competition, false or deceptive advertising, deceptive product labeling, inaccurate or obsolete information on credit reports, and disclosure of the cost of credit.

final pollution. Results from consumption activities; consumer is directly responsible.

finance charge (handling charge). The interest or money charged the borrower for the use of credit.

finance company. Small loan companies that charge high rates of interest to use their money.

financial planning. An orderly program for spending, saving, and investing the money you earn.

financial resources. Sources of income.

fire insurance. Insurance that will cover losses from fire damage to your home and possessions.

First World nations. Free world, industrialized countries.

fiscal drag. To bring expansion to a halt rather than just slow it down.

fiscal policy. The changing of government spending and taxing to control output, recession, inflation, and unemployment.

fiscal year. The government accounting period beginning October 1 and ending September 30.

fixed costs of production. Costs that remain constant regardless of production level.

floating a check. The practice of writing a check on insufficient funds and hoping to make a deposit to cover the check before it is cashed.

follow-up. A final contact made after a job interview and before the interviewer makes a decision.

Food and Drug Administration (FDA). A government agency charged with enforcing laws and regulations to prevent distribution of mislabeled foods, drugs, cosmetics, and medical devices.

formal education. Knowledge gained through attending formal institutions of learning.

formal wedding. A wedding for which all guests and participants wear formal attire.

Form W-4, Employee's Withholding Allowance Certificate. A form completed for income tax withholding purposes.

Form W-2, Wage and Tax Statement. A form that lists income earned during the year and all amounts withheld by the employer in your behalf.

free and clear. A term describing a possession that has no debt of any kind owed against it.

fringe benefits. Optional or extra benefits provided for employees.

full disclosure. To reveal to a purchaser in complete detail every possible charge or cost involved in the granting of credit.

furnished. A residence supplied with basic furnishings and essential appliances.

gems. Natural precious stones, such as diamonds and rubies.

generic. A general term for a product having the same qualities or contents as a well-known brand-name product.

goal. An end toward which efforts are directed.

gold standard. A condition wherein a country redeems money in gold and gold is redeemed at a fixed price.

good credit rating. A rating earned by paying bills on the due dates or within a five-day grace period.

government spending. Purchases of domestic goods and services by all government units.

grace period. The period following the due date of an unpaid premium during which an insurance policy is still in effect.

grapevine. The informal communication channel that exists in all organizations.

gross income. All taxable income received, including wages, tips, salaries, interest, dividends, unemployment compensation, alimony, and so forth.

Gross National Product (GNP). The total value of all final goods and services produced in an economy over a given period of time.

gross pay. The total salary, before any deductions are made.

handling charge. *See* finance charge.

health insurance. A plan for sharing the risk of financial loss due to accident or illness.

hierarchy. The formal communication and power structure of an organization.

high book value. The low book value of a used car, plus the value of the car's added features.

holographic will. A will written in a person's own handwriting.

homeowners insurance. A policy that combines fire, loss and theft, and liability coverage.

human relations. The art of getting along with others.

identity. Who and what you are.

implied agreement. An agreement that is understood, though not necessarily discussed.

importing. The purchase of commodities from foreign countries.

incentive. A way to encourage employees to do more and better quality work.

income distribution. A function that determines the value of a product and the price of the factors of production that make the product.

Index of Leading Economic Indicators. The government's gauge of future economic activity.

industry advertising. Advertising to promote a general product group without regard to where these products are purchased.

inelastic. Demand that does not respond to changes in price.

infant industry. A new or young industry that cannot compete against corporate giants.

inflation. The increased cost of living.

informal wedding. A wedding for which no special clothing is required for the wedding party or the guests.

initiative. A quality that allows you to do things on your own without being told.

innovations. New ideas, methods, or devices that bring about changes.

inside address. The part of a letter that shows the name and address of the person or company to whom you are writing.

insolvent. A poor credit position in which one's liabilities are greater than one's assets.

installment loan. A written agreement to make regular payments on a specific purchase.

insurable interest. A condition of insurance contracts wherein the insured must be in a position to sustain a financial loss if the event insured against occurs.

insurance. A cooperative system of sharing the risk of financial loss.

insured. The person, partnership, or corporation protected against loss by an insurance policy.

interdependence. A condition wherein each person or unit depends on others to do what each can do best.

interest. Money paid by the financial institution to the saver for the use of his or her money; the amount paid for the use of credit; the price paid for using capital.

International Monetary Fund (IMF). An organization that monitors international monetary relations between nations.

intestate. What you are said to be if, when you die, you do not have a will, but own property that will not automatically pass to another person.

investment. The outlay of money in the hope of realizing a profit.

investment tax credit. A tax credit given to businesses for undertaking investment spending.

involuntary bankruptcy. A financial situation that occurs when creditors file a petition with the court, asking the court to declare a debtor unable to pay bills.

itinerary. A detailed schedule of events, times, and places.

job interview. A situation in which a potential employer asks questions about the answers an applicant has provided on the application for employment.

joint endorsement. The signature, on the back of a check, of both persons named as payees on the front of the check.

judgment. An obligation or debt created by decision of the court.

jurisdiction. The legal right and authority of the court to hear and decide a case.

jury. A body of citizens sworn by a court to hear the facts submitted to them during a trial and to render a verdict.

labor. The human factor of production.

labor union. A group of people who work in the same or similar occupations, organized for the benefit of all employees in these occupations.

land. The factor of production that represents resources that are fixed or nonrenewable.

landlord. The owner of the property that is rented or leased to another person.

law of demand. Consumers will buy more at lower prices than at higher prices if everything else is constant.

law of supply. The higher the price, the greater the quantity that will be produced or supplied if everything else is constant.

laws. Rules of conduct accepted by people and enforced to protect people.

layaway. A credit plan whereby merchandise is laid away in your name, and you make regular payments and claim the merchandise when it has been paid for in full.

lease. A written agreement to rent certain property at a certain price for a specified time period.

lease option. A lease agreement wherein each rent payment applies toward the purchase of the item or property leased.

lethal. Deadly or dangerous.

letter of application. A letter that introduces you to a potential employer and gives you a chance to sell your qualifications.

letter of reference. A statement, in letter form, written by someone who can be relied upon to give a sincere report on your character, activities, and experience.

level term life insurance. A type of insurance that is renewable at set intervals, no proof of insurability being required.

liability coverage. A policy that protects the insured against claims for personal injury or damage when the insured is driving his or her car or someone else's car.

lien. A hold or claim one person has against property of another to secure payment of a debt.

life insurance. Protection against the financial disaster that might otherwise result when a family's primary wage earner dies.

life-style. The way people choose to live their lives based on their values.

limited-payment life insurance. A type of whole life insurance on which premiums are higher because the payment period is limited to a specific number of years.

line of credit. A pre-established amount that can be borrowed on demand.

liquidation. A sale held to turn inventory into cash quickly.

liquid effluent. The dumping of industrial sewage into rivers and streams.

liquidity. The quality of being easily converted into cash.

loan sharks. Unlicensed lenders who charge very high and usually illegal interest rates.

lo-balling. Advertising a repair service special at an unusually low price to lure customers, then attempting to persuade the customer that additional services are needed.

lobbying. Supporting legislation and political action that is beneficial to a certain profession.

loss. An unexpected reduction or disappearance of an economic value.

loss leader. An item of merchandise marked down to an unusually low price, sometimes below actual cost.

macroeconomics. The study of how the economy as a whole functions.

Major Appliance Consumer Action Panel (MACAP). A group comprised of representatives of the home appliance industry, which provides assistance in resolving consumer problems in the purchase and use of home appliances.

maker. The person who creates and signs a negotiable instrument agreeing to pay it on a certain date; the person authorized to write checks on an account.

marginalism. A technique used to analyze the results of small changes in quantity.

marginal utility. The added satisfaction that is received when an additional unit is consumed.

marketable. A term describing work of quality such that the employer can use or sell it.

market economy. An economic system characterized by private property ownership, self-interest behavior, consumer sovereignty, and competition.

market power. The ability of firms or buyers to affect price.

market study. Research of the profit potential of a new product or service.

market value. The highest price a property will bring in a competitive and open market.

markup. The amount added by the dealer to the suggested retail price of a car.

mass production. The use of machinery and capital goods to make mass quantities of goods and services.

maturity date. The date on which you must renew a time certificate, cash it in, or purchase a new one.

mediation. A neutral third party assists other parties in reaching a decision.

merger. The joining of two companies to make a weak one stronger, thereby making both more financially sound.

microeconomics. A study of individual market interactions.

minor. A person under the age of legal majority.

mixed economy. An economic system in which both producers and consumers play active roles; a market economy in which there is some government intervention.

monetary base. Bank reserves plus currency held by banks in their vaults and by the public.

monetary policy. Activity by the Fed to influence money supply growth, credit conditions, and the level of interest rates.

money. Anything acceptable in exchange for goods and services.

monopolistic competition. The market situation characterized by many sellers of products that are not exactly the same but are very similar.

month-to-month tenancy agreement. A written or oral agreement to rent certain property at a set price on a month-to-month basis.

multiple listing service. An organization of real estate offices through which all listings from each office are combined into one book. All salespeople within that geographic area have access to all real estate listings and can sell any one of them to a buyer.

multiplier effect. The concept that any change in policy affects total demand and total income by an amount larger than the amount of the change in policy.

mutual assent. Agreement to all terms of the contract by all parties to the contract.

mutual (open-end) fund. An investment wherein someone else is paid to choose and buy various securities for the investor.

NADA Blue Book. The National Automobile Dealers Association book that lists a low book value for a basic used car for six years.

National Bureau of Standards (NBS). An agency within the Department of Commerce that sets measurement, product, and safety standards.

National Credit Union Administration (NCUA). An agency that insures deposits in credit unions.

national debt. Amount of government bonds or other securities sold by the U.S. government.

national income. Total income received in the form of rent, wages, interest, and profits.

national product. Output produced by the factors of production.

negotiable instrument. A document that contains promises to pay monies and is legally collectible.

negotiation. The process whereby an employer meets with union representatives to work out an agreement.

net pay. The amount left after all deductions have been taken out of your gross pay.

net weight. The weight of a product without the container or package.

networking. The process of using connections and sources of information.

no-fault insurance. Insurance that provides for the repair or replacement of your car, regardless of who is at fault at the scene of an accident.

nominal rate. The rate of interest calculated on the principal amount only (does not include compounding).

nondurable goods. Groceries, clothing, and supplies that will be used in a short period of time.

NSF check (not-sufficient-funds check). A check written without sufficient money in an account to cover it.

obstetrician. A doctor who specializes in delivering babies.

obtain accurate information. The second step in problem solving, wherein all alternative solutions and costs are listed.

odd-number pricing. The practice of putting odd numbers on price tags to make an item appear inexpensive.

Office of Consumer Affairs. An agency that represents consumer interests in federal agency proceedings, develops consumer information materials, and assists other agencies in responding to consumer complaints.

oligopoly. The market situation characterized by very few firms.

open-ended credit. Credit wherein the lender places a limit on how much a qualifying customer can borrow during a given period.

opportunity cost. What you must give up to get something else that you also want.

optimizing. Getting the most from all available resources.

overbooked. A term used to describe the situation in which tickets have been sold to more people than can be accommodated.

overdraft. A check that is written but cannot be covered by the funds in an account.

overextension. A situation wherein purchases exceed what can be handled comfortably with present income.

ownership risk. The factor of production that represents management, innovation, and risk-taking.

oxidize. To permanently lose the shine of a car's finish due to exposure to weather and sun.

pawnshop. A legal business in which loans are made against the value of specific personal possessions.

payee. The person to whom a negotiable instrument is made payable.

pediatrician. A doctor who specializes in the care and treatment of diseases of small children.

peril. An exposure to the risk of loss.

personal factors. Those influences in a person's or a family's life that determine spending patterns, preferences, and choices.

personal injury protection (PIP). Automobile insurance that pays for medical, hospital, and funeral costs of the insured and his or her family and passengers, regardless of fault.

personality. Personal qualities and traits that make one unique.

personal resources. Time, money, energy, skills and abilities, and available credit.

pigeon drop. Any method used by experienced con artists to convince vulnerable people to invest in swindles.

placement service. An organization that helps students find employment, usually without charge.

plaintiff. The person filing a legal complaint.

point system. A method used in rating consumers' creditworthiness wherein a credit applicant is given points for employment, amount of income, length of residence, type of residence, and other factors.

pollution. The contamination of the environment with human-made wastes, making it impure and unclean.

poor credit rating. A rating earned by a customer who does not make regular payments, or who misses payments and must be reminded frequently of debts outstanding.

portfolio. A list of investments and securities owned.

Postal Inspection Service. An organization within the United States Post Office that deals with consumer problems pertaining to the illegal use of the mails.

poverty. The state of having insufficient economic resources to care for oneself.

poverty level. A monetary line below which one is considered poor by government standards.

precious metals. Tangible, beautiful, desirable substances of great value such as gold, silver, and platinum.

preferred stock. Stock on which dividends are paid first in the event of company liquidation.

premium. The sum of money the policyholder agrees to pay to an insurance company periodically for an insurance policy.

prenatal expense. A cost that is incurred before a baby is born.

previous balance method. A method of computing finance charges in which the charge is added to the previous balance, then the payment made during the last billing period is subtracted to determine the new balance in the account.

price ceiling. A maximum product price set by the government that is below the market equilibrium price.

price fixing. The practice by some competing producers of conspiring to set the same prices on the same goods or services.

price floor. A minimum product price set by the government that is above the equilibrium price.

primary deposit. A new demand deposit, often called *high-powered money*.

prime rate. The rate of interest lenders offer their best commercial (business) customers.

principal. The amount of money deposited by the saver; the total amount that is financed or borrowed and on which interest is computed.

probability. The chance that a given event that causes loss will occur.

Producer Price Index (PPI). An index showing changes in the average price of goods that are of particular interest to producers.

producers. Citizens and businesses that make products and services available for others to purchase.

product advertising. Advertising to convince consumers to buy a specific good or service.

production possibilities curve. A graph showing combinations of two goods that can be produced with a given level of resources and technology.

productive debt. Money spent in such a way that the debt will paid out of earnings from the investment.

productivity. Output per unit of input.

product market. The composite of all individual markets in which buyers and sellers interact to exchange goods and services.

product rationing. A function that determines who will and will not purchase products.

professional organization. A group that collects dues from members of a profession and provides support services.

profit. The entrepreneur's reward for taking risk.

profit motive. The desire to maximize income while minimizing expenditures.

progressive taxes. Taxes that increase in proportion to income.

proof of loss. The written verification of the amount of a loss that must be provided by the insured to the insurance company before a claim can be settled.

propensity to consume. The proportion of income spent for consumer goods and services.

propensity to save. The proportion of income saved for future purchases.

property settlement agreement. A court-approved document specifying the division of property and assets agreed to by the parties in a divorce proceeding.

proportional share. A percentage of a bankrupt's assets paid to a creditor, based on the total debt owed the creditor.

proportional taxes. Taxes for which the tax rate remains constant, regardless of the amount of income.

prorate. To divide, as to divide a charge, proportionately over a period of time.

purchasing power. The power to buy goods and services, based on the amount of money owned.

pure competition. The market situation in which there are a large number of buyers and sellers interacting at the same time.

pure monopoly. The market situation that occurs when there is only one producer of a particular good or service, and there are no substitutes available for that product.

pyramid sales. Selling schemes, illegal in many states, in which sellers are promised a lot of money quickly and with little effort for selling a product.

quasi-governmental agency. An agency that is governmental in nature, operating as a private, not-for-profit business, such as the Fed.

rate. The interest charge, expressed as a percentage of the principal.

rational expectations. The economic theory that when consumers expect fiscal policy, they take action to protect themselves.

reaffirmation. When debtors agree to pay some or all of their debts after bankruptcy is completed.

real cost inflation. Inflation caused by an increase in the cost of the factors of production.

real estate. Land and anything permanently attached to it.

recall. A procedure whereby the manufacturer of a product stops production and refunds the purchase price of items already sold.

reconciliation. The process of matching your checkbook register with your bank statement.

recorded. Term describing some document or event that has been made a public record.

references. Persons who have known you for at least one year and who can provide information about your character and achievements. References should be over age 18 and not related to you.

referral sale. A selling method wherein a merchant promises a money rebate, prize, or discount if the buyer can provide names of friends and acquaintances who are prospective customers.

regressive taxes. Taxes that decrease in proportion to income increases.

rent. The price paid for land.

reservation. An advance commitment that assures you of service.

reserve requirement. The percentage of each deposit a bank must keep in reserve (not lend to others).

resource allocation. A function that determines which resources are given higher values.

resource market. The composite of all productive resources in which economic resources are purchased and used.

restrictive endorsement. An endorsement that restricts or limits the use of a check.

resume. A concise summary of personal information.

retail stores. Stores that purchase goods from wholesalers and sell directly to customers.

return address. The part of a letter that shows the writer's street address, city, state, ZIP Code, and date of the letter.

revenue. Money collected by the government from citizens and companies in the form of taxes.

risk. The chance of loss.

risk management. Management of personal risks to improve the likelihood of protecting assets and income against loss.

sabbatical. A leave of absence that benefits the company as well as the employee.

sales finance company. A manufacturer-related company that makes loans through authorized representatives.

salutation. A greeting to the receiver of a letter.

Second World nations. Communist countries that enjoy relative economic gains through limited trade and interdependence.

secured loan. A loan that is guaranteed by a pledge of property or other assets to assure the creditor of repayment.

select an alternative. The fourth step in decision making in which you make a decision.

semiformal wedding. A wedding to which guests wear less formal attire such as special occasion suits and dresses.

semi-variable costs of production. Production costs, part of which are fixed, part of which are variable.

seniority. The policy that the last ones hired should be the first ones laid off.

service charge (carrying charge). The amount charged borrowers by merchants or banks for servicing an account or loan.

service credit. Credit for a service rendered (telephone, doctor).

services. Haircuts, repairs, medical care — actions performed by individuals and companies that contain no measurable quantity.

share account. A savings account at a credit union.

shortage. A market situation that occurs when the quantity of a product that consumers wish to purchase at some price exceeds the quantity that suppliers wish to supply at that price.

simple interest. Interest computed on the principal only. The formula for computing simple interest is $I = P \times R \times T$.

simple will. A short one- or two-page document that lists spouse and children and provides how each shall inherit.

social costs of pollution. Society's losses because of pollution such as quality of life, diminished resources, and reduced options.

social costs of cleaning up pollution. Forgone opportunities for new products and services because money is used to clean up pollution.

socialism. An economic system in which government has a substantial influence on productive decisions.

Social Security Act. The first national social insurance program enacted to provide federal aid for the elderly and for disabled workers.

social security number. A permanent work identification number.

space. The physical attribute of production that is concerned with dimensional, geographic, and measurable commitments of productive resources.

special endorsement (endorsement in full). An endorsement that instructs the bank to pay the amount of a check to a third party.

specialization. The production of only one or a limited number of goods and services by a person or group that consumes many goods and services.

stagflation. Rapid inflation together with high rates of unemployment.

standard deduction. The amount that is deducted from adjusted gross income, depending on filing status, when deductions are not itemized.

standard policy. A contract form that has been adopted by many insurance companies, approved by state insurance departments, or prescribed by law.

Statute of Limitations. A law that restricts the length of time in which court action may be taken on various complaints.

stock market. A general term that describes the securities market — the place where supply and demand for investment alternatives meet.

stop payment order. A request that the bank not cash or process a specific check.

straight life insurance. A type of whole life policy on which premiums are paid throughout life and the face value is paid at death.

strike. A process whereby the members of a union refuse to work until an agreement is reached.

subscriber. A creditor who pays an annual fee to a credit bureau for use of its credit reports.

subsidies. Partial and temporary payments to help relieve financial burdens.

sunken cost. The amount already spent, or the amount it costs to have reached equilibrium.

supply. The quantity of goods and services producers are willing and able to manufacture.

supply curve. A graph that illustrates the quantity supplied at various prices.

supply schedule. A list of quantities that will be provided at certain prices.

supply-side economics. An economic theory based on increasing productivity and business investment spending (rather than consumer spending).

surplus. A situation that occurs when the quantity suppliers wish to supply at some price exceeds the quantity consumers wish to purchase at that price.

take action. The final step in decision making in which the decision is implemented.

takeover. A friendly or hostile purchase of massive shares of stock in order to win control of a company.

target audience. A specific consumer group to which the advertisements for a product are directed.

tariff. A tax or duty assessed against imported products.

taxable income. Gross income minus deductions, exemptions, etc.

tax-deferred annuity. A contract wherein you agree to set aside a certain amount of money each month and defer paying taxes on the earnings until a later date.

tax evasion. Willful failure to pay taxes.

tax liability. The amount of taxes due from you, based on your taxable income.

tax shelter. A legal method of avoiding paying taxes on present earnings.

tenant. One who rents or leases a residence from a landlord.

term life insurance. A type of life insurance that protects you for a set period of time.

testator. The person who makes a will.

thank-you letter. A tool to remind the employer of your interest in the job, written after the job interview.

Third World nations. Undeveloped or underdeveloped nations that benefit little from trade with other nations.

time. The period the borrower will take to repay a loan; the crucial timing of production so that a product or service is available for consumption when it is desired by the consumer.

toxic. Poisonous.

trade embargo. A government-enforced prohibition of international trade.

trade-in. An older vehicle used to reduce the price of the new car by the amount of money the dealer will give on the old vehicle.

trade-off. A situation in which you must choose one option over another.

trade quota. A physical restriction on the number of units of a product allowed to enter the country.

traditional economy. Rules of custom and habit are decided by following long-established values and beliefs.

transfer payments. Monies collected from employers and workers and distributed to those who do not work.

travel agency. An authorized agent for all airlines to issue tickets and make reservations in the customer's behalf.

trial court. A court that has the authority to hear a dispute when it is first brought into court.

true annual percentage rate. The effective rate received when money is compounded and interest is received on interest already earned.

trust will. A very complicated will that has specific provisions for holding property, assets, and money for minor children and others.

20/10 Rule. Never borrow more each year than 20 percent of your yearly take-home pay, and never agree to monthly payments that are more than 10 percent of your monthly take-home pay.

unearned premium. The portion of the original premium that has not been earned by the insurance company and is returned to the policyholder when a policy is canceled.

unemployment insurance. Insurance that provides benefits to workers who lose their jobs through no fault of their own.

unfurnished. A rental residence that may or may not include basic kitchen appliances such as stove and refrigerator.

uninsured motorist coverage. Insurance that covers damages caused by the driver of a car that is uninsured.

union. A unit or group of people joined together for a common purpose.

unitary elastic. A decrease in price results in an offsetting increase in demand.

unit pricing. The determination of the cost per unit of items sold in quantity.

universal life insurance. A life insurance policy that combines term insurance with a savings plan.

unlisted telephone number. A telephone number that is not listed in the telephone directory and cannot be obtained through directory assistance.

unsecured debt. No specific asset is pledged, but all of the debtor's resources are considered.

unused credit. The amount of credit above what you owe that you could charge, to a maximum amount.

urbanization. The process of becoming a part of inner-city life.

usury laws. Laws setting maximum interest rates that lenders may charge.

utility. A service such as light, power, or water provided by a public utility company; the satisfaction received from consuming a good or service.

values. The beliefs in life that are important to you.

variable costs of production. Costs that go up and down in direct proportion to production.

variable expenses. Expenses that change according to needs and short-term goals.

voluntary bankruptcy. A financial situation that occurs when a debtor files a petition with a federal court asking to be declared unable to meet his or her debts.

voluntary compliance. The expectation that all employed citizens will prepare and file income tax returns.

wages. The total compensation for employment, including gross pay, insurance, sick pay, fringe benefits, and all other types of direct or indirect compensation.

warranty. An assurance of product quality or responsibility of the seller.

wedding party. The persons who are active participants in a wedding ceremony.

well-baby visits. Regular visits to a doctor during the first year or two of infancy for the purpose of receiving immunizations and checkups.

whole life insurance. Insurance that pays the face amount to the beneficiaries on the death of the insured.

workers' compensation. Benefits paid to workers and their families in the event of injury, illness, or death that occurs as a result of the job or working conditions.

work history. A record of all jobs held and the length of time spent with each employer.

zero population growth. A condition in which for as many babies born and immigrants entering a country, an equal number dies or leaves the country.

INDEX

◆◆◆◆◆◆◆◆◆◆◆◆◆◆◆◆◆◆◆◆◆◆◆◆◆◆◆◆◆◆◆

PHOTO CREDITS